COMPUTING

IN THE INFORMATION AGE

SECOND EDITION

COMPUTING
IN THE INFORMATION AGE

NANCY STERN
Hofstra University

ROBERT A. STERN
Nassau Community College

John Wiley & Sons, Inc.   *New York • Chichester • Brisbane • Toronto • Singapore*

To Melanie and Lori

ACQUISITIONS EDITOR   Beth Lang Golub
DEVELOPMENTAL EDITOR   Johnna Barto
MARKETING MANAGER   Leslie Hines
PRODUCTION EDITOR   Edward Winkleman
DESIGN SUPERVISOR   Ann Marie Renzi
ASSISTANT MANUFACTURING MANAGER   Mark Cirillo
PHOTO EDITORS   Lisa Passmore
                Jennifer Atkins
SENIOR FREELANCE ILLUSTRATION COORDINATOR   Anna Melhorn
COVER AND TEXT DESIGN   Jeanette Jacobs
COVER PHOTOGRAPH   Viesti Associates, Inc.; screen: courtesy of Microsoft

Recognizing the importance of preserving what has been written, it is a policy of John Wiley & Sons, Inc. to have books of enduring value published in the United States printed on acid-free paper, and we exert our best efforts to that end.

The paper in this book was manufactured by a mill whose forest management programs include sustained yield harvesting of its timberlands. Sustained yield harvesting principles ensure that the number of trees cut each year does not exceed the amount of new growth.

Library of Congress Cataloging-in-Publication Data:

Stern, Nancy B.
    Computing in the information age/Nancy Stern, Robert A. Stern.—2nd ed.
        p.   cm.
    Includes index.
    ISBN 0-471-11061-2 (pbk. : alk. paper)
    1. Business—Data processing.   2. Information technology.
I. Stern, Robert A. II. Title
HF5548.2.S7817   1996
658'.05—dc20

95-17400
CIP

Printed in the United States of America

10 9 8 7 6 5 4

PREFACE

We have written *Computing in the Information Age,* Second Edition, for introductory students. While the focus is on business applications, the book, which draws on our experience as instructors and textbook authors, is appropriate for a wide range of course offerings. Our main objective is to explain computing today in a clear and meaningful way and to focus on those concepts likely to have the greatest impact as we approach the next century and the next phase of the information revolution.

A primary goal of this text is student understanding of both the "tools" and the "whys and hows" of computing. We focus on the unique applicability of computers to business and to life, the advantages we gain from knowing how and why to use computers, and the potential of computers to enrich our lives.

While *Computing in the Information Age* is more substantive than a tutorial, it is by no means an encyclopedia. Rather, we have taken great care to provide what we regard as the ideal mix of concepts that belong in the introductory course, along with optional, add-on interactive multimedia software and tutorials to supplement the text for instructors who want a more customized approach.

Balanced Coverage of Both Concepts and Application Software

During the past decade, the focus of introductory courses shifted from the lecture hall to the lab. While teaching students in a laboratory setting how to use software remains important, hands-on learning is but one part of the broader quest toward understanding how computers can enrich our lives, how they work, and how computer information systems can help people make decisions and solve problems.

We believe that introductory computing courses are moving into a new phase. The emphasis now is on a more balanced approach, moving beyond the microcomputer lab and back toward concepts. While the lab remains vital, a useful text for the introductory course must offer a solid foundation of concepts.

Discussions of technology must be integrated with discussions of applications in a meaningful way so that students are not overwhelmed by complex concepts or by an overemphasis on terms. We make concepts understandable as well as concrete by presenting an appropriate mix of technology and applications. When teaching students about computing, we believe that knowing when to stop is at least as important as knowing what to focus on. Books that mention every conceivable subject are not usually the best books. We hope we have achieved an appropriate balance of depth and breadth of coverage.

We integrate application software concepts with our information processing focus so that students learn *why* major productivity tools and other types of programs are important. Once the student understands the applicability of the software, we present a conceptual explanation of *how* each major type of tool is used.

Because instructors tend to have differing ideas about the best package to use, we keep our software discussions generic. A *Getting Started* series on Windows, all the major productivity tools, and the Internet is also available.

Four Organizing Themes

Students must learn to look critically at four main elements—hardware, software, networks (connectivity), and the people who make them work. Only then can they anticipate and appreciate the fruits of the Information Age. We have divided the text into five parts. The first part provides an overview of the four major elements—hardware, software, networks, and people. Each of the four succeeding parts focuses on one of these main elements.

In order to emphasize that all four elements must be integrated for effective computerization, we include applications or brief highlights of each in all chapters. A chapter that focuses on hardware, then, will also include an emphasis on the other three components of computing—as a way of tying together specific subjects and reinforcing the themes. When used in this way, the four elements are highlighted with icons:

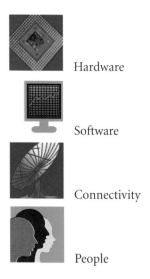

Hardware

Software

Connectivity

People

With these pointers throughout the text students can understand that the concept under discussion is gradually being developed from chapter to chapter. In this way, themes are reinforced as vital elements in all areas of computing.

Changes in Second Edition

Based on our classroom experience and the comments and recommendations of our colleagues, we have tried to enhance the effectiveness of *Computing in the Information Age*. Building on the successful elements of the First Edition, we have made the following changes in the Second Edition:

1. *The text has been significantly streamlined to present concepts in a clear and meaningful way, without overwhelming students with detail and technical discussions.* While we maintain our emphasis on providing students with a solid conceptual foundation to computing, we have minimized some details such as binary arithmetic, feasibility studies in systems analysis, and design of executive information systems. We have also provided a more focused approach to many technical topics such as computer architecture and the structure of networks.

2. *Coverage is balanced by discussing microcomputers both as networked devices and as standalone machines.* As a result, students fully understand that PCs can indeed be personal tools for productivity as well as nodes in a distributed or client-server environment. Also, we emphasize the place of larger computers today so students appreciate that mainframes are the backbone for many organizations' computing needs.

3. *Current issues in computing are emphasized with consideration of how the computer has affected (and will continue to affect) our lives.* Topics such as the infor-

mation superhighway, multimedia, global issues in computing, distance learning, and social concerns about privacy and security are brought to the forefront. Critical thinking questions throughout the chapters, in the margins, and at the end of chapters help the students address social issues.

4. *A thematic approach integrates the four components in computerization: hardware, software, connectivity, and people.* We introduce these themes in the first chapter and include them in every chapter, highlighted by icons in the margins. Hence students will fully understand the need to have all four elements properly balanced in the information system. The Instructor's Manual provides references that assist instructors who wish to use this thematic approach in their lectures.

5. *A wider range of supplements is available to help instructors customize materials to fit the needs of their courses.* Instructors can select from a vast array of *Getting Started* titles for all the major software products. These productivity manuals have been field-tested and widely reviewed. In addition, a CD-ROM that includes a great deal of material is available to instructors to augment material presented in the text and to serve as lecture enhancers. The CD-ROM includes PassPort software, electronic transparencies, additional topics, and multimedia demonstrations that help explain various concepts.

Other Distinguishing Characteristics

In addition to providing a more balanced approach to information processing, *Computing in the Information Age* offers several other features that distinguish it from other texts in the marketplace:

EMPHASIS ON BUSINESS APPLICATIONS (WITH ADDITIONAL DISCUSSIONS OF CONSUMER, EDUCATION, AND GLOBAL ISSUES) This text focuses on computing concepts as well as on real-world examples of how computers are used, mainly in the business world. Emphasis is on hardware used in business, productivity tools and other business software, networks used in commercial organizations, and the people who work in business to design, develop, and use information systems. We also provide a balance by focusing on how computers are used globally, in education, in the home, and in a wide variety of other application areas.

ALL COMPUTERS FROM MICROS TO MAMMOTHS Our book begins with the concept that all computers process data in essentially the same way, keeping in mind that the differences among categories of computers are essentially differences of degree. Since many students enter introductory courses having had some exposure to personal computers, we begin with micro concepts and build up to larger systems in Part One. Then all subsequent chapters reinforce the fact that large computers are simply faster, more expensive, and more powerful than micros. In this way, the distinctions among computers are not rigidly cast, and students gradually lose their fear of "big" machines. They come to understand that with proper connectivity, it does not really matter to users whether they are on a mainframe, mini (midrange), or microcomputer.

Although mainframes can be viewed as quantifiably different from micros, the fact is that certain tasks are best performed on larger machines. We make the analogy that a mainframe is to a micro what a mass transportation system is to a personal car. The former is most efficient for handling the needs of the largest number of users, but it requires users to follow more structured rules and schedules. Many books today emphasize the micro so much that the importance of mainframes is virtually ignored. Using client-server computing as a major topic, we put into perspective the relationships among different types and sizes of computers.

While emphasizing IBM-compatible micros when discussing personal computers, we do not ignore the Macintosh or the Power PC. Indeed, we highlight the features that make these computers ideally suited for some applications.

CONNECTIVITY AND THE HUMAN FACTOR This book goes beyond the traditional units of hardware and software that appear in most books and adds two very important perspectives: *connectivity* and the *human factor*.

Throughout the text we emphasize connectivity and the human factor and, in addition, focus on these topics in more detail in Parts Four and Five. For example, the networking of computers and other devices such as modems, fax machines, and CD-ROM drives has changed the focus of computing; we highlight how these changes have occurred and their anticipated long-term impact. Most importantly, the information superhighway and the Internet—and their significance in society—are discussed in great detail, as is client-server computing.

Similarly, social, ethical, legal, environmental, and global issues continue to be important topics in education, as indeed they should be. We integrate these issues throughout the text and give them special emphasis in Part Five. We also focus on technologies that have the potential to significantly affect an individual's quality of life, such as multimedia, smart devices, and interactive TV.

A BUILDING BLOCK APPROACH Another feature of this text is its layered, "building block" approach to topics and themes. That is, topics are introduced in a simplified way, then further developed at key points throughout the text. For example, the four main topics of the book—hardware, software, connectivity, and people power are introduced in the first unit and expanded upon in subsequent units. Major topics such as the information superhighway, multimedia, and global issues in computing are presented in numerous chapters; each discussion builds upon the previous one and has a specific focus depending on where it is presented. When students complete the text, they will have a full understanding of these major topics from a hardware, software, connectivity, and social perspective.

CRITICAL THINKING EMPHASIS To improve their understanding of the world around them and to become effective decision-makers, students need to learn to think more critically. Our goal is to help students to examine controversies and current events in computing, to analyze the factors affecting them, and to ask the right questions—in short, to encourage critical thinking. We regard our critical thinking emphasis as a way of motivating and empowering students.

Consequently, we present issues and brief analytical problems in computing designed to encourage students to think about social issues in computing and to ask pertinent questions relating to them. Critical thinking questions appear in text margins, in end-of-chapter Critical Thinking Exercises, and in the form of brief cases at the end of each chapter.

A main objective of the text is to help students evaluate products and resources. Obviously, we include the state-of-the-art, but if that were all we did the book would become obsolete very quickly. We also cover techniques used by computer-proficient users, managers, and professionals to evaluate software, hardware, networks, and information systems, providing readers with tools to understand and assess future developments and their probable impact on society. More importantly, products are featured for students to analyze and evaluate as part of their critical thinking training.

Pedagogy

Our unique approach to teaching the student computing concepts, which has been refined and updated, remains the most important pedagogic feature of this text. Furthermore, all chapters have a common structure designed to facilitate comprehension, self-study, and retention:

- **Chapter Outline.** A brief outline showing the organization of the major topics covered in the chapter appears on the first page as a chapter preview.

- **Opening Description.** Each chapter opens with a brief description of an event or issue in computing that motivates the student and emphasizes *why* the chapter topics are important.

- **Learning Objectives.** A list of objectives points the student to the main learning outcomes at the beginning of the chapter. In addition, these objectives reappear in the margin beside the pertinent text discussion *and* in the margin beside the Chapter Summary. The constant reinforcement of these objectives serves as a very effective study aid.

- **In a Nutshell.** Throughout each chapter, these marginal notes highlight crucial material (such as criteria used to evaluate computers) and, where appropriate, present brief summaries of major topics in outline or list form.

- **Looking Back** and **Looking Ahead.** These special boxes provide historical perspective on major innovations (*Looking Back*) and project into the future regarding the impact of new technologies (*Looking Ahead*).

- **Critical Thinking Questions.** The reader is challenged to integrate what they are learning with what they know about life through questions placed in the margins at strategic places.

- **Extensive Illustration Program.** Carefully chosen photographs and specially created screen dumps and illustrations help to clarify ideas presented in the narrative. Detailed captions clearly tie the art to the text. In addition, a photo essay sets the stage for each of the five parts of the book.

- **Self-Tests.** At the end of each major section within each chapter, a short self-test with solutions reinforces understanding and retention of the material just presented.

- **End-of-Chapter Materials.** Each chapter concludes with a series of materials intended to assist students in review and application of the concepts discussed.

  - A *Chapter Summary* provides a concepts-oriented review and is directly related to the learning objectives.

  - The *Chapter Self-Test* assesses the student's understanding of the entire chapter and gives immediate feedback by including solutions.

  - *Key Terms* are presented in a list to serve as a review. If the student cannot recall a term, a page number refers back to where the term was defined in the chapter. The Glossary at the end of the text includes definitions of all key terms.

  - *Review Questions* and *Critical Thinking Exercises* serve as a final test of the student's comprehension of the chapter topics and their implications in real life.

  - A *Case Study* serves as a final challenge for the student. It focuses on an event or recent innovation in computing, along with relevant critical thinking questions, to reinforce concepts covered in the chapter.

SUPPLEMENTS

The text is available with a wide variety of supplements to help customize your course and to reinforce the concepts presented in the text.

GETTING STARTED SERIES An array of software manuals is offered by the publisher to provide support for the lab portion of your course. These include carefully tested, practically oriented tutorials for DOS, Windows, and various productivity packages.

ANNOTATED INSTRUCTOR'S MANUAL (AIM) is a unique resource which integrates the entire text package to help instructors organize the text and supplementary materials into an informative and exciting course. A detailed outline of the text is annotated with suggestions for the use of video, software, transparencies, and/or World Wide Web sites, and an explanation of how to incorporate it into the text coverage. It also includes overviews, lecture introductions and extenders, teaching hints, review question and case study solutions, activities and exercises, points to emphasize, and advice to first-time instructors.

TEST BANK AND COMPUTERIZED TEST BANK Approximately 150 test items per chapter include multiple-choice, true-false, and essay questions. MicroTest is a computerized test bank available for IBM-compatibles.

COLOR TRANSPARENCIES These include 75 full-color acetates of key figures from the text.

STUDENT STUDY GUIDE Intended to help the novice student get through the course, this manual includes chapter outlines, key terms, fill-in exercises, sample test questions, games and exercises, and common misconceptions demystified.

Electronic Supplements

Implementing the tools of the Information Age, we also offer a number of new media supplements to enhance both teaching and learning.

CD-ROM A truly multimedia instrument, this item includes *PassPort: A Multimedia Tour of the Information Age,* electronic slides, and multimedia demonstrations that illustrate basic introductory computing concepts. *PassPort* is a collection of multimedia programs that uses text, graphics, photos, animation, and sound to enhance and extend the information provided in the text. These programs can be used either in a lecture hall that has a projection system, in a computer lab, or individually by students. PassPort extends textbook information by:

1. Introducing productivity tool concepts (*TechTools*)—there are three modules on word processing, spreadsheets, and database management.
2. Providing in-depth explorations of new products through *TechTours* and overviews of new technologies through *TechBytes.*

VIDEOS A selection of news segments from "Nightly Business Report," the longest-running, most-watched daily business, financial, and economic news program on television, is available as a companion to the text. NBR anchors provide lead-ins to tie the video segments directly to text coverage.

COMPUTERIZED STUDY GUIDE The student is offered the option of learning computing by using an electronic study guide.

PRODIGY DEMONSTRATION PACK The popular subscriber service, Prodigy, is introduced on a disk. A discount coupon is also included.

ACKNOWLEDGMENTS

This text has been improved as a result of our own classroom experience. In addition, feedback from our colleagues around the country has helped us to refine the content and presentation of the Second Edition. The manuscript has been reviewed by instructors teaching from *Computing in the Information Age*, First Edition, as well as those using other texts. Other professors participated in a focus group to help the publisher to identify the most effective teaching and learning package. We wish to thank the following reviewers for their invaluable comments, suggestions, and criticism, which have helped us to develop this text:

Bruce Brown
Salt Lake Community College

William R. Cornette
Southwest Missouri State University

Wayne Eirich
Northern Arizona University

Ted Finch
Napier University

Joe W. Fortson
McLennan Community College

Rhonda L. Haller
Jackson Community College

Richard D. Hauser, Jr.
East Carolina University

Sharon Ann Hill
University of Maryland

William R. Kenney
San Diego Mesa College

Marilyn G. Kletke
Oklahoma State University

Lawrence J. Krieg
Washtenaw Community College

Hans Lee
Michigan State University

Anita Lee-Post
University of Kentucky

Marilyn W. Meyer
Fresno City College

Matthew Michelini
Manhattan College

David Nicholas
Cedarville College

Robert O'Brien
CUNY—Baruch

Margaret Porciello
SUNY—Farmingdale

Leonard Presby
William Paterson State College

Sorel Reisman
California State University—Fullerton

Al Schroeder
Richland College

Liang Chee Wee
Luther College

We would like to thank the following people at Wiley for their efforts:

Joe Heider, Publisher
Johnna Barto, Director of Development
Beth Lang Golub, Acquisitions Editor
Leslie Hines, Senior Marketing Manager
Ann Marie Renzi, Senior Designer

Edward Winkleman, Senior Production Editor
Ann Berlin, Vice President of Production and Manufacturing
Andrea Bryant, Supplements Editor
David Kear, Administrative Assistant
Lisa Passmore, Photo Editor
Anna Melhorn, Senior Freelance Illustration Coordinator
Linda Muriello, Senior Production Manager
Stella Kupferberg, Director of Photo Research

We would also like to thank Shelley Flannery and Carol Eisen for their assistance in preparing, copyediting, and proofreading the manuscript; Jennifer Atkins for her assistance in photo research; Rosann Kelly for her technical support; and Elisa Adams for her developmental work.

We welcome your comments, suggestions, and even criticisms. We can be reached through Beth Golub at John Wiley & Sons, 605 Third Avenue, New York, NY 10158, via Internet at ACSNNS@VAXC.HOFSTRA.EDU, and via CompuServe at 76505,1222.

Nancy Stern
Robert A. Stern

BRIEF CONTENTS

Part One   Introduction: The Basics

1. The Basics of Computing: Hardware, Software, Connectivity, and People   4
2. From Micros to Mammoths   29
3. Using Productivity Tools   59

Part Two   Hardware Advances the Information Age

4. Computer Processing   107
5. Input and Output: From Applications to Hardware   140
6. Secondary Storage Devices   182

Part Three   Software Drives the Information Age

7. Application Packages: Beyond Basic Productivity Tools   218
8. Developing Custom Software   256
9. Systems Software   292

Part Four   Connectivity Unites the Information Age

10. Connectivity, Networks, and the Information Superhighway   329

Part Five   People Power Makes the World a Better Place

11. Systems Analysis and Design   371
12. Database Management Information Systems   399
13. Social Issues in Computing   428

Appendix An Overview of the History of Computing   461

Glossary   472
Index   485

CONTENTS

Part One
Introduction: The Basics 2

1. THE BASICS OF COMPUTING: HARDWARE, SOFTWARE, CONNECTIVITY, AND PEOPLE 4

1.1 *Introducing Computer Systems: Input-Process-Output* 5
  The Computer System and How It Processes Data 6
  Software Makes It Work 8

1.2 *Understanding Information Processing* 11
  Computer Systems Automate Information Processing 11
  Connectivity Links Hardware, Software, and People 12
  The Human Factor: People and Computing 13
  The Pros of Computing 14
  Avoiding the Cons of Computing 16

1.3 *Computing in the Information Age* 19
  Hardware Happenings: Computers Make the World Smaller and Smarter 20
  Software Sensations: Computers Make the World More Creative 21
  Information Interchange: Computers Make the World More Connected 21
  People Power: Computer Users Make the World a Better Place 22

2. FROM MICROS TO MAMMOTHS 29

2.1 *Classifying Computer Systems* 30
  Types of Computers 30
  Processing Power 32

2.2 *Getting to Know Your Hardware* 36
  Mainframes 36
  Minis and Midrange Computers 37
  Supercomputers 38
  Microcomputer Categories 39
  The Apple Macintosh, IBM-compatibles, and Power PCs 43
  Multitasking on Micros vs Multiprogramming on Larger Computers 44

2.3 *Choosing and Using Computer Systems* 46
  Information Processing Environments 46
  The Human Factor in Information Processing: Users and Computer Professionals 49
  The Right Time to Buy 53

3. USING PRODUCTIVITY TOOLS 59

3.1 *Understanding Software* 60
  Software Makes It Work: A Review 60
  The People Who Use Application Packages 61
  Types of Productivity Tools, Integrated Packages, and Suites 61

3.2 *Common Features of Productivity Tools* 67
  Loading the Program 67
  Creating and Retrieving Files 68
  Status Lines 68
  Data Entry 69
  Basic Commands and Function Keys 69
  Search and Replace 71
  Macros 72
  Importing Files 72

3.3 *Unique Features of Productivity Tools* 73
  Word Processing Packages 73
  Electronic Spreadsheets 80
  Database Management Systems 88
  Electronic Mail, Groupware, and the Information Superhighway 96

Part Two
Hardware Advances the Information Age 104

4. COMPUTER PROCESSING 107

4.1 *How the CPU Processes Data* 108
  Overview of Components and Operations 108
  Primary Storage or Main Memory 111
  The Arithmetic/Logic Unit 113
  The Control Unit 113
  Registers and Machine Cycles 114

4.2 *How the CPU Represents Data* 115
  The Binary Numbering System 115
  Bits, Bytes, and Words 116
  EBCDIC and ASCII 118
  Error Checking with Parity Bits 119

4.3 *Computer Architecture* 121
  Chip Technology: One-Upman-"Chip" 121
  Clock Speed 123
  Processing Speed 124
  Bus Width and Word Size 125
  Main Circuit Boards and Expansion Slots 126
  Additional Devices for Improving Processing Power 127

4.4 *Methods of Processing Data* 129
  Batch Processing 130
  Interactive Processing 131
  The Main Processing Technique: A Record at a Time 132

5. INPUT AND OUTPUT: FROM APPLICATIONS TO HARDWARE   140

5.1 *Input Devices Create Source Documents and Data Files*   141

A Review of File Processing Concepts   141

Keying Devices   143

Alternatives to Keying   148

5.2 *Source Data Automation Reduces Data Entry Operations*   151

Optical Character Readers   151

Applications Using Data Collection Systems   155

Automation in the Banking Industry   157

Voice Recognition Equipment   160

Digitizers   161

5.3 *Output Devices Produce Information*   162

Types of Output   163

Output Devices   164

Expanding the World of Computers   174

6. SECONDARY STORAGE DEVICES   182

6.1 *Fundamentals of Secondary Storage*   183

Review of File Processing Concepts   184

Criteria for Evaluating Storage Devices   184

6.2 *Magnetic Media for Secondary Storage*   186

Magnetic Disks and Disk Drives   186

Magnetic Tapes and Tape Drives   193

Maintaining Disk and Tape Files   195

Smart Cards, Flash Memory, and RAM Cards: You *Can* Take It With You!   198

6.3 *Optical Storage Alternatives to Magnetic Media*   201

CD-ROM Drives: A Most Valuable Player   201

Networking Compact Disks   206

WORM Drives: Will They "Worm" Their Way into Your Heart?   206

Erasable Magneto-Optical Drives: Doing the "Write" Thing   207

6.4 *Organizing Data Files*   209

Sequential File Organization   209

Random-Access File Organization   209

Part Three
Software Drives the Information Age   215

7. APPLICATION PACKAGES: BEYOND BASIC PRODUCTIVITY TOOLS   218

7.1 *A Review of Application Software*   219

Packaged and Customized Programs   219

Productivity Tools Revisited: Basic Packages, Integrated Packages, and Suites   219

Additional Productivity Programs   220

7.2 *Other Power Tools*   230

Graphics or Illustration Packages   230

Document Viewers   234

Desktop Publishing   234

Statistical Packages   237

Artificial Intelligence Software: Expert Systems, Virtual Reality, and Neural Network Packages   237

Business Packages   240

Packages for Consumer Use   243

7.3 *Choosing and Using Software*   244

The Make or Buy Decision   244

Versions of Software   245

Evaluating Software Products   245

Where and How to Acquire Software   246

The Human Factor: Security and Safety   247

8. DEVELOPING CUSTOM SOFTWARE   256

8.1 *The Software Developer*   257

In-house Software Developers—Analysts, Programmers, and Users   257

Outside Consultants   258

8.2 *Software Development Cycle*   259

Develop the Program Specifications with the Help of the Users   259

Design the Program Logic   259

Code and Translate the Program   263

Test the Program Until It Is Fully Debugged   264

Implement the Program   266

Maintain the Program   266

Complete the Documentation for the Program   266

Software Development: Art or Science?   266

8.3 *Programming Techniques for Standardizing Software Development*   267

Modular Programming   268

Structured Programming   268

Top-Down Programming   270

Reusable Code   271

Object-Oriented Programming   271

Visual Programming   272

8.4 *Five Generations of Programming Languages*   273

Machine Language: The First Generation   273

Assembly Language: The Second Generation   274

High-Level Languages: The Third Generation (3GLs)   274

Fourth-Generation Languages (4GLs)   283

Fifth-Generation Languages (5GLs)   285

9. SYSTEMS SOFTWARE   292

9.1 *Systems Software: Functions and Features*   293

What Systems Software Actually Does   293

9.2 *Microcomputer Operating Systems and Graphical User Interfaces*   296

DOS: PC-DOS and MS-DOS   296

DOS with Windows   299

Windows 95 as a Full Operating System   302

OS/2 Warp   304

Macintosh Operating System   304

Operating Systems for the Power PC   306

Operating Systems for Personal Digital Assistants (PDAs) and Other Pen-Based Computers   306

9.3 Operating Systems That Facilitate Connectivity   308

UNIX—An Operating System for All Categories of Computers   308

Network Operating Systems   309

NextStep   310

9.4 How Operating Systems Maximize Processing Efficiency   311

Multiprogramming and Multitasking   311

Multiprocessing   313

Virtual Memory and the "Virtual Machine" Concept   314

Other Tasks Performed by Systems Software   315

Part Four
Connectivity Unites the Information Age   326

10. CONNECTIVITY, NETWORKS, AND THE INFORMATION SUPERHIGHWAY   329

10.1 Communications and Connectivity   330

Sharing Resources Is the Goal   330

Communications Hardware   331

10.2 Common Application Areas for Networks   339

Distributed Processing   339

Accessing Information from Networks   342

The Information Superhighway   346

Interoffice Electronic Mail and Groupware   346

Telecommuting   347

10.3 Controlling Data Flow with Communications Software   348

Speed of Transmission   348

Direction of Data Flow   349

Serial and Parallel Transmission   351

Data Bits in the Computer Code   352

Parity   352

An Overview of Protocols   352

10.4 Network Configurations   353

The Local Area Network (LAN): A Promised LAN for Sharing Resources   353

LAN Software   353

Network Topologies: Star, Bus, Ring, Hybrid   354

Wide Area Networks (WANs)   356

10.5 Connectivity Leads to a Smaller, Smarter, and More Creative World   357

Facsimile (Fax) Machines   357

Wireless Communications   359

Smart Phones   359

Interactive TV and High-Definition Television   360

Videoconferencing and Distance Learning   361

Part Five
People Power Makes the World a Better Place   368

11. SYSTEMS ANALYSIS AND DESIGN   371

11.1 The Role of the Systems Analyst   372

Making Business Systems More Efficient   372

In-House Analysts vs Outsourcing   373

Job Requirements for Systems Analysts   373

Interfacing with Key Users   373

Understanding the Systems Development Life Cycle   374

11.2 Investigating and Analyzing Existing Business Systems   376

Collecting Data About the Existing System   376

Describing the Elements of an Existing System   377

Using Structured System Charts to Describe an Existing System   379

Undertaking the Feasibility Study   383

Developing Alternative Design Strategies   383

Obtaining Management Approval for a Design Alternative   383

11.3 Designing A New or Revised System   385

Prototyping a System   385

Using CASE—An Automated Design Tool   386

Designing Components of the New System   388

11.4 Implementation   391

Obtaining Management Approval for Implementation   391

Implementing the New System   391

Redesigning Tasks Performed by Users   392

Types of System Conversions   392

Documenting the System   393

12. DATABASE MANAGEMENT INFORMATION SYSTEMS   399

12.1 Database Management Systems: The Driving Force Behind Management Information Systems   400

Database Structures   400

Components of DBMS Software   409

Issues for the Database Administrator   411

12.2 Management Information Systems   413

Facilitating Decision Making at All Management Levels   413

Specialized Management Information Systems   414

13. SOCIAL ISSUES IN COMPUTING   428

13.1 Protecting the Privacy of Users   429

Privacy Issues Relating to E-mail   429

Privacy Issues Relating to Database Access   430

Privacy Legislation   431

Public Interest Groups   432

13.2 *Making Information Systems and Networks More Secure*   433

What Is Computer Crime?   434

Legal Concerns   437

Minimizing Security Problems   437

The Clipper Chip: When Privacy and Security Concerns Clash   437

13.3 *Making Information Systems More Socially Responsible*   440

Managing the Work Environment   440

Do Computers Result in Unemployment or Worker Dissatisfaction?   443

Computer Professionals and Social Responsibility   444

Developing, Promoting, and Supporting Standards   444

The Impact of Computers on the Quality of Life   445

Appendix

AN OVERVIEW OF THE HISTORY OF COMPUTING   461

GLOSSARY   472

INDEX   485

COMPUTING

IN THE INFORMATION AGE

PART ONE

Introduction: The Basics

Computers have given us new options in the ways we use the information and products at our disposal. To understand and appreciate the power of computer systems we consider their four essential and interconnected components: hardware, software, connectivity, and people. Our study begins with a brief introduction to each.

Hardware is the physical component of any computer system, which consists of (1) a central processing unit (CPU) and main memory, (2) devices for entering data (called input devices), (3) devices for displaying results or information (called output devices), and (4) storage devices for storing programs and data for future processing. All categories of computers, from supercomputers to mainframes to minis to microcomputers, process data in the same manner using these four types of hardware. The differences between machines are differences in their processing power, cost, physical size, and number of possible input and output devices. The trend is toward smaller and more portable devices that we can take with us anywhere.

Software is the set of instructions that enable a computer to process data. Most basic to the function of the computer is the operating systems software, which controls and monitors the machine. Applications software allows the computer to perform the specific operations you choose, such as preparing a report, balancing a checkbook, playing a game, sending messages, or creating designs and graphs. It is through our choice of software that we use computers to work more quickly and accurately, giving us more freedom to think and to create.

Hardware and software work together to enable us to accomplish our tasks. But computers need to talk to one another as well, so they can exchange infor-

2

mation and perform a broader variety of applications. Networks and the power of **connectivity** enable organizations and individuals to share computer resources like programs, data, and even relatively expensive hardware like plotters, scanners, and high-quality color printers. The Internet is a group of networks that enable people to communicate with each other all over the world. It also has vast amounts of its own data that can be downloaded to individual computers. The coming information superhighway will expand many computer capabilities as well as the Internet's resources and could significantly change the way we learn and communicate.

None of the great power of computers would even be possible, however, without the **people** who design and manufacture machines, develop software, manage networks, and use their resources. The success of computing depends on people like you, who can understand and control the hows and whys of computers.

Let's begin . . .

CHAPTER 1

The Basics of Computing: Hardware, Software, Connectivity, and People

1.1 INTRODUCING COMPUTER SYSTEMS: INPUT-PROCESS-OUTPUT

The Computer System and How It Processes Data

Software Makes It Work

1.2 UNDERSTANDING INFORMATION PROCESSING

Computer Systems Automate Information Processing

Connectivity Links Hardware, Software, and People

The Human Factor: People and Computing

The Pros of Computing

Avoiding the Cons of Computing

1.3 COMPUTING IN THE INFORMATION AGE

Hardware Happenings: Computers Make the World Smaller and Smarter

Software Sensations: Computers Make the World More Creative

Information Interchange: Computers Make the World More Connected

People Power: Computer Users Make the World a Better Place

W ithin your lifetime, computers and information technology have changed the world more than any machine invented during the entire 200 years of the Industrial Revolution, *including* the automobile. We have moved far beyond the Industrial Revolution into the Information Age, and what an age it is.

To some degree, you probably already are **computer literate:** You are aware of computers and sometimes even use them without knowing it. Every day you interact with devices actually created or enhanced by computing technology— the TV, the telephone, remote controls, cars, even this book. In this sense, you are a computer **user.** The purpose of this book is to increase and refine your computer literacy, especially as it applies to business systems. We will help you understand how computers operate and how they are used in business today. We will take you from computer literacy to computer proficiency. This book is also about the future and how you will use computers in your career and throughout your life.

Study Objectives

We begin in Chapter 1 to describe computers and their uses, or application areas. After completing this chapter, you should be able to:

1. **Explain how computers process data to produce information.**

2. **Describe why organizations use computers for information processing.**

3. **Demonstrate how information processing has been revolutionized by computers.**

▬ 1.1 INTRODUCING COMPUTER SYSTEMS: INPUT-PROCESS-OUTPUT

The main purpose of using computers, regardless of the application area, is **processing** or manipulating data quickly and efficiently so that the information obtained is complete, accurate, timely, economical, and relevant. Computers read incoming data called **input,** process the data, and display outgoing information called **output. Data** itself consists of raw facts; data is processed or operated on in order to produce structured, meaningful **information. Information processing** is a set of procedures used to operate on data to produce meaningful results. The computer actually consists of numerous devices that input data, process it, and produce output information.

Computers have created a revolution in the production, processing, and transfer of information, primarily because of their ability to handle enormous amounts of data quickly. And the changes continue. In a single decade, business computing has changed dramatically. It was once completely dominated by large computers dedicated to producing payrolls and financial reports and dependent on technically trained specialists to satisfy all information processing needs. Now, small, powerful **personal computers (PCs)** are widely available to individual workers who can access information from larger systems and increase their own personal productivity. Computer users today often are not computer professionals; rather, they are people like you who need information to do their jobs effectively. Business users include people who work with computers to process customer orders, prepare budgets, or make decisions about hiring personnel or selecting a marketing strategy.

Study Objective

1. Explain how computers process data to produce information.

▪ IN A NUTSHELL

Input—Data entered into a computer
Output—Information produced by a computer; processed data
Information processing—Procedures that convert input data to output information

In this chapter, we look at the various components of *computer systems*—whether they are large, companywide computers; small, personal computers; or combinations of the two. Think of this chapter as an introduction to computing; we will cover each of its topics in more depth in later chapters.

The Computer System and How It Processes Data

We use the word *system* in many different ways. There are, for example, telephone systems, nervous systems, grading systems, and betting systems. For our purposes, a **computer system** is a group of machines, or **hardware,** that accept data, process it, and display information. The main reason for using computer systems is to process data quickly and efficiently. A computer system performs its information processing operations under the control of sets of instructions called **programs** or **software.** As shown in Figure 1.1, a computer system, regardless of its size, consists of the following components: **input devices;** main memory and the **central processing unit (CPU); output devices;** and **storage devices.**

When people use the term *computer,* or *computer system,* they are really referring to hardware, which is a group of machines. Computer systems come in various sizes from personal computers to much larger systems. Figure 1.2 compares the major components of a typical large computer system to those of a PC. Even though these systems are dramatically different in size, cost, and power, they process data in the same way.

Each business—and computer user—has individual needs, so computer systems are specially equipped, or **configured,** to include components or devices

IN A NUTSHELL

Hardware—A group of machines in a computer system
Software—The instructions that control the operations of the hardware

Figure 1.1 *A computer system consists of the following hardware components: input devices; main memory and the central processing unit (CPU); output devices; and storage devices.*

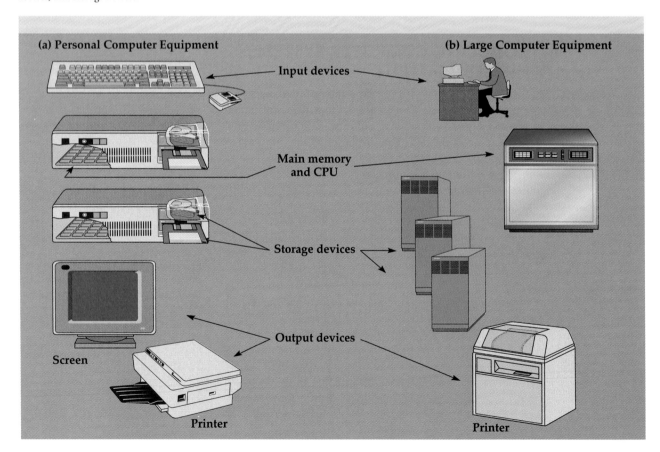

(a) Personal Computer Equipment

(b) Large Computer Equipment

Input devices

Main memory and CPU

Storage devices

Output devices

Screen

Printer

Printer

(a)

Figure 1.2 *Computers of all sizes like (a) a large computer system, and (b) a personal computer have main memory, a CPU, input devices, output devices, and storage devices. Hardware in a computer system differs mainly in terms of size and processing power.*

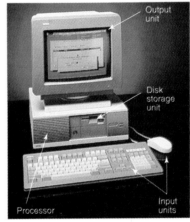

(b)

that meet individual needs. All systems process data, however, in the following way:

INPUT DEVICES READ INCOMING DATA There are many different types of input devices: keyboards, disk drives, page scanners, bar code readers, and voice recognition units, to name a few. Each input device reads a specific form of data; for example, keyboards transmit typed characters whereas scanners "read" typed or handwritten characters from documents or images from graphs, photos, or drawings. Input devices convert data into electronic signals that are transmitted to main memory and processed by the CPU.

Different businesses are apt to have various types of input devices. An insurance company, for example, may use keyboards and disk drives as input devices; a supermarket may use electronic cash registers and scanners that read bar codes on food products or other consumer goods. See Figure 1.3.

MAIN MEMORY AND THE CENTRAL PROCESSING UNIT Main memory stores programs and data for processing and the central processing unit, or CPU, controls all computer operations. The CPU reads data into main memory from an input device, processes the data according to program instructions, and produces information by activating an output device. The CPU is the "brains" of the computer system.

The unit that houses main memory and the CPU must be linked by cables or by communication channels such as telephone lines to all input and output devices in the computer system. A program, or set of instructions for processing data, must be read into main memory by the CPU before data can be entered and processed in order to generate information.

OUTPUT DEVICES PRODUCE OUTGOING INFORMATION Each output device in a computer system accepts information from main memory under the control of the CPU and converts it to an appropriate output form. A printer, for

IN A NUTSHELL

COMPUTER COMPONENTS

1. Input devices
2. Main memory and CPU
3. Output devices
4. Storage devices

(a)   (b)

Figure 1.3 *Organizations have different computing needs. (a) Sometimes basic keyboard/screen units with disk drives suffice, as in many insurance companies. (b) Sometimes applications require different types of devices. Supermarket checkout counters use scanners to read bar codes on consumer goods so that they can be processed by electronic cash registers.*

example, is an output device that prints reports or graphs based on information that the CPU has processed and produced. Similarly, a video monitor is an output device that displays both text and graphics on a screen.

STORING PROGRAMS AND DATA FOR FUTURE PROCESSING Once you turn off a computer, the data and instructions operated on by the CPU are lost. For this reason, separate storage devices are needed to keep the data and instructions in electronic form so they can be used again and again. **Disks** are common storage media for PCs and for larger computer systems. See Figure 1.2 again.

Software Makes It Work

THE STORED PROGRAM CONCEPT Before computer hardware can actually read data, process it, and produce information, it needs a set of instructions—a program—that controls the CPU's operations. Programs, like data, are read into main memory under the control of the CPU. We say that computers are **stored-program devices** because they require a set of instructions to be stored in the computer's main memory before data can be processed.

Computer professionals called **programmers** write programs for each user need or application area. The set of programs that enables the computer system to process data is referred to as *software.* Typically, software is available on disk. A computer system for a medium-sized company, for example, may have hundreds of programs for a variety of application areas such as payroll, accounting, inventory control, and sales forecasting. A home computer system may have dozens of programs for typing reports, playing games, or balancing the checkbook. See Figure 1.4.

Figure 1.4 *PCs are currently found in 60 percent of American homes. They help businesspeople work at home yet stay connected to the office; they help children and adults learn with computer-based training; and they provide access to large databases of information. They improve the quality of life for consumers by helping them perform day-to-day operations like balancing their checkbooks or shopping at home.*

TYPES OF SOFTWARE: SYSTEMS SOFTWARE AND APPLICATION SOFTWARE Computers require two types of software: (1) **operating systems software** to monitor and supervise the overall operations of the computer system and (2) **application software,** such as a word processing or accounting package, to manipulate input data and provide users with meaningful output information.

Operating Systems Software. Computers use a series of control programs, called the **operating system,** that monitors the running of application programs. Some computers have built-in operating systems, but these cannot be easily changed or updated. Most computer manufacturers either provide their own operating system, usually on disk, or allow users to purchase disks containing the more popular operating systems.

The IBM Personal Computer (IBM PC) and computers with similar designs or architectures are called IBM-compatibles. They originally used an older operating system, called **DOS,** which is an abbreviation for *d*isk *o*perating *s*ystem. **Windows,** which began as a **user-friendly** interface that worked along with the DOS operating system, is now available for these computers as a full operating system. There are other operating systems for these machines as well, like OS/2. The Apple Macintosh family of computers has its own operating system similar to Windows. See Figure 1.5. The new Power PC, supported by both IBM and Apple, can use Windows, the Macintosh operating system, and other systems software as well. Large computers also have their own software that controls overall processing.

The Macintosh and Windows systems software permit users to select commands by highlighting graphic symbols or **icons** displayed on a screen. Many people find these more user-friendly, or easier to use, than text-based operating systems like DOS and those for large computers that also require users to type commands.

Each operating system has unique ways to process and store data. A disk that is prepared for one operating system may not work on another system, even if the disk fits into the machine. Application programs are written for a particular operating system as well. WordPerfect for Windows, for example, which is a popular word processing package, cannot be used on a Macintosh—you must obtain the Macintosh version of this software. Programs and data that are designed for different operating systems are often **incompatible;** that is, they cannot be used together. As a result, programs written for one computer are frequently not usable on another computer. Similarly, some hardware devices can be used only with certain computers. Lack of hardware and software compatibility is a common problem for users. We will soon see how the problem of compatibility is being resolved.

Application Programs. Application programs are designed to satisfy user needs by operating on input data to perform a given job, for example, to prepare a report, update a master payroll file, or print customer bills. Typically, application programs are available in one of two forms: (1) **packaged programs** purchased off-the-shelf from a software retailer or (2) **custom programs** designed especially for the unique needs of an individual or an organization.

Figure 1.5 *(a) IBM-compatibles often use a text-based operating system called DOS, which requires commands to be typed or enables users to select commands from a menu. (b) The Macintosh has always had a user-friendly operating system where commands are represented as graphic symbols or icons that are selected by the user. (c) Windows is a user-friendly operating system for IBM-compatibles (older versions of Windows interface with DOS). Windows enables users to select commands represented as icons. Windows makes IBM-compatible computers similar to a Macintosh when selecting commands.*

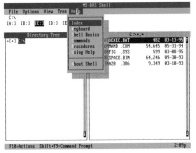

(a)

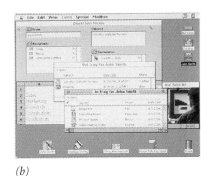

(b)

(c)

Figure 1.6 *Packaged software is usually supplied on disk along with boxed manuals that indicate how to set up the software, how to use it, and what to do if an error occurs.*

Application packages are sold or leased by computer vendors or software developers and are designed for use in organizations or for personal use. Packaged programs allow only limited customization, since they really are intended to be used as is by a broad range of people. Although they may not meet all aspects of every user's needs, application packages are inexpensive compared to custom programs and are supplied with comprehensive user reference manuals called **documentation** (Figure 1.6).

Custom software, on the other hand, is written by programmers within an organization or by outside consultants. Custom programs are designed to meet the precise needs of users, but they are very time consuming and costly to develop.

Users of large computer systems are more likely to be satisfied with custom programs than packaged programs, particularly for major application areas like accounting and inventory; but the time and expense required to develop custom programs often are not justified. As a result, organizations frequently buy packaged programs and then either sacrifice some of their specific needs or have computer professionals modify the package.

One category of application programs, called **productivity tools,** is designed to help PC users perform day-to-day business activities, some of which can assist in decision-making. Productivity tools help users create written documents, maintain information, develop worksheets for preparing budgets and financial statements, and communicate with one another. As the term implies, productivity tools make users more productive by enabling them to complete business tasks more efficiently, search for information faster, and analyze alternatives more effectively.

SOFTWARE DRIVES HARDWARE Computer users should decide on the software they need *before* deciding what hardware to buy. In other words, first determine what you will use your computer for and whether application packages exist that can satisfy your needs. Then find hardware that is compatible with that software. We say that software drives hardware.

Inexperienced purchasers of PCs often buy what they think is "the biggest and the best" hardware only to find that the software they really need cannot run on the PC they own. Experienced computer users know better: They select their software first!

Self-Test

1. Data that has been processed by a computer so that it is in meaningful form is called _____.

2. Instructions that read input, process it, and produce output are part of a _____.

3. List the major components of a computer system and the purpose of each.

4. The software that controls and monitors the overall operations of the computer is called _____.

5. Programs that are developed to satisfy user needs are called _____.

1.2 UNDERSTANDING INFORMATION PROCESSING

Computer Systems Automate Information Processing

We have seen that computer systems—the hardware—consist of input units that read incoming data; main memory and a central processing unit that process that incoming data and convert it to meaningful information; storage devices that store data and programs; and output units that produce information in a usable form. We have also seen that computers are stored program devices: software instructs the computer system to read and process data and to store or produce output.

Organizations began using computers to automate business tasks decades ago. Within each business function, tasks from order fulfillment to preparing payroll checks to listing out-of-stock items all require a set of procedures—a system. The integration of tasks and procedures in each business area is a **business system.** The major business systems or functional areas within organizations are:

- Accounting and finance: systems for keeping the books, generating bills and payrolls, and investing money.

- Human resources: systems for managing employee benefit plans and recruiting new employees.

- Marketing: systems for promoting, pricing, distributing, and selling the organization's products and services.

- Production: systems for controlling inventory, scheduling production, manufacturing, and purchasing.

Computerized information systems enable these various business systems to work together and hence contribute to the organization's goal of earning a profit.

In general, computers are used to more efficiently operate on data that would otherwise be processed manually. Hardware and software enable employees to work more productively, search for information faster, and analyze options

> **Study Objective**
>
> 2. Describe why organizations use computers for information processing.

Solutions

1. information

2. computer program or software

3. input devices that read incoming data; main memory and the CPU, which process the data; output devices that produce information; storage devices that hold programs and data for future processing

4. operating systems software

5. application programs or software

better. Note too that it takes more than hardware and software to computerize a business system. The following sections introduce the other two components of computing: connectivity and people.

Connectivity Links Hardware, Software, and People

A wide variety of computer systems and software is available to satisfy a range of user needs. For each application or type of computer, there are different types of users, in offices, homes, and schools.

In recent years, computing resources have been more effectively harnessed when they are to be shared, where resources include computing power, software, and input/output units. The concept that allows the sharing of resources is called **connectivity** and is achieved by the use of an integrated computer system referred to as a **network.**

Not only do networks make more efficient use of information resources, they also enable hardware and software developed for different types of computers to work together. Thus networks enable an organization to have better control and to more effectively utilize its overall computing resources.

The types of computers linked together in a network depend on the application areas and the processing needs of the organization. Because the capabilities of computer systems change, the tasks they perform also change. Operations performed by a large computer today are apt to be relegated to the faster PCs of tomorrow. Conversely, tasks performed independently by PCs in a network may instead be more efficiently performed by a central computer in the future. The relationship between personal computers and larger systems, then, is dynamic—it changes frequently. As smaller computers become more powerful, larger computers will be used instead to perform other tasks.

Since many users work primarily with PCs, they may think that the era of the big computer is coming to an end. This is a misconception. The tasks performed by large computer systems are apt to change over time, but with the increasing use of networks, larger systems are likely to remain an integral part of an organization's computing facility. Often a large computer in a network or a very powerful microcomputer is used as a file server—a CPU that provides PCs connected to it with the hardware and software resources needed to effectively process data.

Connectivity makes sharing of resources by compatible computers less expensive. See Figure 1.7. For example, an organization can obtain a software developer's permission to allow all computers for which the software is compatible to access it, at a relatively low cost, whenever desired. Suppose an organization has 300 PCs that all use the same application program. It would be much cheaper and more efficient to have all these computers access one program rather than purchasing 300 separate software packages, one for each computer. Moreover, users can share input and output devices as well as software. A facility with 10 PCs may be able to share as few as four printers with no loss of productivity.

With connectivity we can share not only hardware and software resources, but information as well. Large databases with vast amounts of information in a variety of subject areas can be shared by people with access to a network.

The *information superhighway* is a term used to describe an integrated network that will someday enable everyone to access these databases. The *Internet* is an integrated network that currently provides some of this capability.

Figure 1.7 *Some networks enable users within one organization to share information and other resources. Other networks, like those that are used by stock exchanges, enable brokers and organizations throughout the world to access information.*

The Human Factor: People and Computing

We have seen that computer systems operate under the control of software, which provides the necessary instructions for entering data, for processing the data and converting it into information, and for displaying or printing output. Connectivity enables computer systems to share hardware and software resources as well as databases, for greater productivity.

But information resources must be controlled by people. Because information processing procedures differ depending on each application, people—users and computer professionals—must determine an organization's computing needs, implement and control information systems, and supervise the overall computing process. **Systems analysts** are the computer professionals within an organization who are responsible for developing business information systems. Systems analysts work closely with programmers and other computer professionals to develop computerized systems, but they need the help of computer users to guide them through the development phase.

The first goal in computerizing business systems is understanding user needs. Among the computer users in business who require effective information systems to perform their jobs are:

- Managers, who analyze information in order to make decisions. An executive may depend on a profit/loss statement, for example, to decide whether a price increase for a product is warranted.

- Operating staff, who use computers to perform day-to-day tasks, such as billing, answering customer inquiries, and so on.

- Data entry operators, who interact directly with a computer to update the information in a business system. Tellers in banks and cashiers in stores perform data entry operations. See Figure 1.8.

Figure 1.8 *Data entry operators, like those who work for the Internal Revenue Service, key data into computers. Some IRS offices process tens of thousands of income tax returns a day.*

Critical Thinking

How can a computer improve the quality of life? How might it diminish the quality of life?

IN A NUTSHELL

To be useful, information must be current, complete, accurate, and meaningful.

Ideally, systems analysts, programmers and computer users at all levels work together exchanging knowledge and ideas. Computer users must communicate what they need from the system. Systems analysts and programmers must help users understand what they can reasonably expect from the system. Computerizing business systems is a process that begins and ends with computer users.

Computer users and professionals must also be socially responsible. That is, they have an obligation to ensure that computing resources are used in an ethical way—that the privacy of individuals in the company is protected, for example. Social responsibility also means that we should all work toward ensuring that computers enhance the quality of life for every individual.

The Pros of Computing

Organizations spend a great deal of time and money designing, developing, implementing, and maintaining information systems so that they will be effective in providing essential management support. In addition to the costs of hardware, software, and networks there are organizational costs such as those for training users, upgrading systems, and supplying technical support—hidden costs that sometimes constitute the bulk of the total information processing expenses in an organization! Despite these costs, organizations continue to use computers because of the significant benefits they provide. Here are five reasons for using computers:

COMPUTERS ARE FAST Most modern computers process data in speeds measured in billionths of a second, called nanoseconds. Some computers can process hundreds of thousands of data items and perform millions of calculations in seconds or minutes.

COMPUTERS ARE ACCURATE Electronic technology is so precise that when a computer is programmed correctly and when input is entered properly, the accuracy of the output is virtually guaranteed. This is not to say that output from a computer is always correct; rather, when inaccuracies occur, most often they are the result of human error—incorrect input or a programming error—and rarely the result of a computer error.

Looking Ahead

THE INFORMATION SUPERHIGHWAY

People talk about the information superhighway, but few understand where this highway will go or what the rules of the road will be. We believe that the past is the best predictor for the future.

If information and other resources are to be widely available over a superhighway network, development of such a network is likely to take its course like technologies that preceded it. Like computers themselves, as well as fax and copy machines, the highway will probably make stops at businesses where the need is greatest, before it makes stops at every home in the United States. Eventually it will reach each home, but only when the demand is strong enough to make it economically feasible.

The technical capability to connect every computer user in the United States exists today. But remember cable TV, which was tech-nologically feasible long before it became economically practical? It took 20 years for cable TV to become commonplace—it is still far from ubiquitous. Even today, home shopping and pay-per-view movies are widely available, yet relatively few homes take advantage of them. Sometimes we have the technological capabilities to achieve a goal, but the demand or need for the product is not yet sufficient. Interconnectivity via an information superhighway has great potential for improving the quality of our lives—but the road must first be paved—all the rules of the road must be in place before we will have a smooth ride. Major issues such as what will be the mode of communication (telephone, TV, or some combination) are still to be resolved.

COMPUTERS OFFER COMPACT STORAGE Data and information previously stored in a room full of file cabinets can be stored compactly on computer media in a fraction of the space. See Figure 1.9. Moreover, data can be retrieved from storage quickly and in a variety of useful forms.

COMPUTERS ARE ECONOMICAL The overall cost of computers for large applications is often far less than the cost of manual systems. In fact, many of today's business and industrial application areas such as oil exploration, genetic research, and airline reservations systems would not even be feasible manually. The computations required would be too expensive or too time consuming.

COMPUTERS HAVE INTANGIBLE BENEFITS The benefits of information processing often exceed the tangible gains of greater speed and lower cost. Intangible benefits are hard to measure but easy to demonstrate. For example, the quality of computer-produced information may improve the decision-making process and speed the flow of information through an organization. Such benefits can enhance the company's reputation or improve its service by helping employees respond more quickly to customer requests and questions, provide better quality control, and improve the overall delivery of goods and services. See Figure 1.10.

Smart devices can improve the quality of life. On another level, computers in the home and the workplace have the potential to improve the overall qual-

Figure 1.9 *Most organizations use disks of all sizes to store data. A single CD (compact disk) can store 680+ million characters, the equivalent of 340,000 pages of information.*

Figure 1.10 *Sometimes computers are used to perform tasks that would be nearly impossible to perform manually because the cost would be prohibitive. Shown here is the use of computers to control a nuclear facility.*

Figure 1.11 *Computers can help the visually impaired to read and write.*

ity of life in our society. Consider these examples. "Smart" devices with built-in computers can be programmed to maximize energy efficiency and can be controlled by a standard Touch-Tone phone, remote control unit, or a PC. Smart appliances like VCRs and microwaves make day-to-day jobs in the home easier as well. Smart cars make driving safer.

The disabled have benefited greatly from computer technology. Computer scanners convert printed text to verbal output or to Braille for the visually impaired; similarly, telephones and other voice recognition equipment convert speech to printed or displayed output for the hearing impaired. Computerized components in pacemakers, artificial limbs, and other medical wonders have not only improved the quality of life for some people but extended their lives as well. See Figure 1.11.

Avoiding the Cons of Computing

Despite their advantages, computers sometimes prove dissatisfying to users. Hardware and software incompatibility is one reason, although connectivity is helping to alleviate that problem. Another reason for dissatisfaction is too much or too little information, or information that is simply not useful—such as outdated sales figures, inaccurate billing dates, or a listing of client ZIP codes when what is needed is client phone numbers.

Users and computer professionals can work together to overcome most cons of computing. The secret is communication. Users must understand what they reasonably can expect a program or an information system to do, and they must be able to convey their computing needs to the professionals who develop or select computing resources. Professionals must understand what is most important to users, for example, how often sales figures need updating, how to catch billing errors before they are processed, or what data the system should be collecting.

Working together, users and professionals can minimize compatibility problems and overcome the drawbacks of useless information, poorly developed systems, and user resistance to computing, by focusing on the six steps that follow.

MINIMIZE PROGRAMMING AND INPUT ERRORS Computer systems should be designed to minimize downtime, or breakdowns, and information systems should be designed to minimize errors. Both machine breakdowns and errors in processing damage a company's relations with customers and make employees' work more difficult. Mistakes occur as a result of input errors, programming errors, and poor management of the computer system.

Most "computer errors" result from input mistakes. Users and data entry operators need to check the data they enter into the computer to make sure that it is relatively free of errors. Moreover, programmers should include tests in their programs that check input for accuracy. For example, programs can test to ensure that paycheck amounts are within an established range and that birth dates or transaction dates are reasonable. Finally, computer managers need to institute procedures to minimize computer errors.

PROVIDE ADEQUATE CONTROLS AND PROPER SECURITY Security is a major issue in information systems. Computer software and critical data need protection from natural disasters such as fire, flood, and earthquakes, as well as from people who are not authorized to access these resources. Computers are sometimes used as tools for white-collar crime or even for revenge. Computer **hackers** who are unauthorized users make news when they penetrate huge networked systems with schemes that overwork the system or destroy programs or data. The resulting errors and computer failures could be avoided if the computer system and its resources were made more secure.

As the number of computer users continues to grow, the need for proper control and security measures increases dramatically. Networks like the Internet that provide access to users around the world are at great risk. To maintain the integrity of programs and data, users and computer professionals must work together to prevent unauthorized access to their systems and data.

GET USERS MORE INVOLVED IN SYSTEMS DEVELOPMENT One main reason that computers fail to satisfy user needs is poor communication. Either users do not understand an information system's limitations and potential, or systems analysts do not fully understand user needs. Poor communication sometimes results in computer phobia; that is, people fear computers and do not trust the output produced by them. Initially, those fears were coupled with the concern that computers would produce mass unemployment. But the evidence has shown that more jobs are generated by computers than are lost by them, except in certain areas such as automated factories. When computers generate growth in a company, more labor is needed to operate the computer and to develop the information systems.

People who have negative feelings about computing can benefit from a better understanding of what computers can accomplish and how problems can be minimized. Employees should learn, for example, that some of the tedious tasks they currently perform manually are apt to be tasks easily performed by computing. Effective training programs also help users work more efficiently with computers. Here are three ways to get users more involved in what we call **systems development,** which consists of designing and implementing information systems:

Involve Users in Planning. Users are apt to resist a computerized system if they did not work with the systems analysts and programmers in its design. Without the cooperation of users, information systems will almost always fail to meet expectations.

Be Sure Development Goals Are Realistic. In their enthusiasm, computer professionals may underestimate the time and resources needed to build an information system and fail to provide for unanticipated delays and obstacles.

•••••➤ **Looking Ahead**

HACKERS GO LEGIT

The word *hacker* has gone through many meanings. Once it was an honorable term referring to a superior programmer or hardware designer. But in 1983 the movie *War Games* presented the hacker as someone who breaks into computer systems for fun. Even today, some find the challenge of breaking into systems and networks irresistible. A few make their living breaking into systems in order to show business executives the weak points in their information systems and then, for a fee, develop techniques for making the systems more secure. New terms for *hacker* are *cyberpunk* or *cracker.*

Critical Thinking

What are some other reasons why people have negative feelings about computers? What can be done to overcome these feelings?

Such overoptimism can create difficulties for users working within a fixed budget and a projected schedule.

Address Employee Concerns. Many people in organizations resist using computers because they are concerned about invasion of their privacy. A computerized payroll system that contains salary information may be accessible to so many users that many employees fear their privacy is being violated. Medical information for insurance purposes may also be widely available, and an employee's personal health records may be compromised. Employees are also concerned about loss of jobs or physical and mental strain caused by computers. For employees to cooperate in the design and use of computers, they must feel confident that accepted business procedures are being properly followed and that their needs and concerns will be addressed.

MINIMIZE INFORMATION OVERLOAD (MORE IS NOT NECESSARILY BETTER) One result of computerization in many organizations is the proliferation of information and a consequent overload of output, usually in the form of paper. Providing users with a great deal of information may seem a worthwhile goal, but it may, in fact, prove more a burden than a blessing. The objective of computing is to provide meaningful and timely information that users need to perform day-to-day tasks and to help them make decisions. Giving users more than they need can be as ineffective as giving them less than they need.

One of the original objectives of bringing computers into organizations was to achieve the "paperless office"—to virtually eliminate paper documents or at least to significantly minimize them. That goal has yet to be realized. Indeed, far more paper is generated now than before. The business world reports using more than three trillion pages a year! When people have a great deal of information at their fingertips, they are apt to want to capture it on paper, which is not always the best form of output. See Figure 1.12.

The objective of reducing paper in the office is an important one. The technology exists to dramatically decrease the amount of paper generated. As users continue to realize the drawbacks of information overload, output in paper form is likely to be reduced.

PROMOTE AND DEVELOP COMPUTING STANDARDS Because the computing industry changes so rapidly, there are few established standards. As we have seen, computer systems and software within the same office may be incompati-

Figure 1.12 *(a) More is not necessarily better when generating printed output. (b) Sometimes a picture is worth more than a thousand words. The objective is to provide users with the right amount of information to do their jobs.*

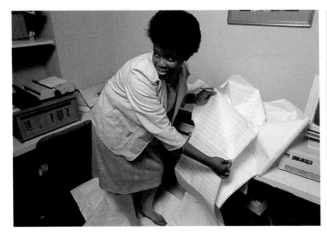

ble, which means they cannot be shared. Some input/output devices can be used only with specific types of computers. Similarly, some software works only on certain types of computers. Even networked software and hardware are not always usable with all types of systems and with all types of programs. Computer professionals and users must work together to promote the need for standards in hardware, software, and connectivity. This is another example of people acting responsibly to ensure effective computing.

INSIST ON COMPLETE AND ACCURATE DOCUMENTATION Hardware, software, and systems that are properly developed are easier to use and maintain. But in the final analysis, the effectiveness of information depends on adequate documentation. User manuals should be clear, complete, and accurate. Information systems are virtually useless if no one knows how to effectively use them.

Self-Test

1. (T or F) When information systems are being developed, it is best to provide users with as much output information as possible in the belief that they will ultimately need all they can get.

2. _____ is a concept that enables different computers to share hardware and software, even if the computers are not compatible.

3. Two basic categories of people who work with computers are _____ and _____ .

4. Computer errors are most often caused by _____ and _____ .

5. (T or F) Computer professionals can more efficiently and effectively perform their jobs if they work independently to generate an information system and then show users how to work with it.

▬ 1.3 COMPUTING IN THE INFORMATION AGE

Our objective in this book is to help you become more proficient in computing, and that involves both showing you how to use computers and increasing your understanding of the elements of computing: hardware, software, connectivity, and people. To assist you in thinking critically about how these elements are related, we focus throughout this book on the ways in which computing affects our lives now and will continue to affect us in the future.

Study Objective

3. Demonstrate how information processing has been revolutionized by computers.

Solutions

1. F—This can be as ineffective as giving users less than they need.

2. Connectivity

3. computer users; computer professionals (systems analysts and programmers)

4. input errors; program errors

5. F—Users and computer professionals must work closely together.

Hardware Happenings: Computers Make the World Smaller and Smarter

Initially, computer systems were the size of large rooms. The trend, however, is toward smaller computing devices with greater power. Today, a PC that fits in the palm of your hand has computing power hundreds of times that of the first electronic computers.

The ability of tiny computing devices to control complex operations has transformed the way many tasks are performed, ranging from scientific research to producing consumer products. Tiny "computers on a chip" are used in medical equipment, home appliances, cars, and toys. Workers use handheld computing devices to collect data at a customer site, to generate forms, to control inventory, and to serve as desktop organizers.

Not only is computing equipment getting smaller, it is getting more sophisticated. Computers are part of many machines and devices that once required continual human supervision and control. Today, computers in security systems result in safer environments, computers in cars improve energy efficiency, and computers in phones provide features such as call forwarding, call monitoring, and call answering.

These smart machines are designed to take over some of the basic tasks previously performed by people; by so doing, they make life a little easier and a little more pleasant. Smart cards store vital information such as health records, drivers' licenses, bank balances, and so on. Smart phones, cars, and appliances with built-in computers can be programmed to better meet individual needs. A smart house has a built-in monitoring system that can turn lights on and off, open and close windows, operate the oven, and more. See Figure 1.13.

In this book we highlight hardware happenings that help computers make the world smaller and smarter. Look for the hardware icon (*shown at left*) that appears at various places in the text. It means that the topic being discussed focuses on hardware happenings.

Figure 1.13 *The homeowner can control lighting, security, sprinklers, climate, and various electrical circuits in a smart house by simply selecting entries from a screen.*

Figure 1.14 *This expert system provides diagnostic testing of an automobile.*

Software Sensations: Computers Make the World More Creative

With small computing devices available for performing smart tasks like cooking dinner, programming the VCR, and controlling the flow of information in an organization, people are able to spend more time doing what they often do best—being creative. Computers can help people work more creatively.

In this book we highlight the ways in which computers are making our world more creative. **Multimedia** systems are software sensations known for their educational and entertainment value—which we call edutainment. Multimedia combines text with sound, video, animation, and graphics, which greatly enhances the interaction between user and machine and can make information more interesting and appealing to people. Multimedia encyclopedias, for example, might contain written material on a subject such as John F. Kennedy along with an audio clip of his inaugural address and a video clip of his funeral cortege. **Expert systems** software is another sensation that enables computers to "think" like experts. See Figure 1.14. Medical diagnosis expert systems, for example, can help doctors pinpoint a patient's illness, suggest further tests, and prescribe appropriate drugs. Look for the software icon (*shown at right*) for topics that focus on how software sensations can expand your creative powers.

Information Interchange: Computers Make the World More Connected

Connectivity enables computers and software that might otherwise be incompatible to communicate and to share resources. Now that computers are proliferating in many areas and networks are available for people to access data and communicate with others, personal computers are becoming *inter*personal PCs. They have the potential to significantly improve the way we relate to each other. Many people today **telecommute**—that is, use their computers to stay in touch with the office while they are working at home. With the proper tools, a hospital staff can get a diagnosis from a medical expert hundreds or thousands of

Critical Thinking

Are employers justified in their fears about telecommuting? Does telecommuting have any potential disadvantages for workers in terms of their quality of life?

Figure 1.15 *Teleconferencing enables health care professionals to offer their opinions on cases where the patient and the test results are at a remote location.*

miles away. See Figure 1.15. Similarly, the disabled can communicate more effectively with others using computers.

Distance learning and videoconferencing are concepts made possible with the use of an electronic classroom or boardroom accessible to people in remote locations. Vast databases of information are currently available to 20 million users of the Internet, the global network accessible to businesses, universities, governments, and home users, all of whom can send mail messages to each other. The information superhighway is designed to significantly expand this interactive connectivity so that people all over the world will have free access to all these resources. Look for the interactive icon (*shown at left*) to see how information interchanges help computers bring the world closer together.

People Power: Computer Users Make the World a Better Place

People power is critical to ensuring that hardware, software, and connectivity are effectively integrated in a socially responsible way. Computers used in social, political, cultural, environmental, and global applications have the potential to significantly affect the quality of people's lives. People—computer users and computer professionals—are the ones who will decide which hardware, software, and networks endure and how great an impact they will have on our lives. They should help to ensure that individual needs are met and that individual rights such as the right to privacy are maintained. Users and professionals must work together to ensure that any adverse physical effects of computer work such as wrist or eye strain are minimized. Ethical, legal, and global issues must be considered. Ultimately people power must be exercised to ensure that computers are used not only efficiently but in a socially responsible way. Look for the people icon (*shown at left*) for discussions of these types of issues.

Self-Test

1. (T or F) Miniature computers are often used in home appliances, cars, and toys.

2. (T or F) Computers are often used in machines to control and supervise tasks.

3. (T or F) A smart machine such as a smart phone is typically one that has a built-in computer.

4. Multimedia incorporates _____ in conveying information.

5. To bring the world closer together, computers must be able to _____ .

CHAPTER SUMMARY

When computer systems were first used for information processing, the Information Age began. Anyone who has gone to school or to work in the past decade already is, to some degree, **computer literate** and may also be a computer **user.** Chapter 1 describes computing basics and computer **applications.**

1.1 Introducing Computer Systems: Input-Process-Output

Computers read incoming **data**—raw facts—as **input, process** these raw facts into meaningful **information,** and produce **output. Information processing** techniques vary depending on the application area. Today, small, powerful **personal computers (PCs)** allow any computer user access to information from larger computers.

Computer systems operate under the control of **programs** or **software. Input devices** accept data from the user and store it in main memory. The **CPU** transforms input data into information, which is produced for the user via **output devices. Storage devices** hold programs, data, and information on **disk** for later use. The set of computer devices in a system is called the **hardware.** Large or small, specially **configured** or not, all computer systems operate in basically the same way: input-process-output. The real differences among computer systems relate to their relative size, cost, and processing power.

Computers are **stored-program devices.** Professional computer programmers write sets of programs for any user need. This software, available on disk, comes in two forms. **Operating systems software** controls computer operations through an **operating system,** such as **DOS** for IBM-compatible PCs, and communicates with users via a user interface. **User-friendly** graphical interfaces with **icons,** such as **Windows,** have become more popular than text-based interfaces.

Application programs for specific information processing tasks may be **packaged** for retail sale or **custom** designed for a unique need. **Productivity tools** are application programs used to perform day-to-day business tasks and

> **Study Objective**
>
> 1. Explain how computers process data to produce information.

Solutions

1. T

2. T

3. T

4. graphics, video, animation, and sound

5. share resources or communicate with one another

to assist users in decision making. Packaged programs usually provide users with comprehensive reference manuals called **documentation.**

Software and hardware **incompatibility** is a major issue in the computing industry. Smart computer users select their software before they decide on their hardware.

1.2 Understanding Information Processing

In organizations, computer systems automate information processing for major **business systems**—accounting, human resources, production, and marketing. Hardware and software enable employees to work more productively, search for information faster, and analyze results better.

Connectivity enables even incompatible software and hardware to share information and resources through the use of a communications **network.**

People control the entire computing process. Computer users at all levels depend on effective information systems to do their jobs. When user needs change, computer professionals—programmers and **systems analysts** among them—modify existing business systems or create new ones in the continuing cycle of **systems development.**

There are many reasons for developing computerized information systems. Computers are fast, accurate, and economical. Computer systems can store vast amounts of information in a compact space, and computing offers tangible and intangible benefits, such as improved productivity and better quality control.

To eliminate or minimize the cons of computing, users and computer professionals work to improve communication. To ensure effective systems development, users must understand what to expect from computerized information processing; professionals must understand users' information needs. Other techniques to avoid the cons of computing include correcting errors in programming or incoming data; providing system security against natural disasters or unauthorized use by **hackers** or others; avoiding information overload; promoting computing standards; and insisting on complete, accurate documentation.

1.3 Computing in the Information Age

To be proficient in computing, you need to develop your skills in using systems and software, and you also need to understand the basic concepts behind hardware, software, and connectivity, and the people who use them. This book explains how these components of computing interrelate and why computers are making the world smaller, smarter, more creative, and more interconnected.

In just two generations, computers moved from the laboratory to the dormitory, home, and office. Even smaller and more powerful personal computers can be carried in a briefcase or pocket while larger computers bring the entire world to your fingertips. **Telecommuting** enables people with computers to stay in touch with their office while at home.

Smart cars, telephones, and children's toys are just the beginning. One day you will use smart cards as money and come home to a smart house. Smart computing devices take some of the drudgery out of work and make life a little easier.

With smart devices at work, you are free to be more creative with your time. Software sensations expand your creativity, no matter what field interests you, personally or professionally, as the potential of **expert systems** and **multimedia** illustrate.

Connectivity brings computing resources to organizations and individuals. As interpersonal machines, PCs have the potential to bring vast databases of

Study Objective

2. Describe why organizations use computers for information processing.

Study Objective

3. Demonstrate how information processing has been revolutionized by computers.

information to the desktop. Computer networks on a global scale help businesses and nations meet their needs for information.

People power is the element necessary for ensuring that computers are used in a socially responsible way that helps to improve our lives. It is the thread that ties hardware, software, and connectivity together.

KEY TERMS

Application, *p. 5*
Application software, *p. 8*
Business system, *p. 11*
Central processing unit (CPU), *p. 6*
Computer literate, *p. 5*
Computer system, *p. 6*
Configured, *p. 6*
Connectivity, *p. 12*
Custom program, *p. 9*
Data, *p. 5*
Disk, *p. 8*
Documentation, *p. 10*
DOS, *p. 9*
Expert system, *p. 21*
Hacker, *p. 17*

Hardware, *p. 6*
Icon, *p. 9*
Incompatibility, *p. 9*
Information, *p. 5*
Information processing, *p. 5*
Input, *p. 5*
Input device, *p. 6*
Multimedia, *p. 21*
Network, *p. 12*
Operating system, *p. 9*
Operating systems software, *p. 8*
Output, *p. 5*
Output device, *p. 6*
Packaged program, *p. 9*
Personal computer (PC), *p. 5*

Processing, *p. 5*
Productivity tool, *p. 10*
Program, *p. 6*
Programmer, *p. 8*
Software, *p. 6*
Storage device, *p. 6*
Stored-program device, *p. 8*
Systems analyst, *p. 13*
Systems development, *p. 17*
Telecommuting, *p. 21*
User, *p. 5*
User-friendly, *p. 9*
Windows, *p. 9*

CHAPTER SELF-TEST

1. Incoming data, or raw facts, is called _____ and information produced by a computer is called _____ .

2. The computer device that actually manipulates and operates on input to produce output is called the _____ .

3. The set of instructions that specifies what operations a computer is to perform is called a _____ .

4. Data and programs are typically stored on _____ for future use.

5. Name an operating system for an IBM-compatible personal computer.

6. Application programs that can be purchased ready to use are called _____ .

7. Telecommuting enables workers to use computers at _____ .

8. Two computer systems that cannot run the same software are said to be _____ .

9. A _____ enables computers to share hardware and software resources.

10. The computer professional responsible for systems development is called the _____ .

11. (T or F) Information is processed to produce data that is meaningful, timely, and accurate.

12. (T or F) Operating systems software supervises the overall operations of the computer system.

13. (T or F) An icon is a type of packaged program.
14. (T or F) Computer programs are known as software.
15. (T or F) Documentation should include guidelines for using a program.

REVIEW QUESTIONS

1. List the basic hardware components of a computer system and briefly describe each.

2. Describe the two basic types of software.

3. Explain the term *connectivity* and describe why it is so important in computing.

4. Why is compatibility important and how does that issue relate to computer industry standards?

CRITICAL THINKING EXERCISES

1. Brigham and Women's Hospital decided to automate its clinical functions to help it provide better care to its patients and reduce costs at the same time. The hospital installed a large network using over 3,300 microcomputers with 120 file servers. A key feature of the custom-designed application software tells doctors when they have prescribed medication that can cause bad reactions if taken with previously prescribed medications. The software also reports the quantity of tests ordered for a patient to help doctors reduce patient costs. The hospital has placed microcomputers in obstetrics and rheumatology examining rooms so doctors can easily recall a patient's medical history and save paper costs.[1]

[1]*Source: Forbes,* April 11, 1994, v153, n8, pS114(4).

Solutions

1. input; output

2. central processing unit (CPU)

3. program or software

4. disk (or another storage medium)

5. DOS or OS/2 (Windows 3.1 is *not* an operating system, but a graphical user interface for DOS; Windows 95 is a full operating system.)

6. application packages

7. home or anywhere away from the office

8. incompatible

9. network

10. systems analyst

11. F—Data is processed and information is produced.

12. T

13. F—It is a graphic symbol on a screen that represents a file or command that can be selected.

14. T

15. T

What are the potential social benefits of such automation? What are the potential disadvantages? How can the benefits be maximized and the disadvantages minimized?

2. Video games are often a person's first exposure to computers. But many people believe that video games are, in general, sexist. Most are marked by fierce warriors and fearless adventurers, with very few heroines. One sociologist who studied these games and their impact on female children found that there were only two types of heroines—"macho" women who act like their macho male counterparts and pretty females in distress who want to be rescued. Both strength and femininity are rarely characteristic of females in video games.

Do you think that these types of video games are likely to have a negative impact on young children, particularly females?

3. Computer systems are like automobiles. To use either, you need not know, in detail, how each component works. In what other ways are computers like automobiles? Think about (1) the reasons why people buy new cars and (2) how manufacturers often tout their products as being unique, when most devices operate in a similar manner.

4. Give some examples of how computers have significantly improved our quality of life. Also give some examples of how computer use has had serious adverse effects on people. Indicate how those adverse effects could have been avoided. Use newspaper or magazine articles for reference if necessary.

Case Study

Multimedia Puts on a Good Show

Can computing help a city get chosen as an Olympic site? Atlanta officials would say yes. They give much of the credit for being selected to host the 1996 Summer Olympics to the multimedia extravaganza they put on for the Olympic selection committee.

Multimedia, a new technology for personal computers, combines text, graphics, animation, high-quality video images, and audio to make presentations, to provide training, and for traditional game playing. With special navigational tools for viewing multimedia presentations, users can interact directly with the program.

Atlanta's program shows the impact multimedia can have on marketing. Developed with the help of the Georgia Institute of Technology, the multimedia presentation program provided the Olympics selection committee with an electronic tour of the city, complete with sights and sounds. The interactive feature enabled the judges to ask questions that were immediately answered on the video screen.

Multimedia is an ideal presentation and educational tool. It has been shown to increase information retention from 20 to 80 percent over simple text presentations. American Airlines uses multimedia to train or retrain thousands of employees in ticketing, cargo, and security procedures.

Some software developers believe the future of multimedia is in the consumer market, potentially as a rival to television. Where the TV viewer is passive, the multimedia viewer is active. Users navigate around presentations and even interact with them, techniques that are not possible with TV. For home reference, Microsoft, the developer of IBM DOS and Windows, publishes a dictionary that pronounces words; a book of quotations that features authors reading their works; an analysis of Beethoven's Ninth Symphony, complete with music; and a critical evaluation of major art works, with visual reproductions.

With so many possible applications, why isn't multimedia more widely used? The main problem is the price: to be effectively used for multimedia, a computer system must be fast and have a very large storage capacity. Relatively expensive audio and video hardware and sophisticated software are needed to synchronize images and sound. Another problem with multimedia, as with so many other computing products, is a lack of standards.

As computer manufacturers vie for a share of the multimedia market, prices have decreased. The Apple Macintosh has been the forerunner in multimedia, but IBM-

Multimedia kiosks like the one illustrated here are used to provide consumers with information. The presentations are interactive, enabling users to request the specific type of information they want. The presentations often incorporate videos, graphics, sound, and animation along with text.

compatibles and Power PCs are catching up. Today, you can purchase a full multimedia system for under $2,000.

Analysis

1. How might multimedia be used as a presentation or teaching tool for business, education, or home use?

2. Besides price, describe three basic differences between multimedia and TV presentations.

3. Can you think of any reasons not mentioned in this case why people may be reluctant to use multimedia resources?

CHAPTER 2
From Micros to Mammoths

2.1 CLASSIFYING COMPUTER SYSTEMS

Types of Computers

Processing Power

2.2 GETTING TO KNOW YOUR HARDWARE

Mainframes

Minis and Midrange Computers

Supercomputers

Microcomputer Categories

The Apple Macintosh, IBM-compatibles, and Power PCs

Multitasking on Micros vs Multiprogramming on Larger
Computers

2.3 CHOOSING AND USING COMPUTER SYSTEMS

Information Processing Environments

The Human Factor in Information Processing: Users and
Computer Professionals

The Right Time to Buy

A re the small personal computers you encounter in your daily life *really* similar to the computers the U.S. government uses to manage the enormous federal tax system? The answer is yes. Computers consist of these basic components: input devices; main memory and a central processing unit; output devices; and storage devices that store programs and data on media such as disk. All types of computers have these basic components and all process data in essentially the same way. The desktop PC and larger computer systems that require a full room (or more) for their components use the same basic instructions for processing data.

Study Objectives

Chapter 2 covers the fundamentals of hardware, computer processing, and connectivity. After completing this chapter, you should be able to:

1. Distinguish between different types of computers.

2. Describe how application areas govern the choice of hardware.

3. Outline what users need to know about hardware and connectivity.

▊ 2.1 CLASSIFYING COMPUTER SYSTEMS

Types of Computers

Study Objective

1. Distinguish between different types of computers.

All computers (1) use input devices to read data into main memory, (2) have a CPU that actually operates on the data in main memory, (3) have output devices that print, display, or otherwise create meaningful information for users, and (4) have storage media for holding programs and data for future processing. But computers vary in characteristics such as size, power, and cost. There are four widely used categories for classifying computers. We list them here, from largest to smallest:

1. **Supercomputers.** When it comes to speed, power, and size, supercomputers are the fastest, largest, and costliest of computer systems. They are used mostly in scientific and industrial research, by the government, and by very large organizations for controlling their networks. Some supercomputers can process data from more than 10,000 users at once. A typical supercomputer costs a million dollars or more.

2. **Mainframes.** The first computers used in business, beginning in the early 1950s, were mainframes. In mid-sized and large companies today, mainframes remain widely used computer systems. They occupy entire rooms and often are available to hundreds or even thousands of users who work at input/output devices called **terminals,** which are located at sites away from the main computer's location. See Figure 2.1. Mainframes are very large and powerful computer systems, but they are often so expensive that companies lease them rather than purchase them outright. They typically cost hundreds of thousands of dollars.

3. **Minicomputers.** Known also as **midrange computers,** minicomputers (or minis), stand midway between micros and larger computers in size, power, and cost. Minis were specifically created as **multiuser systems**—systems that can be shared by many users who access the system using PCs or terminals.

Figure 2.1 *A terminal can be any input/output device not at the same site as the main computer, but most often it is a keyboard/screen device or a PC.*

For example, all the employees in a small business or a single department within a larger company can use a single mini or midrange system for the bulk of their computing needs. That mini or midrange system can function independently or it can be linked to a larger mainframe or supercomputer. These systems range in price from $20,000 to $250,000.

4. **Microcomputers.** PCs, also called micros, are used mainly by one individual at a time and are the smallest, least powerful, and least expensive computer systems. They allow users to increase their productivity with the use of application software or by communicating electronically with larger systems. PCs range in price from hundreds of dollars to thousands of dollars.

● ●➤ *Looking Ahead*

CLIENT-SERVER COMPUTING

The trend in computing today is to have PC power on the desktop for every employee who needs one. Desktop PCs are used in two main ways: (1) as productivity tools and (2) as devices in a network with access to the organization's software and databases and to external databases as well. When PCs operate on data and programs that are stored on a shared central computer, we refer to this as **client-server computing.** The network's central computer or **file server** provides PCs with access to software and hardware and monitors usage of resources.

Because client-server computing provides a method for PC users to maximize the resources available to them, it has become a common method of processing in business and in education. Applications once relegated to larger systems are now performed on PCs in a client-server environment. As a result, many organizations are **downsizing**—using PCs and minis for applications that were previously mainframe-based.

A file server—the central computer in a client-server network—can itself be a PC, as is typically the case in small student labs. Or, where vast databases need to be accessed, the file server could be a mini, mainframe, or even supercomputer. So large computers are not fading away—they are simply assuming new roles. Because the term *downsizing* may signal to some the demise of the large computer, many organizations today say they are *rightsizing*—selecting appropriate-sized computers for the tasks at hand.

Because computers of all sizes are becoming more and more powerful, categories such as microcomputer and supercomputer, and all categories in between, are relative. Supercomputers are simply the fastest, most powerful computers currently available, and microcomputers are at the other end of the spectrum. Today's microcomputers can do the work that it took a room-sized mainframe to accomplish two decades ago; today's supercomputer may well be tomorrow's microcomputer.

As the processing power of computers increases, the lines between categories blur further. The applications best handled by each category of computer are likely to change over time.

New names may lead to new categories, just as minis and micros evolved from mainframes. Even though we use four basic categories of computers in this text, we ask you to keep in mind that these are neither explicit nor consistent distinctions and are not likely to stand the test of time.

Processing Power

Although definitive categories do not exist, larger systems are distinguished from smaller ones with respect to the basic factors of size, cost, and processing power. Processing power is related to how much main memory a computer has for

Figure 2.2 *With newer technologies emerging, categorical distinctions among computer systems are becoming increasingly blurred.*

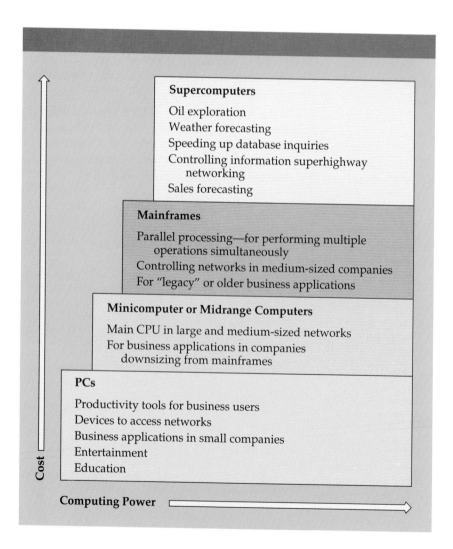

Supercomputers

Oil exploration
Weather forecasting
Speeding up database inquiries
Controlling information superhighway
    networking
Sales forecasting

Mainframes

Parallel processing—for performing multiple
    operations simultaneously
Controlling networks in medium-sized companies
For "legacy" or older business applications

Minicomputer or Midrange Computers

Main CPU in large and medium-sized networks
For business applications in companies
    downsizing from mainframes

PCs

Productivity tools for business users
Devices to access networks
Business applications in small companies
Entertainment
Education

Cost

Computing Power

programs and data, the computer's speed, and the number of input/output devices it can handle. See Figure 2.2. Let us discuss processing power in more depth:

MEMORY SIZE Memory size refers to the primary storage capacity, or **main memory,** available to the CPU. As you work on a computer, each letter, digit, or symbol you enter as data or as part of an instruction is stored in a single storage position called a **byte** of storage.

In larger computers, primary storage capacity is measured in **gigabytes (GB),** or billions of bytes. Today's micros have main memories measured in **megabytes (MB),** or millions of storage positions. In contrast to the latest micros, early PCs had much smaller memories. The main memory of the first Apple and IBM PC computers, for example, was measured in **kilobytes (K),** or thousands of storage positions. Each kilobyte actually equals 1024 bytes, but we typically round a kilobyte to approximately 1000 bytes.

PROCESSING SPEED Processing speed is determined in a number of ways. The speed of the memory and CPU chips is typically measured in **nanoseconds** or billionths of a second for most computers, although the speed of supercomputer chips is faster and can be measured in **picoseconds** or trillionths of a second.

Raw computing power, which factors in both processing speed and memory size, is measured in **MIPS,** or millions of instructions per second. Many PCs operate at 20 to 100 MIPS while mainframes operate at hundreds of MIPS and supercomputers at thousands of MIPS.

There are still other ways to measure processing speed and power. We consider these in Chapter 4. In the end, real power means the ability of the computer to get your jobs done quickly and efficiently.

INPUT/OUTPUT DEVICES (PERIPHERALS) The power of mainframes and supercomputers makes them ideal for large networks and for applications that are shared by many users. Although a PC can use the resources in a mainframe or supercomputer network, microcomputers by themselves are mainly single-user systems. The CPU in most micros is designed to handle one user with one set of input, output, and storage devices or **peripherals,** at any one time. Larger systems can handle multiple users and applications, and can have many more peripherals. Yet micros are basically miniatures of larger systems, and they are the computers that you are most likely to have encountered. Thus, we cover here the basics of computer system peripherals from a PC perspective. Keep in mind that the differences among computer categories are essentially differences of degree with regard to size, cost, and processing power. What is true for micros is likely to be true, on a larger scale, for larger computers.

IN A NUTSHELL

The CPU and main memory are typically stored in a single unit called a *main circuit board.*

IN A NUTSHELL

UNITS OF STORAGE

Byte	One storage position; used to store a character (letter, digit, or symbol), which is part of data or an instruction
Kilobyte (K)	Approximately 1000 storage positions (actually 1024 bytes)
Megabyte (MB)	Approximately 1 million storage positions (actually 1,048,576 bytes)
Gigabyte (GB)	Approximately 1 billion storage positions (actually 1,073,741,824 bytes)

Figure 2.3 *A PC typically has a keyboard, mouse, monitor, printer, disk drives, and a modem, which can be a separate external device or built into the computer. Most newer multimedia computers also have a CD-ROM drive, internal sound board, and speakers.*

Figure 2.4 *Color printers are often used to produce graphs and documents.*

A common input device for PCs and larger systems is the **keyboard,** designed like a typewriter but with additional specialized keys. In many systems, keyboarding is combined with the use of a pointing device, or **mouse.** Both a keyboard and a mouse enable users to enter data and execute instructions. The data entered is visible on the computer **monitor,** a video screen that looks like a television. The monitor displays both input data and instructions, as well as computer responses; it can also display output information. See Figure 2.3.

The majority of PC users want to get their information on paper—a report for school, a bill for services, or the family budget. Most output for larger systems—paychecks, inventory reports, sales forecasts—is paper output too. The most common output device is the **printer,** which can print words and pictures on paper in black and white or color. See Figure 2.4.

PC users store their software and data on magnetic disks that fit into a computer's **disk drives.** Magnetic disks come in many sizes. They may be portable, flexible **floppy disks,** rigid **hard disks** mounted permanently in a disk drive, or removable disk cartridges. Hard disks and disk cartridges have much greater storage capacities than floppy disks, also called **diskettes.** The most frequently used floppy disk is 3½ inches in diameter, but older 5¼-inch disks are still used. The latter type is less durable and has a storage capacity of up to 1.2 MB, while 3½-inch disks are more popular and have storage capacities from 1.44 MB to 2.88 MB or more. Portable compact disks with 680+ MB of storage are also used to store data and programs as are microflopticals with 22+ MB storage capacity. We discuss all forms of disk storage in depth in Chapter 6. We will also be discussing multimedia computers that have sound boards and speakers to generate music, verbal messages, and other sounds.

A device called a **modem** connects the computer system by cable to a standard telephone jack. With a modem, signals from one computer can be transmitted to another over telephone lines. The modem may be built into the computer, as shown in Figure 2.3, or it may be a separate external peripheral connected to the computer by cable.

Special modems called *fax-modems* can also transmit and receive faxes as well as mail messages via computer. With the proper software and a modem, you can communicate with another PC or fax user, with your organization's client-server network, or indeed with people anywhere in the world that have access to the same network as you.

The bigger the system, the bigger its CPU. From minis to supercomputers, larger systems use terminals, which are usually combined keyboard/monitor

IN A NUTSHELL

TOPIC	CHAPTER WHERE YOU'LL FIND IT
CPU	4
Peripherals	5
Storage	6
Connectivity	10

units, as their main input/output device. These larger systems process much greater volumes of data and instructions than do micros. Many other types of peripheral devices are used for high-volume information processing. Often the system must gather data from remote locations far away from the computer system—the drive-in window at a bank branch, the supermarket aisle, even a national park.

Table 2.1 summarizes the four computer categories in order of increasing size, price, and processing power.

Table 2.1 *Categories of Computer Systems*

Micro: *A Gateway personal computer can be used as a stand-alone desktop micro or connected to other machines in a network.*

Mini/midrange: *The VAX is a popular minicomputer manufactured by the Digital Equipment Corporation (DEC).*

Mainframe: *The IBM ES/9000 mainframe is accessible to numerous users with terminals or PCs at remote sites.*

Supercomputer: *The CRAY supercomputer is distinguished by its unique shape and bright colors. The four units shown are processors.*

Category	Micro	Mini/Midrange	Mainframe	Supercomputer
Price range	$500–$10,000	From $20,000 to $250,000	$100,000 or more	$1 million or more
Speed	20–100 MIPS or more	Nanoseconds; hundreds of MIPS	Nanoseconds; hundreds of MIPS	Picoseconds; thousands of MIPS
Memory size	640 K–64 MB or more	Hundreds of megabytes to gigabytes	Dozens of gigabytes	Hundreds of gigabytes or more
Connectivity	Essentially single user; can be networked; high-end PCs may be multiuser systems	Multiuser	Multiuser	Multiuser

Self-Test

1. Which category of computers is the most powerful?
2. Whatever you type on the keyboard will typically be displayed on a _____ .
3. What device enables computers to communicate over telephone lines?
4. What computer medium is most often used for storing data and instructions?

Solutions

1. supercomputers   2. monitor   3. modem or fax-modem   4. disk

2.2 GETTING TO KNOW YOUR HARDWARE

Now we will discuss computer categories in more depth in the sequence in which they were developed. Remember: Computers of all sizes work on the same principle of input-process-output. They differ mainly in cost, size, processing power (speed, memory size, and the number of peripherals)—factors that determine the applications for which each category is best suited. Keep in mind that client-server computing means that resources from larger computers can be shared by smaller ones, subject to the processing capability of the smaller machines.

Mainframes

In the early 1950s the mainframe was the first computer developed for general-purpose use in business. Although downsizing is occurring and the number of mainframes sold each year is decreasing, mainframes remain the primary computers in medium to large companies for processing applications in business areas such as accounting, sales and marketing, production, and human resources.

A mainframe typically costs $100,000 or more, and its main memory, CPU, storage, and input/output devices often occupy a large room. On-site peripherals are connected to the CPU by cables linked beneath an elevated floor in the computer room. Mainframes are operated by a professional computer staff. User needs are handled on a production basis with schedules carefully maintained and controlled. If, for example, payroll checks are prepared by a mainframe, it is likely that a regularly scheduled date and time is allotted for the production run.

Environmental factors such as temperature, humidity, and dust must be carefully set and controlled to keep the mainframe functioning properly. Organizations might expend tens of thousands of dollars to prepare a facility for the hardware and to ensure that the facility is properly monitored. Mainframe computer rooms are usually secured, which means that access is controlled by the computer staff. This minimizes accidents and unauthorized access to equipment, programs, and data.

Mainframes are often used as the central computer or server in organizations that have large client-server networks. In addition to the input/output units located at the same physical site as the CPU, hundreds of remote terminals or PCs may be linked or networked to the mainframe by cables, telephone lines, or other transmission media. The terminals or PCs can be located from within several feet of the CPU to miles away.

Today's mainframes have parallel processors or multiple CPUs that can perform numerous operations all at the same time; this enhances their ability to function as a file server in a client-server network.

Mainframes, in general, as well as most other types of systems, are said to be **upwardly compatible,** which means two things: (1) the higher the model number, the more advanced the computer and (2) any software that can run on a lower model number can also run on a higher number, although the reverse is not necessarily true. An IBM ES/3090, for example, has more capability than an ES/3000. Moreover, any program executable on an ES/3000 will run on an ES/3090, but programs that are used on an ES/3090 may not run on an ES/3000. We will see that the concept of upward compatibility applies to versions of software as well as hardware: Version 2.0 of a software product, for example, is more advanced than 1.0.

Looking Back ◀ ●

WHO INVENTED THE FIRST ELECTRONIC DIGITAL COMPUTER? THE CONTROVERSY RAGES ON

During World War II, the U.S. government was developing new artillery at an unprecedented rate. This created a computational backlog, because the new machines could not be used until range tables were prepared to instruct soldiers how to fire them. Since the calculations necessary for preparing range tables were so extensive, effective use of the weapons was delayed months and sometimes even years. The government was prepared to fund any reasonable project that might speed up the calculations.

At the time, John Mauchly, a physicist at the University of Pennsylvania, had conceived the idea of an electronic digital computer that could perform 5000 additions per second—hundreds of times faster than any existing device. Since the University was already under contract to the government for other war-related work, it was relatively easy to obtain a $500,000 contract for Mauchly's proposed device, called ENIAC, an abbreviation for Electronic Numerical Integrator and Computer. Mauchly became principal consultant on the project, and J. Presper Eckert, Jr., a brilliant young graduate student, became chief engineer.

The ENIAC, developed from 1943 to 1946, was the first electronic digital computer completed in the United States. It was a huge device consisting of 30 units and 18,000 vacuum tubes. Because of its speed and reliability, it resulted in a virtual revolution in the computing field. The accompanying illustration shows some of the units of the ENIAC.

We credit Mauchly and Eckert as co-inventors of the first electronic digital computer completed in the United States, but you may find that other sources claim priority for a different inventor, John Vincent Atanasoff. Priority issues are not easily resolved, and it is often difficult to determine which individuals made the most important contributions. This is so because invention is usually not an isolated act of creativity; rather, it follows an evolutionary path with many significant developments built on one another.

Atanasoff, a mathematical physicist at Iowa State College, developed the Atanasoff-Berry Computer (ABC) in the late 1930s and early 1940s. (Berry was a graduate student who worked with Atanasoff.) The ABC was designed as a special-purpose device that could solve up to 29 simultaneous equations. Atanasoff met Mauchly in 1941 and corresponded with him several times about the ABC. Mauchly even visited Iowa State once to see the model being built.

Although Atanasoff's machine was never fully operational and was designed specifically for solving simultaneous equations,

The ENIAC was the first operational general-purpose computer. Its components are shown here along with some of the people who helped develop it. J. Presper Eckert is in the foreground (left) and John Mauchly is in the center.

many people claim he, not Mauchly, invented the first electronic digital computer.

Atanasoff's claim to priority was strengthened by a lawsuit filed in 1971 by the Honeywell Corporation against Sperry-Univac. In that suit, Honeywell claimed that the ENIAC patent, held in 1971 by Sperry, was invalid because of the prior invention of Atanasoff's ABC machine. Since Honeywell and other computer manufacturers were paying royalties to Sperry for the right to build machines that used ideas intrinsic to the ENIAC, a significant amount of money was at stake. The suit was settled in 1973 when the judge ruled that the ENIAC patent was indeed invalid for numerous reasons, including Atanasoff's prior invention. Thus, from a legal point of view, Atanasoff's device is seen as a precursor to the ENIAC. Historians, however, are divided over the issue; most believe that Atanasoff's influence on ENIAC was minimal and that his device is not really the "first" computer because it was neither a functional machine nor a general-purpose one. What do you think?

Minis and Midrange Computers

In the late 1960s, when mainframes were at their peak and business functions were being widely computerized, many organizations grew dissatisfied with having one central computer for all their needs. The mainframe was often overloaded, so departments had to wait their turn not only for output but for other application areas to be computerized.

Some manufacturers, like the Digital Equipment Corporation (DEC), began to develop minicomputers, which were smaller, less powerful, and less expensive versions of a mainframe that could be used to augment an organization's central computer. Sometimes departments in large companies bought their own minis to help satisfy their individual needs. In the 1970s and 1980s minis and then "superminis" were used extensively either as additions to mainframes or as

Critical Thinking

Some people believe that computer manufacturers place obstacles to compatibility by developing proprietary systems or components that differ slightly from the standard. Why might it be in their interest to do this? What can users do to foster the development of standards for hardware and software so that compatibility problems are minimized?

Figure 2.5 *The AS/400 is called a midrange computer by IBM, but it competes directly with the VAX "supermini" manufactured by DEC.*

IN A NUTSHELL

substitutes for them. An accounts receivable department, for example, might have its own mini for all its information processing needs. In other instances, minis were used to **offload** the mainframe for specific tasks. Offload is a term that means reducing one computer's tasks by having those tasks handled by a second computer. An inventory department might use a mini to provide better control of stock and to make predictions about future needs.

Minicomputer capabilities have continued to increase as their cost has decreased, thereby making them competitive with mainframes in many application areas. Today, a midrange computer, or mini, is essentially a device with the power of a mainframe but smaller and less costly. Note that many people use the terms *midrange* and *mini* as synonyms. See Figure 2.5.

Supercomputers

Supercomputers are the fastest, largest, and costliest computers available. Their speed is in the hundreds to thousands of MIPS range. Supercomputers tend to be used primarily for scientific, "number-crunching" applications at large universities and in weather forecasting, aircraft design, nuclear research, seismic analysis, and the space program. All of those applications require rapid analysis of vast amounts of data. Supercomputers are also used in business environments for controlling very large networks.

THE INFORMATION SUPERHIGHWAY The information superhighway, which will provide computer users all over the world with vast amounts of data from global databases, will be controlled by supercomputers. Prices of these machines are typically several million dollars.

Some manufacturers of large mainframes such as Hitachi, IBM, and Thinking Machines, Inc. build supercomputers. One company, Cray Research, specializes in supercomputers and offers extremely sophisticated hardware and processors. Its best-selling Cray-2 sells for approximately $17 million. At these prices, far more supercomputers are leased than purchased outright.

While mainframes have parallel processors, supercomputers have *massively parallel processors*, which means their numerous CPUs can perform a great number of operations all at the same time. As a result, supercomputers can process data from thousands and even tens of thousands of terminals or remote PCs.

Microcomputer Categories

In the late 1970s and early 1980s, when the first micros were marketed, smaller firms such as Radio Shack, Commodore, Atari, and Apple dominated the market. When the microcomputers produced by these companies became very successful, manufacturers of larger systems like IBM and Hewlett-Packard began to develop micros. Today, there are hundreds of micro manufacturers. Compaq is the current market leader.

Table 2.2 illustrates the main categories of micros. A more in-depth discussion of each type of micro, from largest to smallest, follows.

WORKSTATIONS—THE SUPERMICROS: ARE THEY WORTH THE RISC? A **workstation** is a high-powered supermicro that approaches the processing power of a minicomputer. A workstation can be a multiuser system that can control a small client-server network, or a standalone computer used for creating high-quality graphic images or performing typical business tasks. Supermicro use is increasing as more application software is developed for them.

A workstation or supermicro, then, as you would suspect, is a faster, more expensive version of a standard micro. A standard micro has a large set of complex instructions that it can execute, but surprisingly, many workstations have a *reduced* instruction set. Such a workstation is called a **RISC computer** for

| **Table 2.2** | *Categories of Micros* |

Workstation: *A Silicon Graphics computer.*　**Desktop:** *The desktop computer is still the most popular type of PC.*　**Laptop:** *Laptop computers are often used by people away from the office.*　**Notebook:** *Notebook computers are lightweight and easy to carry.*　**Palmtops and PDAs:** *Palmtop computers and Personal Digital Assistants (PDAs) can be carried in a purse or pocket.*

| | | | Portables | | |
Category	Workstation	Desktop	Laptop	Notebook and Subnotebook	Handheld Personal Digital Assistant (PDA)
Cost	$7,000–$10,000	Hundreds of dollars to $5,000	Hundreds of dollars to $3,000	Hundreds of dollars to $3,000	Hundreds of dollars to $1,000
Size	Desktop or floor mounted	Desktop	Suitcase	Briefcase	Pocket
Weight	30–70 lbs.	30–50 lbs.	Less than 12 lbs.	Less than 7 lbs.	Less than 1 lb.

•••••••••••••••••••••••••••••••••••••••➤ Looking Ahead

THE POWER PC

Sun Microcomputer Systems and Silicon Graphics, Inc. have been the market leaders in work-stations, but the new Power PC is likely to change that. The Power PC is available from both IBM and Apple and is intended to help restore these two companies to their positions of pre-eminence in computing. The RISC-based Power PC brings workstation capability to the desk-top for well under $2,500 as well as cross-platform compatibility—you can run *both* Windows and Macintosh software on these machines. See Figure 2.6.

With the favorable price/performance ratio of the Power PC, the distinction between workstations and desktop PCs is likely to erode.

Figure 2.6 *RISC computers, like the Power PC, can generate high-quality graphics.*

reduced *i*nstruction *s*et *c*omputer, as opposed to most desktops which are CISC computers, an abbreviation for *c*omplex *i*nstruction *s*et *c*omputer. An instruction set consists of the basic instructions that the computer can run or execute. By eliminating complex, infrequently used instructions that can be easily replaced by a smaller instruction set, RISC machines are "leaner and meaner." Although RISC-based machines can be used as workstations in a large network or as the central computer in a smaller network, they are likely to become even more widely used for all business applications.

DESKTOP COMPUTERS: THE MIDDLE GROUND The standard **desktop computer,** still the most widely used PC in business, is typically a single-user device. Advanced operating systems and user interfaces enable the desktop micro to be used for two or more different applications at one time, but most often these applications are under the control of a single user.

PORTABLE MICROS: LAPTOPS, NOTEBOOKS, SUBNOTEBOOKS, AND HANDHELD COMPUTERS **Portable microcomputers** are compact and light-weight enough to be transported easily from place to place. Businesspeople use them when they travel or commute to the office, stay at a hotel, visit a branch office, attend a conference, or work at home. Students use them in class, the library, or virtually anywhere—even the beach (but watch out for sand). Porta-bles can be connected to larger desktop PCs or other computers.

Compaq's original 1982 PC was called a *portable,* but at a weight of 30 pounds, *luggable* might have been a better word. Now standard **laptop comput-**

•••••➤ Looking Ahead

In terms of applications and processing power, desktop computers are currently positioned between more powerful workstations and smaller, portable mi-crocomputers. As both lower-end and upper-end microcomputers increase in power and decrease in price, today's ubiquitous desktop PC may eventually disappear. Wireless communication us-ing handheld computers is likely to be-come a major growth area.

Looking Back ◄

THE FIRST APPLE AND IBM PCS

Steven Jobs and Stephen G. Wozniak are proof that college dropouts can sometimes go far in this world. In Wozniak's garage, the two young men first built an Apple Computer in kit form in 1977. The Apple Computer Company, which began in that garage, went public several years later making both men multimillionaires.

For nine years, Jobs served in various management positions of Apple, including chairman of the board. As the small company gained prominence in the computing field, he was instrumental in building both the Apple II and Macintosh computers.

Jobs left Apple in 1985 to form NeXt Computer, Inc., which now develops operating systems for micros. Wozniak is a consultant and has his own company as well.

IBM introduced its first personal computer system, the IBM PC, in 1981. Apple, Radio Shack, Commodore, and Atari all had personal computers already on the market. Based on the success of these smaller companies, computer giant IBM hoped to sell 250,000 PCs in total. It sold 15 million units of its original PC. As a result, the microcomputer became the most significant technological breakthrough for business since the telephone.

A decade ago there were fewer than 300,000 micros at work in the United States. By the early 1990s, there were more than 60 million. Currently, 60% of all U.S. households have a PC. Worldwide use is estimated at 300 million.

Wozniak (left) and Jobs holding a board from their original Apple computer.

ers that weigh in at about 11 pounds are small enough to fit on an airplane tray table or in a small suitcase. At 7 pounds or less, **notebook computers,** which actually look like notebooks, can fit into a briefcase. **Subnotebooks** are even smaller versions of portable computers with the capability of larger machines. Some portables are pen-based. See Figure 2.7a.

The main objective of portable PCs is to provide the greatest computing power in the smallest area. Most portable computers are almost as powerful as desktop micros and use conventional software. Some are actually components of larger PC systems, which serve as docking stations for the portable when it is home-based. See Figure 2.7b. Application software and even operating systems are built into some portables.

(a)

(b)

Figure 2.7 *(a) Pen-based computers are often used by a field staff for collecting data. (b) A laptop computer can fit into a docking station providing the unit with more processing power and making more peripherals available to the laptop when it is home-based.*

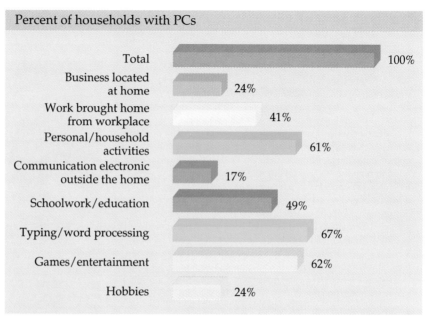

Percent of households with PCs

Category	Percent
Total	100%
Business located at home	24%
Work brought home from workplace	41%
Personal/household activities	61%
Communication electronic outside the home	17%
Schoolwork/education	49%
Typing/word processing	67%
Games/entertainment	62%
Hobbies	24%

What do people do with their home computers? Personal household activities include such tasks as balancing checkbooks, typing, and word processing. (Source: © INTECO Corp., The Interactive Home 1994.)

An even smaller handheld palmtop computing device called a Personal Digital Assistant (PDA) is now available. PDAs do not have the computing power of portables but they have great potential for businesspeople on the move. As their name may imply, these are devices that have basic desktop features including calculators, calendars, notepads, and personal database access. Along with a basic keypad, most of them are **pen-based,** permitting the user to handwrite notes and select commands using a pen rather than a keyboard or mouse. All PDAs can store handwritten notes, but their ability to actually interpret the notes varies greatly. That is, some may simply save your notes while others will understand that your handwritten "PRINT" means you want to create printed output.

Figure 2.8 *(a) The overall growth of PCs in the United States. (b) The growth of portables.*

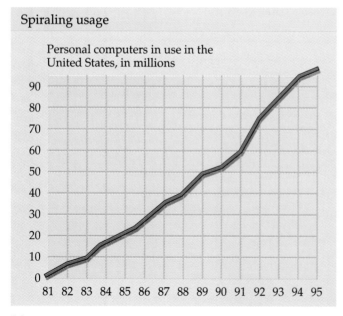

Spiraling usage

Personal computers in use in the United States, in millions

(a)

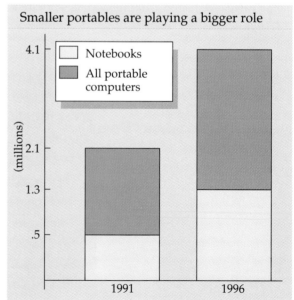

Smaller portables are playing a bigger role

- Notebooks
- All portable computers

(millions)

(b)

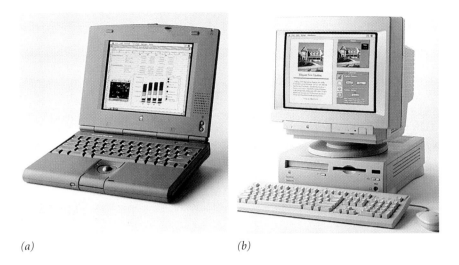

(a)   *(b)*

Figure 2.9 *Apple's Macintosh Powerbook portable and Macintosh Quadra desktop computer.*

The greatest potential of PDAs is in the communications area. Many have wireless communication capabilities enabling users to send faxes, receive electronic mail, page their colleagues, or communicate with other PCs. Apple's Newton MessagePad and Sharp's Expert Pad are among the most popular PDAs. Look for these handheld devices with wireless communication features to greatly enhance our connectivity and bring computing capability to even larger numbers of people. Figure 2.8a shows the growth of PCs over the last decade, and Figure 2.8b shows the growth of portables over the last several years.

The Apple Macintosh, IBM-compatibles, and Power PCs

Apple's original microcomputers, which preceded IBM PCs by several years, were in large part responsible for the huge success of the personal computer. Apple computers are still widely used in education, particularly in elementary and secondary schools, and Apple's newer Macintosh computers are viewed by many as the most user-friendly machines on the market. See Figure 2.9.

The Mac, as the Macintosh is affectionately called, has a graphical user interface. Commands represented by icons are selected by pointing and then clicking a mouse. The Mac's computing power and user-friendly interface have made it popular with both college students and business users.

A different category of computer is called the IBM-compatible. These computers were once copies or clones of the original IBM PC. Today the term *IBM-*

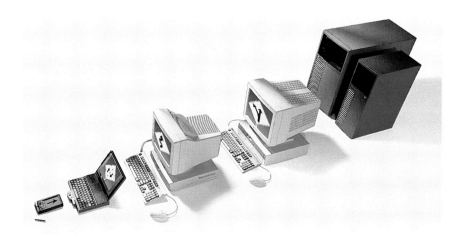

Figure 2.10 *This is a "family" of IBM-compatible computers. The computer on the left is the smallest and least powerful, with each computer (moving right) being larger and having more processing power.*

compatible refers to the overwhelming majority of PCs that, like IBM PCs, have an architecture set by an industrywide standards committee. Compaq, Hewlett-Packard, Dell, AST, and dozens of others make IBM-compatible computers with different sizes and processing power. See Figure 2.10. Note that software developed for IBM-compatibles typically does not run on Macs unless some conversion software is used.

THE POWER PC The competition between IBM and Apple has been one of the computing industry's fiercest rivalries. Facing declining market share, significant inroads by low-cost competitors, and a growing dissatisfaction among users who clamor for compatible products, IBM and Apple have joined forces to develop a new PC called the Power PC, a RISC-based high-end microcomputer.

MULTIMEDIA AS A SOFTWARE SENSATION Many people think the Power PC will have a profound impact on the microcomputer field. It is able to use both IBM-compatible and Macintosh operating systems so that it can run software developed for either machine. Its RISC-based architecture makes it preferable for running multimedia applications, which often require high-speed processing.

Multitasking on Micros vs Multiprogramming on Larger Computers

As we have seen, classifying computers by type is just a guideline to their cost, size, and processing power. Keep in mind that these classifications are not cast in stone and that today's minis are apt to be most similar to tomorrow's micros. There is one area, however, in which there is still a decided difference between micros and larger systems. Micros are still essentially single-user devices, whereas most larger computers can be shared, at the same time, by many users.

Although micros tend to be single-user devices, they often can run more than one program at the same time. The ability of micros to execute more than one program concurrently is called **multitasking.** A manager may, for example, use a word processing package to create a report and while the report is still "open" (i.e., active), the manager could prepare a budget using a different package that is then "cut and pasted" into the report.

DOS, the original operating system for IBM-compatibles, was not designed for multitasking, but newer operating systems like Windows 95 (or later), OS/2, and UNIX are. Older versions of Windows (3.11 and earlier) are graphical user interfaces—not full operating systems—but they do permit multitasking in a DOS environment

The term *multitasking* and the various features of operating systems that enable it to be used will be explained in more depth in Chapter 9. For now, you should know that a micro is essentially a single-user device that can have more than one application running at the same time if it has the proper operating system.

Mainframes and minis, on the other hand, are devices specifically intended to be shared by many users. Their operating systems are sophisticated enough that *different users* can run different applications all at the same time. This multi-user concept is called **multiprogramming.**

HOW PEOPLE USE COMPUTERS Think of mainframes as "mass transportation" devices, with all the features associated with that term; think of micros as automobiles—individualized methods of travel. Mainframes require users to have the appropriate "ticket" for access—a code and a password. Hours of use

ᴵᴺ A NUTSHELL

Operating systems software controls computer processing. The Mac and IBM-compatibles have different operating systems.

ᴵᴺ A NUTSHELL

Multitasking—Ability of PCs to run more than one program for a *single user* at the same time
Multiprogramming—Ability of large computers to serve *different users* at the same time

are determined by the people who provide the service, not the user. But once "on board," you can "leave the driving to them." Micros, on the other hand, are accessible at the user's convenience, but the user is totally responsible for their operation and upkeep.

Recall, however, that many of the features that differentiate computers are becoming less distinct. In fact, this standalone, single-user nature of microcomputers is changing. Some multitasking workstations are becoming more like "vans" or "trucks" or "trailers," which make them more diversified and more like "mass transportation" vehicles.

CONNECTIVITY LEADS TO INTERPERSONAL COMPUTING As we will see in more detail in Chapter 10, many organizations are finding it cost-effective to link, or network, their computer equipment so that hardware and software resources can be shared and computer utilization can be better controlled. In some cases micros are linked to central computers, and in other cases micros are linked to each other. This concept of connectivity, which includes networking and which allows the sharing of resources, means that micros need no longer be predominantly standalone devices.

Today, connectivity enables computers to perform the following types of activities:

1. Send data, programs, messages, and so on to computers of different sizes and different types.

2. Share resources including hardware such as printers, modems, and disk drives.

3. Monitor and control all computer operations to improve overall efficiency.

4. Offload overworked or inoperable computers by rerouting the work flow.

If connectivity and networking continue to enhance the computing field, perhaps instead of calling our micros PCs we will call them ICs, for *interpersonal computers.*

Self-Test

1. A _____ is a high-powered supermicro used for powerful PC processing.

2. What types of computers weigh approximately 1 pound?

3. (T or F) Many portables have the processing power of a desktop micro.

4. Portables often use _____ instead of electricity when operated away from home or the office.

5. Which computers were originally developed to offload the work of mainframes?

Solutions

1. workstation

2. Personal Digital Assistants (PDA)

3. T

4. batteries

5. minicomputers

▨ 2.3 CHOOSING AND USING COMPUTER SYSTEMS

Recall from Chapter 1 that when an organization decides to computerize information processing for its business systems, the systems development cycle begins. Systems development requires the combined expertise of computing professionals and users. Decisions about the design of the system are based not only on the hardware and software available but also on the ways in which the organization uses information. For large production runs such as preparing a payroll, a central mainframe may work best. For other applications, such as developing a departmental budget, microcomputers may be more appropriate.

As smaller computers become more powerful, their applications become more sophisticated. Just as categories and capabilities of micros and larger computers change, so too do the tasks they perform. Many companies are now downsizing or rightsizing—offloading applications from, say, a central mainframe computer to a smaller system so that the larger machine can be used for centralized applications such as controlling the operations in a client-server network. In this section we discuss the types of computers used in business and how they relate to one another.

Information Processing Environments

As we have seen, downsizing is a growing practice among companies. Smaller, smarter computer systems can make more efficient use of resources that can be distributed throughout a company. Originally, a single, central mainframe served all the separate business systems in a company. As minicomputers and then microcomputers became increasingly powerful and inexpensive, managers within individual departments began purchasing their own computer systems. They wanted more access to computing power and more control over their own applications. Because of this trend, computer facilities in many organizations became decentralized.

It did not take long, however, for the disadvantages of decentralization to become evident. Computers in individual departments often could not communicate with one another, with computers in other departments, or with central computers. Companies realized that they needed to link their decentralized systems together in order to distribute information and resources throughout the organization and to better serve top management, which needs to be able to retrieve information from all systems. Thus, distributed processing using a computing network was born. Each of these three methods for organizing computer systems—the centralized, decentralized, and distributed or networked processing environments—has its own advantages and disadvantages, and each fosters different degrees of communication between computer users and computer professionals.

▪N A NUTSHELL

COMPUTING ENVIRONMENT	MOST COMMON COMPUTER CONFIGURATION
Centralized	Mainframe-oriented
Decentralized	Mini- or micro-based
Distributed	Central mainframe or mini networked to PCs

CENTRALIZED AND DECENTRALIZED PROCESSING The following is a summary of the pros and cons of the different computing environments:

Centralized Computing: One Main Computer for the Entire Organization	PROS	CONS
	• Uses one central facility and one computing staff, which are easier to manage and keep secure. • Functional areas can share central data minimizing duplication of effort. • Satisfying computing needs of users can be accomplished in priority order.	• When control is centralized, users often have to wait to gain access or get computing needs satisfied.
Decentralized Computing: Each User Group Has its Own Computing Facility	PROS	CONS
	• Each user group or functional area controls its own computing facility. • Management can more easily assess the effectiveness of computing resources for each user group or functional area.	• Duplication of effort occurs—groups that might otherwise share central data have to develop their own. • Top-level management's control of all computing resources is often lacking.
Distributed or Network Computing: One Central Computer Is Accessible to All Users Who Have Their Own Computers	PROS	CONS
	• Combines advantages of centralized and decentralized computing. • Enables top-level management to assess the effectiveness of computing resources and to plan for future needs.	• Hardware and networking costs are high. • Since access to central computing is dispersed, security and privacy become even more critical issues.

DISTRIBUTED PROCESSING AND CLIENT-SERVER COMPUTING Distributed processing, then, is often used at all levels of computing—from a small company that has only microcomputers linked in a network, to a medium-sized company that has a mini networked to micros, to a Fortune 500 company that has huge mainframe systems linked to minis and micros. See Figure 2.11. Client-server computing is one type of distributed processing.

One advantage of distributed client-server computing is that it is relatively easy and inexpensive for an organization to expand its computing facilities by

Centralized computing means that one facility is used to satisfy all or most of a company's computational needs.

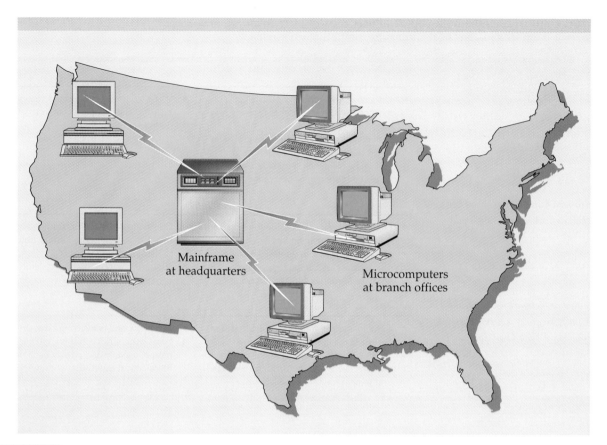

Mainframe
at headquarters

Microcomputers
at branch offices

Figure 2.11 *Distributed processing often has micros linked to a large mainframe. The micros can be in different cities or in the next room.*

simply adding micros as the need arises. Micros are now so common as components in distributed systems that their combined hours in use sometimes doubles or triples that of the organization's mainframe.

Distributed systems are not without disadvantages. Networks demand a high level of technical and organizational skill from the computing staff, because the distributed environment must serve all business systems and all levels of computer expertise. As the network expands, strict procedures and design standards must be implemented when hardware or software is added. Finally, because distributed systems typically have so many users (many of them off-site) with access to so much information, computer professionals and business managers must provide a high level of security against unauthorized use and disruption, whether intentional or accidental.

Sometimes organizations use external facilities to augment their own computers or to replace them. Contracting with outside processing centers to run your organization's programs is called **time-sharing.** Companies that specialize in time-sharing can actually provide user organizations with all their computational needs. This is called **outsourcing.** In outsourcing, time-sharing companies supply hardware and software to organizations for a fee and actually run programs as a service, on a regularly scheduled basis. Outsourcing is becoming increasingly popular for many companies that have their own computers but find them inadequate and do not want to spend additional funds to upgrade their facilities.

ɪɴ A NUTSHELL

CLIENT-SERVER COMPUTING

SERVER

- The main supplier of computer resources
- Controls and maintains the security of databases/programs and other resources

CLIENT

- PC or workstation that requests access to computing resources
- Client performs some or all of the actual processing

THE MICRO-MAINFRAME MIX Despite our emphasis on distributed processing and networks, there is a growing misperception that PCs are replacing mainframes and that larger computers will no longer be needed in the years ahead. The fact is, mainframes have been, and continue to be, the backbone of computing in medium-sized and large organizations. The overwhelming majority of the computing needs in these organizations are still being met by mainframes, just as large transportation systems are the mainstay of urban areas. People who live in urban areas may prefer to use the family car for a Sunday drive or a night out, but they often rely on mass transportation systems to get to work. Personal computers, like personal cars, may make life easier, but when it comes to providing large numbers of people with transportation (or information), they often cannot do the job.

What is likely to change in the next century, then, are the *activities* performed by various-sized computer systems, particularly as more and more companies downsize. As PCs get faster and more powerful, tasks commonly performed today on a mainframe are apt to be offloaded to PCs.

The Human Factor in Information Processing: Users and Computer Professionals

SATISFYING USER NEEDS Employees working at each level within an organization tend to use computers for different purposes. At the first-line management level, both workers and managers use computers for *operational* purposes: to perform specific tasks such as entering orders, paying invoices to vendors, and so on. Middle managers and the people who work for them use computers to do *tactical analysis;* that is, they use the data entered at the operational level to make decisions such as when to order new inventory, when to raise a product's price, and so on. At the top management level, computers assist executives in the *strategic planning* that determines long-term policy for the company.

Two different approaches may be used to computerize a business system so that it becomes an effective information system: the traditional systems approach and the management information systems (MIS) approach. With the traditional approach, information systems are designed to meet the basic needs of each functional area, independent of other departments' systems. Centralized or decentralized computers are often used in companies where the traditional approach to designing information systems is the norm.

With the management information systems approach, the needs of the overall organization are considered first. We call this top-down processing. The specific needs of functional areas are met only after the information needs of all areas have been integrated. Distributed processing is best used for management information systems where a central computer maintains an organization's databases and users have access via a network.

Traditional information systems are based on the assumption that an organization is the sum of its functional areas, or parts. In other words, if each functional area does its work efficiently, the entire organization will run smoothly. Many organizations have used this approach successfully.

Although the traditional approach to information systems is best for satisfying the needs and requirements of operating staff and managers in functional areas, what do you do if you are a top-level executive and need broad-based sales information across all your company's divisions? How do you get a companywide sales forecast? How do you analyze your product mix to develop corporate strategies?

These questions point to a fundamental weakness in traditional information systems: even if an information system is effective in meeting specific departmental objectives, the global information needs of top-level executives may not be met. Department managers may be satisfied with the day-to-day information provided by traditional information systems, but top executives need to look at data and trends across a number of functional areas so they can develop business perspectives and create competitive strategies. Traditional information systems are not designed to provide the cumulative, integrated, historically based information that top-level executives need.

Rather than focusing on the business needs of each functional area, an MIS treats an organization as though it were one complete unit with one set of overall corporate objectives, for example, the objective of gaining an increase in market share of 5 percent while making a profit of 14 percent of sales. MIS developers begin by designing a system around the information needed to meet top managers' companywide goals and then focus on the information needed in each functional area to achieve those goals. In other words, MIS developers view the company as an integrated entity with goals that go beyond the collective goals of all the independent functional areas (Figure 2.12). An MIS depends on a fully integrated database management system to provide needed information to all users.

Both the traditional systems and MIS approaches are widely used today, but with the use of networks and the availability of packaged database management

Figure 2.12 *Each level of management has unique information needs and will access a management information system differently.*

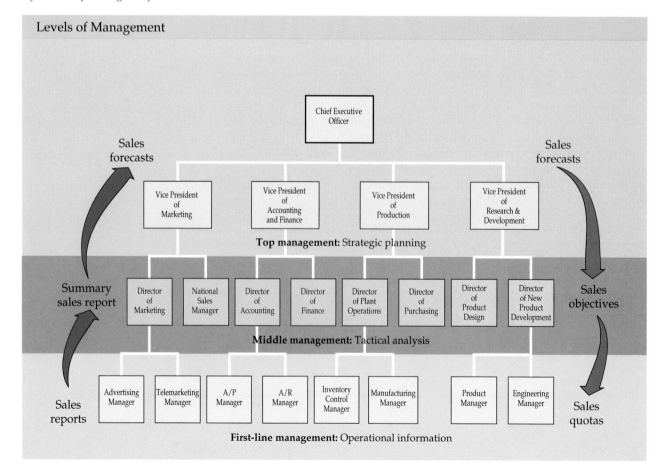

systems, an effective MIS is now easier to develop and more able to satisfy management needs. Specific types of management information systems are discussed in Chapter 12.

MIS STAFF: THE PEOPLE BEHIND THE COMPUTER SYSTEM Centralized and distributed computing facilities are usually maintained by a separate department, whereas decentralized facilities are most often controlled by the departments they serve. In the former case, the computer center's manager may have one of any number of titles (director, manager, or vice president) and the department may be called Management Information Systems, Information Systems, Computer Information Systems, or Information Processing. Regardless of titles, information systems managers are responsible for the entire computer facility and its staff.

Six principal categories of computer professionals are commonly found in computing departments, two of which—programmers and systems analysts—we discussed in Chapter 1. We consider here the personnel in a typical computing department:

1. Systems analysts, who are supervised by a systems manager. Systems analysts are responsible for analyzing existing business procedures, determining basic problem areas or inefficiencies, and designing a more effective information system. The systems manager assigns specific tasks to individual analysts and evaluates their progress.

2. Programmers, who are supervised by a programming manager. The programmer receives the job requirements from a systems analyst and is responsible for writing, testing, and documenting programs that will be part of the information system as a whole. Some companies also have programmer analysts who design information systems and write all the necessary programs as well. The programmer analyst is responsible for the entire information system, including analysis and design and all the programming and implementation.

3. Data entry and computer operators, who are supervised by an operations manager. Operations managers are responsible for the efficient and effective use of computer equipment. An operations manager must ensure that input errors are kept to a minimum and that the computer system is relatively secure from breakdown, natural disasters (earthquakes, fire, power outages), and unauthorized use or misuse.

4. Auditors. Auditors are the accounting and computer specialists responsible for the overall integrity of each information system's programs and data.

5. Database administrator. The database administrator oversees the structure, organization, and control of all the data used for information processing. The database administrator is responsible for efficient design of the files that contain the data and for implementing proper controls and techniques necessary for accessing them.

6. Network manager. The network manager is responsible for ensuring that computing devices linked to one another are being used effectively and efficiently. The role of the network manager is becoming increasingly important as more organizations are relying on connectivity.

Common Organizational Structures. In small companies, the entire staff of computer professionals may consist of just one or two microcomputer specialists who are responsible for every computer-related function, from customizing software packages and designing the information systems to purchasing hard-

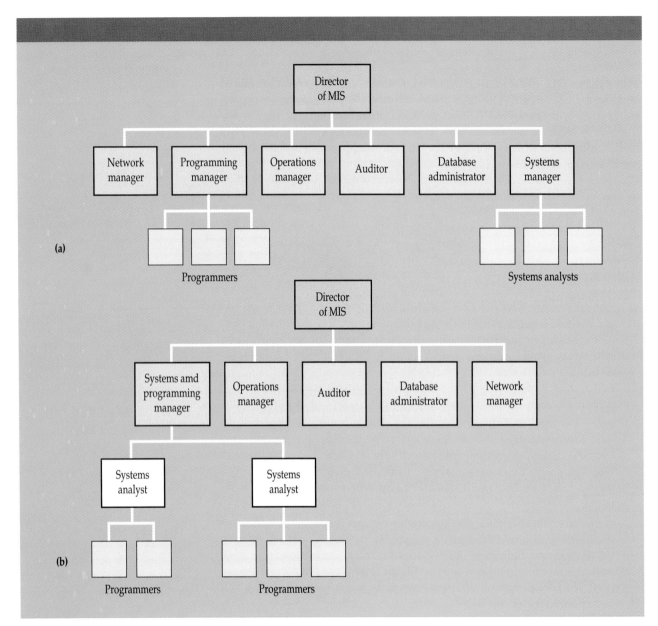

Figure 2.13 *Two common organization structures for MIS departments. When programmers and systems analysts have separate managers, as in the chart on the top, there is more flexibility; but programmers and analysts working in teams, as in the chart on the bottom, makes for better control.*

ware. Large companies, however, usually have a department of people as just described. In such companies, computer facilities are usually organized in one of two basic ways: (1) systems analysts reporting to a systems manager and programmers reporting to a programming manager or (2) programmers reporting directly to systems analysts.

The structure on the top of Figure 2.13 illustrates an organization in which programmers and analysts report to different supervisors and work together as peers designing programs for a new system. Under this structure, analysts have less control over the programmers who work on a specific application, but the advantage is that a more open exchange of ideas is likely to occur between the two groups.

The structure on the bottom of Figure 2.13 illustrates an organization in which programmers report directly to systems analysts. In this case, systems analysts are project managers; they supervise programmers, monitor their progress, and evaluate their programs. With this structure, there is one overall manager for both systems and programming.

The Right Time to Buy

In large organizations, computer professionals control the process of selecting computer systems. Individuals face similar decisions when they buy their hardware. Recall that software drives hardware—you should determine your software needs first and then look at the hardware needed to run that software. Among the basic criteria used to select computer systems are cost, processing power, and size.

When a new computer system becomes available, it is likely to have features that are more advanced or more user-friendly than computers already on the market. Because the hardware is novel, however, it is likely to cost more. Research and development of new products is costly for manufacturers; for buyers, this means higher prices for innovative hardware. Once manufacturers recover their costs, however, and competitors begin to offer similar devices, prices fall, often dramatically. For example, the original desktop IBM PC cost $2,500 in 1981. Adjusting for inflation, the same $2,500 today will buy you a portable microcomputer with network capability, 35 times the processing power, and 1200 times the storage capacity of the original IBM PC.

If you buy a new "hot" product, you will derive the benefits of innovation but at a high price. If you wait for prices to drop, you will save money; but a newer computer with even greater potential benefits—and a higher price—is just around the corner. When laptop PCs weighing 11 pounds were introduced, users who were willing to pay a steep price for portability snapped up these lightweight computer systems. Before they knew it, 7-pound notebook computers that were just as powerful and that cost about the same were available.

If you buy hardware when it is first introduced, you will pay dearly for the benefits it offers. If you wait, you will pay less but outgrow the hardware sooner. People who use their computers only occasionally can live with less power, but users who depend heavily on their computers and use them for complex applications need to upgrade their systems more frequently. If you are a bargain hunter, constantly waiting for the best buy, you may find that you are always shopping but never buying!

Critical Thinking

In the early 1980s when microcomputers were new to corporations, computer stores sold approximately 90 percent of all micros. Ten years later, the same stores sell only about 46 percent of all micros. Many customers now shop at department stores or discount houses or purchase PCs through the mail, and many computer stores are merging or going bankrupt. Why do you think this change has occurred?

Self-Test

1. What are the three information processing environments?

2. What is downsizing?

3. A distributed processing environment usually uses a group of computers _____ to one another.

4. What are the two approaches to computerizing information systems?

Solutions

1. centralized—one main computer; decentralized—each department with its own computers; distributed—a central computer that can be accessed by PCs or minis in each department

2. offloading applications from a central computer to smaller computers

3. networked or connected

4. the traditional systems approach in which each department's needs are most important and the MIS approach where the needs of top-level management are most important

CHAPTER SUMMARY

Chapter 2 focuses on hardware. How hardware works, types of hardware, and the information processing tasks hardware performs all influence decisions about what computer system is appropriate for an organization or individual.

2.1 Classifying Computer Systems

Computer systems are classified by size, cost, and processing power. These factors determine the applications for which each type of computer is best suited. **Microcomputers** are mainly single-user systems. **Minicomputers,** or **midrange computers,** are **multiuser systems,** as are the larger **mainframe** computers. Room-sized mainframes may be connected to thousands of users at **terminals,** other **peripherals,** or PCs. The largest of all computer systems, **supercomputers,** which are used mainly for scientific and industrial research and by the government, often can accommodate as many as 10,000 users at once.

With computers of all sizes becoming more powerful, the boundaries that separate computer categories often change. A supermicro, for example, may be as powerful as a low-end mini. The distinctions between minis and mainframes are also becoming blurred. As computers in all categories grow more powerful, the applications they can process get more sophisticated.

Most computers process data in **nanoseconds**; supercomputers process data in **picoseconds.** Sometimes computer speeds are measured in **MIPS.** In computers of all sizes, **main memory** capacity is measured in **bytes.** The main memory in the early Apple and IBM computers was measured in **kilobytes.** Today's PCs have memory capacities ranging up to several **megabytes,** and larger systems operate with **gigabytes** of main memory. Together, processing speed and main memory capacity determine the overall measure of processing power.

The most common input devices for micros are the **keyboard** and the **mouse,** which enable the user to enter data and instructions to the CPU. A **monitor** displays input and output. **Disk drives** give the CPU access to programs and data stored on **floppy disks** (also called **diskettes**) or on **hard disks.** Compact disks and microflopticals are also used to store data and programs. The most common output device for PCs is the **printer.** With the proper software, computers linked by **modems** or fax-modems can communicate with each other using standard telephone lines. Terminals are the main input/output device for larger systems. Smaller and smarter peripherals for computers of all sizes are constantly being developed.

2.2 Getting to Know Your Hardware

Beginning in the 1950s, mainframes were the first general-purpose computers used in business. They remain the most widely used computer systems in medium- to large-sized companies, where they meet computing needs of major business systems. With prices averaging $100,000, many companies lease or rent a mainframe rather than buy one. Mainframes are valuable business assets that are closely monitored by computing professionals and maintained in secure, specially designed facilities. Often, mainframes are used as the central computer in a large network.

Mainframe use peaked in the late 1960s when DEC and other companies developed minicomputers in response to organizational needs for more computing power within each functional area. Through the 1970s and 1980s, companies bought increasingly smaller, more powerful, less expensive minis and superminis. These computer systems free up computing time on mainframes by **offloading** applications. Many computers made by the same manufacturer are **upwardly compatible.**

In the United States, the government accounts for more than half of all supercomputer use. Cray Research is the primary supercomputer manufacturer. To operate more efficiently, a supercomputer may be connected to a smaller mainframe or minicomputer. The smaller system handles routine tasks and frees the supercomputer for the complex processing applications it does best.

The earliest microcomputers were introduced about 20 years ago. The first micro to gain wide use was developed by Apple Computer Company. Today, Apple's user-friendly Macintosh micros are widely used in schools and businesses. Since 1981 IBM has sold 15 million of its original Personal Computers—60 times the number originally forecast. By current estimates, there are more than 100 million micros in use in the United States alone.

Initially, micros were single-user systems, although more recently developed **workstations**—powerful, multiuser supermicros—can control small networks. Many workstations use **RISC** technology, which uses a reduced instruction set that makes them more efficient. Standard **desktop computers** are still the most widely used micros in business, but **portable microcomputers** are also very popular. Compaq introduced its original **laptop** portable in 1982. Ever since, the goal of more computing power in a smaller package has led to **notebook computers,** and more recently, **subnotebook computers** that weigh just a few pounds. Some notebooks, palmtops, and handheld Personal Digital Assistants are **pen-based systems** that enable the users to handwrite entries.

Currently Compaq is the market leader for IBM-compatibles, but there are hundreds of companies that manufacture these types of computers. IBM and Apple formed a joint venture to develop a powerful computer that could run both Mac and IBM-compatible software. This computer, called the Power PC, is a major competitor of the IBM-compatibles.

Micros are often used for **multitasking,** that is, processing two or more applications at one time. Larger systems are often used for **multiprogramming** whereby two or more users can run different applications at one time.

2.3 Choosing and Using Computer Systems

When an organization or an individual decides to use computers, the decision is based on the hardware and software available and on the way in which the business uses information. As smaller computers have become more powerful and their applications more sophisticated, many companies are **downsizing,** or rightsizing, their computing operations.

A generation ago, mainframes were used by businesses for **centralized processing.** Then some organizations moved to **decentralized processing** to better satisfy individual departmental needs. Today, businesses are moving increasingly into **distributed processing** networks and **client-server computing** to meet their computing needs. Each processing environment has advantages and drawbacks. Regardless of the processing environment, mainframes remain the backbone of information processing in medium-sized and large organizations.

Two approaches to computerizing business systems are possible. In the traditional systems approach, the needs of each department are considered first. In the management information systems approach, the needs of top-level management are considered first. The computing staff responsible for the design, implementation, and control of information systems consists of systems analysts and systems managers, programmers and programming managers, operations managers and operators, auditors, database administrators, and network managers.

In large organizations, computer professionals select computer systems for a company as a whole, but individual users face the same selection process when they buy hardware for themselves. Among the basic criteria used to select

Study Objective

3. Outline what users need to know about hardware and connectivity.

computer systems are cost, processing power, connectivity, and size. Buying the newest, most innovative hardware may yield benefits, but at a high price. Waiting usually means spending less but outgrowing the system sooner.

Sometimes companies use external facilities for their computational needs. **Time-sharing** organizations will sell computer time to companies. When an organization provides a company with all its computational needs this is called **outsourcing.**

KEY TERMS

Byte, *p. 33*
Centralized processing, *p. 47*
Client-server computing, *p. 31*
Decentralized processing, *p. 47*
Desktop computer, *p. 40*
Disk drive, *p. 34*
Diskette, *p. 34*
Distributed processing, *p. 47*
Downsizing, *p. 31*
File server, *p. 31*
Floppy disk, *p. 34*
Gigabyte (GB), *p. 33*
Hard disk, *p. 34*
Keyboard, *p. 34*
Kilobyte (K), *p. 33*

Laptop computer, *p. 40*
Mainframe, *p. 30*
Main memory, *p. 33*
Megabyte (MB), *p. 33*
Microcomputer, *p. 31*
Midrange computer, *p. 30*
Minicomputer, *p. 30*
MIPS, *p. 33*
Modem, *p. 34*
Monitor, *p. 34*
Mouse, *p. 34*
Multiprogramming, *p. 44*
Multitasking, *p. 44*
Multiuser system, *p. 30*
Nanosecond, *p. 33*

Notebook computer, *p. 41*
Offload, *p. 38*
Outsourcing, *p. 48*
Pen-based system, *p. 42*
Peripherals, *p. 33*
Picosecond, *p. 33*
Portable microcomputer, *p. 40*
Printer, *p. 34*
RISC computer, *p. 39*
Subnotebook computer, *p. 41*
Supercomputer, *p. 30*
Terminal, *p. 30*
Time-sharing, *p. 48*
Upwardly compatible, *p. 36*
Workstation, *p. 39*

CHAPTER SELF-TEST

1. The largest type of computer is called a _____.

2. The first computers used in business and the ones most likely to be the central computer in a network for a large or medium-sized business are called _____.

3. _____ are computers that were originally developed to offload mainframes in a large company.

4. (T or F) Micros are usually single-user computers and larger systems are usually multiuser systems.

5. Larger computers differ from small computers in _____.

6. Another term for the primary storage of a computer is _____.

7. Another term for the input/output units of a computer system is _____.

8. A device that enables one computer to communicate with another one over telephone lines is called a _____.

9. When two computers can use the same hardware and software, we say they are _____.

10. A million bytes of storage is called a _____.

11. The most commonly used storage device for saving programs and data is a _____.

12. The _____ can run both Mac and IBM-compatible software.

13. With a (centralized, decentralized) processing environment, it is difficult to determine the actual computer costs to attribute to each department.

14. A _____ processing environment attempts to satisfy the needs of each department as well as the needs of the company as a whole.

15. The most difficult information processing environment to manage and keep secure is (centralized, decentralized, distributed).

REVIEW QUESTIONS

1. College campuses have computer facilities for their financial and accounting systems, computer science instruction, student registration information, statistical analysis and research, and so on. Review your college's bulletin and catalog and see if you can discover whether your campus has a centralized, decentralized, or distributed computer system. You may find that some computers are centralized, while others, such as those for specialized research facilities, are decentralized.

2. The Power PC is likely to have a significant impact on personal computing in the years ahead. Why? What issues should users be concerned about when purchasing a Power PC?

3. Describe the advantages and disadvantages of client-server computing.

4. What are the advantages of downsizing? Are there any possible disadvantages?

CRITICAL THINKING EXERCISES

1. The Clinton administration has eliminated most of the export controls on telecommunications equipment and computers that can be sold to China, Russia, and other Communist countries, effective April 1, 1994. Export controls are still in place for countries the administration believes support terrorism such as Libya, Iraq, and North Korea. Tough export controls still remain for supercomputers. The government's loosening of export controls is estimated to be worth $150 billion in extra revenue by 2004. AT&T executives expect the company to realize at least $500 million in additional sales by 1998 because of the government's actions.[1]

Why do you think export controls on supercomputers are still so tough?

2. Personal Digital Assistants (PDAs) do not yet have the computing power of other portables. Given their current communications capability, what impact on business and industry do you think they are likely to have?

[1]Source: *New York Times*, March 31, 1994, v143 pA1(N) pA1(L) col 6 (30 col in)

Solutions

1. supercomputer
2. mainframes
3. Minicomputers or midrange computers
4. T
5. cost, size, processing power
6. main memory
7. peripherals
8. modem or fax-modem
9. compatible
10. megabyte
11. disk drive
12. Power PC
13. centralized
14. distributed
15. distributed

Case Study

The U.N. Downsizes to Establish an Integrated Management Information System

What happens when an enormous organization like the United Nations must cope with the inadequacies in its information system? A bank of mainframes in its New York headquarters currently stores information on the U.N.'s more than 20,000 employees, but that information exists in 20 different systems, some of which are 30 years old—and the systems are not connected to each other. Administrators who need to obtain payroll figures or cost-of-living data have had to manually search through numerous databases, many of which contain duplicate information or information that is out-of-date.

A further complication is that the U.N.'s $3 billion annual budget is broken down into 90 different currencies. Calculating exchange rates in order to convert everything to U.S. dollars, which is required for the master budget, has been an enormous task. Determining the U.N.'s cash flow at any given time has been an even more insurmountable chore.

Help is on the way, however. A $47 million project is now underway to automate and consolidate many of the administrative functions performed at the U.N. Secretariat in New York. The new system, called the Integrated Management Information System or IMIS, creates a standard format for recording data so that information can be analyzed across the U.N.'s various organizations. For the 400 pilot users, administrative applications are being moved off the mainframes and onto just four client-server workstations, a change that should dramatically improve the quality of information available and ease the decision-making process. Once the system is fully operational for these 400 users, an additional 1700 users in nearly 30 other Secretariat branches and peacekeeping missions around the world will be added.

Two key characteristics of IMIS are its modularity and its security. To achieve modularity, users will be able to automate business transactions that are within their control without negatively impacting the performance of the entire system. If, for example, hazardous duty pay in dangerous peacekeeping areas needs to be added to the entitlements

The United Nations, like many organizations with extensive information processing needs, is downsizing.

procedures, a designated user session could define the rules for this module; in this way, all records related to hazardous duty pay could be updated immediately without the need for separate changes to be made in each branch office.

IMIS allows U.N. employees to more easily access information for a central database. Users will be able to immediately obtain reports on a population or on employees who meet certain criteria. But any system that provides accessibility to sensitive data must be very secure. To ensure that users are authorized, the system will monitor access and have passwords and usernames updated at varying intervals.

Analysis
1. Why is the U.N. downsizing?
2. How does client-server computing impact the decision-making functions at the U.N.?
3. Why do integrated management information systems require extra security?

CHAPTER 3
Using Productivity Tools

3.1 UNDERSTANDING SOFTWARE

Software Makes It Work: A Review

The People Who Use Application Packages

Types of Productivity Tools, Integrated Packages, and Suites

3.2 COMMON FEATURES OF PRODUCTIVITY TOOLS

Loading the Program

Creating and Retrieving Files

Status Lines

Data Entry

Basic Commands and Function Keys

Search and Replace

Macros

Importing Files

3.3 UNIQUE FEATURES OF PRODUCTIVITY TOOLS

Word Processing Packages

Electronic Spreadsheets

Database Management Systems

Electronic Mail, Groupware, and the Information Superhighway

ardware oftentimes steals the limelight with its dramatic impact on information processing. But, as you learned in Chapter 1, software makes computers work, regardless of their size, cost, or processing speed. Software helps computer users perform their day-to-day business tasks in the office, on the road, or at home. An **application package** is a type of prewritten software designed for business or personal use. You can purchase packages such as productivity tools off-the-shelf at computer stores, from other retailers, or by mail.

Study Objectives

In Chapter 3, you will discover how computer users can derive the benefits of improved productivity. After completing this chapter you should be able to:

1. Describe what productivity tools are and demonstrate how they are used in business.
2. Describe the common functions of productivity tools, integrated packages, and suites.
3. List the most important features of productivity tools.

3.1 UNDERSTANDING SOFTWARE

The driving force behind computing is not hardware; it is software. The experienced computer user selects a computer system not so much for its high-powered processing but for the application areas it serves best. Users must, of course, know how to operate their hardware, but understanding the hows and whys of using software is far more important.

Software Makes It Work: A Review

Computer systems operate under the control of programmed instructions, or software. In Chapter 1 you learned that one set of programs, the operating systems software, controls computer operations and allows users to interact with their hardware. Computer users work with application programs to complete day-to-day business tasks more efficiently, search for the information they need faster, and analyze their options more effectively.

Application software can be purchased as a package, or it can be custom-designed, that is, written specifically for individual users. Both packaged and custom software are used with computer systems of all sizes. Larger organizations with more specific computer needs and more extensive computer staffs often invest in custom software while PC-based organizations are apt to have a limited computer staff and are therefore often best served by off-the-shelf packages.

One main objective of software—either in the form of packages or custom programs—is to help employees increase their productivity. Regardless of whether users have PCs, larger systems, or client-server networks at their disposal, they rely on software to help them become more productive.

Programs are stored on storage media, such as disks, in the form of program files. The data to be processed by programs is also stored on disk as data files. Both program and data files must be loaded into main memory (primary storage) for the CPU to operate on them.

IN A NUTSHELL

TYPES OF SOFTWARE

1. Operating systems software: controls operations of a computer system
2. Application software: transforms raw data into meaningful information to satisfy user needs
   - Packaged: designed for a wide range of users
   - Custom: designed for a specific user's needs

The People Who Use Application Packages

Employees at every level have access to computers in organizations these days. Those who use software, particularly productivity tools, fall into three main groups:

1. *Users* who are business managers, executives, or employees who need computer-produced information to summarize and analyze data, and to help them make decisions. They are sometimes referred to more specifically as *end users.*

2. *Software specialists* who customize the software so that the information produced is in the proper format. These specialists know precisely what the software can accomplish and how it can best be used to satisfy individual needs. Sometimes these specialists are computer professionals who work with end users to obtain the desired output. Sometimes end users are computer proficient enough to do the job themselves.

3. *Data entry operators* who actually enter the data.

Depending on the software and on the application area, these three functions may be performed by separate individuals, or they may be performed by one person. In the first case, managers may make decisions based on information produced by others. The software may have been tailored to their needs by computer professionals and the input entered by data entry operators. Often, however, computer-proficient managers who analyze data in different ways to prepare output actually customize the software and enter the data themselves, and then use the results. So a single individual may wear three different hats when using a software product—that of data entry operator, software specialist, and end user. Such end users are often called power users.

Types of Productivity Tools, Integrated Packages, and Suites

In this chapter, we focus on a type of application software called productivity tools. These tools are widely used to perform operations that are an integral part of day-to-day business activities and that help make office workers more productive.

Our goal is to explain why productivity tools are so widely used rather than to teach you how to use specific products. A conceptual understanding of the significance of these tools comes first. Then we recommend you turn to the *Getting Started* tutorials available with this book; they teach you how to use specific packages. These hands-on tutorials assume that you are at a computer and can step through the procedures specified as you read the tutorial. The emphasis in this text, however, is on *why* each type of tool helps to increase productivity, not on *how* to use any specific tool. Our *PassPort* multimedia disks, also available with this text, include interactive training modules on the productivity tools discussed here.

Many application packages qualify as productivity tools. We discuss four of the main ones here. (Other packages are discussed in Chapter 7.)

WORD PROCESSING Employees whose jobs once required many hours a day of typing and retyping documents now spend less time at the keyboard because they use electronic **word processing**. If you use a standard office typewriter, you must either patch or completely retype your document whenever you need to make a change or correction. Word processing software saves considerable time

> ### Study Objective
>
> 1. Describe what productivity tools are and demonstrate how they are used in business.

Critical Thinking

Do computers used for word processing actually improve the quality of writing?

Unquestionably computers reduce drudgery by minimizing the need for reentering text. Some experts, however, think that the ease with which a document can be revised results in too much drafting and editing. Beyond a few drafts, the quality does not improve greatly.

Although grammar checkers are helpful for catching errors in wording, many people find that changes suggested by the package are not always improvements.

Some proponents, however, contend that word processing makes the physical act of writing so much easier that users spend more time being creative. The result is an improved document. Do you agree? Do you see any potential disadvantages to depending on word processing packages?

and energy; it records the words or text electronically and makes them easy to change. Word processing also minimizes the need for retyping every time you want a new version of a document. It allows you to rearrange words, sentences, and paragraphs and insert or delete text with a few simple keystrokes. Word processing is so widely used that the typewriter faces extinction.

A word processing software package produces letters, reports, and other text referred to as **documents** that look better and convey information more effectively, whether their purpose is to inform, entertain, or persuade. Some people believe that by freeing users to concentrate on their writing—what they want to communicate—word processing also makes documents read better. As one professional writer said of her word processing program, "Once I learned it could do the two most time-consuming tasks, inserting and deleting text, I was free to spend my time creating and thinking."

SPREADSHEET AND GRAPHIC ANALYSIS The **electronic spreadsheet** package is one of the most important and widely used business tools to come along in the era of microcomputers. Ledger sheets, **worksheets,** or spreadsheets have always been used by accountants; when produced by an electronic spreadsheet package, they are a powerful analytical tool available to anyone with access to a computer. See Figure 3.1.

Electronic spreadsheets use a column and row format for representing data. The user enters data in the boxes, or **cells,** formed where columns and rows intersect. Formulas can also be entered in cells to carry out mathematical functions.

A common use for spreadsheets is budgeting. Of course it is useful to know how much you will spend in an entire year, but it is also important to have the total amount for each budget category "spread" across 12 months, so you know how much money you need each month.

One reason electronic spreadsheets are so popular is that they will automatically recalculate results when a change to data is made. If you entered a value erroneously, you can reenter that value and the computer will automatically perform all recalculations in cells where the initial value was used in a formula. If you review your budget for the next 12 months and decide you need to reduce your expenses by moving to a cheaper apartment and by not taking a trip you

Figure 3.1 *The spreadsheet combines three manual tools commonly used for working with numbers: the ledger sheet, the pencil, and the calculator.*

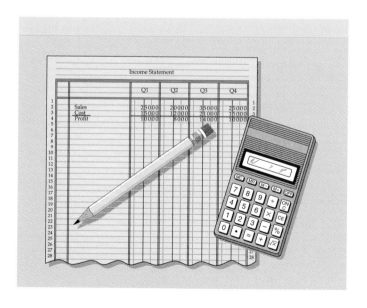

had planned, you could simply make changes to the rent and vacation entries and have the computer generate new totals in seconds.

Many users think that the real power of spreadsheet packages lies in the ability they give users to *predict* the effects of a possible or hypothetical change in numbers. What will happen if sales increase by 5 percent? If profits fall by $1 million? What will happen to the family budget if you get that raise?

Having the power to analyze possible changes gives users more control over planning and setting goals. Electronic spreadsheets allow businesses to project the effects of different courses of action on company goals. This "what-if" feature of spreadsheet packages is what launched productivity tools into widespread use in business. In essence, spreadsheets did for software what the PC did for hardware.

Spreadsheets are also capable of graphing results and displaying them pictorially. For instance, a sales manager can compare monthly sales of the top three salespeople during a year by analyzing three columns of numbers. Many people, however, find that looking at a graph that displays the same information is easier and has more impact. Figure 3.2 illustrates the difference between representing the same data in a spreadsheet and in graphic form.

DATABASE MANAGEMENT SYSTEMS Walk into almost any office and you will find large numbers of filing cabinets with drawers full of file folders. Storing all this data electronically using an application package not only saves space but makes accessing and analyzing the data easier and faster.

A concept central to electronic filing—and to a great deal of this book—is the database. A **database** is a group of related files where a **file** is a major collection of data in a specific application area. For example, all the payroll files, personnel files, and salary history files in a company might be defined as a database. Because they are interrelated, **database files** can be linked together and used in many ways. A manager, for example, can link the personnel and payroll databases to print an address list of all the workers in a specific department and their salaries. See Figure 3.3 for a database illustration.

IN A NUTSHELL

USES OF ELECTRONIC SPREADSHEETS

1. To represent data in column-and-row format
2. To perform automatic recalculation in cells that include formulas
3. To create graphs based on data in the worksheet
4. To create templates or worksheet shells that can be reused when new data is compiled (e.g., budgets, trial balances, etc.)
5. To perform what-if analysis—to test the impact of projected changes

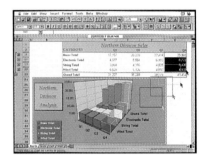

Figure 3.2 *Spreadsheet packages display information in column-and-row format and as graphs for reporting purposes. They also enable managers to perform "what-if" analyses.*

Looking Back

HISTORY OF THE SPREADSHEET

The VisiCalc spreadsheet package was the single most important software product of the early 1980s. It has been heralded as the one application package that convinced businesses of the potential of PCs as productivity tools.

Dan Bricklin, a Harvard MBA student, got the idea for an electronic spreadsheet when he saw his professor erasing values from a worksheet he had drawn on the blackboard and trying to do all the necessary recalculations while class was in session. In 1978, Bricklin, with the aid of another Harvard MBA student, Dan Fylstra, and an MIT student, Bob Frankston, developed VisiCalc, an abbreviation for *Visible calc*ulator. VisiCalc was the first software package to minimize the need for recalculating budgets and schedules by hand.

VisiCalc was initially available for the Apple PCs only; it sold 200,000 copies its first two years, exceeding even Apple's sales predictions. VisiCalc was considered so appealing that it actually spurred people to buy computers: 20,000 Apple computers were sold primarily because people wanted VisiCalc. This is further proof that software drives the market.

Today there are dozens of spreadsheet packages that include many VisiCalc features.

Dan Bricklin, at right, and his colleague Robert Frankston designed VisiCalc, the first electronic spreadsheet package.

A screen in a database management system called dBASE for Windows shows the record layout for each customer.

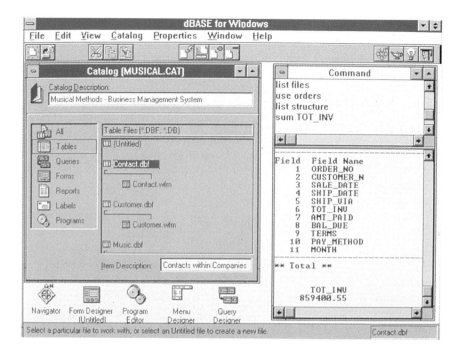

USES OF DATABASE MANAGEMENT SYSTEMS (DBMS)

1. To create database files
2. To enable database files to be displayed, edited, and updated
3. To enable users to inquire about data in the files and to obtain statistics and other summary data
4. To provide printed reports based on data in the database files
5. To join or link data in two or more database files for obtaining more comprehensive information

A **database management system (DBMS)** is the software used in an information system. The DBMS creates database files, edits and updates them as needed, and provides reports and responses to inquiries based on data in the database files.

ELECTRONIC MAIL, GROUPWARE, AND THE INFORMATION SUPERHIGHWAY Electronic mail (**e-mail**) establishes person-to-person connectivity. E-mail enables computer users to send, store, and retrieve messages by computer at any time of day or night from any location or to broadcast messages to multiple users. See Figure 3.4.

Electronic mail enables users to send messages to one another and to reply to, forward, print, store, or delete messages received.

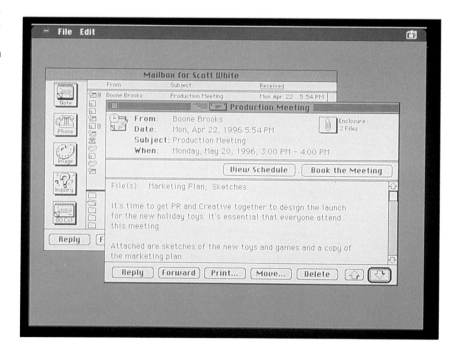

Looking Ahead

INFORMATION INTERCHANGE USING COMPUTERS

1. All people with access to a computer will be able to communicate with each other, either one-on-one or as members of teams or groups.
2. Vast amounts of public and private information will be available online including newspapers, library resources, government documents, etc.
3. Wireless commmunications will enable people to retrieve information from virtually any place in the world.

E-mail can be simple messages from one employee to another or messages flowing across the globe on an international network. Such messages can be basic text or contain multimedia elements such as sound, video, graphics, and animation.

Groupware is a term for software run on a network that allows teams of people to work on joint projects. Groupware can be used in a meeting with team members sitting at a conference table and typing their ideas on a PC. It can also be used individually by members of the team who are in different locations making their own comments or annotations to a file shared by all members. It includes not only e-mail capability but forms routing, project management tools, outliners, and so on.

E-mail and groupware are just the tip of the iceberg in what is shaping up as a communications revolution. The **Internet** is a global collection of over 12,000 networks supported by academic institutions, businesses, and governments. It enables users not only to communicate with one another using e-mail but to access data from vast databases on thousands of subjects. Currently, the Internet is also available to subscriber organizations, but the U.S. government is committed to ensuring all Americans access to these services. *Information superhighway* and *cyberspace* are catchall terms to describe networks like the Internet that will be accessible to all people for sending and receiving data and messages. Productivity is greatly enhanced by an individual's ability to have immediate access to all types of databases and to other users. Users can be employees within a company with networked PCs or with terminals that are linked to mainframes. Users can also be consumers who subscribe to services that provide e-mail capability.

Table 3.1 indicates some of the popular productivity tools that are available.

INTEGRATED PACKAGES AND SUITES Some products combine features of the four productivity tools into a single **integrated package.** The way you select and execute commands with each productivity tool in an integrated package is the same, so you need learn only one methodology. In addition, you have the ability to easily combine data from two or more tools. A spreadsheet created by

Critical Thinking

When predicted enhancements are added to e-mail and groupware software and the information superhighway becomes a reality, it is likely that the ways in which people communicate with one another and receive information will be revolutionized. These changes have the potential for significantly impacting society and the quality of life of individuals. Discuss some ways in which these aspects of computing are likely to impact your life. Do you think that people who can afford computers will become part of an "information elite" and that those who cannot afford computers will be "informationally disadvantaged"?

WORD PROCESSING	SPREADSHEETS
Word	Excel
WordPerfect	Lotus 1-2-3
Ami Pro	Quattro Pro

DATABASE MANAGEMENT	COMMUNICATION TOOLS
Paradox	Access to the Internet and other e-mail services
dBASE	Lotus Notes
Access	Novell Groupwise

Table 3.1 *Common Productivity Tools*

IN A NUTSHELL

PRODUCTIVITY ENHANCEMENTS

1. **Word processing** reduces the time it takes to create and edit documents.
2. **Electronic spreadsheets** enable users to set goals, make plans, and analyze results.
3. **Database management systems** enable users to integrate information, extract information, and report on trends.
4. **Communication tools** enable users to electronically send and retrieve data and messages.

the spreadsheet component of an integrated package, for example, can easily be added to a report being prepared by the word processing component. Microsoft Works and Claris Corp.'s ClarisWorks for the Mac are examples of integrated packages. The term "Works" has become a generic word for this type of software.

Integrated packages were once very popular because they offered word processing, spreadsheet, database, and e-mail capability in a single product for a relatively low cost. But integrated packages have traditionally been limited in their capabilities—the features of each component are not as great as those of individual products.

A more recent software trend is for manufacturers to offer their popular, full-blown productivity tools packaged together at a very low cost in what is called a **suite** of products. Microsoft Office, for example, is a suite that includes Microsoft Word, Excel, Access, Microsoft Mail, and a multimedia presentation graphics package called PowerPoint that is used for creating electronic slides. Sold separately, the software costs hundreds of dollars more than the suite. We discuss these types of packages in more depth in Chapter 7.

Self-Test

1. (T or F) Software should be selected before hardware.
2. (T or F) Most PC users purchase application packages rather than write their own custom programs.
3. (T or F) Productivity tools are a part of operating systems software.
4. Define and describe four productivity tools.
5. What is the difference between an integrated package and a suite?
6. What is the Internet?

Solutions

1. T
2. T
3. F—They are types of application software.
4. a. word processing package for entering, editing, and printing documents
   b. spreadsheet package for representing data in column-and-row format, for calculating automatically, for graphing results, and for determining the impact of potential changes ("what-if" analysis)
   c. database management package for creating, editing, and updating files and for producing reports and answering inquiries about the status of those files
   d. e-mail and groupware for electronic communication among users
5. An integrated package is a single software product that has word processing, spreadsheet, DBMS, and e-mail features. It is usually not as sophisticated as the individual productivity tools. A suite consists of the separate, full-blown productivity tools packaged as a unit. An integrated package is *one* software tool; a suite consists of separate packages.
6. The Internet is a global collection of networks supported by academic institutions, governments, and businesses. Users with access to the Internet can send each other e-mail messages and access thousands of databases.

3.2 COMMON FEATURES OF PRODUCTIVITY TOOLS

Productivity tools, like most software products, are supplied to users in a package that includes programs on disks. Most programs are supplied on a series of 3½-inch disks, which are usually copied to a hard disk. Large programs may be available on CD-ROM, a compact disk with a very large storage capacity. For older computers, software is also available on 5¼-inch disks. Before purchasing software, be sure you understand what type of hardware you will need to use it. Requirements such as CPU type and size of main memory are usually prominently displayed on the outside of the package.

The software package routinely includes a user's manual or set of manuals with step-by-step procedures for using the product. Most software must be installed, which means it must be configured to run with your specific computer. Nowadays the step-by-step setup procedures are clear and include screen displays to show you what to expect when you install a program and how to respond to the questions asked. If you are using a productivity tool that has already been installed, then you can skip installation details and begin by learning how to use the product.

Loading the Program

All programs must be read, or loaded, into main memory from disk before they can process data. Once a program has been loaded, an initial screen display introduces the product and provides some licensing information describing your right to use the software. See Figure 3.5 for an example. A message is usually

Study Objective

2. Describe the common functions of productivity tools, integrated packages, and suites.

IN A NUTSHELL

The operating system must be loaded into the computer before you can run an application program.

Figure 3.5 *This is an initial Lotus screen display.*

Welcome to the Lotus 1-2-3 Install Program

Welcome to the Install program. This program installs 1-2-3 and configures it for your system.

Thank you for your decision to use Lotus 1-2-3.

Government users: This software is subject to Restricted Rights, as set forth in the Lotus License Agreement.

Copyright © 1994 Lotus Development Corporation. All rights reserved.

Your name: [   ]

Company name: [   ]

Attention network administrators: Select the option below if you are installing the application on a file server.

☐ **Install on a file server**

[Next >]   [Exit Install]   [Help]

displayed on this screen telling you how to move to the main screen. Typically, you are asked to press a key to continue. After you press the key indicated, a main screen appears. That screen enables you to begin using the product, usually by selecting items from a menu.

Creating and Retrieving Files

All software products enable users to input data in order to create files. Most often, you begin using a productivity tool by creating a data file. Word processing packages create document files, spreadsheet packages create spreadsheet files, DBMS packages create database files, and e-mail packages create message files. The files created can be displayed or printed, and they can also be saved on disk or other storage medium for future reference or processing.

To save a file you must give it a **filename.** Rules for forming filenames vary, but for most packages a filename of one to eight characters (letters and digits) will be acceptable. The package adds a three-character file extension, which is separated from the filename by a period; this file extension identifies the file as one created by the specific product. PAYROLL.DBF, for example, is a data file created by dBASE, a DBMS product; BUDGET.WK4 is a data file created by the Lotus spreadsheet package. File extensions make it easier to identify files on a disk. All files with a .WK1 extension, for example, are Lotus spreadsheet files. Filenames should be as meaningful as possible to help identify the application area. PAYROLL, for example, is a better name than DATA1, which is not very informative. Newer operating systems like Windows 95 have fewer restrictions for defining filenames.

Status Lines

When a productivity package is loaded into main memory and the main screen is displayed, status lines appear at the top or bottom of a screen. See Figure 3.6. The status line or lines provide information about the file you are currently

Figure 3.6 *The Microsoft Word for Windows status line at the bottom of the screen includes details about the position of the cursor within the document and the size of the display. It also specifies that the current default is CAPS (uppercase) mode and that the NumLock key (NUM) has been pressed.*

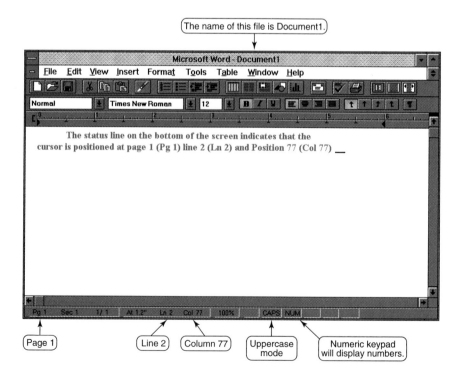

working on. It might also include some details regarding date and time, and existing settings or **defaults** for the product. Some packages, for example, start up in uppercase mode; this means that whatever you type appears as uppercase letters. If so, the status line often includes the term CAPS. To change the setting, or default, you press the Caps Lock toggle key on the keyboard. A toggle key is like an on/off switch: pressing it once changes the setting; pressing it a second time resets the key to its original value. Consult *Getting Started with DOS* or *Getting Started with Windows* for a detailed discussion of the computer's keyboard.

Data Entry

When you begin entering data, a cursor on the screen tells you where you are. The status line also indicates the position of the cursor, as you saw in Figure 3.6. You can change the location of the cursor, which sometimes blinks, by using the cursor control keys ($\uparrow, \downarrow, \rightarrow, \leftarrow$) or a mouse to navigate around the screen when you are entering data. There are other cursor control keys as well that work with some packages: PgUp scrolls up a set number of lines (which is a page on a screen); PgDn scrolls down a set number of lines; Home takes you to the first entry on the screen or the first line of the file; End takes you to the last entry on the screen or file. Some products, particularly word processing and electronic mail packages, provide you with a full, free-form screen so you can enter data anywhere you like. Other products, particularly spreadsheet and DBMS packages, require you to enter data according to more specific data entry rules.

All packages permit you to correct data entry errors. If you realize your mistake immediately, you can always use the Backspace key to delete a character and move the cursor one position to the left. Each time you press the Backspace key, the character at the cursor is erased and the cursor repositioned.

As you type, your text or data appears on the screen and the cursor moves to the next position. Many packages require you to press the Enter key when you are ready to actually transmit the data to the computer. Suppose you press the Enter key and *then* realize you made a mistake. To correct errors in data that has already been transmitted to the computer, you typically use the cursor arrows or a mouse to move back to the error point and then make the required changes. You can replace erroneous characters or insert new characters. The INS, or Insert, key is a toggle key that controls whether your corrections will add a character (insert mode) or replace an existing character with another (replacement or typeover mode). Changing *cot* to *cat,* for example, is accomplished by moving the cursor to the *o* and replacing it with an *a* when you are in replacement mode. Alternatively, you can add characters, like changing *cot* to *coat* when you are in insert mode.

Basic Commands and Function Keys

As noted, you begin using most packages by entering data to create a file. To perform operations such as saving a file, retrieving a file, or printing a file, you must select the appropriate **command.** Commands are most often selected from **menus,** which usually appear at the top of the screen. You use the cursor control keys or a mouse to highlight the menu item desired and then select it by pressing the Enter key or clicking the mouse. Sometimes there is a main menu that, when selected, provides you with submenu items or pull-down menu items. See Figure 3.7 for typical menu items.

ɪɴ A NUTSHELL

Use either the cursor control keys or a mouse to navigate around a screen.

Figure 3.7 *Typical menu items and icons used in a word processing package.*

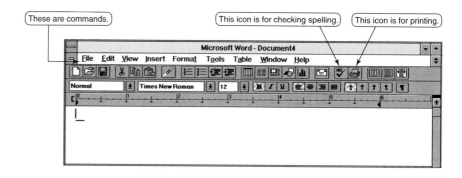

As an alternative, most packages also enable you to use **function keys** labeled F1–F12 to execute some commands. With some packages, pressing the F10 function key, for example, may be the same as highlighting the Save command and selecting it. Menu items that are selected with a mouse can also be selected by using a combination of keystrokes. In Figure 3.7, for example, the File menu item has an underscore under the F (i.e., File). This means that instead of clicking in on File with the mouse to select this command, you can press the Alt key and, while it is depressed, press the F key. All other menu items can be selected by pressing the Alt key and then the underlined letter in the command.

As you begin to use a productivity tool, you may need help. Windows-based software includes a Help command on the menu line. Selecting Help provides a Table of Contents of help items as well as offering a way to search for help on any topic. DOS-based software usually uses the F1 function key for **context-sensitive help,** which consists of screen displays that pertain specifically to what you are currently doing in the package. Say you select a file command and then you ask for context-sensitive help by pressing the F1 function key. A screen display will appear indicating file command options. To leave (exit) the help screens, or any other menu item, you usually press the Escape, or Esc, key. Help screens can be printed as well as displayed, for ease of reference.

IN A NUTSHELL

To get started with any software package, learn how to:
1. Load the program.
2. Name a new file that you will create or retrieve an existing file.
3. Enter a new file.
4. Edit or make changes to a file.
5. Select and execute commands.
6. Save the file.
7. Print the file.
8. Exit the program.

Figure 3.8 *A block of text can be cut, copied, or moved using a word processing package. This is sometimes called "cutting and pasting."*

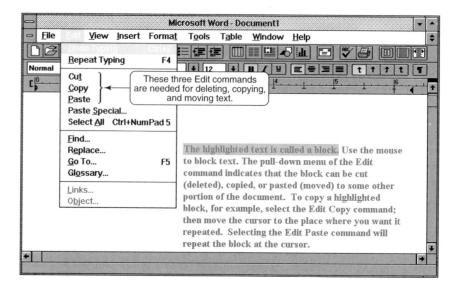

A command common to most productivity tools enables you to define or highlight a section of a data file called a **block** and move it, copy it to another place in the file or to another file, or delete it. We call this **cutting and pasting** blocks of data. See Figure 3.8.

Search and Replace

Another time-saving feature of productivity tools is called the **search and replace** command. Rather than scrolling through a file looking for a specific data item, you can execute a command that will take you directly to that item. This feature positions the cursor at the item being searched and enables you to change or replace it. In document files, you can find specific terms or topics using the search and replace command without having to read the entire file. Figure 3.9 shows

(a)

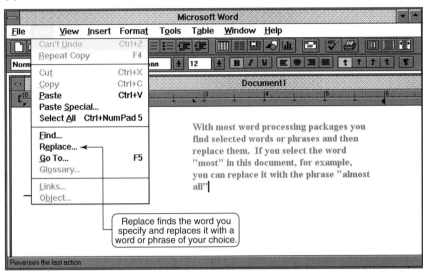

(b)

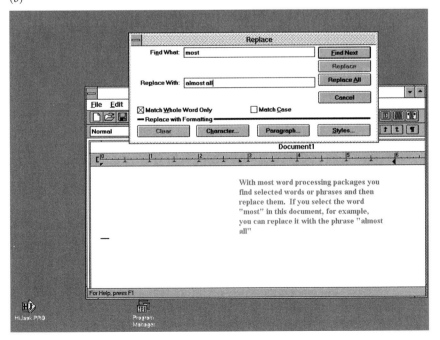

Figure 3.9 (a) *Selecting the replace command.* (b) *After the command is executed the word "most" will be replaced by "almost all" and the paragraph will be realigned if necessary.*

how a search and replace command can take you to the first occurrence of a data item selected, the last occurrence, or all occurrences—a *global search and replace*.

Commands are available with most productivity tools to format data to be printed. Formatting is used to print headings, set margins, select type fonts, specify page numbers, highlight entries with boldface or italic, and so forth.

Macros

Many productivity tools enable users to add customized sets of instructions called **macros** to facilitate the creation and use of data files. Macros are usually used to save keystrokes or to make the data entry operation easier. Macros can be inserted in a word processing file, for example, so that it is automatically formatted according to your predefined specifications or so that it contains a graphic image or special heading. You might write a macro to establish a file format that you will use to create numerous files, so you do not need to individually select the formatting commands from menus each time. In a spreadsheet file, you might create a macro that automatically produces a graph and prints it, according to your specifications, with just a touch of a key rather than having to select items from several menus.

Importing Files

When you import a file, you copy data already created into the file you are currently working on. Perhaps you are working on a word processing document file and decide to add a copy of a letter that you wrote previously. Most packages permit you to do this. Most also provide some compatibility across product lines thereby enabling you to add spreadsheet files to word processing files, for example. See Figure 3.10.

Figure 3.10 *Productivity tools often have multiple uses. Most word processing packages can import a spreadsheet or a database into a document.*

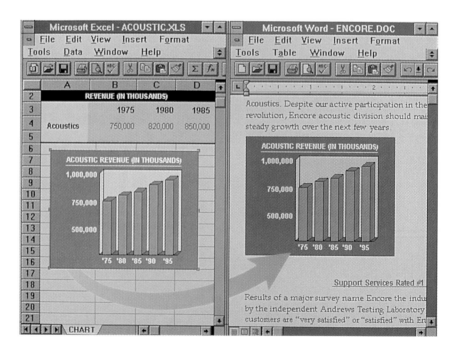

Self-Test

1. Software packages are used to _____ files. To operate on the data, we typically select _____ from _____ or use _____ keys.

2. Most productivity tools enable you to use _____ arrows to move around the screen.

3. The _____ line usually indicates date, time, name of a file, and default settings.

4. (T or F) Often files can be created by a spreadsheet package and imported into a word processing document.

3.3 UNIQUE FEATURES OF PRODUCTIVITY TOOLS

The overall look and feel of productivity tools is similar from one type of package to another. Here we focus on why specific tools are so useful. You may find that some of the so-called unique features of each productivity tool are not that unique at all, and what is stated here as pertaining to a spreadsheet package may be available with your word processing package or DBMS. As newer versions of packages are developed, they tend to offer many more features common to most productivity tools.

Study Objective

3. List the most important features of productivity tools.

Word Processing Packages

The one use of computers that makes the biggest difference for the greatest number of people, regardless of their particular interest or field of expertise, is word processing. Once people become adept at using a computer for word processing, they pack away their typewriters and invariably wonder how they managed without word processing for so long. A word processor is like a car, copy machine, or portable telephone: Once you learn how to use it, it becomes a tool you feel you cannot live without.

In this chapter we emphasize word processing packages for general-purpose computers. Some computers are, however, special-purpose word processors; that is, they perform no other function but word processing. Such special-purpose systems are called dedicated computers.

UNDERSTANDING THE CAPABILITIES A word processing package is a program or set of programs used to enter, edit, format, store, and print documents where a document is a letter, report, or any type of text. Documents are created and then printed and/or stored or saved. Later, they can be retrieved and mod-

---

Solutions

1. create (or edit); commands; menus; function

2. cursor control

3. status

4. T

ified. They can also be printed at any time, with as many copies as you need. All word processing packages make it relatively easy to alter or edit a text on the screen while it is being created or later when you are reviewing it. This minimizes the drudgery of typing because the document does not need to be rekeyed every time changes are made. Making on-screen changes to a document is called **text editing.** You simply use a mouse or the appropriate cursor arrow keys to return to a portion of text that needs to be changed and then make the changes.

Each time you make a change to the document the word processing package automatically reformats it so that it is perfectly aligned. There is no need for using "white out," for physically cutting and pasting paragraphs to reorganize the document, or for making handwritten corrections. Moreover, you need not use copy machines to make duplicates since you can print as many extra copies as you need.

Organizations use word processing packages to increase productivity by helping employees communicate better in written form. Documents prepared by word processing packages tend to read better because the user does not have to worry about making mistakes. Typos or spelling errors are so easy to correct that users can focus on the message being conveyed rather than on pressing the correct keys. In addition, the user can easily reorganize a document to determine the structure that best conveys the message. Moreover, the message conveyed in the document can be enhanced stylistically by highlighting, formatting, or changing type fonts. As a result, word processing documents have the potential to convey more meaningful messages.

As noted, if you make insertions or deletions in a document the program automatically realigns the paragraphs according to the margin specifications you establish. Margins, line spacing, and page lengths can be set, reset, and changed for different parts of the document. Left margins are usually justified, which means that they are precisely aligned. Right margins can be ragged or right-justified, whichever you prefer. See Figure 3.11.

Figure 3.11 *Margins in a document can be ragged right or right-justified.*

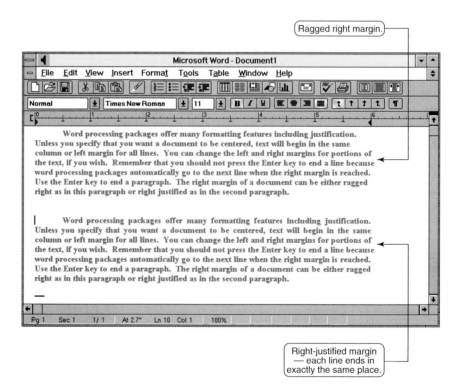

Besides data entry and text editing capability, word processing packages have several other important features:

• Most word processing packages include a spelling checker for finding errors and a thesaurus for providing synonyms. You typically invoke the spelling checker feature to look for spelling errors after a document has been completely entered. If a word is unrecognizable to the package, it will be listed as a spelling error. Correctly spelled words that are similar to the one typed will appear on the screen. See Figure 3.12. If one of the displayed words is the correct version of what you typed, you can replace the misspelled word with the correct one by highlighting the word you want and pressing a single key to select it. If your original entry is correctly spelled but is a special term not in the package's dictionary, you can add it to the dictionary so that

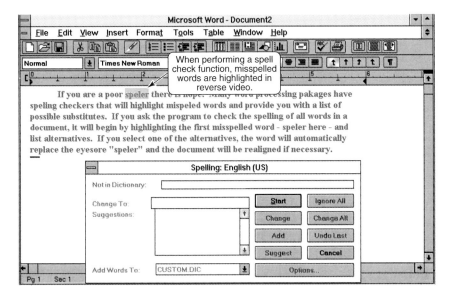

Figure 3.12 *Most word processing packages can check the spelling of words, suggest alternatives for misspelled words, or add unrecognized words from a document to the dictionary so that these words will not be flagged in the future as spelling errors.*

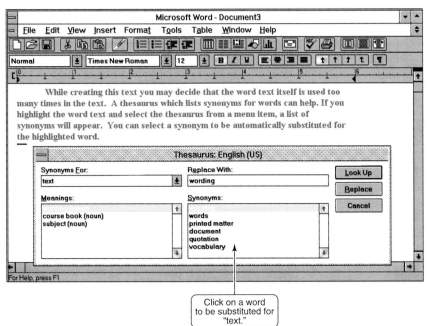

Figure 3.13 *Most word processing packages have a thesaurus from which you can select synonyms for highlighted words. Grammar checkers are also included with most word processing packages.*

it won't be flagged as an error in the future. Synonyms from the thesaurus can also be automatically inserted into a text and properly aligned with a few keystrokes. See Figure 3.13. Some word processing packages have grammar and style checkers as well, and even small encyclopedias and almanacs so information can be added to or "pasted" into a document.

- Most word processing packages can create a bibliography, index, and table of contents automatically.

- The text in all word processing files can be blocked so it may be deleted, copied, or duplicated in another place. Copying standardized portions of text into a contract, will, or other document with a word processing package is called **boilerplating** and is a common technique used by legal firms. See Figure 3.14.

Figure 3.14 *Boilerplating enables you to import standard clauses, like terms of an agreement, procedures to follow if a problem arises, instructions, and so on, into documents. Each clause can be stored in a separate file and accessed as needed.*

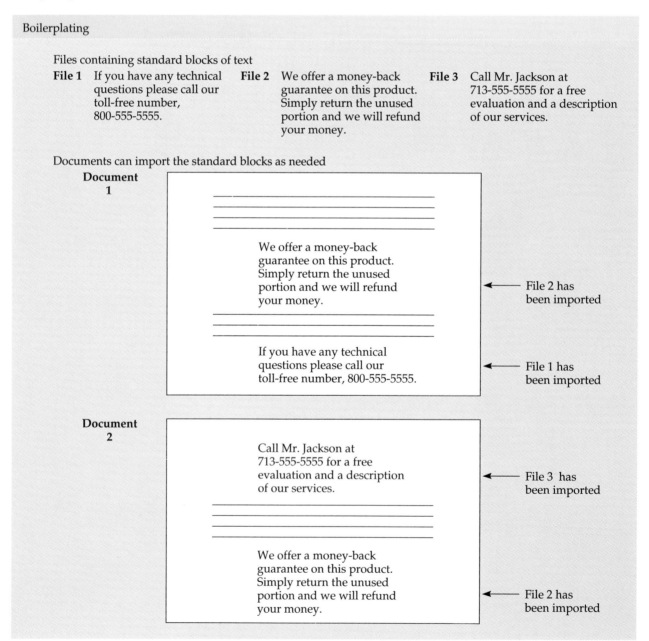

Boilerplating

Files containing standard blocks of text

File 1 If you have any technical questions please call our toll-free number, 800-555-5555.

File 2 We offer a money-back guarantee on this product. Simply return the unused portion and we will refund your money.

File 3 Call Mr. Jackson at 713-555-5555 for a free evaluation and a description of our services.

Documents can import the standard blocks as needed

Document 1

We offer a money-back guarantee on this product. Simply return the unused portion and we will refund your money.

If you have any technical questions please call our toll-free number, 800-555-5555.

File 2 has been imported

File 1 has been imported

Document 2

Call Mr. Jackson at 713-555-5555 for a free evaluation and a description of our services.

We offer a money-back guarantee on this product. Simply return the unused portion and we will refund your money.

File 3 has been imported

File 2 has been imported

- A document file and a name-and-address file can be merged to produce form letters that look personalized. See Figure 3.15.

Many word processing programs enable users to add to documents graphics, photos, or images that have been scanned in; spreadsheets or other files, even video and sound, can also be added. With a sound file added to your document,

Figure 3.15 *A name-and-address file can be merged with a document file to create personalized letters.*

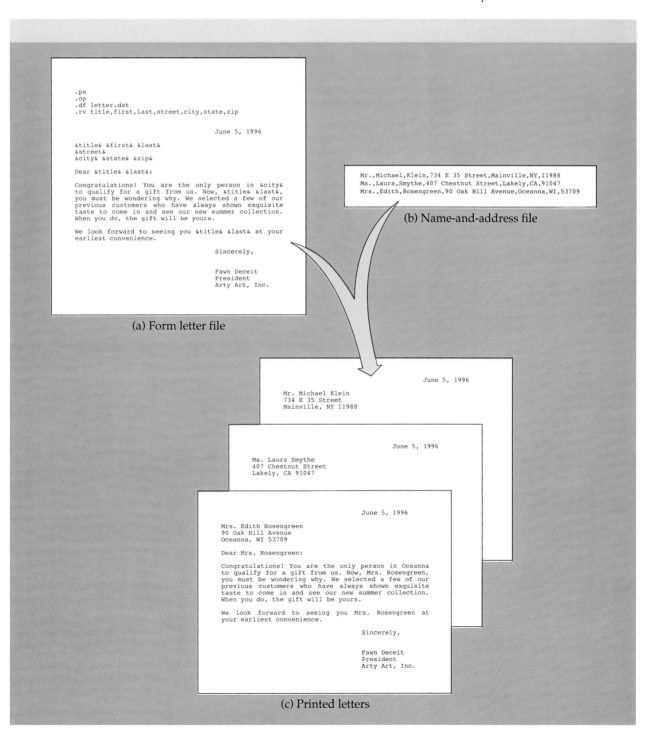

(a) Form letter file

(b) Name-and-address file

(c) Printed letters

 **Looking Ahead**

AROUND THE GLOBE

New word processing packages are becoming multilingual. They can convert blocks of text to different languages, or display or even verbally "read" a document to a user in a number of foreign languages.

for example, you can send verbal messages that add some explanation or personal commentary.

The status lines of word processing packages may have date and time, name of file, and defaults, but they are also likely to have the document's current page number, the current line number, and the column where the cursor is positioned (where the character you type will appear on the screen).

The page, line, and column numbers on the status line change as you type as does the position of the cursor, which sometimes blinks. Remember that you use the cursor control keys or mouse to return to any previous point in a document to make corrections.

WORD PROCESSING COMMANDS In the next section we will discuss how you enter text into a document using the keyboard. But first keep in mind that the package's commands enable you to perform various functions before, during, and after you type the document. Depending on the product, you may be able to use function keys to accomplish many tasks, select commands from a menu, or click on an icon. Often, the Ctrl, Alt, and Shift keys are used with the function keys to execute additional commands.

Most often, Windows-based productivity tools use **pull-down menus** to accomplish specific tasks. See Figure 3.16. To select a command and then a pull-down menu item associated with that command, you may move or drag the mouse to highlight the command and then press or "click" the left mouse button to select it. Alternatively, you can use the cursor arrow keys ($\rightarrow$ and $\leftarrow$) to highlight a command and then press the Enter key to select it. Once the command has been selected, you can use the mouse or the $\downarrow$ or $\uparrow$ cursor keys to highlight the pull-down menu item. Clicking the mouse or pressing the Enter key selects the highlighted pull-down menu item. Often icons appear on a Toolbar line, which can be activated with a click of a mouse. These icons are shortcuts to accomplishing a task.

Commands available with most Windows-based word processing software include:

MENU LINE COMMAND	SOME SELECTIONS AVAILABLE FROM PULL-DOWN MENU
File	Open, Save, Close, Print
Edit	Cut, Copy, Paste, Find, Replace, Go To, Undo changes
Insert	Page break, page numbers, picture, date and time
Format	Type font, heading indentation, line spacing, right justification, convert to other language
Tools	Spelling check, grammar check, thesaurus
Help	An index of items can be selected or a search for a specific topic can be performed

Typically, pressing a specific function key or selecting File Save from a pull-down menu will save your document file on disk; pressing another function key or using the mouse to click on an icon will center a heading or other text on a line, and so forth.

ENTERING TEXT IN A DOCUMENT You begin by loading the word processing package into main memory and then executing the command to create a new document. You type a document as you would with a typewriter. As you type, the cursor moves one position to the right on the screen where the next character you key will appear.

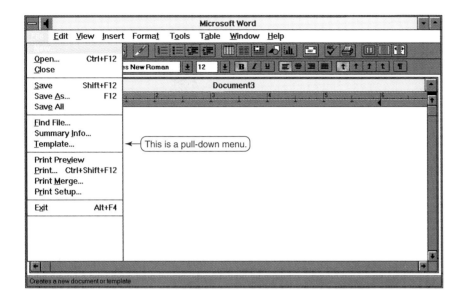

Although word processing is very much like typing, there is one important distinction. You do *not* press the Enter key at the end of each line as you would press the carriage return key or reset the carriage on a typewriter. Word processing packages automatically proceed from line to line as you key. This saves a considerable amount of time since you do not need to constantly look at the document or listen for a ring that warns you that you are near the end of a line. With all word processing packages, you use the Enter key only when you want to end a paragraph, *not* a line.

If the cursor is near the end of a line and a full word cannot fit on that line, the package automatically performs a **word wrap;** that is, it brings the last word on the current line down to the next line. If the right margin of the document is to be ragged, then blanks appear at the end of the first line. (Look at Figure 3.11 again.) If the right margin is to be right-justified as left margins are, then **microjustification** occurs. This means that the spacing between words on each line is adjusted to make the right margins "flush" as they are on the left. If right justification is selected, then, some words may have more spaces between them than others. See Figure 3.17. Sometimes the microjustification required to achieve right justification results in large spaces between words. If you prefer, you can have the computer automatically hyphenate long words rather than simply perform word wrapping. This minimizes the large gaps between words in a right-justified document.

To make corrections, you can use the backspace key to delete to the error point or you can use the cursor control keys or a mouse to move the cursor to the error point and insert or replace characters. Each time you add or delete characters or words, the word processing package automatically reformats so that the document looks perfect.

Word processing packages enable you to type page after page of material. Since a screen displays only about 24 lines of text, you may need to scroll forward or backward to see other parts of a document you are entering or editing. Use the PgDn key to scroll forward one page and the PgUp key to scroll back one page.

All word processing packages have similar types of commands, such as retrieving, formatting, and printing. The methods used for executing the commands are, however, package specific.

ᴵᴺ A NUTSHELL

The cursor arrow keys and the mouse enable you to move around the text without erasing characters; the backspace key erases as it backspaces.

Figure 3.17 *With word wrap, words that do not fit on a line are automatically moved to the next line. For right-justified text, microjustification results in the realignment of words on each line so that they are flush-right. This is done by adding spaces between words.*

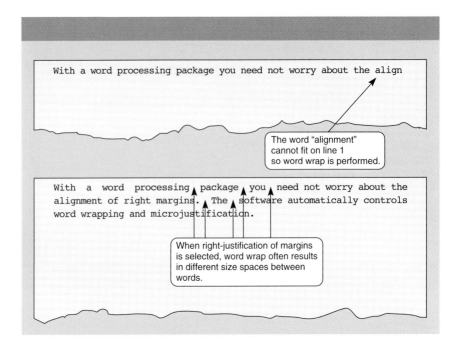

UNIQUE FEATURES OF WORD PROCESSING PACKAGES

1. Spelling checker, thesaurus, grammar checker, small encyclopedia, or almanac are available.
2. Bibliography, index, and table of contents can be created automatically.
3. Different type fonts, styles, and formats may be used in a document. See Figure 3.18.
4. Personalized letters may be created by merging a document file with a name and address file.

Figure 3.18 *Most word processing packages can display and print documents using a number of different type fonts and sizes.*

Many word processing packages enable you to display on a screen just what you would see if the text were printed. This feature is called **WYSIWYG** (wizzy-wig), a tongue-in-cheek term for *what you see is what you get.*

In Chapter 7, we discuss *desktop publishing* software. These packages use word processing files to create printed documents that are of such high quality that they appear to be typeset. Currently, desktop publishing packages are noted for including extensive formatting and printing options to achieve a published look, whereas word processing packages are noted for extensive text editing capabilities. Newer packages, however, incorporate both word processing and desktop publishing features.

Electronic Spreadsheets

Spreadsheet packages create worksheet, or spreadsheet, files that represent data in column and row form. Accounting worksheets are used for budgets, income statements, and ledgers but many other documents, such as schedules and tables, can represent data in column-and-row form as well.

UNDERSTANDING THE CAPABILITIES Spreadsheets are used for reporting, graphing, analyzing, forecasting, or projecting. Spreadsheets enable you to:

1. Prepare worksheets and reports that are formatted properly and are arithmetically correct.
2. Make corrections or changes easily and perform automatic calculations. Numeric data can be changed without affecting the validity of the results. Formulas are automatically recalculated each time a numeric entry used in a formula is changed.
3. Determine the effects of hypothetical changes to data. We call this what-if analysis.
4. Reuse formats or worksheet "shells." An empty worksheet shell can be created that contains labels and formulas but no data. Such shells are called **templates.** The worksheet templates can be used to create different spreadsheets, each

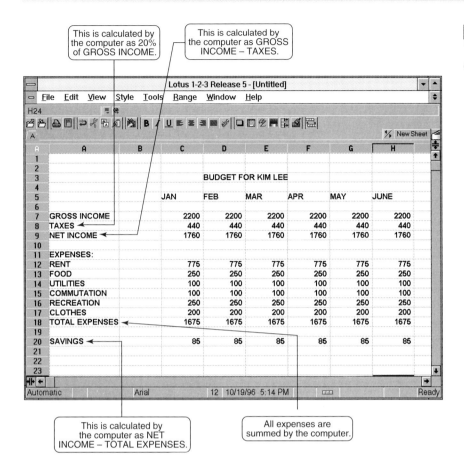

This is calculated by the computer as 20% of GROSS INCOME.

This is calculated by the computer as GROSS INCOME – TAXES.

This is calculated by the computer as NET INCOME – TOTAL EXPENSES.

All expenses are summed by the computer.

Figure 3.19 *Budgets that have figures "spread" over months or quarters are often created using a spreadsheet package.*

with different data. Consider the budget in Figure 3.19, which was prepared by a spreadsheet package. This budget can be reused in a number of ways.

a. For Kim Lee's budget next year, using the same formulas.

b. For distribution to others so they can use the same format for entering their own data. If Jerry Johnson thinks he has the same expenses and no others, he can use Kim Lee's spreadsheet format as a template. He can enter his own values for wages, rent, food, clothing and leisure and have the computer generate totals.

c. For projections or what-if analysis. If Kim Lee estimates that her wages will increase by 10 percent next year, that her rent will increase by 15 percent, and that her other expenses are likely to increase by 5 percent, she can use her spreadsheet format as a template to make the necessary changes. See Figure 3.20.

d. Similarly, if Jerry Johnson is considering a new job in a different city, he can enter the new job's wages and estimate his other expenses to see instantly what impact such a change would have on his financial position.

To facilitate reusability, a spreadsheet should include formulas or should *copy* data from other cells where possible. In our budget only one column of values needs to be entered. If you expect all values to be the same for each month, FEB–JUN data would not need to be keyed. Rather you would copy the JAN entries using a copy command. In this way, an actual change, anticipated change, or hypothetical change needs to be made only to the one column. All other cells will then reflect the change.

5. Modify a worksheet as needed. Suppose you like the format of Kim Lee's budget but you have other expenses. You own a car and you have a small life

Figure 3.20 *Budgets, like any worksheet, can be used to view the outcome if certain projections are made, or if you want to see the impact of hypothetical changes. When spreadsheets are used for evaluating anticipated changes so that decisions can be made, we call this "what-if" analysis.*

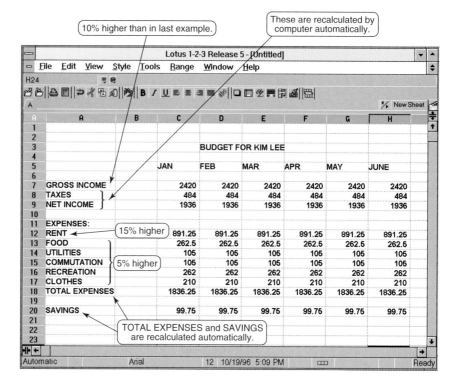

insurance policy. You do not pay rent because you live with your parents. You want your budget to include figures for JAN–MAR only. This does not mean that you must create an entirely new spreadsheet. You can easily modify the existing spreadsheet by deleting the entries for APR–JUN. You can add rows for car payments, car insurance, parking, gas, and tolls and for life insurance premiums. When changing columns and rows, however, formulas sometimes need to be adjusted as well. See Figure 3.21.

Figure 3.21 *You may use an existing spreadsheet's format as a template or "shell" for your own individual needs. Here, Jerry Johnson used Kim Lee's budget as a template and made modifications as necessary.*

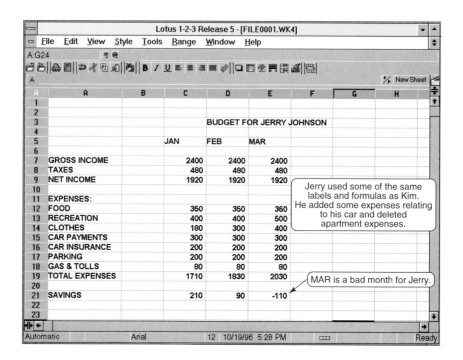

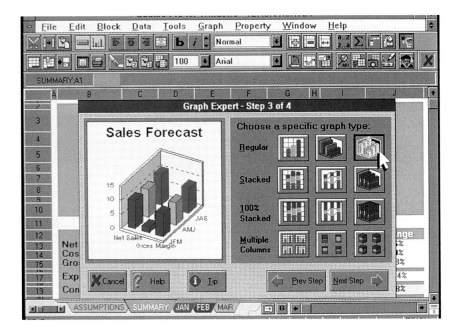

Figure 3.22 *A sales forecast created by a spreadsheet package.*

6. Print and graph results. Sometimes data is easier to analyze when it is in graphic form.

Figures 3.22 and 23 are sample worksheets created by spreadsheet packages. We illustrate them here just to familiarize you with the various types of data that lend themselves to being represented in spreadsheet form. Spreadsheets can be used in all of the basic functional areas of a business. In all cases, data is entered and formulas established by the user to enable the package to automatically perform calculations and recalculations if changes are made.

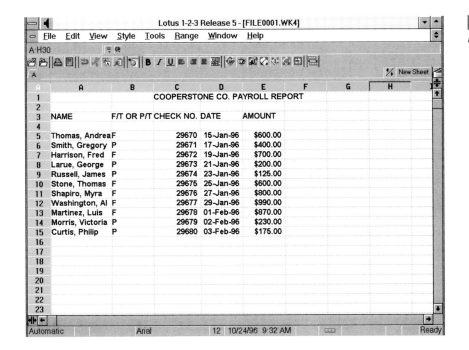

Figure 3.23 *A payroll report created by a spreadsheet package.*

Figure 3.24 *An income statement created by a spreadsheet package.*

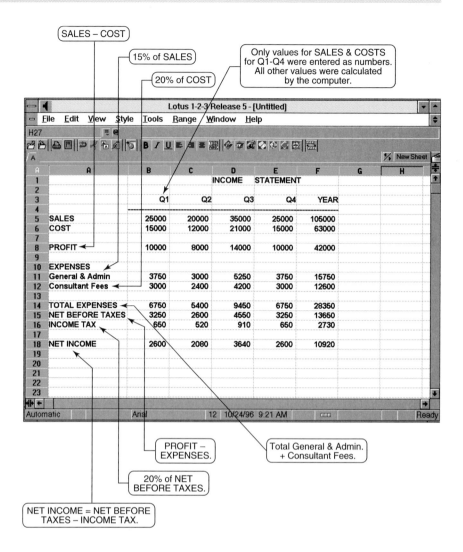

SALES – COST

15% of SALES

20% of COST

Only values for SALES & COSTS for Q1–Q4 were entered as numbers. All other values were calculated by the computer.

PROFIT – EXPENSES.

Total General & Admin. + Consultant Fees.

20% of NET BEFORE TAXES.

NET INCOME = NET BEFORE TAXES – INCOME TAX.

ENTERING DATA IN CELLS AND USING COMMANDS We will refer to the Income Statement in Figure 3.24 to illustrate how spreadsheets are designed. The worksheet consists of columns and rows. A column is a vertical section identified by letters A–Z, AA–AZ, BA–BZ, and so on. A row is a horizontal section identified by a number from 1, 2, 3, and so on. Data is entered into worksheet locations called cells, which are the boxes formed by the intersection of columns and rows (see Figure 3.25). Cell location B3, for example, refers to a cell in the B column on row 3. The number of cells in a worksheet depends on the package but most have millions of cells available.

You enter identifying labels, numeric data, or formulas in cells. You should always enter a formula when feasible rather than calculating the results yourself. By entering formulas rather than doing calculations yourself, you minimize errors. In addition, any necessary recalculations will be automatic.

When you begin, cell location A1 will be highlighted with a shaded rectangle. This shaded rectangle is called a cell pointer and it indicates the active or current cell. It serves as the cursor point. If you enter data, that data would automatically be placed in the cell highlighted by the cell pointer.

You may use the cursor arrows keys on a keyboard or a mouse to move the cell pointer to different locations. In addition, the PgDn key moves the cell pointer down 20 or so rows (one full screen display), PgUp moves it up 20 or

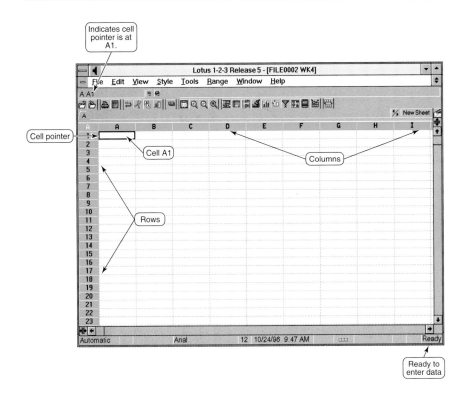

Figure 3.25 *Rows, columns, and cells in a spreadsheet.*

so rows, Home brings it to cell location A1, and End brings it to the last filled cell location or to the last physical cell location, depending on the package. Many spreadsheet packages also have a "GO TO" function key that enables you to move directly to specific cell locations.

Spreadsheet packages enable you to enter data but they also have commands for operating on that data in a wide variety of ways. Some of the more common commands are discussed next.

Save, retrieve, and print the spreadsheet. In addition to the standard formatting commands that set margins, lengths, and so on, a spreadsheet can be printed in compressed format so that more columns appear on a single page. A spreadsheet can also be printed sideways, or in landscape mode, so that the entire spreadsheet appears as one contiguous unit—not in pieces. Moreover, for checking purposes, each cell value or formula can be made to print on a separate line. See Figure 3.26. To print a file, you select the appropriate print command and then choose various options.

Change the size of cells in individual columns or in all columns. Most spreadsheet packages have a default or preestablished cell size—usually nine characters, which can be changed by the user. Sometimes you may want a column with more characters. For example, the first column in a spreadsheet typically contains labels for identifying rows of data, where a label may require more than nine characters.

Insert, move, or delete rows or columns.

Copy formulas. Consider the spreadsheet in Figure 3.24. We can enter the formula that subtracts COST from SALES in cell location B8 and then repeat a similar formula for cells C8 through F8. Or we can copy the formula. When copying

Figure 3.26 *An Income Statement like the one in Figure 3.24 can be displayed or printed in cell-formula mode, with the contents of each cell printed on a single line. The cell formulas here are for part of the full spreadsheet.*

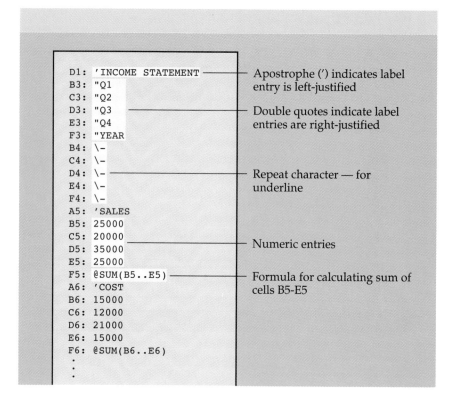

```
D1:  'INCOME STATEMENT ────── Apostrophe (') indicates label
B3:  "Q1                       entry is left-justified
C3:  "Q2
D3:  "Q3 ─────────────────── Double quotes indicate label
E3:  "Q4                       entries are right-justified
F3:  "YEAR
B4:  \-
C4:  \-
D4:  \- ──────────────────── Repeat character — for
E4:  \-                        underline
F4:  \-
A5:  'SALES
B5:  25000
C5:  20000
D5:  35000 ────────────────── Numeric entries
E5:  25000
F5:  @SUM(B5..E5) ──────────── Formula for calculating sum of
A6:  'COST                      cells B5-E5
B6:  15000
C6:  12000
D6:  21000
E6:  15000
F6:  @SUM(B6..E6)
  .
  .
  .
```

a formula, the spreadsheet assumes you want automatic adjustment for columns and rows. So if the formula at B8 is +B5−B6 and you copy it to C8, the computer makes a column adjustment and enters +C5−C6 in C8. This process is called relative addressing. If a copy command is to use *fixed cells* in all formulas, then relative addressing can be overridden; this process is called absolute addressing. See Figure 3.27 for an illustration of absolute and relative addressing.

Figure 3.27 *Relative addressing, absolute addressing, and mixed addressing.*

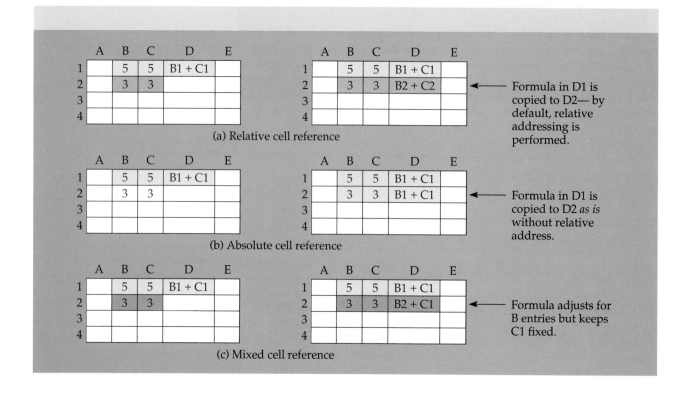

(a) Relative cell reference

Formula in D1 is copied to D2— by default, relative addressing is performed.

(b) Absolute cell reference

Formula in D1 is copied to D2 *as is* without relative address.

(c) Mixed cell reference

Formula adjusts for B entries but keeps C1 fixed.

Use functions. Spreadsheets have built-in functions that can be used to evaluate or operate on data. The user does not need to actually enter formulas that are already stored. For example, to find the sum of cell locations E1 to E7 and place the result in E8, you can enter the formula $+E1+E2+E3+E4+E5+E6+E7$ in cell E8, or you can enter a function in E8 called the @SUM function: @SUM(E1 . . E7). The dots (. .) mean "through." You can type this as you see

(*a*)

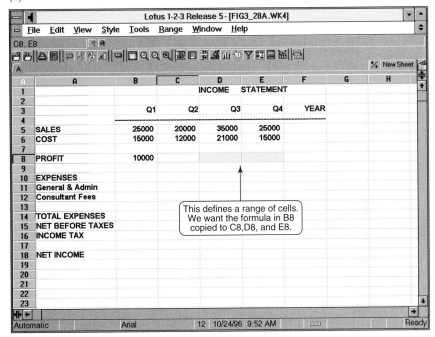

(*b*)

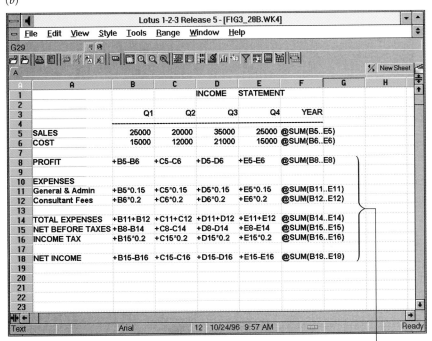

Figure 3.28 (*a*) *When copying formulas, you must indicate the range of cells where the copied formula is to be placed.* (*b*) *The formulas are entered in the B column and in cell F5 and then copied to the relevant cells. This is how the spreadsheet looks in formula mode after all copy commands have been executed.*

• ➤   *Looking Ahead*

SPREADSHEETS

- The playing field is shrinking. That is, fewer companies are challenging Lotus 1-2-3, Borland's Quattro Pro, and Microsoft's Excel.
- Ease of use continues to be the main selling point.
- Access to data in database files is increasingly important in spreadsheets. Tools for analyzing information in an organization's database have been added to spreadsheets.
- Spreadsheets will either have groupware and e-mail features or be linked to other products that have them.

As with all software, the key innovations of today are becoming the standards of tomorrow.

it or you can use the cursor or mouse to highlight the block of cells E1 . . E7 that needs to be summed. See Figure 3.28.

Some other common arithmetic and statistical functions are:

@AVERAGE(range)	Finds the average value in a range of values
@MAX(range)	Finds the highest value within a range of values
@MIN(range)	Finds the lowest value
@COUNT(range)	Counts the number of items in a range
@SQRT(number)	Finds the square root of a number

Financial functions, mathematical functions, date and time functions, and database functions are also available with most spreadsheet packages. Financial functions are particularly useful because they perform complex operations such as calculating interest rates, balances, and amortizations. The user need only enter the variables and the package will generate the results using built-in functions.

Graph. Numeric data in a spreadsheet can be graphed to provide a pictorial representation of the data for analysis or decision making. Graphs are usually in bar, pie, or line form. Graphs can be displayed, saved, retrieved, and printed. If your monitor or printer has the capability, graphs may be displayed or printed in color. Legends, borders, titles, and other data can be added to the graph. See Figure 3.22.

Create database files and functions. Spreadsheets can be used to create simple database files. We discuss packages specifically designed for processing database files next.

Database Management Systems

UNDERSTANDING THE CAPABILITIES A database management system (DBMS) is a set of programs that creates database files and enables users to edit and update the data and to inquire and report from the files. DBMS programs allow you to manage data using a computer. You may add, delete, change, sort, or search for data in a database using a DBMS. Your college or university may use a DBMS to store information about you and your courses on a computer. The information in a database is stored in database files on disk rather than in manual file folders. A DBMS enables you to enter and use the information in your database file just as you would use data in file folders, except that the computer quickly performs searches, sorts, calculations, and printing. The examples presented in this section are just illustrations. They could, however, be used by many businesses in their day-to-day operations.

The many uses or applications for a DBMS include:

- Mailing lists (membership and subscription lists).
- Accounting (bookkeeping and accounting information).
- Scientific research (experimental data, scientific journals).
- Business information (customers, vendors, inventories).
- Personal use (record, tape, or book library).
- Library and government databases (scientific, academic, and federal publications).

A wide variety of database management systems is available for use not only with micros but with larger computers as well. Micro-based database management systems sell for several hundred dollars or less, while those for larger systems are much more expensive, mainly because they have far greater capability. Most mainframe-based DBMS products are leased rather than purchased. It is not uncommon, for example, for a highly sophisticated DBMS to lease for tens of thousands of dollars per year or more. Although this seems expensive, in the end it is usually cheaper for an organization to lease a DBMS than to develop its own programs.

We will see in Chapter 12 that there are various ways in which data can be organized in a DBMS. For now, you should know that a database management system is used for creating, editing, and updating data and for answering inquiries and producing reports in a timely fashion. A DBMS can be used to integrate or join files so that data can be shared, and help keep access to files secure.

USING A DBMS As we have seen, most word processing and spreadsheet packages require you to select commands from menus or use function keys. With a DBMS you may similarly select commands from a menu. Some DBMS products offer the user a choice of modes: either selecting commands from a menu or actually typing commands on your own (command mode). See Figure 3.29 for a sample database.

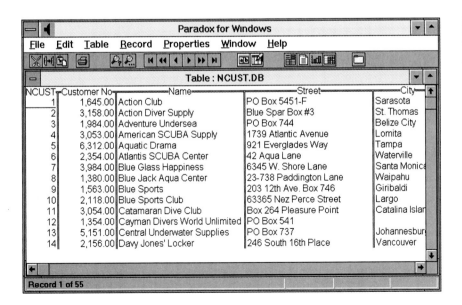

Figure 3.29 *This is a screen display of a customer database created using Paradox for Windows.*

Databases Are Widely Used on Computers from PCs to Mainframes. Users with PCs may have their own personal databases on disk. Users connected to client-server networks may access their organization's databases stored on a disk maintained by the server.

Entering Data in a Database. Before a database can be constructed or retrieved you need to know how to structure data. A database file is a collection of information in a specific subject area. Database files differ from what are called **flat files** in that database files can be joined, or interrelated, while each flat file must be processed separately. We have payroll files, inventory files, accounts receivable files, and so forth. A file is subdivided into **records** and each record is a unit of information pertaining to one item in the file. A payroll file, for example, consists of payroll records; each record pertains to a specific employee. Similarly, an accounts receivable file consists of individual customer records. Each record includes specific elements called **fields.** An employee record within a payroll file, for example, may have a Social Security number field, an employee name field, and a salary field. See Figure 3.30.

Keep in mind that a DBMS is capable of *joining* two files by using a key field that appears in both files. Suppose a company has an employee file and a sales file, each with records identified by the Social Security number of the salespeople. The two files can be joined using Social Security number as a key field to determine the commissions of all salespeople based on their sales.

Creating a Database File. Before actually creating a database file, you begin by naming it and then specifying the format of records within that file. To specify a format, you indicate the following five characteristics.

1.   The sequence in which fields are to be entered in a record. The first field specified is the first one in the record, and so on.

Figure 3.30 *Fields are contained within records, and all records are contained within a database file. Before creating a database file using a DBMS, you must define the format of each record. This is a layout of how fields have been defined for records within an employee database file.*

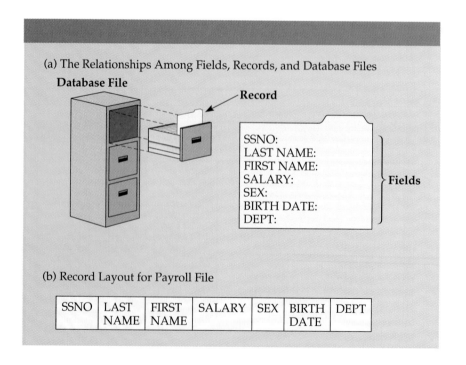

(a) The Relationships Among Fields, Records, and Database Files

Database File

Record

SSNO:
LAST NAME:
FIRST NAME:
SALARY:
SEX:
BIRTH DATE:
DEPT:

Fields

(b) Record Layout for Payroll File

SSNO	LAST NAME	FIRST NAME	SALARY	SEX	BIRTH DATE	DEPT

2. Each field's name. Each DBMS has rules for forming field names. Most often, a field name must begin with a letter and contain some combination of letters and digits. With some DBMSs, blanks between words are not permitted; words can always be run together or separated by an underscore, such as LASTNAME or LAST_NAME. Rules for forming field names are typically displayed on the screen or are available from a help screen.

3. The field type. Each DBMS offers a number of field types including:

   a. Character or alphanumeric: for alphabetic fields or fields that can contain any characters including letters, digits, and symbols, such as an address field.

   b. Numeric: for fields used in arithmetic.

   c. Date: for fields using a date format such as mo/yr, mo/dd/yr, dd/mo/yr.

   d. Logical or binary: for fields designating either/or, yes or no, on or off (e.g., salaried/hourly or male/female could be designated this way).

4. The width or size of fields. When all records are to be the same fixed length, then each field must be given a size that is large enough for all or most entries. A last name may be 20 characters, for example. Fields can be filled with spaces if each position does not include a significant character. Some DBMSs, like Paradox for Windows, have users establish size for character fields only; other types of fields have their sizes established for each record as the data is entered.

5. Decimal positions. The number of decimal positions must be specified if a field has been designated as numeric.

Once the format for records in a database file has been established, you save the format. You can always add fields later on if the need arises. After the format has been saved, you can enter data as input. When you are ready to enter input, the DBMS provides you with an outline of what each record should look like. See Figure 3.31.

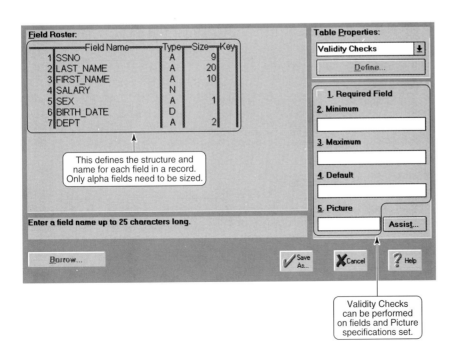

Figure 3.31 *This is how you would define fields within an employee record.*

Figure 3.32 (*a*) *An onscreen form (or template) representing field layouts for an employee record.* (*b*) *Users might find it easier to enter data using this "form" rather than the format shown in* (*a*). *A DBMS enables you to define your own screen layout for data entry.*

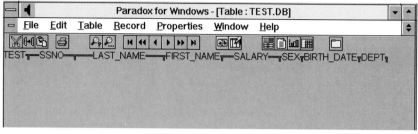

(*a*)

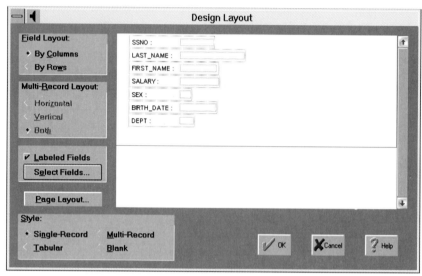

(*b*)

Correcting Data Entry Errors. Full-screen text editing is usually available with a DBMS; this means that while you are entering a record and it is displayed on the screen, you can return to previously entered fields using the cursor arrows or mouse to position the cursor to add data, delete data, or replace data. The rules for making corrections are similar to those for word processing packages.

When fields are defined, validity tests can also be specified to set up acceptable ranges for each field. Look at Figure 3.31 again. A salary field, for example, may be established with a range specified so that only salaries from a minimum of $15,000 to a maximum of $125,000 will be accepted. Similarly, other fields, like Social Security number, for example, may be established so that they *must* contain a specified number of characters (e.g., 9). If the user presses the Enter key before nine characters are entered, a message can be displayed. Similarly, some fields can be set up so that the user *must* enter data. Other fields may be protected for security purposes, so what the user enters is not displayed on the screen.

The method for entering data into a database file can usually be made more user-friendly for data entry operators. The DBMS designer can build a screen display that highlights and clarifies the entries to be made and establishes parameters or acceptable ranges for each field. See Figure 3.32.

Executing Database Commands. Once you have entered data into a database file, you can save it. A DBMS enables users to browse through a file or display a file to look for errors. The file may be edited or corrected when it is viewed. Users routinely update files by modifying existing records—replacing old values with new ones. Files can also be updated by appending or adding new records and deleting inactive or old records. Most DBMS products also enable the file's structure to be modified by adding or deleting new fields or changing the format of existing fields.

After a file has been created and edited, users can inquire about the status of records. Figure 3.33 illustrates the full file used in the examples in Figures 3.34 and 3.35, which contain answers to queries about the database.

A DBMS can also be used to generate reports. The user specifies the sequence in which output information is to appear, the actual information desired, the format, the headings, and any totals. See Figure 3.36.

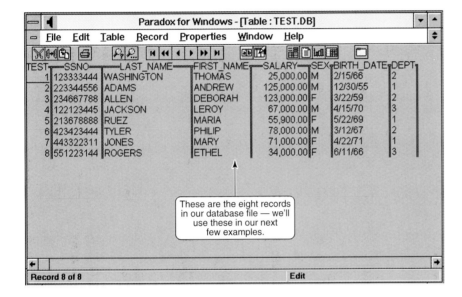

Figure 3.33 *A database file of eight employee records created using Paradox for Windows.*

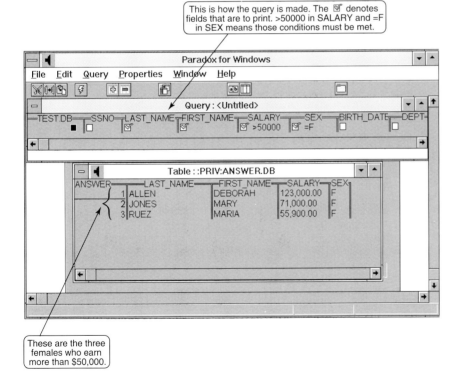

Figure 3.34 *Results of an inquiry: What are the first and last names and salaries of all females who earn more than $50,000?*

Figure 3.35 *Results of an inquiry: What is the average salary?*

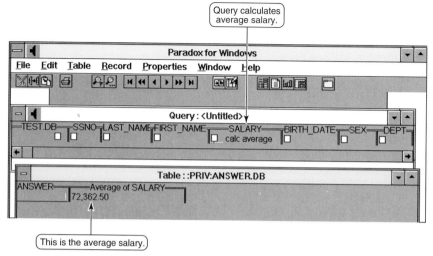

Figure 3.36 *A DBMS is often used to print reports. First the user fills in answers to questions. Then the DBMS generates the report.*

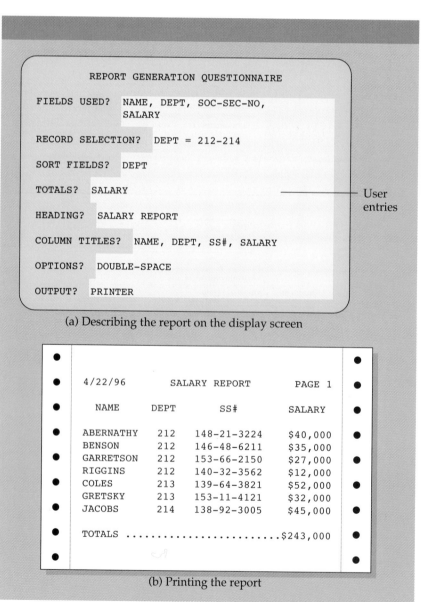

Both inquiries and reports can be generated from joined files in a database. Suppose you want to print the names, balance due, and items purchased by each customer in an accounts receivable file, along with product information for each purchased item, which can be obtained from a separate product file. You would use the item number as the key field in both files. The files can be joined and the required data extracted to generate the report. See Figure 3.37.

Files in a database can be sorted into any sequence for ease of retrieval. Files can also be organized with an index for quick retrieval of specific records. An index enables the computer to look up the location of records by key fields just the way you might look up the location of a book's topic from an index. We discuss indexing in more detail in Chapter 6.

In summary, database management systems are popular for four reasons:

1. They make data entry, editing, and updating relatively easy.

2. They allow records within files to be accessed quickly.

3. They enable users to create well-designed reports and to obtain quick responses to inquiries.

4. They enable managers and other users to generate desired output in a timely fashion without the need for a computer professional to write a program.

QUERY LANGUAGES One notable feature of DBMS products is that the language used to report from a database file or to answer inquiries is English-like and does not require knowledge of the actual procedures used by a computer to process data. Each DBMS has a **query language,** that is, a method of accessing records quickly and providing users who may not be computer proficient with necessary information.

A problem with query languages, however, has been that they tend to be different for each package; that is, query languages, like many computer products, are not standardized. As a result, users with knowledge of one query language cannot always transfer that knowledge to other products.

Figure 3.37 *The join feature allows files to be combined on a key field.*

Customer File				Product File		
Name	Current Balance	Item Number		Item Number	Item Description	Item Price/Unit
Mike Toony	60.00	100038		100038	Band saw	300.00
Jerry Layman	278.37	14066		14066	Shelving	37.95
Robert Steele	47.95	21373		21373	Hammer	9.50

Joined File				
Name	Current Balance	Item Number	Item Description	Item Price/Unit
Mike Toony	60.00	100038	Band saw	300.00
Jerry Layman	278.37	14066	Shelving	37.95
Robert Steele	47.95	21373	Hammer	9.50

Figure 3.38 *The query language SQL enables users to obtain data from different databases. In this instance, records for customers from California who are older than 20 are highlighted.*

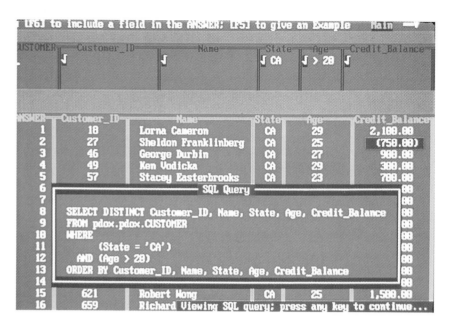

One way in which products get standardized is by persistent user demand. If users only buy products that are compatible with others, they can drive manufacturers toward standardization. During the past decade, one query language has emerged as a particularly user-friendly method of access. This query language is called SQL (for *s*tructured *q*uery *l*anguage). It has become so popular and widely used it is considered a de facto standard—a standard in fact although not formally designated as such. Now most DBMS products have their own proprietary query language but also enable users to make inquiries in SQL. Thus SQL users can make inquiries into database files created by a wide variety of database management systems. See Figure 3.38.

Electronic Mail, Groupware, and the Information Superhighway

Electronic mail or e-mail packages enable users to send messages, text, files, graphics, and faxes from one computer to another. Users can communicate with one another using e-mail in a number of different ways.

E-mail messages can be informal and read like verbal messages left on an answering machine, or they can be formal documents. The sender can transmit a message to one or more recipients and indicate whether the message is urgent. Once completed, the message can be transmitted any time that the network is active or whenever the user wants it sent; similarly, the message can be read by the recipient whenever he or she accesses the network. When users log on to a network, they are told if there is mail waiting. Messages, which can be scanned by subject or by degree of urgency, can be read, saved, forwarded, or responded to. See Figure 3.39 for an e-mail screen display.

Users may have access to a subscriber service that has an electronic mail (e-mail) facility so that all subscribers can communicate with one another. Some of these services, like CompuServe, Prodigy, and America Online are called subscriber services because they charge a fee to users. Anyone with a PC, a modem, and a communications software package can subscribe.

Users within an organization may be networked and have access to e-mail over the network so that all employees with a computer can communicate with one another.

Looking Ahead

E-MAIL, INTERNET, AND THE INFORMATION SUPERHIGHWAY

- Increasing numbers of individuals will be able to communicate with each other, but there will be a need to control or limit "junk" e-mail—unsolicited and unwanted broadcasts or advertisements.
- Increasing volumes of information from databases will be available at your desktop, but we will need better methods for efficiently accessing them. Currently users must scroll through thousands of files or filenames to locate information that may be useful to them.

- Users will be able to access and store the equivalent of a library of information on their PCs, but the need for security to prevent illegal access to networks will become even more critical. With illegal access comes the potential for damaging or destroying files you worked so hard to create.

Groupware extends the e-mail concept by enabling people to work together on shared projects and to communicate with each other more effectively in developing and improving those shared projects. In other words, groupware helps employees in workgroups manage information. It helps users collect, organize, process, and customize shared information. The most popular groupware products are Lotus Notes and Novell Groupwise.

As we have seen, the Internet is a computer network that enables users within governments, academic institutions, and businesses to send messages around the world to each other. There are currently more than 12,000 networks linked to the Internet. If you are a private individual who has no affiliation with an Internet organization, you can still access the Internet by subscribing to a service such as America Online. In addition to offering e-mail connectivity, subscriber services provide access not only to the Internet but to thousands of other databases with information on medicine, law, news, travel, and so on.

To access a subscriber service you need a communications package that permits the transfer of data over telephone lines. Kermit and ProComm are examples of such products. For sending messages over an organization's internal network, you need an e-mail package. E-mail packages for PCs include Lotus cc:Mail and Microsoft Mail.

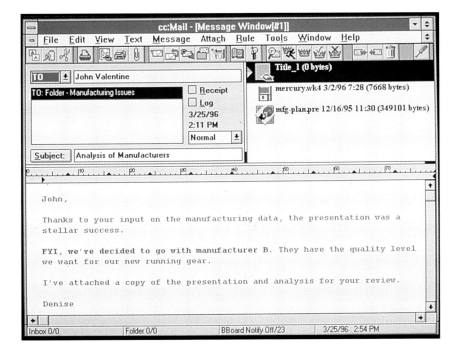

Figure 3.39 *A sample electronic mail screen display.*

The information superhighway will extend Internet facilities so that people all over the world will be able to more easily send and receive e-mail and access databases.

Self-Test

1. Right margins in a word processing document can be _____ or _____ .

2. Sometimes a word that is being typed using a word processing package cannot fit on the current line and is automatically brought down to the next line. What is this process called?

3. Name three types of data users can enter in spreadsheet cells.

4. (T or F) Formulas can be copied from one cell or range of cells to another cell using a spreadsheet package.

5. (T or F) A DBMS can be used to inquire about records in a database file and to report from the database file.

6. Name six criteria often used for evaluating productivity tools.

7. What is the term that describes copying a portion of text to other texts?

CHAPTER SUMMARY

Software is the driving force that makes computers work. **Application packages** are a type of prewritten software designed for business or personal use that can be purchased off-the-shelf. Some of the most important application packages used in business are known as productivity tools.

Study Objective

1. Describe what productivity tools are and demonstrate how they are used in business.

3.1 Understanding Software

Software is typically stored on disk and is supplied as program files. Disks can also store data files; these files contain data created by a software product and can be used for future processing.

Software users fall into three basic categories: users who need the output information to perform their jobs, software specialists who help customize software for individual use, and data entry operators who actually key in the input. Power users are those who wear all three hats; that is, they do the job of software specialists and data entry operators as well as analyze output.

The tools most widely used to increase employee productivity are called productivity tools. **Word processing packages** are used for entering, editing, and

---

Solutions

1. right justified; ragged right
2. word wrapping
3. labels; numeric data; formulas
4. T
5. T
6. speed, cost, compatibility, technical support, ease of use, quality of the documentation
7. blocking, or cutting and pasting blocks of text

printing **documents. Electronic spreadsheet** packages are used to create **worksheets** (spreadsheets), which represent data in column-and-row format and automatically calculate results. Once a format is established, the spreadsheet can be reused with different numeric values. Spreadsheets allow users to predict the outcome of hypothetical changes to data and to graph results. **Database management system (DBMS)** software is used for creating, editing, and updating **files** in a **database** and for inquiring about the status of those files or for reporting from files. A spreadsheet package can create independent or **flat files,** while a DBMS creates files that can be linked or joined. **Electronic mail (e-mail)** packages enable computer users to send, store, and retrieve messages at any time. **Integrated packages** combine the features of all four productivity tools. A **suite** is a group of popular productivity tools supplied by one vendor for a reduced price. The suite of products usually has a similar command structure.

3.2 Common Features of Productivity Tools

Productivity tools include some common features shared by most software. They create files and enable users to retrieve them if the files need to be changed or reused. Each file is given a **filename** and a file extension that identifies the program that created the file.

The main screen of each productivity tool has a status line containing information such as date and time and current settings, or **defaults,** for the product.

Data is initially entered, or typed, using the keyboard. Packages enable users to make corrections using the cursor arrow keys or mouse to return to an error, which can then be corrected. Data is operated on with the use of **commands** that are typically selected from **menus,** which are sometimes displayed as **pull-down menus** when a command is selected. **Function keys** may also be used to execute commands. Sometimes pressing a function key provides the user with **context-sensitive help.**

Typical commands include saving, retrieving, and printing files. A section of a data file called a **block** can be moved, copied, or placed at another point in the file or added to a different file. This process is called **cutting and pasting.** Productivity tools can also be used to find specific items in a data file and to make replacements; this process is called **search and replace.**

Many productivity tools permit you to write special instructions called **macros** to execute a series of commands either repeatedly or whenever the need arises. Many tools also allow files created by one productivity tool to be imported, or added, to files created by another productivity tool.

3.3 Unique Features of Productivity Tools

Word processing packages are used for **text editing** documents, that is, making on-screen changes to documents. In addition, they can format documents, check for spelling, and incorporate standard blocks of text (called **boilerplating**). Most have an electronic thesaurus for selecting synonyms. A bibliography, index, and table of contents may be created automatically and personalized letters may be prepared easily.

Word processing packages automatically perform **word wrap:** They bring words down to the next line if there is no room on the current line. If the space left at the end of a line is excessive, spacing among characters can be adjusted automatically to achieve a more even look—a process called **microjustification.**

Some word processing packages can display text on the screen just as you would see it if printed, even if the text has formatting codes. This feature is called **WYSIWYG** for *what you see is what you get.* Word processing files are also used in desktop publishing, where high-quality output is created that looks as if it is typeset.

Study Objective

2. Describe the common functions of productivity tools, integrated packages, and suites.

Study Objective

3. List the most important features of productivity tools.

Spreadsheet packages use locations called **cells,** which are formed where columns and rows intersect. Cells are used to store labels, numeric data, and formulas. Special functions can operate on data in cells. Graphic output can also be produced. A spreadsheet shell called a **template** can be created with only labels and formulas (no data); users then create many different worksheets using that shell or template, each with different data entered.

A DBMS creates **database files** consisting of **records.** Each record is a unit of data in a file. Records consist of **fields** of data. Every DBMS has a **query language,** which is a method for inquiring about the status of records.

E-mail message files are similar to files created by other productivity tools. They can be corrected as they are entered and operated on with commands like print, save, and retrieve. **Groupware** is software that enables users to work in teams. The **Internet** and subscriber services enable users to communicate with each other and to share resources including thousands of databases.

KEY TERMS

Application package, *p. 60*
Boilerplating, *p. 76*
Block, *p. 71*
Cell, *p. 62*
Command, *p. 69*
Context-sensitive help, *p. 70*
Cutting and pasting, *p. 71*
Database, *p. 63*
Database file, *p. 63*
Database management system (DBMS), *p. 64*
Default, *p. 69*
Document, *p. 62*

Electronic mail (e-mail), *p. 64*
Electronic spreadsheet, *p. 62*
Field, *p. 90*
File, *p. 63*
Filename, *p. 68*
Flat files, *p. 90*
Function key, *p. 70*
Groupware, *p. 65*
Integrated package, *p. 65*
Internet, *p. 65*
Macros, *p. 72*
Menu, *p. 69*

Microjustification, *p. 79*
Pull-down menu, *p. 78*
Query language, *p. 95*
Record, *p. 90*
Search and replace, *p. 71*
Suite, *p. 66*
Template, *p. 80*
Text editing, *p. 74*
Word processing, *p. 61*
Word wrap, *p. 79*
Worksheet, *p. 62*
WYSIWYG, *p. 80*

CHAPTER SELF-TEST

1. What are the four major categories of productivity tools?
2. Name the four files created by each of these tools.
3. A package that combines the features of the four productivity tools and adds some features of its own is called a(n) _____.
4. The intersection of a column and a row in a spreadsheet is called a _____.
5. (T or F) Once a spreadsheet is set up, you cannot insert new rows or columns, so it is important to get it right the first time.
6. @ SUM is an example of a special kind of formula called a _____.
7. (T or F) Some keys on the keyboard are assigned special tasks by each software package.
8. (T or F) All software packages have default settings that assume certain initial values; the user can override such defaults.
9. To end a paragraph in a word processing file, press the _____ key.
10. The _____ keys are used to move the cursor around the screen.

11. (T or F) The structure of a database file can be changed by the user even after data has been entered.

12. Global changes to a file means that _____.

13. A _____ of text can be moved, copied, or deleted from files. The term _____ is used to denote the concept of importing sections of standard text into a current document.

14. (T or F) Records in a database file that meet user-specified criteria can be displayed or printed.

15. (T or F) Electronic mail files can be sent to more than one recipient without having to reenter the message.

REVIEW QUESTIONS

1. What is the purpose of help screens in application packages?

2. What are the benefits of using a word processing package over simply typing a document on a typewriter?

3. What types of page formatting tasks can be performed by most word processing packages?

4. Assume you have created a document in which you repeatedly referred to the date of an upcoming meeting as being March 24. The meeting has been changed to March 28. What would be an efficient way of changing each occurrence of March 24 to March 28?

5. Suppose you are a teacher. What type of productivity tool might you find most useful to maintain student grades? Why?

6. List three tasks that can be performed by a database management system.

7. Based on magazine reviews, brochures from computer stores, manuals, or other information, compare the graphics features of the latest versions of two leading spreadsheet programs. One of these should be Lotus 1-2-3; the other

---

Solutions

1. word processing; spreadsheet; DBMS; e-mail
2. document files; spreadsheet, or worksheet, files; database files; message files
3. integrated package
4. cell
5. F
6. function
7. T
8. T
9. Enter
10. cursor control arrow
11. T
12. changes are made to the entire file
13. block; boilerplating
14. T
15. T

should be either Microsoft Excel or Borland's Quattro Pro. How many kinds of graphs does each offer? What kinds are available in each? (Good sources for reviews include *InfoWorld, PC, PC World,* and *PC Computing,* which should be available in campus and public libraries.)

CRITICAL THINKING EXERCISES

1. What if You Have a Technical Question?

Because of declining profits resulting from decreased software costs, many software companies have reduced their technical support services. Major competitors once offered unlimited toll-free phone support. Today, such support is limited to 180 days—at best. The clock starts ticking when you make your first call. When free support has expired, most companies will provide additional technical support for a fee.

Do you think reduced technical support will impact sales?

2. At least half of U.S. and U.K. executives lack basic personal computer (PC) skills, according to a study conducted by Robert Half International. The reasons cited ranged from "fear" to "time pressures."

The survey asked 100 top executives in both the United States and the United Kingdom, "In your opinion, what percentage of the nation's top executives is not computer literate?" The answers were 55 percent of executives in the United States and 51 percent of executives in the United Kingdom lack computer skills.[1]

a. Why do you think many executives lack PC skills?

b. What can be done to overcome the problem?

3. Over 7,000 elementary school students in Minnesota and Northern California, including the Los Alamitos Elementary School in San Jose, CA, are connected from home to their schools through an online network test program. The network is maintained by French telecommunications company 101 Online, a subsidiary of Meta International, and is accessed through microcomputers or Minitel terminals and telephone lines. Parents can look at their child's homework assignments and attendance record, or communicate with teachers through e-mail. Students are often assigned homework on the network, which may include sending e-mail to pen pals at other schools, checking the stock market, or finding local weather reports. The network, which is free to the test families for six months, is targeting families that do not have microcomputers but may be interested in having online access to the children's schools.[2]

Do you think that this type of computing use will help children learn more and retain more? Explain your answer.

[1]*Source:* Half of top executives are computer illiterate, Linda Rohrbough, Computer Select, April 1994: Articles, *Newsbytes,* Dec. 22, 1993, pNEW12220028.

[2]*Source:* Computer links parents to schools (Meta International subsidiary 101 Online offers 101 Online information service), Michelle Quinn, Computer Select, April 1994: Articles, *New York Times,* March 30, 1994, v143, pB7(N), pB10(L), col 1 (18 col in).

Case Study

With Electronic Communications, Does the Medium Influence the Message?

The proliferation of electronic communications in the office has brought with it a host of questions that users must deal with in the next few years, but the thorniest of these may not have much to do with hardware specifications or software capabilities. They may have to do with etiquette. Office workers quickly learn the proper way to deal with each other in the face-to-face situations that come up each workday. But communications via e-mail and groupware is another scenario altogether, one for which no manuals have yet been written.

A few rules have surfaced, however, and new ones are being tested all the time. Most experts agree, for example, that bad news should still be delivered face to face, instead of being entrusted to the "cool" media of electronic communications. Anger and hostility, never in vogue in the office, do not belong on e-mail either. Known as "flaming," the practice of sending inflammatory messages across electronic pathways is frowned upon. Phone mail is best for delivering fast updates on familiar situations and coming to quick agreement when few people are involved in the decisions. E-mail can handle both uncomplicated announcements and complex ideas; it is also ideal for technical information that needs to be "written down" or saved for accuracy and comprehension.

Depending on your point of view, e-mail may not be so good for emotional messages that should be reconsidered before being sent. Some e-mail proponents, however, say that it fosters an open writing style that is more personal and casual than traditional forms of communication. Indeed, office romances have been known to blossom over networks where people are often less inhibited than they would be in face-to-face encounters.

Groupware has the potential to speed up the bonding process by which a collection of people become a cohesive team. By facilitating fast communication among all parties, increasing access to important information, and allowing members to participate in group or individual training as a project proceeds, groupware often pays for itself in very little time. It cannot replace the

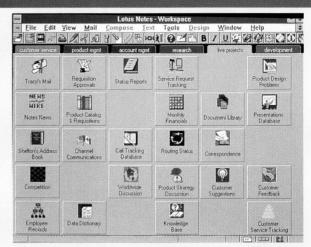

Groupware and e-mail can enhance the flow of information among co-workers and even impact the way people communicate with each other.

team leader, however, who still plays a vital role in resolving conflicts, mediating disputes, and smoothing over the difficulties that can arise among team members who do not get along.

As standards for e-mail and groupware products are formulated and come into wide use, the integration of multimedia packages is expected to grow, and to bring its own array of etiquette questions with it. Voice, video, and animation can, for example, have sexual connotations which some people might find offensive.

Analysis

1. Do you think that the casual, informal style of writing that is fostered by the use of e-mail will have a positive or negative impact on office communications?

2. What are some of the advantages of groupware as defined in this case?

3. Should an office worker send personal messages over e-mail? Explain your answer.

4. Describe some ways in which multimedia could add some content to an e-mail message.

PART TWO

Hardware Advances the Information Age

The tasks computers perform not only minimize human effort, they also help improve the quality of life. Smart appliances include microwaves that cook to perfection and sewing machines that sew any stitch automatically. Smart tools, from magnetic resonance imaging devices to voice synthesizers, push the limits of medical diagnosis and care. Smart homes have computing devices to provide comforts from security to automatic climate control. Smart cars, phones, and cameras have built-in microprocessors that make them more efficient as well as easier and more enjoyable to use.

Some very **large and complex computers** perform sophisticated tasks that require data from many remote locations to be gathered and processed instantly. Even most **smaller computers** are powerful enough to enable individual users almost anywhere to collect and process data from virtually any source in the world.

General-purpose computers require specific instructions, supplied in the form of programs, to accomplish their functions. In contrast, **special-purpose**

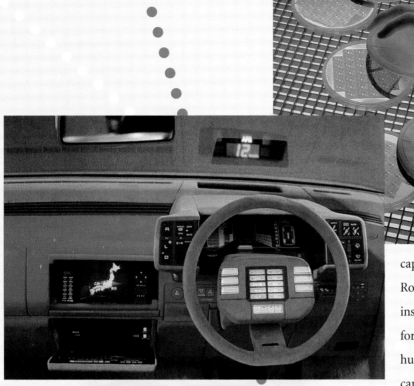

computers such as robots have built-in capabilities to perform very specific tasks. Robots can work with enough precision to insert chips into a circuit board. They can perform scientific experiments too dangerous for humans to undertake, like exploring a volcano's crater. They can even embark upon interplanetary explorations, as did the Rover vehicle that recently landed on the surface of Mars.

Computing need not be purely functional and utilitarian; both hardware and software can be **customized** to express the user's personal style. Consumers can use computers for gathering specific information or simply to learn more about the world. **Multimedia computers** not only provide their output in the form of words but also use

sound, video, animation, and high-quality graphics to make information more dynamic and ultimately more usable.

TOURISM INFORMATION

CHAPTER 4
Computer Processing

4.1 HOW THE CPU PROCESSES DATA

Overview of Components and Operations

Primary Storage or Main Memory

The Arithmetic/Logic Unit

The Control Unit

Registers and Machine Cycles

4.2 HOW THE CPU REPRESENTS DATA

The Binary Numbering System

Bits, Bytes, and Words

EBCDIC and ASCII

Error Checking with Parity Bits

4.3 COMPUTER ARCHITECTURE

Chip Technology: One-Upman-"Chip"

Clock Speed

Processing Speed

Bus Width and Word Size

Main Circuit Boards and Expansion Slots

Additional Devices for Improving Processing Power

4.4 METHODS OF PROCESSING DATA

Batch Processing

Interactive Processing

The Main Processing Technique: A Record at a Time

Regardless of their size, cost, and power, all computers process data in essentially the same way. Micros are simply smaller, less expensive, and less powerful versions of larger systems. Remember that in order for data to be processed, a program must first be loaded into the computer system. The program indicates what type of input is to be read, what processing is to be performed, and what output is to be created.

In Chapter 4 we focus on main memory and the central processing unit, or CPU, of a computer system.

Study Objectives

After completing this chapter you should be able to:

1. **Describe the properties of the CPU that make it the heart of the computer system.**
2. **Explain how data is stored in a computer.**
3. **List the factors that affect a computer's processing power.**
4. **Describe the common methods of processing.**

■ 4.1 HOW THE CPU PROCESSES DATA

Overview of Components and Operations

Chapter 1 introduced a computer system as a group of hardware devices that read data as input, follow programmed instructions to process that data, and produce information as output. A computer system is defined in terms of its central processing unit. The VAX minicomputer manufactured by the Digital Equipment Corporation (DEC), for example, has a VAX CPU; the AS/400, a midrange computer from IBM, has a CPU that identifies it as an AS/400.

Peripherals, or input/output units, are linked to the CPU, which controls their operation. Because of the wide variety of hardware available, users must set up, or configure, a computer system with the type of input, output, and storage devices that will satisfy their specific needs. For example, one system may be configured with three printers and two disk drives, whereas another may need a sound board, CD-ROM drive, scanner, and five disk drives. Hardware linked to a CPU can be obtained from the computer manufacturer or from a manufacturer who specializes in producing specific input/output (I/O) devices. A larger system may have dozens or even hundreds of input/output devices. A PC is limited to a relatively small number of such devices depending on the number of I/O connections, or **ports,** it has. See Figure 4.1.

Networking Peripherals. The CPU can be linked to peripherals in two ways: (1) by cable if the devices are in the same physical location as the CPU and (2) by communication facilities such as telephone lines or special cables if the I/O devices are not at the same local site as the processor.

Networks enable PCs to share peripherals. In school labs, for example, there are apt to be many more computers than printers. This is because students spend most of their time using computers to process data; printing is the last activity performed after all processing has been completed. On average, it may take 1½ hours to complete a computer assignment and only three minutes to print the

Typical IBM-Compatible

The Back of the System Unit

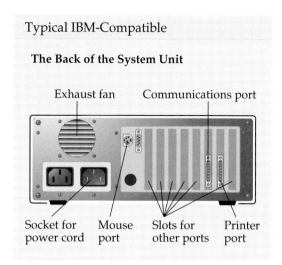

Exhaust fan   Communications port

Socket for   Mouse   Slots for   Printer
power cord   port   other ports   port

Figure 4.1 *Ports allow input/output and communication devices to be connected to other parts of the computer system.*

output. If each PC had its own printer, the peripheral would be idle most of the time. To save money, most PC labs have only a few printers that are networked to dozens or hundreds of computers. Output to be printed is queued under network control so that students can retrieve their printouts from some central location.

The operations typically performed by a CPU are:

1. CPUs control the reading of programs and input files.
    a. The CPU activates input units to read programs and data.
    b. The CPU controls the transmission of program and data files from disk to main memory (primary storage).
2. CPUs process data according to the instructions in a program.
    a. Data can be processed arithmetically—numbers can be added, subtracted, multiplied, and divided.
    b. Logical tests can be performed on data (e.g., comparing the contents of two fields) to determine a course of action.
    c. Data can be transmitted or copied from one area of primary storage to another.
3. CPUs control the creation of output. The CPU activates an output unit and controls the transmission of outgoing information to that unit.

ɪɴ A NUTSHEʟʟ

CPU OPERATIONS
1. The CPU controls transmission of data from input devices to memory.
2. The CPU processes data that is in main memory.
3. The CPU controls transmission of information from main memory to output devices.

Although CPUs for all types of computers have become much more sophisticated in recent years, the basic operations they perform have remained fairly constant.

Because all computer operations are under the control of the CPU, it is often referred to as either "the brains" of a computer or "the heart" of a computer. Now let us look at the CPU in detail. A CPU has the following functions:

1. It interfaces with main memory for storing data and programs.
2. It controls each operation through the **control unit.**
3. It performs arithmetic and comparison operations in its **arithmetic/logic unit.**

Main memory is on the same circuit board as the CPU so that the control unit and the arithmetic/logic unit of the CPU can interface directly with main memory.

Most computers use **integrated circuits,** also called **chips,** for their CPUs and main memory. A chip is approximately $\frac{1}{16}$ to $\frac{1}{2}$-inch square and about $\frac{1}{30}$

Figure 4.2 *A Pentium micro-processor chip. A chip is a tiny piece of silicon that can consist of millions of electronic elements. The new Intel Pentium™ chip is the latest in a line of improvements in speed and processing power for IBM-compatibles.*

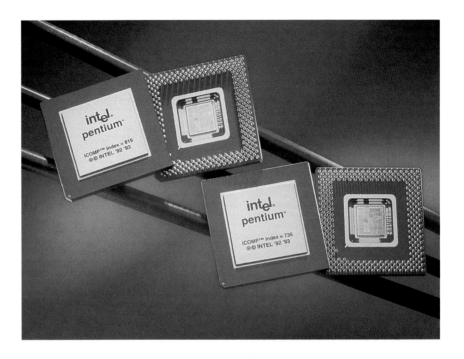

of an inch thick. It can hold from a few dozen to millions of electronic components such as transistors and resistors. A single chip or series of chips no bigger than a child's fingernail can contain all of a computer's memory and CPU components. See Figure 4.2.

The CPU of a PC is called a **microprocessor.** The CPU along with main memory is typically contained on a single board called a main circuit board, which consists of a series of chips. The CPU of larger systems is stored on a series of boards called processors. We will discuss types of chips in more detail later in this chapter.

Chips for all types of computers are made from silicon, a sand found in quartz rocks. Silicon itself is considered a semiconductor, which means it is a poor conductor of electricity. A thin sliver of silicon on a chip is coated with an electromagnetic emulsion that is etched in a way that leaves electrical-conducting material behind in paths that form circuits. Silicon chips carry out many operations very quickly; for example, they store and retrieve data, perform calculations, and compare numbers—all in fractions of a second.

IN A NUTSHELL

The CPU is the microprocessor. The CPU and main memory are on the main circuit board.

Looking Back ◄ ••

TED HOFF AND THE HISTORY OF THE MICROPROCESSOR

In 1969, a small Japanese firm called Busicom contracted with Intel, then a small California firm, to build an ordinary calculator that could be programmed. The task fell to Marcian E. (Ted) Hoff. Hoff did more than computerize a calculator. He developed the Intel 4004 chip, which became known as the first general-purpose microprocessor, or "computer on a chip." Intel later became the leading producer of microprocessor chips. In 1982, *U.S. News and World Report* listed 12 Milestones of American Technology. Along with the light bulb, the telephone, the airplane, and others, Ted Hoff's microprocessor made the list.

Ted Hoff developed the first general-purpose microprocessor chip.

The CPU controls the reading of data into primary storage, the processing of data, and the writing of data from primary storage. Because access to primary storage is controlled by the CPU, we consider some of its features here before we discuss the CPU itself in more detail.

Primary Storage or Main Memory

Data and instructions are stored as a series of characters in a computer where a **character** can be a letter, digit, or symbol. Each character is stored in a single storage position of main memory, called a byte of storage.

The total amount of primary storage, or number of bytes in main memory, is referred to as the computer's memory size. The primary storage capacity, or main memory, of a computer depends on its size. A supercomputer, for example, has a greater memory size than a mainframe. Similarly, micros have a smaller storage capacity than more powerful computers. See Table 4.1.

Computer memory sizes are measured as follows:

Measuring Memory Sizes (numbers are rounded)

Kilobyte (K) = 1000 bytes (actually 1024 bytes)
Megabyte (MB) = 1,000,000 (one million) bytes
Gigabyte (GB) = 1,000,000,000 (one billion) bytes
Terabyte (TB) = 1,000,000,000,000 (one trillion) bytes

You may wonder why the main memory of larger computers needs to be so great. It is not only because programs and files are often sizable. Another reason is that most computers are capable of running more than one user program at a given time; this increases the need for very large storage capacities.

Sometimes a computer's primary storage needs to be increased; that is, what was originally considered to be sufficient memory turns out to be inadequate. In such cases, memory chips can be added to increase a computer's storage capacity. Each computer type has a range of memory sizes so that it can be configured with one size memory to which storage can be added. Each computer has a maximum primary storage capacity, however.

The main memory of a computer that uses integrated circuits is said to be **volatile,** which means that its contents are lost if the computer loses power or is turned off. That is one reason why data and programs must be saved on an auxiliary storage medium, such as a disk, that is **nonvolatile.**

There are two forms of main memory: random-access memory (RAM) and read-only memory (ROM).

RANDOM-ACCESS MEMORY (RAM) Random-access memory **(RAM)** is the part of primary storage that is used to store programs and data during processing. The capacity of the computer's memory determines the number and size of programs and data that can be operated on at a given time. When the user quits the application, the memory it took up becomes available for other programs.

IN A NUTSHELL

THE TWO TYPES OF MAIN MEMORY
RAM—Stores user programs entered as input
ROM—Stores instructions that were permanently etched into the chips

Micros	From 640 K to 64+ MB (most micros range from 4 to 64 MB)
Minis/midranges	From hundreds of megabytes to gigabytes
Mainframes	From hundreds of megabytes to hundreds of gigabytes
Supercomputers	From hundreds of gigabytes to terabytes (trillions of bytes)

Table 4.1 *Typical Memory Sizes*

Figure 4.3 *Each RAM chip for PCs has a storage capacity typically in the 1 to 16+ MB range. These are, from left to right, a 16 MB, 4 MB, and 1 MB chip.*

The term *random-access,* when applied to memory, means that the control unit accesses data directly without the need to search through each storage location in sequence. The speed with which a CPU accesses data from RAM is called the *access rate,* and the speed with which it transfers data into and out of RAM is called the *transfer rate.* We will see that these speeds are two criteria used to evaluate the processing power of a CPU.

User programs must be loaded into RAM in order to be processed; that is, they are stored on disk, accessed by the CPU, and then transferred to RAM as needed (see Figure 4.3).

READ-ONLY MEMORY (ROM) Not all main memory in a computer is volatile. When you turn your computer on or load a software program into it, your computer must have some preset instructions available to tell it what to do. These permanent, nonvolatile instructions are programmed into **read-only memory (ROM).** Another name for chips that contain ROM is **firmware.** ROM chips have many functions. For example, they provide commands that indicate what the CPU should do when the power is turned on, they check to see that the cable to the printer is connected, and they tell the control unit what each key on the keyboard means. In summary, a computer's main memory consists of both RAM and ROM, but most of it is used for RAM.

Storing Programs in ROM. Any program, however, *could* be stored in ROM. This would save time because you would not need to load the program by moving disks in and out of the system. ROM, however, tends to be more expensive than the volatile memory chips used for primary storage. In addition, software vendors would have to create new chip circuitry and new ROM chips every time they updated their programs, and users would have to open the computer system's chassis, or case, and replace chips when they wanted to upgrade their programs. Despite these disadvantages, many smaller computers do have some software in ROM. Some portables, for example, have word processing and spreadsheet packages stored in ROM for ease of access.

Figure 4.4 *An EPROM memory chip nestled between a piece of germanium and a piece of silicon from which it is made. Exposing the transparent quartz crystal's "window" to ultraviolet rays will erase the chip's contents so it can be reprogrammed if necessary. ROM, PROM, EPROM, and EEPROM chips resemble each other—but only the latter two have a window for erasing.*

PROM, EPROM, EEPROM. ROM itself has three subcategories called PROM, EPROM, EEPROM (see Figure 4.4). Each can be custom-made or preprogrammed for the user by the computer manufacturer or software developer. Each can contain programs, as we have seen, or data. For example, an insurance company might have actuarial tables in ROM and an accounting firm might have tax data in ROM.

PROM means *programmable read-only memory.* PROM chips contain instructions and data that cannot be easily changed.

Erasable programmable read-only memory (EPROM) chips enable changes to be made to the data or instructions in ROM. For the contents of EPROM chips to be changed, the chips must be removed from the computer. EPROM chips

IN A NUTSHELL

TYPES OF ROM

PROM	Programmable read-only memory
EPROM	Erasable programmable read-only memory
EEPROM	Electronically erasable programmable read-only memory

have a transparent quartz crystal covering the circuitry. Subjecting this "window" to ultraviolet rays erases the contents.

Electronically erasable programmable read-only memory (EEPROM) is the most advanced form of ROM. Changes can be made to the chips under software control. Thus, there is no need to remove the chips. EEPROM is the most useful form of ROM, but it is also, not surprisingly, the most expensive. It is widely used in point-of-sale systems in which prices and taxes are recorded in read-only memory. When necessary, the information can be re-recorded using a special software package.

We next consider the two main units of the CPU, the arithmetic/logic unit and the control unit, and how registers are used in each.

Intel's new form of memory for RAM and ROM is called *flash memory*. It occupies less space on a circuit board and it is nonvolatile—it can retain its contents even after the power is shut off. Many notebook and subnotebook computers use flash memory cards and flash disks. See Figure 4.5. Flash memory is also used in smart cards, which we discuss later. Flash memory is becoming an alternative to EPROMs and EEPROMs because it is more easily updated.

The Arithmetic/Logic Unit

The arithmetic/logic unit (ALU) is the section of the CPU that actually operates on data. All arithmetic and logic operations are executed in the ALU. Arithmetic includes the basic operations of addition, subtraction, multiplication, and division. Logical operations are used to compare two items of data to determine if one is larger than, equal to, or smaller than the other.

The Control Unit

The control unit handles the transmission of data into and out of the CPU and supervises its overall operations. Transmission between the control unit, ALU, and main memory occurs on a special electronic path called a **bus.** The speed of a bus and the number of characters that it can handle during a processing

Critical Thinking

What are the advantages and disadvantages of including software on ROM in portable PCs? Hint: Think about factors like weight, compactness, and ease of use. Also think about the ease of upgrading the software.

Figure 4.5 *Hewlett Packard's flash memory and flash disk cards.*

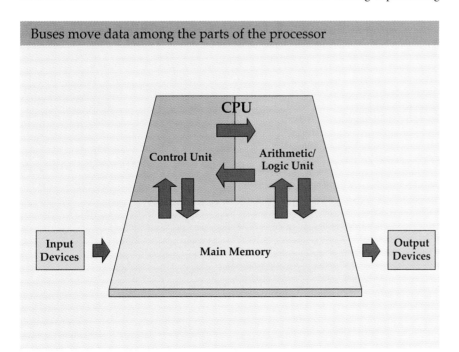

Buses move data among the parts of the processor

Figure 4.6 *The bus (⇔) is an electronic path along which data is transmitted between input/output devices and main memory, and between main memory and the components of the CPU—the control unit and the ALU. A computer's processing power is dependent on the speed of the bus and the number of characters it can handle in a processing cycle. Data from input devices and information transmitted to output devices also travel along buses.*

cycle are factors that affect the overall processing speed and efficiency of the computer. There are also buses that transmit data from input devices to main memory and from main memory to output devices. See Figure 4.6.

Registers and Machine Cycles

To enhance the processing capability of a CPU, the ALU and control unit contain special storage areas called **registers.** Their function is to hold instructions, data values, and main memory addresses of both the instructions and data. There are four basic types of registers.

1. Instruction register—high-speed circuits within the control unit that hold an instruction to be executed.

2. Address register—high-speed circuits within the control unit that hold the address of data to be processed or of the next instruction to be executed.

3. Storage register—high-speed circuits most often in the ALU that temporarily store data retrieved from main memory prior to processing.

4. Accumulator—high-speed circuits most often in the ALU that temporarily store the results of arithmetic and logic operations.

The processing of a single instruction occurs during a **machine cycle.** It involves accessing data from main memory, using registers in the control unit and ALU to operate on that data, and transmitting results back to main memory. A machine cycle consists of two parts: an **instruction cycle** during which the control unit fetches the instruction from primary storage and prepares it for processing, and the **execution cycle** during which an instruction is actually executed and results produced. See Figure 4.7.

Several basic operations are performed during the instruction cycle:

• The control unit fetches the instruction from main memory.

• The control unit interprets or decodes the instruction.

• The control unit places the part of the instruction that indicates the operation to be performed in the instruction register and places the part of the

Figure 4.7 *A machine cycle consists of two parts: an instruction cycle and an execution cycle.*

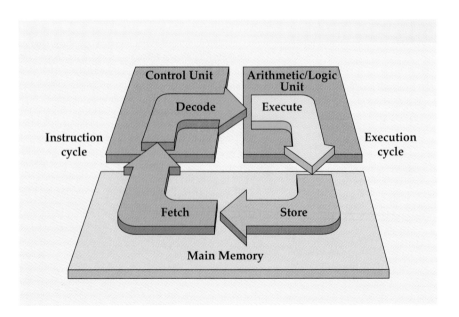

instruction that indicates where the corresponding data is located in the address register.

The basic operations performed during the execution cycle are as follows:

- Using information in the address register, the control unit retrieves the data from main memory and places it in the storage register.
- Using the information in the instruction register, the control unit instructs the ALU to perform the required operation.
- The result of the operation is stored in an accumulator and then transmitted back to main memory.

As you can see, many operations are performed during a machine cycle, but because computers are so powerful, a machine cycle can be as short as a nanosecond or microsecond.

Self-Test

1. The _____ is the CPU component that manages the processing of data.
2. Logical operations such as the comparison of two numbers are performed by the _____.
3. (T or F) During processing, data or instructions are held in temporary storage areas called registers.
4. (T or F) RAM is volatile and ROM is nonvolatile.
5. The CPU of a microcomputer together with main memory are contained on the _____.

4.2 HOW THE CPU REPRESENTS DATA

The Binary Numbering System

We have seen how data is stored and processed by a computer system. In this section, we consider how data is actually represented within the computer. Computers are capable of storing data and instructions in primary storage as characters, but each character must be converted into a coded form that permits high-speed processing.

When we refer to the electronic computers of today we usually mean **digital computers,** that is, computers that process data in discrete form as countable numbers. Another category of computers is analog computers; they process

Solutions
1. control unit
2. arithmetic/logic unit (ALU)
3. T
4. T
5. main circuit board

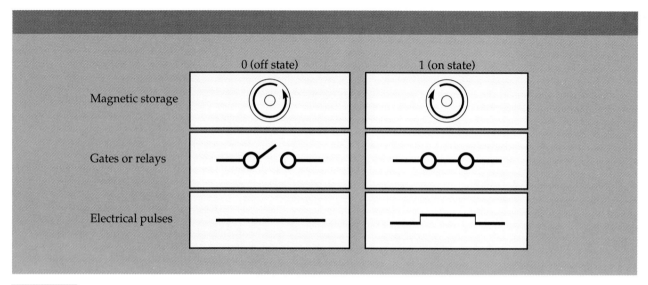

Figure 4.8 *How a computer uses the binary numbering system. 0 is an off state and 1 is an on state.*

entities related to speed, height, or length such as voltage fluctuations or frequencies. A thermostat, for example, is a simple analog computer. In this text we concentrate on digital computers.

All digital computers use some variation of the **binary numbering system** for representing characters, where a character is defined as a letter, digit, or special symbol. Our decimal system is based on 10 digits (0–9); in contrast, the binary numbering system has only *two* digits: 0 and 1. This system is ideal for computer processing because the 1 is used to denote the presence of an electrical pulse, signal, or a closed computer circuit permitting current to flow through and a 0 is used to denote the absence of such a signal or an open circuit that does not permit current to flow through. Figure 4.8 illustrates the way digital computers use the binary numbering system.

Bits, Bytes, and Words

Through a combination of on-off pulses (1's and 0's) it is possible to represent any decimal digit. These on-off pulses are called bits, an abbreviation for *b*inary dig*it*. In the decimal numbering system, the position of each digit has a value as follows:

...	10^2	10^1	10^0

positional value—in exponential form

...	100	10	1

positional value—as a factor of 10

3	8	6

◄—— any digit 0–9 can be used in each position

The number 386 is actually $3 \times 100 + 8 \times 10 + 6 \times 1$.

Note that $10^0 = 1$; in fact, any positive number to the 0 power is 1. $10^1 = 10$; $10^2 = 100$; and so on. This is how positional values are established.

In the binary numbering system, each position has a value as follows:

...	2^3	2^2	2^1	2^0

positional value—in exponential form

...	8	4	2	1

positional value—as a factor of 2

8	4	2	1

◄—— any digit 0–1 can be used in each position

The decimal number 9, for example, would be represented in binary form as:

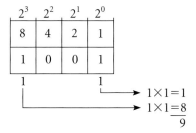

That is, $1 \times 8 + 1 \times 1 = 9$.

Since each digit will be either 1 or 0, we say that a binary digit or **bit** is either "on" (1) or "off" (0).

Recall that each storage position in main memory is called a byte. If each byte contained only four digit bits, representing the decimal numbers 8-4-2-1, it would be possible to represent any of the decimal digits 0 to 9. That is, with 8-4-2-1 we can denote the decimal digits 0 to 9 as well as numbers 10 to 15 (see Figure 4.9). In short, 4 bits in each byte are used to designate a single decimal digit. An "on" or 1 bit means that current flows through and an "off" or 0 bit means that current does not flow through.

But what about the representation of alphabetic characters or special symbols? How can they be depicted using binary digits? To represent these characters, the computer frequently uses an 8-bit code with *four zone bits* as well as *four digit bits:*

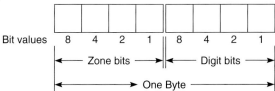

The four leftmost bits are called zone bits. The four rightmost bits are called digit bits.

The smallest unit of data in a computer code is the bit. A group of 8 bits is called a byte. Typically, one character is represented in 1 byte. A group of con-

Decimal Digit	BITS			
	8	4	2	1
0	0	0	0	0
1	0	0	0	1
2	0	0	1	0
3	0	0	1	1
4	0	1	0	0
5	0	1	0	1
6	0	1	1	0
7	0	1	1	1
8	1	0	0	0
9	1	0	0	1
10	1	0	1	0
11	1	0	1	1
12	1	1	0	0
13	1	1	0	1
14	1	1	1	0
15	1	1	1	1

Figure 4.9 *The binary equivalents of decimal digits 0 to 15.*

Figure 4.10 *Eight bits make up one byte, which can represent a character. Currently, newer PCs have 64-bit word sizes.*

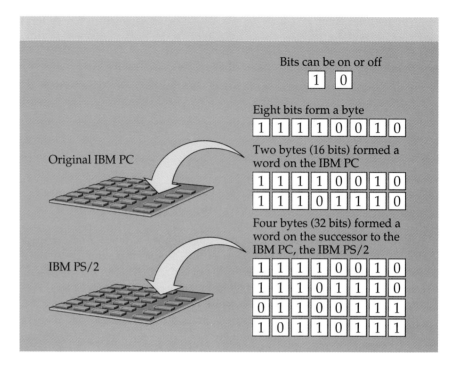

Bits can be on or off

```
1  0
```

Eight bits form a byte

```
1 1 1 1 0 0 1 0
```

Two bytes (16 bits) formed a word on the IBM PC

```
1 1 1 1 0 0 1 0
1 1 1 0 1 1 1 0
```

Four bytes (32 bits) formed a word on the successor to the IBM PC, the IBM PS/2

```
1 1 1 1 0 0 1 0
1 1 1 0 1 1 1 0
0 1 1 0 0 1 1 1
1 0 1 1 0 1 1 1
```

Original IBM PC

IBM PS/2

secutive bytes is a **word,** the term for a unit of data that can be processed at one time. The more bytes in a computer's word, the faster it can process data. A computer with a word size of 32 bits can process 4 bytes as a unit, while a faster 64-bit computer can process twice as many bytes as a unit.

Figure 4.10 illustrates the relationship of the three binary units—bit, byte, and word. The term *word* in this context should not be confused with its usual meaning. Here, it is a unit of data that corresponds to the number of bits that can be transferred to a register in the CPU's control unit during a single operation. The number of bytes in a word varies from system to system. As noted, the larger the word size, the faster the computer. Word sizes range from 8, 16, 32, to 64 bits, with newer computers having the larger word sizes. The next generation of PCs are apt to have 128-bit word sizes.

EBCDIC and ASCII

We consider now the two most frequently used computer codes, EBCDIC and ASCII, both of which make use of binary representation. One computer code, **EBCDIC,** which stands for *Extended Binary Coded Decimal Interchange Code* and is pronounced *eb-ce-dick,* is commonly used to represent letters, digits, and special symbols. In EBCDIC, each storage position or byte consists of eight data bits; four are used to specify the zone and four are used to specify the digit.

The four zone bits are used to indicate whether a character is a letter, unsigned number, positive number, negative number, or special character. The four digit bits are used to represent the numbers 0 to 9. For example, 1111 in the zone bits designates a character as an unsigned number; 1100 in the zone bits indicates that the character will be one of the uppercase letters A through I. If 1100 appears in the four zone bits, the digit bits then will indicate which specific letter from A through I is being represented. The digit bits can represent 0 through 9 as 0000, 0001, 0010, 0011, . . . 1001.

EBCDIC is used by many computers, especially IBM mainframes and their compatibles. **ASCII** is an even more common computer code widely used by most micros. ASCII stands for *A*merican *S*tandard *C*ode for *I*nformation *I*nterchange and is pronounced *ask-ee.* Some computers and terminals use a 7-bit ASCII code; others use an 8-bit ASCII code similar to EBCDIC. These three codes—EBCDIC, 8-bit ASCII, and 7-bit ASCII—are illustrated in Figure 4.11. In all the codes, combinations of binary digits 0 and 1 represent characters.

IN A NUTSHELL

COMPUTER CODES

ASCII—7- or 8-bit
EBCDIC—8-bit

Error Checking with Parity Bits

During processing, data is constantly being transmitted from one part of the computer to another and often from one computer to another. Data is trans-

Character	EBCDIC	8-bit ASCII	7-bit ASCII	Character
0	1111 0000	0101 0000	011 0000	0
1	1111 0001	0101 0001	011 0001	1
2	1111 0010	0101 0010	011 0010	2
3	1111 0011	0101 0011	011 0011	3
4	1111 0100	0101 0100	011 0100	4
5	1111 0101	0101 0101	011 0101	5
6	1111 0110	0101 0110	011 0110	6
7	1111 0111	0101 0111	011 0111	7
8	1111 1000	0101 1000	011 1000	8
9	1111 1001	0101 1001	011 1001	9
A	1100 0001	1010 0001	100 0001	A
B	1100 0010	1010 0010	100 0010	B
C	1100 0011	1010 0011	100 0011	C
D	1100 0100	1010 0100	100 0100	D
E	1100 0101	1010 0101	100 0101	E
F	1100 0110	1010 0110	100 0110	F
G	1100 0111	1010 0111	100 0111	G
H	1100 1000	1010 1000	100 1000	H
I	1100 1001	1010 1001	100 1001	I
J	1101 0001	1010 1010	100 1010	J
K	1101 0010	1010 1011	100 1011	K
L	1101 0011	1010 1100	100 1100	L
M	1101 0100	1010 1101	100 1101	M
N	1101 0101	1010 1110	100 1110	N
O	1101 0110	1010 1111	100 1111	O
P	1101 0111	1011 0000	101 0000	P
Q	1101 1000	1011 0001	101 0001	Q
R	1101 1001	1011 0010	101 0010	R
S	1110 0010	1011 0011	101 0011	S
T	1110 0011	1011 0100	101 0100	T
U	1110 0100	1011 0101	101 0101	U
V	1110 0101	1011 0110	101 0110	V
W	1110 0110	1011 0111	101 0111	W
X	1110 0111	1011 1000	101 1000	X
Y	1110 1000	1011 1001	101 1001	Y
Z	1110 1001	1011 1010	101 1010	Z

Digits 0–9

Letters A–Z

Figure 4.11 *The bit configurations of the EBCDIC, 8-bit ASCII, and 7-bit ASCII codes.*

Figure 4.12 *Parity bits are added to each byte to keep the number of "on" bits even (as shown here) or odd, depending on whether you use an even- or odd-parity computer.*

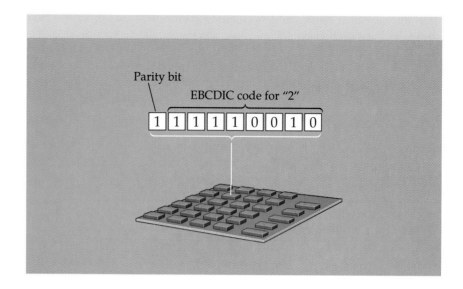

Parity bit

EBCDIC code for "2"

1 1 1 1 1 0 0 1 0

IN A NUTSHELL

SUMMARY: DATA REPRESENTATION

1. Computers use some form of the binary numbering system.
   a. Combinations of 0s and 1s represent all characters.
   b. 0 = off state.
   c. 1 = on state.
2. 8 bits = 1 byte, which stores one character.
   a. 4 bits represent the zone and 4 bits represent the digit (8-4-2-1).
   b. An additional parity bit may be used to minimize transmission errors.

mitted as electronic impulses, some in the on state and some in the off state, so slight irregularities in the electrical power supply occasionally cause errors in transmission to occur. One way to verify that data has been accurately transmitted might be to send it twice and compare the two transmissions, but that would double processing time and costs. Using a **parity bit** is an alternative solution to detecting transmission errors.

The parity bit is a single bit attached to each byte; the computer code itself determines whether the parity bit is a 0 or a 1. There are even-parity and odd-parity computers. In **even-parity** computers, an even number of bits must always be on at any given time; in **odd-parity** computers, an odd number of bits must always be on. In even-parity computers, if the number of 1 bits in any byte is odd, the parity bit is automatically turned on or set to 1 so that there is always an even number of 1 bits on. If the number of 1 bits is even, the parity bit is set to 0. This means that when all the 1 bits are added up, there is always an even number of them. Figure 4.12 shows the EBCDIC code for the number 2, including the parity bit for even-parity computers.

When a transmission is sent to a computer that uses even parity to do error checking, the receiving computer checks to see that there are always an even number of 1, or on, bits. If a byte contains an odd number of on bits, it requests retransmission. Computers using odd parity work in exactly the same way except that the parity bit is used to ensure an odd number of 1 bits.

Parity checking is guaranteed to detect an error only if just one bit is transmitted incorrectly. If, however, two bits were transmitted incorrectly, the error would not be detected, because the number of 1 or "on" bits would still be even for even-parity computers and odd for odd-parity computers. Although the chance for double transmission errors is very remote, some systems do protect against it. To guard against the possibility of multiple errors, a longitudinal parity can be used. With this technique, a check byte is added to the end of each record or stream of data that is transmitted. Each bit of the check byte is used to preserve the appropriate parity of every bit position in each byte of the record.

Parity checking is most often used to detect errors, not to correct them. A number of encoding schemes are now available that both detect and correct single or multiple errors when large volumes of data are transmitted over communications lines. Because they are much more elaborate than parity checks, these encoding schemes require additional processing at the receiving end. Their major use is for the long-distance transmission of data to a site where retransmission would be difficult—the transmission of data to a space probe, for example.

Thus far we have described the technical detail of data transmission. Next, we will take a look at how data is processed at the operating level.

Self-Test

1. All computers use some variation of the _____ numbering system to represent data.

2. A character of data is _____.

3. The word *bit* stands for _____.

4. Each _____ of storage holds one character of data.

5. The two most commonly used computer codes are _____ and _____.

6. A _____ bit is used in computer codes for error checking.

4.3 COMPUTER ARCHITECTURE

One of the most important ways to compare computer systems is to look at processing power—what technology does a computer use to process data and how fast can it operate? Several measurements are used to define processing power, some of which we discussed in Chapter 2. A relatively small difference in a computer's processing speed may significantly reduce execution time, particularly if the computer is being used for reading and writing many large-volume files.

The following sections describe some of the criteria used for evaluating computer **architecture,** that is, the design of the computer system. Our emphasis is on microcomputer architecture, but, in general, the same criteria apply to larger computer systems. Keep in mind that differences in types of computers are really differences in power, speed, and size. Figure 4.13 illustrates how the cost of one aspect of computer power—memory size—has decreased over time.

> ### Study Objective
> 3. List the factors that affect a computer's processing power.

Chip Technology: One-Upman-"Chip"

Motorola and Intel have been the leading manufacturers of microprocessor or CPU chips. Apple's Macintosh computers use the Motorola 68000 family of microprocessor chips (68000-68040), and IBM micros and their compatibles have traditionally used Intel chips.

Solutions

1. binary

2. a letter, digit, or special symbol

3. binary digit

4. byte

5. ASCII; EBCDIC

6. parity

Figure 4.13 *This graph shows how the cost of memory is declining over time while the chip capacity is increasing. In general, the price of RAM has dropped 20% per year over the past 20 years, while its capacity has doubled every two years over the same period.*

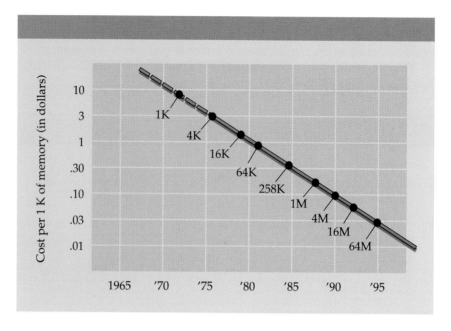

Inspecting wafers etched with new chips at a Motorola manufacturing plant.

In 1994, Intel chips dominated with 74% of the market, but in recent years other manufacturers of chips used in IBM-compatibles have begun to challenge Intel.

The original IBM PC used the 8086 Intel chip; that was followed by the 8088 Intel chip used in later IBM PCs and their compatibles. Computers with 80286 chips were newer, faster, and more efficient; these chips were used in IBM ATs and their compatibles. The IBM PS/2 family of computers and their compatibles also use, on the low end, the 80286 chip, often abbreviated as the "286" chip. In the midrange, IBM-compatibles use 80386 or "386" chips, and on the higher end they use 80486 or Pentium (the equivalent of 80586) chips. Most Intel-based computers today use 80386, 80486, or Pentium chips.

Intel **coprocessors** are special chips that can be added to or built into micros to speed up certain kinds of operations. One common chip is the math coprocessor, which is used to increase the processing speed of mathematical operations for number-crunching applications such as statistical analysis. These are designated as 8087, 80287, or 80387 chips corresponding to the 8086, 80286, and 80386 chips. Many newer 80486 and 80586 chips have math processors built into them.

The IBM-Apple alliance has resulted in a new category of computer called the *Power PC,* which uses a Motorola chip. This new type of computer has more processing power than Intel computers and Macs. It costs about the same as Macs and IBM-compatibles, but it is a RISC workstation that is significantly more powerful. See Figure 4.14.

CISC VERSUS RISC COMPUTERS Traditional Intel and Motorola PCs are CISC machines, which means they are *c*omplex *i*nstruction *s*et *c*omputers, with complex instructions built into the hardware. Workstations and the Power PC are RISC machines, which means they are *r*educed *i*nstruction *s*et *c*omputers. The computer architecture of RISC computers reduces chip complexity by using simpler instructions built into the hardware. RISC computers must use software routines to perform complex instructions performed in hardware on CISC computers. RISC computer chips are faster and can be built more economically. Until the Power PC was introduced, however, RISC and CISC computers had to use different software—that is, they were not compatible.

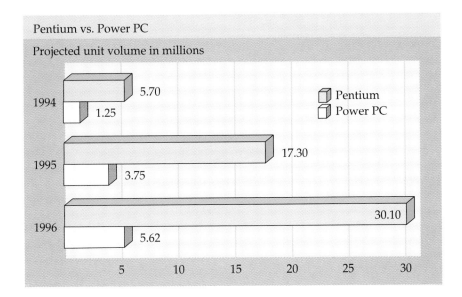

Pentium vs. Power PC

Projected unit volume in millions

1994 — Pentium 5.70, Power PC 1.25
1995 — Pentium 17.30, Power PC 3.75
1996 — Pentium 30.10, Power PC 5.62

Figure 4.14 *Although market-research firm Dataquest projects sales of about 5.6 million units for the Power PC by 1996, it expects the Pentium to maintain an approximate 5-to-1 lead in sales with 30 million units sold. Source:* Dataquest.

Tremendous advances in CISC architecture have been made over the years by Intel and some of its competitors. However, the physical limitations of the new, high-performance CISC design result in significantly bigger and more complex chips like the Pentium, which are much more expensive and which must run at higher temperatures to perform the same tasks as comparable RISC chips. Power PCs offer a significant advantage in price as well as performance.

Processing power, then, is dependent on chip technology. It is also dependent on clock speed, processing speed, bus width, and word size. We discuss each here:

Clock Speed

Every CPU has a clock, which generates clock pulses that synchronize the computer's operations. Processing actions occur at each "tick" of the electronic clock. The speed of the clock determines the speed at which the CPU can process data.

●●●●●●●●●●●●●●●●●●●●●●●●●●●●●●●●➤ **Looking Ahead**

CHALLENGING INTEL

With Motorola chips being used in Power PCs as well as Apple's Mac computers, Intel's dominance of the market will continue to be challenged. Power PCs have greater power at a lower price than Pentium computers, newer P6 computers, or even high-powered 486 computers—called *DX4* machines.

But other challenges exist. Manufacturers such as Cyrix, AMD, Digital Equipment, and MIPS Technology have developed chips to compete with Intel and Motorola. In December 1994, users of Intel Pentium chips discovered that arithmetic operations were performed incorrectly under certain circumstances. Intel initially claimed that the problem was minor; only after considerable public pressure did they agree to replace the chips. This incident further eroded Intel's market dominance.

SUCCESS OF POWER PC DEPENDS ON SOFTWARE

How will Intel computers fare against the Power PC? It really depends on the software developers. While all Power PCs can run Windows-based products in a slow, emulation mode, these machines need software specifically developed for their architecture in order to achieve their maximum capability. If software developers believe computers like the Power PC will become dominant, they will begin to offer Power PC–based products. This, ultimately, will determine the success of the Power PC.

Table 4.2 *Comparison of Popular Chips*

Name and Date Introduced	Manufacturer	Word Length (in bytes)	I/O Bus Width (in bytes)	Clock Speed (MHz)	Systems Using Chip	MIPS
8088 (1979)	Intel	16	8	4–8	IBM PC and XT	.3
68000 (1979)	Motorola	32	16	8–16	MacintoshPlus Macintosh SE Commodore Amiga	1.6
80286 (1982)	Intel	16	16	8–28	IBM PC/AT IBM PS/2 Model 50/60 Compaq Deskpro 286	2.66+
68020 (1984)	Motorola	32	32	16–33	Macintosh II	5.5
Sparc (1985) (RISC)	Sun Microsystems	32	32	20–25	Sun Sparc-station 1 Sun Sparc-station 300	20+
80386DX (1985) DX means double speed	Intel	32	32	16–33	IBM PS/2s IBM-compatibles	11.4+
68030 (1987)	Motorola	32	32	16–50	Macintosh IIx series Macintosh SE/30	12
80486DX (1989)	Intel	32	32	25–66	High-end IBM PS/2 models and IBM-compatibles	54+
68040 (1989)	Motorola	32	32	25–40	Macintosh Quadras	35+
RISC 6000 (1990)	IBM	32	32	20–150+	IBM RISC/6000 Workstation	56+
MicroSparc (1992)	Sun Microsystems	32	32	50–150+	Sun Sparc-station LX	59
Pentium (1993)	Intel	64	64	60–150+	HP Net Server Compaq Deskpro 5/60M	100+
Alpha AXP (1993)	DEC	64	64	150+	Digital	300+
604, 605, 607 (1994)	Motorola	64	64	150+	Power PC	300+

IN A NUTSHELL

The internal clock speed of a PC, measured in megahertz, determines how quickly instructions are retrieved from memory and processed.

Speed is measured in megahertz (MHz) where 1 MHz is a million pulses per second. Computers with higher clock speeds can process data faster than those with lower clock speeds. Notice in Table 4.2 that the range in IBM-compatibles varies from 8 MHz for the older IBM PC to 150+ MHz for Pentium, P6 (the planned upgrade for the Pentium), and RISC computers.

Processing Speed

Everything that happens in a computer, then, is timed by a clock that ticks millions of times every second. Clock speed is a raw measure of internal speed.

Processing speed is the time required to perform operations in the CPU as well as the time required to access data in memory. Both the instruction cycle and the execution cycle determine processing speed. Processing speed is measured in microcomputers in *microseconds,* or millionths of a second. For example, the older IBM PC family can perform about 20+ million instructions per second (MIPS). Mainframes, minis, and newer PCs operate at speeds measured in nanoseconds, or billionths of a second. See Figure 4.15. At the high end of the scale, processing speeds for supercomputers are measured in picoseconds, or trillionths of a second. The Cray-2 supercomputer can process data at hundreds of millions—or even trillions—of operations per second.

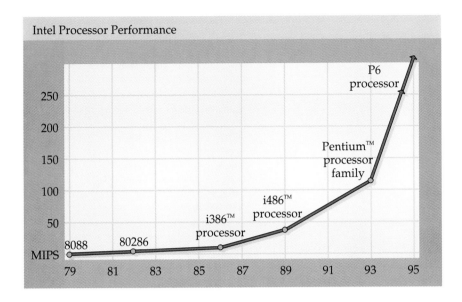

Intel Processor Performance

Figure 4.15 *Not only is the performance of Intel processors increasing dramatically from one processor to the next, the time between generations is decreasing as well. Source:* Intel.

Bus Width and Word Size

Clock speed is actually a misleading term since it is only one way to measure the speed of a computer. One other important way of measuring speed is indicating how fast data is transmitted within the CPU. This is controlled by the bus width.

Buses, as you recall, are the electronic tracks on which data moves from memory to the control unit and to the arithmetic/logic unit. Buses also connect input/output components to main memory and the CPU. The more bytes the bus can handle, the more data passes through and the greater the processing speed and power. Remember that 1 byte, which stores a character, is equal to 8 bits. Some computers have a word size that is larger than their bus size. A computer with a 32-bit word size, for example, but only a 16-bit bus size, is really limited to processing 16 bits at a time. This is analogous to cars with the capability to achieve 120 mph speeds that must travel on a highway with a 60 mph speed limit.

A bus, then, is the way a microprocessor gets information to peripherals, main memory, and the CPU. The original IBM PC was balanced in that the speed of the microprocessor matched the speed of the machine's bus—an ISA bus pioneered by IBM. ISA is an abbreviation for *Industry Standard Architecture*. ISA components were used in most IBM-compatibles in the 1980s, first in an 8-bit and then a 16-bit version. But microprocessor speeds got faster and more powerful, and the bus lagged behind. When IBM introduced its PS/2 family of computers, it also introduced its 32-bit MCA bus, an abbreviation for *Micro Channel Architecture*, which was proprietary, meaning that competitors would have

IN A NUTSHELL

WHY CALL IT A BUS?

It was named for the vehicle "bus" because just as all bus stops on a transportation route are available to everyone, so, too, are all signals on the electronic bus available to all devices communicating with the CPU and main memory.

IN A NUTSHELL

MEASUREMENTS OF PROCESSING SPEEDS		USED FOR MEASURING SPEEDS IN
Microsecond	Millionth of a second	Micros
Nanosecond	Billionth of a second	Mainframes
Picosecond	Trillionth of a second	Supercomputers

Table 4.3 *Factors Impacting Computer Power*

Chip Technology	RISC vs. CISC; Intel vs. Motorola
Clock Speed	The system clock generates electronic pulses that synchronize processing. Faster clock speeds mean more operations can be performed in a fixed period of time.
Bus Width	Determines how much data can be transferred from one component to another. A 32-bit bus can transfer twice as much data at one time as a 16-bit bus.
Word Size	The number of bits that can be manipulated at one time. A computer with a 32-bit word size can manipulate twice as much data at one time as a system with a 16-bit word size.

to pay IBM a fee to use this bus. The MCA bus was not only expensive for competitors, it was not compatible with the ISA bus. As a result, the industry developed a new standard in 1988 called EISA, an abbreviation for *Extended Industry Standard Architecture*, which was a 32-bit bus that successfully competed with the MCA bus.

Although EISA provides a 32-bit bus rather than a 16-bit bus, it still runs at the slow 8 MHz speed of the ISA bus in order to be compatible with ISA devices. Because of this limitation, local bus architectures such as the VL-bus and PCI bus have become dominant in new machines; they provide speeds for the transfer of data to and from peripherals that begin to match today's high-speed CPUs. The increasingly popular PCI bus, an abbreviation for *Peripheral Component Interconnect*, can be used with non-Intel computers. Table 4.3 summarizes the major factors affecting computer power.

Main Circuit Boards and Expansion Slots

A microcomputer's microprocessor (CPU), main memory, battery-operated clock, and other circuits are interconnected on a **main circuit board** sometimes called the **motherboard** (note the sexism!). Most micros have an open architecture, which means that the user is able to open the system's cabinet and add components to the main circuit board. In such computers, this board has a series of **expansion slots** into which add-on units can be inserted. For example, random-access memory cards that fit into an expansion slot of the main circuit

Looking Ahead

COMING SOON
- The Intel 486 chip will be the minimum technology used in most corporate environments, with Pentium, P6, and Power PC computers becoming increasingly popular.
- Continued improvement in data translation, data conversion, and networking will allow incompatible computers to communicate more easily with one another.
- Both VL-bus and PCI bus computers will thrive.
- RISC workstations will become even more widely used.
- Notebooks and subnotebooks will become increasingly popular as laptops.
- Wireless communications for sending and receiving e-mail, faxes, and information from databases will become a key technology.

(a)

Figure 4.16 *(a) A main circuit board rests in the system unit, which also houses disk drives. (b) The main circuit board contains the CPU, memory, and the circuitry necessary to process data. Add-on memory boards can be used to increase primary storage capacity.*

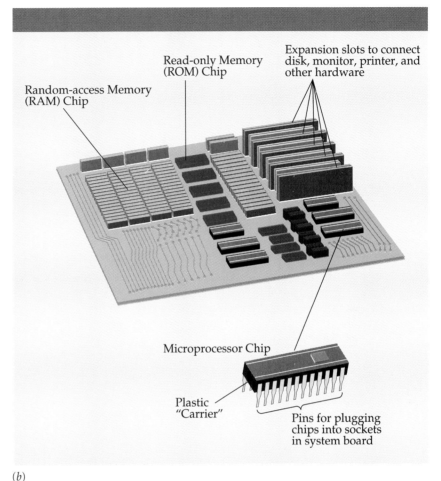

Random-access Memory (RAM) Chip

Read-only Memory (ROM) Chip

Expansion slots to connect disk, monitor, printer, and other hardware

Microprocessor Chip

Plastic "Carrier"

Pins for plugging chips into sockets in system board

(b)

board are widely available to increase the primary storage of micros that have an open architecture. See Figure 4.16.

Additional Devices for Improving Processing Power

Most computers can perform multitasking, which means running more than one application concurrently. Even more sophisticated computers perform multiprogramming, which enables multiple users to share a computer. Many computers—even micros—also have parallel processors; in effect, these are multiple CPUs that permit more than one instruction to be executed simultaneously.

Cache memory is a type of memory that is capable of doubling the speed of a computer. It is based on a technique of storing and retrieving the most frequently used data in readily accessible form so that retrieval is made more efficient. It is used extensively in minicomputers as well as in some micros, usually for storing the most frequently referenced data and instructions. It also has great potential for supercomputers and larger mainframes. Figure 4.17 shows an enlargement of a cache memory chip.

A 486 computer called the DX4 has double the cache size of traditional 486 computers and a faster clock speed. Together, these advantages can bring Pentium-class performance to 486 computers for hundreds of dollars less.

IN A NUTSHELL

SOME SELECTION CRITERIA FOR COMPUTER SYSTEMS

1. Software availability (How well suited is the computer for user applications?)
2. Cost
3. Speed
4. Size
5. Main memory capacity
6. Architecture
7. Number and type of input/output units
8. Vendor or manufacturer's reputation for quality
9. Vendor or manufacturer's support and service
10. Quality of the documentation or user's manuals

Figure 4.17 *An enlargement of a cache memory chip.*

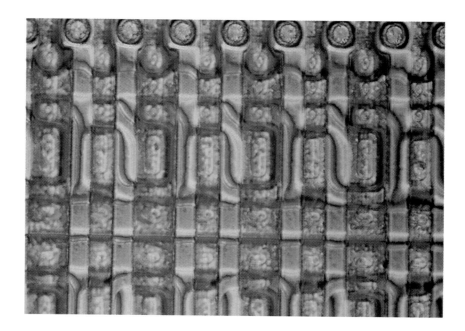

Figure 4.18 *PCMCIA cards are standard credit card–sized devices that add flash memory, hard disk memory, sound, network, and fax-modem capability to a notebook or subnotebook computer.*

Looking Ahead

PCMCIA CARDS PROMOTE PORTABILITY

The cost for PCMCIA add-ons is still about twice as much as that for comparable desktop accessories. But efforts are being undertaken to make PCMCIA slots standard on all PCs including desktops. This would mean that you could simply pop out the hard drive of a subnotebook and slip it into a desktop!

PCMCIA (WHAT A MOUTHFUL!) There is typically no physical problem adding peripherals to desktop computers as long as there are slots for them. But adding peripherals to notebook and subnotebook computers is another matter since there is simply no room for new components in their small cases.

The Personal Computer Memory Card International Association (PCMCIA) developed a design standard for peripherals and communication devices for very small computers including notebooks, subnotebooks, and Personal Digital Assistants (PDAs). These are credit card–sized devices that add flash memory, sound, network adapters, hard disk space, and fax-modem capability to these small machines. See Figure 4.18. We discuss PCMCIA technology again in Chapter 6.

Self-Test

1. One megahertz is equal to _____.

2. A nanosecond is _____.

3. A unit of data that corresponds to the number of bits that can be transferred to a register in the CPU's control unit is called a _____.

4. (T or F) The larger the word size, the faster the computer.

5. In addition to megahertz and nanoseconds another term for measuring the speed of a computer is _____.

6. The electronic paths on which data moves between the CPU and memory are called _____.

4.4 METHODS OF PROCESSING DATA

You can now breathe a sigh of relief—we are done with the technical features of the CPU and main memory! Keep in mind that the preceding discussion was designed to familiarize you with types of computers, but architectures change very frequently, as does the performance and processing power of machines. When evaluating computers, think in terms of broad ranges and categories.

Study Objective

4. Describe the common methods of processing.

Solutions

1. one million clock ticks per second

2. one billionth of a second

3. word

4. T

5. MIPS (million instructions per second)

6. buses

Next we discuss the two primary methods for processing data: in batch mode and interactively. We also indicate that regardless of the processing methods used, computers typically operate on one record at a time.

Batch Processing

Businesses usually produce all payroll checks for each pay period *at the same time*. This is an example of **batch processing**: holding all data until output is to be produced and then processing the data collectively at one time.

First, let us consider how data is collected so that it can be processed in batches. When a large volume of data needs to be stored, terminals or PCs connected to the main CPU are used for entering data. This type of data entry is called an **offline** operation. For example, payroll information might be keyboarded at several different corporate branch sites in separate offline operations and stored on disks. The disks collected from each site could be transmitted to the computer center at corporate headquarters every Thursday, for example, where they would be merged so that paychecks could be printed on Friday in a batch-processing operation.

In a small company that uses microcomputers, the payroll data could be entered on any microcomputer and stored on disks that are processed in batch mode at a later date. The payroll example in Figure 4.19 illustrates batch processing on a microcomputer.

Batch processing is a good way to make effective use of expensive computer time. First, it is generally more efficient to process the data in a large file all at the same time. Second, there may be a practical advantage to batch processing when preprinted forms such as checks are used for output and have to be specially loaded in the printer.

There are, however, disadvantages to batch processing as well. When data is updated in batch mode, it is less timely; it would be, after all, current only at the

Figure 4.19 *In batch processing, the computer stores all data until output is needed and then performs all operations at one time.*

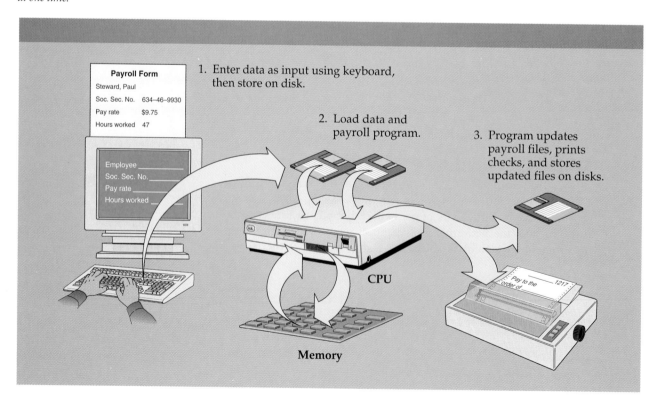

Payroll Form
Steward, Paul
Soc. Sec. No.   634–46–9930
Pay rate $9.75
Hours worked   47

Employee _____
Soc. Sec. No. _____
Pay rate _____
Hours worked _____

1. Enter data as input using keyboard, then store on disk.

2. Load data and payroll program.

3. Program updates payroll files, prints checks, and stores updated files on disks.

CPU

Memory

time the entire batch is processed. After that, changes that are stored on disk are not processed until the next update cycle. Batch processing is not appropriate, therefore, for an application that needs to process or report on current data immediately.

Examples of appropriate tasks for batch processing are producing transcripts of grades at the end of the semester, or producing stock inventory reports at the end of the day. If an inventory manager relies on yesterday's inventory report produced in a batch processing operation, he or she must keep in mind that changes in stock made during the current day will *not* be reflected in the report. In summary, if there is no great need for up-to-the-minute accuracy on reports, then batch processing is the most efficient method for producing those reports.

If there is a need to process data as soon as it is transacted or entered, then batch processing would not be suitable.

Interactive Processing

It may be that payroll files need to be current only at the end of a payroll cycle when it is time to produce checks. If so, then the files can be effectively processed in batch mode. Some applications, however, require immediate processing. Airline reservation systems, for example, must update their files as the data is transacted. Airlines need to know at all times how many seats have been sold so ticket agents will stop selling tickets when a flight is booked. An airline reservations system, therefore, is an example of a system that uses interactive processing (Figure 4.20).

INTERACTIVITY IS REQUIRED TO KEEP FILES CURRENT ALL THE TIME
In **interactive processing** data is processed immediately, as soon as it is transacted, so that updated information can be quickly provided to all users of the system. In airline reservations systems, there are terminals at many sites—in travel agencies, at airports, and so forth. Although the terminals are off-site, at

Figure 4.20 (a) An airline reservation system is an example of interactive, or real-time, processing. (b) The computer completes each task immediately, keeping all records current and available.

(a)

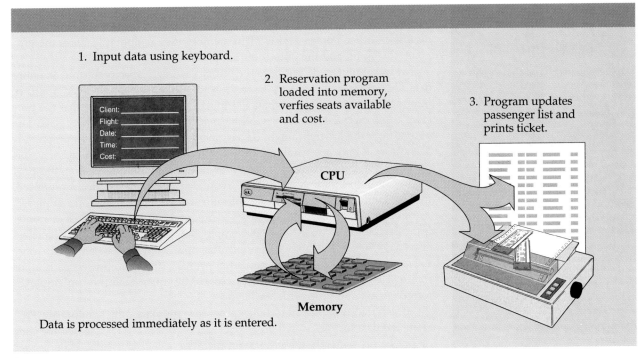

1. Input data using keyboard.

2. Reservation program loaded into memory, verfies seats available and cost.

3. Program updates passenger list and prints ticket.

Client: _____
Flight: _____
Date: _____
Time: _____
Cost: _____

CPU

Memory

Data is processed immediately as it is entered.

(b)

IN A NUTSHELL

BATCH PROCESSING

- Data is collected offline.
- Data is processed at fixed intervals, not immediately.
- Processing is efficient, but not timely.

INTERACTIVE PROCESSING

- Data is processed immediately as it is transacted.
- The computer itself as well as the program and files pertaining to the application must always be available, not just available at fixed intervals.

Critical Thinking

Suppose you make a purchase with your department store's credit card. A clerk keys in your transaction and gives you a receipt. Because the clerk used a keying device for entering data, you might assume that the transaction was processed interactively—but you may be wrong. The data entered may be transmitted from the clerk's terminal to a disk in an offline operation, and the disk itself may not be processed until later on. When you make your purchase you have no real way of knowing whether the processing is interactive. How can you definitely determine if the store does, in fact, use interactive processing? What risks would the store be assuming if it used batch processing instead? What benefits would it derive from batch processing?

remote locations, they communicate directly and instantly with the central computer via communications lines such as telephones and satellites (see Chapter 12). These systems immediately update ticket information on all flights.

Updating information interactively is called an **online** operation. The person at the remote terminal is said to be "online" with the main computer. For interactive, online processing, the central computer must be linked to all terminals at all times, and a program must always be stored in main memory so that the CPU can process the data being entered from the various terminals. A form of interactive processing called **transaction processing** enables a user to input data and complete a transaction on the spot.

PRIVACY AND SECURITY ARE CONCERNS WHEN INTERACTIVE SYSTEMS ARE USED Many interactive systems such as those for banking, making hotel and airline reservations, and purchasing items have improved the quality of our lives. As a rule, if cost were not a factor, most of us would agree that interactive systems would generally be preferable to batch systems. But interactivity brings with it social problems like a greater potential for invading privacy or making illegal changes to data. Once a computer and its databases are available to users at remote sites, the risks of security violations increase dramatically. An interactive airline reservations system, for example, increases the risk that someone might use your credit card number to purchase tickets. It also brings with it the threat that the government or other organization might be able to keep track of your whereabouts. Users as well as software and hardware developers must work closely to minimize the dangers associated with interactive processing.

The Main Processing Technique: A Record at a Time

Regardless of the memory technology used by a computer, software is supplied to users on a secondary storage medium, usually disk. In order to process data, the program must be read, or loaded, into main memory so that each instruction can be executed. Programs read input data, perform some operations, and produce output information. Input can be entered from a terminal or first stored on disk or other storage device. Main memory then temporarily stores the program, the input, and the output during processing.

Most computers do not have the primary storage capacity to store an entire data file especially if it is very large. Instead, programs typically read a *unit* of information at a time rather than all input. Suppose, for example, that the program to be executed reads a payroll file, which contains all employee data. The output from the program might be paychecks for all employees. The program is likely to read *only one* employee record at a time, process it, and create a paycheck for that employee. Then it reads the next record and processes it; this procedure continues until all records in the file are read and all checks produced. In this example, a record is the unit of information pertaining to one employee.

In this way, primary storage needs to hold only one record of data at a time. If the payroll file consisted of 10,000 employee records each with 150 characters of data, 10,000 × 150 storage positions for input would not be required—only 150 storage positions would be needed in primary storage to process each input record. The input area would be replaced 10,000 times, each time an employee record is read and processed. See Figure 4.21.

Recall that main memory holds programs and data only temporarily. Program and data files are stored on auxiliary storage devices like disk because they cannot be permanently stored in main memory, which is volatile. If the power supply is cut off (e.g., there is a power outage), whatever program and data are in main memory are lost.

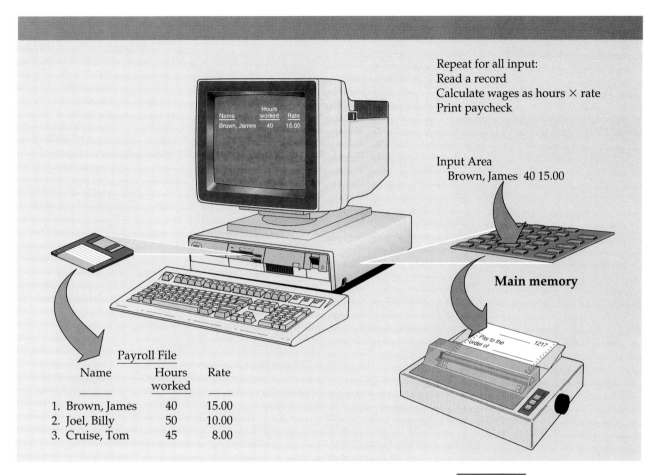

Repeat for all input:
Read a record
Calculate wages as hours × rate
Print paycheck

Input Area
    Brown, James 40 15.00

Main memory

Payroll File

Name	Hours worked	Rate
1. Brown, James	40	15.00
2. Joel, Billy	50	10.00
3. Cruise, Tom	45	8.00

Figure 4.21 *Computers read one record at a time and process each record before reading and processing the next one.*

Self-Test

1. If bills are prepared by computer once a month, we call this a _____ operation.

2. (T or F) When terminals are used to process data then online operations are required.

3. The process of keeping a file current is called _____.

4. (T or F) When batch processing is used to update files, the file is always current.

5. Transaction processing means that _____.

Solutions

1. batch

2. F—Not necessarily.

3. updating

4. F—The file is only current as of the last update cycle.

5. data is processed by computer when it is transacted

CHAPTER SUMMARY

All computer systems consist of various input/output devices, main memory, a central processing unit, and secondary storage. This chapter focuses on the CPU and how it processes data.

4.1 How the CPU Processes Data

A computer system is defined in terms of its CPU. Peripherals, or input/output (I/O) devices, are linked to the CPU, which controls all operations. While large computer systems can have numerous I/O devices, the number of I/O devices a PC can have is limited by the number of I/O connections, or **ports,** it has. The CPU can be linked to peripherals in two ways: (1) by cable or (2) by communications facilities such as telephone lines, if the devices are not at the same physical location as the CPU.

All computer operations are performed under the control of the CPU. Thus, the CPU is referred to as either the "brains" or the "heart" of a computer. The CPU has three basic features: (1) it interfaces with main memory (primary storage) for storing data and programs; (2) it has a **control unit** for controlling each operation; (3) it has an **arithmetic/logic unit (ALU)** for performing arithmetic and comparison operations. CPUs for PCs are called **microprocessors**.

Most computers use **integrated circuits,** or **chips,** for their CPUs and main memory. The CPU of a PC along with main memory is typically contained on a single board called a **main circuit board.**

Primary storage consists of storage positions called bytes. Each byte can typically store one **character** such as a letter, digit, or symbol. A computer's memory size refers to the number of bytes in the CPU. Sometimes it is possible to enhance a computer's primary storage by adding memory boards to increase the storage capacity up to some established limit for that type of computer.

The main memory of a computer that uses integrated circuits is said to be **volatile;** that is, its contents are lost if the computer loses power or is turned off. **Nonvolatile** secondary storage devices such as disk are used to save data and programs after processing.

There are two forms of main memory: **random-access memory (RAM)** and **read-only memory (ROM).** RAM is that part of primary storage that stores programs and data during application processing. The CPU accesses data from RAM at a speed referred to as the access rate; the speed with which the CPU transfers data into and out of RAM is called the transfer rate. ROM, also known as **firmware,** refers to read-only memory chips that contain permanent, nonvolatile instructions that have been programmed into them. The three categories of ROM are PROM (programmable read-only memory), EPROM (erasable programmable read-only memory), and EEPROM (electronically erasable programmable read-only memory).

The arithmetic/logic unit (ALU) is the section of the CPU in which all arithmetic and logic operations are performed. The transmission of data between the control unit, ALU, and main memory occurs on a special electronic path called a **bus. Registers** are special storage areas in the ALU and control unit that are used to hold instructions, values, and main memory addresses relating to the instructions and data being processed.

The processing of a single instruction occurs during a **machine cycle,** which consists of two parts: (1) an **instruction cycle** during which the control unit fetches the instruction from primary storage and prepares it for processing and (2) the **execution cycle** during which the instruction is actually executed and the results produced.

4.2 How the CPU Represents Data

Digital computers process data in discrete form as countable numbers. Internally, all digital computers use some variation of the **binary numbering system** for representing characters, where a character refers to a letter, digit, or special symbol. In the binary numbering system, there are only two possible digits: 0 and 1. In computer systems, the 1 denotes the presence of an electrical pulse or signal in the computer circuitry, and a 0 denotes the absence of such a signal. The smallest unit of data in a computer code is the **bit** (*bi*nary dig*it*)—a single on or off signal. A **word,** or group of consecutive bytes, refers to a unit of data that can be processed at one time.

The two most frequently used computer codes are **EBCDIC** (*E*xtended *B*inary *C*oded *D*ecimal *I*nterchange *C*ode), in which each byte consists of eight data bits, and **ASCII** (*A*merican *S*tandard *C*ode for *I*nformation *I*nterchange), which may be a 7- or 8-bit code. EBCDIC is used by many computers, especially IBM mainframes and their compatibles. ASCII is the code most widely used by micros.

When data is transmitted from one part of the computer to another or from one computer to another, parity bits are often used to detect transmission errors. The **parity bit** is a single bit attached to each byte. An **even-parity** computer means that when all the 1 bits in a byte are added up, there must be an even number of them. Similarly, in an **odd-parity** computer, the parity bit is used to ensure an odd number of 1 bits in each byte.

Study Objective

2. Explain how data is stored in a computer.

4.3 Computer Architecture

Architecture refers to the computer's design. The word size specifies the number of bits processed by the computer at one time. Generally, the larger the word size, the faster the computer. **Coprocessors** are special chips that can be added to or built into some micros to speed up certain kinds of operations. Processing speeds of computers are measured in microseconds, nanoseconds, or picoseconds. The most widely used measure of a microcomputer's CPU performance is the clock speed, which is measured in megahertz (MHz).

The main circuit board of a computer contains the microprocessor, clock, main memory, and other circuits that are all interconnected. If a micro has an open architecture, that means that the user can open the system's cabinet and add components to the main circuit board or **motherboard.** In such a computer, the main circuit board has a series of **expansion slots** for inserting add-on units.

Cache memory is a type of memory that can double the speed of a computer; it is based on a scheme of storing and retrieving the most frequently used data in readily accessible form.

Study Objective

3. List the factors that affect a computer's processing power.

4.4 Methods of Processing Data

Batch processing refers to the storing of all data until output is to be produced and then processing the data all at once. Data entry for a batch processing application is sometimes performed in an **offline** operation. This means that the data is entered on computers or terminals that are not connected to the main CPU. Batch processing may be a good way to make effective use of expensive computer time for some applications, but a major disadvantage of batch applications is that the data is less timely—it is only up-to-date at the time the entire batch is processed. With **interactive processing** data is processed immediately, as soon as it is transacted. Updating information interactively is referred to as an **online** operation. **Transaction processing** is a form of interactive processing that enables a user to input data and complete a transaction on the spot.

Study Objective

4. Describe the common methods of processing.

KEY TERMS

Architecture, *p. 121*
Arithmetic/logic unit (ALU), *p. 109*
ASCII, *p. 118*
Batch processing, *p. 130*
Binary numbering system, *p. 116*
Bit, *p. 117*
Bus, *p. 113*
Cache memory, *p. 127*
Character, *p. 111*
Chip, *p. 109*
Control unit, *p. 109*
Coprocessor, *p. 122*

Digital computer, *p. 115*
EBCDIC, *p. 118*
Even parity, *p. 120*
Execution cycle, *p. 114*
Expansion slot, *p. 126*
Firmware, *p. 112*
Instruction cycle, *p. 114*
Integrated circuit, *p. 109*
Interactive processing, *p. 131*
Machine cycle, *p. 114*
Microprocessor, *p. 110*
Motherboard (main circuit board), *p. 126*

Nonvolatile memory, *p. 111*
Odd parity, *p. 120*
Offline, *p. 130*
Online, *p. 132*
Parity bit, *p. 120*
Port, *p. 108*
Random-access memory (RAM), *p. 111*
Read-only memory (ROM), *p. 112*
Register, *p. 114*
Transaction processing, *p. 132*
Volatile memory, *p. 111*
Word, *p. 118*

CHAPTER SELF-TEST

1. CPU is an abbreviation for _____.

2. All computer systems have the same components: _____, _____, _____, and _____.

3. The CPU transmits data from an input device into _____, where it is stored during processing.

4. The part of the CPU that does math and logic functions is the _____.

5. Data moves between the CPU and main memory on an electronic path called a _____.

6. (T or F) If data is stored in volatile memory, it will be lost if the power goes off.

7. Some microcomputers have an internal hard disk that can hold large amounts of data. Is this primary storage or secondary storage?

8. Is the data on an internal hard disk volatile or nonvolatile?

9. RAM stands for _____.

10. Is RAM volatile or nonvolatile?

11. _____ memory is a type of memory capable of doubling the speed of a computer.

12. ROM stands for _____.

13. There are three kinds of ROM memory: _____, which stands for _____; _____, which stands for _____; and _____, which stands for _____.

14. Numbering systems in which the place of a digit within a number determines the number's value are called _____.

15. The numbering system that uses base 2 is called _____, and the numbering system that uses base 10 is called _____.

16. Two commonly used coding systems are ASCII and EBCDIC. The one used by IBM mainframes is _____; the one used by most microcomputers is _____.

17. The two basic types of processing are _____ and _____. When an entire transaction is completed on the spot, including output, this is a type of interactive processing called _____ processing.

18. Since numbers are frequently represented within the computer as a series of on-off switches, the _____ numbering system is well suited to computer processing.

19. (T or F) All numbers must be entered into the computer in binary form.

20. (T or F) Some numbers can be expressed in base 2 but not in base 10.

21. (T or F) In general, more binary digits are necessary to represent a number than are necessary in the decimal numbering system.

22. $2^2 =$ _____.

23. $2^5 =$ _____.

24. $2^3 =$ _____.

25. $10^2 =$ _____.

Solutions

1. central processing unit

2. input devices; the central processing unit and main memory; output devices; and secondary, or auxiliary, storage

3. primary storage or main memory

4. arithmetic/logic unit (ALU)

5. bus

6. T

7. secondary storage

8. nonvolatile

9. random-access memory

10. volatile

11. cache

12. read-only memory

13. PROM, programmable-read-only memory; EPROM, erasable programmable read-only memory; EEPROM, electronically erasable read-only memory

14. positional numbering systems

15. binary; decimal

16. EBCDIC; ASCII

17. batch processing; interactive processing; transaction processing

18. binary, or base 2

19. F—Decimal numbers as well as binary numbers can be entered as input. Decimal numbers will, however, be converted into binary form or some variation of binary form before they are processed.

20. F

21. T—For example, 16 in base 10 uses two digits but requires five in binary (10000).

22. $2 \times 2 = 4$

23. $2 \times 2 \times 2 \times 2 \times 2 = 32$

24. 8

25. 100

REVIEW QUESTIONS

1. List and briefly describe the components of the CPU.

2. What is the function of primary storage and how does secondary storage differ from it? What do RAM and ROM stand for?

3. Define batch processing and interactive processing.

4. Find out how much memory the computer you use has. Has it been upgraded beyond the amount that it came with originally?

5. What kind of microprocessor chip does your computer use? (You may have to check your computer's documentation.) Is it slower or faster than a Power PC in clock speed? in word size?

6. Consult newspapers or journals written five to ten years ago to see whether you can find projections regarding computer capability in the 1990s. Compare and contrast the predictions with the current state of the art.

7. Suppose you want to spend $2,000 or less for a computer. First determine what software you want to run on it. Make a list of the hardware you would like. Then look at newspaper ads for computers. Select the best buy for your money and your needs. Does the ad specify information on chip technology, clock speed, bus type, and word size? Are there terms used in the ad with which you are not familiar?

8. Suppose you could afford any PC you want. Which one would you purchase? Why? How would you make your decision?

CRITICAL THINKING EXERCISES

1. Macs have traditionally been the student's choice, but not the choice of businesses. However, Apple would like its Macs to make greater inroads into the office of Fortune 500 companies. For this, it will need to change its image. How would you suggest Apple accomplish this?

2. American schools spent over $2 billion on educational technology in the past year and the ratio of students to computers is about 16:1 compared with 125:1 ten years ago. The Organization for Economic Cooperation and Development in Paris predicts that by the year 2005, each child's desk will have its own PC.

Explain how you think computers could be used to improve children's understanding of social issues.

3. Suppose you go to a computer store with the intention of buying a specific computer. You have done your homework—researched the type of software and machine you want and the store with the least expensive price. The salesperson tells you the machine you want is okay, but she has one with a better price/performance ratio. What will you do—listen to her, do more research, or follow your original course of action? Explain.

Case Study

The Smart Card in Your Wallet

What can hold all the power of the original Apple computer and can fit in your pocket? The answer is, the *smart card*. An innocuous-looking object the size of a commercial credit card and made of the same plastic material, the smart card has an embedded microprocessor chip that can hold a wealth of information—and do it securely. "Chemical, physical, and electronic defenses make our chip impenetrable," says Walt Curtis of National Semiconductor. On the surface of most cards is a visible contact plate that enables the card and a card reader to exchange information—you don't "swipe" the smart card as you do a bank or credit card.

Smart cards are nothing new in Europe, where the French have been using them to make telephone calls on pay phones for years. When the amount of credit embedded in the card runs out, it is discarded. Eighty million Germans carry health insurance information on their smart cards and British hospitals keep X-rays and MRI scans on optical memory cards, which do not have microprocessors like smart cards but which have enormous memory.

The challenge in the United States is no longer a technological one. What manufacturers must do now is get potential users of smart cards to work together, so that hospitals and patients, travel agents and airlines are educated about the benefits of the card and are willing to use it. The range of potential applications is great. A smart card could hold digital airline tickets, room keys, even digital cash! It could also store medical, drug, and insurance records, school transcripts and driver's licenses, even the contents of your wallet. Wouldn't you rather carry an electronic wallet that held your bank card, credit cards, keys, railroad tickets, and checkbook? Some predict it could happen in as little as two years.

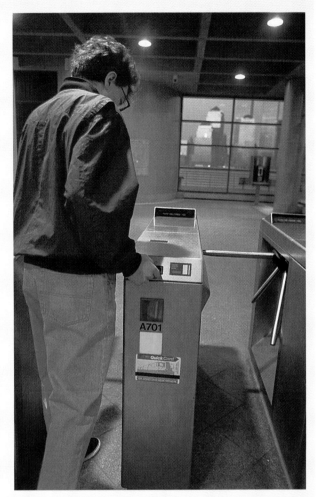

A smart card can be used for paying fares in a transportation system.

Analysis

1. Discuss some additional uses of electronic cards or smart cards that could improve the quality of our lives.

2. What are some of the risks of using electronic cards not discussed in the case?

CHAPTER 5
Input and Output:
From Applications to Hardware

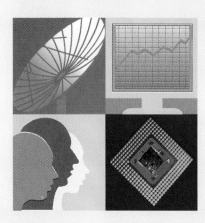

5.1 INPUT DEVICES CREATE SOURCE DOCUMENTS AND DATA FILES

A Review of File Processing Concepts

Keying Devices

Alternatives to Keying

5.2 SOURCE DATA AUTOMATION REDUCES DATA ENTRY OPERATIONS

Optical Character Readers

Applications Using Data Collection Systems

Automation in the Banking Industry

Voice Recognition Equipment

Digitizers

5.3 OUTPUT DEVICES PRODUCE INFORMATION

Types of Output

Output Devices

Expanding the World of Computers

e have seen in the previous chapters that computers, regardless of their size, cost, and processing power, operate on data in essentially the same way. The factors that determine how those computers will be used are software, connectivity, and people. In addition, each organization, and each application area within it, needs special computer peripherals for accomplishing its objectives.

Study Objectives

Chapter 5 covers the types of input and output devices or peripherals commonly used in computer systems for business-related applications. After completing this chapter you should be able to:

1. Describe how input devices have evolved to meet user needs for error-free source documents.
2. Show how source data automation actually improves productivity.
3. List advantages and disadvantages of each class of output device.

5.1 INPUT DEVICES CREATE SOURCE DOCUMENTS AND DATA FILES

A Review of File Processing Concepts

Most often, computers process data that is organized into files where a file is a collection of records in a specific application area. Typically, a master file is created in functional areas such as payroll, accounting, and marketing. Each master file contains all important data pertaining to its corresponding application area. For example, a master payroll file contains salary information about employees, and a master accounts receivable file contains information about customers. Database files created by database management systems can be linked together to provide management with more comprehensive information.

Master files are usually created using a keyboard as an input device; that is, data is first keyed and then stored on disk. We will see, however, that keying operations are not the only ones used to create master files.

After master files are created, they must be updated so they are current. To accomplish this, the computer must read as input any changes to be made and incorporate them into the master file. Changes to a file are referred to as transaction data. The update procedure may be performed either (1) online, that is, interactively as the change occurs or (2) in batch mode—later on at fixed intervals. With batch processing, transaction data is keyed, saved on disk, and used periodically to update the master file.

Study Objective

1. Describe how input devices have evolved to meet user needs for error-free source documents.

ıN A NUTSHELL

An update procedure keeps a file current.

ıN A NUTSHELL

File	Collection of records in a specific application area
Types of files	
Master	Contains key data in each application area
Transaction	Contains changes to be made to the master file
Update Procedure	Uses transaction data to keep the master file current

Up-to-date master files provide managers and the operating staff with the output they need to perform their jobs. As we will see, output is usually produced in the form of printed reports or screen displays, but other types of output, such as audio responses, are sometimes preferred. Printed reports can be created on a regularly scheduled basis or on demand when the need arises. Regularly scheduled printed output such as checks or invoices are produced at fixed intervals. Printed or displayed output is created on demand when quick responses to inquiries are required.

In general, input is most often keyed and output is most often printed on paper or displayed on a screen. There are, however, many other types of input/output devices besides keyboards, printers, and screens. In this chapter we discuss a wide range of peripherals for computer systems of all sizes, and the application areas that use them. Our discussion covers micro, mini/midrange, and mainframe peripherals in specific application areas so that you learn not only what devices are available but also how they are used.

In business, input data frequently comes from documents such as purchase orders, vendor invoices, or payroll change requests. Such documents are prepared in the department where the original action occurs—at the source of a transaction—so they are called **source documents** (Figure 5.1). A purchase order, which originates in the purchasing department, and a payroll change request, which typically originates in the human resources or payroll department, are examples of source documents.

To increase productivity and to minimize input errors, systems analysts and users should try to limit the number of times data needs to be recorded manually. For example, in a company that does not have efficient input procedures, an employee salary increase might involve as many as three inputs. First, the department manager fills out a handwritten form authorizing the raise. Next, the handwritten request goes to the human resources department for verification. The human resources department then types up a list of all salary increases, which is sent to the payroll department where the information is keyed into the computer. In a more efficient computer environment, the originating department enters the salary increase on its own terminal or PC, which is networked to the company's central computer. The human resources department verifies the request electronically, and the payroll department processes the raise without ever reentering the data. If data is keyed only once during the entire process, the risk of input errors is reduced and the processing speed is significantly increased.

IN A NUTSHELL

Input/output units connected to a CPU are called peripherals.

Figure 5.1 *Source documents are often used to update master files so that printed output in the form of checks or statements can be produced.*

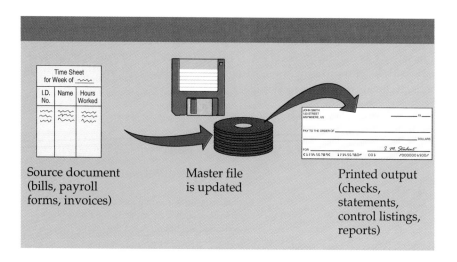

Source document
(bills, payroll
forms, invoices)

Master file
is updated

Printed output
(checks,
statements,
control listings,
reports)

Figure 5.2 illustrates basic input devices found in business. Some are used to process large amounts of data—payroll, order processing, and inventories—whereas others are special-purpose devices, such as supermarket scanners, that are needed in specific application areas where they dramatically improve productivity.

There are two basic types of input devices: those that create a source document along with an input file, and those that read previously created source documents to produce an input file. First, we look at input devices that require a data entry procedure for creating a source document and transmitting the data to a CPU in the form of an input file. Next, we consider source data automation, which focuses on techniques other than keying for electronically converting existing source documents to computer files. See Figure 5.3.

Keying Devices

When data must be entered into a computer, it is most often keyed by a data entry operator. A single keying operation accomplishes two things: (1) it creates a source document and (2) it enters the data as input to a computer. When an airline reservations clerk keys data to create an airline ticket (the source document), that data is also used to update flight information on disk. Similarly, when a clerk keys in a payroll change, that data is transmitted directly to a central computer to update the payroll master file. See Figure 5.4.

Sometimes, however, source documents are created in one procedure, and they are entered as input to a computer in a separate procedure. For example, consider an application in which employees transact their business at a client's premises. These employees may fill out purchase orders that later serve as source documents for the purchasing department. To be processed by computer, the handwritten or typed source documents may need to be keyed in as input to a computer in a separate operation. Independent keying procedures, in which an

---

Looking Back

THE PUNCHED CARD: DO NOT FOLD, STAPLE, BEND, OR MUTILATE

Herman Hollerith developed the 80-column punched card for storing data for the 1890 U.S. census. See (a). He also developed electrical accounting machines that could sort and tabulate the punched-card data. See (b). Hollerith's cards and equipment helped pave the way for computers by reducing the time it took to complete a census by 50 percent. After several mergers, his Tabulating Machine Company became known as the International Business Machines (IBM) Company.

Hollerith's census data was recorded on cards in the form of punched holes. These cards, which were the same size as a dollar bill, served as the model for those adopted by the computing field in the 1950s when punched card data became the most popular form of input. The warning "do not fold, bend, staple, or mutilate" was commonly found on these cards to emphasize how fragile they were. Compare that to today's 3½-inch floppy disk, which can store the equivalent of 18,000 cards of information or more and has been known to withstand being machine-washed when accidentally left in a shirt pocket!

An exhibit at the Smithsonian Institution features a touch screen station to describe the 1890 census process that used punched cards to record data. The station prompts visitors for information about their age group, gender, and current residence. The data is then compared to actual 1890 census data, and visitors receive a profile of who they were likely to have been in 1890. A suburban teenage male

(a)   (b)

(a) A punched card, which was designed to be the size of a dollar bill and (b) Hollerith's tabulating machine.

from Kansas in 1996, for example, would probably have lived on a farm in 1890. At the same time the system gives the profile to the visitor, the information is used to update the person's bar code, which was created when he or she entered the exhibit. The Smithsonian also has on display Hollerith's original tabulating machine.

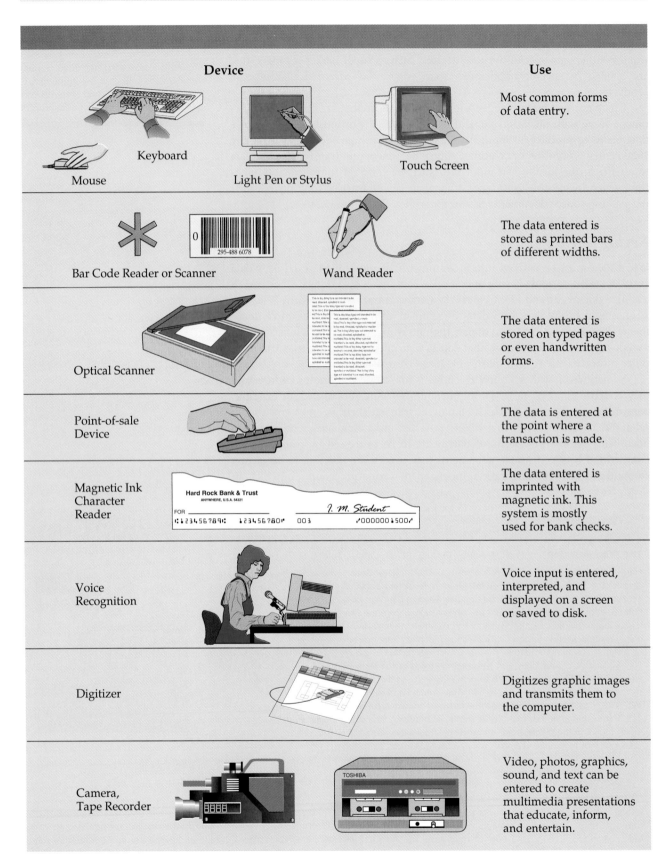

Device	Use
Mouse / Keyboard / Light Pen or Stylus / Touch Screen	Most common forms of data entry.
Bar Code Reader or Scanner / Wand Reader	The data entered is stored as printed bars of different widths.
Optical Scanner	The data entered is stored on typed pages or even handwritten forms.
Point-of-sale Device	The data is entered at the point where a transaction is made.
Magnetic Ink Character Reader	The data entered is imprinted with magnetic ink. This system is mostly used for bank checks.
Voice Recognition	Voice input is entered, interpreted, and displayed on a screen or saved to disk.
Digitizer	Digitizes graphic images and transmits them to the computer.
Camera, Tape Recorder	Video, photos, graphics, sound, and text can be entered to create multimedia presentations that educate, inform, and entertain.

Figure 5.2 *Examples of input devices. Each input device reads in a different form of data for processing by the CPU.*

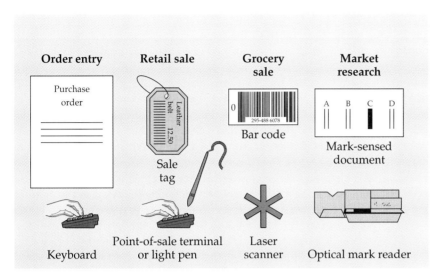

Figure 5.3 *Here are some samples of source documents and devices that can be used for entering them as input.*

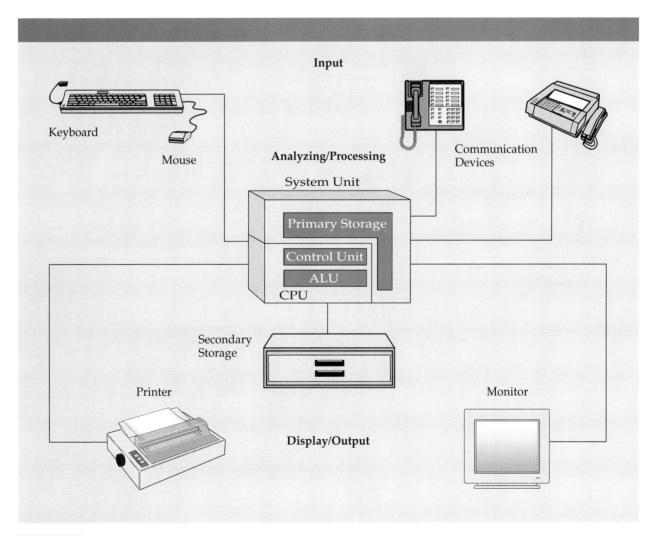

Figure 5.4 *The heart of a computer system. A computer is actually several different devices that together make up a computer system—input devices, secondary storage devices, and output devices all controlled by the system unit containing the CPU and primary storage.*

input file is created, are called offline operations. In an offline operation, data entry is not under the control of the main CPU; that is, conversion of source documents into an input file is performed in a separate procedure that keys the data onto disk. Such a procedure results in duplication of effort: first the source document is created at the point of transaction, and later the data is keyed onto disk. Although it may be inefficient, this is sometimes the most practical and inexpensive procedure. One method for minimizing duplication is to provide the field staff with handheld data collection devices that have a keyboard, pen, or voice recognition unit that can convert the input data directly to disk or other machine-readable form—as it is being transacted.

Some organizations, like express delivery services, find it cost effective to use newer techniques such as pen-based computing for entering data at the point of transaction, and others find traditional manual procedures that require a separate conversion of source documents to disk to be less expensive and more reliable.

In cases where source data needs to be reentered to be read by a computer, the method of input is commonly the keyboard. The keyboard is typically linked to a monitor or video display terminal so that the data being entered can also be viewed on the screen. Data that is entered by means of a keying operation is stored in a transaction file, most often on disk. As we have seen, such a file can be processed in batch mode or interactively.

The keying operation, which is just like typing, is a labor-intensive activity that tends to be costly, time consuming, and prone to errors. Methods to minimize keying errors are user-friendly screen displays and error-control procedures.

USER-FRIENDLY SCREEN DISPLAYS FOR REDUCING ERRORS Selecting entries from a menu minimizes errors and makes it easier for data entry operators to interact with a computer. See Figure 5.5. In this figure, items are displayed on the screen and users select the entry of their choice. To select Sports Hotline from the Daily Gazette in Figure 5.5, for example, the user can press the digit 5 on the keyboard. Alternatively, the ↓ cursor arrow key can be pressed four times to highlight the fifth item and then the Enter key pressed to select it. In

Figure 5.5 *You can select the entry you want from this user-friendly screen display by keying in a number from 1 to 6, using the cursor arrow keys to highlight the number 1–6, or using a mouse.*

the next section, we will see that a mouse can be dragged until it highlights the fifth item and then its left button clicked to select it. The use of a mouse is an alternative to keying for selecting items from a menu.

After an entry is selected from a main menu, the selection process may continue with additional prompts that ask the user to choose more specific entries from submenus. A **prompt** is a request to supply a response or to input a value. If the submenu appears as a superimposed drop-down menu, it is called a *pull-down menu*. You can use the cursor arrows to highlight an item or command in the pull-down menu. Once you have highlighted an item, you select it by pressing the Enter key. As we saw in Chapter 3, some pull-down menus permit you to press a key or combination of keys to select an item. After the required items or commands have been entered, you are typically prompted to key the actual input.

User-friendly screen displays can have entries that are highlighted with the use of color, boldface, reverse video (where background and foreground colors are reversed), or a blinking cursor. Programmers can reduce the risk of input errors and make screens more user-friendly by writing instructions that perform the following actions:

1. Prompt for input with detailed messages that clearly explain what the input should look like: "Enter Code (1-5)."

2. Ensure that fields are actually keyed in and are completely filled. For example, a program can ensure that a department number is keyed as two digits by causing any other entry to make the computer beep or wait for an appropriate entry.

3. Protect sensitive fields such as salaries or passwords from being read by others. Such fields can either remain blank on the screen even when keyed by a data entry operator, or they can appear with special symbols (like #) to mask the values being keyed.

4. Ensure that fields are entered within valid ranges or with valid values. Unit prices, for example, would be accepted only if they fall within price limits established at the company.

ERROR CONTROL PROCEDURES Programs that create input files typically include many error-control procedures, in addition to user-friendly displays, to minimize errors. Although the number of errors can be reduced with such procedures, they can never be eliminated entirely. For example, a program can be written to ensure that a salary falls within an acceptable range. But if a transposition error were made in a salary field so that 45000 was entered instead of 54000, it is unlikely that a program could detect the error.

For this reason, *manual verification* by a staff of employees should be part of any error control procedure. A printout called a **control listing** or **audit trail** includes all changes actually made to files. Users should compare the control listing to the changes that should have been made. If errors are found on the control listing, the data must be corrected.

Most methods of data verification, even those that are programmed, rely on the human factor. For example, after data for an individual record has been entered, the program may display the data in final form and ask the data entry operator to verify that what is displayed is correct. Well-designed interactive screen displays enable the operator to return to any previously entered data and make corrections if necessary.

Even with help from programs in the form of menus, interactive screen displays, and error-control procedures, keying errors do occur. Alternatives to keying operations are often used to minimize such errors and to reduce the cost and time of data entry.

Alternatives to Keying

Instead of using a keying operation, many data entry operators use a mouse, touch screen, light pen, or even a joy stick for entering input. Later in this chapter, we will see that the newest data collection systems accept virtually any form of source document without the need for a separate input procedure. See Figure 5.6.

MOUSE A mouse is a small, handheld device that usually contains a ball-type roller on the bottom and one or more buttons on the top (Figure 5.7). Apple's Macintosh was the first PC to make the mouse popular. It is now a common tool for most micros and many larger computer systems as well. Because a mouse is easy to use and reduces the need for typing, it is considered a user-friendly input device.

The mouse is normally used to select choices from a menu. You *drag* the mouse to highlight the item desired and then *click* in, usually with the left button, to select the item. This selection method is often much faster than using cursor control arrow keys for highlighting an entry and then pressing the Enter key to choose it. See Figure 5.8 for an illustration of how menu items can be selected by a mouse.

A mouse does not eliminate the need to use a keyboard for entering text, although it does reduce some keying operations, particularly for selecting commands or making choices. In word processing applications, for example, the text is entered using the keyboard, but it may be formatted by using the mouse to make selections from menus that offer choices in type font and page layout. The mouse may also be used to select print options from a menu that offers choices about which pages to print and how many copies are needed. Alternatively, cursor control arrow keys can be used to highlight the desired symbol or icon; pressing the Enter key instead of clicking the mouse selects the entry. We will see in Chapter 7 that graphics packages make particularly good use of the mouse, which can actually trace or draw patterns.

There are many types of mice. On the underside of the standard mechanical mouse is a ball. As the mouse is moved, the ball rolls up, down, left, and right across a flat surface and a signal is sent to the computer that drives the cursor up, down, left, and right, corresponding to the motion of the mouse. An optical mouse is a different type that rolls over a desktop pad with a reflective grid. The optical mouse emits a light as it is dragged, which correspondingly moves the cursor to match the mouse's position on the grid. Mice that use balls and rollers and emit a light for positioning a cursor are also common. With all mice, one or more buttons on the top of the mouse are pressed to select, or click on, the user's commands when the cursor is at the desired position.

Portable computers often use rollerballs or trackballs as pointing devices because they are part of the computer itself, or they can be attached to the keyboard. Sometimes these are called mice and sometimes they are simply called pointing devices. A rollerball has rubber-coated control balls for smoother, quieter dragging and clicking. A trackball is a stationary unit that contains a movable ball which, when rotated with the fingers or palm of the hand, moves the cursor on the screen. Both the rollerball and the trackball are often easier to use than the mechanical or optical mouse. Figure 5.9 illustrates different types of pointing devices.

Figure 5.6 *A handheld system can be used for keeping track of inventory.*

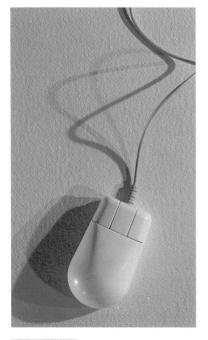

Figure 5.7 *A mechanical mouse.*

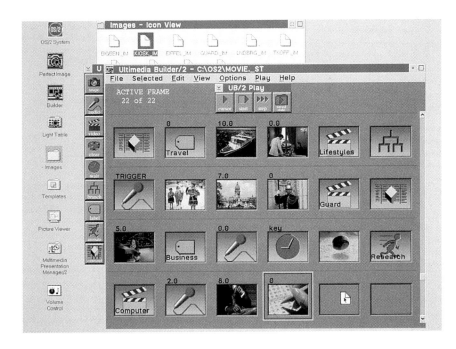

Figure 5.8 *Sample menu items that can be selected by a mouse. You use the mouse to point to the desired icon and then click in to select the item. Similarly, the mouse can be used for moving the cursor to a specific point in a text or for highlighting a portion of text for editing.*

●●●●●➤ **Looking Ahead**

NEW MICE ARE EVEN MORE USER-FRIENDLY

- Newer mice reduce the risk of wrist-strain injuries.
- Mice are now available in left-handed as well as right-handed versions.
- The speed of a mouse is now easier for users to control.
- Cordless mice, which are battery operated and use radio transmitters, are becoming popular.
- Some mice can be programmed to automatically select commands such as File Save or File Retrieve.

Many applications rely on the use of a mouse or other pointing device to select entries represented as symbols, or icons, on a screen. Icons, such as the ones shown previously in Figure 5.8, can depict commands that the user may wish to select for performing some task.

Icons create a user-friendly environment from which people can select visual, self-explanatory commands without having to key or remember complex instruction formats. Icons can replace the clutter on a screen, make displays more user-friendly, and make it easier for users to select entries with a mouse, other pointing device, or even a keyboard. Some operating systems and interfaces, like the Macintosh System 7.5 and Windows for IBM-compatibles, make extensive use of icons that are best selected with a mouse.

TOUCH SCREEN A **touch screen** enables you to select entries and enter choices or commands by simply using your finger to make contact with the screen to highlight the desired item. A touch screen is similar in concept to buttons in elevators where you select the desired floor by touching the corresponding floor number. Instead of using a mouse to click on an entry to select it, you actually

(a)

(b)

Figure 5.9 *There are many different types of mice or pointing devices. (a) Portable PCs often have a rollerball. (b) The Glide Point is an easy-to-use touch surface that permits smooth, full-screen cursor control with the sweep of a finger.*

Figure 5.10 *Many people consider touch screens to be the most user-friendly and intuitive interfaces available. There is no need to enter keyboard commands or manipulate a mouse.*

Figure 5.11 *Light pens are used to select menu items by touching the desired item on the screen with the pen. Here, a nurse extracts hospital records using a pen.*

Figure 5.12 *A joy stick is often used for playing games or simulating certain actions, such as driving a car or flying a plane.*

select the desired entry with a touch of your finger. IBM and other manufacturers make touch screens for PCs as well as for terminals. Some touch screens can simply snap on to existing video monitors. Figure 5.10 illustrates a touch screen application. Information kiosks at central locations often enable visitors to get tourist information by pressing a touch screen. Your school may have touch-screen kiosks for getting information on locating a building, finding out your professor's office hours, or viewing your transcript.

Touch screens are also often used to select purchases in department stores that have wedding registries. A customer keys in the bride and/or groom's name; the screen then displays items for which the engaged couple is registered. The customer selects purchases by pressing the screen where the appropriate item is displayed.

PEN-BASED COMPUTERS A **light pen** or stylus works just like the touch of your finger on a touch screen. Instead of using your finger to select items, you use a special pen. See Figure 5.11.

Many handheld portable computers have pens as well as keyboards. The pen can be used instead of a mouse for highlighting and selecting items. It can also be used to make handwritten entries. Most of these computers have at least limited handwriting recognition capability.

JOY STICK A **joy stick** is similar to a mouse in that it positions and moves a cursor. It is used primarily for playing games although trackballs are also commonly used for this purpose. See Figure 5.12.

Many information systems require source documents to be keyed into a computer. Sometimes, a mouse, touch screen, or light pen is used in place of, or in conjunction with, keying for selecting entries, thereby minimizing data entry costs and errors. In the next section, we focus on techniques that minimize the need for manually converting source documents to machine-readable form.

Self-Test

1. A _____ is an originating document that is entered as input to a computer system.

2. (T or F) Most applications use keying devices for entering data into a computer system.

3. What are the two methods used for updating master files?

4. What are the advantages of selecting applications from menus?

5. The file that contains changes to be made to a master file is called a _____ file.

6. Name three alternatives to keying devices that are popular in business.

5.2 SOURCE DATA AUTOMATION REDUCES DATA ENTRY OPERATIONS

In organizations with many branch locations or with an extensive field staff, source documents may be created offline (i.e., not under the control of a central computer). These offline operations usually require a clerk or typist to create a source document, or a data entry operator to create a disk file from a source document where up-to-date information is not required at all times. Offline data entry operations tend to be less costly alternatives to online data entry, where the data being entered as input is under the direct control of the main CPU and is immediately available to update existing files.

When source documents are created manually, the data from them often needs to be rekeyed into a computer, which results in duplication of effort and which increases the risk of errors. To minimize this duplication, the source document created offline in a manual procedure may be read by special scanners that automatically convert the input to machine-readable form. **Source data automation (SDA)** is the process of computerizing the procedure that converts source documents to machine-readable form. Its objectives are to minimize labor-intensive tasks such as keyboarding and to reduce errors. The most common devices for converting source documents to machine-readable form are optical character readers (OCR), but there are other devices as well. We begin our discussion of source data automation with OCR devices.

> **Study Objective**
>
> 2. Show how source data automation actually improves productivity.

Optical Character Readers

Where large volumes of manually created forms or source documents need to be read by computer, special input devices that physically scan the document and convert it to machine-readable form are more suitable than manual rekey-

---

Solutions

1. source document

2. T

3. online, or interactive, processing; batch processing

4. less keying and fewer errors

5. transaction

6. mouse; touch screen; light pen

Figure 5.13 *A scanning device at the supermarket checkout counter reads the Universal Product Code (UPC) on packages. The computer then looks up the price and computes the total cost of a purchase. It also updates inventory records.*

Critical Thinking

Bar code readers eliminate the need for including prices on grocery items. The computer automatically looks up prices from its database so that unit pricing is not necessary—except for providing the shopper with the cost for each product and a way of checking the bill! Some supermarkets have tried to eliminate unit pricing because it requires costly manual labor—they claim they will pass on the savings to the consumer. Consumer groups have been effective in many states in getting legislation passed requiring items to be stamped with the price. Do you think unit pricing should be required by law—or do you think the cost of consumer goods will decrease without it?

ing. **Optical character readers (OCRs)** form a class of input devices that can read or scan data without the need for a keying operation. They are widely used with PC-based systems for scanning documents; they are also popular in large organizations where the need to minimize keying is great. OCR input devices include bar code readers, wand readers, optical mark readers, as well as optical scanners that read documents.

BAR CODE SCANNERS AND WAND READERS Most grocery stores rely on optical **bar code readers** for their checkout procedures. These devices read, or scan, the zebra-like bars that you see on most food packages and other consumer goods. The black-and-white bars of different widths form a code called the **Universal Product Code (UPC)** that identifies the manufacturer of the product as well as the product itself.

The bar code reader is usually a laser scanning device that converts the product data into electrical impulses (see Figure 5.13). An electronic cash register at the transaction site uses the UPC information to retrieve the product's price from a computer. The bar code data need not be keyed or otherwise converted to a machine-readable form because the scanner reads it directly, minimizing the time it takes to complete a transaction and reducing data entry errors. In addition, inventory and accounts receivable data can be updated immediately as products are purchased.

You are probably familiar with bar codes on consumer products sold in supermarkets or department stores. But bar codes have much wider applicability. Laboratories encode blood samples with bar codes. Factories use bar code readers for scanning inventory. The New York City Marathon, as well as many other races, has been assigning individual bar codes to runners who must wear them on their shirts. As a runner finishes the marathon, a device scans the bar code to record the runner's name and order of finish. Figure 5.14 illustrates another application for bar codes.

The handheld **wand reader** is also a popular scanning device for reading bar codes. Some wand readers can scan data encoded with special OCR typefaces. Wand readers that scan OCR codes are often used as alternatives to bar code readers. The character data scanned is readable by people as well as by machines.

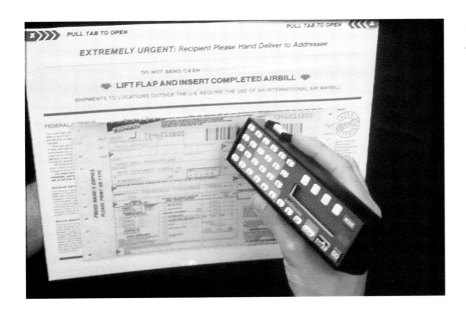

Figure 5.14 *Bar codes can be read from FedEx packages. These codes are used to keep track of each package from its source to its destination.*

Hospitals, libraries, and factories use wand readers for scanning data. Many retail stores include special OCR typefaces on their inventory tags. The wand reader can be connected to a point-of-sale terminal or electronic cash register for generating a sales receipt.

OPTICAL MARK READERS An **optical mark reader,** sometimes called a mark sense reader, detects the presence of pencil marks on predetermined grids. As a student, you are probably familiar with one type of mark-sense source document: the computer-scored test answer sheet (Figure 5.15). You mark the answers

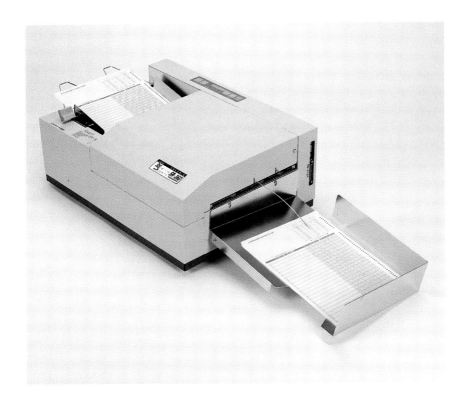

Figure 5.15 *An optical mark reader is used to compute the score on answer sheets filled in by students.*

to multiple-choice questions by filling in a square or a circle that surrounds the letter or number of choice. Identifying data such as student name can also be specified by filling in the circles or squares corresponding to letters.

Other applications of optical mark readers include payment forms and surveys or questionnaires that request the customer or respondent to fill in answers to inquiries. Grids must be filled in carefully—no stray pencil marks—for data to be interpreted correctly by an optical mark reader.

OPTICAL SCANNERS FOR TYPED OR HANDWRITTEN DATA With an **optical scanner,** source documents such as reports, typed manuscripts, or even books can be entered directly to a computer without the need for keying. An optical scanner converts text and images on paper into digital form and stores the data on disk or other storage media. Optical scanners are available in different sizes and for different types of applications. Small handheld units for PCs cost hundreds of dollars and can process a few pages a minute. More sophisticated scanners for larger computers can process hundreds of pages a minute at a cost of thousands of dollars or more, depending on the speed and capability of the device.

The publishing industry is a leading user of optical scanning equipment. Publishers scan printed documents and convert them to electronic databases that can be referenced as needed. Similarly, they can scan manuscripts instead of retyping them in preparation for the process that converts them into books or magazines. Considerable time and money are saved, and the risk of introducing typographical errors is reduced. In addition, publishers who need to reprint previously published articles in different formats can scan the original documents.

Scanners that can interpret handwritten input are available, but they are subject to errors. To minimize mistakes, handwritten entries should follow very specific rules. Some scanners will flag handwritten entries that they cannot interpret or will automatically display for verification all input that has been scanned. (See Figure 5.16.)

Because handwritten entries are subject to misinterpretation and typed entries can be smudged, misaligned, erased, and so forth, optical scanners have an error rate considerably higher than error rates for keyed data. Nevertheless, scanners are widely used by organizations whose documents have been prepared offline and need to be converted to machine-readable form at a later date. Despite the 8% to 10% error rate of some scanning operations, many users would rather make corrections resulting from these errors than spend the time and money to rekey documents and risk additional errors. Scanners are becoming increasingly more reliable. Some are sophisticated enough to read not only

·····➤ Looking Ahead

"SCANNING" THE WORLD WITH OCRs

- New OCR devices will read handwriting and poorly reproduced text with improved accuracy.
- Advanced OCR systems will use expert systems to "learn" or decipher the characteristics of new type fonts or handwritten data that may be difficult to read.

Figure 5.16 *Handwritten entries to be scanned must follow precise rules.*

Rules	Acceptable	Unacceptable
1. Make letters big	REDFORD	REDFORD
2. Use block letters	ROBERT	Robert
3. Carefully connect lines	571	571
4. Close loops	9086	9086
5. Do not link characters	ROBERT	ROBERT

(a)   (b)

Figure 5.17 *Many scanners can scan images as well as text and can be a desktop unit or a handheld unit. Many units can scan color images as well as black-and-white illustrations. (a) This desktop scanner is used by law enforcement agencies to scan photos of missing children. (b) Handheld units can scan forms such as a tax return.*

text but visuals such as photos, illustrations, and graphs, which can then be incorporated in files as they are or modified as needed. (See Figure 5.17.)

Applications Using Data Collection Systems

If insurance salespeople or other field staff employees transact business at the client's premises, the data entry problem is compounded by the need to collect data from many locations or transaction sites. Similarly, in a large store, sales-clerks typically complete transactions in their own departments; then data from these transactions needs to be collected before it can be processed. Data collection devices are designed to (1) record data electronically and (2) collect it from various sites.

POINT-OF-SALE TERMINALS A common input device for data collection with which you may be familiar is the **point-of-sale (POS) terminal,** which can be a bar code reader like the ones we discussed previously or a keyboard device. Broadly defined, a point-of-sale system uses remote terminals in retail establishments to enter data at the locations where business is transacted. For example, stores have POS terminals located strategically in each department (Figure 5.18). At the point of sale, the purchase is recorded and the POS terminal produces a sales slip for the customer. For a purchase made by credit card, the POS terminal transmits the data to the central computer, which verifies the account number and updates the account. The POS terminal also calculates sales totals and may be used to keep track of inventory. Other retail businesses that commonly use POS terminals are fast-food restaurants, supermarkets, and hotels.

A POS terminal can be a keying device, a bar code reader, or any type of data collection device suitable for specific retail applications.

TELEPHONES, FAX MACHINES, PORTABLE DATA COLLECTION DEVICES, AND WIRELESS COMMUNICATION EQUIPMENT Some computer systems are equipped to accept input data directly from any Touch-Tone telephone. For example, many banks allow their checking account customers to pay bills by telephone. The customer responds to prerecorded instructions that request the

Figure 5.18 *Point-of-sale terminals, which include electronic cash registers, are used in retail stores to enter sales information, update inventories, and print customer receipts.*

Figure 5.19 *Portable keying devices can be used in many types of applications. Here, a law enforcement agent uses a portable keying device to write tickets.*

account number to be entered, the company to be paid (usually identified with a code number), the amount to be paid, and the date on which to make payment. In this case, the phone is simply a remote keying device for data collection.

Automatic Telephone and Fax Services Many organizations have computerized telephone systems that serve as electronic receptionists. They lead you through a maze of options that require you to provide a Touch-Tone response. In this way, you can reach the person you want to speak to, obtain the information you want, place an order, and so on.

A facsimile machine (fax) can also transmit input directly to a computer over telephone lines. Some organizations, like the AAA Travel Service Center, have fully automated fax-back systems where a recorded message asks you to press specific keys on your telephone to define your inquiry. The information you are requesting is then faxed back to you—all without operator intervention.

Portable Devices Portable or handheld keying and scanning devices are widely used as well. See Figure 5.19. Some of these devices store the data collected on disk in an offline operation and others use a standard telephone or wireless communication equipment to send input data directly to a CPU in an online operation. A salesperson working at a client's premises (or any remote location not at the same site as the main CPU), for example, can enter orders using a portable keying or scanning device. Some portable devices simply store data for future batch processing. Others generate source documents or transmit data over telephone lines to a CPU that receives the order and updates files.

PEN-BASED SYSTEMS: THE WRITE STUFF Many PC manufacturers today offer pen-based portables. The pen can be used for data collection, or as in Personal Digital Assistants (PDAs), for taking notes, selecting commands, sending handwritten faxes over wireless communication lines, and so on. Salespeople who are part of a field staff find pen-based systems convenient to fill out orders displayed on a screen and store the data on disk. See Figure 5.20. Pen-based systems can also serve as general-purpose computers; input to be entered can be either keyed or handwritten.

A pen-based system has wider applicability than a system with a touch screen or a mouse because it has a stylus (or pen), which has the following three features:

1. Users can make handwritten entries that can be text-based as well as sketches and drawings.

2. Users can insert an entry using a caret (^) to mark the entry point. Text can be marked for deletion by drawing a line through it. The ability to mark text makes a pen more useful than a mouse for some types of applications.

3. Users can actually enter text as handwritten characters. These pen-based systems may have keyboards as well, along with disk drives for storage.

As with optical readers, the problem of high error rates with pen-based systems has yet to be entirely resolved. Even though individual printed characters can be recognized with reasonable accuracy, the normal handwriting of most of us may not always result in an acceptable level of recognition.

Figure 5.20 *Pen-based computers can be used to fill out order forms in a supermarket or complete applications for clients.*

Automation in the Banking Industry

The banking industry has specific information processing needs that are often met by specialized input devices. Some of the input devices used by banks are magnetic ink character readers, automatic teller machines, and debit cards.

MAGNETIC INK CHARACTER READER DEVICES When checks are printed for a bank's customers, they contain magnetically encoded digits on the bottom that identify the customer's account and each check number. After the check has been used in a transaction and returned to the bank, the amount of the check is encoded on the bottom. Banks use **magnetic ink character readers (MICRs)** to read the magnetic ink numbers printed at the bottom of checks. Figure 5.21*a* is an example of specially encoded bank checks and 5.21*b* illustrates a MICR device.

When magnetically encoded checks are returned to the bank, they can be processed in large batches very quickly by these high-speed MICR devices that read, sort, and store the data on disk or other medium. In the United States alone, billions of checks are processed with MICR devices each day. These units read digits only and some special characters, but not alphabetic characters. Limiting the number of acceptable characters in this way increases the speed of the device.

Laser printers capable of printing magnetic ink characters that can be read by MICR devices are now widely available. With these printers, users can print checks—with company logos and all—on the spot as the need arises.

AUTOMATIC TELLER MACHINES The **automatic teller machine (ATM)** is an interactive input/output device in which data entered at the point of transaction can automatically and immediately update banking records in an online operation. Customers use an ATM to deposit cash or checks, withdraw cash, or electronically transfer money from one account to another. ATMs make banking more flexible because they are usually available 24 hours a day and do not require any intervention from a teller or other bank employee. To protect the customer's funds, the bank provides plastic cash cards that have magnetic stripes

ɪN A NUTSHELL

SPANNING THE GLOBE

Pen-based computers are expected to be among the fastest growing machines in the international market with an anticipated annual growth rate of 68% through the year 2000. One of the reasons for this projected growth is that Asian communities, which have rejected keyboard-based computers, prefer pen input because it is easier to use for their languages.

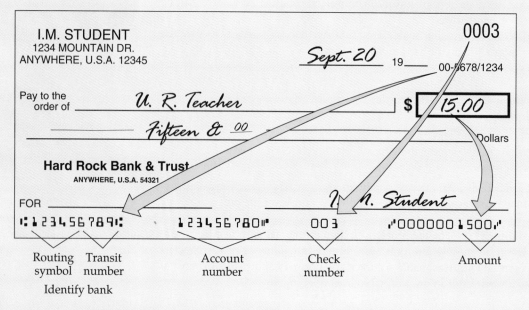

Cancelled checks have magnetic numbers imprinted along the bottom, identifying the bank, account number, and check amount.

I.M. STUDENT
1234 MOUNTAIN DR.
ANYWHERE, U.S.A. 12345

Sept. 20   19____   00-5678/1234

Pay to the order of _____ U. R. Teacher _____ $ 15.00

_____ Fifteen & 00 _____   Dollars

Hard Rock Bank & Trust
ANYWHERE, U.S.A. 54321

FOR _____   I.M. Student

⑈123456789⑈   123456780⑈   003   ⑈0000001500⑈

Routing   Transit   Account   Check   Amount
symbol   number   number   number

Identify bank

1. Checks are fed into large, high-capacity MICR reader/sorter devices.
2. MICR characters on checks are read electronically.
3. Check data is stored on disk for processing.
4. Checks are sorted by bank number and returned to your bank.
5. If you wish, a bank may sort checks by account number and return them to you with the monthly statements.

(a)

Figure 5.21 (a) Canceled checks have magnetic numbers imprinted on the bottom identifying the bank, account number, and check amount. An operator encodes the check by keying the amount of the transaction when the check is returned to the bank. (b) A MICR check-processing device can process 2400 or more checks per minute.

(b)

Figure 5.22 *Standard automatic teller machines have become an everyday convenience for many people. Some ATMs, like this one, have enhanced capabilities.*

encoded with account information; the customer inserts the card into the ATM and then keys in a password called a personal identification number (PIN). The information entered by the user is compared to that on the magnetic stripe. If the account number and PIN are valid and the account is active, the customer is able to proceed with the transaction. See Figure 5.22.

DEBIT CARDS A **debit card** looks like a credit card and is also used to make purchases; but with debit cards, transactions are immediately posted to your account.

Because debit cards result in the immediate withdrawal of funds from an account, they are far less popular than credit cards, which post transactions and bill customers at the end of the month.

SMART CARDS Smart cards differ from credit, ATM, and debit cards. The smart card actually contains a microprocessor and has the ability to store millions of characters of data—and the ability to alter balances based on transactions made. It can be used in place of cash—you buy a card for a fixed amount and use it to make purchases. Because the balance on the card can be changed, there is no need to contact the bank to verify a purchase. Rather, the amount of purchase is deducted from the value of the card. When the card's value is down to 0, simply throw it away. Such cards could move us very quickly to a cashless society.

Smart cards are used widely in Europe for making calls from a public telephone. You purchase a telephone card for a specific denomination. Insert the card in a public telephone, make your call and the phone charges will be deducted from the card. When the card no longer has any value, you can discard it.

IN A NUTSHELL

SMART CARDS FOR STORAGE

A smart card can contain up to 20 MB of storage; this far exceeds the capacity of credit cards, which usually store less than 100 characters. Credit cards, however, are much cheaper to manufacture.

Critical Thinking

Some people think smart cards with cash values provide individuals with a greater degree of privacy than traditional credit and debit cards. Credit cards enable banks and credit companies to keep track of your purchases while smart cards with cash values leave no electronic trail—you buy the card, use it for purchases, and remain anonymous in each transaction, making it more difficult for the government—and others—to follow your movements. Would you feel more secure using a smart card rather than a credit card?

Figure 5.23 *A supersmart card with a keypad can be used for bank transactions.*

Some supersmart cards are available with keypads so that you can check the status of your account as well as make purchases. See Figure 5.23.

Because smart cards can be used for storing data as well as entering input, we discuss them in more depth in Chapter 6.

Voice Recognition Equipment

Probably the most user-friendly input device is one that can accept human speech as input and correctly interpret the spoken word. **Voice recognition equipment** enables computers to interpret words and phrases. For example, a factory worker can enter inventory data which is then stored on disk, by speaking into a device while opening boxes and analyzing their contents. A laboratory technician can record results of a blood workup by speaking into a voice recognition device while viewing the blood samples in a microscope. A quality control expert can specify the results of an automotive inspection by speaking into a voice recognition device as the inspection is being performed. A security system may use voice recognition equipment to identify authorized personnel based

Figure 5.24 *A voice recognition device can be used by the physically disabled for executing instructions or even for selecting items from a menu.*

IN A NUTSHELL

COMPARISON OF CREDIT, DEBIT, AND SMART CARDS

Credit Card	Stores credit card information used to verify the card's validity or to post a transaction when a purchase is made
Debit Card	Stores account information; used to immediately deduct amount of purchase from your bank account; an ATM card is a type of debit card
Smart Card	Can store a lot of personal or other information; can contain a microprocessor so that it may be sold to a user for a set cash value that is reduced each time a purchase is made

on their responses to computer-generated queries. A voice pattern, like a finger-print, is a distinctive trait that can uniquely identify an individual. In each case, the voice recognition equipment not only records the input but interprets it as well and stores it in machine-readable form. See Figure 5.24.

Voice recognition devices improve productivity by enabling data entry operators to use their hands for other operations such as verifying products, stamping cartons, and making handwritten entries. Telephone companies, shop-at-home facilities, and customer service centers rely heavily on this technology. Some organizations have automated their routing and operator services to such an extent that the need for operator intervention has been greatly minimized and in some instances eliminated entirely.

VOICE RECOGNITION AND TELEPHONE COMPANIES Some telephone companies have limited voice recognition capabilities. For example, if a taped message tells you that you have a collect call, you may be able to decline by simply responding "no" when asked if you wish to accept the charges—your response is interpreted by a voice recognition device. Some telephone companies have automatic directory assistance using more sophisticated voice recognition equipment to interpret the name as you speak it. The system looks up the phone number for that person or organization and using an audio response unit provides you with the telephone number—all without operator assistance. Sprint has a service that enables you to insert a credit card into a phone, and instead of using a Touch-Tone phone to call your mother, you simply say "Mom" when asked for the party you wish to contact. A voice recognition unit finds "Mom" and her phone number in its database and automatically dials the number.

The bill for phone fraud—the illegal use of telephone credit card numbers for making long distance calls—is staggering. Some telephone companies are using voice recognition technology to prevent phone fraud by using devices that compare callers' voices to stored voice-print templates of the rightful card owners. You call up and say a password; if your voice and password do not match the template, your call is cancelled.

Currently, voice recognition systems exist that can recognize thousands of words regardless of the accent, dialect, or tonal qualities of the speaker. Some can even "learn" the meaning of new words. Some have a high degree of reliability even when there is background noise. But voice patterns differ widely from person to person, so this technology still has a high error rate. As voice-based equipment becomes more reliable, however, its applicability is likely to increase.

In summary, voice recognition devices, like pointing devices, light pens, touch screens, and handheld data collection devices, minimize the need for keying data. This makes them ideally suited for people who do not like to type, whose other tasks prevent them from using their hands, or who have eye-hand coordination problems or other physical disabilities.

TALKING TO COMPUTERS Note, too, that many sound boards for PCs commonly used to output sounds, music, and voice messages now have limited voice recognition capability as well. With these boards, you can program your computer to execute a command when you orally enter a specified phrase.

Digitizers

One fast-growing application of computers today is for drawing illustrations or creating graphic images. Artists, engineers, and designers need specialized equipment to create their designs so that they can be stored, analyzed, and manipulated by the computer. Professional quality illustrations can be drawn with a pen on a sensitized surface called a **digitizer tablet.** As the pen makes contact with the surface, differences in electrical charges are detected, and the image being drawn is stored electronically in the computer. The digitizing tablet contains a grid of sensor wires, and as the pen moves over the grid, it makes contact with specific points on it. In this way, continuous movements of the pen are translated into digital signals. See Figure 5.25.

Figure 5.25 *A digitizer is used for drawing illustrations and converting them into machine-readable form. Maps, for example, are commonly converted into machine-readable form using a digitizer. Digitizers are also used extensively for computer-aided design applications.*

Self-Test

1. (T or F) Offline data entry operations tend to be less costly alternatives to online data entry.

2. Besides keying, the most common devices for converting source documents to machine-readable form are _____.

3. Most grocery stores use _____ readers for their checkout procedures.

4. (T or F) The Universal Product Code on a grocery item or other consumer goods typically includes the price for that item.

5. A _____ system uses remote terminals in retail establishments to enter data at the locations where business is transacted.

6. (T or F) Magnetic ink character readers (MICRs) can read any letter or digit that is magnetically encoded.

7. (T or F) The automatic teller machine (ATM) is an example of an interactive input/output device.

Study Objective

3. List advantages and disadvantages of each class of output device.

5.3 OUTPUT DEVICES PRODUCE INFORMATION

We use computers because we need them to produce some form of useful information, or output. To be useful, output information must meet the criteria of completeness, conciseness, accuracy, timeliness, cost-effectiveness, and relevancy.

In Chapter 1 we discussed the distinction between data and information, and this is a good time to review it. Individual data items—such as today's date or the record of the sale of a box of nails—are typically entered into the computer, which uses application programs to process them in a meaningful way. Each application is designed to produce a particular kind of output, for exam-

Solutions

1.   T

2.   optical character readers (OCR devices)

3.   optical bar code

4.   F—It specifies a code for the manufacturer of the product as well as for the product itself. This data is used to retrieve the price from a computer. To change a price, only the computer entry need be updated, *not* the UPC on every product.

5.   point-of-sale (POS)

6.   F—They can read only digits and some special characters, but not alphabetic characters.

7.   T

ple, a summary of all sales for a given day. This output, or processed data, is information. Output differs from raw data, or input, in that it can be used for decision making.

If you manage a store's inventory, for example, it is not enough to know how many boxes of nails were sold today. You also need to know how many boxes are on hand at the end of the day, the average number of boxes sold per day, the projected date by which all the boxes of nails will be sold, and how long it takes to restock nails by ordering from your nail vendor. This *information* allows you to decide when to reorder nails.

Types of Output

We use output devices daily, usually without even noticing that a computer program is controlling the application. Many libraries, for example, have converted their card catalogs from drawers stacked with file cards to disk from which specific entries can be displayed on a computer screen. To determine whether your library has a certain book, you simply follow a few on-screen instructions. You may type an author's last name or a subject, and the related titles and catalog codes in the library's collection appear on the screen. In this case the computer is producing **soft copy,** or screen display, output. Computers can also produce **hard copy,** or printed output. Some libraries, for example, have the capability of printing a bibliography of titles on a subject. You key in a few parameters and the computer gives you a printed list of all the books that meet the criteria you set.

There are endless varieties of special-purpose output such as airline tickets, ATM transaction slips, library overdue notices, and a book manuscript from a word processor. Most routine business output, however, can be classified into two categories: responses to inquiries and reports.

RESPONSES TO INQUIRIES Inquiries usually involve on-demand searches of a database for a particular piece of information. For example, a human resources department might need to know the date of employment for Lamont Jones, whose Social Security number is 342-00-0228. Or a customer service representative might need to determine whether an item ordered is currently in inventory. Responses to inquiries are usually made interactively with the output either displayed, printed, or perhaps verbally transmitted to the user.

REPORTS Printed reports are produced either on demand (unscheduled) or periodically. Special reports may be generated on demand whenever the need arises; usually they are produced in response to a request by management. Periodic reports are printed on a regular basis. Reports can be classified into three groups: exception, summary, and transaction. For example, a marketing manager might notice an unaccountable increase in sales in a geographic area and request a listing of individual orders for that area to determine whether the increase represents a trend. This would be an on-demand **exception report.** An example of a scheduled exception report is a weekly listing of all salespeople whose expense accounts are not within the expected range. Exception reports are usually generated to alert managers to situations that require their attention.

Summary reports are produced periodically—daily, weekly, monthly, quarterly, yearly—or on demand. These include sales summaries, end-of-month inventory listings, a company's financial statements, cost analyses—all the standard working reports needed by an organization's functional areas. Summary reports are used by the operating staff and by managers for decision making.

TYPES OF REPORTS

On demand or scheduled
- Exception
- Summary
- Transaction

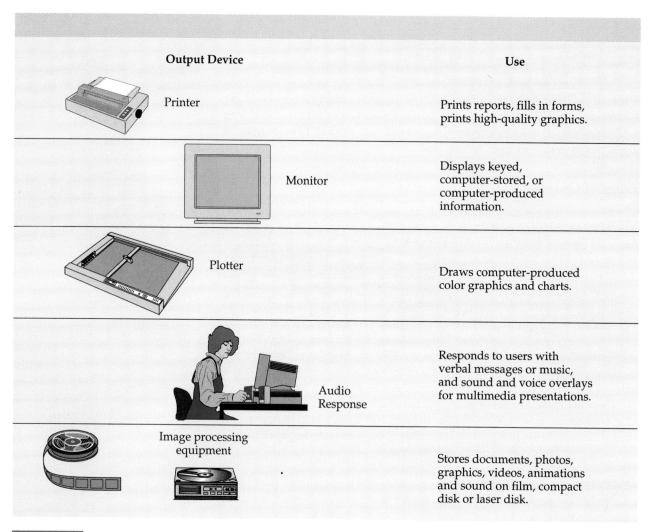

Output Device	Use
Printer	Prints reports, fills in forms, prints high-quality graphics.
Monitor	Displays keyed, computer-stored, or computer-produced information.
Plotter	Draws computer-produced color graphics and charts.
Audio Response	Responds to users with verbal messages or music, and sound and voice overlays for multimedia presentations.
Image processing equipment	Stores documents, photos, graphics, videos, animations and sound on film, compact disk or laser disk.

Figure 5.26 *Examples of common output forms and devices.*

Transaction reports contain detailed information of business transactions and are routinely used by the operating staff. Examples of transaction reports include complete listings of payroll checks, orders received, invoices scheduled for payment, and stock transactions.

Most output devices are designed to produce information either as hard copy printouts or soft copy visual displays. Figure 5.26 shows some of the more common ones. Next we will discuss hard copy and soft copy output devices in detail; then we will describe two other forms of output devices: those for audio output and for image processing.

Output Devices

MONITORS Soft copy screen output is usually associated with some form of interactive processing in which input is entered or a request is made and output is displayed. When performing an interactive inquiry or search, you typically choose an option from a menu; then the screen displays more detailed submenu options; and when your exact request has been entered, the computer retrieves the information you need.

A variety of screen display devices, also called video display terminals

(VDTs), are available, and the technologies used to produce them can be quite sophisticated. Early PC monitors or screens were usually either black and white or black and green, but today's monitors can produce high-quality graphics in many colors.

CRTs. One common form of display monitor is the **cathode ray tube (CRT),** which is still used extensively with microcomputers and as terminals. CRTs resemble the picture tube in your TV. They contain an electron "gun" that fires a beam of electrons, lighting up tiny points of phosphor that glow for a short period of time. Every character you see on the screen is made up of many of these points of light called **pixels.** Early models of CRTs, for example, consisted of 640 × 480 pixels; more recent models today have 1024 × 768 pixels. The gun constantly scans the screen, relighting the pixels so rapidly that the screen characters appear to be glowing continuously. The quality of what you see on the screen is determined by how many pixels your monitor is designed to display. The more pixels, the better the **resolution,** or crispness, of the characters on the screen.

Older, less expensive CRTs that display only one color are called monochrome monitors, and they are typically either green or amber against a black background. Color monitors are far more desirable not only because they make viewing text more appealing, but also because they are better for graphic applications. The cost of color monitors has decreased considerably in recent years, which has made them even more popular.

Today's color monitors are often called VGA or Super VGA (SVGA) monitors. VGA is an abbreviation for video graphics adapter. Figure 5.27 shows the high quality of graphic images displayed on SVGA monitors. Super VGA screens offer the best quality images. Their resolution is 800 × 600, 1024 × 768 pixels, or more. Super VGA screens with 1024 × 768 or more resolution can display 64 K, 256 K, and even 16 million colors. NEC and Sony are major manufacturers offering 14-inch SVGA screens for a few hundred dollars. Larger screens cost substantially more. A 17-inch screen, for example, is in the $1,000 range and a 21-inch screen is in the $2,000 range.

Although CRT screens are well suited for desktop PCs and terminals, portable PCs need screens that are smaller and lighter. Such screens use flat-screen technologies that often do not have the high resolution of desktop monitors.

Flat-Screen Technologies. You may have noticed that the monitor on your personal computer is actually deeper than it is wide or tall; this is the shape required for the CRT's electron gun inside. It is not, however, a practical shape or weight for portable computers. Thanks to new flat-screen technologies, portable computers like laptops, notebooks, and personal digital assistants can have high-resolution screen displays. Although most current flat screens are monochrome, color flat screens are available but tend to be expensive.

The most common flat screen is the liquid crystal display (LCD), in which a current passes through liquid crystals sandwiched between two sheets of polarized material. Characters on the screen are created when crystals arrange themselves so that light does not shine through; the image is dark against a lighted background. An LCD display is used on digital wristwatches and pocket calculators. Many LCD screens get their light source from the back of the screen, so they are called *backlit panels.* Such screens often have sharper characters and brighter backgrounds. Another flat-screen technology, called electroluminescent (EL) display, is available but it sometimes requires too much power for battery-operated laptops.

Some of the newest laptops use gas-plasma displays, even though they too

Figure 5.27 *Super VGA monitors offer the best quality images.*

IN A NUTSHELL

TYPES OF MONITORS

MONITOR	STANDARD RESOLUTION	NUMBER OF COLORS SUPPORTED
VGA	640 × 480 pixels	16
SVGA	800 × 600 pixels	256
	1024 × 768+ pixels	64 K to 16 million

require more power than LCDs. They have very good resolution and graphics capability, and some have color displays as well (Figure 5.28). Gas-plasma displays sandwich a neon/argon gas mixture with grids of vertical and horizontal wires. Pixels are located at the points where horizontal and vertical wires cross.

The Human Factor: Ergonomics, Radiation, and Other Health-Related Issues. **Ergonomics,** or human engineering, is the science related to human-machine relationships. For computer users, ergonomics focuses on the overall effects of sitting at a computer for much of the work day. Chapter 13 includes an entire section on ergonomics.

Controversy rages over monitors and their potentially adverse impact on the health of users because of the threat of radiation exposure. Antiradiation screens can help, but they block electric fields at only low frequencies and they do not block magnetic fields at all. (Some experts consider magnetic fields to be the more serious hazard.)

The issue of whether radiation from monitors is really dangerous has yet to be resolved, so experts advise users to sit at least 18 inches away from their screens and to stay 4 feet away from the sides and back of other monitors in the

Figure 5.28 *An IBM notebook computer with a gas-plasma display screen.*

workplace. To minimize the effects of screen glare, employees who work at monitors should have a 15-minute break every 2 hours.

Other health hazards include repetitive stress injuries, back pain, eye strain, and wrist and hand disorders, which cause many people to be uncomfortable and less productive. Some people even find it necessary to leave their jobs.

Ergonomic keyboards are designed to reduce repetitive stress injuries. The Kinesis Ergonomic keyboard is contoured and enables users to define the positioning for each key. Apple has an adjustable split keyboard that can be spread to as much as a 30-degree angle and includes wrist rests that detach while the user is typing. Figure 5.29 illustrates an ergonomically designed keyboard.

Computer users will be more comfortable and more productive if their work environment includes (1) adjustable chairs, tables, screens, and keyboards; (2)

Figure 5.29 *The contours of an ergonomic keyboard reduce wrist injuries.*

improved lighting; and (3) minimal external noise. Chapter 13 discusses ergonomics in more detail.

IMPACT PRINTERS Various types of printers are available for hard copy output. They are classified either as **impact** (strike-on method) or **nonimpact printers.** Both kinds are used with all types of computers. Inexpensive impact printers are commonly used with microcomputers and more expensive, high-speed impact printers are used with large mainframes. Nonimpact printers for large and small computers can produce high-quality output faster than most impact printers, but at a higher price. Nonimpact printers include laser, thermal, and ink-jet printers.

Serial Printers. Like typewriters, impact printers use some form of strike-on method to press a carbon or fabric ribbon against paper to create a character. At the inexpensive end are **serial printers.** These printers, which are designed for microcomputers or terminals for larger systems, are slow: they print one character at a time. Serial printers are usually designed for feeding paper by either tractor feed or friction feed, although some may include attachments that allow for both methods.

Tractor-feed printers use **continuous-form paper** (Figure 5.30) that feeds through the device without interruption. Continuous-form paper has small holes on either side that fit onto sprockets on the printer, which feed the paper through at the required speed. The paper can be preprinted for specialized business tasks. For example, many companies produce their bills and checks on continuous forms that are preprinted with the company logo and the desired format. Pressure-sensitive mailing labels are also available on continuous forms so that they can be printed in batches. Most business forms that go through a computer's printer are some type of continuous form—either standard stock paper or special preprinted forms such as invoices, purchase orders, or shipping labels. These forms are perforated so that they can be separated, and many are chemically treated so that multiple copies can be created.

Friction-feed impact printers feed a sheet at a time through the mechanism as do many nonimpact printers. They are used for high-quality output such as correspondence and reports, often on a company's letterhead paper.

The two types of serial printers are dot-matrix and character printers:

Dot-matrix Printers. **Dot-matrix printers** are impact printers that create characters from a rectangular grid of pins. The pins strike against a carbon ribbon to print on paper. The characters are rather crude, but readable. As we will see, line printers as well as serial printers can be of the dot-matrix type. Many offices use a form of dot-matrix printer that is called a near-letter-quality printer because it overprints in a slightly offset pattern that fills in the lines to create much better quality type. Figure 5.31 illustrates output from a standard dot-matrix printer in both draft and near-letter-quality form.

Character Printers. Character printers most often use a daisywheel mechanism to print characters. **Daisywheel printers** print fully formed characters from a flat disk that has petal-like projections containing individual characters (Figure 5.32). They are the slowest type of printer, but they produce crisp, letter-quality output. Many offices use daisywheel printers as serial printers for their correspondence because the quality of the output is similar to that of standard typewriter output. The daisywheels themselves are interchangeable so that a variety of typefaces can be used on the same printer. They are limited in their graphics capability, however.

Figure 5.30 *Output is typically printed on continuous forms that are perforated so that the pages can be easily separated.*

(a)

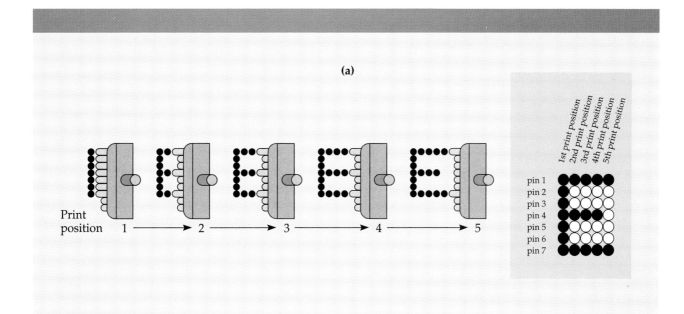

Print position 1 → 2 → 3 → 4 → 5

1st print position
2nd print position
3rd print position
4th print position
5th print position

pin 1
pin 2
pin 3
pin 4
pin 5
pin 6
pin 7

(b)

Computers   Computers

Figure 5.31 (*a*) *How a dot-matrix printer prints characters. The letter E is formed with seven vertical and five horizontal dots. As the print head moves from left to right, it fires one or more pins into the ribbon, which makes a dot on the paper.* (*b*) *Printed output from a dot-matrix in draft and near-letter-quality form.*

Figure 5.32 *A daisywheel printer uses a revolving, petal-like print head to produce clear, precise letters.*

Line Printers. At the more expensive end, designed to be used with large computer systems, are high-speed **line printers;** they print one line at a time and also use continuous-form paper. Types of line printers include band printers, chain printers, and drum printers as well as dot-matrix printers previously discussed.

Some line printers use a flexible, stainless-steel print band that is photoengraved with print characters and prints one line at a time. The band rotates horizontally until the characters to be printed are properly aligned. Band printers are popular because they are inexpensive compared to other line printers, produce high-quality output, run at high speed, and have removable bands that allow type fonts to be changed easily.

Chain printers are line printers that have one print hammer for each print position in a line. The chain revolves horizontally past all print positions. As a character on the chain passes the position where it is to print, the hammer presses the paper against the ribbon to produce a character image. Chain printers have two disadvantages: they are relatively expensive and some have chains that are difficult to change.

Drum printers use a cylindrical steel drum embossed with print characters. Each column on the drum contains all the characters, and the columns and

Figure 5.33 *Chain, drum, and band printers. These impact printers all use some form of strike-on method to print. (a) The chain printer hammer strikes as the chain rotates past the paper, while (b) drum printers create lines of type by rotating column sections of the drum. (c) With band printers, the band spins horizontally around the hammer and when the desired character is at the desired position, the corresponding hammer hits the paper.*

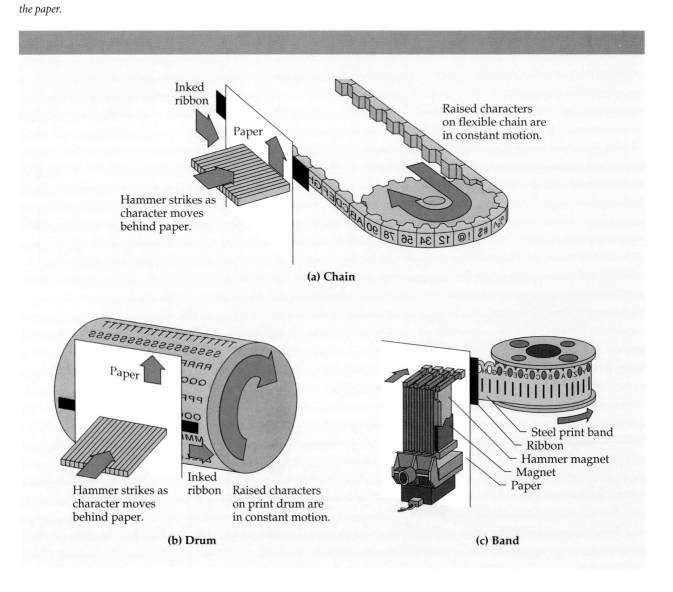

ıN A NUTSHELL

TYPES OF DESKTOP PRINTERS

	Type	Category	Quality	Speed	Cost
Impact	Dot-matrix	Serial	Draft to near-letter-quality	30 to 500+ cps	$100 to $2,000
	Character or Daisywheel	Serial	Letter	10 to 90+ cps	$400+
Nonimpact	Thermal	Serial	Near-letter-quality	11 to 80+ cps	$200
	Ink-jet	Serial	Near-letter-quality	35 to 400+ cps	$500 to $2,000
	Laser	Page	Letter	8 to 200+ ppm	$500 to $10,000

cps = characters per second; ppm = pages per minute; 48 cps = 1 ppm

---

drum rotate at high speed to print a line at a time. Many organizations have replaced their drum printers with newer band printers, which are more versatile and tend to last longer. Figure 5.33 shows how the chain, drum, and band print mechanisms work.

The disadvantages of all impact printers (in contrast to nonimpact printers discussed next) are that they are slower, noisier, and more often subject to mechanical breakdowns. Nevertheless, because they are relatively inexpensive, they continue to be popular.

NONIMPACT PRINTERS Three commonly used nonimpact printers are thermal printers, ink-jet printers, and laser printers. Note that nonimpact printers cannot produce carbon copies; only a strike-on method can make a visible impression on backup sheets.

Thermal printers create whole characters on specially treated paper that responds to patterns of heat produced by the printer. Thermal printers are less popular than ink-jet and laser printers because they are slow; in addition, the

ıN A NUTSHELL

low   IMPACT PRINTERS   slow

Serial Printers

- character printers
- dot-matrix printers

Line Printers

- band printers
- drum printers
- chain printers

NONIMPACT PRINTERS

Page Printers

- laser printers
- ink-jet printers
- thermal printers

← quality →

← speed →

high   fast

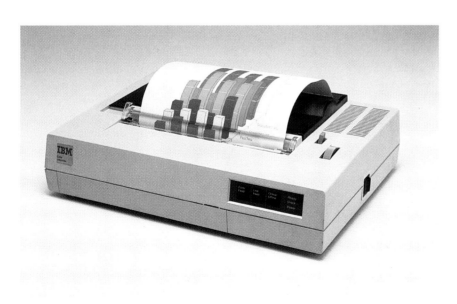

Figure 5.34 *An ink-jet printer with color output. Ink-jet printing is particularly well-adapted to color printing.*

paper is expensive and the image deteriorates over time. Newer thermal transfer printers use a heat-and-wax method that produces high-quality output in color and on untreated paper.

Ink-jet printers, for both microcomputers and large computer systems, shoot tiny dots of ink onto paper. Since any color ink can be used, these printers are well suited for graphics applications. Figure 5.34 shows an ink-jet printer with examples of its color output.

Laser printers were first introduced as high-speed printers for large mainframe systems, but their versatility, high-quality output, and decreasing cost have made them popular for computer systems of all sizes. Laser printers beam whole pages at a time onto a drum; then the paper passes over the drum and picks up the image with toner, like that used in xerographic copiers. At the high-priced end, color laser printers that cost tens of thousands of dollars and produce near-photographic-quality images are being used in the graphics industry for color reproduction of books and magazines. At the lower end, laser printers are available for micros for hundreds of dollars. Hewlett-Packard and Xerox are major manufacturers of laser printers for the PC market.

One application that has developed largely because of the availability of laser printers for micros is desktop publishing, which uses personal computer systems to produce professional-quality publications. Desktop publishing is discussed in more detail in Chapter 7.

DO-IT-ALL DOCUMENT PROCESSORS Some ink-jet and laser printers can be purchased with plug-in modules that can scan, fax, and copy documents. The cost of these optional modules begins at approximately $500. Okidata and Lumina are major manufacturers of such do-it-all document processors.

CAPTURING GRAPHIC IMAGES Graphic images have the visual power to summarize or represent data in a way that is often more meaningful and informative than words alone. In some instances, a graphic image may be the only form that output can take, for example, a customized design of an automobile. Sometimes output is produced graphically because a picture really is worth a thousand words.

Graphic output is usually displayed on a screen and then directed to another medium only if it is needed in hard copy form. Most printers are capable of producing high-quality graphics, many even in color. In general, graphic images require far more storage than text does, so that computers used for graphic applications often have more primary storage and secondary storage than those used strictly for processing text.

Plotters are printing devices specially designed to produce very high-quality drawings in color. Pen plotters move pens containing different colors of ink over paper. Electrostatic plotters use electrostatic charges to produce images on paper. Plotters have many applications, particularly for presentation graphics (charts and graphs for business meetings) and engineering drawings. See Figure 5.35.

AUDIO OUTPUT USING VOICE RESPONSE UNITS AND SOUND BOARDS Not all output from computers is visual. **Voice response units** provide verbal responses by means of a voice simulator or a series of prerecorded messages. Some automobiles give you computerized voice messages if you leave your key in the ignition or your parking lights on, or if you trip the security system. In many banks audio response units respond to tellers or to customers at home who need to determine whether an account has funds to cover a check. The teller or customer keys in the account number and the amount of the check using a

Figure 5.35 *Plotters can be desktop devices or very large floor models, as in this illustration.*

Touch-Tone phone. The computer then determines whether there are enough funds in the account and selects the appropriate verbal response to "speak" to the teller or to the customer at home.

Voice simulators are a practical aid for blind people. Figure 5.36 shows a word processing application designed to give audio feedback to typists who cannot visually verify the accuracy of their keyboarding.

Many telephone companies have voice response units for directory assistance. You call an operator who keys the name and address of the person whose number you want; then the voice response unit gives you the number. Locator services like this have widespread applicability: they can tell customers where the nearest store stocking a desired product can be found—users need only call and key in their ZIP codes. Such services, for example, can give an oral message specifying the nearest theater that is playing a movie you keyed in. As we have seen, many such services combine voice recognition—for interpreting the request—with audio response for providing the information desired.

Sound or audio **boards,** used extensively with PCs, can generate a wide range of sounds, including music, in addition to voice responses. We will see later that you may find them in multimedia applications where audio output enhances presentations and the learning process. See Figure 5.37. Note, too, that sound boards are not just for output—many of them enable users to speak into a microphone and can interpret certain phrases or commands as if they were keyed.

MICROFILM AND OPTICAL DISKS FOR IMAGE PROCESSING SYSTEMS

Many organizations need high-speed devices for recording and storing images of documents for future processing by computer. When data to be stored includes illustrations, photographs, special forms, signatures, and so on, **image processing** systems are used to scan and store the data. Many insurance companies, for example, have image processing systems that scan claim forms and store the data on microfilm, compact disk, laser disk, or other media. In this way, they are better able to handle a large volume of similar claims, for example, those related to common disasters such as earthquakes and hurricanes. See Figure 5.38. Banks often scan and store credit reports using image processing techniques.

Microfilm and microfiche, collectively referred to as microforms, have been in use for many years to store images and documents. These are miniaturized photographic copies of documents that require a relatively small storage space.

Figure 5.36 *A voice response unit for the visually impaired.*

•••••▷ **Looking Ahead**

THE DOCTOR IS ALWAYS IN

Hospitals are experimenting with techniques for creating effective hospital-physician networks. Doctors and their office managers can use Touch-Tone phones to obtain information from a hospital and to have the information forwarded to various locations. The system is linked to both a voice response unit that provides the doctors with the facts they need and to a facsimile (fax) machine for transmitting the information to other locations. Physicians can call from their car phones, offices, or virtually anywhere.

Figure 5.37 *A sound board can create different types of sound and music.*

Figure 5.38 *Using image processing techniques, computers can store, for example, loan applications, insurance claim reports, or real estate listings that include graphic images as well as text.*

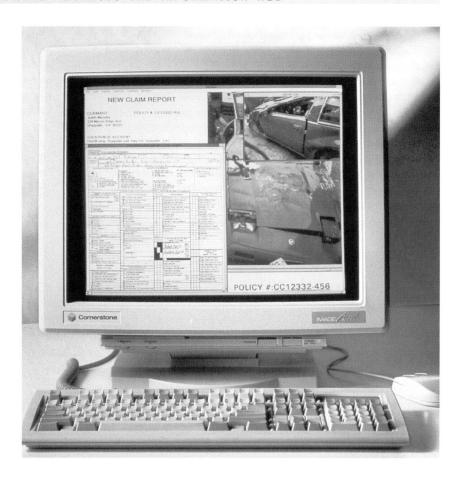

Computer output microforms, which can store illustrations as well as text, are one early type of image processing medium.

Optical disks, however, are becoming more popular than film-based systems for storing high-volume data and pictures. Libraries that once used microfilm now use the newer optical disk technology to store images of newspapers and magazines that they would otherwise be unable to keep because of space limitations. Even University Microfilms International is using optical disk image technologies rather than microfilm for storing some documents. Currently, it offers Business Periodicals Ondisk, a full-text image database that provides access to several hundred business journals on optical disk. (Maybe it is time for University Microfilms to change its name!) Today, many image processing systems store documents on optical disk or other optical media, which we discuss in the next chapter.

Expanding the World of Computers

MULTIMEDIA SYSTEMS Multimedia is the integration of text, graphics, animation, sound, and video into an interactive product typically used for presentations, education, entertainment, or combined educational/entertainment applications, called *edutainment.* Multimedia is one of the most exciting and fastest growing areas in computing today.

Researchers have found that people retain 20% of what they see, 40% of what they see and hear, and 70% of what they see, hear, and do. Multimedia applications are visually exciting, have interesting sound and visual effects, and enable the user to interact as well, making such applications more likely to impress, educate, and entertain.

Multimedia techniques are currently being used for dynamic presentations in industry, for on-the-job training tutorials, for teaching subjects such as reading and foreign languages, and for games. The number of such applications has increased greatly in the last few years and that trend is likely to continue, making the PC look more and more like an interactive TV.

Multimedia applications require special software and hardware. Multimedia software enables users to develop their own presentations and tutorials. Such software also includes clips of videos, animations, sounds, famous speeches or lines in a movie, photos, and other illustrations that users are free to incorporate in their applications. Full multimedia application packages such as encyclopedias, travelogs, medical references, music guides, chess games, and so on are widely available for under $100. We discuss multimedia software tools in depth in Chapter 7.

The hardware used for these applications includes:

1. A sound board for playing sounds, music, and voice messages.

2. A video board for capturing or inputting video clips from a VCR, TV, or camcorder when developing your own applications. Video boards not only input videos but accelerate the speed at which any video presentation can play.

3. A CD-ROM drive for delivering multimedia software as well as delivering "clips" of sound, video, animation, graphics, CD photos to be used in tutorials, presentations, and other applications developed by a user. CD-ROM storage devices are discussed in detail in the next chapter.

4. A color scanner for inputting color illustrations and photos when developing your own applications.

Multimedia components are also being added to existing software. Many word processing packages enable users to include sound, video, graphics, and animation in the documents. To play any of these components, you click on an icon that appears within the document. Many database files also include the ability to store multimedia information. A database for a real estate company, for example, may include a video of the house for sale, blueprints of the rooms, videos of the neighborhood, sound files describing various features, and so on. Some software products like Lotus for Windows include a multimedia tour or tutorial as an introduction to the product.

VIDEOCONFERENCING Videoconferencing uses networked video and audio software and hardware to enable users at different locations to see and hear each other. Audio can be provided by special videoconferencing equipment, through the telephone, or through the computer. Increasingly, specially equipped PCs communicating over phone lines are being used for desktop videoconferencing. Such PCs need an audio board, video capture board, speakers, microphone, and camera, all of which can often be purchased for under $2,000. Videoconferencing helps bring people closer together. There is less need to travel to interact with others, and groups can work even more effectively than with the use of e-mail, faxes, and telephones alone. The information superhighway will also make videoconferencing easier and less costly.

Factors making videoconferencing more popular are its improved ability to compress videos and sound files, reduced cost of the equipment and phone lines, and better standardization of products and interfaces.

Self-Test

1. (T or F) In computer systems, the word *data* is simply another term for information.

2. Screen display output is referred to as (<u>soft copy/hard copy</u>).

3. Printed output is referred to as (<u>soft copy/hard copy</u>).

4. A(n) _____ report is a listing of all events or data items that fall outside a set of management-determined parameters.

5. (T or F) The more pixels a monitor can display, the better the resolution of the characters on the screen.

6. Ergonomics, or human engineering, is the science that concerns itself with _____ relationships.

7. The two major classifications of printers are _____ and _____.

CHAPTER SUMMARY

Information systems rely on input/output devices to meet their computational needs. There are a wide variety of such devices available for specific user needs.

5.1 Input Devices Create Source Documents and Data Files

Computers process raw data as input and produce information as output. Information is "processed data"—data that has been manipulated, operated on, and formatted in a way that helps users make decisions and take action. Raw data that is entered as input from **source documents** must be entered into a storage medium to be processed. Some source documents must be rekeyed so that they can be read by a CPU; others are already machine readable. Separate keying operations to create an input file are called offline operations.

In business today, data is typically entered via a keyboard and is stored in a file, usually on disk. To minimize errors, a **control listing,** or **audit trail,** may be prepared as a printout so that users can manually check all changes made to files.

Alternatives to keying include several user-friendly input devices. A mouse, for example, can be moved around the computer's screen to position the cursor. A mouse is useful for responding to a **prompt** or for selecting submenu items, which often appear as pull-down menus. Other alternatives to keyboarding include **touch screens** and **light pens.** A **joy stick,** popular for playing games, can also position a cursor. All these devices minimize the need for keying.

5.2 Source Data Automation Reduces Data Entry Operations

Source data automation is the process of computerizing the procedure that converts source documents to machine-readable form. A number of devices can read

Study Objective

1. Describe how input devices have evolved to meet user needs for error-free source documents.

Solutions

1. F—Data refers to input; information refers to output, or *processed* data.
2. soft copy
3. hard copy
4. exception
5. T
6. human-machine
7. impact; nonimpact

various types of input directly and then convert them to machine-readable form. **Optical character readers (OCRs)** scan data. They include **bar code readers,** which read the **Universal Product Code (UPC)** on merchandise or other types of bar codes; bar code readers can be scanners or **wand readers,** which read bar codes as well as specially typed characters; **optical mark readers,** which read pencil marks made on special forms; and **optical scanners,** which scan text and graphics from typed or handwritten entries.

Applications for source data automation are varied. Data collection systems use **point-of-sale (POS) terminals,** telephones, facsimile equipment, and portable devices for collecting data at the point that a transaction is made. Pen-based systems are ideal for portable data collection. Banks have **magnetic ink character readers (MICRs)** that read the magnetic ink numbers on checks; **automatic teller machines** that act as interactive input/output units; and **debit cards** that maintain transaction records.

Voice recognition equipment is perhaps the most user-friendly input device because it interprets spoken messages. Another device growing in popularity is the **digitizer tablet,** which converts illustrations into machine-readable form.

Study Objective

2. Show how source data automation actually improves productivity.

5.3 Output Information and Output Devices

To be useful, output must be timely, complete, concise, and relevant. Standard business output falls into two categories: inquiries and reports. Printed output is either scheduled or produced on demand, usually in the form of **exception reports, transaction reports,** or **summary reports.**

Study Objective

3. List advantages and disadvantages of each class of output device.

Output hardware includes printers for **hard copy** output and screens for **soft copy** output. Screens are usually associated with interactive output; they present menus of choices from which the user can make selections. One kind of screen, or monitor, is the **cathode ray tube (CRT),** which can be either monochrome or color. Each tiny point of light is called a **pixel,** or picture element. The more pixels, the better the **resolution,** or crispness, of the image. VGA or Super VGA screens with high resolution are very popular today.

Laptop computers take advantage of flat-screen technologies such as electroluminescent displays, liquid crystal displays, or gas-plasma displays. **Ergonomics,** or human engineering, is the science of human-machine relationships; it focuses on topics such as the possible adverse effects caused by working with computers and the ways to alleviate these effects.

Impact and **nonimpact** printers produce hard copy output. Impact printers can be **serial printers**—slower mechanical devices such as **dot-matrix** and character or **daisywheel printers** for micros—as well as high-speed **line printers** such as band printers, chain printers, and drum printers for mainframes. Both often use **continuous-form paper.**

Nonimpact printers currently in use are primarily **thermal printers, ink-jet printers,** and **laser printers.** The availability of high-quality laser printers has led to a whole new industry called desktop publishing. **Plotters** are printing devices specially designed to produce color graphics for presentations and engineering drawings.

Not all computer output is visual. Two forms of audio output are currently available: a **voice response unit** simulates the human voice or plays prerecorded messages in response to input, and a **sound board** plays a variety of sounds including music.

Image processing is a new technology that encompasses computer output microforms, optical storage, and other high-volume media to capture not only text output but photos, illustrations, documents, and signatures.

Two relatively new application areas of computing that provide dynamic forms of output are multimedia systems and videoconferencing. Multimedia systems are used for education, entertainment, and presentations to provide not only text-based output but integrated sounds, graphics, animation, and video. Videoconferencing uses networked video and audio software and hardware to enable users at different locations to see and hear each other.

KEY TERMS

Audit trail,   *p. 147*
Automatic teller machine (ATM),   *p. 157*
Bar code reader,   *p. 152*
Cathode ray tube (CRT),   *p. 165*
Continuous-form paper,   *p. 168*
Control listing,   *p. 147*
Daisywheel printer,   *p. 168*
Debit card,   *p. 159*
Digitizer tablet,   *p. 162*
Dot-matrix printer,   *p. 168*
Ergonomics,   *p. 166*
Exception report,   *p. 163*
Hard copy,   *p. 163*
Image processing,   *p. 173*
Impact printer,   *p. 168*

Ink-jet printer,   *p. 172*
Joy stick,   *p. 150*
Laser printer,   *p. 172*
Light pen,   *p. 150*
Line printer,   *p. 170*
Magnetic ink character reader (MICR),   *p. 157*
Nonimpact printer,   *p. 168*
Optical character reader (OCR),   *p. 152*
Optical mark reader,   *p. 153*
Optical scanner,   *p. 154*
Pixel,   *p. 165*
Plotter,   *p. 172*
Point-of-sale (POS) terminal,   *p. 155*
Prompt,   *p. 147*

Resolution,   *p. 165*
Serial printer,   *p. 168*
Soft copy,   *p. 163*
Sound board,   *p. 173*
Source data automation (SDA),   *p. 151*
Source document,   *p. 142*
Summary report,   *p. 163*
Thermal printer,   *p. 171*
Touch screen,   *p. 149*
Transaction report,   *p. 164*
Universal Product Code (UPC),   *p. 152*
Voice recognition equipment,   *p. 160*
Voice response unit,   *p. 172*
Wand reader,   *p. 152*

CHAPTER SELF-TEST

1. What is the difference between data and information?

2. A blinking cursor or an actual message called a _____ signals the user that a computer response is required.

3. A purchase order that must be read by the computer or converted to machine-readable form is called a _____.

4. If a submenu appears as a superimposed drop-down menu, it is called a _____ menu.

5. Input devices that can read printed characters directly from a source document are called _____.

6. Name several ways in which screen output can highlight entries.

7. (T or F) A printout called a control listing or audit trail includes data that a program has found to be erroneous.

8. (T or F) In general, laser printers are faster than line printers.

9. Impact printers that form characters using pins in a rectangular pattern are called _____ printers.

10. (T or F) Daisywheel printers produce letter-quality output.

11. The bar code on consumer goods is called the _____.

12. (T or F) Laser printers use a technology similar to that of copy machines.

13. What are two advantages of impact printers?

14. (T or F) Plotters are used to reproduce photographic images.

15. The computer device that creates output as a microform is the _____ unit.

REVIEW QUESTIONS

1. Describe two handheld input devices and indicate how they might be used in business.

2. List three ways of detecting input errors.

3. Define the following terms related to screen displays: CRT, pixel, resolution, and monochrome.

4. Describe three types of flat-screen technologies.

5. For impact printers and nonimpact printers, list at least two advantages and three disadvantages.

CRITICAL THINKING EXERCISES

1. Consider the following:

A poll of over 200 businesses conducted by market researcher Dataquest found that 64 percent of the firms surveyed were very unlikely to buy desktop videoconferencing equipment this year—or next. While the market for Fortune 500 boardroom-style videoconferencing remains healthy, demand for videoconferencing in general is low for small and medium-sized firms.

Even with the introduction of systems for less than $2,000 per seat, users appear unimpressed. Given the current business and economic climate, lower-cost communication technologies such as network document sharing, e-mail, and fax seem sufficient for most companies.

Do you think videoconferencing will become a high-demand item as costs decrease? Explain your answer.

Solutions

1. Data consists of raw facts; information is processed data.

2. prompt

3. source document

4. pull-down

5. optical character readers (OCR) or optical scanning devices

6. color; boldface; reverse video; a blinking cursor

7. T

8. T

9. dot-matrix

10. T

11. Universal Product Code (UPC)

12. T

13. They are relatively inexpensive and they can produce multiple "carbon" copies.

14. F

15. computer output microfilm

2. Consider the following:

The goal of establishing a paperless office is not a practical one, despite the recent advances in electronic information systems and document management software. A more realistic goal is that of reducing paper usage by 50%. This can be accomplished by educating the work force as to the available alternatives. The key is to familiarize office workers with the many inexpensive software solutions that exist to facilitate the electronic storage, transmission, and management of documents. In addition, technologies such as inexpensive notebook computers are now available that enable workers to carry data home with them without utilizing paper documents. The crucial factor is that most people still associate the reading habit with paper systems and paper media. In all likelihood, they will continue to maintain this cultural bias well into the next century.

Do you think the next generation of Americans will be as dependent on paper as we are?

Case Study

Videoconferencing: Boon or Boondoggle?

Until recently, videoconferencing was a luxury affordable only to the very largest corporations. It required acoustically sealed presentation centers with built-in conferencing equipment that cost several hundred thousand dollars. Today, videoconferencing is moving from these corporate theaters to networks and desktops because the cost of equipment and software has fallen dramatically.

High-quality desktop videoconferencing for a reasonable cost is eagerly awaited by many companies. They believe that the ability to communicate face-to-face with business partners, clients, and other associates who are in different parts of the world while sitting at one's desktop PC will revolutionize the way we do business.

Some think the revolution is here. For $1,500 per station, distant users can see live video of one another, work together on an interactive monitor, share applications, hold meetings, transfer data and faxes—all over a standard phone line. The $1,500 package includes a color video camera linked to a PC, video and audio capture capability, and the requisite software. But the use of relatively inexpensive phone lines, rather than high-speed communication linkages, has a negative impact on the quality of the transmissions and their speed. As a result, many companies still await reasonably priced systems that run over high-speed networks. Other companies hesitate to make an investment because of the lack of standards and compatibility among videoconferencing systems.

The technology is undoubtedly growing very quickly, the price is decreasing, and potential users abound. Imagine not having to travel to meetings and being able to communicate face-to-face with others at remote locations while you are at your PC. Desktop videoconferencing is already

Desktop videoconferencing enables people with PCs to communicate with each other interactively.

here for some and on its way for many others who are awaiting further improvements.

Some people, however, are not only skeptical about the potential advantages of videoconferencing—they are downright negative. They fear we are already overburdened by too much useless information and that videoconferencing will only make this trend worse.

Some believe it is already too difficult to get out of a business meeting, and it may be especially hard to escape a videoconference. Some skeptics have suggested that video-conference participants will still find ways to idle away meetings, just as employees sometimes do in person. In fact, you might not even need to attend the meeting at all if you can arrange for a video of yourself to appear on your screen at the right moment, looking attentive and thoughtful. Of course, your fellow participants might all be doing the same thing, or they might be watching a tape of last night's game in a corner of their screen. On a more serious note, some people fear that the ease with which videoconferences can be set up will rob executives of the only free time they have in their already meeting-laden days. One writer, Arlan Levitan, advises executives to get familiar with "the most critical component of any videoconference system"—the *off* switch.

Analysis

1. Describe some of the potential benefits of videoconferencing not discussed in this case.

2. Do you think the potential benefits of this technology justify the cost? Explain your answer.

3. Do you agree that videoconferencing could decrease office productivity as suggested in the latter part of the case? How might a company minimize such risks?

CHAPTER 6
Secondary Storage Devices

6.1 FUNDAMENTALS OF SECONDARY STORAGE

Review of File Processing Concepts

Criteria for Evaluating Storage Devices

6.2 MAGNETIC MEDIA FOR SECONDARY STORAGE

Magnetic Disks and Disk Drives

Magnetic Tapes and Tape Drives

Maintaining Disk and Tape Files

Smart Cards, Flash Memory, and RAM Cards: You *Can* Take It With You!

6.3 OPTICAL STORAGE ALTERNATIVES TO MAGNETIC MEDIA

CD-ROM Drives: A Most Valuable Player

Networking Compact Disks

WORM Drives: Will They "Worm" Their Way into Your Heart?

Erasable Magneto-Optical Drives: Doing the "Write" Thing

6.4 ORGANIZING DATA FILES

Sequential File Organization

Random-Access File Organization

I n recent years, computers have become faster, more powerful, and more accessible to individuals and organizations. It is likely that the amount of data and information available in our society will continue to multiply at an ever-increasing rate.

Television shows and movies often provide a futuristic version of what is available to users of large computer systems. In these accounts, the mere click of a few keys brings to the screen an individual's entire life history with photos, fingerprints, and forms such as a driver's license, birth certificate, and marriage license. In another type of movie, scientists scan the records of thousands of databases to pinpoint diseases, determine drug therapies, locate potential donors for transplants, and so on. Although the widespread availability of such information may not yet be a reality, technologies for storing and retrieving the necessary data are making such uses more feasible.

In Chapter 4 we considered the power of computers and the ways in which the CPU processes data. In Chapter 5 we focused on the wide variety of input and output devices for various application areas. A computer's ability to provide information to users, however, relies heavily on the secondary storage units it has to store programs and data.

Study Objectives

After reading this chapter you should be able to:

1. Explain why secondary storage is a crucial component of a computer system.
2. Identify the different types of disks and disk drives.
3. Show why disks have replaced tapes as secondary storage in most systems.
4. List the advantages of optical storage devices.
5. Describe the major ways of organizing data files.

6.1 FUNDAMENTALS OF SECONDARY STORAGE

In Chapter 4 we saw how data is processed by the CPU. Programs are loaded into primary storage (also called main memory), input data is read, and output is produced as information. But primary storage in most computers is temporary, or volatile, which means that when the power supply is shut off, any programs and data in main memory are lost. Storage of programs and data for future processing requires a peripheral device, such as disk, called **secondary storage** or **auxiliary storage.** Secondary storage is *nonvolatile;* that is, all information is saved even after the power is shut off. In this chapter we discuss secondary storage media with storage capacities and retrieval mechanisms that allow fast and easy access of information.

Magnetic units such as disk and, to a far lesser extent these days, tape are traditional storage media for data and programs. Other magnetic media such as memory cards are becoming popular as well. Optical media such as compact disks and magneto-optical disks have very large storage capacities and sophisticated methods of access that enable them to augment or, in some instances, replace magnetic media. See Figure 6.1.

Study Objective

1. Explain why secondary storage is a crucial component of a computer system.

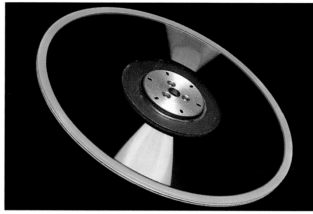

(a)   (b)

Figure 6.1 *Photos of secondary storage. (a) 3½-inch magnetic disks. (b) Optical disk.*

Review of File Processing Concepts

Secondary storage units store data that was originally entered using an input device such as a keyboard. Typically, the data is stored in the form of a file. Let us review some file processing concepts before we study specific secondary storage media.

Recall that a file is a major collection of data in a given application area. Within a file, each individual unit of data is called a record. A payroll file, for example, consists of employee records and an accounts receivable file consists of customer records. Each record contains characters organized into fields. A payroll record may have a Social Security number field, name field, salary field, and so forth. In Chapter 12, we will see that database management systems can be used to link or join files so that data from them can be processed in an integrated manner.

Files are processed in either batch mode or interactively. In batch processing, each record in a file is read and processed in sequence from the first to the last record. If a file is routinely processed in batch mode, then it can be organized simply for sequential processing. All storage media can process records in sequence but we will see that tapes, once widely used for secondary storage, can *only* be processed in sequence.

Sometimes records need to be processed interactively. If managers must access or make inquiries about records as the need arises and in no particular sequence, an information system based on sequential access of records will be very inefficient. Similarly, if a point-of-sale system updates accounts receivable records as transactions occur—that is, randomly—the records to be processed are not likely to be in sequence by customer number. Disks and optical media can process files randomly but tapes cannot. Tapes, then, are typically used for backup purposes—to store copies of files most commonly processed on disk.

CRITERIA FOR EVALUATING
SECONDARY STORAGE MEDIA

Storage capacity
Access time
Transfer rate
Cost
Size

Criteria for Evaluating Storage Devices

We consider five major criteria for evaluating secondary storage media and drives: the storage capacity, the access time needed to locate data, the transfer rate for data, the cost, and the size of the storage unit itself.

Storage capacity, measured in kilobytes (K), megabytes (MB), gigabytes (GB), or terabytes (TB), indicates the amount of data that the storage medium can hold. The storage capacity for a PC's hard disk is typically several hundred megabytes or even a gigabyte whereas the storage capacity for larger disks and some optical media may be as much as hundreds of gigabytes. Only older diskettes have storage capacities measured in kilobytes; most diskettes can store from 1 to 2 MB, at least. All other media have much greater storage capacities.

Note, too, that compression programs like Stacker enhance the storage capacity of magnetic disks by enabling users to store more data in fewer bytes. Using a compression program, a 350 MB hard disk might be able to store 700 MB of data in compressed form. Some operating systems include compression software for maximizing the efficient use of disk space.

Access rate, which is the time needed to locate data on a secondary storage device, is measured in thousandths of a second (milliseconds). It varies from dozens to just a few milliseconds for magnetic media, but it is often somewhat slower. Some top-performing disks can access data in less than one millisecond for optical media—up to a few hundred milliseconds.

Data on a secondary storage medium is not available for processing until it is copied from the storage unit to main memory, where the CPU has access to it. **Transfer rate** refers to the speed at which data is transferred (that is, copied) from the secondary storage unit to main memory, and it is measured in megabytes per second. Transfer rates typically range from one to several MBs per second.

Both access time and transfer rates are far slower than a computer's processing speed, so any technique that speeds up these rates makes a computer more efficient. As noted in Chapter 4, a cache stores frequently accessed data and instructions in a special area that is available for more immediate processing. A cache uses operating system software and innovative technological mechanisms to improve access time and data transfer rates. It has been available for many years on larger systems and is now widely used with microcomputers as well.

The cost of a secondary storage unit directly relates to the three factors mentioned above: storage capacity, access rate, and transfer rate. Smaller capacity disk drives for micros typically cost hundreds of dollars; mainframe disk drives may cost thousands of dollars. When a computer system processes large amounts of data, saving even ten thousandths of a second per record can add up to significant amounts of time, a benefit that may more than outweigh a higher price.

The physical size of the storage unit is important because it affects the space requirements for the organization's computer facility. A series of compact disks housed in a desktop unit that stores as much data as several stand-alone or floor-mounted magnetic disk units not only requires less space but is easier to maintain.

IN A NUTSHELL

Note that after a "transfer" operation, the data is still stored on the secondary storage medium. The word *copy* would be a more accurate term.

Self-Test

1. (T or F) Data recorded on secondary storage media is nonvolatile.

2. (T or F) When a file is read from secondary storage into primary storage, it is erased from secondary storage in the process.

3. What is the most widely used magnetic storage medium?

4. The time it takes to locate data on a secondary storage device is called _____.

Solutions

1. T

2. F

3. disk

4. the access rate

6.2 MAGNETIC MEDIA FOR SECONDARY STORAGE

In this unit we focus on disks as the main magnetic medium for secondary storage. We include tape concepts as well, since tape is commonly used for backup; we also discuss some of the newer magnetic storage media. Secondary storage media that use optical technology, such as CD-ROMs and flopticals, are discussed later in this chapter.

Magnetic Disks and Disk Drives

A magnetic disk, often simply called a disk, is a Mylar film or aluminum platter coated with a magnetic substance such as ferrous oxide. Data is stored in concentric rings called tracks. Each character of data is represented as bits (*bi*nary di*gits*) that appear as magnetic fields on the tracks.

Micros use floppy disks (also called diskettes) or hard disks to store programs and data files. Mainframe systems use either fixed disks, like those in PCs, or removable disk packs. Both types consist of a series of disks or platters, but, compared to PCs, they have greater storage capacity, faster access rates for reading data, and faster rates for transferring data from primary storage to disk and back again. All disks need a peripheral called a disk drive for reading from and writing to the disks.

Although mainframe disks were developed first, we will begin with what is probably more familiar to you, the floppy disk. Then we will discuss the types of hard disks for micros and, finally, their mainframe equivalent.

MAGNETIC DISKS AND DISK DRIVES FOR MICROS

Floppy Disks. The primary function of floppy disks is to store programs and data files for microcomputer processing. Two sizes predominate today: the older 5¼-inch and the newer 3½-inch. The 5¼-inch diskettes, which became popular with the original IBM PC, had a capacity of 360 K, but now they have capacities of from 360 K to 1.2+ MB. Since most typed pages contain approximately 2000 characters, a 1.2 MB 5¼-inch diskette can store the equivalent of 600 typed pages.

The Macintosh was the first popular computer to use 3½-inch diskettes, beginning in 1984. The most current IBM-compatibles also use 3½-inch disks with a capacity from 720 K to 2.88 MB or more. These diskettes have a rigid plastic casing that provides much better protection than the original, flexible 5¼-inch floppy diskettes that actually "flop."

Other sizes of diskettes are available for some types of computers with special disk drives. Although the 3½-inch and the older 5¼-inch disks are still the most widely used, standardization remains a serious industrywide problem. For example, 1.2 MB 5¼-inch diskettes cannot be read by older diskette drives designed for 360 K floppies. Similarly, older 3½-inch diskette drives designed to read 720 K diskettes cannot read 1.44 MB or 2.88 MB diskettes.

How Diskettes Store Data. Inside a disk jacket, or sleeve, is a thin, flexible plastic disk that has a metal oxide coating capable of retaining magnetic bits of data. The 5¼-inch disks are enclosed in a flexible paper jacket, while 3½-inch disks are enclosed in rigid plastic, which makes them more durable.

Figure 6.2 illustrates how data is stored on diskettes. Each diskette contains two surfaces, or sides. On each surface there are a number of tiny concentric cir-

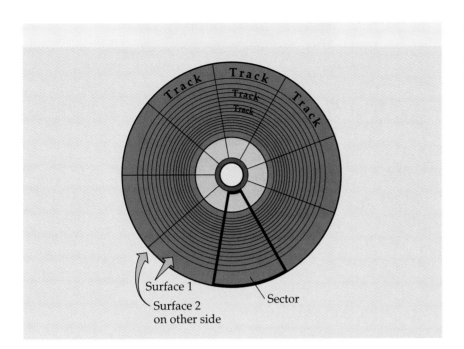

cles called tracks, and the tracks are segmented into wedge-shaped sectors. Even though tracks get successively smaller toward the hub of the diskette, each track contains the same amount of data. Data is just recorded more densely in tracks closest to the center.

Most microcomputer diskettes are **soft-sectored;** that is, the sectors are not already defined on the diskettes when you purchase them. Because sector definition differs among operating systems, sectors are defined for the first time when you format, or initialize, your new diskettes. Your computer's operating system contains the program that formats diskettes so that files can be saved, or written, to the diskettes. Some diskettes designed for specific micros can be purchased already formatted so that you need not format them first. Whenever you format a diskette that was used previously, you erase everything that is on it.

Taking Care of Diskettes. Diskettes are fairly durable, but they can be damaged or erased, making your data unusable. Figure 6.3 illustrates five rules for protecting the data on the older 5¼-inch diskettes.

With a single command, it is possible to erase all data on a diskette. For example, the DOS command ERASE *.* deletes all files. To prevent data on diskettes from being erased accidentally, you can write-protect it. Figure 6.4 shows a 5¼-inch diskette with a write-protect notch that can be covered with a gummed tab and a 3½-inch diskette with a built-in write-protect tab that can be positioned to cover the notch. Covering the notch on 5¼-inch diskettes write-protects them so that you cannot write onto them; that is, any instruction to write data on the diskette will result in a "write error." Positioning the tab so that it *does not* cover the notch on 3½-inch diskettes write-protects them. Diskettes containing programs supplied by software developers sometimes have the write-protect notch permanently covered on 5¼-inch diskettes (often the diskette is supplied with no notch at all). Similarly, 3½-inch write-protected diskettes may have their notch permanently uncovered. This minimizes the risk that users may accidentally write over an important program.

1. Keep disks away from magnetic fields.

2. Store flexible 5 1/4" disks inside paper sleeves.

3. Use a felt-tip pen to write on labels. Ballpoint pens will scratch the disk inside.

4. Keep food and liquid away from disks.

5. Don't leave disks in heat or sun.

Figure 6.3 *These five simple rules will protect your disks and their data from the most common sources of damage.*

How Diskette Drives Access Data. A **read/write head** is a mechanism for reading data from, or writing information onto, a disk. Diskette drives that process double-sided floppy disks have two read/write heads, one for each side of the diskette. (Older, single-sided disk drives have a read/write head that can access only one side of the diskette.)

Files are stored on diskettes at diskette locations called addresses. A diskette address consists of a surface number, track number, and sector number. When a particular program or data file is to be accessed or read, the address of the file

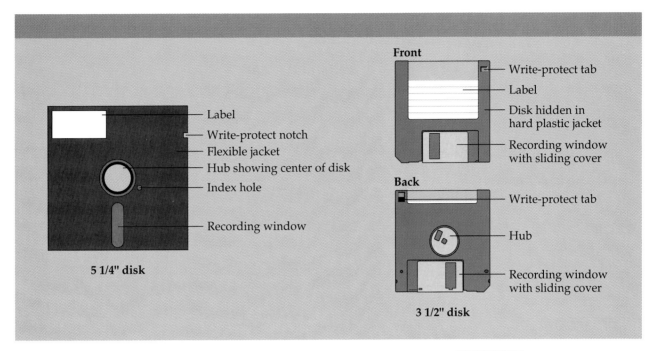

5 1/4" disk

Label
Write-protect notch
Flexible jacket
Hub showing center of disk
Index hole
Recording window

Front
Write-protect tab
Label
Disk hidden in hard plastic jacket
Recording window with sliding cover

Back
Write-protect tab
Hub
Recording window with sliding cover

3 1/2" disk

Figure 6.4 *The 5¹/₄-inch and 3¹/₂-inch floppy disks have similar features. However, sliding panels and a hard case give the newer, more popular 3¹/₂-inch disk more protection.*

is looked up from a file allocation table, which keeps track of each file's location. The disk drive then whirls the disk inside its sleeve to locate the correct sector, while the arm moves the appropriate read/write head to the track containing the data. The same thing happens when you write to a disk: the disk drive locates an available surface/sector/track address on which to write the data.

Hard Drives for Micros. Microcomputers have one or two floppy disk drives, which may be housed in the system unit or which may be separate external devices. You insert diskettes into these drives as shown in Figure 6.5, which puts the read/write head in contact with the disk so that it is ready for reading or writing data (for 5¹/₄-inch disk drives, close the lever first). When there are two diskette drives in a system unit, the drive on the left or top is usually labeled as drive A, and the one on the right or bottom is called drive B.

Many microcomputers also have a large-capacity internal hard disk, usually called drive C on IBM-compatible computers, although it can be designated by other letters as well. Macintosh computers identify the drives by icons instead of letters—a more user-friendly approach. Hard disks have a capacity several times that of a diskette; the smallest hard disks today hold 80+ MB, while the larger ones currently available hold from hundreds of megabytes to several gigabytes.

Hard disks are made of a rigid metal substance coated with a metal oxide. Data is stored on a hard disk in surfaces, sectors, and tracks—just as on diskettes. See Figure 6.6. Hard disks are sealed into sterile containers, because the distances from the read/write heads to the disk are so small that even something as tiny as a cigarette smoke particle can affect the mechanism. When foreign substances get between a read/write head and the disk, a **head crash** may occur: the head makes direct contact with the disk and destroys its surfaces. Computer users dread this occurrence because everything on the disk is likely to be lost. We will see later on in this chapter that disks are periodically copied to tape or other disks, which are stored as backups in case something happens to the originals.

Hard disks are typically internal—built into the system. An *external* hard disk drive or a second internal drive could be added to a computer as well. An

Figure 6.5 *Insert a disk into the slot in the disk drive (then close the lever or gate to secure it in place if you are using a 5¹/₄-inch disk). Here, a 3¹/₂-inch disk is being inserted into a drive.*

(a)

Figure 6.6 *(a) Fixed disks, or internal hard disks, are made of a rigid material, and hold many times more data than a floppy disk. (b) Inside view of a hard disk drive.*

IN A NUTSHELL

Most disk storage units can be purchased for an average price of less than a dollar per megabyte.

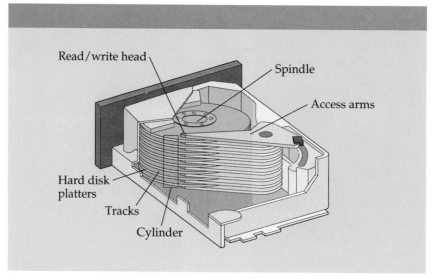

(b)

external drive means that you need more desk space to accommodate an extra piece of equipment, but the drive has the advantage of being portable; you can unplug it from one computer and move it to another.

Hard disks for micros have many advantages over diskettes. To begin with, the computer's operating system can be copied onto the hard disk. If you have an IBM-compatible PC, for example, you would start your computer directly from the hard disk without inserting an operating system diskette in drive A. In other words, when you "boot," or turn your computer on, the operating system is loaded automatically from the hard drive.

Another benefit of a hard disk is that you can copy your application programs directly to it, thereby eliminating the need to swap large numbers of diskettes into and out of floppy disk drives. Many operating systems and programs today require a hard disk.

For each application on your hard disk, it is best to create a *subdirectory,* which is a separate, labeled area on the disk. Such divisions make it easier to find your way around this large data storehouse and help keep related files together. After data on a disk is no longer needed, it can be erased and written over. Hard disks have very large storage capacities. In addition, hard disk drives can transfer disk data to main memory at speeds from 1 to 5+ MB per second.

At one time, only mainframes could process large databases because such databases simply would not fit on diskettes. Now that hard disks for PCs have large capacities, many databases can be managed quite satisfactorily on microcomputers. Similarly, hard disks with large storage capacities enable users to store and run more sophisticated programs that require considerable storage.

HARD DISKS AND CLIENT-SERVER COMPUTING As software and hardware get more sophisticated, the need for greater secondary storage capacity increases. It is not unusual for a program to require 20+ MB of disk space, for example. Moreover, user files are increasing in size, especially if they incorporate multimedia features such as audio, graphics, animation, and video, all of which use a great deal of disk space. One way to minimize the need for disk space is to store files on a network controlled by a file server and copy them to each user PC on an as-needed basis. This could significantly decrease the need for disk space on each individual PC. Instead, the network controls the transfer of data from its high-capacity disk drives. Copying files from a central computer or file server to

Figure 6.7 *Disk cartridge and drive. This external cartridge drive is portable, as is the disk, which stores 150 MB of data.*

an individual's PC is called **downloading.** Copying files from individual PCs to a central computer or file server is called **uploading.**

ALTERNATIVES TO HARD DISKS

Disk Cartridge Drive. Although hard drives have the advantage of very large storage capacities, diskettes have the advantage of portability. Data and programs on a diskette can be used with any computer that is compatible with the diskette's format. Data and programs on internal hard disks need to be downloaded to diskettes to be transported or used on other machines.

Disk cartridges accessed by disk cartridge devices combine the advantages of diskettes and hard disks: they have storage capacities comparable to hard disks but they are removable and, thus, are portable. See Figure 6.7. To compete with disk cartridges, some manufacturers have introduced removable hard disks.

As noted previously, to save disk space, many files are compressed, that is, stored in condensed form. Special programs can be purchased that compress files to save space and automatically decompress them when you want to read them. Note that because compressed disks must be uncompressed before the data can be processed, they have slower access rates. Sometimes programs are provided to users in compressed form to reduce the number of diskettes required. Utility programs, supplied by the manufacturer, convert compressed programs to usable form before you try to run them.

MAGNETIC DISKS AND DISK DRIVES FOR LARGER SYSTEMS

Larger computer systems use hard disks as their major storage medium. As you might expect, disks for the larger systems have far greater storage capacities than microcomputer disks and are larger in size as well. Data on magnetic disks for larger systems is assigned an address just as data on floppy disks for micros. Data is addressed by surface number, track number, and cylinder number, although the *number* of surfaces, tracks, and cylinders is much greater on larger hard disks. A sector on a floppy is similar in concept to a cylinder on a hard disk. See Figure 6.8. A typical micro's disk may have 80 or so tracks, and a disk for a mainframe may have 200 or more tracks.

Because large computer systems need access to enormous amounts of data, a mini or mainframe computer is able to instantly access any disk drive attached

Critical Thinking

Suppose you have a computer at the office with a hard drive and a disk cartridge drive. You have a computer at home with a dual diskette system, but you want to add a storage medium with at least a 100 MB capacity. Would you purchase a hard drive or a disk cartridge drive? Why?

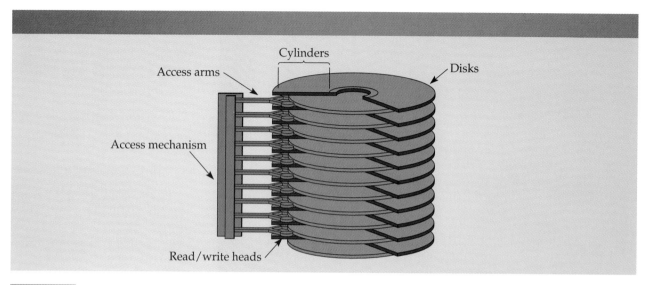

Figure 6.8 *A fixed-head disk device for larger computers.*

to it, and it may have as many as 100 or more disk drives available at one time. Consider, for example, the storage needs of the U.S. Social Security system, which has records on virtually every man, woman, and child in the country.

Most hard disks currently in use for larger systems are fixed disks that cannot be removed from the **fixed-head disk drive.** They are similar to the internal hard disks on microcomputers. Fixed-head disk drives are most often separate, standalone peripherals linked by cable to the CPU.

An older type of disk for minis and mainframe computers that is still popular today is a removable **disk pack.** It consists of *removable* sets of hard disks, typically 10½ to 14 inches in diameter, mounted together on a center spindle like a group of phonograph records (Figure 6.9). Data is recorded on both sides of each disk, except that the top and bottom surfaces of the disk pack are not used because they are more exposed and susceptible to being damaged. A disk pack consisting of 11 disks or platters, for example, has 20 usable surfaces. Disk packs are being replaced by fixed disks because of the potential for deterioration in data when an individual disk is moved on and off the system.

Figure 6.9 *Disk packs are sets of disks mounted together on a spindle. The packs are enclosed in a sterile case that can be easily mounted or removed from the computer system.*

READ/WRITE HEAD DESIGN FOR DISK DRIVES Disk files can be accessed randomly as well as sequentially by directly activating one of many read/write heads and positioning the head at the appropriate location on the disk. Some disk mechanisms for large systems use movable read/write heads. In this design, all the heads in a stack of disks are attached to a single access mechanism that moves directly to a specific disk address when data is to be read or written. A drive with movable read/write heads is relatively slow, because all the access arms must move together.

Fixed-head disk drives contain one or more hard disks and stationary access arms with separate read/write mechanisms for each of the tracks on the disks. The disk, rather than the head, whirls around to bring the correct sector to the arm. The correct track of the disk is then positioned at the read/write mechanism for retrieving or writing data, depending on the application.

Some disk devices combine the technologies of both movable- and fixed-head access to produce a high-capacity, rapid-access drive.

Magnetic Tapes and Tape Drives

Although magnetic disk is the principal storage medium today, not long ago magnetic tape held that preeminent position. We consider next some of the reasons why tape is no longer widely used except as a backup medium.

THE WANING OF TAPE AS A PRINCIPAL STORAGE MEDIUM A magnetic tape drive is a high-speed device that is very similar in concept to a cassette or tape recorder. The drive can read (play) data from a magnetic tape and also write (record) data onto a tape by means of a single read/write head. Figure 6.10 illustrates magnetic tapes and tape drives.

Magnetic tape was once used extensively in business as a secondary storage medium, but its popularity has waned in recent years mainly because disks have all the advantages of tape and none of the disadvantages. Disk drives have a series of read/write heads so that the one closest to the data to be accessed can be activated to locate it. This results in faster access time for disks, especially for high-speed, random-access applications. Tapes have a single read-write head and can, therefore, be accessed only sequentially. Thus, their access time is slow; moreover, it is inefficient to access records that are not in sequence. In addition, disk records can be read, updated, and rewritten in place, whereas tape records that need to be updated must be written to a new tape. Consider a tape cassette you

IN A NUTSHELL

WIDELY USED FORMS OF MAGNETIC DISK

Diskettes
- 5¼-inch—320 K to 1.2+ MB
- 3½-inch—720 K to 2.88+ MB

Hard Disk
- Fixed disk (PCs)
- PC hard disk capacities typically range from 100 MB to 1+ GB
- Disk pack
- Disk cartridge capacities are similar to hard disk capacities

Study Objective

3. Show why disks have replaced tapes as secondary storage in most systems.

Figure 6.10 (a) Magnetic tapes. (b) Magnetic tape drives.

(a)

(b)

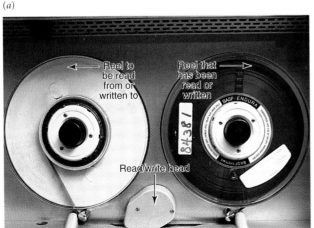

ᴵᴺ A NUTSHELL

AN OVERVIEW OF MAGNETIC TAPE

TYPE OF TAPE	USE	CAPACITY
Reel-to-reel magnetic tape	Larger systems	200+ MB
¼- to ½-inch cassette tapes	Micros	80 MB to 5+ GB
8-mm cartridge tape	Micros	5+ GB
Digital audio tape	All sizes of computers	3+ GB

The prices of ¼- to ½-inch cassette tape drives range from several hundred to one or two thousand dollars. The prices of most other drives are several thousand dollars. The tapes themselves usually cost well under $100.

recorded with your favorite songs on it. If you wanted to add a recording to the middle of the cassette tape, you would need to rerecord the first half onto a new cassette, add the desired record, and rerecord the rest of the tape. Computer tapes need to be processed the same way.

TAPE AS A BACKUP MEDIUM If tapes are so limited as a storage medium, why do we discuss them at all? First, some organizations still use them for file processing. But more importantly, tapes are popular as a backup medium; they store copies of important files in case the master disks become unusable or are lost.

Don't Forget to Back Up. Because of the potential for errors, natural disasters, computer crimes, and other problems that could corrupt data on a disk, it is imperative that all computer users back up their files regularly.

Standard reel-to-reel magnetic tapes often serve as backup media for large computers, while cassettes and cartridges function as PC backup media. Because of their large storage capacity and relatively low cost, digital audio tape can be used as backup for all types of systems. See Figure 6.11.

The contents of a micro's hard disk can be copied to tape in minutes or at most an hour or two. Disks for larger systems require a little more time for

Critical Thinking

Many PC users do not regularly back up data and programs on their disks. They are simply unwilling to spend the time it would take each day to perform a backup procedure. They know the risks: a disk failure would require them to spend hours or days re-creating data files and reinstalling programs. Do you think the risk they are taking is worth it?

Figure 6.11 *Cartridge tapes and digital audio tapes, and their respective drives.*

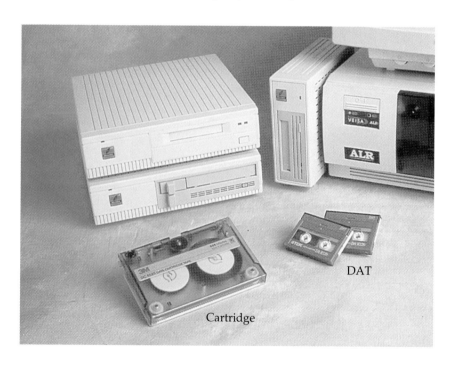

DAT

Cartridge

	Access Rate	Transfer Rate	Storage Capacity
Removable Disk Pack	15 to 100 milliseconds*	150,000 to 2 million characters per second	65 million to 32 billion characters
Fixed Disk	5 to 30 milliseconds*	200,000 to 2 million characters per second	To 2 billion characters
Floppy Disk	70 to 500 milliseconds*	60,000 to 100,000 characters per second	360,000 to 1.4 million characters
Tape	10 milliseconds* to several seconds	18,000 characters per second	8 MB to 5+ GB
CD-ROM (to be discussed in the next section)	195 milliseconds to .5 seconds	150,000 to 600,000 characters per second	680+ MB

*millisecond = 1/1000 of a second

Table 6.1 *A Comparison of Disk and Tape Storage Media*

backup. Some computer systems automatically back up disks to tape at a pre-determined hour of the day or just before the system is turned off.

See Table 6.1 for a comparison of access rate, transfer rate, and storage capacity of disks and tape.

Maintaining Disk and Tape Files

Data is represented on both disk and tape as magnetized bits. These bits of data are extremely small and not visible to the human eye. As a result, large volumes of data can be stored on a relatively small surface area. Data that can be displayed on an 80-character line of a monitor, for example, can typically be stored on $\frac{1}{20}$ inch or less of magnetic tape or disk.

The average tape reel can store up to hundreds of millions of characters. Disks for mainframes have storage capacities ranging from hundreds of millions to billions of characters or more. After a file has been processed on disk or tape and is no longer needed, the same disk or tape may be used repeatedly to store other information by erasing and writing over the old file.

REPRESENTATION OF DATA

Computer Code. Data is stored on disk and tape as magnetized bits corresponding to the CPU's own code—either ASCII or EBCDIC. A disk stores the bits that represent a character consecutively along the surface of a track, while a tape uses a series of tracks for representing a single character. See Figure 6.12. Note that the term *track* has different meanings for disk and tape. Tracks on a disk are concentric, with those closest to the center representing the same amount of data, but more compactly. Each track on a tape stores one bit.

Tape and Disk Density. Millions or billions of characters can be recorded as magnetized bits on a single magnetic disk or tape. The primary reason for this large storage capacity is the fact that bits are exceedingly small, and hundreds or thousands of them can be placed in an inch or less. The actual number of characters that can be represented in an inch of disk or tape is called its **density.** Since each character is represented by a series of bits in a specific position, disk and tape densities are measured in bits per inch (bpi). Bits on a tape are laid out

Figure 6.12 *Comparison of how characters are stored on magnetic tape and magnetic disk. (a) This illustrates how bits are recorded on tape tracks. (b) This illustrates how bits are recorded on disk tracks.*

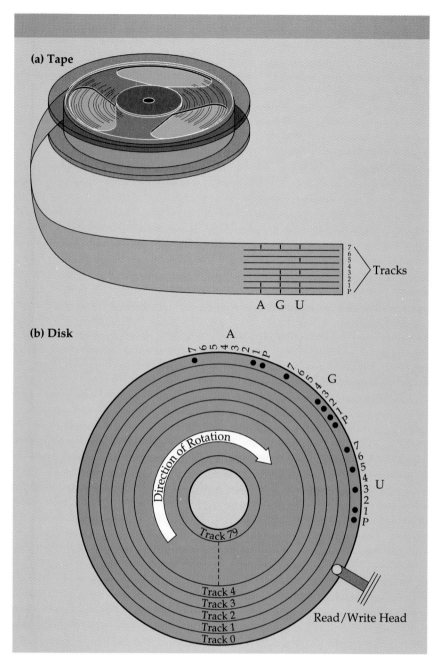

in parallel tracks so that "bits per inch" is really equivalent to "bytes per inch." The most common tape densities are 1600 and 6250 bpi. Disk densities vary widely. Data on tracks closest to the center of a disk is stored more densely than data on outside tracks. In general, disk densities vary from 6400 bpi to tens of thousands of bpi.

SAFEGUARDING FILES Most organizations have hundreds or even thousands of magnetic disks and tapes, each utilized for specific applications. These disks and tapes are usually stored in a separate room sometimes called a storage library or media room.

Because data recorded on these media is not "readable," that is, not visible to the naked eye, it is often difficult to maintain control of all the disks and tapes. If a master accounts receivable disk were inadvertently erased, the mistake would destroy the existing accounts receivable information. The result could be an expensive and time-consuming re-creation process. Moreover, if there is a fire, theft, or other catastrophe that results in loss of data, many files could be affected. Several control measures have been implemented in most organizations to prevent such occurrences or to reduce the extent of damage should they occur:

Write Protection. Diskettes can be write protected to ensure that someone does not accidentally write over needed files. 3½-inch disks have a tab that the user slides to write protect it. 5¼-inch disks have a notch that must be covered to write protect it. Files on all magnetic media can be established with a "read only" attribute, which means that you cannot write over or delete the file without first changing the attribute. Changing a "read only" attribute on a file requires a special program.

Using External Labels. Gummed external labels should be placed on the surface of each disk or tape (see Figure 6.13) to identify the files on it. These labels are clearly visible to anyone, so the chances of accidentally erasing a valuable disk or tape are reduced.

Controlling Access. Most companies have access control procedures that permit only authorized personnel to use disks and tapes. Sometimes a media librarian is hired specifically to maintain control of disks and tapes in a library. The result is less misuse and misplacing of disks and tapes. See Figure 6.14. Individual PC users should store their disks in desktop disk storage containers, many of which have locks.

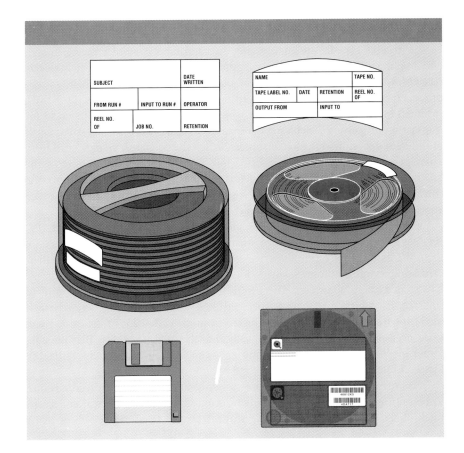

Figure 6.13 *External labels are used to identify magnetic storage media.*

Figure 6.14 *Media librarians usually select tapes from a cartridge library, but in this illustration a robot designed to make cartridge selections is used instead.*

Maintaining Backup Files. Since files on magnetic media can be erased, damaged, misplaced, or stolen, it is essential to maintain backup copies of all important files. If backup copies are available, the re-creation process, should it become necessary, will not be as costly and time-consuming.

Smart Cards, Flash Memory, and RAM Cards: You Can Take It With You!

Newer magnetic media are augmenting disk and tape as storage media in specific application areas. We saw in Chapter 5 that a smart card, which closely resembles a credit card, is a piece of plastic that contains a built-in microprocessor and has a memory capacity, which can be as much as 20+ MB. Invented in France in 1977, these cards now are used throughout the world for transaction processing. Telephone companies in many countries sell smart cards of different denominations to consumers. When the consumer makes a call from a pay phone, the smart card is inserted into the phone and the amount of the call is subtracted from the card's balance. When the balance reaches zero, the consumer purchases a new card. In some European countries, people pay for viewing television programs with smart cards.

In Canada and the United States, pilot projects are underway in which drivers pay highway tolls by means of smart cards. When participating truckers in British Columbia, for example, arrive at designated toll booths, they insert their card and the toll is automatically deducted from the card's credit account.

Some systems allow consumers to transfer cash from their bank accounts to smart cards, which then have a specified cash value. Each time a purchase is made, the transaction amount is deducted from the cash value of the card. There is no need for an online service to verify that the card is valid or that the customer is within his or her credit limit as is the case for most credit cards. See Figure 6.15.

Smart cards are also used in some schools. Students pay a sum in advance to be on a meal plan; the smart card records the cost of each meal and keeps track of the balance available to the student. Access to laser printers in many

Figure 6.15 *In Paris, people pay for their newspapers with a smart card.*

schools is also controlled by smart cards. You purchase a card with a fixed value and each time you use the laser printer you insert the card in a device that subtracts the price of each page printed. When the value of the card is depleted, you purchase a new one.

The U.S. government has begun to replace food stamps with smart cards; the dollar amount to which a recipient is entitled is changed on the card each time he or she makes a purchase.

Every day, new applications for smart cards are being introduced. They can store medical and drug records for patients and driver information on an electronic driver's license. They can control access to secure sites: a smart card can store passwords, digital fingerprint data, even photos, to identify individuals seeking access to an area.

There are credit card–sized memory modules that can be used as disks or to add random access memory to a computer. When used as added RAM they are called RAM cards or memory cards. These are ideal for laptops, notebooks, and palmtops because they are so small, but they can be used in larger PCs as well. These memory modules require small batteries to retain their contents. Flash memory cards, a type of EEPROM chip, are also used as disks or memory modules, but they hold their contents without power.

IN A NUTSHELL

MEMORY CARDS FOR PORTABLES

TYPE OF CARD	CHARACTERISTICS
Flash memory cards	Highly reliable, fast access time, expensive
RAM cards	In comparison to flash memory cards, they have more electrical components, slower access time and transfer rates, and smaller capacities

Figure 6.16 *PCMCIA cards can provide additional types of RAM for portables.*

The Personal Computer Memory Card International Association card (PCMCIA) standardizes credit card–sized packages for memory and disks, and is widely used in laptops and notebooks. PCMCIA cards are also used for modems, fax cards, and network connections. See Figure 6.16.

ɪɴ A NUTSHEʟʟ

PCMCIA Card	Standardized credit-card unit for main memory add-ons, disks, input/output units on a laptop or palmtop
TYPES OF PCMCIA MEMORY CARDS	
Flash Memory	Used for main memory add-on or disk; derived from EEPROM; data is retained even if the power is off
RAM or Memory Card	Used for main memory add-on; needs a battery

Self-Test

1. Name two advantages of hard disks over diskettes.

2. A _____ has the capacity of a hard disk, but is portable.

3. Files are often compressed in order to _____.

4. All files should be _____ periodically in case something happens to the original.

5. (T or F) Data recorded on a smart card can be changed.

6. _____ cards are used in portables as alternatives to heavier hard disks.

Solutions

1. Larger storage capacity and faster processing speed

2. disk cartridge

3. save space on a disk

4. backed up

5. T

6. RAM, memory, or PCMCIA

6.3 OPTICAL STORAGE ALTERNATIVES TO MAGNETIC MEDIA

As the variety of computer applications increases, the need for auxiliary storage devices with greater and greater capacities also increases. Typical hard disks for PCs can store hundreds of megabytes or even gigabytes of data, and disk packs for mainframes can store hundreds of gigabytes. Even now, the hard disk storage capacity of micros is beginning to approach that of disk packs for larger systems.

In Chapter 5, you learned that optical, or laser, technology is used in scanners and laser printers. It is used for secondary storage as well. Three types of optical storage media are currently available.

1. CD-ROMs: read-only compact disks
2. WORM CDs: Write-Once, Read-Many compact disks
3. Erasable CDs: erasable compact disks, which use a combined magneto-optical technology

Of the three, CD-ROM is currently the most widely used as a storage medium. **CD-ROMs** have read-only capability, and they are popular for storing sophisticated programs and multimedia software. Write-once, read-many disks are not yet standardized and are available in a variety of sizes. Erasable CDs have the greatest potential for augmenting or even replacing hard disks, but they are still expensive—several thousand dollars or more. We will also discuss floptical disks, which use magneto-optical technologies.

CD-ROM Drives: A Most Valuable Player

A compact disk with read-only memory is a silver platter, 4.72 inches in diameter. It looks just like a standard audio compact disk and is read by a drive very similar to that used for audio disks. See Figure 6.17. In fact, most CD-ROM drives can play audio CDs! Data on CD-ROM is stored in binary form and is read by a laser beam. The data is stored as microscopic pits on the disk; the presence of a pit represents a binary 1 and the absence of a pit represents a 0.

> **Study Objective**
>
> 4. List the advantages of optical storage devices.

Figure 6.17 *CD-ROM drive with a caddy, or case, containing a compact disk (CD). For some drives, CDs must be in a caddy in order to be accessed.*

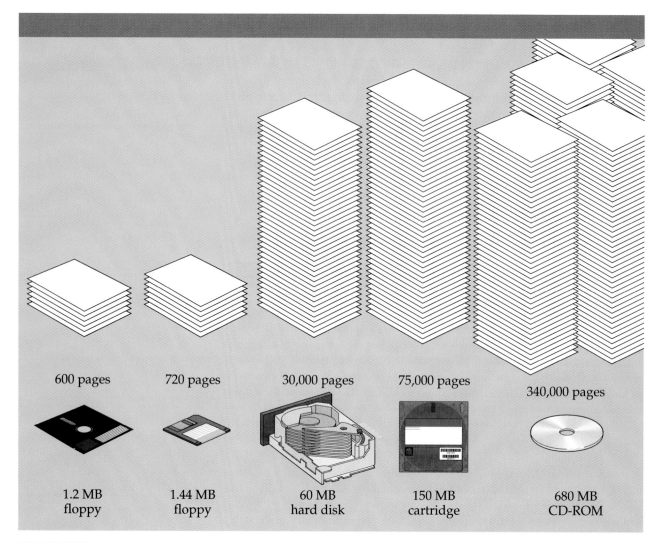

600 pages	720 pages	30,000 pages	75,000 pages	340,000 pages
1.2 MB floppy	1.44 MB floppy	60 MB hard disk	150 MB cartridge	680 MB CD-ROM

Figure 6.18 *Comparing storage capacities. Assume that one double-spaced typewritten page is the equivalent of 2 K (two kilobytes) of information. Shown here are the storage capacities (in pages) of various secondary storage devices.*

ın A NUTSHELL

OPTICAL STORAGE COMPARED TO HARD DISK

PROS
1. Larger storage capacity
2. More reliable
3. Removable

CONS
1. Currently most widely available as a read-only medium
2. Slower access speed and transfer rate than hard disk drives

CD-ROMs can store 680+ MB of data, equivalent to many hard disks or to hundreds of floppy disks or more. A single CD-ROM can incorporate the data contained in several full-sized books. The files can be in text form exclusively or can also contain images and sound in document or multimedia files. Figure 6.18 compares a CD-ROM's storage capacity with those of PC disks.

CD-ROMs can be accessed quickly but the speed of retrieval of CD-ROM drives is less than that of most magnetic disk drives. Because they use laser technology, CD-ROM drives are more reliable. The CD-ROMs themselves are removable, which makes them more versatile for data retrieval than hard disks. Some CD-ROM drives are double spin, triple spin, or quadruple spin for two to four times the processing speed.

CD-ROMs, MULTIMEDIA, AND VIRTUAL REALITY Because CD-ROMs can hold 680+ MB on a single compact disk, they are ideal for storing multimedia software—games, presentations, and educational products that contain high-quality graphics, animations, video, and sound, all of which use a great deal of storage space. Figure 6.19 illustrates a screen display of a multimedia game on CD-ROM called Travelrama. Figure 6.20 illustrates an entry from a CD-ROM multimedia encyclopedia describing a butterfly. The user can control the visual demonstration of the butterfly emerging from its chrysalis by clicking on the control buttons, which are similar to those on a cassette player.

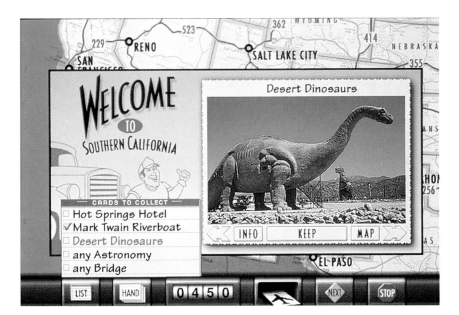

Figure 6.19 *This is a screen display from a multimedia game on CD-ROM called Travelrama. Players "travel" around the United States collecting picture postcards—and learn about geography along the way.*

CD-ROM drives are relatively fast—they can transfer data from a compact disk at speeds from 150 milliseconds, although double-, triple-, and quadruple-spin drives correspondingly double, triple, and quadruple that transfer rate. This is still only about half as fast as the transfer rates for high-speed disks.

The latest recommendations for multimedia equipment, called MPC2, as specified by the PC Marketing Council in 1993, include a CD-ROM drive. The full recommendations for multimedia capability are shown in Table 6.2.

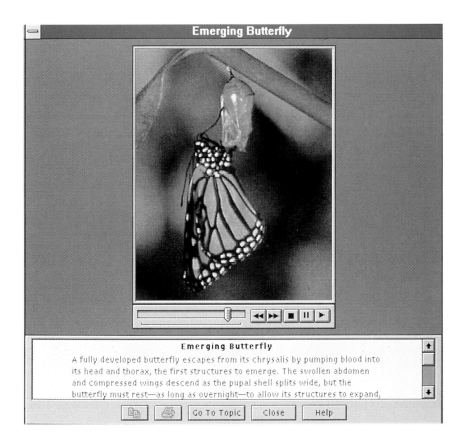

Figure 6.20 *A multimedia encyclopedia like Encarta can visually demonstrate a butterfly emerging from its chrysalis.*

Table 6.2 *PC Marketing Council's Recommendations for Multimedia Computers*

	Minimum Requirements
RAM	4 MB (8 MB recommended)
Processor	486 25 MHz
Hard disk	160 MB
CD-ROM	300 KB transfer, 400 ms access time
Sound	16-bit
SVGA monitor	640 × 480 × 64 K

CD-ROMs with multimedia components often include **virtual reality** components as well. With virtual reality, a user actually becomes part of the action. Through the use of a headset or goggles, gloves, and even a "walker pad," users not only see and hear a story line develop on the screen in multimedia; they also have the sensation of actually being there. They feel as though they are interacting directly with the characters and the environment. See Figure 6.21.

Newer CD-ROM multimedia games are played using virtual reality. Users can find themselves stranded on a desert island, locked in combat with aliens, or faced with other adventures that require them to search for solutions. Popular movies like the *Star Trek* series and *Raiders of the Lost Ark* are available on CD-ROM with the user as the hero! Simulation applications for playing baseball, golf, and tennis are entertaining and often helpful—many include virtual reality techniques for making users believe they are actually playing the game.

Books like *The Last of the Mohicans, Moby Dick*—and even the *Bible*—are available on CD-ROM with virtual reality components that enable "readers" to be a part of the action.

College tours might be arranged using a CD-ROM and virtual technology. A prospective student wearing special goggles could experience a "virtual" walk through a campus.

CD-ROM is used extensively for published databases where mass production of data on a secondary storage medium is needed. The process of creating a database on a CD-ROM is similar to that used for creating an album on an audio compact disk. A master is produced and disk copies are manufactured by stamping them the way audio CDs are stamped. Numerous encyclopedias, for

Figure 6.21 *Virtual reality applications and simulations supplied on CD-ROMs often use headsets and gloves, which give people the sensation that they are in a different environment interacting with other players or characters as well as with the set.*

Figure 6.22 *Some graphics packages like CorelDRAW that use a large amount of storage for representing images are available on CD-ROM.*

example, are stored on a single CD-ROM and sell for less than $100. Microsoft's Bookshelf has a CD-ROM with a collection of common office reference tools including a dictionary, thesaurus, almanac, atlas, and encyclopedia. Material from this product can be "cut and pasted" into any document you are working on.

Many other publications and collections are available on CD-ROM. Computer Select, for example, contains abstracts and articles from hundreds of computer journals along with computer product and vendor information. Each year, more and more publication services offer a series of journals in specific subject areas on CD-ROM. You may even be able to take some of your library's resources home by checking out CD-ROMs that store thousands of articles or scores of books and that provide the ability to quickly search through the database to locate specific topics.

And the uses of CD-ROM continue to expand. Telephone directories for entire sections of the United States are available on a single CD-ROM. Many companies rely on CD-ROMs for documentation, tutorials, and other company-wide information. Los Angeles County, which has one of the largest libraries in the country, stores its catalog of 5 million titles on a CD-ROM. A search for a specific title takes far less time than it would using a card catalog or microfilm. Accountants in large firms have CD-ROMs containing all the tax information they need. By accessing a single CD-ROM, job seekers can obtain information about employment opportunities throughout the country.

Some software, particularly graphics packages that use a large amount of storage for representing images, is available on CD-ROM as well as diskettes (see Figure 6.22).

Several companies are experimenting with CD-ROMs that include demos and trial versions of software. If, after trying the software, you want to purchase it, you can make a phone call (or have your computer dial a number), supply your credit card information, and receive a code that unlocks the full software on the CD. The manuals are supplied electronically—also on the CD! There is no wait for delivery and everything is contained on a single CD. Microsoft's CD-ROM Sampler and Apple's Mac Productivity Edition are two examples of CD-ROMs which contain software that a user can experiment with before purchasing.

IN A NUTSHELL

DIGITAL LENNON: THE MARRIAGE OF MUSIC AND MULTIMEDIA

Warner Brothers Consumer Products and Compton's NewMedia have teamed up to produce "Imagine," a CD-ROM based on the life of John Lennon. The product includes home videos and art never before released to the public, as well as Lennon's music, including many unpublished works.

Source: Advertising Supplement to *New York Times*, June 5, 1994, p. 7.

In summary, numerous games, educational products like encyclopedias and atlases, edutainment software with high-quality audio and visual effects, and standard software are widely available on CD-ROMs. These are just some of the applications for CD-ROMs. The list is likely to grow exponentially in the years ahead.

Most CD-ROMs are for sale; others with date-sensitive data are available by subscription. Suppose you subscribe to Computer Select. The first month's CD contains publications for the past 12 months. Each month you receive a new CD-ROM with that month's publications added. The previous disk can be discarded or saved as a backup. There is no need for you to integrate the new data with the old the way you would if the data were in print form. Moreover, unlike data stored in print form in a library or other central location, your CD-ROM is available any time day or night. Many new magazines are delivered on CD-ROM on a subscription basis.

CD-ROM drives are typically several hundred dollars but high-speed, quadruple-spin drives can cost more. Many new PCs, especially those designed for multimedia applications, come equipped with a CD-ROM drive as well as a hard disk drive.

KODAK PHOTO CD A recent advance from Kodak enables users to have 35 mm slides or negatives digitized and stored on a CD-ROM. The Photo CD consisting of these slides or negatives is created by photo finishers that have a Kodak Picture Imaging Workstation. Each photographic image uses six MB of storage on a single Photo CD, so that each CD can store approximately 100 photos. There are two types of Photo CD players—one that displays the images on a TV and one that displays the images on a PC. Computer users with a Photo CD drive can convert their photos to either an IBM-compatible or a Mac graphic format and paste them into documents or files or into their multimedia presentations. See Figure 6.23.

Networking Compact Disks

CD-ROM drives are often networked so that many users can access them concurrently. Instead of multiple drives, many systems have CD-ROM servers that stack and retrieve a group of compact disks for large numbers of users (see Figure 6.24). Servers automatically shift from one disk to another without physically replacing disks.

The District-of Columbia Public Library has installed a Pioneer "jukebox" as a server to provide users with access to its three CD-ROMs that contain a U.S. residential and business telephone directory. The appeal of the jukebox is that the librarian does not need to manually insert a different compact disk each time a person seeks information about a geographic location in a different database. A jukebox can access multiple compact disks, sometimes even hundreds of disks. Some servers can make a terabyte (1 trillion bytes) of data available. Networks in universities, businesses and government agencies commonly make CD-ROMs available to authorized users through file servers.

WORM Drives: Will They "Worm" Their Way into Your Heart?

WORM—write-once, read-many—CDs, developed in 1985, are now available in different sizes, but 5¼-inch and 12-inch are the most common. A 5¼-inch WORM CD can store 1+ GB of data and a 12-inch version can store 3+ GB of data. At present, WORM CD drive designs remain nonstandardized and expensive.

•••••➤ Looking Ahead

- Storage capacities for all magnetic, optical, and magneto-optical media will increase 30 times, yielding the equivalent of 10 GB on one side of a 5¼-inch CD. Consequently, more search and retrieval and navigational tools will be available with graphics and voice capability to augment and perhaps even replace straight text.
- CD-ROMs may be eclipsed by card-sized read/write optical recording media.
- Optical and magneto-optical storage media will augment rather than replace magnetic disks.
- As networks become more prevalent, they will make available data on optical drives, as well as magnetic disks. The location of the data and the method of access will be transparent (that is, unnoticeable) to the user.

Figure 6.23 *The Kodak CD Unit enables users to create multimedia presentations using their own photos. The presentations can be displayed on a TV or PC screen.*

WORM disks are used by companies that need to maintain vast archives. Such archives are created once by a user organization and then permanently stored on WORM CDs. They are commonly used to replace microfilm or microfiche systems. WORM drives, like CD-ROM drives, use a laser that changes the physical state of a disk. In contrast, however, WORM drives do not physically pit the surface so they do not lend themselves to mass duplication.

Image Processing Optical disks such as WORM CDs have made it possible for complete image processing systems to emerge. As we have seen, document management by image processing allows full documents including graphics, photos, and signatures to be captured, stored, processed, and retrieved. Of course, such systems are quite expensive; they require midrange computer capacity (or more) and typically cost $100,000+. But for banks, as an example, storing checks, deposits, and withdrawals along with loan applications in an image processing system can actually save money as well as time and storage space. Similarly, insurance companies store their claim applications and insurance policies in such systems.

Optical storage media, like CD-ROM and WORM disks, are a necessary part of multimedia systems as well as image processing systems because of their storage capacity. Nontextual material like photos, signatures, and other graphics require a great deal of storage space.

Figure 6.24 *A multiple or stacked CD-ROM unit that can be used as a server.*

Erasable Magneto-Optical Drives: Doing the "Write" Thing

Although most storage technologies are either purely magnetic (disk and tape) or purely optical (WORM CDs), erasable CDs make use of combined optical and magnetic principles. They were introduced in 1988 and are called **magneto-optical (MO) disks.** They have several benefits:

- Removability (like floppies and disk cartridges).
- Random-access capability similar to that of hard drives.
- Reliability similar to CD-ROMs.
- Capacity similar to digital audio tape.

The MO drive writes data to a disk as a pattern of magnetized fields by means of both a laser and a magnet. As the disk rotates, the MO drive turns the laser on and off. The laser selectively heats specific spots as they pass, which changes their magnetic polarity. The MO drive reads data by means of the laser only. It interprets these magnetized fields on the reflected light.

MO disks are a good choice as a backup storage medium. Tapes can also be

Critical Thinking

A few years ago, Lotus Development Corporation announced MarketPlace: Households, a database on CD-ROM. This database contains names, addresses, and financial information—including income estimates—for 120 million U.S. households. The product was the target of protests, and Lotus agreed to cancel its production.

Do you think Lotus did the right thing? Under what conditions or limitations should such products be made widely available?

Looking Ahead

MEDICAL MEMORY CARDS

As an experiment, the U.S. Department of Veterans Affairs in Troy, New York, is testing optical memory cards and read/write devices to store medical records for veterans. If the initial installations are successful, additional test locations will be added. If the system is implemented fully, optical cards may be used by millions of veterans throughout the VA's network of hospitals and clinics.

The hope is that the medical records card will improve health care delivery to veterans while reducing problems caused by inaccessibility to prior records and test results. Patients will carry the optical card and have it updated during each medical visit. In this

way, physicians will have immediate access to medical history data, which can provide life-saving information.

Known as the LaserCard, this data storage device is the size of a credit card and can store up to 4.11 MB of data. Medical reports, x-ray images, ultrasound and CAT scans, and other test results can be stored on and retrieved from the card. Access to the card's information can be protected through security codes and software. Also, the patient's photograph, voice print, and signature can be stored on the LaserCard for identification and security purposes.

used for backup but tapes need to be converted to disk before data can be accessed randomly. MO disks are "mirror images" of hard disks. MO drives can read and write randomly, but at a slower rate than hard drives.

MO storage media are also removable, which makes them ideal for situations in which security is an issue or where there is a need for transportability. And MO drives are reliable because the read/write heads do not whirl across the disk as they do with hard drives; they are relatively safe from head crashes, which can destroy a disk if the read/write head accidentally makes contact with it.

The technology does, however, have limitations:

- High cost.
- Lack of a standard size.
- Not as much storage as a hard disk (although there is potential for far more storage than hard disks).
- Slower access time than a hard disk.

A typical MO disk drive can store 2.6 GB for 5¼-inch disks and costs under $1,000. A hard drive of similar capacity is approximately half the cost. Although MO disks are not yet standardized, they have the greatest potential for augmenting or replacing magnetic disks, mainly because data can be written, deleted, and rewritten to MO disks.

FLOPTICAL DISK DRIVES A floptical or microfloptical disk is a floppy disk that uses optical tracking to greatly increase storage capacity. A floptical has approximately 14 times the capacity of a comparable 3½-inch diskette—22 MB. This increase is achieved by having more tracks of data on each side of the diskette and using an optical tracking system that is precise enough to enable reading and writing of very narrow tracks. The technique used for recording data is the same used for conventional magnetic floppy disks. Most 3½-inch floptical disk drives can read and write both the 22 MB flopticals as well as the 720 KB and 1.44 MB diskettes.

Self-Test

1. The most common form of optical disk is the _____, which has a vast amount of storage capacity but is limited because _____.

2. CD-ROMs are currently used mainly to store _____.

3. WORM disks are used for _____.

4. A device that is capable of stacking compact disks and retrieving data from any one of them quickly is called a _____.

5. Why are some CD-ROMs purchased by subscription?

Solutions

1. CD-ROM; it is a read-only medium

2. multimedia software and large databases

3. write-once, read-many applications (such as storing company archives or other data that needs to be recorded only once)

4. jukebox, CD-ROM server, or stacked CD-ROM drive

5. If data is date sensitive and newer versions are needed often, then CD-ROMs are typically made available by subscription.

6.4 ORGANIZING DATA FILES

Because disks are still the most widely used storage medium for database files and because high-speed accessing of such files is so important to information systems, we consider next some of the processing techniques commonly used for accessing disk files.

Sequential File Organization

We have seen that sometimes files are processed sequentially by reading record 1, then record 2, and so on, until all records have been processed. Records processed sequentially are typically in sequence by a key field such as Social Security number, customer number, or part number. When a file is in sequence by a key field and the only way we need to process the data is in sequence, then sequential files are created.

Files that are always processed in batch mode are usually organized for sequential processing. Consider a master payroll file that is accessed once a week for updating. If the changes to the master are in sequence by a key field (e.g., Social Security number) and the master file is also in sequence by the same key field, then sequential file updating is not only feasible, it is most efficient. That is, a program would read one record from each file, compare key fields, and, on a match, update the master file.

Note that the only way to process sequential files is sequentially; if records in these files need to be accessed in a different order, they must be sorted first. For example, the payroll file that is in sequence by Social Security number is fine for updating purposes. But when payroll checks need to be printed, the file is likely to be sorted first, alphabetically by employee name within department so that the checks can be more easily distributed. Keep in mind that sequential files are almost always accessed in batch mode.

Suppose, however, a manager wants to inquire about the status of individual employee records. Sequential access would be extremely inefficient for such processing. Say the manager needs to know the salary of an employee with a Social Security number of 987-32-6577. The manager could surmise that the record is near the end of the file since the file is in sequence by Social Security number, but that record can only be accessed by reading past all the preceding records.

Random-Access File Organization

INDEXED FILES If inquiries need to be made from a file in which the records being accessed are in no particular sequence, sequential processing is not the best technique. For example, on an average day, the vice president of marketing may ask for information about 20 salespeople where the requests are in no specific sequence. Similarly, the VP of finance may want to know how many employees in a specific department earn more than $80,000, and the VP of human resources may want to know the names of employees eligible for retirement during the following year. In each case, the requests are random. These users need a technique to access records *directly* without having to read them sequentially.

The indexed method for organizing records in a file allows random access of the records. An **indexed file** is one that is created sequentially; but, in addition, an index is created that keeps track of the physical location on disk of each record. To each record's key field, the index associates a unique disk address that identifies the record location by its surface number, track number, and sector (or cylinder) number. That index is in sequence and can be "looked up" any time a record needs to be accessed. If you are seeking a record with a key field of 9222, you do not sequentially search the file by reading record 1, seeing if its key field is 9222, then reading record 2, and so on. Rather, the computer "looks up" in the index the disk address of the record with a key field of 9222 and goes directly to the surface, track, and sector on the disk that stores that record. Think of how you might look for a topic in a book. You can sequentially search for the topic by scanning page 1 of the book, then page 2, and so on. Or you can look up the topic in the book's index, find its page number (its address), and go directly to that page. If you have to perform numerous searches on random topics, it is far more efficient to use an index rather than a sequential search.

DIRECT FILES Although randomly accessing indexed files is faster than sequentially accessing them when the search criteria are in no specific sequence, looking for indexed records still requires a search procedure. In a **direct file,** the computer accesses records by converting a key field, through some arithmetic calculation, into an actual address that identifies the surface, track, and sector (or cylinder) number. There is no need to search an index. As a simplified example, assume that in a three-digit key field called Account Number, the first digit provides the surface number and the last two digits provide the track number. This scheme would use 10 surfaces (0–9) and 100 tracks (0–99) for storing the data. Direct file access is faster than indexed access because there is no need to look up an address from an index. But sometimes the direct access method requires more extensive programming, because the programmer must determine the best mathematical formula for converting key fields to addresses.

If the key fields are in sequence, however, and most of the records have consecutive key fields (e.g., 001, 002, 003, and so on), the key field need not be converted to an address at all. That is, the record with a key of 001 may be placed at the first disk location, the record with a key of 002 may be placed at the second, and so on. This is the simplest type of direct file organization. To access a record with a key of 987, the computer goes to the 987th location on disk. Using key fields directly as disk locations is feasible only for records that have key fields with consecutive values (e.g., customer number *not* Social Security number).

Self-Test

1. When records are always processed by reading the first, then the second, and so forth, the process is called _____ access.

2. When records need to be accessed from a disk in no particular sequence, then _____ processing is required.

3. Disk files to be accessed randomly use either the _____ or _____ method of file organization.

CHAPTER SUMMARY

Every computer system consists of a CPU and various input/output devices. In addition, every system must have one or more secondary storage units to store programs and data for future processing.

Solutions

1.   sequential

2.   random

3.   indexed; direct

6.1 Fundamentals of Secondary Storage

When data is processed by the CPU, programs are loaded into primary storage, input data is read, and output is produced as information. Primary storage, however, is usually volatile in nature. A peripheral device such as disk, referred to as **secondary storage** or **auxiliary storage,** is required to store programs and data for future processing. Secondary storage is nonvolatile, which means that all information is saved even after the power is shut off.

There are five major criteria for evaluating secondary storage devices: (1) **storage capacity,** which indicates the amount of data the storage medium can hold and is measured in kilobytes, megabytes, or gigabytes; (2) **access rate,** which is the time needed to locate data on a secondary storage device and is measured in thousandths of a second; (3) **transfer rate,** which is the speed at which data is transferred, or copied, from the secondary storage unit to main memory and is measured in megabytes per second; (4) cost of the secondary storage unit; and (5) the physical size of the storage unit.

Study Objective

1. Explain why secondary storage is a crucial component of a computer system.

6.2 Magnetic Media for Secondary Storage

Micros use floppy disks (also called diskettes), hard disks, or portable **disk cartridges** to store programs and data files. Mainframes use either fixed disks or removable disk packs. Disks are ideal for the **uploading** and **downloading** of files. All disks use a peripheral called a disk drive for reading data from the disks and writing to them.

Data is stored on a magnetic disk in concentric rings called tracks. On diskettes, the tracks are segmented into wedge-shaped sectors. Most diskettes are **soft-sectored,** which means that sectors are not already defined on a diskette when it is purchased; rather, sectors are defined when the disk is formatted. Diskette drives that use double-sided floppy disks have two **read/write heads,** which are mechanisms for reading data from, or writing information onto, the diskette. Records are stored on diskettes at locations called addresses; an address consists of a surface number, track number, and sector number.

In addition to having one or two floppy disk drives, many micros have a large-capacity internal hard disk. A **head crash** occurs when the read/write head makes direct contact with the disk. In such a case, the data stored on the disk is usually lost. Disk cartridges combine the advantages of diskettes and hard disks: they have storage capacities as large as hard disks but they are removable and, thus, are portable. Some hard disks are external, which makes them portable, too.

Most of the larger computer systems have fixed disks that are similar to the internal hard disks on micros. A **fixed-head disk drive** contains one or more hard disks and stationary access arms with separate read/write mechanisms for each of the tracks on the disks. A **disk pack** is an older type of disk common to some minis and mainframe computers. It consists of *removable* sets of hard disks.

The popularity of magnetic tape as an auxiliary storage medium has waned in recent years because disks have all the advantages of tape and none of the disadvantages. Disks are ideal for applications in which data must be accessed quickly and randomly. Tapes, however, can be accessed only sequentially. Tapes function well as a backup medium.

The number of characters that can be represented in an inch of disk or tape is called **density.** Disk and tape records are frequently blocked.

There are other magnetic media besides disk and tape. A smart card is a piece of plastic that has a built-in microprocessor and memory. A smart card is purchased for a given amount; each time a purchase is made, the amount of the purchase is subtracted from the card's balance on hand. A memory card is a

Study Objective

2. Identify the different types of disks and disk drives.

Study Objective

3. Show why disks have replaced tapes as secondary storage in most systems.

credit card–sized memory unit. This type of memory is ideal for laptops and notebook computers because it can replace heavy hard drives and increase battery life. Some manufacturers of laptops, palmtops, and Personal Digital Assistants offer RAM cards, which are similar in concept to memory cards.

6.3 Optical Storage Alternatives to Magnetic Media

Three types of laser, or optical, storage media currently are available: (1) **CD-ROMs** (read-only compact disks); (2) WORM CDs (write-once, read-many compact disks); (3) erasable CDs (erasable compact disks). Of the three, CD-ROM is the most widely used as a storage medium, especially for storing databases and **virtual reality** software. Erasable CDs, called **magneto-optical disks,** make use of combined optical and magnetic principles.

6.4 Organizing Data Files

The two major methods of organizing data files are (1) sequential file organization and (2) random-access file organization. Sequential files can only be accessed sequentially. Random-access files—either indexed or direct—allow records to be accessed directly without having to read them sequentially. When an **indexed file** is created, an index is established that keeps track of the physical location on disk of each record. This index can be "looked up" any time a record needs to be accessed. With a **direct file,** the computer accesses records by converting a key field, through some arithmetic calculation, into an actual address.

Study Objective

4. List the advantages of optical storage devices.

Study Objective

5. Describe the major ways of organizing data files.

KEY TERMS

Access rate, *p. 185*
Auxiliary storage, *p. 183*
CD-ROM, *p. 201*
Density, *p. 195*
Direct file, *p. 210*
Disk cartridge, *p. 191*
Disk pack, *p. 192*

Downloading, *p. 191*
Fixed-head disk drive, *p. 192*
Head crash, *p. 189*
Indexed file, *p. 209*
Magneto-optical (MO) disk, *p. 207*
Read/write head, *p. 188*
Secondary storage, *p. 183*

Soft-sectored diskette, *p. 187*
Storage capacity, *p. 184*
Transfer rate, *p. 185*
Uploading, *p. 191*
Virtual reality, *p. 204*

CHAPTER SELF-TEST

1. A disk pack consists of a series of platters or disks. How many recording surfaces does each disk platter have?
2. Data is recorded on a disk in concentric _____.
3. (T or F) Because a disk has a series of recording surfaces and numerous read/write heads, it is possible to access disk records more quickly than tape records.
4. A _____ is a direct-access medium used with microcomputers.
5. A disk is best used for _____ processing in a(n)_____ mode.
6. For direct access of disk files, two methods of file organization are _____ and _____.
7. (T or F) Disks cannot be processed sequentially.
8. (T or F) An existing indexed disk record may be altered and then rewritten onto the same physical space on the disk.

9. (T or F) Disks and tapes usually have programmed labels.

10. (T or F) CD-ROMs are used extensively for multimedia applications.

11. (T or F) It is generally a good idea to copy a master disk file onto a tape for backup purposes.

12. (T or F) Sequential data files can be used for batch processing operations.

REVIEW QUESTIONS

1. What are some advantages of optical storage devices over magnetic storage devices?

2. Why are tapes no longer as popular as they once were?

3. Discuss the three principal types of memory cards. Can you think of everyday applications for them?

4. Indicate some possible application areas for compact disks not discussed in the text.

CRITICAL THINKING EXERCISES

1. Older disk drives designed to process 5¼-inch disks with a 360 K capacity cannot process 5¼-inch disks with a 1.2 MB capacity. Similarly, older disk drives designed to process 3½-inch disks with a 720 K capacity cannot process 3½-inch disks with a 1.44 MB capacity. Disk cartridge drives designed to process 44 MB cartridges cannot process 90 or 150 MB cartridges. Indeed, some cartridge drives that read/write to 90 MB disks cannot write to the older 44 MB disks. Why are manufacturers so insensitive to the problem of incompatibility? What can users do to minimize these problems?

2. CD-ROMS can be used with TVs for edutainment, or with PCs for edutainment as well as traditional computer applications. What are some of the things you can do with PC-driven CD-ROMs that are not possible using a TV? Which medium—TV or PC—do you think will see the greatest growth for CD-ROMs in the next few years? Is interactive TV likely to replace PCs?

Solutions

1. two—except for the first and last disks, each of which has only one recording surface

2. tracks

3. T

4. floppy disk or hard disk

5. random; online

6. indexed; direct

7. F

8. T

9. T

10. T

11. T

12. T

3. What are the pros and cons of "reading" a CD-ROM "book" with multimedia effects and virtual reality components as compared to traditional, passive, page-turning?

4. Businesses have been slow to acquire multimedia equipment because they believe that multimedia has more entertainment value than "real" value. Can you think of some ways in which multimedia tools could be helpful in business?

Case Study

CD-ROMs Abound in Diverse Application Areas

Microsoft was the first to release a multimedia business productivity tool, Microsoft Works for Windows, Multimedia Edition. The $199 CD-ROM includes (with Works) digital sound, animation, and pictures in tutorial and reference sections. During the setup phase, a video introduces the program's word processing, spreadsheet, database, drawing, and charting functions as it guides the user through installation. The online tutorial is a collection of more than 40 lessons with multimedia movies, sound, and animation.

Career Opportunities, a new career guide CD-ROM from Quanta Press, is a computer-searchable version of three books: *The Federal Career Guide*, which covers government jobs, *The Occupational Outlook Handbook*, which covers jobs in the private sector, *Your Military Today*, which covers civilian-related military employment. These books, with more than 10,000 pages in printed form, are widely used by career and guidance counselors. The cost for the CD-ROM is approximately $100.

DeLorme Mapping sells its *Street Atlas USA* on CD-ROM. The atlas contains over a million color maps that show every street in every city, town, or rural area in the United States. To find a specific location, you can enter a phone number, zip code, or place name. Any map or portion of a map can be printed or imported to a word processing or graphics package that accepts Windows images. The cost is under $100.

Judging from the growing list of reference works, games, illustrated children's books, software, and other multimedia products that use CD-ROM as the preferred storage medium, we can expect production of these disks and their drives to continue their upward swing. Multimedia products themselves have no formal standard. Simi-

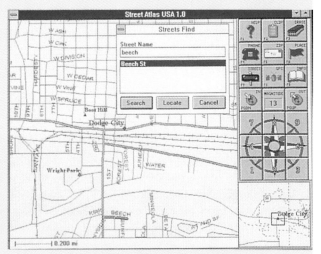

An illustration of a street map stored on a CD-ROM.

larly, standards are lacking for CD-ROM drives and their search-and-retrieval techniques. But there are now only a few preferred formats rather than dozens, and standardization is likely to be achieved soon.

Analysis

1. What are the advantages of CD-ROM as a storage medium compared to conventional hard or floppy disks? What are the disadvantages?

2. Cite some advantages and disadvantages of CD-ROM-based references as compared to printed books.

3. Which reference works would you like to see issued on CD-ROM? How could they be enhanced with multimedia? Would you like to see your textbooks on CD-ROM?

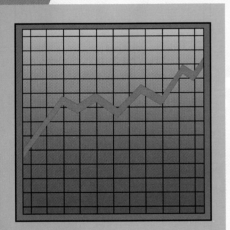

PART THREE

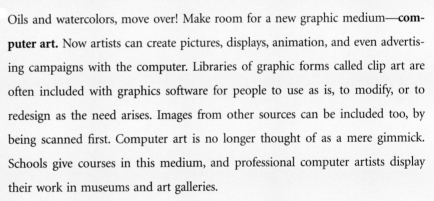

Software Drives the Information Age

Oils and watercolors, move over! Make room for a new graphic medium—**computer art.** Now artists can create pictures, displays, animation, and even advertising campaigns with the computer. Libraries of graphic forms called clip art are often included with graphics software for people to use as is, to modify, or to redesign as the need arises. Images from other sources can be included too, by being scanned first. Computer art is no longer thought of as a mere gimmick. Schools give courses in this medium, and professional computer artists display their work in museums and art galleries.

The architects of the ancient world might have produced more than seven wonders if computers had been available in their time. Today's architects, engineers, and designers use high-quality graphics and **computer-aided design (CAD)** packages to automatically compute and display the dimensions of buildings and to experiment with designs as well. More precise than other graphics packages, these programs also help users create the kind of complex plans and drawings used not only in architecture but also in fields like manufacturing and production—and even in filmmaking.

Electronic music is one of the newest artistic forms. Musicians—both amateur and professional—can create new music or enhance existing compositions.

Interactive CD-ROMs are already available that contain music videos as well as information about the artists.

Creative **multimedia** presentations provide information in a newly dynamic way that integrates audio, video, graphics, and text. As an innovative educational tool, multimedia also brings animated, visually appealing, and interactive lessons to the MTV generation.

Researchers in **artificial intelligence** develop games, simulations, and even robots that examine and try to imitate human thinking and creativity. **Virtual** which an interactive computer environment imitates a real-world setting. Using specially designed devices like data gloves, we can learn how to play sports and games, practice specialized skills like flying an airplane, and even design and visualize entire towns.

CHAPTER 7
Application Packages: Beyond Basic Productivity Tools

7.1 A REVIEW OF APPLICATION SOFTWARE

Packaged and Customized Programs

Productivity Tools Revisited: Basic Packages, Integrated Packages, and Suites

Additional Productivity Programs

7.2 OTHER POWER TOOLS

Graphics or Illustration Packages

Document Viewers

Desktop Publishing

Statistical Packages

Artificial Intelligence Software: Expert Systems, Virtual Reality, and Neural Network Packages

Business Packages

Packages for Consumer Use

7.3 CHOOSING AND USING SOFTWARE

The Make or Buy Decision

Versions of Software

Evaluating Software Products

Where and How to Acquire Software

The Human Factor: Security and Safety

n Part Two we looked at the types of hardware that make computerization effective in a wide variety of application areas. Remember, though, that software drives hardware, and software needs must be considered before hardware acquisitions are made.

In Part Three we focus on software. We begin with application packages—off-the-shelf software used by many organizations and individuals for all or most of their information processing needs.

Study Objectives

After reading this chapter you should be able to:

1. **Describe how application packages have progressed to include more functions.**
2. **Discuss the capabilities of today's "power tools."**
3. **Demonstrate how to select the right software package for a particular application.**

▬ 7.1 A REVIEW OF APPLICATION SOFTWARE

Application software consists of programs that are designed to satisfy specific user needs. User needs exist in various application areas, including those for business, education, and personal use. The following are common application programs for business:

1. Spreadsheet programs to create a budget.
2. Payroll programs to update a master payroll file.
3. Accounts receivable programs to print customer bills.
4. Inventory programs to answer inquiries about the quantity on hand for each item in stock.

Packaged and Customized Programs

Application software can be purchased as a package or it can be custom designed specifically for individual users. Both packaged and custom software are used with computer systems of all sizes. Packages tend to be most popular in PC-based organizations, which are apt to have a limited computer staff. Larger organizations with more specific computer needs and a full computer staff often invest in custom software, although they sometimes purchase or lease packages to augment their own software.

Productivity Tools Revisited: Basic Packages, Integrated Packages, and Suites

In Chapter 3, we studied the features and uses of word processing, spreadsheets, database management packages, electronic mail, and groupware. All are common tools intended to enhance productivity. Integrated packages (e.g., Microsoft Works, ClarisWorks, and PFS:WindowWorks) are low-cost programs that include word processing, spreadsheet, database management, and some e-mail functions in one software product. In addition to cost, an advantage of an integrated package is that it employs one basic type of user interface; that is, the

---

▪N A NUTSHELL

TYPES OF SOFTWARE

1. Systems software supervises processing.
2. Application software satisfies user needs. Application software can be:
   - Packaged
   - Custom-designed

Packages are cheaper than custom programs but they do not always fully satisfy all user needs.

command structure and menu system for all its components are the same. A disadvantage of integrated packages is that they do not include many of the options of full-blown productivity tools.

In addition to integrated packages, the major software manufacturers offer **suites,** which are sets of full-blown productivity tools sold as a unit for a greatly reduced price. Microsoft Office, for example, includes Word, Excel, Access, and a presentation graphics package called PowerPoint for approximately $500. Lotus has SmartSuite, which includes the Ami Pro word processing package, Lotus 1-2-3, Approach (a Lotus DBMS), cc:Mail (an e-mail package), Freelance Graphics (a multimedia presentation graphics package), and Lotus Organizer (a desktop tool). Novell's PerfectOffice includes WordPerfect, Quattro Pro, and Paradox. Note that most schools offer these products with an educational discount, which further reduces the cost. While the cost of these suites is relatively low, each requires a great deal of disk space—typically 50+ MB! See Table 7.1 for a comparison of these suites.

Microsoft, Lotus, and Novell are willing to offer their suites at relatively low cost because it simplifies their training and support services. Currently 60% of Microsoft's productivity tools are sold as suites while only 25% of Lotus's products and 15% of Novell's are sold as suites.

Additional Productivity Programs

In addition to the four basic tools already discussed (word processing, spreadsheets, database management, and e-mail), there are many other products designed to increase the productivity of users in an organization. We consider some of the more common ones here.

DESKTOP ACCESSORIES, SYSTEM OPTIMIZERS, AND OTHER UTILITIES

In addition to word processors, spreadsheets, and database management systems, there are a number of other products that improve productivity. Originally, if you needed an electronic calendar, or a program to optimize disk space and memory usage, or virus protection software, you had to purchase a separate software product for each function. Then Microsoft and other developers of operating systems software began to "bundle" some of this software with their new operating systems. This made it more difficult for other software manufacturers to sell single-function packages.

Today, many products have features for improving productivity. See Figure 7.1. We discuss these features on the next two pages.

Table 7.1 *What's in That Box?*

	Novell PerfectOffice	Lotus SmartSuite	Microsoft Office
Word Processor	WordPerfect for Windows	Ami Pro	Word
Spreadsheet	Quattro Pro for Windows	1-2-3 for Windows	Excel
Database Manager	Paradox for Windows	Approach	Access or FoxPro
Presentation Graphics	WordPerfect Presentations	Freelance	PowerPoint
E-Mail/Groupware	Groupwise	cc:Mail	Microsoft Mail
Personal Information Manager	InfoCentral	Organizer	None

All three suites have "professional" versions as well, which include more sophisticated packages for an added cost.

Desktop accessory— Software that functions as an object normally found on an office desk such as a calculator, calendar, notepad, and address book. Most **desktop accessories** have icons that the user can click on with a mouse to invoke the specific function.

System optimizer— Software that improves the performance of hardware or software. Optimizers provide information about the status and efficiency of system components and have diagnostic and repair capability as well. Optimizers can signal the user when memory is low. They can determine and improve access time and transfer rates for disks and main memory performance. They can be used for file management as well.

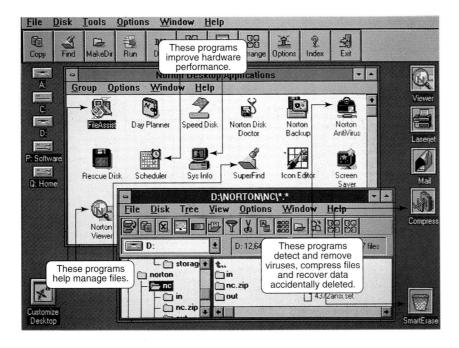

Figure 7.1 *Norton Desktop for Windows includes a number of utilities that can improve productivity.*

Other utilities— Utilities can compress files so that more data can be stored on a disk; they can detect and remove viruses, provide automatic backup procedures, built-in password protection, and programs that convert files and images from one format to another. Some utilities have an "unerase" option that enables them to recover data accidentally deleted. This is possible because when files are deleted with a delete or erase command they are not physically removed from the disk; only the reference to the file is deleted. The unerase command, then, can call back the reference to the file.

Although many operating systems include most of these features, software specifically designed for the above purposes often has "bells and whistles." Such software is typically loaded into memory prior to application software and can be activated at any time by pressing a combination of control keys or clicking on an icon with a mouse.

Many of these programs are called memory-resident or *terminate and stay resident* (TSR) programs. Once they are loaded, TSR programs remain accessible even while other programs are running.

Common tools in this category are Symantec's Norton Desktop for Windows, Central Point Software's PC Tools for Windows, and Hewlett-Packard's Dashboard. In addition to those mentioned here, there are many other tools that are designed to enhance user productivity and creativity.

Screen Savers Add Creativity to Your PC. Another utility that is sometimes bundled with other products or sold separately is called a *screen saver*. A screen saver was originally developed to protect a monitor that might have an image displayed on it for a long period of time while the computer was inactive. After a while, the image could be burned or etched into the phosphor coating of the monitor. To prevent this, screen savers were introduced that display moving images after a display screen has been left idle for a fixed period of time. Users can select the type of moving images they prefer such as flying toasters, fish in an aquarium, etc. Many of these screen savers have password protection capability so that the screen saver remains active until a password set by the user is entered. See Figure 7.2.

Figure 7.2 *A popular screen saver display.*

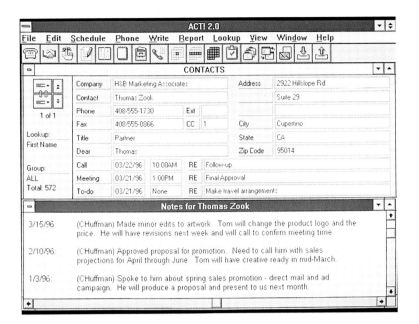

Figure 7.3 *A Personal Information Manager (PIM), like Act!, enables users to keep track of projects and to store, organize, and search for data.*

Once again, some operating system software comes with screen savers but many separate screen savers such as the After Dark program are used by millions of people.

Even though the risk of burning images on an inactive monitor is very remote today, these screen savers enable users to add a little creativity to their screens and some basic security, and these remain desirable goals in computing.

PERSONAL INFORMATION MANAGERS (PIMs) AND PROJECT MANAGEMENT SOFTWARE Personal information managers (PIMs) not only help eliminate the clutter on a desktop screen but also help users store, organize, and search for data regardless of whether it is in a report, database file, memo, table, or note. If a manager is having a meeting with an executive from another company, a PIM can be used to gather information about the company and the executive from database files and from any memos, letters, or notes that could relate to the meeting. See Figure 7.3.

Popular PIM software includes Polaris's Pack Rat, CrossTies (by CrossTies Software Corp.), and Symantec's ACT. In addition to PIM software, there are handheld or palmtop computers specifically developed to serve as PIMs.

Personal Digital Assistants (PDAs). As the new generation of handheld computers, PDAs are most often used for their high-level PIM capability. Using communication equipment and wireless paging systems, PDAs such as Apple's Newton include desktop organizers and offer the ability to retrieve information from home or office PCs and from company databases. These devices have both keyboards and pens. The pens can be used for writing notes or selecting items.

Electronic pocket organizers, which are palm-sized or handheld devices from firms such as Casio and Sharp, have calendar, calculator, notepad, and phone capabilities like simple desktop accessories. These sell for as little as $200.

Many PIMs for desktop PCs also have project management capability, which enables users to keep track of the progress of projects. There are also project management software tools that are designed exclusively for this purpose.

Critical Thinking

It is common knowledge among computer professionals that some of the most popular packages are not necessarily the best. Despite evidence that newer products have better features, companies continue to use and purchase some of the older and less sophisticated software. They claim that the cost of a transition, which may include retraining an organization and rewriting applications, outweighs any innovative features. What do you think?

As the name implies, **project management software** is for managers who need to keep track of the progress of projects under their control. Like spreadsheet software, project management packages allow you to perform a type of what-if analysis. You can, for example, evaluate a number of different scheduling scenarios before you start a project. Once the project is underway, you can track its progress, reallocate tasks or personnel, or make changes to optimize resources as the need arises. Project management software lets you keep track of whether the project is proceeding on time and within budget. Tasks can be prioritized and built-in alarms can be set to warn of impending deadlines or remind users to check scheduled dates.

Many project management packages feature on-screen graphics. They may also include an outliner: software that assists writers in developing outlines for documents they are preparing. Such tools do not replace planning and evaluation by managers; rather, they perform some of the routine tasks, thereby freeing managers for the more important tasks at hand. Microsoft Project and Symantec Time Line are among the more common packages.

COMMUNICATIONS SOFTWARE FOR E-MAIL, GROUPWARE, AND ACCESSING THE INTERNET In Chapter 2 we saw that communications hardware such as modems and telephone lines can be used to send and receive data from one computer to another. Communications software allows you to set the parameters that enable computers to send and receive messages and files. Some communications packages common in business are SmartCom, Kermit, and ProComm. We will discuss how these packages actually enable transmission of data from one computer to another in Chapter 10. Frequently e-mail, groupware, and Internet packages function in conjunction with communications packages if messages are transmitted over telephone lines or some other communications link.

Many newer PC-based e-mail packages include communications software. They also include word processing features such as spell checkers and grammar checkers for editing electronic mail messages. Some communications packages will automatically generate a recorded reply should a message arrive when the recipient is away; they can also place messages in "folders" established by the recipient, or forward messages if they contain specified keywords. Lotus cc:Mail and Microsoft Mail include these features.

A relatively new focus in business today is on total quality management, which emphasizes teamwork and improved quality control. Groupware, which includes communications software, is designed to facilitate the processing of data by teams. Groupware enables users to (1) collect information from a variety of sources including documents, tables, graphics and databases, (2) share updated information with numerous colleagues, and (3) process and pass documents from one person to another, with each person able to add information directly to the document.

Groupware Helps Resolve Incompatibility across Platforms. Many groupware products function across different platforms including DOS, Windows, Macintosh, and Unix. Full document management capabilities and search and retrieval techniques across platforms are provided. Groupware products can also set up integrated in-boxes for e-mail, faxes, schedules, online services, and even voice mail. This means you can have one "in-box" that includes all your messages and the information you have requested integrated where appropriate. If, for example, you receive a phone call or e-mail message with information about an account and later get a fax related to that same account, both transmissions can be linked together for ease of reference. Groupware also provides extensive

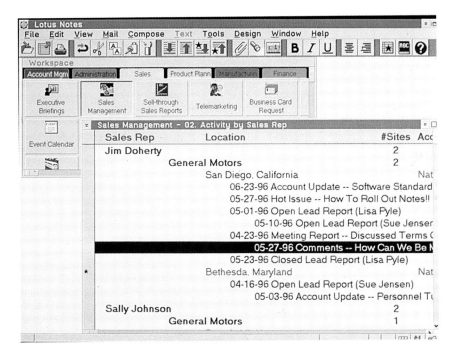

Figure 7.4 *A sample Lotus Notes screen display.*

data conferencing capabilities that enable users to work simultaneously on a shared whiteboard (better than a blackboard). Users are able to conduct real-time conferences, using a groupware product. In a videoconference, for example, information can be brought to the conference as needed. Groupware, then, can be used in environments where office workers use different types of hardware, different communications software and services, and different videoconferencing equipment, thereby helping to resolve the problems normally associated with incompatible systems. See Figure 7.4 for an illustration. Lotus Notes, Microsoft Exchange, and Novell's Groupwise are popular groupware packages.

Some communications software is designed to facilitate the retrieval of data from the Internet. These are called Internet user interfaces or Internet front-end packages. Mosaic, for example, is offered free of charge to Internet users by the National Center for Supercomputer Applications at the University of Illinois. Mosaic provides an easy method for searching through Internet services for key items of special interest to users, and enables users to view full-color images as well as text or to play sound and video files that might accompany text stored on the Internet. This package, and others like it, makes Internet access much more user-friendly and far less daunting than scrolling through files and resources and attempting to download items of interest.

Mosaic has been very successful as an Internet front-end package. In fact, many people believe that this product is, in part, responsible for the increased traffic over the network which is now doubling every four months. Some believe that such continued heavy use of the Internet will result in gridlock. The future of the information superhighway, which will be built on the Internet concept, may require a restructuring of the method of access so that traffic jams are minimized.

Mosaic is not the only Internet user interface or front-end, but its availability as free software has made it the most popular one to date. Other packages include Pipeline, Netscape, and Spry Inc.'s Internet-in-a-Box, which also provides communication capability and facilities for navigating through the Internet. See Figure 7.5.

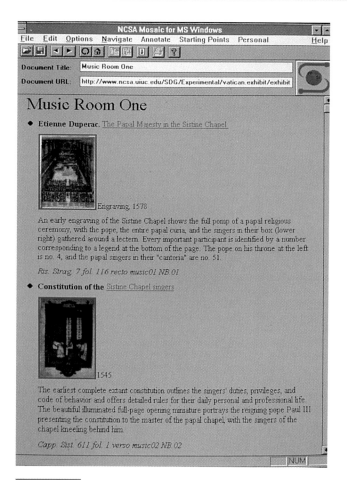

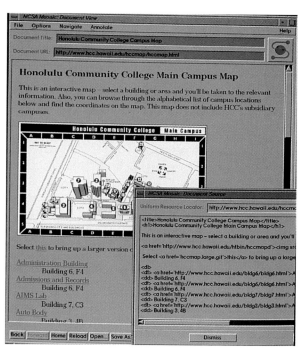

Figure 7.5 *Mosaic screen displays.*

MULTIMEDIA PACKAGES: PRESENTATION GRAPHICS, AUTHORING TOOLS, AND SOFTWARE FOR CREATING VIDEOS As we have seen, multimedia is the use of text, graphics, animation, sound, and video in interactive applications for making presentations, for playing games, and for education with pizzazz (edutainment). It is one of the most exciting and innovative areas in computing today.

Consider a multimedia encyclopedia, which is typically stored on a CD-ROM. See Figure 7.6. If you look up the word "heart," you are likely to find not only a text-based explanation and graphic illustration but a series of icons that provide additional information via sound bytes, animation, and video clips. If you click on the animation icon, you may find an animated clip describing how blood passes through the heart. If you click on the sound icon, you may get a verbal explanation of the animation along with the actual sound of a heart pumping blood. If you click on the video icon you may get a movie illustrating open heart surgery. Such multimedia educational tools are likely to be far more interesting and informative than traditional text-based products.

Multimedia tools are widely used for providing basic information as well. Multimedia kiosks in major tourist areas, for example, offer users information about cities and their attractions. A touch screen is typically provided to enable users to select items of interest.

Your school may have a multimedia kiosk that provides a wide variety of information about its resources. Suppose you have a specific interest in physical fitness. You can navigate through the information provided by touching the screen or using a mouse or other pointing device to select items like "gym" or

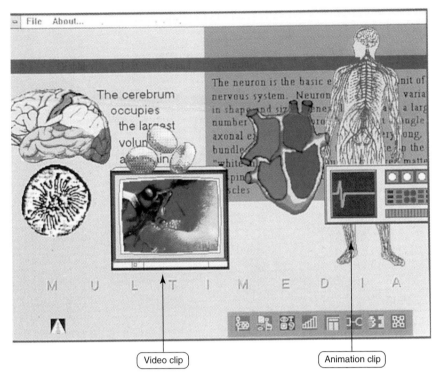

Figure 7.6 *Multimedia screen display that provides text, video, and animated clips about the heart.*

"athletics" or "exercise equipment." The information provided might be a video of the exercise facilities available along with a verbal description and an animated map showing you how to find them. Using a mouse or a touch screen to select desired items reduces the need to wade through page after page of information. See Figure 7.7.

One main characteristic of multimedia packages is their ability to link sections of a presentation together and, within each section, to link various components such as text, graphics, animation, sound, and video. This concept is referred to as **hyperlinking.** See Figure 7.8. With hyperlinking, you can move from one presentation to others without having to use sequential paging. Using our previous "heart" presentation from a multimedia encyclopedia, we could go from a discussion of the heart to a discussion of the blood with one click of a mouse and from there to a discussion of white blood cells with another click of the mouse. There is no need for scrolling through pages or looking up entries in an index. Multimedia objects such as sound and video clips that can be hyperlinked are called hypermedia. Context-sensitive help uses hyperlinking to enable users to easily locate the specific item they need help with.

Figure 7.7 *A consumer uses an information kiosk at a music store to hear the CD or cassette he or she wishes to purchase.*

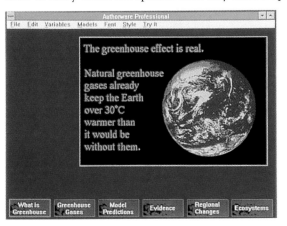

Figure 7.8 *This multimedia screen provides information about the greenhouse effect. Clicking on any item at the bottom of the screen, such as "Ecosystems," provides a hyperlink to another topic related to the greenhouse effect.*

Figure 7.9 *This electronic slide with a graphic image, different type fonts, charts, and attractive colors was created using a presentation graphics package.*

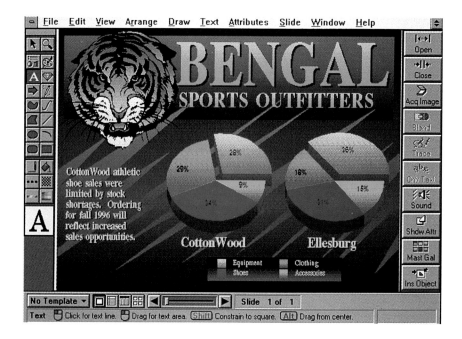

Multimedia components can be found in word processing, DBMS, spreadsheet, and e-mail packages. These enable users to include sound, graphics, animation, and video along with their document, database, worksheet, or message files.

Presentation graphics packages enable users to create computerized slide shows or electronic transparencies displayed on a screen; these packages also include multimedia components. Using graphic templates and basic graphs as background, users can add text with different type fonts, sounds, animation, and video to enhance their presentations. Some multimedia sounds, animation, and video are supplied as "clips" with the package, but users can also create their own. Asymetrix's Compel, Microsoft's PowerPoint, and Macromedia's Action are examples of popular presentation graphics packages. See Figure 7.9.

Figure 7.10 *This employee training screen display with a video that introduces the training module and its hyperlinks to various topics was created using Toolbook.*

To create multimedia applications that provide fully interactive hypermedia linkages such as those used in encyclopedias, training packages, and games requires a **multimedia authoring package** such as Asymetrix's Toolbook, Macromedia's Authorware, and Macromind Director. See Figure 7.10. Using these tools, on-the-job multimedia training packages have been developed, for instance, to teach student pilots how to fly an airplane and to teach interns how to perform medical procedures.

Multimedia authoring packages are also used for electronic games, encyclopedias, and other types of databases. See Figure 7.11.

A full multimedia teaching tool called Passport, developed using Toolbook, is available with this text. It has multimedia tutorials on productivity tools as well as presentations on new areas in computing such as virtual reality and handwriting recognition. A multimedia electronic slide show summarizing the concepts in this book is also available.

Runtime Versions of Multimedia Software. Both multimedia graphics packages and authoring tools are available either on CD-ROM or on a series of diskettes. These programs need to be installed on a hard drive, require a great deal of storage space, and typically operate in a Windows environment.

Users who have developed presentations often wish to install them on portable computers and show them at locations away from the office—at group meetings, at a client's desk, etc. If the full software used to develop the product were required to run the presentations, the portable computer on which the presentations are made would need to have the full software installed. This is often impractical since hard disk space requirements are so great. Moreover, if the presentations were to be distributed to many users, each user would need to purchase a copy of the software to run them.

To resolve these problems, many software manufacturers provide a **runtime** version of their products. This is a subset of the full-blown product that is used for running applications created by the package. The runtime version cannot be

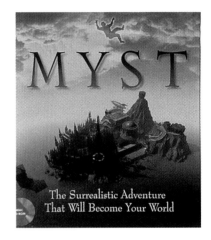

Figure 7.11 *Myst, a multimedia computer game with surrealistic images, is available on CD-ROM. It was created using a multimedia authoring tool. Over one million copies have been sold.*

(a)

(b)

Figure 7.12 *(a) Computer software can be used to edit videos or movies. (b) More than half of the dinosaurs shot for* Jurassic Park *were the "pigment of a computer's imagination."*

used for creating new applications, only for running existing applications. Most multimedia authoring tools and presentation graphics packages permit users to make free copies of runtime versions of the software.

Software for Creating Videos. Users who wish to create video clips or even full-motion videos using a computer need video capture hardware to enter the video as input, video software for manipulating and editing images, and video compression hardware for storing the videos compactly.

Video software typically requires QuickTime for Macintosh and Windows or Video for Windows for recording and playback. Products like Adobe Premiere have extensive editing capabilities.

Movies like *Forrest Gump* use video editing techniques to provide clips in which two people, such as Tom Hanks and President Kennedy, are made to appear as if they are interacting with each other. See Figure 7.12 for other illustrations.

Self-Test

1. Name the two main types of application software.

2. Name three components of an integrated package or suite.

3. A software package that contains a telephone directory, calendar, calculator, and notepad, among other things, is called a _____.

▉ 7.2 OTHER POWER TOOLS

Application packages frequently perform tasks that would otherwise take users many hours to perform. Such tasks are often prone to errors and are costly, especially when substantial manual labor is involved. We discuss here some of the more commonly used application packages that make processing more efficient and produce more accurate and useful output.

Graphics or Illustration Packages

Study Objective

2. Discuss the capabilities of today's software "power tools."

In recent years, businesses have taken to heart the old adage that one picture is worth a thousand words. They are illustrating ideas and information by using programs that interpret information visually (Figure 7.13). **Graphics software** is a general term that refers to programs with tools for drawing, charting, and presenting illustrations. Simple packages can capture screen displays and produce printed copies, film, or 35-mm slides. Some graphics packages convert numeric data into bar, pie, line, and other types of graphs. Some graphics packages also contain a database of graphic displays or **clip art** that you can add to documents. Figure 7.14 displays some common clip art. Graphics packages can also produce animated output and three-dimensional graphics. We have already discussed presentation graphics packages used for multimedia presentations.

Solutions

1. packaged (off-the-shelf) and custom (specially prepared) software

2. spreadsheet software, word processing software, and database management system software (It usually has e-mail and may have other components as well.)

3. desktop accessory

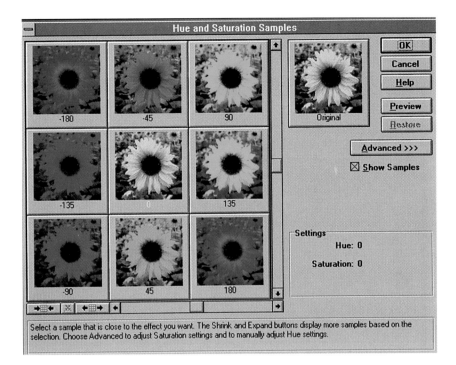

Figure 7.13 *Output produced by a graphics package.*

Here we will discuss graphics packages designed primarily to produce high-quality pictures and images. Freelance Plus, PowerPoint, Compel, Harvard Graphics, and Aldus Persuasion are presentation graphics packages that have far more capability for illustrating text and graphics, as well as sound, animation, and video, in presentation form. Many of these packages are available for both the Mac and IBM-compatibles; typically, the IBM-compatible version requires the use of Windows.

ILLUSTRATION PACKAGES The first Macintoshes featured two built-in **illustration packages:** MacDraw and MacPaint. People were amazed at how easily they could create illustrations with this software. In the 1990s, illustration packages have become increasingly sophisticated. Only recently, however, have business users begun to take this software seriously, largely as a result of the importance that high-quality illustrations have in desktop publishing and in

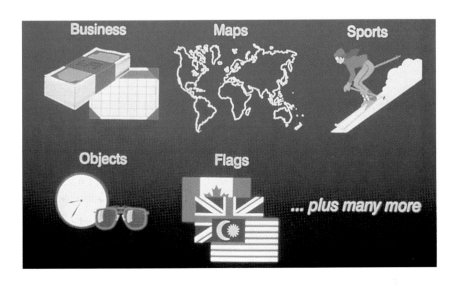

Figure 7.14 *Clip art available from DrawPerfect's Figure Library can be added to any document or file.*

presentations. There are two categories of illustration packages: painting programs and drawing programs.

Painting Programs. Painting programs, such as MacPaint for the Macintosh and PC Paintbrush and CorelDRAW for IBM-compatibles, create **bit-mapped graphics,** which consist of patterns of dots. Bit-mapped graphics are similar to the output of a dot-matrix printer: each character is actually a grouping of small dots arranged to form desired shapes. The smaller and closer together the dots, the better the quality of the output. On the other hand, the more an image that is bit-mapped is enlarged, the coarser or less clear it becomes.

Most bit-mapped graphics are created manually by using a mouse to move the cursor on the screen or by using a tablet that digitizes drawings. Optical scanners can also be used to digitize graphics and photos that already exist on paper. Once a graphic has been scanned, it can usually be edited or refined.

Drawing Programs. As the demand for higher-resolution output has grown, so has the popularity of drawing programs. These programs differ from painting programs in that they use combinations of lines, arcs, circles, squares, and other shapes or objects rather than dots to create visuals. These programs use **vector graphics** as opposed to bit-mapped graphics. Vector graphics can be resized—either enlarged or reduced—without altering their clarity.

Some type fonts are created using bit-mapped graphics but these are not scalable; that is, their sizes cannot be changed easily. Scalable type fonts using vector graphics are more popular today than bit-mapped type fonts.

The more sophisticated drawing programs, such as Adobe Illustrator (Figure 7.15), Aldus Freehand, and Micrografx Designer, offer a great deal of flexibility in creating illustrations. The exact thickness of lines can be specified; objects can be shaded to give them a three-dimensional appearance that was formerly only possible with painting programs; and images can easily be scaled, rotated, duplicated, or revamped for special effects. Micrografx Designer (Figure 7.16), in particular, is a highly sophisticated drawing program with many of the capabilities of the computer-aided design packages that engineers use. We discuss these in the next section.

Figure 7.15 *Vector graphics programs use computer-generated lines, shapes, and dot patterns. No matter how much an image is enlarged, it remains crisply drawn.*

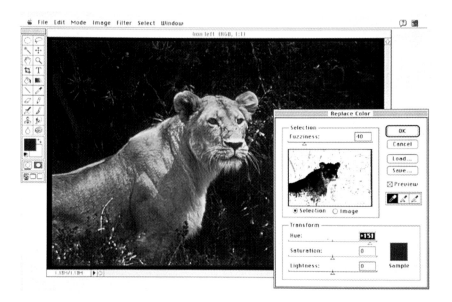

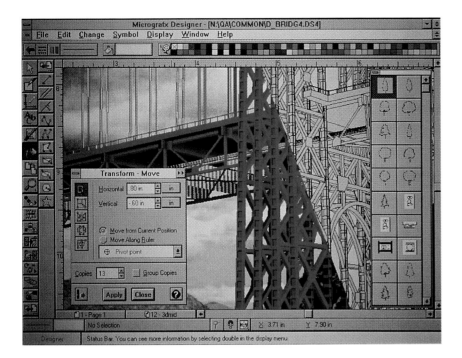

Figure 7.16 *Micrografx Designer combines features typically used in computer-aided design programs with those used in illustration packages.*

Drawing programs require more planning, patience, and skill than painting programs. However, large drawings normally take less disk space than large paintings and take less time to print. Painting programs allow for more spontaneity, but they are far less precise.

Most managers use the graphics created by illustration programs but leave the input procedures to data entry operators and the design of the output to computer professionals. In most business and professional settings, the illustration packages are used in graphic design or desktop publishing departments. If a scanner is available, managers may have their company logos or signatures scanned. The logos and signatures can then be electronically integrated into letters, memos, and other documents. Managers also like graphing and charting programs because they make information accessible in attractive and instructional charts and they can produce slides.

Figure 7.17 *AutoCAD is the most widely used computer-aided design package. It can be used for designing various products including bridges.*

CAD/CAM Computer-aided design (CAD) packages, as the name implies, are used to design products with the assistance of a computer (Figure 7.17). CAD packages are essentially drawing programs, but they offer additional features specifically required by the architects and engineers for whom they were created. CAD programs use objects to create complex drawings, but they allow a degree of precision unavailable in most other graphics packages. For example, they automatically calculate and display the dimensions of an illustration. In addition, they allow you to place objects in precise locations by specifying *x* and *y* coordinates. CAD programs also allow you to store a library of symbols on disk. You can insert, scale, and rotate figures as needed.

Computer-aided manufacturing (CAM) products help engineers design the manufacturing components in a factory or production facility. CAD/CAM software integrates computer-aided design with computer-aided manufacturing. The products designed in the CAD system are directly inputted to the CAM system.

Because of their complexity, many CAD/CAM packages are used on minicomputer or mainframe computers for designing intricate products such as automobiles, airplanes, or weapons systems. In fact, CAD/CAM packages were

Figure 7.18 *In this example of morphing, a car is transformed into a tiger.*

Document viewers provide cross-platform and application-independent document exchange capabilities.

once the primary province of larger systems; now they are available for micros as well. (AutoCAD is the most popular package for micros.) Most illustration packages discussed in the previous section were derived from CAD/CAM software.

CAD, CAM, and CAD/CAM packages assist in designing products; they are not a substitute for human skill. Rather, their goal is to provide support to product designers by performing some basic operations, thereby enabling the professionals to focus on the more creative aspects of their jobs.

Illustration, drawing, and CAD/CAM packages have **morphing** capability, which enables one type of image to be transformed into another. For example, a car can be visually displayed as it is transformed into a tiger, suggesting great power and speed. See Figure 7.18. Morphing techniques are commonly used in advertisements and videos.

Document Viewers

We have seen that documents and presentations can include text with different type fonts, graphics, photos, animations, sound, and video. Software packages create files in different, often incompatible formats. Platforms such as IBM-compatibles and Mac use some software packages that create files that cannot be read by other types of computers. To combine clips, documents, or presentations created by different products and different types of computers can be an awesome task. To transmit such products across a network can also be difficult.

Conversion software, called **document viewers,** enable users to import files created using different packages and even different platforms and standardize them for transmission over a network or for creating one integrated product. Adobe Acrobat and WordPerfect Envoy are examples of document viewers.

Desktop Publishing

Individuals and organizations use **desktop publishing (DTP)** software to design and print documents with a wide variety of type styles and sizes called type fonts. See Figure 7.19. In these documents, text and graphics can appear on a single page. DTP combined with a laser printer enhances the quality of the printed output to the point where the document appears to be professionally typeset—just like this book. DTP products are ideal for creating newsletters, advertising pieces, even full-length texts.

The advantages of desktop publishing for producing typeset-quality documents are similar to the advantages of word processing for preparing manuscripts or documents. Desktop publishing software makes the task of producing output much easier and more efficient. Traditionally, the user who needs printed material submits a typewritten manuscript to a typesetter. The next step is for a designer to determine how the publication will look. The manuscript is then keyboarded using elaborate codes to format the text according to the designer's specifications. If these steps are followed, the manuscript will have been keyed twice, once by the authors and once by a typesetter.

Intermediate output is produced next in the form of long strips known as galleys. The galleys are checked by professional proofreaders and then sent to the user to be read again. After all corrections and changes have been made by the typesetter, a further round of proofreading takes place. Finally, revised galleys are cut apart and pasted up in page format, leaving space for artwork. Now we have come to the page stage. The user checks a copy of these pages, called page proofs, not only for any errors in type that were overlooked, but for the acceptability of

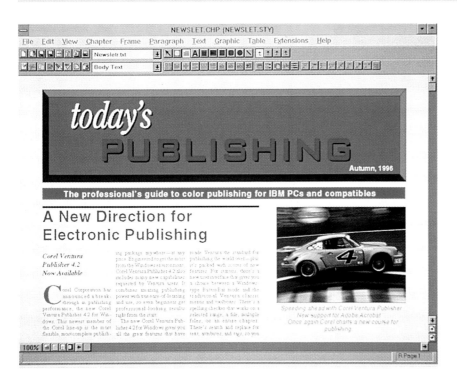

Figure 7.19 *Desktop publishing packages can produce typeset-quality output with graphics and a variety of type fonts.*

the layout. All further corrections are typeset and pasted in the pages; depending on the quantity and type of corrections, some pages may need to be completely redone. The final pasteup is sent to the camera department, where plates for the printing press are made. The user checks a proof of this final stage to make certain that everything is in its proper place. Finally, the publication is sent to a press to be printed.

The many steps involved in this traditional method of publishing provide opportunities for errors. Moreover, the process is time consuming, both for the typesetter and for the user.

In contrast, desktop publishing (DTP) software allows the user to control all aspects of the publication process, including designing the publication, setting the type, proofreading, inserting graphics, and producing the final copy. Moreover, the time needed and the cost necessary to produce the document are greatly reduced. Only one typing operation is required to develop the manuscript. DTP packages can utilize text that has been prepared by virtually any word processing package.

With DTP, text and sophisticated graphics can be easily integrated into a single document. Graphics—ranging from simple lines and geometric shapes to drawings and photographs—can be placed anywhere on the page, enlarged or reduced, and trimmed to fit the available space.

Desktop publishing software also allows complex pages to be formatted on the computer screen in ways not commonly available with most word processing packages. Different typefaces, styles, and sizes can be viewed on the screen just as they will appear when the document is printed. This feature is referred to as WYSIWYG, which, as noted in Chapter 3, is an acronym for *what you see is what you get*. WYSIWYG enables the user to experiment with various screen displays before deciding on a page format. Most DTP packages also include dozens of preformatted page designs, or templates, that can be used as "shells" for creating newsletters, reports, and other documents.

IN A NUTSHELL

Page layout with pizzazz is the main goal of desktop publishing.

Many desktop publishing packages use a universal code provided in a program called PostScript, developed by Adobe Systems, Inc. PostScript is a page description language that allows users to embed printing codes in documents; the codes tell printers capable of interpreting PostScript how to format each page. The advantage of PostScript is that it is a desktop publishing standard. When PostScript is used, typesetting and formatting codes will always be interpreted in the same way by all printers that support PostScript, including laser printers and phototypesetting machines. For example, if you are using PostScript and choose the typeface called Times Roman for your newsletter, the document produced on a PostScript printer will look the same no matter what printer or phototypesetting equipment is used. This means that you can proof your newsletter on a laser printer, which is relatively inexpensive, and then have the final version produced on more expensive phototypesetting equipment.

The concept of desktop publishing was made popular by a product called PageMaker, developed by the Aldus Corporation for the Macintosh. PageMaker soon had competition from other programs such as Ready-Set-Go! and Quark Xpress. Although desktop publishing was originally used primarily on the Macintosh, it was not long before the Xerox Corporation released Ventura Publisher, the first full-fledged desktop publishing program for IBM-compatibles. Within a few months after Ventura was announced, Aldus introduced an IBM-compatible version of PageMaker as well.

PageMaker has remained a popular package partly because it was the first commonly utilized desktop publishing program, and partly because similar versions run on the Macintosh and on IBM-compatibles. Not only does PageMaker include good page design tools, but it has the ability to integrate graphics easily. Moreover, files created with the IBM-compatible and Macintosh versions share a common structure, so they can be used by both systems. PageMaker is easy to learn and best suited for producing short documents and graphic-intensive publications. On the IBM-compatibles, the use of the Windows graphical user interface is required with PageMaker and most other desktop publishing packages.

Virtually all DTP packages provide a screen that resembles an artist's board into which text and pictures can be placed. Typically, a mouse or other pointing device is used to highlight desired images and to place them in the document.

Using Clip Art in Publications and Presentations May Violate Copyright Laws. Desktop publishers and authors of multimedia applications should be aware of copyright issues and ensure that they are using text, graphics, and other material with proper authorization to avoid legal problems. Scanning a photo into a document, for example, may be a violation of the law. Even if you use "clips" supplied on CD-ROM or diskette called clip art, you need to heed the licensing agreements. If you use pickup material from another source in a commercial publication, for example, you may be violating the law. As a general rule, it is relatively safe to assume that something published more than 75 years ago is no longer covered by copyright laws. Note, however, that you may still have problems: Leonardo DaVinci's Mona Lisa is in the public domain, but a photo of it that you scanned from a magazine may not be—the copyright belongs to the photographer or to someone the photographer assigned it to. The best advice is: If you want to include something in a publication, try to get the permission from the copyright holders. You may be surprised at how easy it can be.

• • • • • ➤ **Looking Ahead**

Originally, desktop publishing products had limited word processing capability and word processing packages had limited page layout and graphics capability. But the distinction between these two types of software is blurring. Today, high-end word processing packages have capabilities found in DTP packages and DTP packages have sophisticated word processing capability. In the future, it is likely that a single package will satisfy both text editing and page composition needs.

Now that Aldus and Adobe—two DTP leaders—have merged, we can expect DTP products to have even more capability.

Statistical Packages

Traditionally, statistical analysis of large volumes of data has been a time-consuming, error-prone task. Because of the computer's speed and accuracy, number crunching was one of its earliest uses. **Statistical packages** such as Minitab, SPSS, and SAS can perform virtually any statistical operation, such as determining standard deviations and variances, to help managers analyze data (Figure 7.20). Versions of these statistical packages are available for all types of computers from micros to larger systems. Many of the functions in statistical packages are now commonly found in spreadsheets, so people often choose to use a spreadsheet for their statistical analysis rather than learn a new package.

Artificial Intelligence Software: Expert Systems, Virtual Reality, and Neural Network Packages

Artificial Intelligence (AI) refers to devices, software, and applications that appear to exhibit human intelligence or behavior. AI applications have the ability to learn or adapt to additional information.

For many years, artificial intelligence techniques were used for playing games like chess. In recent years, AI applications have grown dramatically in a wide variety of fields that can be defined in terms of facts and rules (e.g., financial credit evaluations). Expert system software and neural network software are widely used AI products. Many people believe that by the year 2000, as a result of more sophisticated AI techniques, people will be talking to their computers instead of using a keyboard and mouse.

An expert system is software intended to model or simulate the performance of a human expert in a technical field. It performs the role of a consultant or

Looking Back ◄••••••

The term *artificial intelligence* dates back to the 1940s. The British mathematician Alan Turing defined an AI machine in 1950 as follows: "A machine has artificial intelligence when there is no discernible difference between the conversation generated by the machine and that of an intelligent person."[1] Turing challenged scientists to create a machine that could convince people they were conversing with another human, not a machine. This is known as the *Turing Test*.

[1]Source: *Electronic Computer Glossary,* The Computer Language Co., Inc., 1993.

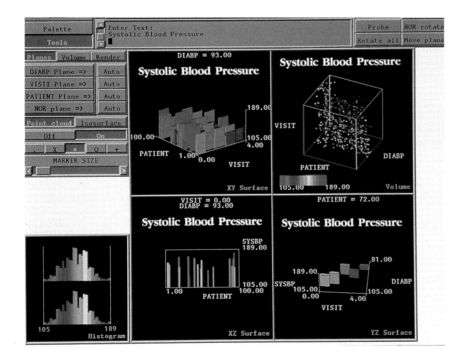

Figure 7.20 *Analysis of blood pressure performed by a statistical package.*

Looking Back

ONE OF THE FIRST EXPERT SYSTEMS

MYCIN, developed at Stanford University in the early 1970s, was designed to store the knowledge of experts in the field of infectious diseases. Originally it contained approximately 200 rules but subsequently was expanded. MYCIN had limited success at diagnosing various diseases.

At a later date, the knowledge base was removed from the program, leaving an empty "shell" that contained the inferencing and control mechanisms so that physicians could create their own knowledge base. This first expert system shell was called EMYCIN, for Essential MYCIN.

IN A NUTSHELL

Expert systems are sometimes called knowledge-based systems.

adviser to users. An expert system can help diagnose specific problems, outline courses of action to take, or suggest approaches to a solution. One of the first expert systems to be utilized was a medical diagnosis system called MYCIN, developed at Stanford University in the early 1970s. Today, expert systems are used not only for medical diagnosis but for predicting weather, analyzing financial plans, processing credit applications, managing order processing and scheduling, establishing inventory reorder levels, diagnosing problems in machinery, and making purchasing decisions. Help-desk personnel often use knowledge-based systems to provide information to customers. In areas where help desks receive frequent calls from people with similar questions or problems, these systems prove very helpful.

To create an expert system, a systems analyst called a knowledge engineer interviews experts in the specific field and translates their knowledge, called the knowledge base, into a series of rules in the form of if-then relationships. When set up, the expert system begins by asking questions of the user; when the system has enough information, it draws a conclusion by means of a component of the software called an inference engine. In summary, expert systems use:

1. Knowledge in the form of a database.
2. Rules in the form of if-then relationships (e.g., *if* patient has a lung infection and a fever, *then* the diagnosis is pneumonia).
3. Human interaction: users respond to queries.
4. An inference engine to draw conclusions.

Expert systems are best suited for providing advice or support to the decision maker. They are not substitutes for human expertise, because human factors such as intuition, creativity, and experience are not easily built into such systems.

EXPERT SYSTEM SHELLS Expert system shells have been developed as generic expert systems. The shells enable users to enter their own knowledge base and inferences to form application-specific expert systems. An expert system shell has an established human interface in the form of dialogs and displays and an inference engine in the form of rules. The knowledge base for these shells can be supplied by the users themselves or by other technical experts.

Expert systems and shells are capable of probabilistic reasoning; that is, even if there is uncertainty or incompleteness of data, predictions can be made. In addition, expert systems allow the user to obtain explanations about how con-

Looking Ahead

THE NERVOUS SHOCK ADVISOR

Knowledge engineers at the University of British Columbia working with IBM have built an expert legal system that provides attorneys with advice on legal cases involving nervous shock, emotional distress, and emotional suffering. The system, called the Nervous Shock Advisor, advises lawyers about whether people who say they have suffered emotional distress have a viable claim. The system bases its conclusions on judgments reached in previous court cases.

After asking the attorney for specific facts about the case, the Nervous Shock Advisor:

• Searches a legal database and determines whether the claim is valid.

• Lists the factors used to arrive at its conclusion and presents a confidence level value for each factor.

• Supplies references to relevant court cases that either support its conclusion or go against it.

• Gives references to cases that demonstrate the arguments that the defendant (that is, the opposing side) might use to present his or her side of the case.

If the system determines that the plaintiff has no case, it tells the lawyer what elements are lacking.

The system was designed to help lawyers prepare a case by presenting the basic elements that support successful litigation.

Figure 7.21 *A virtual reality boxing game. Anyone, including a handicapped person in a wheelchair, could play this game against a simulated opponent. A head-mounted display unit enables users to feel as if they are actually making contact with another boxer. The user can even hear the roar of the crowd.*

clusions were reached and why specific data was necessary. At any point in an analysis, the user can interrupt the consultation and ask why certain information was needed and how a conclusion was reached.

In business, expert systems are used for many purposes.

- Evaluating stocks.
- Determining seating capacity and airplane utilization for various airlines.
- Marketing and planning to help establish prices, provide sales forecasts, and make profitability estimates.
- Diagnosing equipment failure.

1st Class, Exsys, and VP-Expert are expert system shells that can be used with PCs as well as larger computers. In Chapter 11 we will see how expert systems function in decision support systems and executive information systems.

VIRTUAL REALITY Virtual reality is a way of enabling people to participate interactively in 3-D environments created by computer. Imagine the difference between viewing fish in an aquarium and snorkeling or scuba diving among fish in their habitat. That is the difference between computer graphics and virtual reality. Virtual reality games and simulations often include the use of a data glove and a head-mounted display unit, which enables users to feel as if they are actually interacting with objects when in fact those objects are illusions created by computer. Virtual reality software games such as tennis, racquetball, and baseball are currently available. Virtual reality software for taking a simulated trip to some exotic land, or participating in some fantasy such as space exploration, is also available. See Figure 7.21.

NEURAL NETWORKS A neural network is designed to take a pattern of data and generalize from it. For example, using the daily temperatures in Honolulu, Hawaii over a five-year period, a neural network can describe seasonal temperature variations and predict the impact of global warming. Neural networks

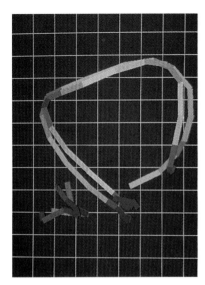

Figure 7.22 *This is a screen display of a "visual ear" used in speech therapy. The visual ear is a computer system based on neural networks that display a "map" of the various sounds associated with a word (the word here is "wait"). The blue line is the "standard" form of the word and the red is a representation of the sound produced by the hearing-impaired person undergoing speech therapy. If there is a large variance between the two lines, the person modifies his or her speech accordingly.*

include a sophisticated form of trial and error, using different modeling techniques until the input yields the actual output. Neural networks can improve their trial-and-error performances (e.g., "learn"). Common neural network applications include:

Business— Sales forecasting, stock market prediction, signature verification, handwriting recognition
Industry— Robotics
Security— Fingerprint recognition
Medicine—Image processing, diagnosing, and therapy (see Figure 7.22)

Neural network applications are either packaged software or special-purpose computers built to be *trained,* not programmed. They are developed to closely resemble the human brain in theory and design.

Neural network packages include handwriting recognition software such as Hewlett-Packard's AccuPage. California Scientific Software's BrainMaker can be used to manage investments by recognizing patterns and trends influencing stock prices. Open Sesame! is a general-purpose assistance package designed to improve user performance with a Mac. The program runs in the background, gradually learning the user's personal work habits and then offering to automate actions it has observed. For example, if Open Sesame! notices that you tend to delete outdated files (empty the Trash, on a Mac) before turning off the computer, it will offer to automate this task. See Figure 7.23.

Business Packages

Some business packages can be used by different types of companies, from small to large. For example, a particular accounting package may be used by a small boutique as well as a large department store chain or a fast-food franchise. Other business packages are designed to meet the highly specialized needs of a specific industry or business. Let us consider the following general and industry-specific software.

GENERAL BUSINESS PACKAGES SUCH AS ACCOUNTING SOFTWARE Some small businesses function well using spreadsheet packages for all of their financial and accounting needs. Other businesses, however, need software that is specifically designed to computerize the overall accounting function. A typical accounting program consists of several modules that work interactively. The three most commonly used modules are those that manage the general ledger, accounts receivable, and accounts payable functions. Depending on the nature of the business, inventory or payroll modules may also be added. Other common features of accounting packages include a systems manager program that integrates the modules, specialized report writers, and charting and graphing routines.

A good accounting program includes error-detection procedures and extensive audit trails that enable users or auditors to trace transactions from the general ledger stage through to individual accounts. Such a program should also provide automatic year-end closings, that is, create complete financial statements that summarize the activity for the year.

Accounting software comes in entry-level, midrange, and high-end configurations that are aimed at small, medium-sized, and large businesses, respectively. In other words, horizontal accounting packages are designed for computer systems from micros to mainframes, and they are priced to reflect their com-

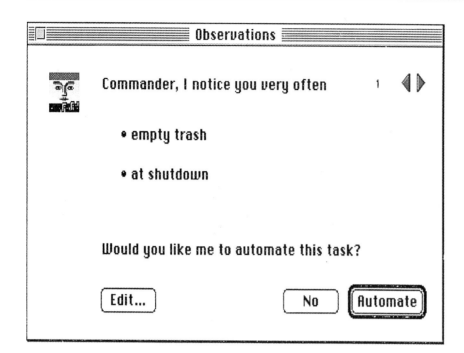

Figure 7.23 *Open Sesame! automates a Macintosh work environment by tracking what you do and when you do it. For example, if it notices that you regularly drag unused files to the trash, it will offer to automatically perform this event on a regularly scheduled basis.*

plexity. Some software publishers have a line of accounting software and upgrade policies that make it possible to start out with one version and move up to a more sophisticated version as the need arises. Peachtree, Computer Associates, and DacEasy have many general business packages including accounting software. See Figure 7.24.

In most cases, an accountant or clerk enters data. In larger businesses, networked versions of accounting programs make it possible for several people to enter data or to handle specific duties, such as billing and writing checks, from different workstations.

Although the modules of an accounting program come ready to run, they usually can be tailored to suit the needs of a particular business. Most packages automatically produce statements, invoices, and paychecks, although a certain amount of formatting is necessary to match the actual output required with the specific forms provided.

Packages such as the accounting software discussed here can be used in a wide variety of organizations. Other types of general business packages include payroll, inventory, and sales management software.

INDUSTRY-SPECIFIC SOFTWARE SUCH AS MEDICAL PACKAGES Many packages have been developed to meet the specialized needs of an industry such as the medical profession (see Figure 7.25). One example is software used to perform the business tasks in optometrists' offices. The software might schedule appointments, maintain patient records, send bills, and keep track of employees' work schedules. It is designed to take into account the specific needs of optometrists, as compared with other groups of professionals such as lawyers, or even more closely related groups such as dentists.

Keep in mind that there are general and specific business packages for both PCs and larger systems. In fact, all types of software packages discussed here are available for both micros and larger systems. Many types were designed originally for mainframes, but versions for micros soon followed. Today, most micro-based software is off-the-shelf, whereas both custom and packaged software are

Figure 7.24 (*a*) *An accounting package like this one allows small businesses to computerize their accounting procedures.* (*b*) *This is a diagram of the steps involved in computerizing accounting procedures.*

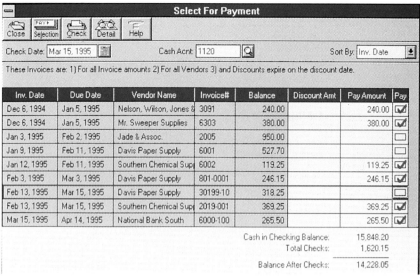

Inv. Date	Due Date	Vendor Name	Invoice#	Balance	Discount Amt	Pay Amount	Pay
Dec 6, 1994	Jan 5, 1995	Nelson, Wilson, Jones &	3091	240.00		240.00	☑
Dec 6, 1994	Jan 5, 1995	Mr. Sweeper Supplies	6303	380.00		380.00	☑
Jan 3, 1995	Feb 2, 1995	Jade & Assoc.	2005	950.00			☐
Jan 9, 1995	Feb 11, 1995	Davis Paper Supply	6001	527.70			☐
Jan 12, 1995	Feb 11, 1995	Southern Chemical Sup	6002	119.25		119.25	☑
Feb 3, 1995	Mar 3, 1995	Davis Paper Supply	801-0001	246.15		246.15	☑
Feb 13, 1995	Mar 15, 1995	Davis Paper Supply	30199-10	318.25			☐
Feb 13, 1995	Mar 15, 1995	Southern Chemical Sup	2019-001	369.25		369.25	☑
Mar 15, 1995	Apr 14, 1995	National Bank South	6000-100	265.50		265.50	☑

Cash in Checking Balance: 15,848.20
Total Checks: 1,620.15
Balance After Checks: 14,228.05

(*a*)

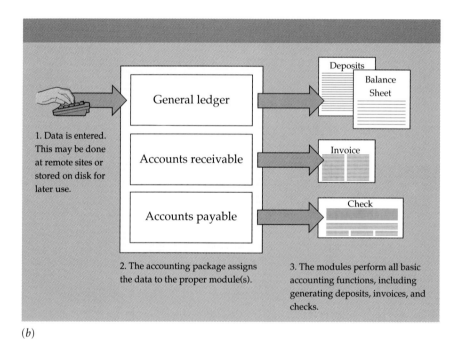

(*b*)

common with mainframes. Because PCs lend themselves to individual use by people with little or no computer background, packaged software is ideal. Mainframe-based companies with more sophisticated processing needs tend to rely more heavily on custom software.

A Step Closer to Information at Your Fingertips. The Timex Data Link watch uses a wireless optical scanning system to receive data from Microsoft software. Hold the watch up to the screen, press a button on the watch to scroll through the personal information like appointment locations and telephone numbers and download the data whenever you need it.

Using a microchip developed by Timex with Motorola, the watch can store about 70 messages. See Figure 7.26.

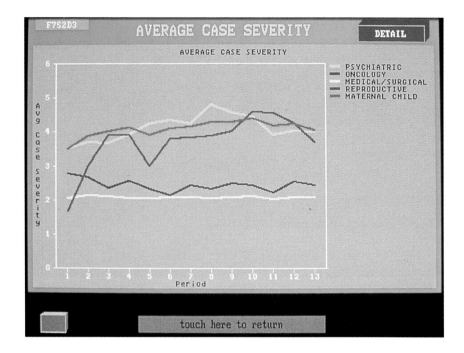

Figure 7.25 *Software for hospitals includes maintaining and reporting on patient data.*

Figure 7.26 *The Timex Data Link can download appointments, phone numbers, time settings, alarms, and To-Do lists from your PC.*

Packages for Consumer Use

Many of the packages we have discussed are employed extensively by home users as well as office workers. Multimedia games, music, videos, encyclopedias, travel guides, and so on are commonly found on home PCs. Word processing, desktop publishing, and graphics packages are almost as prevalent in the home as in the office. Packages like Microsoft's Quicken and Computer Associates' Simply Money are specifically designed as personal financial managers. See Figure 7.27. They enable users to computerize their checkbook processing and provide port-

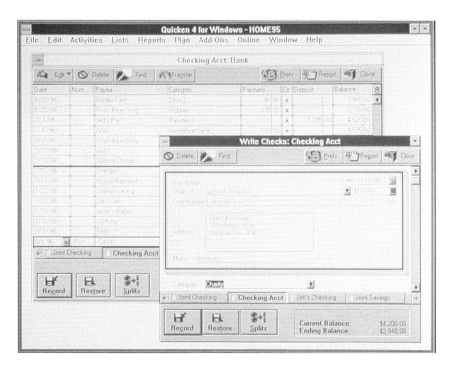

Figure 7.27 *Quicken is used by consumers for writing checks and maintaining checking account information.*

folio management for investors. With access to an online subscriber service, users can track, analyze, and even purchase stocks, bonds, mutual funds, and bank CDs. Quicken comes in a Deluxe version that includes features such as full-motion video tutorials and the *Wall Street Journal Video Guide to Money and Markets.* Microsoft's Bob is a new family information manager with a consumer-oriented "social interface" that replaces the business-oriented Windows display. Home applications use scenes such as the livingroom to designate types of software. Bob has security features that can be used to keep kids away from the household finances.

Self-Test

1. Packages that can produce typeset-quality output with text and graphics appearing on a single page are called _____.
2. (T or F) Most word processing packages have the same capability as desktop publishing software when it comes to formatting text on the computer screen.
3. Multimedia allows you to link not only text but _____.

7.3 CHOOSING AND USING SOFTWARE

Thus far we have discussed some of the widely used software packages. In this section, we consider what users need to know when selecting specific products.

The Make or Buy Decision

Users along with computer professionals need to decide whether to "make or buy"—whether to acquire existing software or to develop custom software for any given application. Many factors should be considered before making such a decision. Consider first the benefits of off-the-shelf software:

- Packaged software is less expensive than custom software. The development costs and the time it takes to complete a top-notch product are considerable; but the manufacturer sells each package for a fraction of its total cost in anticipation of a large number of sales. Thus, an off-the-shelf package that cost millions of dollars to develop may be sold for hundreds of dollars to thousands of people. As a result, both users and developers benefit.

- Packaged software is immediately available, already tested, and thoroughly documented. Users need not wait for development and testing.

- Packaged software is typically supported by features such as tutorials, documentation, manuals, and hot line telephone numbers that provide technical support.

Although application packages have such benefits and some are quite flexible, they rarely satisfy all of an individual's needs. Since such products are

---

Solutions

1. desktop publishing (DTP) software

2. F—Desktop publishing software allows you to view different typefaces and type styles and sizes on the screen just as they will appear when the document is printed.

3. graphics, sound, animation, video

IN A NUTSHELL

TO MAKE OR BUY SOFTWARE?

	PROS	CONS
PACKAGED PROGRAMS	1. Immediately usable on acquisition 2. Widely tested 3. Less expensive for each user 4. Well documented with numerous support features	1. Likely to meet most, but not all, of a user's requirements 2. After acquisition, user is dependent on outside support (e.g., telephone hot lines) rather than having programmers available if modifications are needed or problems arise
CUSTOM PROGRAMS	1. Specifically designed to satisfy individual user needs 2. More easily modified if the need arises 3. Developers readily available to support implementation and modification if needed	1. More expensive to develop and maintain because costs are not shared among many users 2. Takes more time to implement

designed for many types of users, they cannot easily be individualized. On the other hand, they are likely to be more useful for a greater number of users.

Although we use the terms *make* or *buy* when determining whether to acquire packages, a great deal of mainframe software, particularly the more expensive types, is apt to be *leased* rather than purchased. The user pays an annual fee for the right to use the product. Each year, the product is upgraded and the new versions are made available.

Versions of Software

Popular software products are updated with some frequency. Sometimes the new versions have only modest changes and sometimes the changes are significant. Version numbers provide information about the level of the update. Version 2.0, for example, is a significant improvement over 1.0, whereas version 2.2, which has the same integer as 2.0, is likely to have only minor improvements. Software products, like hardware products, are upwardly compatible. A file created using a product with version 1.0 will typically be usable with all newer versions, but files created under newer versions may not be usable with older ones.

When acquiring software, be sure you get the most recent version. Ask about the upgrade policy as well. Some companies sell newer versions to current users at greatly reduced prices.

Evaluating Software Products

CRITERIA The most important factor in evaluating software is, of course, how well the product meets your needs. Remember, though, to consider these additional factors in evaluating application packages.

1. Compatibility with existing hardware and software.
   - Can it be run as is with existing equipment?
   - Can files from other programs be read, or imported, into the package?
   - Can files from the new package be written, or exported, to files created by other programs?
2. Speed.
3. Quality of documentation.

4. Ease of learning.
   - Are online tutorials available?
   - Are the help menus helpful?
5. Ease of use.
   - Are pull-down menus available?
   - Are icons available for selecting commands?
6. Error-handling ability.
7. Technical support.
   - Are there hot lines?
   - Is telephone support available 24 hours a day?
   - Is technical support free?
   - Who pays for the phone call?
8. Upgrade policy.
   - When new versions of the software become available, can users of the previous versions purchase the product at a discount?
   - Can data created using older versions be used without change?
9. Cost of the package.

When you need to evaluate software products, consider the following:

CHECK REVIEWS IN PUBLICATIONS Many magazines like *PC World, PC Week,* and *InfoWorld* provide periodic reviews of software products. There are also technical publications like the Seybold series and *DataPro* that specialize in analysis of hardware and software. Internet newsgroups often contain individual comments regarding popular packages.

PERFORM BENCHMARK TESTS Benchmark tests, or performance tests, can help you determine the efficiency of a product. These tests involve running various programs and measuring the time it takes for the computer to perform the tasks. Computer journals publish results of benchmark tests on different types of software. They enter the same data into a variety of products and compare the results. Using these articles, you can select the product that best meets your needs based on the criteria most important to you.

CHECK OUT THE MANUFACTURER When it comes to software development, reputation is extremely important. It is wise to consult other users of the product. They can provide information about the quality of the product and its documentation, the availability of technical support, and so on.

Where and How to Acquire Software

THE MARKETPLACE As with hardware, there are numerous sources for acquiring application packages; Table 7.2 lists the most common sources. Recall that typically the manufacturer produces the product but a separate vendor or retailer may sell it (you can usually purchase software directly from the manufacturer as well).

SHAREWARE AND PUBLIC DOMAIN SOFTWARE Some software packages are expensive. To spend $500 or more for a micro-based productivity tool, for example, is not uncommon. Some mainframe packages cost tens of thousands of dollars to purchase; others are leased at hefty annual fees. With this in mind, be aware that there are packages in virtually every computing category that can be obtained for little or no cost.

Critical Thinking

Software users realize the importance of technical support. Some software companies provide free telephone support (800 numbers) for a fixed period of time (e.g., 90 days); when the fixed time period has lapsed, they require the user to dial a long distance number or a 900 number for continued support. How do you think the companies enforce this? Do you think the reduced telephone costs are worth the goodwill they might lose by making customers pay for calls?

	Pros	Cons
Mail order	Tends to be inexpensive since the mail-order house has very little overhead	Technical support from the vendor is minimal (although the manufacturer may provide technical support).
Discount stores	Often as inexpensive, or almost as inexpensive, as a mail-order house	Very little support is provided.
Computer, electronic, or retail stores	Tends to be moderately expensive (list price or a little less)	Technical support may be available if personnel are familiar with the product.
Directly from manufacturer	List price	Technical support from the manufacturer is typically available to all users regardless of the source of acquisition. Note that manufacturers put all customers on a mailing list for upgrades if the customer sends in a registration card that accompanies the product.
Online Subscriber Services	You can order software or, in some cases, download programs	Beware of viruses when downloading software!

Table 7.2 *Where to Get Application Packages*

Public domain software, or freeware, refers to noncopyrighted programs that developers make available free of charge. Kermit, a widely used communications package, is in the public domain. **Shareware** is software on the honor system. It is distributed free on a trial basis. If you decide to use it regularly, you should register and pay for it. Then you will receive technical support and upgrade details.

Some shareware and public domain programs are really quite good—desktop managers, utilities, and games are among the most popular. Major computer magazines typically include ads from mail-order houses indicating how such products can be obtained; usually you need to pay the distributor's costs of a few dollars. Also, electronic bulletin boards and subscriber services such as CompuServe or Prodigy provide lists of products that can be downloaded to a microcomputer at no charge. Computer clubs often provide shareware and public domain software as well. The Internet is a widely used source for accessing and downloading public domain software.

The main disadvantages of most shareware and public domain software are (1) they are prone to viruses, which we discuss in the next section, and (2) they frequently have inadequate documentation.

The Human Factor: Security and Safety

LICENSING AND COPY PROTECTING SOFTWARE Most software that is sold or leased is accompanied by a licensing agreement that specifies how the product should be used. When the program is first loaded into the computer, the licensing agreement asks for confirmation that the user agrees to its terms.

Licensing agreements indicate the number of copies users are legally permitted to make. Some licenses explicitly permit users to make as many copies of the software as they need. Others ask the user to make a single copy for backup purposes only. Still others permit copies to be made but ask that only one be used at a given time; that is, you can make one for home, one for the office, and one for school, but you should only use one at a time. The license prohibits someone from using your office copy while you are using your copy at home.

If an organization has many users who need access to a product at the same time, the organization may be able to obtain a **site license.** With a site license, the manufacturer or vendor agrees to sell or lease the rights to a fixed number of copies of the software for a set price. Site licenses are particularly useful in organizations that have networks.

Some software manufacturers enforce their licensing agreements by **copy protecting** their software. Copy-protected disks contain some programmed feature that limits the number of copies that can be made. Sometimes a hardware feature is used instead of software for copy protection. In such a case, the hardware device must be connected to the computer for the software to run. Most software manufacturers, however, do not copy protect their software; rather, they rely on the user's honesty and integrity to adhere to the licensing stipulation.

Making copies of software in violation of the licensing agreement is not only dishonest, it is illegal. In fact, some organizations have actually been sued for such violations, and the software manufacturers typically win such lawsuits. Despite existing laws and efforts by some manufacturers to have them enforced rigorously, it is estimated that software "piracy" costs the computing industry over $2 billion per year!

From a practical point of view, it is fairly easy for individual users to make extra copies of software—especially software that is not copy protected—for themselves or others. Even if the software is copy protected, other packages are available that have been designed to override copy-protection features. Moreover, the likelihood of an individual being sued for copyright infringement is remote.

The issue becomes one of ethics rather than legality. Illegally (or unethically) copying software is not much different from illegally using someone else's property. The main difference is that when you copy software illegally, you are less likely to get caught. Illegal copying of software is not unlike duplicating licensed videos or copying pages from a book.

COMPUTER VIRUSES Hackers are computer-proficient hobbyists who take pride in violating systems, breaking codes, or otherwise using computers in unauthorized ways. News stories relate tales of individuals who successfully gain access to systems, sometimes just for fun and sometimes for more malevolent reasons. Often they are caught and punished, but sometimes a crime is not even recognized as such for months or years. Although we may be amused by some of the antics of hackers who gain unauthorized access to computers, the government views them as criminals. Indeed, sometimes they pose a real threat to data security and integrity, and even to society as a whole.

Some hackers have moved from breaking into systems to wreaking havoc with software. They add some instructions to operating systems or application software that can not only destroy the product but also "infect" every file on disk. These **viruses** have been known to cripple entire computer systems for long periods of time. Viruses abound and just as soon as a new one is introduced, an anti-virus program for it is marketed. It might be more efficient if the hackers who create and spread the viruses would develop a "vaccine" along with it. Maybe someday they will.

Viruses, like any infection, can be prevented if people are careful and always protect themselves. Treat your disks as you would your body, like a temple. Do not bring in anything unless you know where it has been. Always use protection—in the form of an anti-virus program. Get tested often to prevent the spread of the disease. And—most importantly—use common sense.

Critical Thinking

Copyright infringement suits relating to software are numerous. Lotus sued Borland several years ago because Borland's Quattro Pro menu was very similar to the Lotus 1-2-3 menu. Lotus won. Stac Electronics sued Microsoft claiming that Microsoft's DOS 6.0 data compression software used code that was the same as code in its popular Stacker product. Stac Electronics won. Should software developers be permitted to copy or slightly alter components of existing software in order to create better products?

As a computer user, you should be aware of the danger of computer viruses just as you are aware of the danger of any infectious disease. Take precautionary steps to minimize the risk to your system. One practical step you can take is to avoid copying other people's files. You do not know where they have been and you do not, therefore, know whether they carry a virus. Although this may sound like a lesson in health education, it is relevant to computing. Many organizations have not only increased security to prevent viruses but they have pur-

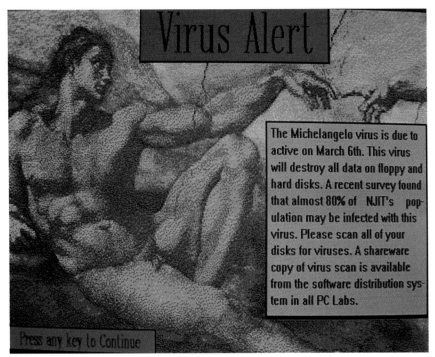

(a)

Figure 7.28 *Anti-virus program screen displays. (a) This screen display shows how you would detect a virus. (b) This screen display shows how you would remove a virus from your system.*

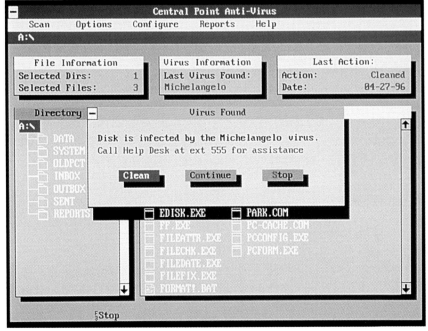

(b)

chased *anti-virus* programs—software designed to detect viruses and eliminate their threat. See Figure 7.28. Organizations and individuals with their own computers should consider the following strategy suggested by the National Computer Security Association, Washington, D.C., to prevent PCs from being infected by a virus.

1. Back up disks frequently. Maintain two or three sets of backups. Be aware that if a virus is "timed" to go off after a three-month period, for example, it could also be on your backup disks. If a virus is detected, a virus removal program should be used to remove the virus code from the disk or corrupted files. As a last resort, your hard disk may need to be reformatted and files reinstalled if the virus code cannot be removed. This recovery procedure can, however, be time consuming, especially if you have many programs on your hard disk.

2. Test new software on a specially designated "test" PC. If there is a virus present, testing on a test PC will ensure that it is not copied to and shared among working PCs throughout your office.

3. Use a virus detector program like VirusScan.

4. Before running files downloaded from subscriber services, the Internet, or publicly accessible bulletin board services, test them for viruses.

Ethical issues in computing including those related to software will be discussed again in Chapter 13.

Self-Test

1. (T or F) Off-the-shelf packages are generally more expensive than custom software.

2. (T or F) Version 2.0 of a software product is a significant improvement over 1.0, whereas version 2.2 is likely to have only modest improvements over 2.0.

3. A test that helps to determine the efficiency of a software product is called a _____ test.

4. Software that is available for minimal cost to anyone and that may be freely copied is called _____.

5. (T or F) Making copies of software in violation of the licensing agreement is illegal.

6. A _____ is a set of instructions that when added to an operating system or application program can destroy the product and even infect every file on disk.

Solutions

1. F

2. T—Version 2.2 has the same integer as 2.0.

3. benchmark

4. shareware or public domain software (freeware)

5. T

6. virus

CHAPTER SUMMARY

7.1 A Review of Application Software

Systems software supervises overall processing; application software satisfies user needs. Application software can be purchased or leased as a package or it can be custom-designed, that is, written specifically for individual users. Integrated packages include word processing, spreadsheet, database management, and some e-mail functions—the four basic productivity tools. An integrated package employs one basic type of user interface; that is, the command structure and menu system for all its components are the same. A ROM-resident package is software that is hardwired into the computer. A **suite** is a set of full-blown productivity tools sold at a reduced price.

Desktop accessories typically include features such as on-screen calculators, electronic card files, notepads, and automatic dialing from the program's phone directory (if a modem is attached). Some desktop accessories are TSR programs (*terminate and stay resident*), which means that when they are loaded into main memory, they remain there even though other software is in use.

Utilities and system optimizers enable users to manage data and program files on their disks. A system optimizer is an example of a utility program, which is software that performs relatively standardized tasks that are often needed by all or most computer users.

Project management software allows users to set up schedules and allocate personnel and resources for projects. The project's progress can be monitored, and personnel and resources reallocated as needed.

Personal information managers (PIMs) combine features of project management software and desktop organizers for a manager's personal use.

Communications software allows the user to set parameters that allow computers to communicate with one another.

Multimedia software enables users to create presentations, educational and training products, and games with text, graphics, sound, animation, and video. **Hyperlinking** is the linking of sections and components in such software. **Presentation graphics packages, multimedia authoring packages,** and video software are used for creating multimedia applications. **Runtime** versions of multimedia software can be used for running applications, not creating new ones.

7.2 Specialized Application Packages: The Power Tools of Today

Desktop publishing (DTP) software integrates text and graphics in documents and creates sophisticated page layouts that are professional looking and of typeset quality.

Graphics software refers to programs with tools for drawing, charting, and presenting illustrations. **Clip art** is a database of graphic displays that can be added to documents, printed, or modified. A major type of graphics program is illustration software. Painting programs and drawing programs are types of **illustration packages.** Painting programs create **bit-mapped graphics,** which consist of patterns of dots. Drawing programs create visuals by combining lines, arcs, circles, squares, and other shapes, rather than dots, to produce **vector graphics.**

Computer-aided design (CAD) packages are highly sophisticated drawing packages that engineers and architects use to create complex drawings. **Computer-aided manufacturing (CAM)** packages help engineers design the manufacturing components in a factory or production facility.

Study Objective

1. Describe how application packages have progressed to include more functions.

Study Objective

2. Discuss the capabilities of today's software "power tools."

Document viewers enable files and clips created by different products and on different computers to be standardized for viewing or transmitting over a network.

Statistical packages perform analysis of data, such as determining standard deviations and variances.

Artificial intelligence refers to computing applications that simulate human thinking. Three types of applications fall within this category: (1) An expert system is software designed to model or simulate the performance of a human expert in a technical field. (2) Virtual reality is a way of enabling people to participate interactively in 3-D environments created by computer. (3) Neural networks take patterns of data and generalize from them.

There are business packages designed to meet specific business needs for organizations of all sizes. Examples include accounting, payroll, and sales packages. There are business packages designed to meet the unique needs of a specific type of business such as a medical office, dental office, or grocery store. There are also packages such as financial software and calendar generators that are designed for personal use.

Study Objective

3. Demonstrate how to select the right software package for a particular application.

7.3 Choosing and Using Software

Users, along with computer professionals, need to decide whether to acquire off-the-shelf software or to develop custom software for any given application. **Benchmark,** or performance, **tests** can be used to determine the efficiency of a software package.

Public domain software consists of noncopyrighted programs that developers make available free of charge. **Shareware** is software that can be obtained with little or no cost; often the developer asks the user to pay a small fee to help share handling and packaging costs.

Licensing agreements indicate the number of copies users are legally permitted to make. With a **site license,** the manufacturer or vendor agrees to sell or lease the rights to a fixed number of copies of the software for a set price. Some software manufacturers enforce their licensing agreements by **copy protecting** their software to limit the number of copies that can be made.

Hackers are computer-proficient hobbyists who use computers in unauthorized ways. Some hackers or unethical programmers introduce **viruses** into systems by adding instructions to operating systems or application software that can destroy the product and infect files on a disk.

KEY TERMS

Benchmark test, *p. 246*
Bit-mapped graphics, *p. 232*
Clip art, *p. 230*
Computer-aided design (CAD), *p. 233*
Computer-aided manufacturing (CAM), *p. 233*
Copy protection, *p. 248*
Desktop accessory, *p. 221*

Desktop publishing (DTP), *p. 234*
Document viewers, *p. 234*
Graphics software, *p. 230*
Hyperlinking, *p. 227*
Illustration package, *p. 231*
Morphing, *p. 234*
Multimedia authoring package, *p. 229*
Presentation graphics package, *p. 228*
Project management software, *p. 224*

Public domain software, *p. 247*
Runtime, *p. 229*
Shareware, *p. 247*
Site license, *p. 248*
Statistical package, *p. 237*
Suites, *p. 220*
Vector graphics, *p. 232*
Virus, *p. 248*

CHAPTER SELF-TEST

1. (T or F) Desktop publishing allows you to create documents that are similar in quality to typeset documents.

2. (T or F) Text editing is usually easier to do in a desktop publishing package than with word processing software.

3. What are the two types of graphics used in drawing packages?

4. Graphing and charting programs are commonly referred to as "business graphics" or _____ graphics.

5. What do we call specialized drawing software that helps architects and engineers create complex designs?

6. (T or F) Communications software is simplified word processing software that can be used to write short letters and memos.

7. (T or F) PageMaker is an example of a DTP package.

8. (T or F) The purpose of desktop accessories is to provide an interface between the user and the operating system.

9. Multimedia software combines text with _____.

10. (T or F) CAD programs use bit-mapped graphics.

11. What do we call software that can be used freely by anyone, without charge?

REVIEW QUESTIONS

1. Suppose you are a manager and want to acquire a desktop publishing package. What sources would you use to select three packages that are likely to satisfy your needs? Prepare a list of questions you would ask vendors who sell these three products.

2. Suppose you are a sales manager and wish to computerize your sales records. Prepare a list of questions you would ask your staff to determine whether to purchase software from (1) a mail-order firm, (2) a discount software house or electronics company, or (3) a traditional retail store.

CRITICAL THINKING EXERCISES

1. The United States controlled 40% of the world software market in 1994, but the trend toward client-server computing may begin to allow less-developed countries to compete more effectively. The migration of business applications from expensive mainframes to easy-to-operate microcomputers and networks enables lower-budget organizations to develop software. The decline in mainframe and

---

Solutions

1. T

2. F

3. bit-mapped graphics; vector graphics

4. presentation

5. computer-aided design (CAD) programs

6. F

7. T

8. F

9. animations, graphics, sound, and video

10. F

11. public domain software or freeware

minicomputer hardware and software sales has caused layoffs at IBM, DEC, Wang, and other computer industry giants, while software firms such as Computer Associates International, Symantec, and Microsoft Corp. have grown quickly. Commercial software industries are emerging in countries such as Venezuela, Hungary, India, Mexico, Russia, and the Philippines. While 85% of software used in the United States comes from domestic firms, the U.S. software industry may soon lose its predominance in the global software market.[1] Why is it predicted that less-developed countries might increase their market share of software and what might U.S. firms do to retain their preeminence?

2. When human beings are fully responsible for decisions, accountability in the case of an error is clear. If a mortgage agent approved a loan to an applicant who later defaulted or a doctor prescribed medication for a patient who had an adverse reaction, or an emergency medical service attendant failed to use a respirator on a patient who later died, responsibility is clear. But who is responsible if the expert system CLUES makes a poor loan decision or the medical expert system MYCIN makes a mistake? How should accountability—both legally and morally—be determined in such instances?

3. Multimedia educational products are likely to be more entertaining and interesting than text-based products, but do you think that people learn more using them? What about retention—are users more likely to retain the information they get from multimedia educational tools?

4. The American Stock Exchange (AMEX) has developed the Market Expert Surveillance System (MESS) to help the Equities Surveillance department investigate possible violations of insider trading rules. Detecting insider trading involves reasoning based on numerical calculations and on logic. MESS includes rules related to market manipulation and unusual activity, but it focuses primarily on insider trading. Data is obtained from a mainframe on stock prices and volumes surrounding the date in question, which is usually the date of a company announcement. The data is downloaded to a file that is read by a Lotus spreadsheet, with which the analyst interacts. A Screen Sculptor program provides forms for selecting the conditions about the news announcement that apply in a specific case. MESS backward-chains through its 160 rules to arrive at its recommendations.[2] What are the potential benefits—and risks—from using such a surveillance system?

---

[1]Can the U.S. stay on top?, Jones, T. Capers, *Information Week,* Jan. 10, 1995, n. 458, p. 47(1).

[2]Market expert surveillance system, Lucas, Henry C., Jr., *Communications of the ACM,* Dec. 1994, v. 36, n. 12, p. 26(8).

Case Study

Multimedia Messaging

An advanced multimedia messaging system from AT&T now combines voice messaging and voice response, allowing users to send and receive voice, text, and visual messages using the same technology. Called INTUITY, this system can convert messages from one form to another, add voice messages to faxes, receive video messages, and select and forward voice mail, among other multimedia functions, all with a desktop computer.

According to AT&T, the system is easy to operate both in the office and on the road, so that, for instance, a business traveler could call the office from a pay phone and get her e-mail messages read aloud to her as voice mail. Another advantage is that the system allows communication to take place at any time, so that users can leave messages in any form—text, audio, or video—regardless of whether the recipient is there to read, hear, or see them at the time.

Accessibility, flexibility, and simplicity will be the key features of the system, and AT&T is already planning for improvements that will make the system even better in the future. While it is now designed to integrate desktop and personal computers with electronic mail and telephone lines, plans for the future include enabling users to hear voice messages on their personal computers and to use voice activation to operate the system. The voice messaging function will also become available in several languages and will eventually include telecommunications devices for the deaf.

AT&T's multimedia messaging system called INTUITY enables people to send and receive images and video messages, as well as faxes and e-mail.

Analysis

1. Do you think voice and video messages, as compared to text, really enhance communications? Explain your answer.

2. Describe some of the ways that multimedia can help the handicapped, in addition to the one described in this case.

Source: On and about AT&T, *Edge*, v. 9, n. 286, p. 14, Jan. 17, 1994.

CHAPTER 8
Developing Custom Software

8.1 THE SOFTWARE DEVELOPER

In-house Software Developers—Analysts, Programmers, and Users

Outside Consultants

8.2 SOFTWARE DEVELOPMENT CYCLE

Develop the Program Specifications with the Help of the Users

Design the Program Logic

Code and Translate the Program

Test the Program Until It Is Fully Debugged

Implement the Program

Maintain the Program

Complete the Documentation for the Program

Software Development: Art or Science?

8.3 PROGRAMMING TECHNIQUES FOR STANDARDIZING SOFTWARE DEVELOPMENT

Modular Programming

Structured Programming

Top-Down Programming

Reusable Code

Object-Oriented Programming

Visual Programming

8.4 FIVE GENERATIONS OF PROGRAMMING LANGUAGES

Machine Language: The First Generation

Assembly Language: The Second Generation

High-Level Languages: The Third Generation (3GLs)

Fourth-Generation Languages (4GLs)

Fifth-Generation Languages (5GLs)

G etting computers to accomplish the tasks users want done requires four basic components: hardware to enter and process data, and to produce the necessary information; software to drive the hardware; people to control the overall operations; and connectivity to enable all components to interact with one another effectively.

Users and computer professionals first try to acquire off-the-shelf, or packaged, software to accomplish the needed tasks. Such software is often readily available, inexpensive, and well documented. But sometimes people need specially prepared software with features that are not available as a package. In this chapter we consider some of the main programming languages used to write custom programs, and their features.

Study Objectives

After reading this chapter, you should be able to:

1. **Describe the advantages of custom software.**

2. **List the steps in the software development cycle.**

3. **Explain the reasons why standardized program development is so important.**

4. **Show how the development of programming languages has enhanced the software development process.**

▨ 8.1 THE SOFTWARE DEVELOPER

When an organization decides to have software specifically developed for its needs rather than to purchase or lease packages, the company's requirements are likely to be unique or very specific; in such instances, modifying existing packages will not suffice. In such a case, either company employees or outside consultants need to develop the software.

In-house Software Developers— Analysts, Programmers, and Users

Organizations with an in-house computing staff often have their own employees develop software. An organization's own staff is familiar with company policy and operating procedures. Moreover, as computing professionals, they have the expertise to develop, implement, and document software.

In most medium-sized to large organizations, systems analysts supervise software development undertaken by programmers. The systems analyst and the future users of the software work closely with programmers to develop a clear understanding of each program's purpose.

The systems analyst focuses on user needs and determines not only how these needs can be met, but also on how the new software can be integrated efficiently into information systems. Since *users* are the people most knowledgeable about the tasks that the software must perform, their needs must be considered first. Users, however, are not computer professionals, so they do not always know how to define their computing needs. To ensure effective computerization, the systems analyst serves as a kind of liaison between users who understand business problems and programmers who actually develop the software.

In some companies, a computer professional called a **programmer analyst** may serve as both programmer and systems analyst. This person possesses pro-

Study Objective

1. Describe the advantages of custom software.

▪ɴ A NUTSHELL

TYPES OF SOFTWARE

1. Operating system software
   - Controls the operations of the computer
   - Manages and monitors computer activities
2. Application software
   - Designed to satisfy specific user needs
   - Some programs are available off-the-shelf in packaged form
   - Other programs are customized for individual users

IN A NUTSHELL

IN-HOUSE DEVELOPERS VS SOFTWARE DEVELOPMENT FIRMS

IN-HOUSE DEVELOPERS

1. Programmers are familiar with the company but not necessarily with the application area.
2. Because programmers are employees, the company has better control of the development process.
3. After programs are implemented, programmers are usually still available to answer queries or make modifications if the need arises.

OUTSIDE CONSULTANTS

1. Programmers are hired based on their familiarity with a specific application area or with the type of company.
2. The price for the software is set in advance, typically on a contract or fixed-fee basis.
3. Once a program is accepted, it may be more difficult to track down the developer if modifications are necessary.

---

gramming and systems analysis skills and is responsible for integrating new software into an information system. Similarly, users at smaller companies sometimes take on an added role of assisting developers or even doing some program development themselves if they are computer proficient.

Outside Consultants

A company may need customized programs but may not have an in-house computing staff. Even if it has an in-house computing staff, the staff may be committed to different projects or may lack technical expertise in a particular area. In such instances, freelance software development firms act as outside consultants.

One main reason for using outside software consultants is that many of them have expertise in a particular application area. Some developers may specialize in areas such as payroll, accounting, or inventory. Other developers may specialize in a type of business such as production, accounting, or retail sales. If an outside consultant has expertise in the area being computerized, the software developed is likely to better suit the needs of the company.

Another reason for hiring outside consultants is that it is often less expensive than assigning the work to an in-house staff. The cost of the project is negotiated in advance, and overhead and fringe benefits are not part of the price.

Critical Thinking

A major complaint of some users is that the custom software developed for them does not really meet their needs. Can you think of measures that could be taken to minimize the risk that the software developed is unsatisfactory? What clauses might you include in a contract with freelance programmers to improve the chances for success?

Self-Test

1. The two ways in which application programs can be obtained are by _____ and _____.

2. Who develops custom programs?

3. Name the three categories of employees who determine program specifications.

Solutions

1. purchasing packages; developing customized programs

2. in-house software developers or outside consultants

3. the user, systems analyst, programmer (Sometimes a programmer analyst wears two hats, that of a programmer and systems analyst.)

8.2 SOFTWARE DEVELOPMENT CYCLE

All programs should be designed in a systematic and scientific manner. We refer to the design steps as the **software development cycle.** Table 8.1 illustrates these steps in the cycle.

Software development is considered a cycle because the process is apt to be repeated. After programs have been written and used for a period of time, they may become outdated, or users may find that their needs have changed. When these situations occur, the development cycle is repeated and new software is produced to meet the changing needs. Keep in mind that this development cycle applies to the creation of software packages as well as to custom programs. Now we will detail each of the cycle's seven steps.

Study Objective

2. List the steps in the software development cycle.

Develop the Program Specifications with the Help of the Users

First, the tasks to be accomplished by the software must be defined clearly. Does this seem self-evident? You would be astounded at the amount of software that is written without a clear understanding of user needs. In many cases, the systems analysts simply did not define the problems to be solved in a precise way. An important first step, then, is to have software developers and users agree on program specifications that indicate what the software is to accomplish.

Design the Program Logic

Once the problem is clearly defined by the user and systems analyst and is described as a set of program specifications, the programmer or software developer can begin to design a program. First, developers create an algorithm, which is similar to a recipe: It is a sequential listing of all the steps needed to obtain the desired output from the input to be processed. The steps must be logical; that is, they must be listed in the order in which they are to be performed. For example, here is an algorithm for preparing a customer invoice:

1. Read the account number, the unit price of the item purchased, and the quantity purchased.
2. Calculate the bill by multiplying the unit price by the quantity purchased.
3. Print the account number and the total bill.
4. Repeat the process for all customer invoices.

Each of these steps accomplishes a given task or tasks; collectively they meet the program's requirements.

1. Develop the program specifications with the help of the users.
2. Design the logic to be used in the program.
3. Code the program and translate it into machine language.
4. Test the program until it is fully debugged.
5. Install, or implement, the program.
6. Maintain the program.
7. Document the program.

Table 8.1 *Software Development Cycle*

In addition to planning the logical steps in a program, the programmer should include error-control procedures. For example, our sample algorithm will multiply the unit price by the quantity purchased. A full program should include procedures that first ensure that the numeric data necessary for performing calculations has been entered and that it has reasonable values. In this case, the unit price should be within the actual range of acceptable unit prices (e.g., < 500 and > 2.50).

A number of problem-solving tools can be used to plan the overall logic of a program. The three most common tools are flowcharts, pseudocode, and hierarchy charts. We begin with flowcharts; these were once the most popular planning tools but have since been replaced in many organizations by a combined use of pseudocode and hierarchy charts.

FLOWCHARTS A **flowchart** is a pictorial representation of the logic flow to be used in a program. It illustrates the major elements of the program and how they will logically integrate. A flowchart is to a program what a blueprint is to a building. Before architects begin to build a building, they draw a blueprint to ensure that all components fit together effectively and efficiently. For the same reasons, many programmers choose a flowchart as their problem-solving tool before writing a program. As with architectural blueprints, the diagrams should

Figure 8.1 *Dividing a program into modules, or subprograms, for specific procedural tasks simplifies program structure. These modules can then be used to build other programs. In this flowchart, a gross pay is being calculated.*

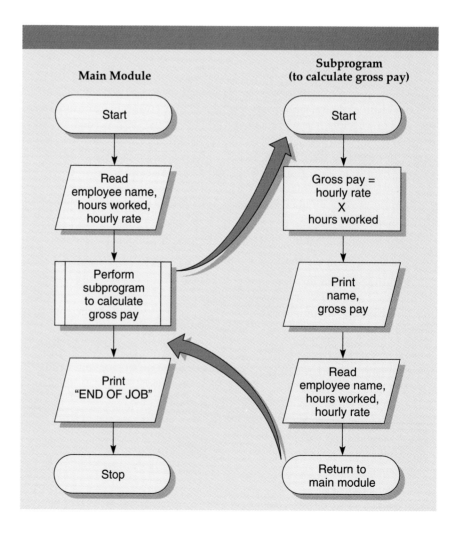

be discussed with users before any actual development work begins to minimize misunderstandings that may result in dissatisfaction later. The flow lines in a flowchart depict the logical flow of instructions in a program. Examine the flowchart in Figure 8.1, which shows the process for calculating an employee's gross pay. The program developed using this flowchart will read data, transfer control to a subprogram that calculates the gross pay, and print the results.

Figure 8.2*a* illustrates a flowchart template, which contains flowchart symbols that programmers can trace when drawing a flowchart. Figure 8.2*b* lists and describes each of the symbols. Each symbol denotes a type of operation. The programmer writes a note inside each symbol to indicate the specific function to be performed.

PSEUDOCODE The use of flowcharts as a planning tool has waned in recent years because flowcharts for large, complex programs are often cumbersome to draw and difficult to understand. Also, it is difficult to make modifications to a flowchart without completely redrawing it. Finally, because a flowchart is frequently very long, the logical structures can be difficult to follow. For these reasons, programmers are now more likely to use an alternative design tool called **pseudocode** (literally, "false code"), which consists of English-like statements (as opposed to symbols) to plan a program's logic. Pseudocode need not indicate *all* the processing details, but it should carefully describe the overall *flow of program logic*. Pseudocode is popular because it can easily represent all the programming structures that programmers need and because its English-like terms are easy to learn and understand.

Figure 8.3 illustrates pseudocode for depicting program logic. Compare the flowchart in Figure 8.1 to the pseudocode; both are describing the same program logic, but in different ways. A programmer commonly uses one or the other as a planning tool, depending on the preferences of the organization. The programs illustrated throughout this chapter will use the logic described in these figures as their basic starting point.

IN A NUTSHELL

Flowcharts use *symbols* to plan and illustrate logic while pseudocode uses *words*.

Figure 8.2 *(a) A flowchart template. (Continued on the next page.)*

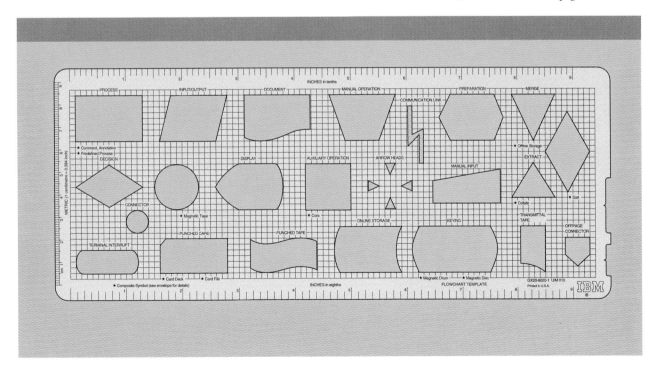

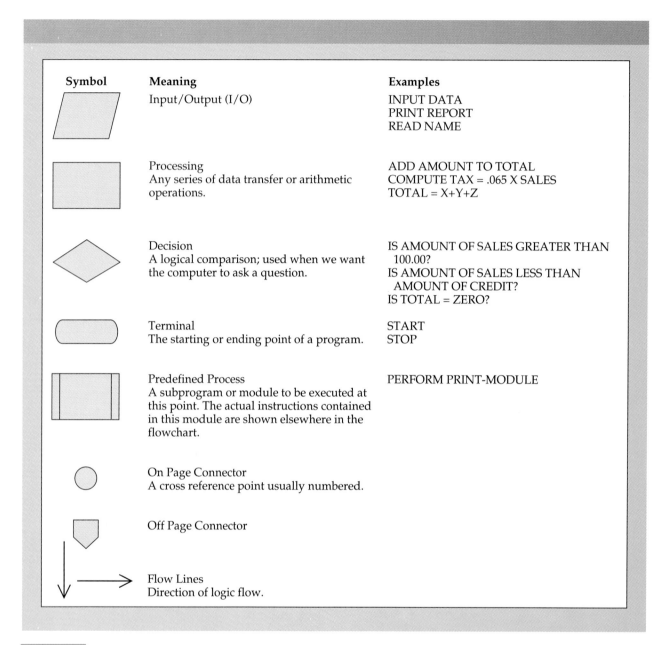

Symbol	Meaning	Examples
	Input/Output (I/O)	INPUT DATA PRINT REPORT READ NAME
	Processing Any series of data transfer or arithmetic operations.	ADD AMOUNT TO TOTAL COMPUTE TAX = .065 X SALES TOTAL = X+Y+Z
	Decision A logical comparison; used when we want the computer to ask a question.	IS AMOUNT OF SALES GREATER THAN 100.00? IS AMOUNT OF SALES LESS THAN AMOUNT OF CREDIT? IS TOTAL = ZERO?
	Terminal The starting or ending point of a program.	START STOP
	Predefined Process A subprogram or module to be executed at this point. The actual instructions contained in this module are shown elsewhere in the flowchart.	PERFORM PRINT-MODULE
	On Page Connector A cross reference point usually numbered.	
	Off Page Connector	
	Flow Lines Direction of logic flow.	

Figure 8.2 *(continued) (b) Each symbol in a flowchart refers to a specific computer operation.*

HIERARCHY CHARTS Flowcharts and pseudocode are tools for designing program logic. **Hierarchy charts,** sometimes called **structure charts,** illustrate how programs are segmented into subprograms, or modules, and how the modules actually relate to one another. We will see later on that subdividing a program into modules makes software easier to develop, use, and reuse in other applications.

Figure 8.3 *In pseudocode, English words are used to express program logic.*

START
    READ Name, Hours, Rate
    PERFORM subprogram to calculate Pay
    PRINT Name, Pay
STOP

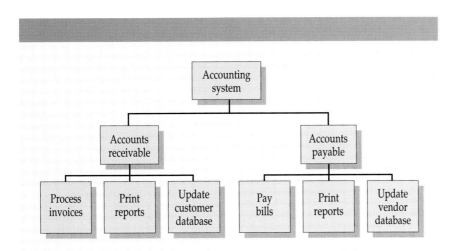

Figure 8.4 *Hierarchy charts break a large task down into smaller tasks, which then become subprograms, or modules.*

Figure 8.4 is a hierarchy chart for an accounting system. Each box represents a major subprogram, or **module,** in the system. The accounting program is subdivided into two modules: accounts receivable and accounts payable. The next level in the hierarchy chart represents separate modules within each subprogram. Each of these modules may then be divided further so that complex hierarchy charts can consist of many levels. Note, however, that a hierarchy chart does not focus on the detailed design elements for each module. Rather, it helps to ensure that all program components fit together logically.

In summary, programmers typically draw a flowchart or write pseudocode to design the program logic. For larger programs, they prepare a hierarchy chart to keep track of the way modules interrelate in the overall design.

Code and Translate the Program

The planning tools just described are used to develop an acceptable program design. Once the design and the logic are agreed on by the programmer, user, and systems analyst, the programmer writes, or codes, the instructions in one of a wide variety of programming languages. The programming language that is selected depends on the resources available, the expertise of the programmer, and the application. As you will learn later in this chapter, there are many programming languages, each best suited for a particular set of tasks.

To actually be executed, however, a program must be in **machine language,** the computer's own internal language. Each type of computer has its own machine language that is designed to be as efficient as possible. The one com-

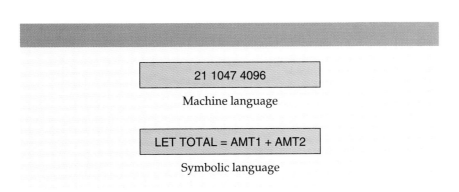

Machine language

Symbolic language

Figure 8.5 *Machine language code is complex because it uses actual machine addresses and operation codes, so that there is no need for translation.*

monality among machine languages is complexity: they all use actual storage addresses and complicated operation codes (Figure 8.5) to process data.

Because of the complexity of machine languages and the fact that they are different for each type of computer, most programs are *not written* in machine language. They are written instead in symbolic languages, such as Visual Basic or C++, which are much easier for programmers to use. **Symbolic languages** use instructions, such as INPUT or +, instead of complex operation codes. They allow the programmer to assign actual names to storage locations.

A program written in a symbolic language is not, however, executable in that form. It cannot be executed until it has been first translated, or converted, into machine language. The computer itself performs this translation process by means of a translator program. This translator reads a symbolic program as input and converts it to output, which is the machine language equivalent. The symbolic program is called the **source program,** and the translated program in machine language is called the **object program.**

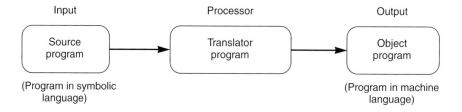

Test the Program Until It Is Fully Debugged

Debugging means finding and correcting all coding and logic errors, or "bugs," in a program. Debugging begins even before the program is translated. The first debugging procedure is **desk-checking** the program. This is the process in which the programmer manually traces through the program, from beginning to end, visually checking for coding errors, called **syntax errors,** which can be simple typing mistakes or violations in the rules of the symbolic language. Most syntax errors can be located by carefully desk-checking a program. Keying INPUTT instead of INPUT, for example, may cause a syntax error. If syntax errors are not caught before the program is entered into the computer, the language's translator program will generally find them and print an error message. Keep in mind that programs cannot be fully translated into machine language until all syntax errors have been corrected.

The first step, then, in the debugging process is to eliminate all syntax errors. But programs without syntax errors are not necessarily completely correct. The program may be coded perfectly but still generate incorrect output or no output at all. Incorrect output is typically the result of logic errors. A **logic error** may occur because there is a mistake in the sequencing of instructions or because the wrong instructions were used. Mistakes in logic result in run-time errors, which means that the output is incorrect or that the program run was terminated. A main debugging task, then, is to ensure that the program runs and the output is correct.

Program testing is crucial in pinpointing logic errors. A program with a logic error may produce correct results most of the time, but incorrect results when some unanticipated input is entered. For example, a payroll program may correctly calculate paychecks for employees who work up to 40 hours per week, but it may incorrectly calculate paychecks involving overtime pay. A logic error causes this program to process data incorrectly when hours exceed 40. Such a logic error will be detected only if test data includes situations requiring overtime pay.

Some newer programming languages have **interactive debuggers** that help programmers find errors by stopping at certain breakpoints and displaying various program components. This enables software developers to step through the logic as machine instructions are being executed.

All logic errors must be detected and corrected before a program can be implemented. The following three techniques help to eliminate logic errors:

1. Prepare test data with great care.
   Make certain that the test data used as input during the debugging phase incorporates all possible types of input, that the program includes tests for specific conditions, and that the test data includes all realistic values. Programs must be written to anticipate any conceivable condition and to process data accordingly. If not, then Murphy's Law is sure to apply: If it is possible for something to go wrong in a program, eventually it will go wrong.

2. Compare computer output with manual output.
   Using the test data, manually compute the results expected from a program run. Compare actual computer output to the expected output. If there is a discrepancy between what should happen in a program and what actually does happen, then the problem must be found and resolved. Whenever an error occurs, the program must be corrected, retranslated, and tested again to ensure that it produces correct output. A program normally requires many test runs before it is fully debugged.

3. Perform a structured walkthrough.
   For long or complex programs, it is often helpful to have a programming team manually "walk through" the logic of a program to ensure that the sequence in which modules are executed is correct and to verify that the program will run efficiently.

Testing a program with all types of input and including many error-control routines minimizes the risks that errors will go undetected.

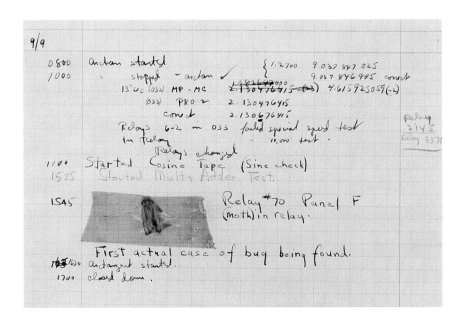

Implement the Program

After a program has been thoroughly tested and debugged, it is ready to be implemented. Typically, custom programs are implemented so that they can run on a regularly scheduled basis. A payroll program, for example, may need to be run weekly, whereas a program that produces customer bills might be run monthly.

Before a new program can be implemented, a conversion plan must be carefully developed and monitored to ensure a smooth transition from the old set of procedures to the new one. The staff must also be thoroughly trained to assist in the conversion and to ensure that implementation on a regularly scheduled basis proceeds smoothly.

A program is usually implemented as part of an overall, integrated information system. An accounting information system, for example, is likely to have several programs *all* of which will require an integrated implementation process. We discuss implementation techniques for information systems in Chapter 11.

Maintain the Program

Studies have shown that only about one-quarter of a programmer's time is spent in developing new software. The remaining three-quarters is spent maintaining existing software. Software maintenance falls into two broad categories: (1) correcting errors and making the software easier to use and more standardized and (2) making modifications to accommodate changing needs.

Increasing the ease of use of a program and eliminating even minor bugs improve user satisfaction. Many businesses hire **maintenance programmers** whose main responsibility is to make such improvements to existing software. If a program is designed properly at the start, modifications will be minor.

All organizations have changing needs, and software is continually being modified to meet those needs. For example, an accounting department may need to have a program modified to incorporate new accounting procedures or changes in the tax laws. Often, users may want the software to perform additional tasks that were not in the original specifications. Thus, new modules may need to be developed to enhance existing software.

Complete the Documentation for the Program

Documentation, which explains every facet of a program to the user, should be prepared on an ongoing basis—as the software is being developed, tested, and implemented. Some documentation is built into the program itself as comments, but most documentation takes the form of printed user manuals. Some parts of the manual explain how to use the program; other parts are written for the technical staff and explain the actual methodology of the program in case it needs modification (Figure 8.6). Before a software project is considered complete, the documentation must be finalized and distributed to users.

Software Development: Art or Science?

Programmers systematically follow the previously described steps in the program development cycle when they develop custom software. Such a step-by-step procedure suggests that the process of software development is basically scientific. In fact, those who focus on the scientific and technical aspects of programming refer to program development as **software engineering.**

Figure 8.6 *A complete software package or custom program includes disks, user manuals, and detailed documentation.*

But many computer professionals still refer to the "art," rather than the "science," of programming. They believe that there are elements in the process that go beyond the systematic, technical ones. Most people believe that to develop good software, programmers need to be creative, to communicate well, to make decisions based on experience, and to use their intuition—all nonquantifiable and nonscientific elements.

The science and art perspectives on programming may seem incompatible. But proponents of both views agree that techniques used to systematize aspects of the development process combined with a creative approach to the subject are apt to make programs easier to write, read, maintain, and modify.

Self-Test

1. What two program design tools are used specifically to describe the logic to be included in a program?

2. A program design tool used specifically to interrelate modules in a program is called a _____.

3. Why are programs typically written in a symbolic language rather than machine language?

4. A program written in a symbolic language must be _____ before it can be run.

5. Finding and correcting errors in a program is called _____.

6. A rule violation in a program is called a _____ error.

7. How are logic errors in a program typically detected?

8.3 PROGRAMMING TECHNIQUES FOR STANDARDIZING SOFTWARE DEVELOPMENT

The cost of software has been rising dramatically in recent years, so much so that organizations are actively seeking ways to minimize the time it takes to complete the software development process. One way to reduce costs is to train programmers to develop software that uses a standard form. Designing a program so that it consists of modules of related instructions is one method of achieving standardization.

In recent years, techniques have been developed to help standardize programming. These widely used techniques minimize differences in the way pro-

Study Objective

3. Explain the reasons why standardized program development is so important.

Solutions

1. flowcharts, pseudocode

2. hierarchy chart (or structure chart)

3. Machine language is cumbersome and requires knowing complex operation codes and keeping track of actual storage addresses.

4. translated

5. debugging

6. syntax

7. By executing the program with test data

grammers approach problem solving. Programs that are standardized are easier to code, debug, maintain, and modify. We describe next the most commonly used techniques for standardizing programs.

Modular Programming

In modular programming, each segment of a program is written as an independent series of steps that is often called a module, routine, subroutine, or subprogram. These program segments are each called in, or executed, by a main module. Review Figure 8.1 on page 260, which has two modules, a main module and a subprogram module.

Each component of a modular program accomplishes a specific task and can be written and tested independently. Indeed, some modules can even be used in more than one program. A module that evaluates and prints input errors, for example, may be reusable in several programs.

Structured Programming

Another method of standardization is to have all programmers use structured design techniques when developing a program. In the past, nonstructured programs contained a number of transfer or GO TO operations that were used to run instructions in different modules. With GO TOs, transfers from one module to another could be made anywhere, that is, backward or forward, like the haphazard arrangement of spaghetti in a bowl. This type of program, which is difficult to debug and to understand because GO TOs take you to different points, has been called "spaghetti code" and is viewed today as an improper and nonstandard style. **Structured programming** is a design technique that integrates, or ties together, program modules in a standard way.

Structured programs most often utilize three logical control constructs to indicate the order in which instructions or modules are executed regardless of the programming language being used. Structured programming technique helps to standardize the logic used in all programs.

Structured programs have a main module from which all subordinate modules are executed. There are no branch points (GO TOs) that make the logic difficult to follow. All program steps can be executed using just three logical control constructs: sequence, selection, and iteration (looping). See Figure 8.7 on pages 269 and 270.

SEQUENCE (FIGURE 8.7a) Each instruction in a program is executed in sequence—as it appears—unless another logical control construct is used.

SELECTION (FIGURE 8.7b) Instructions can be executed *selectively.* IF a given condition is true or is met, THEN specific instructions or modules will be executed. IF the condition is false or is not met, THEN a different set of instructions is executed:

IF condition
THEN
      ←statements to be executed if the condition is met
ELSE
      ←statements to be executed if the condition is not met

Another term for this selection control structure is the IF-THEN-ELSE structure.

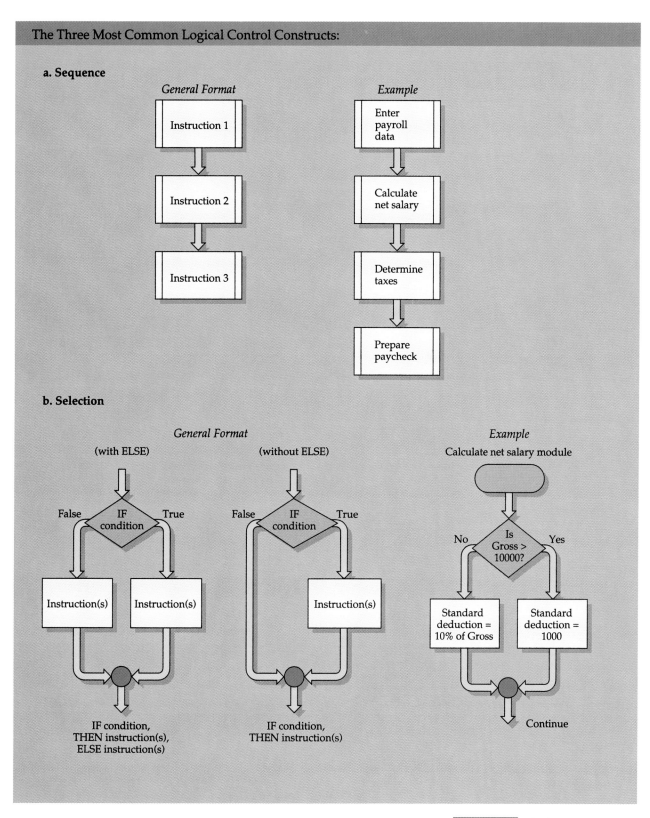

The Three Most Common Logical Control Constructs:

a. Sequence

b. Selection

ITERATION OR LOOPING (FIGURE 8.7c) A module or series of modules can be run or executed from another module. Module B, for example, can be executed from module A either once or repeatedly. Iterative techniques are executed

The Three Most Common Logical Control Constructs:

c. Iteration or Looping

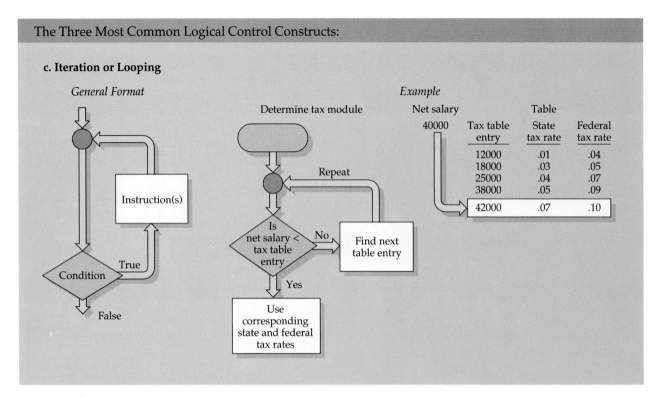

Figure 8.7 *Continued.*

in most languages with a DO or PERFORM loop. We may say, for example, DO (a module) 100 TIMES. Or we may say DO (a module) WHILE COUNTER < 100. If COUNTER begins at 0 and is incremented by 1 each time through the loop, then the module would be executed 100 times.

Top-Down Programming

Top-down programming means that proper program design is best achieved by developing major modules before minor ones. In a top-down program, the main module is coded first, followed by intermediate and then minor ones. By coding programs stepwise in this top-down manner, programmers can give the general

Figure 8.8 *A top-down approach to programming where a main module executes subordinate modules and so on.*

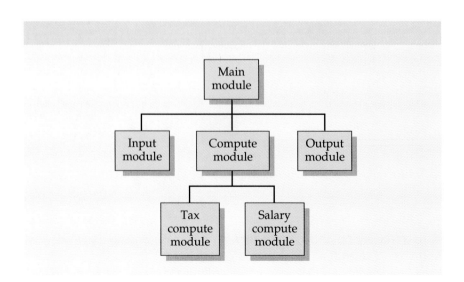

organization of a program primary attention while leaving details for minor modules, which are coded last. Top-down programming is analogous to designing a term paper by developing the outline first. Your outline gets increasingly detailed only after you have established the main organization or structure. See Figure 8.8.

Reusable Code

Because structured programs consist of modules, it is possible to use a single module or a combination of modules in more than one program. An editing routine or a tabulating procedure, for example, may be suitable for many different programs. **Reusable code** can significantly reduce programming and debugging time.

Object-Oriented Programming

As computer use increases, so too does the need for custom software. In fact, the overall demand for such software is rising 12 percent annually, but the number of programmers is only increasing 4 percent annually. As a result, techniques like those mentioned here, which reduce development time and cost by making programs easier to write, debug, and maintain, are becoming even more important. **Object-oriented programming (OOP)** is specifically designed to make program components reusable and to reduce the time it takes to develop those components.

Conventional programs focus on the computer as a machine or engine, and on data as the raw material that the computer processes. The programmer is the technician who controls the machine. The programmer lists all the processing steps the computer must take to obtain the needed output from the input. In contrast, an object-oriented program defines both the data and the set of operations that can act on that data as one unit called an *object*. An object is an entity designed to closely resemble real-world objects. In a check-writing program, for example, a check is an object that has these attributes: amount, check number, date, and recipient. It responds to these instructions: write, cash, sign, and record.

Reusability is achieved because objects belong to classes and objects within a class have the same format and respond to the same instructions as all other objects in the class. If a check belongs to a document class, then it inherits all attributes from the document class and can respond to all instructions written for that class. **Inheritance** is a major feature of object-oriented programming. As another example, a horse is an object belonging to the class of mammals. It "inherits" the characteristics of a mammal (body hair, live birth, nursing its young, and so on). However, it also has characteristics that distinguish it from other mammals, such as its size and shape, the way it moves, and the kinds of sounds it makes.

When a programmer creates a new object, he or she only needs to add the object's new features; the inherited ones are already there and need not be restated. To see how inheritance makes the programmer's job easier, assume you are writing a space-war game. Both sides—the Federation and the Ferengi—have fighting spaceships, but of slightly different types. In addition, each side has nonfighting ships, such as space shuttles and cargo barges. The object *ship* has certain characteristics: *x-y* coordinates, shields, warp speeds, and loyalty (Federation or Ferengi). The object *fightingship* has everything *ship* has, plus photon torpedoes. The object *shuttlecraft* has everything *ship* has except shields and warp speeds. There is no need to redesign ship attributes each time a ship is used; new attributes to make fightingship or shuttlecraft need only be added to ship attributes.

• • • • • ▶ Looking Ahead

Many industry experts believe that in the years ahead software companies will sell segments of reusable code that can be linked together to form a cohesive program in much the same way that Lego blocks are interconnected.

The major goals of object-oriented programming are to improve programmer productivity and increase software reusability, thereby reducing the cost of software development and maintenance.

Object-oriented programming incorporates the assumption that certain aspects of data can be contained in the program itself and, indeed, can be treated by the programmer as fixed. The concept is similar to "real-world processing" by humans. A person who drives a car need only know how to perform certain operations on the car (steer, accelerate, brake, and so on). The fixed aspects of a car (how the carburetor works, how the engine works) are of no real concern to the driver when driving. Object-oriented programming attempts to model programming after such real-world concepts. The programmer defines certain objects (an engine of a car) and uses them in a program without focusing on how they function. In this way, programmers need not duplicate code that can be the same from one program to another (an engine can be used in more than one type of car). See Figure 8.9.

Many computer professionals agree that object-oriented programming can greatly reduce the time needed to implement new software. In addition, because new software builds heavily on existing objects, the code is more likely to be reusable and error-free. The next few years will determine whether the full potential of object-oriented programming is as great as many computer professionals believe it to be. If it is, expect tremendous improvements in the speed of software development and the quality of the final product.

Visual Programming

Object-oriented programming has been enthusiastically embraced by the computing field as one of the best solutions for improving program efficiency with reusable code. But the fact is that the anticipated implementation and availability of object-oriented code has yet to be realized. It may still become the concept that will dominate in the twenty-first century, but another concept that incorporates objects has become a popular technique of the 1990s.

Visual programming is an object-oriented concept that makes use of Windows-type menus, buttons, and other graphics as objects to create programs that are visually appealing, reusable, and relatively easy to code.

We will see later on that Visual Basic and Visual C are two examples of visual programming languages. A large supply of objects written in both languages can be purchased to provide functionality in telecommunications, spreadsheets, database management, and multimedia applications.

IN A NUTSHELL

Visual programming and object-oriented programming are designed to reduce application development time by enabling users to create software that consists of objects as building blocks that can be easily integrated and reused in different programs. Languages such as Visual Basic combine visual programming and object-oriented techniques.

Self-Test

1. A self-contained program segment that can be written and tested independently and even reused in other programs is called a _____.

2. What are the three logical control constructs used in a structured program?

3. Programs in which major modules are coded stepwise before minor modules are said to use _____ programming techniques.

Solutions

1.   module (subroutine, subprogram, routine)

2.   sequence, selection, iteration

3.   top-down

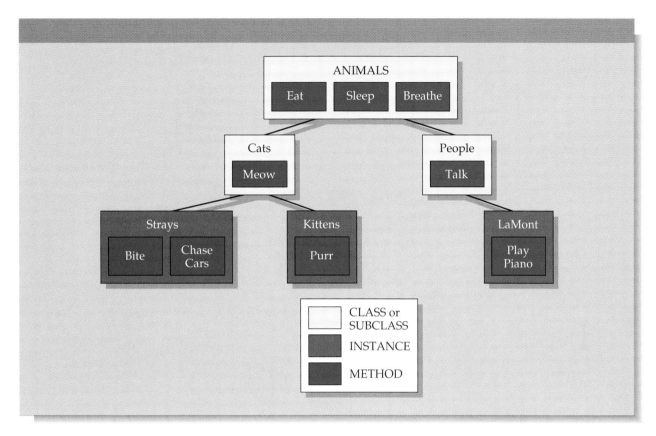

Figure 8.9 *Object-oriented programming enables procedures or methods to be combined with data to form objects. The ability of objects to inherit class characteristics facilitates the development of reusable code.*

8.4 FIVE GENERATIONS OF PROGRAMMING LANGUAGES

Traditionally, types of programming languages have been categorized chronologically by "generations," each with specific features. Even though newer generations may have features that are viewed as superior to those of older generations, sometimes older generation languages are still uniquely suited for specific tasks. You will see, however, that programs are now rarely written in a first- or second-generation language. Most are written in a third- or fourth-generation language. Fifth-generation languages currently are more significant in their potential than in their actual use.

Machine Language: The First Generation

Machine language, as we have seen, is the computer's internal language, which executes directly without translation. Machine languages are referred to as first-generation programming languages because they were the earliest type developed. Initially, in the 1940s and early 1950s, all programs had to be coded in these languages.

Programming in machine language, however, is time consuming and is conducive to making mistakes. Also, machine language is different for each type of computer; if an organization decides to acquire a new computer, all programs must be in the new computer's machine language to be executed. Thus, we say that machine languages are wholly *computer dependent* and are therefore nonstandard. Because of the complexity and widely disparate formats of machine languages, few programmers actually code in them today.

Study Objective

4. Show how the development of programming languages has enhanced the software development process.

But, as we saw in the last section, all programs must be in machine language to be executed, that is, actually run. What programmers do is write programs in other languages, which need to be translated by the computer into machine language for execution.

Assembly Language: The Second Generation

In the 1950s, when computers were first used commercially, the complexity of machine language programming paved the way early on for a second generation of languages called **assembly languages.** In assembly language, the complex operation codes required for execution can be assigned names such as ADD, SUB, and MULT that are easy to remember. Also, the actual storage addresses where data is located can be defined with names such as AMT1 and AMT2 for ease of reference.

Aside from being able to name operations and storage addresses, assembly languages are very much like their corresponding machine language. This means that to be a proficient assembly (or machine) language programmer, you need to understand the machine's architecture, that is, how it physically processes data. Moreover, since each type of computer has its own individual architecture with its own machine and corresponding assembly languages, the structure of one such set of machine language instructions may be totally different from that of another set. Assembly languages, therefore, like machine languages, are computer dependent. We say that assembly language programs are not **portable:** you cannot run an assembly language program written for one category of computers on another type of computer unless they have the same architecture.

Programs written in assembly languages have special codes that make them easier to write than programs written in machine language. But these programs will not execute unless they are translated into machine language by a special program called an **assembler.** An assembler reads the assembly language program as input and then converts it, as output, into a machine language version called the object program.

Despite the complexity of assembly languages, they are still used for some applications today. Because they are so similar to machine language, they result in very efficient code—that is, the program uses relatively little storage, leaving more space for other user programs. When maximizing the efficient use of the computer is a major goal of a program, such as is the case with systems software, assembly language is still favored.

High-Level Languages: The Third Generation (3GLs)

Computer use in businesses grew dramatically in the 1950s as did the need for programmers and application software. Machine and assembly language programming, however, was just too difficult for many people, slowing down the development process. Computer manufacturers, as well as user groups, began to develop third-generation languages (3GLs) that would be both easier for programming and portable. If users decided to upgrade their equipment or acquire more current hardware, they would not need to revise all their software.

These languages are called high level because they are relatively easy to learn and not at all like machine language; rather, they are more like the English language. High-level programs, however, require a computer-based translation process that is very complex. In general, the easier it is to program, the higher the level and the more complex the translation process. Most translator programs for high-level languages are called compilers, but some are called interpreters. We discuss both of these types of translators later in this chapter.

High-level languages, like their predecessors, are called **procedural languages.** This means that the program must specify the *precise set of instructions* necessary to accomplish a given task. We will see that many programs written in newer fourth- and fifth-generation languages are **nonprocedural;** that is, they need not follow precise rules. Think of ordering a piece of pie in a restaurant. In a procedural language, you need to specify the ingredients, how to bake the pie, how to serve it, and so on. In a fourth- or fifth-generation nonprocedural language, you can simply say, "Get me a slice of apple pie."

The most commonly used third-generation languages, in order of their development, follow. These are by no means the only ones; there are hundreds of them, some with a very extensive user base. Those discussed here, however, have had the greatest impact.

FORTRAN In the 1950s, most of the people actually writing programs were scientists or engineers. The types of problems they wanted to solve required a great deal of computation. It is not surprising, therefore, that the first widely used

Figure 8.10 *This FORTRAN program calculates each employee's paycheck amount.*

```
C  ***                      PAYCHECK PROGRAM                          ***
C  ***                                                                ***
C  *** This program calculates an employee's paycheck based on the    ***
C  *** number of hours the employee worked and base pay per hour.     ***
C  ********************************************************************

program Paychk

character * 12 Name
real Gross, Hours, PayRat
C
C  Prompt the user for the employee's name, hours worked, and rate of
C  pay per hour.
C
print*, '     PAYCHECK PROGRAM'
print*
print*
print*, 'Enter the employee''s name:   '
read*, Name
print*, 'Enter the hours worked:'
read*, Hours
print*, 'Enter the hourly pay rate:'
read*, PayRat
C
C  Calculate gross pay.
C
Gross = Hours * PayRat
C
C  Print the results of the paycheck calculations for this employee.
C  Then quit.
C
print*, 'Employee Name        ', Name
print*, '   Hours Worked       ', Hours
print*, '   Pay Rate           ', PayRat
print*, '   Gross Pay          ', Gross

stop
end
```

high-level language was scientifically oriented. **FORTRAN,** an acronym for *Formula Trans*lator, was developed by IBM in the 1950s and is the oldest high-level language. The fact that it is still used today attests to its impact on the field.

Although FORTRAN is ideal for the complex math of scientific and engineering applications, it is *not* well suited for typical business applications that require relatively simple arithmetic operations but a large volume of input/output operations. Although originally developed for large mainframe systems, FORTRAN has been implemented on microcomputers in recent years. Figure 8.10 shows a simple FORTRAN program. This program inputs hours worked and hourly rate and calculates weekly wages. We will illustrate the same program in different third-generation languages so that you can see the main features of each language.

COBOL During the 1950s, the business community began to realize that computers could solve many of its information processing needs. But FORTRAN was not ideally suited for business processing. Consider the procedure for preparing a bill. The number of steps involved may not be large or involve complicated math, but the customer base may be so big that the input/output procedures are quite complex.

In 1959 a group of computer professionals formed an organization called CODASYL (*Co*nference on *Da*ta *Sy*stems *L*anguages) and held a series of meetings to establish guidelines for the development of a business-oriented language. The objectives of this language were to be machine independent, easy to maintain, and English-like. The language developed was **COBOL,** an acronym for *Co*mmon *B*usiness *O*riented *L*anguage. It was released in 1960.

In the 1960s, the American National Standards Institute (ANSI) was charged with the task of developing standards for programming languages. The first ANSI version of COBOL was approved in 1968. All major computer software manufacturers agreed to adhere to this standard. As a result, COBOL is portable, which means that COBOL programs can run on many different kinds of computers with only minimal changes—an important feature for large businesses that need a variety of hardware. COBOL is a standard language—all compilers include the same basic instruction set. Some compilers have additional features as well, such as object-oriented enhancements.

COBOL remains the most widely used language for business programs developed for mainframes. It has been estimated that 70 to 80 percent of all mainframe applications are still coded in COBOL and many micro-based applications are written in COBOL as well. The frequent predictions of its impending demise seem to be greatly exaggerated. Figure 8.11 shows a structured COBOL program that can process any number of input records.

RPG RPG, an abbreviation for *Report Program Generator*, was also developed in the 1960s as a language that enabled users to produce their own reports. In concept, RPG was a precursor to more recent languages that use English-like structures to generate printed output from databases. RPG is still a very popular language for the IBM AS/400 midrange computers.

BASIC During the 1960s, many people believed that languages such as FORTRAN and COBOL were difficult to learn. In addition, these languages were batch oriented and not really intended for newer, interactive methods of processing. In the early days, the programmer submitted both the program and the test data to the computer center for execution in batch mode at some later time. As terminals became popular in the 1960s, these batch methods for executing programs were viewed as slow, inefficient, and limited in applicability.

IN A NUTSHELL

Both FORTRAN and COBOL are available on PCs as well as larger computers but most applications written in these languages remain mainframe based.

```
IDENTIFICATION DIVISION.
PROGRAM-ID. SAMPLE.
ENVIRONMENT DIVISION.
INPUT-OUTPUT SECTION.
FILE-CONTROL. SELECT EMPLOYEE-DATA    ASSIGN TO DISK.
              SELECT PAYROLL-LISTING ASSIGN TO SYSLST.
DATA DIVISION.
FILE SECTION.
FD  EMPLOYEE-DATA            LABEL RECORDS ARE STANDARD.
01  EMPLOYEE-RECORD.
    05   EMPLOYEE-NAME-IN     PICTURE X(20).
    05   HOURS-WORKED-IN      PICTURE 9(2).
    05   HOURLY-RATE-IN       PICTURE 9V99.
FD  PAYROLL-LISTING          LABEL RECORDS ARE OMITTED.
01  PRINT-REC.
    05                       PICTURE X(21).
    05   NAME-OUT            PICTURE X(20).
    05                       PICTURE X(10).
    05   HOURS-OUT           PICTURE 9(2).
    05                       PICTURE X(8).
    05   RATE-OUT            PICTURE 9.99.
    05                       PICTURE X(6).
    05   WEEKLY-WAGES-OUT    PICTURE 999.99.
WORKING-STORAGE SECTION.
01  ARE-THERE-MORE-RECORDS   PICTURE XXX VALUE 'YES'.
PROCEDURE DIVISION.
100-MAIN-MODULE.
    OPEN INPUT EMPLOYEE-DATA
         OUTPUT PAYROLL-LISTING.
    READ EMPLOYEE-DATA
         AT END MOVE 'NO ' TO ARE-THERE-MORE-RECORDS.
    PERFORM 200-WAGE-ROUTINE
         UNTIL ARE-THERE-MORE-RECORDS = 'NO '.
    CLOSE EMPLOYEE-DATA
          PAYROLL-LISTING.
    STOP RUN.
200-WAGE-ROUTINE.
    MOVE SPACES TO PRINT-REC.
    MOVE EMPLOYEE-NAME-IN TO NAME-OUT.
    MOVE HOURS-WORKED-IN TO HOURS-OUT.
    MOVE HOURLY-RATE-IN TO RATE-OUT.
    MULTIPLY HOURS-WORKED-IN BY HOURLY-RATE-IN
         GIVING WEEKLY-WAGES-OUT.
    WRITE PRINT-REC.
    READ EMPLOYEE-DATA
         AT END MOVE 'NO ' TO ARE-THERE-MORE-RECORDS.
```

At the same time, two professors at Dartmouth College, John Kemeny and Thomas Kurtz, wanted to teach students in nontechnical disciplines to write interactive programs on large time-sharing systems. They created **BASIC** (*Beginner's All-purpose Symbolic Instruction Code*); the acronym is far more suitable than the full name! BASIC is easy to learn and is appropriate for small businesses with a limited programming staff. Because BASIC is widely implemented on microcomputers—the type of computer most common in schools from elementary to the college level—it is the language students are likely to learn first. Figure 8.12 shows a short BASIC program that, like our previous programs, calculates an employee's net pay.

Figure 8.11 *This is an excerpt from a COBOL program. Note that the COBOL program is more comprehensive than the others—it operates on any number of data items, whereas the others just operate on one set of data. The PROCEDURE DIVISION illustrates the actual instructions.*

Figure 8.12 *This is the same payroll program written in BASIC.*

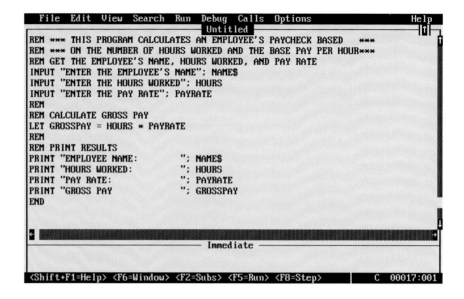

```
 File  Edit  View  Search  Run  Debug  Calls  Options              Help
                          Untitled
REM *** THIS PROGRAM CALCULATES AN EMPLOYEE'S PAYCHECK BASED   ***
REM *** ON THE NUMBER OF HOURS WORKED AND THE BASE PAY PER HOUR***
REM GET THE EMPLOYEE'S NAME, HOURS WORKED, AND PAY RATE
INPUT "ENTER THE EMPLOYEE'S NAME"; NAME$
INPUT "ENTER THE HOURS WORKED"; HOURS
INPUT "ENTER THE PAY RATE"; PAYRATE
REM
REM CALCULATE GROSS PAY
LET GROSSPAY = HOURS * PAYRATE
REM
REM PRINT RESULTS
PRINT "EMPLOYEE NAME:       "; NAME$
PRINT "HOURS WORKED:        "; HOURS
PRINT "PAY RATE:            "; PAYRATE
PRINT "GROSS PAY            "; GROSSPAY
END

                          Immediate
<Shift+F1=Help> <F6=Window> <F2=Subs> <F5=Run> <F8=Step>      C  00017:001
```

Although BASIC is used mainly on micros, it is available on mainframes as well. One problem with BASIC, however, is that there is no standard that has been embraced by users as the one to follow. Even on IBM-compatibles, numerous versions abound. In addition, mainframes have versions that are not entirely compatible with the micro versions.

LANGUAGES DESIGNED SPECIFICALLY FOR STRUCTURED PROGRAMMING: PASCAL AND MODULA-2

Pascal. In the mid- and late 1960s, the concept of structured programming to make programs easier to code and debug became a priority among computer scientists. As a result, many computer educators came to believe that structured programming techniques should be taught to computer students from the beginning. In 1971 Niklaus Wirth, the main proponent of structured programming, developed **Pascal** to meet the need for an easy to learn, highly structured language. Figure 8.13 contains a short Pascal program. Wirth named Pascal after the seventeenth-century mathematician Blaise Pascal, who developed the first mechanical calculator.

Many computer scientists embraced Pascal as a major improvement over languages such as COBOL and BASIC, which were, at the time, essentially non-structured. Because Pascal was designed to be a truly structured language, it became the introductory programming language for computer science students at most universities. Pascal was not, however, intended to be powerful enough for major business applications; that is, it cannot handle large quantities of business data nearly as efficiently as languages such as COBOL. But it can perform complex mathematical operations, so it remains popular with engineers and scientists.

Modula-2. Niklaus Wirth created Pascal to be primarily a teaching language. As its use spread to business, its shortcomings became more apparent. Wirth then developed **Modula-2** as an expansion and improvement over Pascal. Introduced in 1980, Modula-2 is better suited for handling the large quantities of data that are processed in business applications. Because Modula-2 retains the original emphasis on structured programming concepts that were first introduced in

```
program Paycheck (input, output);

{ *** This program calculates an employee's paycheck based on  ***
  *** the number of hours the employee worked and the base pay ***
  *** per hour.                                                ***  }

var
   Name : string;
   Hours, PayRate, GrossPay : real;

begin    { Paycheck }

   { Prompt the user to enter name, hours worked and hourly rate. }
   write ('Enter the employee''s name: ');
   readln (Name);
   write ('Enter the number of hours worked: ');
   readln (Hours);
   write ('Enter the hourly pay rate: ');
   readln (PayRate);

   { Calculate gross pay.}
   GrossPay := Hours * PayRate;

   { Print the results of the paycheck calculations for this employee.
     Then quit. }

   writeln ('Employee Name:       ', Name);
   writeln ('Hours Worked:        ', Hours:8:2);
   writeln ('Pay Rate:            ', PayRate:8:2);
   writeln ('Gross Pay:           ', GrossPay:8:2);

end.    { Paycheck }
```

Figure 8.13 *This Pascal program also calculates employee pay.*

Pascal, and because it has commercial applicability as well, some universities use it in computer science courses. But relatively few translators are currently available, so its future in both schools and business remains unclear.

C: THE HIGH-LEVEL ALTERNATIVE TO ASSEMBLY LANGUAGE PROGRAMMING The **C** language was developed in 1972 by Dennis M. Ritchie at Bell Laboratories. C incorporates the advantages of both assembly language and high-level languages and is therefore often referred to as a "middle-level" language. It is a structured language that uses high-level instruction formats, but it also allows the programmer to interact directly with the hardware, as in assembly language. These combined capabilities make C well suited as the main language for writing operating systems that require extremely efficient code. In addition, instructions written in C, unlike those written in assembly languages, are portable. The UNIX operating system, which we will discuss in the next chapter, was written in C.

The C language is more difficult to learn than other structured languages like Pascal. Even so, because of its power and wide implementation on microcomputers, it is popular among systems programmers for developing systems software and utilities. Figure 8.14 shows the employee pay program we have been illustrating written in C. C++, an object-oriented version of C, is discussed later in this section.

ADA In 1978 the U.S. Department of Defense, dissatisfied with the languages available at the time, held a design competition to select a programming language standard for its software. As the world's largest purchaser of computer hardware and software, the department realized it could save billions of dollars in development by standardizing its software language. The winning language was named for Augusta Ada, the Countess of Lovelace, who designed what we would call "programs" for computing engines originally conceived by Charles Babbage in the nineteenth century.

Ada is a general-purpose language based on the structured concepts first used in Pascal. It is extremely powerful and sophisticated and can be used to

Figure 8.14 *This C program is not as readable as the others, but its translation to machine language is easier for the computer.*

```c
/***                         PAYCHECK PROGRAM                          ***/
/***                                                                    ***/
/*** Program Paycheck calculates an employee's paycheck based on the ***/
/*** number of hours worked and base pay per hour.                    ***/
/**********************************************************************/

main()
{
char    Employee_Name[40];
float   Gross_Pay;
float   Pay_Rate;
float   Hours_Worked
int     Temp;
char    c;
/* ---------------------------------------------------------------- */

    /* Prompt the user for the employee's name, hours worked, and rate
       of pay per hour. */
printf ("                         PAYCHECK PROGRAM\n");
printf ("Enter the employee's name: ");
    /* read characters into name array, one at a time   */
for (Temp = 0; (Temp < 40) && ((c = getchar()) != '\r') && (c != '\n');
    Temp++) Employee_Name[Temp] = c;
Employee_Name[Temp] = '\0\';    /* put in end of string character */
printf ("\n");                  /* write a new line to screen      */

printf ("Enter the number of hours worked: ");
scanf ("%f", &Hours_Worked); /* read number of hours from standard input*/
printf ("Enter the hourly pay rate: ");
scanf ("%f", &Pay_Rate);   /* read pay rate from standard input       */

    /* Calculate gross pay. */

Gross_Pay = Hours_Worked * Pay_Rate;

    /* Print the results of the paycheck calculations for this employee.
           Then quit. */

printf ("\n\n");
printf ("Employee Name        %s\n",    Employee_Name);
printf ("   Hours Worked      %8.2f\n", Hours_Worked);
printf ("   Pay Rate          %8.2f\n", Pay_Rate);
printf ("   Gross Pay         %8.2f\n", Gross_Pay);

}
```

program parallel processes, which greatly improves computer performance. Learning the language well enough to take advantage of its full potential can, however, take several years.

C++, VISUAL BASIC, AND OTHER OBJECT-ORIENTED PROGRAMMING LANGUAGES SmallTalk, developed in 1972 by Alan Kay at Xerox's Palo Alto Research Center, is one of many languages specifically designed to enable users to implement object-oriented programming. In object-oriented programs, a programmer uses objects instead of the operation codes and data names or symbolic addresses that are common to most languages. Two other object-oriented languages popular for developing graphical user interfaces, multimedia, and database management systems are **C++** and object-oriented Pascal, modifications of C and Pascal, respectively.

An object in a program can be a dialog box, a window, or a menu. Operating systems with graphical user interfaces such as OS/2 and Windows can be considered object oriented because they make use of these types of objects. If a window with scroll bars and dialog boxes is to be a component of a program, for example, the programmer can simply use the windows created by a graphical user interface without even knowing how these were created.

Looking Back ◀ •••

THE FIRST COMPUTER AND THE FIRST PROGRAMMER

Charles Babbage, a nineteenth-century Englishman, is often called the father of the modern computer. Although he did not actually build an operational computer himself, his ideas became the basis for modern computational devices.

In 1822, Babbage began work on a device called the Difference Engine, which was designed to automate a standard procedure for calculating the roots of polynomials. The calculations were used for producing astronomical tables that were required by the British Navy for navigational purposes. Despite his foresight, Babbage did not complete his original project. Instead, he abandoned the Difference Engine to work on a more powerful device, the Analytical Engine, which was remarkably similar in concept to twentieth-century digital computers.

The Analytical Engine was designed to use two types of cards: one, called operation cards, to indicate the specific functions to be performed, and the other, called variable cards, to specify the actual data. This idea of entering a program (or set of instructions) on cards, followed by data cards, is one method used by the first generation of modern computers for implementing the stored-program concept.

Babbage conceived of two main units for his Analytical Engine.
1. An area he called a *store* within the device, in which instructions and variables would be placed. Today we call this the *memory* of the computer.
2. An area he called a *mill* within the device, in which arithmetic operations would be performed. Today we call this part of the device the *arithmetic/logic unit.*

Lady Augusta Ada Byron, the Countess of Lovelace and daughter of the poet Lord Byron, worked closely with Babbage in the design of programs for the Analytical Engine. She wrote a demonstration program for the Analytical Engine, prompting many to refer to her as the first programmer. The programming language Ada was named for her.

Charles Babbage (1791–1871).

Augusta Ada (1815–1853).

Babbage's Analytical Engine.

IN A NUTSHELL

LANGUAGES

FEATURES	ADA	BASIC	COBOL	FORTRAN	PASCAL, MODULA-2, AND C	C++ AND VISUAL BASIC
Scientific	X	X		X	X	X
Business	X	X	X			X
Standardized	X		X		X	X
English-like		X	X		X	X

Visual Basic and other visual programming languages are also object oriented. Visual Basic is a version of Microsoft's QuickBASIC used for developing Windows applications. User interfaces are developed by dragging objects from the Visual Basic Toolbox onto the application's form. Objects are activated using icons, buttons, and menus selected from a toolbar. Visual C++ is Microsoft's version of C++, also designed for developing Windows applications.

Visual programming makes application development easier and faster even for nonprogrammers. Studies have shown that Visual Basic enables programmers to reduce by 33% to 80% the amount of code required to create an application when compared with more conventional programming techniques. See Figure 8.15.

INTERPRETERS AND COMPILERS Third-generation languages use translators called compilers or interpreters, which are more sophisticated than assemblers. An **interpreter** translates a program written in a high-level language one statement at a time as the program is actually being run on the computer. Each statement is translated and executed before the interpreter proceeds to the next statement. This process continues until the end of the program is reached. A **compiler** translates the entire source program into machine language in one

Figure 8.15 *This is an example of a Visual Basic application in which a text can be entered and portions can be changed to bold or italic or underlined. Parts of the text can also be cut, copied, or deleted. The visual objects you see are drawn from Windows elements.*

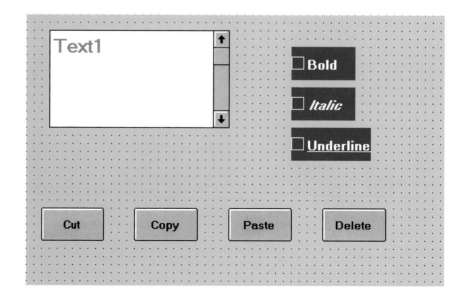

process, thereby creating an object program. Another program, referred to as the linking loader or linkage editor, prepares the object program for execution.

Most high-level programming languages use compilers, but some languages, for example BASIC, also have interpreters. Interpreters do not take up as much space in the computer's primary storage, but they are slower than compilers. Compilers are capable of creating an object program that can be stored in executable form; so if the program is to be run again, it need not be retranslated each time. Thus, programs that are to be run on a regularly scheduled basis are nearly always written in high-level languages that can be compiled, as opposed to languages that require interpreters.

Fourth-Generation Languages (4GLs)

Recall that first-, second-, and third-generation languages are all procedural languages because the programmer must write each step and must use logical control structures to indicate the order in which the instructions are to be executed. Fourth-generation languages (4GLs), on the other hand, are nonprocedural languages. This distinction can be compared to the way in which you might instruct someone to cook a meal. The nonprocedural method is simply to state the needed output: fix a meal of chicken, rice, and salad. The procedural method, on the other hand, involves specifying each step—from preparing the shopping list to washing the dishes.

A nonprocedural language is easier to code, but it gives you less control over how each task is actually performed. For example, if you simply state "wash the dishes," the dishes might be washed by hand or in a dishwasher; the decision would be beyond your control. When you use nonprocedural languages, remember that the instructions are easier, but the methods employed and the order in which each task is carried out are left to the program itself.

ɪɴ A NUTSHELL

TYPES OF TRANSLATORS AND THEIR FEATURES

ASSEMBLER

- Uses symbolic operation codes and storage addresses, which are easier to remember than the codes of machine language
- Requires programmers to understand the machine language of the computer
- Results in very efficient code
- Used for developing operating systems, utilities, and background programs where efficient use of the CPU is most important

COMPILER

- Is the most common type of translator program

- Translates the entire symbolic program into machine language in one cycle
- Translates each symbolic instruction written by the programmer into machine language instructions

INTERPRETER

- Translates and executes each instruction as it is read
- Translates a program each time it is to be executed (Compiled and assembled machine language code can be saved so that the translation process need not be repeated.)

Instructions for 4GLs do not focus on *how* to perform a function but on *what* is actually to be done; the software itself generates the required operations. As a result, 4GLs sacrifice computer efficiency so that programs are easier to write. They require more computer power and processing time than their procedural counterparts. As the power and speed of hardware increase and the cost of the hardware decreases, the need for emphasizing efficient code becomes less important. The result is the blossoming of user-friendly 4GLs.

Fourth-generation languages are generally used to enable managers and executives with minimal programming skills to access data from existing databases. 4GLs provide users with the capability of retrieving information from a database using a query language, generating reports and graphics from a database, and actually generating source code that manipulates data in a database.

QUERY LANGUAGES Query languages allow users to retrieve information from databases by following simple syntax rules. For example, you might ask the database to locate all customer accounts that are more than 90 days overdue. Examples of query languages are Structured Query Language (SQL) and Query-By-Example (QBE). Look at the following example of SQL for querying an employee database and increasing salaries of some employees by 1000; the operations performed are fairly straightforward:

SQL Example

```
UPDATE EMPLOYEE
SET SALARY = SALARY + 1000
  WHERE JOBCODE = 3 OR JOBCODE = 6
```

This increases salaries of employees with a job code of 3 or 6 by $1,000.

REPORT GENERATORS **Report generators** produce customized reports using data stored in a database. The user specifies the data to be in the report, how the report should be formatted, and whether any subtotals or totals are needed. For example, you might ask the system to create a list, arranged by account number, of all the company's customers located in Oklahoma. Often, report specifications are selected from pull-down menus, which makes report generators very user-friendly. Examples of report generators are Easytrieve Plus and Nomad.

APPLICATION GENERATORS A user can access a database with query languages and report generators but generally cannot alter the database with these tools. **Application generators** create programs that allow data to be entered into a database. The program prompts the user to enter the needed data. It also checks the data for validity. Visual Xbase and CA-Realizer are examples of application generators. Many database management systems have their own application generators sold as add-ons.

In summary, fourth-generation programming languages are suitable for writing short, simple programs for accessing and manipulating data in a database. They do not require the training of a professional programmer. They do have a major limitation: Because they are nonprocedural, the person generating the program does not have as much control over the specific processes used as he or she would with high-level languages such as COBOL or Pascal. Chapter 12 covers databases, query languages, report generators, and application generators in more depth.

IN A NUTSHELL

FEATURES OF 4GLs

- Easy to learn, understand, and use even by those with little computer training
- Convenient for accessing databases
- Focuses on maximizing human productivity rather than minimizing computer time
- Nonprocedural
- Available as packaged software that is then used to develop custom applications

Fifth-Generation Languages (5GLs)

Fifth-generation languages (5GLs) are also nonprocedural languages. They are most often used to access databases or to build expert systems. In concept, 5GLs are intended to be **natural languages,** which resemble as close as possible normal human interaction. The user need not employ any specific vocabulary, grammar, or syntax when making a query or issuing a command. Artificial intelligence techniques that enable computers to duplicate or imitate the functions of the human brain are part of 5GLs. These techniques help the computer interpret requests or commands. Currently, 5GLs are still in their infancy; only a few are available commercially. Expert systems developed using fifth-generation languages can help predict the weather, diagnose diseases, and determine where to explore for oil.

LISP, a 5GL, was developed in 1958 by John McCarthy at MIT. Although it is one of the oldest programming languages, it has been used extensively in one of the newer technologies: artificial intelligence research. Figure 8.16 illustrates a Prolog program. Prolog, another 5GL, was developed in 1972 in France by

An expert system includes a knowledge base and an inference engine designed to enable the computer to simulate the decision-making process of an expert.

Figure 8.16 *An excerpt of a Prolog program.*

```
Predicates                          Goal:angers(chocolate, zelda).
  likes(person, thing).             True
  dislikes(person, thing).          Goal:healthy(alcohol).
  angers(thing, person).            False
  healthy(thing).                   Goal:unhealthy(vodka).
  unhealthy(thing).                 False
                                    Goal:

Clauses
  likes(walter, chocolate).         Goal:likes(steve, chocolate).
  likes(steve, chocolate).          True
  likes(diana, chocolate).          1 Solution
  likes(earl, chocolate).           Goal:likes(zelda, chocolate).
  likes(karla, chocolate).          False
  likes(wendy, jogging).            1 Solution
  likes(zelda, jogging).            Goal:
  likes(bruce, alcohol).
  likes(zelda, alcohol).
  likes(walter, salads).            Goal:likes(Who, chocolate).
  likes(diana, salads).             Who = walter
  likes(wendy, salads).             Who = steve
  dislikes(isaac, chocolate).       Who = diana
  dislikes(wendy, chocolate).       Who = earl
  dislikes(bruce, chocolate).       Who = karla
  dislikes(walter, jogging).        5 Solutions
  dislikes(steve, jogging).         Goal:
  dislikes(diana, jogging).
  dislikes(earl, jogging).
  dislikes(isaac, jogging).
  dislikes(bruce, jogging).
  dislikes(walter, alcohol).
  dislikes(diana, alcohol).
  dislikes(steve, alcohol).
  dislikes(earl, alcohol).
  dislikes(karla, alcohol).
  dislikes(isaac, alcohol).
  dislikes(wendy, alcohol).
  dislikes(steve, salads).
  dislikes(earl, salads).
  angers(chocolate, zelda).
  angers(jogging, karla).
  unhealthy(chocolate).
  unhealthy(alcohol).
  healthy(jogging).
  healthy(salads).
```

Looking Ahead

PROGRAMMING IN A NETWORKED ENVIRONMENT

Programming languages that make it easy to access data from databases are likely to become the most popular in the years ahead along with languages that facilitate the development of multimedia applications. These include object-oriented languages like C++ and Visual Basic, 4GLs, and 5GLs.

Alain Colmerauer and Philippe Roussel. It quickly became popular throughout Europe as it improved and expanded. There are several implementations of Prolog for microcomputers.

The clauses in Figure 8.16 define a database of information. The predicates indicate rules. The goals indicate queries that the computer answers based on the rules and the contents of the database. As noted, 5GLs are appropriate not only for developing expert systems, but also for making natural language inquiries from databases.

Currently, most expert or knowledge-based systems are coded either in LISP or Prolog although some are written in C or C++ as well. Recent efforts to improve artificial intelligence languages have attempted to combine the best features of LISP and Prolog. Fifth-generation languages are likely to have great impact in the near future.

See Figure 8.17 for a review of the five generations of programming languages.

Figure 8.17 *The generations of programming languages.*

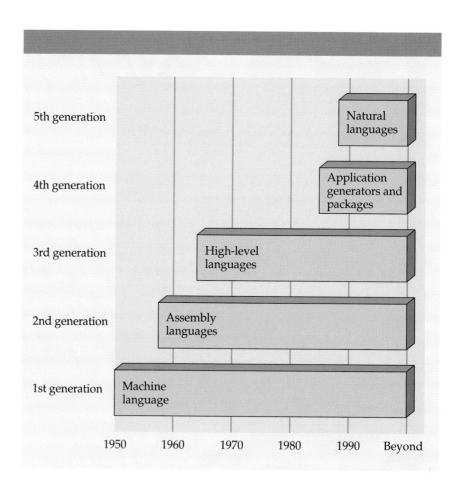

Self-Test

1. (T or F) A program written in a high-level language is more user-friendly than one written in an assembly language.

2. (T or F) Most third-generation languages are portable, which means they are not machine dependent.

3. A language commonly used for business applications, particularly on mainframes, is called _____.

4. A high-level language initially designed for students in an interactive environment is _____.

5. What are nonprocedural languages?

6. Name two ways in which fifth-generation languages are typically used.

CHAPTER SUMMARY

8.1 The Software Developer

Organizations sometimes find that off-the-shelf software does not completely fulfill their needs. One alternative is to have software specifically developed to accomplish the required tasks. In most medium-sized to large organizations with an in-house computing staff, systems analysts supervise programmers who undertake software development. In smaller companies, a **programmer analyst** may serve as both programmer and systems analyst. Some companies hire outside consultants or software development firms.

Study Objective

1. Describe the advantages of custom software.

8.2 Software Development Cycle

The term **software development cycle** refers to the steps involved in creating a program. These include (1) developing the program specifications, (2) designing the logic to be used, (3) coding the program and translating it into machine language, (4) testing the program, (5) installing, or implementing, the program, (6) maintaining the program, and (7) documenting the program.

Study Objective

2. List the steps in the software development cycle.

The three most commonly used tools for planning the logic of a program are flowcharts, pseudocode, and hierarchy charts. A **flowchart** is a pictorial representation of the logic flow to be used in a program. Each flowchart symbol denotes either a particular operation or a series of operations to be performed by a program unit called a subprogram or **module.** An alternative design tool is **pseudocode,** which consists of English-like statements instead of symbols. **Hierarchy charts** (sometimes called **structure charts**) illustrate how programs are segmented into subprograms (or modules) and how the modules relate to one another.

A program must be in **machine language,** the computer's own internal language, in order to be executed. Most programs are written in **symbolic languages,** which use instructions such as INPUT or + instead of complex operation codes. To be executed, a symbolic program, also called the **source program,** must be translated into machine language. The translated program is referred to as the **object program.**

Debugging a program means finding and correcting all logic and coding errors, or "bugs." **Desk-checking** is the process in which a programmer manu-

---

Solutions

1. T

2. T

3. COBOL

4. BASIC

5. They are languages designed for users to obtain information from the computer without necessarily specifying the precise steps or sequence in which operations are to be performed.

6. for designing expert systems; for accessing databases

ally traces through a program visually checking for **syntax errors,** which are coding errors. A program without syntax errors, however, does not necessarily produce correct output. There may be **logic errors,** which are errors that occur because of mistakes in the sequencing of instructions or the use of wrong instructions. **Program testing,** or executing a program with different sets of data, is a technique used to pinpoint logic errors. Some newer programming languages have **interactive debuggers** that help programmers find errors by stopping at certain breakpoints and displaying various program components. A **maintenance programmer** is a computer professional who modifies existing programs to make them more current or efficient.

Software engineering is a name sometimes given to the program development cycle by those who focus on the scientific and technical aspects of programming.

8.3 Programming Techniques for Standardizing Software Development

Study Objective

3. Explain the reasons why standardized program development is so important.

Structured programming is a program design technique that integrates program modules in a systematic way. A structured program has a main module from which all subordinate modules are executed. There are no branch points. All program steps are executed by means of just three logical control constructs: sequence, selection (IF-THEN-ELSE), and iteration (looping). In a top-down program, the main module is coded first, followed by intermediate and then minor modules.

Reusable code refers to a module or combination of modules that can be used in more than one program. Object-oriented programming is a technique designed to make program components reusable and to reduce the time it takes to develop those components. An **object-oriented program** defines both the data and the set of operations that can act on that data as one unit called an *object.* **Inheritance** refers to the fact that all objects within a class share the same attributes. **Visual programming** is a type of object-oriented programming that includes objects that can be used to customize Windows-based applications.

8.4 Five Generations of Programming Languages

Study Objective

4. Show how the development of programming languages has enhanced the software development process.

Machine languages are referred to as first-generation languages because they were the earliest type developed. They are wholly computer dependent and thus nonstandard. They are highly efficient, but they are not user-friendly: they make use of complex operation codes and reference actual machine addresses that store data.

The second generation of programming languages is **assembly languages.** These languages use symbolic instruction codes and symbolic names for storage areas but are similar to machine languages in other ways. Assembly language programs require a translation process by which a program called an **assembler** converts an assembly program into machine language. Assembly language programs are not **portable;** that is, they only run on computers that have the same architecture.

Third-generation languages are more symbolic and easier to use than first- or second-generation languages. They are also portable. These languages are called high-level because they are relatively easy to learn and not at all like machine language; rather, they resemble the English language. High-level programs require a complex translation process to convert the source program into machine language. High-level languages, like their predecessors, are called **procedural languages;** this means that the program must specify the precise set of instructions to accomplish a given task. Some of the most commonly used third-generation languages are **FORTRAN, COBOL, BASIC, Pascal, Modula-2, C, C++, Ada,** and **Visual Basic.** Much of the software developed by the U.S. Department of Defense is written in Ada and is used in embedded systems, which are computer systems built into other systems. Visual Basic is becoming a dominant language for the 1990s.

An **interpreter** translates a program in a high-level language one statement at a time into a machine language as the program is being run on the computer. A **compiler** translates an entire source program into machine language in one process.

Fourth-generation languages are **nonprocedural languages;** that is, they need not follow precise rules. Programs written in these languages are easier to code but give users less control over how each task is actually performed. They are designed so that users as well as programmers can easily access databases. Query languages allow users to retrieve information from databases by following simple syntax rules. **Report generators** produce customized reports using data stored in a database. **Application generators** create programs that allow data to be entered into a database.

Fifth-generation languages, which build expert systems, are intended to be **natural languages**—those that resemble as close as possible normal human interaction.

KEY TERMS

Ada, *p. 280*
Application generator, *p. 284*
Assembler, *p. 274*
Assembly language, *p. 274*
BASIC, *p. 277*
C, *p. 279*
C++, *p. 281*
COBOL, *p. 276*
Compiler, *p. 282*
Debugging, *p. 264*
Desk-checking, *p. 264*
Flowchart, *p. 260*
FORTRAN, *p. 276*
Hierarchy chart, *p. 262*
Inheritance, *p. 271*

Interactive debugger, *p. 265*
Interpreter, *p. 282*
Logic error, *p. 264*
Machine language, *p. 263*
Maintenance programmer, *p. 266*
Modula-2, *p. 278*
Module, *p. 263*
Natural language, *p. 285*
Nonprocedural language, *p. 275*
Object-oriented programming, *p. 271*
Object program, *p. 264*
Pascal, *p. 278*
Portable, *p. 274*
Procedural language, *p. 275*
Program testing, *p. 264*

Programmer analyst, *p. 257*
Pseudocode, *p. 261*
Report generator, *p. 284*
Reusable code, *p. 271*
Software development cycle, *p. 259*
Software engineering, *p. 266*
Source program, *p. 264*
Structure chart, *p. 262*
Structured programming, *p. 268*
Symbolic language, *p. 264*
Syntax error, *p. 264*
Visual Basic, *p. 282*
Visual programming, *p. 272*

CHAPTER SELF-TEST

1. (T or F) Programs must be coded before the program specifications are determined.

2. In large information processing departments, a _____ usually oversees each new project, whereas a _____ does the actual coding of the program.

3. A programming tool called a _____ uses special symbols to plan the program logic, while _____ uses English words to plan the logic.

4. Today, second-generation languages, also called _____ languages, are often used to develop systems software.

5. (T or F) In structured programming, programmers attempt to avoid using iteration.

6. _____ errors are grammatical mistakes in programs; _____ errors are caused by incorrect or incomplete processing steps.

7. Programming languages that are _____ can be executed on many different computers with minimal changes.

8. The language _____ has the advantages of both assembly languages and high-level languages and is often used for developing operating systems.

9. Programs written in a _____ language can be executed without first being translated.

10. (T or F) The programmer who uses the top-down approach divides a program solution into smaller and smaller parts.

11. A translator called a _____ translates and executes programs written in a symbolic language one statement at a time; in contrast, a translator called a _____ translates the entire source program into an object program that may be executed at any time.

12. What is the language most commonly used for business programs that need to access large files of data?

13. What was the first widely used high-level language for scientific and mathematical applications?

14. Which language did Niklaus Wirth develop to teach structured programming techniques to students?

15. (T or F) Fourth-generation languages such as SQL are often used to query databases.

16. (T or F) Programs are tested only after the installation and conversion process is completed.

17. What languages are most commonly used in artificial intelligence and expert systems?

REVIEW QUESTIONS

1. Describe the steps in the software development process.

2. What is structured programming and why is it so important today?

3. What is the difference between source and object code?

4. What is debugging?

5. Describe the differences between compilers, assemblers, and interpreters.

6. Why is documentation important?

Solutions

1. F
2. systems analyst; programmer
3. flowchart; pseudocode
4. assembly
5. F
6. Syntax; logic
7. portable
8. C
9. machine

10. T
11. interpreter; compiler
12. COBOL
13. FORTRAN
14. Pascal (and Modula-2)
15. T
16. F
17. Fifth-generation languages such as Prolog and LISP

CRITICAL THINKING EXERCISES

1. Based on the following, do you think rewriting COBOL programs in C or C++ is a good idea?

Some organizations that are making the switch from COBOL programs to C or C++ programs are regretting it. So far, there have been very few studies evaluating the cost-effectiveness of such a move and the impact on overall productivity, but some managers have begun to express their belief that the disadvantages are outweighing the benefits. They are finding that the information systems professionals who recommend abandoning COBOL are often the ones who emphasize quick-coding over programming quality. They are also finding that the switch from COBOL results in less user involvement in the program development process, because COBOL code is more clearly understandable to users.

2. Computer professionals often make a distinction between "programming" in languages such as BASIC and COBOL and "using" application packages such as Lotus 1-2-3 and Paradox. Indicate the ways in which writing a program differs from using an application package.

Case Study

Visual Programming

It appears that visual programming may live up to its promise and that in addition to being one of the most talked-about developments in programming, it might be one of the most useful.

Writing in *DEC Professional,* Kenneth L. Spencer praises such visual programming tools as Visual Basic for speed and productivity—and fun! He found that applications developed with visual programming tools required much less code—from 33% to 90% less—than with older programming languages, and that means that much less development time is required, which reduces software costs as well. New applications can be produced in weeks instead of years thanks to the reduction in the amount of "dreary" coding required. Instead of spending 80 to 90% of coding time on screen and error handling, the programmer can increase the functionality of the application by adding customized routines.

As Spencer describes it, Visual Basic is a powerful programming language in an easy-to-use graphical environment. Like other visual programming tools, it is "event-driven" instead of character or text-driven, which means that events, or subroutines, are triggered by clicking on items or icons selected from a drop-down list or menu. All the programmer needs to do is put the procedures to be executed in the desired place.

In other words, Visual Basic lets you draw and edit objects and then write the underlying code that links them in an application. Windows controls including dialog boxes, scroll bars, and toolbars can be added directly to an application. Screen displays can be "pizzazzed" up with graphics, animation, interesting type fonts, and all sorts of colors.

Don't be turned off by the word "Basic"—Visual Basic

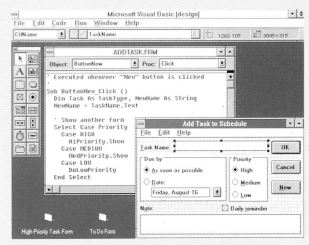

Sample Visual Basic program to determine the priority of a task to be added to a schedule.

is *not* old BASIC. There are no GO TOs or line numbers commonly associated with the nonstructured versions of BASIC. Rather, Visual Basic is a far more powerful programming language with access to a vast array of tools available for Windows. Visual Basic code is very structured and often looks more like C or Pascal than BASIC.

Analysis

1. What are some of the advantages of visual programming as described in this chapter?

2. Suppose your organization currently uses C++ for its programming needs. How would you go about determining whether a shift to Visual Basic would be appropriate?

CHAPTER 9
Systems Software

9.1 SYSTEMS SOFTWARE: FUNCTIONS AND FEATURES
What Systems Software Actually Does

9.2 MICROCOMPUTER OPERATING SYSTEMS AND GRAPHICAL USER INTERFACES
DOS: PC-DOS and MS-DOS

DOS with Windows

Windows 95 as a Full Operating System

OS/2 Warp

Macintosh Operating System

Operating Systems for the Power PC

Operating Systems for Personal Digital Assistants (PDAs) and Other Pen-Based Computers

9.3 OPERATING SYSTEMS THAT FACILITATE CONNECTIVITY
UNIX—An Operating System for All Categories of Computers

Network Operating Systems

NextStep

9.4 HOW OPERATING SYSTEMS MAXIMIZE PROCESSING EFFICIENCY
Multiprogramming and Multitasking

Multiprocessing

Virtual Memory and the "Virtual Machine" Concept

Other Tasks Performed by Systems Software

Whether application software is purchased off-the-shelf or custom-designed for an individual user, it is the driving force in a computer environment. But before the application programs can be run, a computer requires a set of control programs. These control programs supervise overall processing and establish an interface between the computer and the user. It is systems software that provides the control and interface.

Study Objectives

After reading this chapter you should be able to:

1. Identify the functions of operating systems and explain how users access them.

2. Name and describe some common operating systems for micros.

3. Describe the impact on the computing industry of the portability of the UNIX operating system and of the availability of network operating systems.

4. Outline some common features of operating systems.

9.1 SYSTEMS SOFTWARE: FUNCTIONS AND FEATURES

What Systems Software Actually Does

Application software today is much more sophisticated and diverse than programs were only a few years ago. Software packages are available to perform tasks as diverse as creating typeset-quality publications that contain complex graphics or keeping track of daily appointments. If no package can manipulate data in ways that a user desires, then custom products can be developed.

Study Objective

1. Identify the functions of operating systems and explain how users access them.

Not only must application software perform complex tasks, it must also be user-friendly. As application programs become easier to use, so too does the systems software that includes the operating system and acts as an interface between us and the hardware. The systems software that has become available for micros is not only user-friendly, but it also is capable of running several applications concurrently.

The most important demand we make of the systems software for our computers is that it allow us to use our time as efficiently as possible. Of late, the services provided by systems software are becoming more diversified. Some of this software can provide a detailed accounting of how computer resources are being used. Some have antiviral programs built in for protection, along with other utilities that make it easier to use the computer system and enable it to run more efficiently.

The operating system is the main component of systems software, but, as we will see, there are other components as well. Operating systems have two basic functions: to efficiently manage the computer's resources and to execute the user's instructions. The part of the operating system that manages the computer's resources—including the CPU, primary storage, and peripheral devices—is commonly called the **kernel** (or the **supervisor** or control program). It is the kernel that monitors the keyboard—it determines when a key has been

▪N A NUTSHELL

COMPONENTS OF
SYSTEMS SOFTWARE

1. Operating system kernel and user interface
2. Utilities—e.g., virus scanner, file transfer conversion program, undelete option, error detection, systems monitoring
3. Language translators—e.g., BASIC

depressed and what action to take. The kernel also performs basic functions such as switching between tasks. The operating system controls the transfer of data from secondary storage to main memory and back again.

The **user interface,** or operating environment, is the part of the systems software that permits you to communicate with the hardware, for example, to instruct the system to execute a particular application package or to save a file. On larger systems, on some micros, and on networked systems, the user interface controls access through user IDs, passwords, and access codes. Figure 9.1 illustrates how the parts of the operating system interact with the user and the computer hardware.

As you would expect, systems software for micros is less sophisticated and has fewer capabilities than similar software for larger systems. The systems software for a large computer may manage many terminals at different sites and allocate resources to multiple users. On the other hand, systems software for a stand-alone PC is usually intended for single users. In addition, systems software for a micro may include one or two translator programs (e.g., for BASIC), whereas systems software for larger systems may have numerous translators.

Systems Software Can Facilitate Interactivity. Connectivity is so important in today's world because it enables computers with different architectures and different systems software to communicate with each other and to make use of each other's resources.

In contrast to application software, systems software is often supplied by the computer manufacturer or a vendor, along with the hardware. If the price of the hardware includes the systems software, we say it is **bundled** with the computer. Sometimes application packages are also included in the bundle. If you prefer a different operating system or other systems software programs that are compatible with your computer but are not bundled with it, or if you want a newer version of the operating system you currently have, you can purchase the programs separately. As with any packaged software, outlets for such purchases include computer manufacturers, stores, or mail-order houses that advertise in computing magazines and newspapers. Prices of an operating system or other systems

Figure 9.1 *An operating system consists of a user interface that accepts user requests and interprets the various activities or applications to be performed, and a kernel that controls the execution of these activities.*

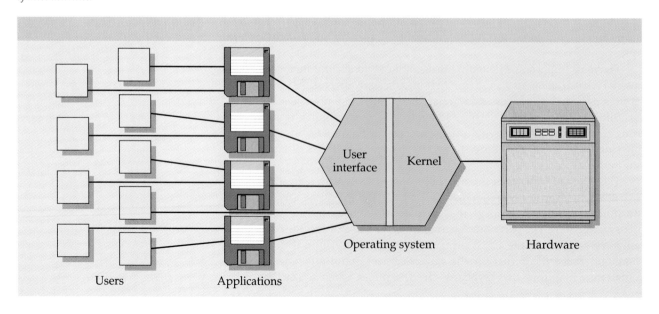

Users   Applications   User interface   Kernel   Hardware

Operating system

ɪɴ A NUTSHELL

TYPES OF SOFTWARE

Systems software	The programs that enable the computer to process data quickly and efficiently; consists of many different types of programs.
Operating system software	The part of systems software that actually controls computer operations; consists of programs that monitor and supervise computer processing.

software components vary widely, but most are under $100. UNIX, another operating system, varies in price from hundreds of dollars to thousands of dollars depending on the computer. Operating systems for mainframes typically cost thousands of dollars.

Because it needs to control and maximize the efficient use of hardware, systems software must be written for each computer's architecture. Hence, such software is not often portable, or usable with other types of computers. Systems software for the Macintosh, for example, cannot be used on an IBM-compatible without a conversion program. Mainframes have systems software that is dramatically different from such software for PCs. Most systems software for mainframes was written almost exclusively in a computer's assembler language. More recently developed systems software programs, however, are written in the C programming language, because C permits direct addressing of a computer's memory and it is portable. The newest systems software is often written in C++, an object-oriented version of C, that is capable of providing graphical user interfaces.

Systems software is written by **systems programmers**—software developers with knowledge of computer architecture. Systems programmers write instructions that use as little RAM as possible so that there is more main memory available for application software.

A multitude of operating systems are currently available as part of systems software. Some of these operating systems, such as DOS and the Macintosh operating system, are designed to be used with specific microcomputers. Others, such as IBM and IBM-compatible mainframe operating systems, can be implemented only on large computers. Still others, such as UNIX, are applicable to all levels—microcomputers, minicomputers, midranges, mainframes, and even supercomputers. UNIX, in fact, is available for many different "platforms," that is, computers developed by different manufacturers or computers of different sizes. Its use on DEC superminis, for example, as well as IBM mainframes and PCs, makes UNIX viable as a candidate for a general-purpose, standardized operating system or as the main operating system in a networked environment.

Self-Test

1. The _____ software controls the overall operations of a computer and enables it to run as efficiently as possible.

2. The main component of systems software is the _____ system.

3. (T or F) Systems software often includes utilities such as antiviral programs.

4. Operating systems are written by _____ programmers.

5. The operating environment or _____ is the part of the systems software that enables users to communicate with the hardware.

▮▮▮ 9.2 MICROCOMPUTER OPERATING SYSTEMS AND GRAPHICAL USER INTERFACES

The microcomputer world is dominated by two families of operating systems: the DOS/Windows and OS/2 operating systems used with IBM-compatibles, and the Apple Macintosh operating system.

DOS: PC-DOS and MS-DOS

The disk operating system IBM initially chose for its personal computer is known by the acronym PC-DOS (Personal Computer Disk Operating System). It was developed by Microsoft Corporation, which also offers a generic version called MS-DOS (Microsoft Disk Operating System) for IBM-compatible computers. We will refer to both of these operating systems simply as DOS.

DOS was introduced in 1981 when the first IBM PC was unveiled. To date, over 150 million copies have been sold and there are literally tens of thousands of applications written for DOS-based or IBM-compatible computers.

DOS tells the computer how to format, read, and write information on either floppy disks or hard disks. It manages peripheral devices such as the printer and the keyboard. It also controls the execution of applications software. In addition, it establishes several parameters, such as the number of files that can be contained in a disk directory, the number of bytes that can be on a disk, and the number of bytes of memory usable by a program.

To boot or start up an IBM-compatible microcomputer, DOS is loaded from the hard drive, which is typically called the C drive. (Each disk drive of an IBM-compatible micro is assigned a letter.) DOS loads the COMMAND.COM file, which performs diagnostic tests on hardware. You then see an A> or C> prompt, depending on which drive has the operating system software in it. For most versions of DOS, operating system commands are entered at what is called the command line—the line with the disk drive prompt. For example, to see the names of the files stored on the disk in drive A, type the operating system command DIR at the A> prompt (A> DIR) and press the Enter key.

DOS has been updated many times to take advantage of technological improvements. Each new version of DOS is assigned a version number. The higher the number, the more sophisticated and more recent the version. For example, when DOS 2.0 was released, it was a major improvement over DOS 1.0. DOS 2.1, on the other hand, contained minor improvements over 2.0.

Solutions

1. systems

2. operating

3. T

4. systems

5. user interface

Looking Back ◀ •••••••••••••••••••••••••••••••••••••••

DOS VERSIONS

VERSION	DATE	FEATURES
1.0	1981	The original version; provides date and time stamping for each file created, has a simple line editor and some utilities, and includes a BASIC translator
2.0	1983	Provides support for subdirectories and color and handles more functions
3.0	1984	Provides support for high-density 5¼-inch disks and hard disks up to 32 MB; adds network support
3.3	1987	Provides support for IBM PS/2 computers
4.0	1988	Includes a menu-driven user interface shell; provides support for hard disks over 32 MB
5.0	1990	Provides Windows interface and better memory management; uses less RAM; permits easy upgrading from lower DOS versions
5.02	1992	Includes standard fonts for European compatibility, power management and file transfer
6.0	1993	Includes built-in disk compression called Double Space and various utilities for antivirus, backup, undelete, and file transfer
6.1	1993	Includes different utilities than MS-DOS 6.0
6.2	1993	Includes 6.0 bug fix
6.21	1994	Does not include the Double Space disk compression program as a result of Stac Electronics's successful patent infringement lawsuit against Microsoft
6.3	1994	Includes new disk compression features significantly different from the features found in Stac Electronics's Stacker program
7.0	1995	Improved multitasking and memory management; includes Stacker 4.0 hard disk compression; detects more than 2000 viruses

Through the 1980s, DOS was essentially a command-driven operating system that was not at all user-friendly. You needed to type precise commands such as COPY A:*.* B: to copy all files from the A drive to the B drive. Moreover, DOS was essentially a one-task-per-machine type of operating system—it did not lend itself to multiprogramming. Compared to Apple's Macintosh operating system, it seemed antiquated. See Figure 9.2.

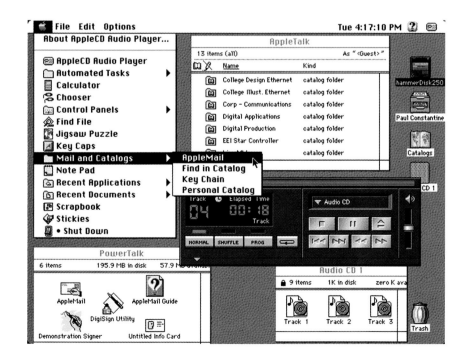

Figure 9.2 *The Macintosh operating system—with its user-friendly screen displays.*

IN A NUTSHELL

COMMON DOS COMMANDS (FOR ALL VERSIONS)

COMMAND	FUNCTION
DATE	Allows current date to be set or changed
TIME	Allows current time to be set or changed
FORMAT	Initializes diskettes
VER	Displays the DOS version number
DIR	Displays any disk's directory
TYPE	Displays the contents of a file
COPY	Copies files
DISKCOPY	Formats a disk and copies all files from one disk to another
CHKDSK	Checks for a disk's available space and specifies whether there are faulty files on the disk
RENAME or REN	Renames files
DEL or ERASE	Deletes files
MKDIR or MD	Creates new directory
CHDIR or CD	Changes the current directory
RMDIR or RD	Removes empty directories

In 1990, DOS 5.0 gave users the most significant update in years. It was the first version of DOS to take advantage of the extended memory beyond 640 K, which is now available on 80386, 80486, and Pentium computers. Extended memory is controlled by disk caches; DOS 5.0 (and higher) automatically recognizes caches so that there is no need for a formal installation procedure.

Despite its advances, DOS 5.0 was the first version of DOS that needed *less* RAM than its predecessors, actually about 5 K less. Unlike most of the older versions of DOS that required you to type specific commands, DOS 5.0, as well as DOS 4.0 before it, allowed you to select commands from a menu if you preferred (see Figure 9.3). In this respect, DOS 4.0 and 5.0 were more user-friendly than their predecessors. DOS 5.0 was also the first version available separately through retail PC stores; previous versions were bundled with the computer.

A disadvantage of DOS 4.1 and lower versions was that if you had a hard disk and had to reinstall the operating system onto the hard disk, you had to reformat the disk and reload all files—a time-consuming and tedious task.

Figure 9.3 *DOS 4.0–6.2 have a user-friendly shell with features such as a pull-down menu that were unavailable in earlier versions. This figure illustrates the DOS 6.0 View pull-down menu.*

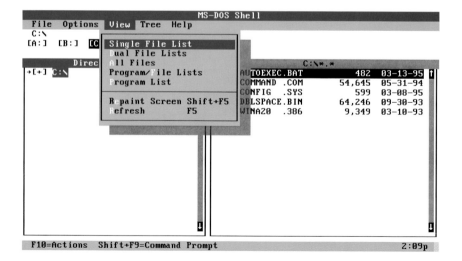

Beginning with DOS 5.0, you may upgrade a previous version of DOS *without* having to reinstall it.

DOS 5.0 and more recent versions have other advantages for users. They offer online help and enable applications to be launched by using a mouse. With DOS 5.0 and more recent versions, tasks can be performed that were previously available only with add-on systems software packages like Norton Utilities. With older versions of DOS, if you needed to find a file but didn't know what subdirectory it was in, you had to change to each subdirectory, then type DIR to see what was in the individual subdirectory. If you have many subdirectories, this is a tedious process. DOS 5.0 can search subdirectories for specific files with a single command. Also, UNDELETE, like Norton Utilities' UNERASE, can restore files that were accidentally erased.

DOS once had a very basic text editor called EDLIN, but it was difficult to use. Beginning with DOS 5.0, the "clunky" EDLIN was superseded by a new mouse-driven, full-screen text editor called EDIT with cut and paste capabilities, clip art, and pull-down menus. DOS 5 through 7 also provide an interactive version of the BASIC programming language called QBASIC, which has a much better interface, translator, and help menus than previous versions of the language. (*Getting Started with Structured BASIC* is a supplement to this text that includes coverage of QBASIC.)

DOS with Windows

Throughout the years, a number of improved user interfaces have been created in an attempt to make DOS easier to use. These improvements include software features that are more graphic than text oriented. Graphical user interfaces use icons (i.e., symbols) to represent various objects. The most popular user interface that works in conjunction with DOS is Microsoft Windows. With this interface, each application is opened in a window and several windows can be opened at once, allowing you to switch from one application to another.

The early versions of Windows including Windows 3.1 and Windows 3.11 for Workgroups, which are still widely used, were not full operating systems. They provided an operating environment or graphical user interface (GUI). That is, Windows 3.11 and earlier versions operate under the control of DOS and provide a kind of bridge between the user and DOS—a responsive and user-friendly bridge. Many people believe that Windows used in conjunction with DOS makes an IBM-compatible micro as user-friendly as a Macintosh.

Windows frees you to work as you would at your desk; you can, for example, spread out several "windowed" documents for reference and to work on simultaneously. This feature enables you to perform some multitasking operations not previously available with older versions of DOS. The most recent versions of DOS and Windows enable programs to access more than 640 K of memory, which was once a limitation of IBM-compatible micros.

Windows has pull-down menus from which you select commands. To select a command, use the cursor keys to highlight it and press Enter, or use the mouse to point to it and then click on the entry. With Windows, then, there is no need to memorize operating system commands.

Because Windows 3.1 (and 3.11) for IBM-compatibles is an operating environment or user interface and not an actual operating system, DOS must be loaded in first when the computer is turned on. With the Mac, the Windows interface is actually part of the operating system so that no other program is required for starting up. There is, however, one advantage to the IBM-compatible version: Windows 3.1 (and 3.11) for IBM-compatibles is supplied with a

IN A NUTSHELL

The most important feature of any operating system is the availability of high-quality applications that are developed specifically for that operating system at a reasonable price.

number of desktop programs such as Write, a word processor, and Paintbrush, a graphics tool. The Mac counterpart to these two products, MacWrite and Mac-Draw, must be purchased separately.

One primary objective of Windows 3.1 is to permit the user to perform multitasking, that is, to run more than one application concurrently including its own desktop programs. With multitasking, there is no need to leave or "close" one application in order to load or "open" a second application. The concept is analogous to a desk that has several elements (e.g., a calculator, calendar, phone book) available at the same time. It is not uncommon for a person preparing a budget to suddenly need to call someone to make an appointment before returning to the budget. With multitasking, the spreadsheet for the budget, the calculator, the calendar, and the phone book are all available to the user at the same time.

There are several desktop programs that are supplied as accessories with Windows. Any of these Windows programs can be run either alone or in conjunction with others. By selecting an icon, you can run the application represented by the symbol at any time. To select the icon, you point to it with a mouse and then click the left mouse button. See Figure 9.4a. The programs include the following:

1. Calculator.

2. Calendar—For displaying a view of your calendar in month or day format and for setting alarms to "beep" at specific times. See Figure 9.4b.

3. Notepad—For writing brief notes.

4. Card File—For creating "index" cards.

5. Clock—For displaying the time in digital or analog form.

6. Paintbrush—For drawing or modifying illustrations.

7. Write—For simple word processing.

8. Clipboard—For saving a portion of any application so that it can be "pasted," or copied, to another application. A full spreadsheet or a portion of a spreadsheet, for example, can be stored in the clipboard and pasted to a document prepared by a word processor. The clipboard serves as a temporary holding area for transferring information from one application to another.

A wide variety of applications are designed specifically to run in conjunction with Windows. The following are applications that must run in a Windows environment: Microsoft Word, a word processing package; Toolbook, a multimedia authoring tool; Aldus PageMaker, a desktop publishing package; and CorelDRAW, a graphics package. In addition, many software packages like Lotus 1-2-3 and WordPerfect have both DOS and Windows versions as well as Mac versions.

Applications that run under Windows have been developed to take advantage of Windows features and to work with other Windows applications in a multitasking environment. They are generally more graphical in their presentations and use of icons. Windows also provides a memory management system that interfaces more efficiently with applications.

Non-Windows applications can often be used in a Windows environment, even though they were not specifically designed for that purpose, but sometimes they cannot be active along with another program. Users need to experiment to find out how well given applications work in the Windows environment if they are not specifically designed for it.

In addition to having multitasking capability, a user-friendly screen display, and a set of desktop accessories, Windows permits users to size and position

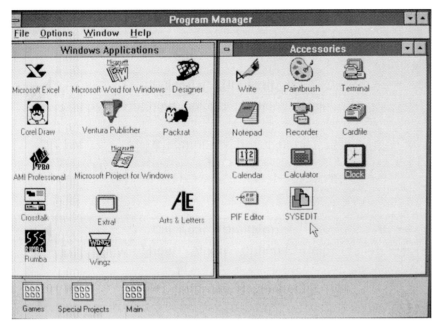

(a)

Figure 9.4 (a) Microsoft Windows presents the user with typical graphical user interface features: windows, icons for files, and pull-down menus. (b) If you double-click on the Calendar icon, a window such as this appears. It will display the hours for the current day.

(b)

windowed applications to suit individual tastes and needs. Another advantage is its ability to move text or graphic data from one application to another easily and efficiently by means of its clipboard feature. Other versions of the Windows graphical user interface, which run under DOS, include Windows NT, a "power" version, and Windows for Workgroups, a groupware version.

IN A NUTSHELL

WHY USE WINDOWS FOR IBM-COMPATIBLES?

- Instead of typing in cryptic commands, you can simply use a mouse to select icons that execute commands.
- You can run more than one application at a time.
- You have at your disposal desktop applications such as a built-in calculator, clock, calendar, and so on which make your computer simulate a real desktop.
- You may need it to run many of your application packages.
- You can easily copy or move text and graphic data from one application to another.
- Many different type fonts are available with Windows.
- Your hard disk becomes an extension of main memory, enabling you to effectively use more than 640 K of storage, even if your computer's primary storage capacity is only 640 K.

- You can display programs and data in windows that can be sized, moved to a different place on the screen, overlaid on top of other displays, or "tiled" next to one another. This provides visual features that text-based programs simply cannot match.
- You can easily group tasks and programs into logical categories and identify them with an icon for easy access.
- You can use your mouse not only to select objects, but also to drag them to different locations on the screen. For example, if you want a wider column in a spreadsheet, you can drag it and size it any way you want.

Windows 95 as a Full Operating System

The DOS/Windows interface has been a successful combination for many years, and each version has been incrementally better than the previous one. Windows 95 is a totally new product that is itself a full operating system. See Figure 9.5.

Unlike the previous versions of Windows, Windows 95 takes full advantage of the 32-bit architecture in newer PCs. This means that the computer will perform faster in a Windows environment. With its totally redesigned interface Win-

Figure 9.5 *Windows 95 screen display.*

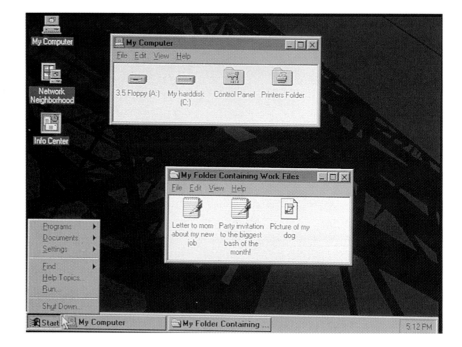

IN A NUTSHELL

WHAT'S NEW IN WINDOWS 95

1. Windows is a full operating system that includes DOS
   No more A> B> C> etc. prompts: DOS is built in and runs in the background.
2. An enhanced user interface
   File Manager and Program Manager have been combined into a more intuitive program called Explorer.
3. Long Filenames
   No more eight-character filename limitation—you now have 255 characters in which to create clearly labeled names.
4. Increased Compatibility
   Windows adds support for drivers, software, and hardware. You can keep your existing software and you can add new resources with a minimum of installation worries.
5. The Information Superhighway
   TCP/IP protocols are built into Windows that facilitate Internet access.

---

dows 95 also offers true multitasking. It provides "Plug and Play" support designed to make installing and upgrading peripherals easier—devices need only be plugged in and they will be configured with appropriate drivers automatically. The Windows 95 Configuration Manager coordinates all hardware device drivers and resources in your PC. Multimedia systems that use sophisticated hardware benefit greatly from this Plug and Play capability, although some cynics refer to "Plug and Play" as "Plug and Pray."

Until now, the number of characters in a filename was limited to eight, with a three-character limit on filename extensions. Windows 95 does not have this limitation. See Figure 9.6.

Windows 95 is designed to compete directly with IBM's newest OS/2 and with Taligent's operating system for the Power PC.

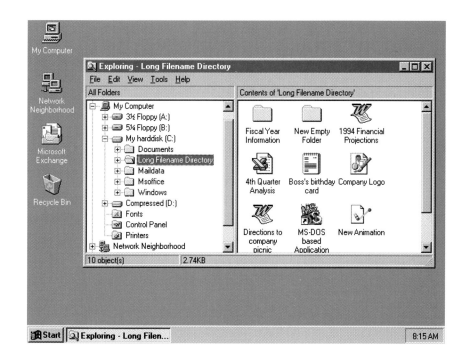

Figure 9.6 *Windows 95 Explorer screen display.*

Windows 95 will run existing DOS and Windows 3.1 applications in a slower way, called emulation mode, that requires a computerized translation before programs can be executed.

OS/2 Warp

In 1987, IBM announced a new line of personal computers, the PS/2 (Personal System/2) series. The original versions of the OS/2 operating system were written for these 80286 PS/2 computers and were developed jointly by IBM and Microsoft. The current versions are IBM products. In fact, IBM with its current version called OS/2 Warp, and Microsoft with its DOS and Windows products are direct competitors for the IBM-compatible computers that use Intel or Intel-based chips. See Figure 9.7.

Currently there are 7 million users of OS/2 and 47 million users of Windows. Many more software products are available as Windows-based programs than as OS/2-based products, but OS/2 can run Windows and DOS software as well.

For many years, OS/2 Warp has had many of the features now available with Windows 95: It takes advantage of 32-bit architecture, it offers true multitasking, it has Plug and Play capability, it supports long filenames, and its latest user interface, the Workplace Shell, is similar to the Mac interface.

Macintosh Operating System

Unlike IBM-compatibles, the original Macintosh always provided a graphical, rather than a text-based, interface between the user and the system. The Mac operating system is also unlike the original DOS in that there never was a need to memorize a variety of commands; the Macintosh presents such commands in a menu. This approach proved to be so popular that the IBM world, first with Microsoft Windows and more recently with OS/2, adopted a similar look for its interfaces.

Figure 9.7 *OS/2 screen display.*

●●●●●●●●●●●●●●●●●●●●●●●●●●●●●●● ➤ *Looking Ahead*

WHICH OPERATING SYSTEMS WILL DOMINATE?

The operating system war between IBM and Microsoft has heated up recently with the arrival of Windows 95 and the competition for Power PC market share. The new operating system from Taligent is still another product competing in this market. All these operating systems are likely to survive, further reducing the potential for standardization that so many users seek.

When you first turn on a Macintosh, you see a "desktop" with icons representing various files. See Figure 9.8. Related files can be placed in "folders," which are similar to subdirectories. Finder, which manages a single application, and MultiFinder, which manages multiple applications, are the Mac's graphical user interfaces that allow you to open and manipulate the files on the desktop. Most often, the actions needed to perform a specific function are obvious. For example, if you want to delete a file, you use the mouse to place the file in the trash can. You select additional commands from pull-down menus, which are displayed when you select a main menu item.

The graphics capabilities of the Macintosh are very popular with publishers, designers, journalists, and educators. The Mac's acceptance in business and industry, however, has been slow, largely because Mac could not run DOS applications until recently. In addition, the original Macintoshes, unlike IBM-compatible micros, did not allow for easy expansion. Most DOS-based computers have expansion slots that allow you to customize the system to meet your specific needs; in contrast, adding more peripheral devices to the early Macintoshes was a difficult task. The newer Macintoshes, however, such as the Quadra, have numerous expansion slots, and special circuit boards can be added to allow them to run DOS software.

The Mac's latest version of its operating system is 7.5. For the first time, Apple will license this operating system so that other computers can use it. This

ⁱⁿ A NUTSHELL

There are emulators or translators such as Soft PC that enable a Mac to run IBM-compatible, DOS-based software. This provides some cross-platform capability but emulators tend to be slow.

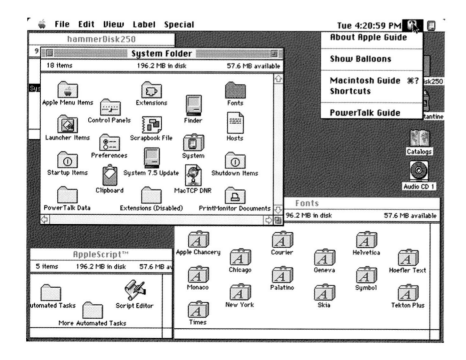

Figure 9.8 *On a Macintosh, items are selected from menus. To select an entry, use the mouse to position the cursor on the menu item. Click the left mouse button. Then release the button to execute the command.*

is likely to further heat up the battle between the Mac operating system and Windows 95.

System 7.5 includes PowerTalk, which has an updated Finder, and sophisticated groupware and communications capability. Its built-in e-mail facility includes directory services and digital signatures that enable e-mail recipients to verify the identity of a sender by checking signatures. Communications capability includes links to paging systems and the ability to keep track of e-mail efficiently and effectively.

System 7.5 includes an OpenDoc data-sharing facility, an AppleScript language for automating routine tasks, and QuickTime for developing and playing multimedia applications using sound, video, and animation.

Operating Systems for the Power PC

In 1991, Apple and IBM formed a joint-venture company called Taligent, Inc. which was to develop a cross-platform operating system for Power PCs, IBM-compatibles, and Macs. Since then, Hewlett-Packard has bought a 15% interest in the new company.

Taligent, Inc. has developed some innovative operating system components that can be used with OS/2 and Apple's System 7 and 7.5. A full operating system is scheduled to be released in 1996.

Taligent components consist of frameworks, which are collections of object-oriented libraries or reusable code that form the foundation for user applications. There are frameworks for handling graphics, database access, networking, and multimedia, just to name a few. Frameworks facilitate collaborative work by enabling users to share objects such as e-mail messages and databases.

Taligent also has a highly interactive user-friendly interface called People, Places, and Things, which refers to three objects in the interface. A business card is an example of a People object. A Thing object could be a telephone that a user can drag to the business card to telephone that person. Place objects may be locations that a user can click on to access services.

So far, no common operating system has emerged for the new Power PC. Software developers who want their products to run on this RISC-based machine have to either gamble and select one or two operating systems they think are likely to dominate or create numerous versions of their products.

Apple's Power Mac can run a version of the Mac's System 7.5, only some of which has been optimized for the Power PC chip. It can also run Windows 95. IBM's Power PC can also run an enhanced version of OS/2 called OS/2 Heavy, Windows 95, Windows for Workgroups, and IBM's version of UNIX called AIX. To run DOS and DOS/Windows 3.1 software on the Power PC, you need an emulator such as Soft PC. Novell has developed a version of its network operating system NetWare for this machine. The new Taligent operating system will run on all versions of the Power PC.

Operating Systems for Personal Digital Assistants (PDAs) and Other Pen-Based Computers

Personal Digital Assistants (PDAs), the handheld or palmtop pen-based computers, have their own operating systems, each with a different focus. So far, PDAs have not sold very well—under 200,000 in 1995. They are expensive—

Figure 9.9 *This screen displays the Magic Cap desktop manager for PDAs.*

surveys show that at about $1,000 they cost twice what buyers want to spend. Some, but not all, provide applications similar to those for desktops. The handwriting recognition capability of the machines is still not adequate. Finally, their wireless communication features are bulky and expensive. When the handwriting and communications components improve and the cost decreases, PDAs are likely to capture a larger share of the market.

The main operating systems have different features as well:

Microsoft's WinPad	Designed for PDAs that are used primarily for business applications. WinPad provides a window to a user's desktop PC.
General Magic's Magic Cap	Originally designed for Motorola's Envoy PDA, this operating system has sophisticated wireless communication capabilities with linkages provided over radio or phone lines. See Figure 9.9.
Apple's Newton Message Pad	Designed for Newtons that are used over networks. This operating system also has sophisticated handwriting recognition capability.
Geowork's GEOS	Similar in concept to the Newton Message Pad, it provides wireless communication and handwriting recognition capability.

Self-Test

1. Name and describe the two versions of DOS for IBM-compatibles.
2. What is the most popular graphical user interface used with DOS?
3. Name another IBM operating system that has its own graphical use interface.

4. What micro has always had a graphical user interface that makes it seem very user-friendly?

5. (T or F) Windows helps IBM micros perform multitasking more effectively.

6. Name two operating systems for PDAs.

▇▇▇ 9.3 OPERATING SYSTEMS THAT FACILITATE CONNECTIVITY

UNIX—An Operating System for All Categories of Computers

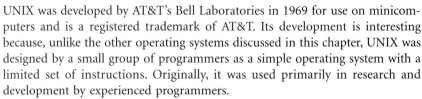

UNIX was developed by AT&T's Bell Laboratories in 1969 for use on minicomputers and is a registered trademark of AT&T. Its development is interesting because, unlike the other operating systems discussed in this chapter, UNIX was designed by a small group of programmers as a simple operating system with a limited set of instructions. Originally, it was used primarily in research and development by experienced programmers.

UNIX has two advantages. Unlike most operating systems, it is available on many different types and sizes of computers. Its portability stems from the fact that it was written in the programming language C rather than in an assembly language. Because of its portability, it is referred to as an open system. In addition, UNIX was one of the first operating systems designed to provide smaller computers with multiprogramming capability.

As more sophisticated microcomputers are developed to support multitasking and multiuser environments, UNIX is becoming the operating system of choice. Microsoft has a version of UNIX called XENIX for microcomputers, IBM supports a version called AIX for its computers, and Apple's version is called A/UX. There are UNIX operating systems for Sun RISC workstations and most minis and mainframes as well. Because of the variety of implementations and its popularity among programmers (many of whom were trained to use it on university computer systems), UNIX is now widely available in business and industry and is expected to gain even more popularity in the years ahead.

The original goal of UNIX was to build an interactive programming environment that had features to help programmers develop software more efficiently. For example, UNIX provides a wide variety of utility programs called tools. The user interface is contained in a **shell,** or separate software module, and is not part of the operating system itself. There are a number of commonly used UNIX shells.

A major complaint about UNIX is that it is not particularly user-friendly. Its commands are often cryptic and difficult to remember (see Table 9.1). How-

Study Objective

3. Describe the impact on the computing industry of the portability of the UNIX operating system and of the availability of network operating systems.

▪ᴺ A NUTSHELL

UNIX has two main features: portability and multiuser connectivity.

```
                    cmdtool - /bin/csh
1264 libF77_p.a          80 libolgx.a
3168 libIV.so.3.0       112 libolgx.so
   8 libV77.a           112 libolgx.so.3.1
  48 libV77.so.1.1       86 libolgx_p.a
   8 libV77_p.a           2 test.f
 480 libXaw.a
(Marge:CQ-SERVER) -> /bin/rm -rf *
(Marge:CQ-SERVER) -> ls -Fs
total 0
(Marge:CQ-SERVER) -> pwd
/export/home/marge/tmp
(Marge:CQ-SERVER) -> ls -Fs
total 0
(Marge:CQ-SERVER) -> cp ../lib/* .
(Marge:CQ-SERVER) -> /bin/rm -rf *
(Marge:CQ-SERVER) -> mkdir tmp
(Marge:CQ-SERVER) -> cd tmp
~/tmp/tmp
(Marge:CQ-SERVER) -> cd ..
~/tmp
(Marge:CQ-SERVER) -> rmdir tmp
(Marge:CQ-SERVER) ->
```

Sample UNIX screen display.

Solutions

1. PC-DOS is for IBM micros and MS-DOS is for IBM-compatibles.

2. Windows

3. OS/2

4. Macintosh

5. T

6. Newton Message Pad, Magic Cap, WinPad, GEOS

UNIX COMMAND	DESCRIPTION
pwd	Lists the current directory
ls	Lists files and subdirectories in current directory
cp	Copies files or directories
mv	Renames a file
mkdir	Creates a subdirectory
rmdir	Removes a subdirectory
tput clear	Clears the display screen
lp	Queues and prints data files
cat	Displays contents of a text file

Table 9.1 *Common UNIX Commands*

ever, many computer manufacturers supply user-friendly shells such as Motif and Open Look to make these systems easier to use. Another major complaint is that there are many versions of UNIX, all slightly different.

Because the UNIX operating system is available on a broad spectrum of computers, it is becoming widely used in networks where many different types of systems are linked to one another. Currently, most Internet access tools are UNIX-based. For example, TCP/IP is a UNIX-based communication package for networking incompatible systems. TCP/IP is an abbreviation for Transmission Control Protocol/Internet Protocol. File transfers and e-mail over the Internet are typically handled by TCP/IP.

Network Operating Systems

Special network operating systems like Novell NetWare for IBM-compatibles and Mac computers and AppleShare for Mac networks not only perform standard operating system tasks but also monitor shared resources so that effective uti-

Critical Thinking

Suppose your organization had a number of IBM-compatible PCs and you were asked to standardize with a single operating system. What questions would you ask users before making your decision?

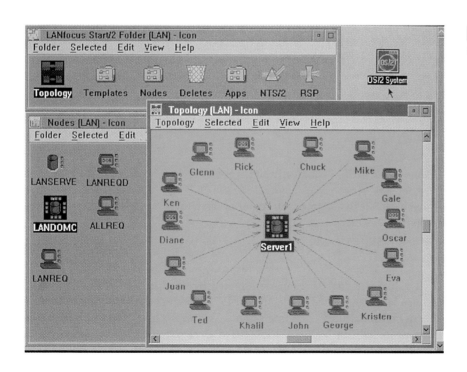

Figure 9.10 *OS/2 network screen display.*

Table 9.2 *A Review of Operating Systems Software for Microcomputers*

SYSTEM	FEATURES
Macintosh operating system	The first operating system to have a user-friendly interface, called the Finder, which allows the user to select commands from pull-down menus. Objects such as files are represented by icons. A multi-tasking version called MultiFinder is now available.

Systems for IBM Micros and Compatibles

SYSTEM	FEATURES
DOS 1.0–4.1	First operating system for IBM and IBM-compatible PCs and PS/2s. It is command driven; that is, commands are entered without benefit of menus or prompts. It also has strict memory limits. DOS 4.0, 4.1 and higher include an optional command menu shell, mouse support, direct support of expanded memory, and support for hard disks larger than 32 MB.
DOS 5.0–7.0	An operating system with multitasking capability, memory management beyond 640 K, virus scanner, and some extra disk-handling features. It provides for easy upgrade from previous versions of DOS.
Microsoft Windows 3.1: A Graphical User Interface for DOS	Allows several programs to be open at a time, each in its own window. Windows 3.0, 3.1, and higher have a true multitasking environment and eliminate the 640 K RAM limitation imposed by DOS 4.1 and lower versions.
OS/2	IBM's operating system introduced with the PS/2 family of micros. PS/2s can use DOS with Windows, the original OS/2 with Presentation Manager, which is a graphical user interface similar to Microsoft Windows, or OS/2 Warp.
Windows 95	The first version of Windows that is a full operating system.

Other Operating Systems for PCs

SYSTEM	FEATURES
UNIX for PCs	IBM's AIX and Apple's A/UX are UNIX operating systems for PCs. Uses standard commands and is available on a wide variety of computers of all sizes. IBM's AIX is also the standard operating system for IBM's midrange AS/400.
Network operating system	Novell Netware, AppleShare, and Windows NT are operating systems designed to more effectively share resources in a networked environment.

lization of all hardware and software is achieved. Windows and OS/2 Warp also have network versions. See Figure 9.10.

Table 9.2 reviews the various types of operating systems software for micro-computers.

NextStep

NeXt Computer, Inc., a company founded by Stephen Jobs (who along with Stephen Wozniak formed Apple, Inc., in 1976), has developed the first fully operational object-oriented operating system. NextStep is a UNIX-like product that runs successfully on high-end RISC-based workstations. NeXt is promoting its operating system for IBM-compatible computers with 486 or Pentium chips.

NextStep has an impressive graphical user interface (GUI), good text editor and file viewer, and multimedia electronic mail capability, and is designed for use in a network environment.

Its object-oriented technology enables you to easily enhance system features and have them "inherited" by all applications that rely on those features. For example, if you add color scanning capability to your optical character recognition (OCR) equipment, all applications that use the OCR object will automatically have color scanning ability.

NextStep is a high-end operating system that is expensive (about $700) and has significant hardware needs. Sixteen megabytes of RAM is required (32 MB is actually recommended) and you must have at least 250 MB of hard disk space.

Insignia Solution's Soft PC enables DOS and Windows applications to run with NextStep.

More than 100,000 copies of NextStep have been sold to date and the expectation is that this operating system will remain competitive for high-end, RISC-based workstations.

Self-Test

1. Why is UNIX such a popular operating system?

2. What are some disadvantages of UNIX?

3. What does IBM call its version of UNIX for IBM micros?

4. What type of operating system is Novell NetWare?

5. _____ is a UNIX-based communication tool that handles file transfers and e-mail over the Internet.

9.4 HOW OPERATING SYSTEMS MAXIMIZE PROCESSING EFFICIENCY

One of the primary purposes of an operating system is to ensure that a computer's resources are used as efficiently and effectively as possible. In this section we discuss some of the ways this is accomplished.

Study Objective

4. Outline some common features of operating systems.

Multiprogramming and Multitasking

Most larger computer systems are capable of running many programs concurrently by means of a technique called multiprogramming. With multiprogramming, several application programs are placed in the computer's primary stor-

---

Solutions

1. UNIX can be used on a variety of computers; that is, it is portable.

2. It is command driven and not particularly user-friendly; there are different versions that are not compatible.

3. AIX

4. It is a network operating system designed to enable resources to be effectively shared among different computers.

5. TCP/IP

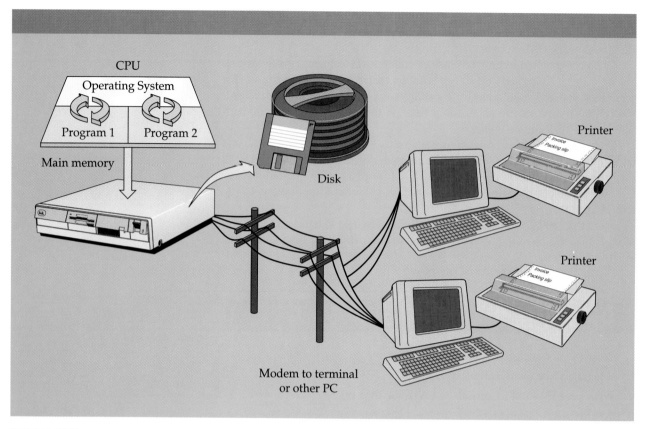

Figure 9.11 *An operating system with multiprogramming capability enables one or more users to communicate with one or more programs and one or more peripherals.*

SPECIFIC FUNCTIONS PERFORMED BY AN OPERATING SYSTEM

- Works with ROM to boot the computer.
- Performs diagnostic tests to ensure that the components are functioning properly.
- Controls access to the computer.
- Provides an interface between the user and the computer.
- Manages data and controls transfers between secondary storage and main memory.
- Activates peripherals as needed.
- Makes utilities and other systems software available.

age at the same time and the CPU, under control of the operating system, divides its time between these programs. See Figure 9.11. The operating system enables the CPU to execute one program for a brief period of time and to then switch to another, and so forth, until each program is completed. New programs are then loaded into available portions of main memory, and the multiprogramming process is repeated. All of these tasks are performed in such a way that users may not even know that other people are running programs at the same time.

On computer systems intended for interactive use, the operating system allows the CPU to juggle its time among various users and respond to requests quickly. In this way, numerous users have access to a CPU, all at the same time, and none of them is adversely affected by the fact that they are operating in a multiuser environment.

When a computer system performs multiprogramming operations, it must divide primary storage into separate areas. An application is placed in a separate area in primary storage called a **partition.** An operating system with multiprogramming capability ensures that partitions are kept separate, so that one application will not interfere with the others that are being processed concurrently. Generally, such an operating system also assigns priorities to the various tasks submitted to the CPU, in order for important tasks to be executed before those of less urgency. For example, the requests of upper-level management are often assigned a higher priority than those of data entry personnel; similarly, large, routine accounting jobs may be assigned a lower priority than a simple query to a database that needs to be handled quickly.

Multiprogramming is accomplished through a series of **system interrupts,** which cause execution of a program to be temporarily suspended when resources and devices are being used by other programs. Although it may look as if programs are executed continuously from start to finish, in fact the operating system constantly interrupts these programs to effectively use existing resources.

Once confined exclusively to mainframes, multiprogramming is becoming increasingly common on smaller computers. Originally, the ability of larger computers to perform multiprogramming was the one characteristic that separated them from micros. As the speed and capacity of micros increase, however, this distinction is beginning to fade.

Multitasking is really a variation of multiprogramming that was implemented first on high-end microcomputers and now is widely available on most computers. Multitasking allows *one user* to access *several programs* at the same time. You can tell the computer to print a word processing file, sort a database, and recalculate data in a spreadsheet; all operations will be performed concurrently if the operating system allows multitasking. Figure 9.12 illustrates how multiprogramming and multitasking are achieved.

In summary, multitasking permits a single user to perform many tasks all at one time. Multiprogramming, however, is usually applied to situations in which several users want to access different programs and data—or even the same programs and data—at the same time.

Multiprocessing

Multiprocessing involves linking two or more CPUs to optimize the handling of data (Figure 9.13). While one CPU is executing one set of instructions, another CPU can be executing a different set. This technique differs from multiprogramming, which executes only one program at a time but switches quickly

Figure 9.12 *Multitasking, a variation of multiprogramming, allows a user to access several programs at the same time. Multitasking is for single-users; multiprogramming is performed in a multiuser environment.*

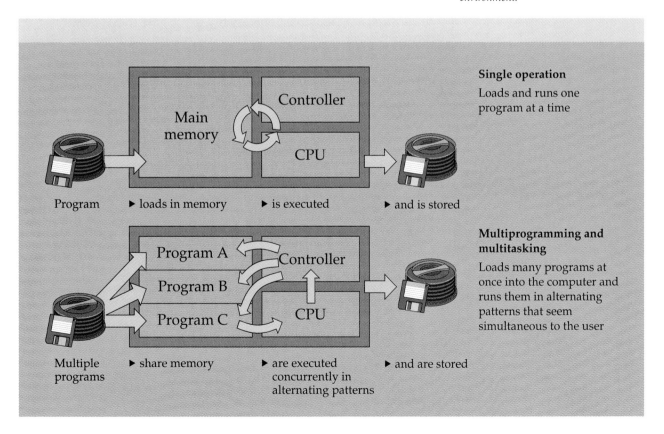

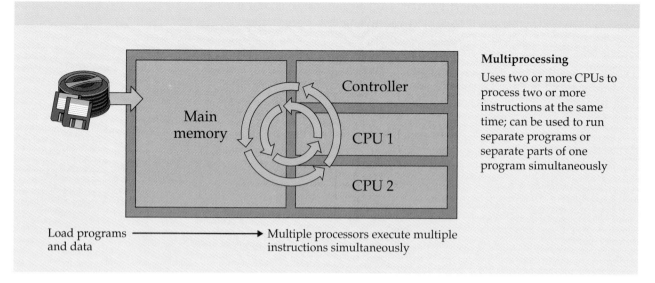

Multiprocessing
Uses two or more CPUs to process two or more instructions at the same time; can be used to run separate programs or separate parts of one program simultaneously

Load programs and data ⟶ Multiple processors execute multiple instructions simultaneously

Figure 9.13 *Multiprocessing enables a computer to actually run two programs simultaneously—using two processors.*

among the different programs currently in memory. In multiprocessing, the system can actually execute several programs simultaneously because parallel processors or multiple CPUs are being used.

Virtual Memory and the "Virtual Machine" Concept

Virtual memory, sometimes called **virtual storage,** enables the computer system to operate as if it has more main memory than it actually does. An application program is segmented into a series of modules (called pages) that are stored outside main memory on a high-speed, direct-access device such as a disk. When the CPU is ready to execute a specific page, the operating system moves that page from secondary storage into main memory and moves a page in main memory back to secondary storage. This process, which is referred to as **swapping,** is illustrated in Figure 9.14. Swapping enables very large programs to be

Figure 9.14 *In virtual memory, disk storage supplements the computer's main memory, and parts of a large program are swapped back and forth.*

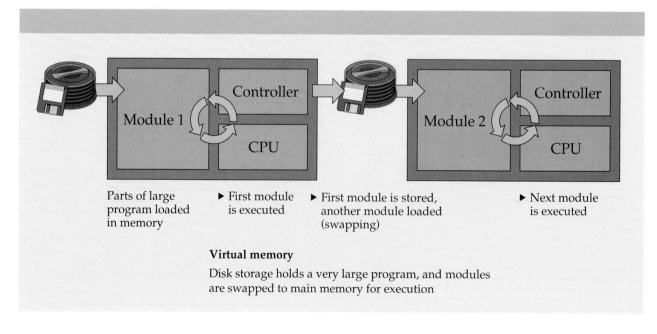

Parts of large program loaded in memory ▶ First module is executed ▶ First module is stored, another module loaded (swapping) ▶ Next module is executed

Virtual memory
Disk storage holds a very large program, and modules are swapped to main memory for execution

executed in a relatively small area of main memory because the entire program is not loaded in at the same time. Virtual memory is common on larger systems and is widely available on many microcomputer systems as well.

Virtual memory is distinct from *real memory,* which is actual RAM. Recall that cache memory is memory set aside for the most frequently used data. An operating system that supervises virtual memory as well as cache memory can significantly improve the overall efficiency of a computer.

The concept of a **virtual machine (VM)** takes virtual memory one step further. The real machine, usually a mainframe, simulates a number of virtual machines, each capable of having its own operating system (Figure 9.15). So even though in reality there is only one computer system, it operates on data as if there were a number of separate systems. The CPU automatically chooses the appropriate operating system for each application program. It appears to an individual user as if an entire CPU and its peripherals are dedicated completely to his or her specific needs. Because the concept of virtual machines allows a computer system to execute several operating systems simultaneously, it provides a great deal of flexibility. For example, several application packages that each require a different operating system can be executed on the same hardware.

Other Tasks Performed by Systems Software

MEMORY MANAGEMENT Systems software controls and manages the use of main memory. **Memory management,** a component of systems software, specifically refers to four tasks.

1. Allocating memory to programs.
2. Protecting memory so that one program does not have access to the storage space used by another.
3. Giving higher priority to some programs.
4. Making the most effective use of a computer's memory.

More advanced memory managers produce audit trails that track programs, the storage they use, the devices they access, and the time it takes them to run. Such information helps in scheduling, allocating, and monitoring computer resources.

Figure 9.15 *A virtual machine has a second operating system, so one computer can act like two.*

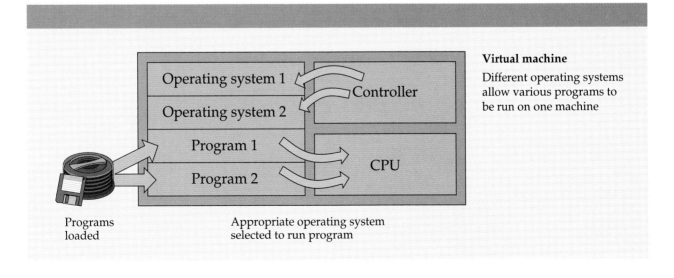

Programs loaded

Appropriate operating system selected to run program

Virtual machine

Different operating systems allow various programs to be run on one machine

INTERFACING WITH TRANSLATORS Translator programs are sometimes provided as part of systems software. Even if they are separate, the systems software controls how they access source programs, translate them, and prepare them for execution. Recall that the three types of translators are called assemblers, compilers, and interpreters; compilers are the most common.

Compilers and assemblers convert the entire *source program* written by an application programmer into an *object program*, which is the machine language equivalent of the source program. If there are no syntax errors, the program is ready to run. But the object program must be linked to the CPU; that is, it must be assigned primary storage space so that it can run. See Figure 9.16. Any special routines that the program needs must also be linked to it. Special functions such as square root computations or input-output error routines are typically linked to an object program by the systems software. The **linkage editor** is a systems software program that performs the necessary operations.

A program that uses an interpreter as a translator does not normally need a linkage editor, because the program is executed directly, one instruction at a time. The disadvantage of interpreting a program, however, is that the entire program cannot be stored in machine language form and then linked as necessary; instead, the program must be translated again each time it is run.

PERFORMING UTILITY FUNCTIONS A utility is a systems software program that performs "housekeeping" tasks commonly required by many different types of application programs. Such tasks are the same regardless of the application area, so computer manufacturers often bundle utilities with systems software so that users do not need to write their own programs or buy additional software. In this section we discuss some tasks performed by utilities. Keep in mind that operating systems may perform some essential functions very well, but their utilities may be limited. If they are, users may need to purchase separate utilities.

Figure 9.16 *A linkage editor places programs into a partition before execution. It links the programs to the CPU for execution.*

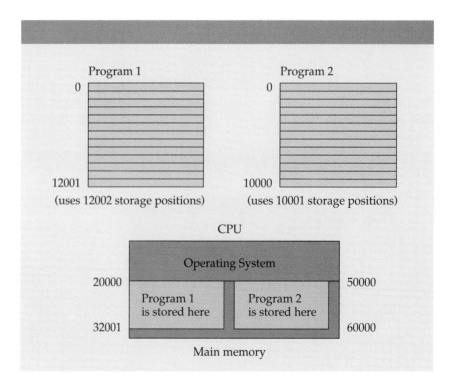

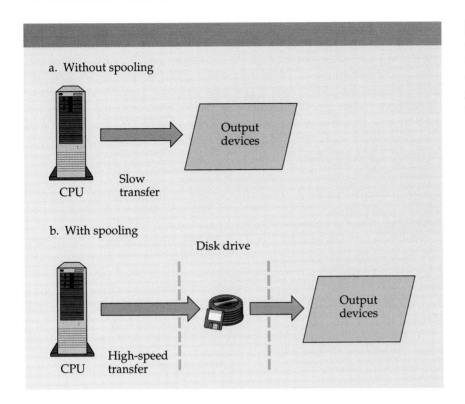

Figure 9.17 *Spooling directs output to be printed to a disk or buffer area where the transfer of data can be completed very quickly; the actual printing then can be performed while the CPU is doing other things.*

Sorting. In many applications, files must be sorted into sequence by key fields. Sometimes a payroll file, for example, may need to be in sequence by Social Security number; other times the sequence required may be by last name or department number. Often, multiple sorts are necessary: the file may need to be accessed by department number and within department by last name and then first name. In other words, all records need to be in alphabetic order within department. Sort utilities can perform single or multiple sorts on any fields specified. They can also sort into ascending sequence (from low to high) as well as descending sequence (from high to low).

Spooling. One function of systems software is to establish a queue (a waiting line) for processing programs. Each program in a queue is executed according to a priority system established by the computing center. Output from application programs that have been queued is generally created on disk, because a disk can be accessed—read from or written to—very quickly in batch mode. The output data is transferred at high speed to printed form in an offline operation called **spooling.** Figure 9.17 shows how spooling is performed. Spooling, which increases the efficiency of the system, is usually controlled by systems software, but sometimes application software includes spooling techniques. Input, as well as output, can be spooled to increase efficiency.

In a single-user environment, the DOS PRINT command accomplishes spooling. It establishes a temporary print area called a **buffer** where a queue of files waits to print. The PRINT command feeds the printer a file at a time in background mode while other programs can be run. In a multiuser environment, spooling enables output from programs being executed at different terminals to be queued and printed in a sequence established by the operating system.

In a networked environment spooling is essential for facilitating the output process for multiple users.

Text Editing. Sometimes users must create special files that the systems software needs to interface with the computer. For example, you might need to instruct the operating system to establish buffer areas if you want output spooled. The buffer area would be created in a special systems file. A word processing package could be used to create such a file, but typically word processing packages include special formatting or control characters that are not understood by systems software. For that reason, systems software often comes with its own basic *text editor* for creating the simple files the operating system needs for controlling overall processing.

Using Device Drivers. **Device drivers** are special utility programs that enable application programs to receive data from, and send data to, specific hardware devices. When you acquire a software package for your PC, you typically need to install it before you actually run it. Installation means, among other things, selecting the appropriate device drivers that will enable you to use the program. When you are installing a software package, you will be asked some hardware-specific questions such as the type of computer, monitor, disk drives, and printer that you are using. Each time you select a piece of hardware, a device driver is added to your systems software to enable the package to interact with it.

The process of adding device drivers for each software package you install is not very efficient. It would be much better if the systems software automatically selected the device drivers needed for all your applications programs. Newer versions of operating systems do just that.

Performing Data Compression and Decompression. One way to save space on a disk is to code data so that it is in compressed form. Some operating systems automatically compress data when files are saved and decompress the data when the files need to be read again.

Data compression is accomplished by encoding data so that unnecessary blanks and duplications are eliminated. Compression factors are at least 2:1, but some packages such as Stacker can compress at much higher ratios, which means that you can store far more data on your disks. Compressed files must be decompressed before they can be used by the computer.

EXECUTING BATCH FILES WHEN STARTING UP Systems software enables you to establish a file that will always be executed immediately after the computer is turned on or after you log on. You may want this file to contain a set of program names that you always want executed before you do anything else. Many systems call this an AUTOEXEC.BAT file for "automatically executed batch file." This file can display any defaults or parameters you want to know about, such as date, time, number of current users, and amount of memory available. This startup file can turn off default displays such as log-on messages, help menus, or listings of directories if you prefer not to see them each time. It can automatically execute some programs immediately, for example, a virus test program, a personal information manager, or a specific utility.

Since the systems software executes this batch file automatically, you can include commands in this file that will customize the user interface to best suit your needs. You can also use this file to load in any programs you want without having to key in commands each time you start a computing session. Batch files are typically created by a programmer or user with the system's text editor or by a word processor that can create straight ASCII text.

MAINTAINING SUBDIRECTORIES AND A FILE ALLOCATION TABLE When you boot up or log on to a computer system, you are typically in the main directory, called the **root directory,** of the default drive. But if all program and data files were in this root directory, it would be difficult to find them or to maintain order, especially if the default drive is a hard drive or fixed disk with millions of storage positions. Files, then, are typically stored on disks in **subdirectories** where each subdirectory contains related files. A subdirectory is like a tab in an address book—it enables you to quickly locate items in a particular section. Address books have tabs that are alphabetic; similarly, computers have subdirectories that include files of a particular type. See Figure 9.18.

Figure 9.18a shows just the name of the subdirectories. Figure 9.18b shows not only main subdirectorties but any sub-subdirectories within them. Without subdirectories, all files would be in the root directory and the command to list the directory would list *all* files. Some operating systems, graphical user inter-

```
A:\>dir

 Volume in drive A has no label
 Directory of  A:\

123           <DIR>        7-12-96    10:25p
DBASE         <DIR>        7-12-96    10:25p
EMAIL         <DIR>        7-12-96    10:25p
WP            <DIR>        7-12-96    10:25p
DOS           <DIR>        7-12-96    10:27p
         5 Files(s)   1455104 bytes free

A:\>
```

(a)

```
A:
 ├──123
 ├──DBASE
 │      ├──WORDART
 │      ├──MSGRAPH
 │      ├──MSDRAW
 │      ├──EQUATION
 │      └──GRPHFLT
 ├──EMAIL
 ├──WP
 │      ├──TROPICAL
 │      └──EXAMPLES
 └──DOS
```

(b)

> •••••➤ **Looking Ahead**

NEW FEATURES FOR OPERATING SYSTEMS

1. Printers differ widely in their capabilities. Typically, they need to be installed (or set up) for each program or package. Newer operating systems include features so that printers, as well as other devices, can be installed automatically.
2. The user interface will become more standardized so that the way you access commands will be the same for most operating systems.
3. New operating systems control the ways in which data and programs are exchanged among computers.
4. More utilities are being bundled with systems software. Virus detection and protection programs, programs that convert files from one format to another, and desktop organizers are just three of the many add-ons being supplied with newer operating systems.

Figure 9.18 *How subdirectories are displayed with DOS (a) using the* dir *command and (b) with a tree command.*

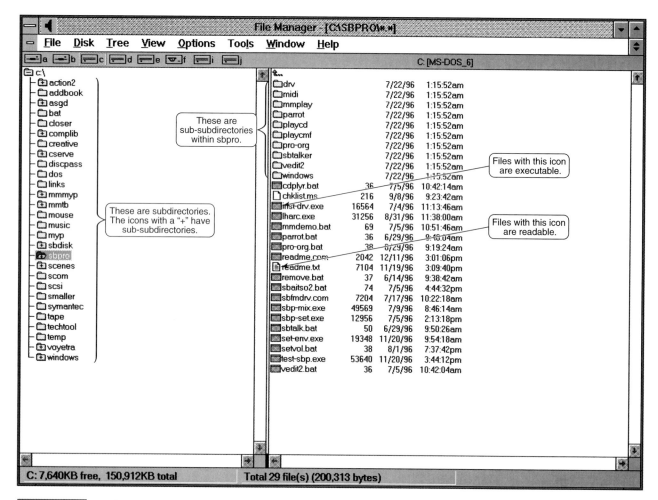

Figure 9.19 *Windows provides a display of subdirectories and other information.*

faces, and utilities enable you to view the contents of files in subdirectories in an even more useful and accessible manner. See Figure 9.19.

Systems software for all sizes of computers enables you to establish subdirectories and to use them effectively. It also sets up a **file allocation table** for disk drives that permits fast access of files within subdirectories. The file allocation table contains the disk address for each file and is searched, like an index, when you look for a file. When you erase or delete a file from a disk, the file is not actually erased—it is the *reference* to the file in the file allocation table that is eliminated so that it is no longer accessible. The space on the disk where the deleted file is actually located is designated as free space and will eventually be used when another file is saved. Since it is possible to accidentally erase or delete files, many operating systems, user interfaces, and utilities have an "unerase" command that finds the original reference to the file in the file allocation table and restores it so that it is accessible again.

Self-Test

1. What do we call the type of processing whereby multiple CPUs optimize the handling of data?

2. Name two types of memory controlled by an operating system that maximize the efficient use of computer resources.

3. What is the term used for producing output using a temporary print area called a buffer where a queue of files can be stored while they wait to print?

4. A program that can create and edit simple files is called a _____.

5. Why are subdirectories used?

CHAPTER SUMMARY

Software drives hardware. In this chapter we focus on systems software that controls the overall operations of the computer and ensures that application programs are executed properly.

9.1 Systems Software: Functions and Features

Systems software includes the operating system and acts as an interface between users and hardware. The operating system, which is the main component of systems software, has a **kernel,** or **supervisor,** which monitors resources; it also oversees the running of user programs. The **user interface** is the part of systems software that permits you to communicate with the hardware in an operating environment.

Systems software is written by **systems programmers** who are software developers capable of writing efficient code for computers with a specific architecture. Systems software can be purchased separately, but it is usually **bundled,** that is, supplied with the hardware by the manufacturer or vendor.

Systems software uses several features to maximize computer efficiency. It controls multiprogramming, which **partitions** a computer's primary storage into separate areas so that several programs can be entered and run simultaneously. By means of a series of **system interrupts,** execution of some programs can be temporarily suspended so that others can use the resources and devices of the computer.

Study Objective

1. Identify the functions of operating systems and explain how users access them.

9.2 Microcomputer Operating Systems and Graphical User Interfaces

IBM micros use the PC-DOS operating system and IBM-compatibles use the MS-DOS operating system. Windows began as a graphical user interface that was used with these DOS operating systems to provide a more user-friendly environment, to effectively manage a computer's resources, and to run programs that actually require the Windows environment. Windows 95 and newer versions are full operating systems. IBM's newest version of OS/2, called OS/2 Warp, is an alternative to Windows.

The Macintosh, which has an operating system with a graphical user interface built in, popularized the concept of user-friendly interfaces. Personal Digital Assistants and other pen-based systems have their own operating systems. Operating systems for PDAs include WinPad, Message Pad, and GEOS.

Study Objective

2. Name and describe some common operating systems for micros.

Solutions

1. multiprocessing

2. virtual memory, cache memory

3. spooling

4. text editor

5. to place related files together in an area that is easily accessible

Study Objective

3. Describe the impact on the computing industry of the portability of the UNIX operating system and of the availability of network operating systems.

9.3 Operating Systems That Facilitate Connectivity

UNIX is an operating system that can be used on a wide variety of computers. Its user interface called a **shell** is separate from the operating system and is non-standard. UNIX is expected to grow in popularity. Most Internet access tools are UNIX-based.

Network operating systems like Novell NetWare and AppleShare are also widely used where different types of computers share resources.

Study Objective

4. Outline some common features of operating systems.

9.4 How Operating Systems Maximize Processing Efficiency

Systems software controls multitasking, which enables several applications to be active at the same time. Systems software also controls **multiprocessing** whereby two or more CPUs are linked so that different instructions can be run simultaneously.

Some systems software uses **virtual memory**, also called **virtual storage**, techniques that enable a computer to operate as if it had more primary storage than it actually does. With virtual memory, an application program is segmented into a series of pages; **swapping** techniques move the pages from secondary storage into main memory and back again. The **virtual machine** concept enables one real machine to operate as if it had a number of virtual machines each capable of having its own operating system.

Other principal tasks performed by systems software include **memory management,** which allocates and controls the effective use of a computer's memory; interfacing with translators; and performing utility functions. **Spooling** is a utility function that enables data you want printed to be stored in a temporary print area called a **buffer.** The buffer establishes a queue of files to be printed and prints them while other processing is being performed. Text editing is another utility function whereby a text editor creates simple files. Two other tasks performed by systems software are executing batch files when a computer is turned on and maintaining a **root directory,** which is a main directory, and **subdirectories** for organizing files and a **file allocation table** for quickly accessing files on a disk. Systems software also enables you to use **device drivers,** which are special utilities needed for interfacing with certain types of hardware such as a sound board or CD-ROM drive. Systems software also has a **linkage editor** that enables the computer to store a program and any external modules needed in main memory so that it can be executed.

KEY TERMS

Buffer, *p. 317*

Bundled, *p. 294*

Device driver, *p. 318*

File allocation table, *p. 320*

Kernel, *p. 293*

Linkage editor, *p. 316*

Memory management, *p. 315*

Multiprocessing, *p. 313*

Partition, *p. 312*

Root directory, *p. 319*

Shell, *p. 308*

Spooling, *p. 317*

Subdirectory, *p. 319*

Supervisor, *p. 293*

Swapping, *p. 314*

System interrupt, *p. 312*

Systems programmer, *p. 295*

User interface, *p. 294*

Virtual machine (VM), *p. 315*

Virtual memory, *p. 314*

Virtual storage, *p. 314*

CHAPTER SELF-TEST

1. (T or F) To carry out multiprocessing, a computer system must have two or more CPUs.

2. With virtual memory, a technique called _____ is used to move program modules from secondary storage to main memory as they are needed.

3. (T or F) The UNIX operating system was originally designed to be used on mainframes.

4. Both Windows and the user interface for the Macintosh use _____, which are symbols representing various objects or functions.

5. (T or F) The newest version of Windows is a complete operating system for IBM-compatible PCs.

6. What is the graphical user interface for the Mac called?

7. (T or F) Some applications can only be run in a Windows environment.

8. (T or F) UNIX is an operating system that can run on a wide variety of computers.

9. The _____ is the part of the operating system that allocates computer resources.

10. _____ permits more than one program to be active in a CPU at the same time.

11. The version of DOS used on IBM-compatible micros is called _____.

12. (T or F) With virtual machines, more than one operating system can be used at the same time.

Solutions

1. T
2. swapping
3. F
4. icons
5. T
6. Finder or MultiFinder
7. T
8. T
9. kernel
10. Multitasking
11. MS-DOS
12. T

REVIEW QUESTIONS

1. Explain the differences between multiprocessing, multiprogramming, and multitasking.

2. Explain the differences between virtual memory and cache memory.

3. What is a memory manager?

4. What is a linkage editor?

5. What features does Windows add to a DOS operating environment?

6. Under what conditions would you change the standard operating system for your IBM-compatible from DOS to UNIX?

CRITICAL THINKING EXERCISES

1. Consider the following: "I have always believed that Macintoshes had superior hardware and a better operating system than IBM-compatible PCs. However, I've almost always chosen and recommended IBM-compatible PCs over Macs for business applications because they run more software."[1]

What is your preference—an IBM-compatible Intel-based computer or a Mac?

2. One columnist wrote, only half-facetiously: "I plan to earn a Nobel Peace Prize by ending the operating system wars. These are the skirmishes among partisans of Windows, OS/2 and plain old DOS about the best way to run a computer. (For now let's ignore the side battles involving NeXt, UNIX, and the Apple Macintosh alternative universe. Dealing with them will net me my second Nobel Prize.)

Half the time we discuss these struggles as if they represent the inevitable clash of titanic business systems: Microsoft vs IBM, the West Coast youngsters versus the aging empire of the East. The rest of the time we're wrapped up in hair-splitting arguments about which system will repaint its screen 2 milliseconds faster than its rivals."[2]

What is the author's opinion of the controversy over operating systems?

[1]Kevin O'Connor, "Apple closes the gap on the PC," *PC User,* April 20, 1994, n. 233, p. 34.

[2]Adapted from James Fallows, *Windows Magazine,* March 1994, p. 53.

Case Study

"Killer Apps" May Decide the Future of Operating Systems

Computer users generally select their hardware based on their software needs, which are best served by one or another operating system such as DOS, Windows, or Macintosh. In the future, however, portable operating systems such as those described in Section 9.3 of this chapter may create entirely new criteria for selecting hardware, since these operating systems can migrate from one computer system to another. It may no longer be necessary for users who need to change their operating system to change their hardware as well. They can simply switch to the needed operating system and keep right on going.

For those who think such a simple switch is still too much trouble, however, there has always been the hope that an innovative software developer would produce an applications package so formidable that it would drive the choice of hardware and operating system alike, and no further decisions would need to be made. Lotus 1-2-3 did this for the IBM-compatible and DOS. Similarly, Aldus Page-Maker established the Mac as the preeminent platform for graphical and desktop publishing applications. But these "killer" applications packages are more than a decade old

and although there are reports of truly amazing new applications, no new "killer app" has appeared. Ed Foster, writing in *InfoWorld,* says the hope for such a "killer app" is futile.

Foster suggests, tongue in cheek, that computer manufacturers might instead create a must-have computer game. "If IBM comes up with a Super Mario–type hit exclusive to OS/2 [for example]," he writes, "millions of American kids will become part of IBM's sales force." No matter how likely or unlikely such a scenario seems, Foster concludes that, at least from the standpoint of information systems managers, that long-hoped-for "killer" applications package should really be the one that best allows companies to develop their own applications and frees them from dependence on software suppliers.

Analysis

1. What features in an operating system are most important to you?

2. If you purchased a Power PC, which operating system would you get? Why?

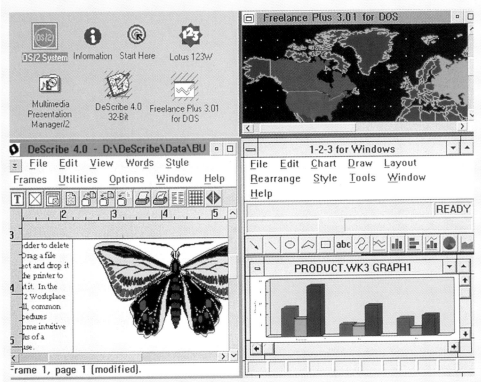

Here are screen displays of various products that can be used with many different operating systems. The future of operating systems depends on the number and quality of the applications they can run.

PART FOUR

Connectivity Unites the Information Age

If you want to stay in touch, even when you're getting away from it all, the computer can help. Today virtually every corner of the world is reachable by some kind of **communications system.** Scientists stationed in remote Antarctica are equipped with communications devices that link them with their home base, and astronauts in space are closely monitored in a constant communication stream from earth. In a very real sense, computers are bringing us closer together.

When you're away from your office, a **modem** will allow you to access information through a telephone line or wireless network. Computers can be connected to one another by cable, telephone lines, satellites, microwave relays, and even radio waves, so we can combine and use their power and resources no matter where the hardware is physically located.

The pony express could carry a letter 2000 miles in only eight days in 1860. Now it takes seconds to transmit and receive messages and other information by computer. Vast **networks** of computers collect, monitor, and process data, connecting users from all parts of the globe. **E-mail** allows us to send and receive all sorts of data, including documents, graphs, charts, pictures, and even sound

and video images. E-mail users can communicate with others no matter where they are and access external **databases** containing huge amounts of information.

The **Internet** and **subscriber services** such as Prodigy and CompuServe will enable us to communicate with people from all over the world, retrieve files and databases on every topic imaginable, and become part of user groups that address our specific interests, hobbies, and professions. The Internet has brought us one step closer to the **information superhighway,** which will provide interactive access to information in a way that promises to truly enrich our lives.

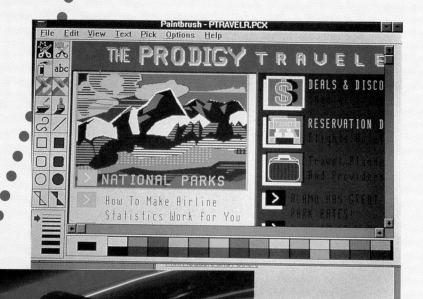

The telephone, patented in 1876, is still going strong as new applications develop that depend on it. Direct dialing provides voice, data, and even video access. Touch-Tone phones have made it easier to electronically access information, to process college applications, and even to apply for U.S. citizenship. Distance learning centers make it possible for people to take courses using advanced technology where instructors might be hundreds of miles away.

Network television provides information and entertainment to viewers everywhere. **High-definition TV** makes available even higher quality images and sound that can be further enhanced by computer. **Interactive TV** connects consumers to a host of information services and may someday revolutionize the way we shop and transact business.

CHAPTER 10
Connectivity, Networks, and the Information Superhighway

10.1 COMMUNICATIONS AND CONNECTIVITY

Sharing Resources Is the Goal

Communications Hardware

10.2 COMMON APPLICATION AREAS FOR NETWORKS

Distributed Processing

Accessing Information from Networks

The Information Superhighway

Interoffice Electronic Mail and Groupware

Telecommuting

10.3 CONTROLLING DATA FLOW WITH COMMUNICATIONS SOFTWARE

Speed of Transmission

Direction of Data Flow

Serial and Parallel Transmission

Data Bits in the Computer Code

Parity

An Overview of Protocols

10.4 NETWORK CONFIGURATIONS

The Local Area Network (LAN): A Promised LAN for Sharing Resources

LAN Software

Network Topologies: Star, Bus, Ring, Hybrid

Wide Area Networks (WANs)

10.5 CONNECTIVITY LEADS TO A SMALLER, SMARTER, AND MORE CREATIVE WORLD

Facsimile (Fax) Machines

Wireless Communications

Smart Phones

Interactive TV and High-Definition Television

Videoconferencing and Distance Learning

We have seen how hardware, software, and people work together to create effective information systems. With connectivity, such systems can be made available to a wide variety of users who may be employees within a single organization, people from different organizations, or any individuals who need access to central databases.

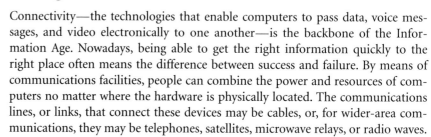

Study Objectives

After reading this chapter you should be able to:

1. Identify the communications linkages that contribute to effective connectivity.
2. Describe the ways in which connectivity can be achieved in organizations.
3. Explain how transmission specifications and protocols control the flow of data in networks.
4. Describe common network configurations.
5. Identify new technologies that contribute to connectivity.

▨ 10.1 COMMUNICATIONS AND CONNECTIVITY

Sharing Resources Is the Goal

Study Objective

1. Identify the communications linkages that contribute to effective connectivity.

Connectivity—the technologies that enable computers to pass data, voice messages, and video electronically to one another—is the backbone of the Information Age. Nowadays, being able to get the right information quickly to the right place often means the difference between success and failure. By means of communications facilities, people can combine the power and resources of computers no matter where the hardware is physically located. The communications lines, or links, that connect these devices may be cables, or, for wider-area communications, they may be telephones, satellites, microwave relays, or radio waves.

When trainers for Olympic athletes in colleges and universities around the country seek broad-based physiological information for their athletes, they use computers in their offices to tap into a specialized sports database located in Colorado. Similarly, salespeople with small, inexpensive microcomputers in Iowa access the power and resources of a multimillion dollar mainframe facility in New York through a telephone link. Immediate pricing estimates and inventory information enable them to complete their sales quickly. Some real estate appraisers have doubled their earnings simply by accessing a national electronic database of public and private real estate records to do research and analysis in minutes that once took them hours.

Such capabilities are possible because of advances in data communications that enable computers to work together no matter where they are located. Computers near each other, either in the same room or building, can send data directly to one another through cables or telephones. Computers stationed at a considerable distance from each other use a special data communications technology called **telecommunications** that can transmit data via communications facilities such as satellites. Highly advanced communications technologies now quickly send—to almost anywhere in the world—not only textual data but also photographs, illustrations, and video images.

The main feature of communications applications is that computers and input/output devices can be in different rooms, different buildings, or even in different geographical locations, and still communicate with each other. Keep in mind that the term *connectivity* as used in this text has a broad meaning: it refers to the linking of all equipment such as telephones, fax machines, and televisions as well as computers.

Communications Hardware

A REVIEW OF NODES AND HOSTS IN A NETWORK A network is the type of configuration that enables devices to communicate with one another. Often, one or more central computers interface with a variety of input/output devices at remote locations. In such a network, each device is called a node. A node may be an input/output device such as a terminal, PC, or other computer. Some networks have a series of nodes linked to a central computer. In this case, the central computer is called the host. Other networks have a ring of computers that communicate with one another where there is no need for a host computer. When a host computer is used primarily for distributing hardware and software resources to PCs it is called a file server. Hosts can also be used for collecting information that updates central databases.

Nodes in a network can be any device such as a terminal, laptop, desktop, workstation, or even larger computer. If your school's computing center has a file server, which transmits software like a spreadsheet package or a DBMS to PCs, then the host or file server can be a workstation or standard PC and the nodes can also be PCs. See Figure 10.1. Point-of-sale systems in retail establishments use POS terminals to transmit accounts receivable and inventory data to a host. A terminal can really be any type of input/output unit that is not located at the same site as the host, but usually it is a keyboard/monitor unit.

COMMUNICATIONS CHANNELS The linkages between nodes and a host (if there is one) in a network are called **communications channels.** The simplest type of channel is a direct cable. When devices are connected by cables, we say they are hardwired. A common alternative to cables is the telephone line. By means of a modem, nodes connected to a telephone can communicate with another node and/or the host, each of which must also have a modem linking it to a telephone line. So any two computer devices located anywhere in the world that have access to telephone lines can communicate with one another. For faster communications over longer distances, satellite and microwave lines, as well as specially prepared or "conditioned" telephone lines, are used. Wireless communications via light beams or radio waves is the newest technology.

The types of communications linkages that are available today include (1) hardwired cables, (2) telephones, (3) microwave stations, (4) satellite stations, and (5) radio or infrared waves. To share resources in a wide variety of areas, often more than one type of linkage is used.

Figure 10.1 *A node can be a desktop PC or a workstation in an office. In this illustration, a university's PCs access a library network.*

Hardwired Cables. Hardwired terminals are directly linked to a CPU or host by cable. Terminals are commonly hardwired when they are relatively near the host and their locations are not expected to change, because moving a hardwired terminal requires rewiring.

A principal advantage of hardwired terminals is that they have immediate access to a central processor as soon as they are turned on. There is no need, as with a telephone line, to "dial up" the computer. Networks may be hardwired with three basic types of cable: twisted-pair cable, coaxial cable, and fiber optic cable.

ɪɴ A NUTSHELL

HARDWIRED COMMUNICATIONS CHANNELS

TWISTED-PAIR CABLE	*COAXIAL CABLE*	*FIBER OPTIC CABLE*
• Most common type of hardwired cable for small networks • Inexpensive • Least reliable because it is subject to "noise" on the line resulting from electrical interference	• Used for high-quality data transmission • More expensive than twisted-pair cables • Sturdy • High speed	• High speed • Highly reliable • Transmits signals by light impulses rather than electrical impulses • Not subject to electrical interference

Twisted-pair cable is the typical telephone wire used in your house, and it is the most common type of hardwired cable for small networks. It consists of bundles of pairs of copper wires that are twisted to give them physical strength (Figure 10.2). Twisted-pair cable is relatively inexpensive and has low maintenance costs. A major disadvantage of this type of wiring for communications, however, is that it is highly susceptible to electrical interference (called "noise") both from within and outside the system. Noise is a major source of transmission errors. For protection from interference, shielded twisted-pair wiring is available at a slightly higher cost.

A **coaxial cable** is used in place of standard twisted-pair cables for high-quality data transmission. Although it is more expensive than twisted-pair cable, coaxial cable is sturdy enough to be laid without the wiring conduits or mechanical support elements that twisted-pair cable wiring requires. If conduits for twisted-pair cables are *not* already in place, coaxial cable may be cheaper to install and more flexible to use. Illustrated in Figure 10.2, coaxial cable consists of a central cylinder surrounded by a series of wires that transmit data at high speeds. Coaxial cable is commonly laid under the floor or in the ceiling of com-

Figure 10.2 *The three common types of cable are twisted-pair cable, coaxial cable, and fiber optic cable.*

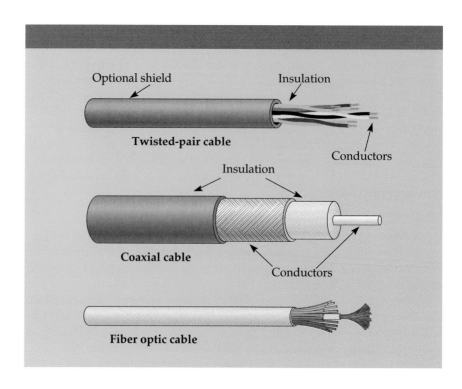

Figure 10.3 *Bundles of threadlike glass fibers in a fiber optic cable carry encoded light beams to transmit voice and data messages virtually without interference.*

puter centers. It is so sturdy that telephone companies often bury it underground or lay it across sea bottoms to provide high-quality phone transmission.

Fiber optic cables are highly reliable communications channels. Data can be transmitted at very high speeds with a relatively low error rate. While standard cables transmit signals electrically in the form of moving electrons, a fiber optic channel transmits by means of light impulses that travel through clear, flexible tubing half the size of a human hair. Unlike wire cables, fiber optic cables are not subject to electrical interference. Technological innovations continue to drive down the costs of installing, using, and manufacturing fiber optic cables, so they are becoming competitive with traditional cabling. Most long-distance telephone companies now use fiber optic cables. See Figure 10.3.

Ethernet is one commonly used standard for hardwiring devices in a network. It provides the cabling, hardware, and data transmission specifications for the network. For less than $500 per node, Ethernet enables users to share resources at transmission rates of millions of characters per second.

Telephones for Data Communications. Standard telephones commonly connect computers and terminals that are separated by long distances. Using a telephone, nodes located anywhere in the world can have access to a host computer. Salespeople can call in and place orders from the field and send transaction data directly to a central processor. For example, a salesperson uses his or her terminal or micro to "dial" the host computer's phone number; if the computer line is free, the salesperson will have direct access to the host.

Telephone lines have several disadvantages as a transmission medium. They are slower and have higher error rates than hardwired cables because they were specifically designed to handle voice transmission signals, not computer signals. In addition, as we all know, long-distance telephone rates are expensive.

To send computer data, which is in digital form, over the phone, users need additional interface equipment such as a modem or a communications controller to convert the signals.

Modems. Data in a computer is formatted as digital signals—on-off elec-

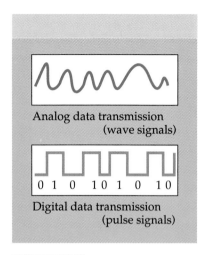

Figure 10.4 *Analog signals are transmitted in wave form and digital signals are transmitted in pulse form.*

Figure 10.5 *Telephone lines currently transmit only analog, or wave, signals. Modulator-demodulator units called modems convert digital signals to analog form so that data can be transmitted over phone lines. A modem at the receiving end converts the analog signals back to digital form.*

tronic pulses. Because telephone lines were designed to transmit the human voice, they transmit data as analog signals, that is, as continuous waves, not discrete pulses (see Figure 10.4). For communication between computers to take place over a telephone line, the digital signal, or pulse, must be converted to an analog signal, or wave, before it can be transmitted. After traveling over telephone lines, the analog signal is then converted back to a digital signal so that it can be used by the receiving computer. See Figure 10.5.

The process of converting a digital signal to an analog signal is called modulation. Demodulation is the process of converting the analog signal back to a digital signal. The device that accomplishes both modulation and demodulation is a modem, short for *mo*dulator-*dem*odulator. There are two basic kinds of modems: direct-connect modems and acoustic couplers. As the name implies, direct-connect modems are attached directly to computers. They can be either an internal device on a circuit board inside the computer or an external device in a unit separate from the computer. Both internal and external modems work in the same way. They connect to the phone line, or jack, with a standard telephone wire. See Figure 10.6. PCMCIA cards can be used in place of internal modem boards on laptop computers.

If you are using a telephone without a jack (e.g., a pay phone or cellular phone), an **acoustic coupler** will allow you to transmit and receive computer data or faxes over telephone lines. The acoustic coupler has two cups into which a telephone handset is placed. The acoustic coupler transmits the computer's data through the mouthpiece and receives data through the earpiece of the handset.

An acoustic coupler is an older interface that is not as common today as direct-connect modems. Still, it is useful for transmitting data from locations that have internal phone systems where there is no phone jack, for example, hotels or other business establishments or public telephones. Acoustic couplers are also useful for transmitting data from different types of telephones commonly found outside the United States. Sometimes acoustic couplers are built into a terminal or microcomputer, enabling the device itself to be used in conjunction with a telephone handset. A salesperson, for example, who routinely obtains rate information from the central office or transmits orders to the central office from a pay phone or cellular phone would benefit from an acoustic coupler built into his or her PC.

We will see that the speed of transmission for direct-connect modems and acoustic couplers is measured in bits per second (bps). Roughly speaking, these devices can transmit and receive from 240 to hundreds of thousands of characters per second.

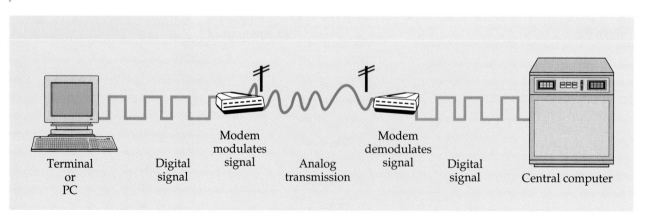

Terminal or PC   Digital signal   Modem modulates signal   Analog transmission   Modem demodulates signal   Digital signal   Central computer

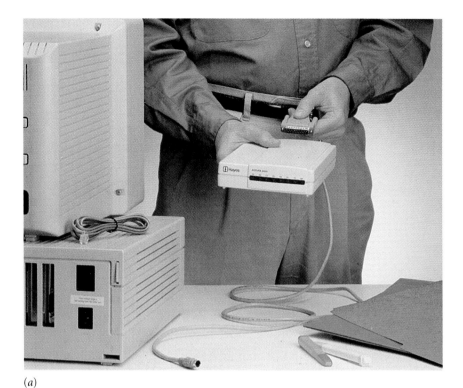

Figure 10.6 (*a*) *This external modem plugs into its own power outlet.* (*b*) *Here, a modem is connected to a telephone line by plugging the wire into the telephone wall jack.*

(*a*)

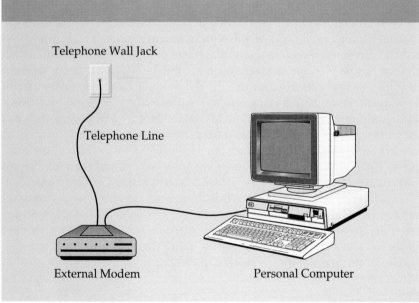

Telephone Wall Jack

Telephone Line

External Modem

Personal Computer

(*b*)

Communications controllers. When PC users communicate with hosts or other devices using a telephone, all they need is a modem. But if an application calls for collecting messages from several devices at one location for batch transmission across communications lines, more powerful devices with additional capabilities are more efficient than modems. Multiplexers and front-end processors provide control and monitoring functions and have built-in modems as well for transmitting a high volume of data over telephone lines. Point-of-sale department store systems, for example, which have numerous terminals in a branch store, would use a multiplexer for communicating with the central computer at the main office.

IN A NUTSHELL

TYPES OF MODEMS

- Direct-connect
  1. Internal—on a board, fits into a slot
  2. External—separate unit, plugs into the computer
- Acoustic coupler: external—either a separate unit or part of a micro; handset of telephone, rather than telephone wire, fits into it

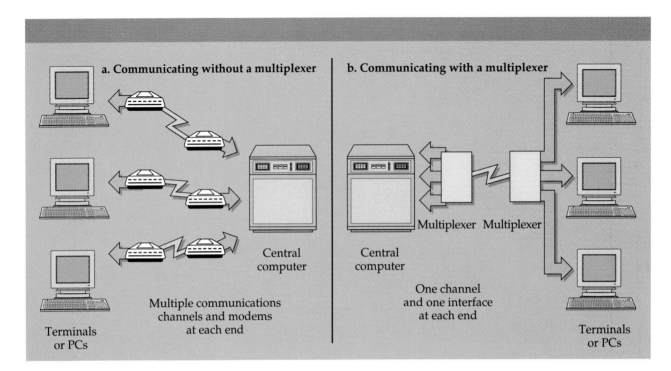

a. Communicating without a multiplexer

b. Communicating with a multiplexer

Terminals
or PCs

Multiple communications
channels and modems
at each end

Central
computer

Central
computer

Multiplexer Multiplexer

One channel
and one interface
at each end

Terminals
or PCs

Figure 10.7 *For some applications, each terminal has its own modem and telephone line to connect it to a central computer. Alternatively, a multiplexer can combine transmissions so that many terminals can send data over a single line.*

A **multiplexer** is a hardware device that collects messages from many nodes at one physical location and transmits them in batch mode at high speeds over a single communications channel, as illustrated in Figure 10.7. Similarly, a multiplexer can be used for message switching, which means that it can receive a collection of responses from a host CPU and transmit each response back to the appropriate node. Multiplexing minimizes two major sources of inefficiency. First, most interactive communication is intermittent: You enter data, then wait for a response. If the channel uses a long-distance telephone line, these delays can be very expensive. A multiplexer can maximize the efficient use of the channel by batching transmissions from many users. Second, without multiplexing, each time a node is added to the network a new channel or communications link is required. With multiplexing, new devices can simply be connected to the multiplexer, which is itself connected to the communications channel. A department store with several branches, for example, does *not* have each POS terminal linked to its host at a central office. Rather, each POS terminal is linked to a multiplexer at the branch office, and all transmissions to the host are controlled by that multiplexer. The result is a considerable saving of telephone costs and CPU time.

When many terminals are connected directly to a central computer, the host must spend an inordinate amount of time monitoring and coordinating the flow of data rather than processing that data. For example, the host needs to keep track of which terminals are sending data; it must check data and coordinate message switching; it might need to prioritize transmissions, and so on. While it is performing these tasks, actual processing of applications is suspended. **Front-end processors** are specialized micros or minis that offload the activities performed by the host computer so that it can run more effectively. Front-end processors ensure that data is routed appropriately and that it is free of errors; they also perform some of the housekeeping and control tasks that would otherwise be performed by the host.

Telephone carriers. In 1968, the Federal Communications Commission (FCC) handed down the now-famous Carterfone decision, which required AT&T

to allow independent equipment manufacturers to use public telephone networks. By 1972, competing companies were permitted to launch their own communications satellites. Today, a wide variety of companies provide many different types of services using telephones for networking. In addition to switched lines that connect telephones via switching centers, many telephone companies offer **value-added services:** extra services beyond those normally provided for voice messages.

A leased telephone line is one such value-added service that telephone companies provide for a fixed fee. It is a private line dedicated to a specific organization for its individual communications needs. A leased line may handle digital data only, or it may be capable of handling both voice and digital data just as a standard telephone line does. When leased lines have been designed specifically for data transmission, they produce less static and fewer transmission errors than regular telephone lines—and they are more secure from wiretapping and other security risks. Most importantly, the central processor is always accessible through the leased line, and the line usually transmits data at faster speeds than a standard telephone line.

Microwave and Satellite Transmission. Most networks use either hardwired cables or telephones for networking. Some, however, transmit and receive data over very long distances by microwave signals. Microwave networks are usually more expensive, and sometimes less reliable. They tend to be used where cables are not practical, for transmission across waterways or highways, for example, or in sparsely populated areas or over rough terrain.

Microwave and satellite signals travel in a straight line. Therefore, they require transmission stations to redirect them around the earth's curved surface. The stations boost the signals and then transmit them again. Microwave and satellite transmissions also require interfaces to convert analog signals to digital form.

Microwave stations. A microwave station transmits data, such as radio signals, through the air rather than through wires. Microwave stations primarily transmit data at high speeds over very long distances. Normally, the stations are placed at high points—on mountaintops and on tall buildings—where they can transmit to other stations without interference. You may be familiar with the dish antennas of microwave stations that are typically located on the roofs of buildings or on hilltops (Figure 10.8). More than half of the standard telephone transmissions make use of microwave technology.

Figure 10.8 *(a) Microwave transmission towers receive signals sent from other stations. Stations are used to amplify signals and transmit them directly to other stations. (b) Microwave transmission towers send signals that are relayed in space.*

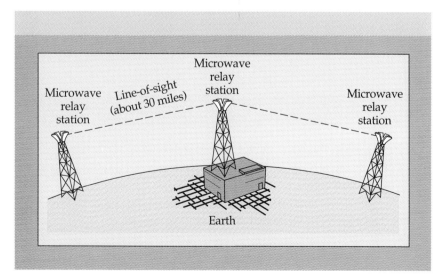

(a)

(b)

(a)

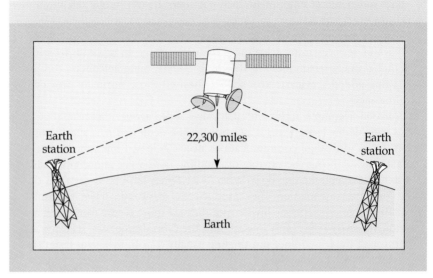

(b)

Figure 10.9 *(a) Satellite receiving dish. (b) Satellite stations orbit around the equator tens of thousands of miles above the earth.*

Satellite stations. Communications satellites in space, orbiting tens of thousands of miles above the earth, also serve as microwave relay stations (Figure 10.9). They orbit around the equator at a speed that makes them appear stationary to microwave transmitters on the ground. These satellites are used for high-volume data transmission as well as for television broadcasting and telephone transmission. A satellite can beam transmissions to other satellites, which relay signals back to stations on earth. Hundreds of satellites are currently in orbit.

Other Wireless Transmission. Networks that use radio or light waves to connect PCs and other devices such as printers move us one step closer toward full connectivity. Cellular phones, paging systems, and radio modems can be used with Personal Digital Assistants (PDAs) or other portables used for electronic communications. See Figure 10.10.

The primary benefits of wireless networks are reduced cabling costs and improved portability. Reporters covering a major news event may need a network that can be set up quickly, without the need for cables. People like traders on financial exchange floors or data collection employees have more freedom of movement if they can use wireless, handheld computers. The primary disadvantage of wireless networks is their cost, which is sometimes twice the price of conventional network stations. A second problem is interference.

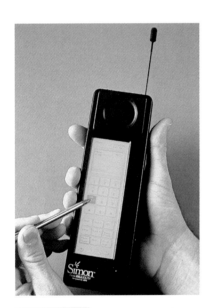

Figure 10.10 *Simon is a PDA that can phone, fax, e-mail, or page someone, as well as contain a personal directory, keyboard, scheduler, clock, calendar, and notepad.*

Self-Test

1. (T or F) Microcomputers cannot be used as terminals in a network.

2. (T or F) A multiplexer can reduce the overall cost of transmitting data over communications lines.

3. (T or F) Remote terminals can be placed strategically at different locations, but they must be in the same building as the computer.

4. (T or F) Front-end processors can be used to make host computers run more efficiently.

5. Networks use _____ placed strategically at key locations to enter input and/or receive output.

10.2 COMMON APPLICATION AREAS FOR NETWORKS

Although there are a variety of application areas for networks, we will focus on the following: distributed processing, accessing information from online subscriber services and other networks, electronic mail, and telecommuting. Connectivity is achieved by using networks for transmitting computer information and for conducting other office functions as well, such as those performed by networked fax machines or voice-mail systems. We will also consider the future of the proposed Information Superhighway.

Study Objective

2. Describe the ways in which connectivity can be achieved in organizations.

Distributed Processing

The transmission of computer power throughout an organization from a central facility to each user site is called distributed processing. The most common distributed systems have micros, minis, midranges, or terminals linked to a host computer, usually a mainframe, in order to improve productivity and to provide users with immediate access to files. Many business tasks such as receiving customer orders and sending merchandise can take several days to complete when manual (uncomputerized) procedures or batch procedures with a central computer are used instead of distributed systems. The two most common distributed processing activities are (1) remote data entry and inquiry and (2) client-server computing.

REMOTE DATA ENTRY AND INQUIRY In remote data entry and inquiry applications, nodes serve as input devices for entering transaction data. Transaction data is data needed to update a master database file. Entering data on a terminal located where a transaction actually occurs, such as in point-of-sale systems in fast-food restaurants or supermarkets, is called **remote data entry.** Remote data entry applications have a host that may not be physically at the same site as the terminals or nodes. See Figure 10.11.

Remote data entry systems can be designed for either interactive or batch processing. Recall from Chapter 4 that in interactive processing the computer reads input data as it is entered and uses it to update the master files immediately. In batch processing, the computer stores the data and processes it all together at a scheduled time. In a batch system, the data entered is first stored in a file on a secondary storage medium such as disk. The computer then

IN A NUTSHELL

Distributed processing enables users at remote sites to do processing locally and to access a central computer as well.

Solutions

1. F—Nodes in a network can be any type of computer or terminal.

2. T

3. F—Nodes, for example, can use modems to communicate with one another and/or the host.

4. T

5. terminals, PCs, or nodes

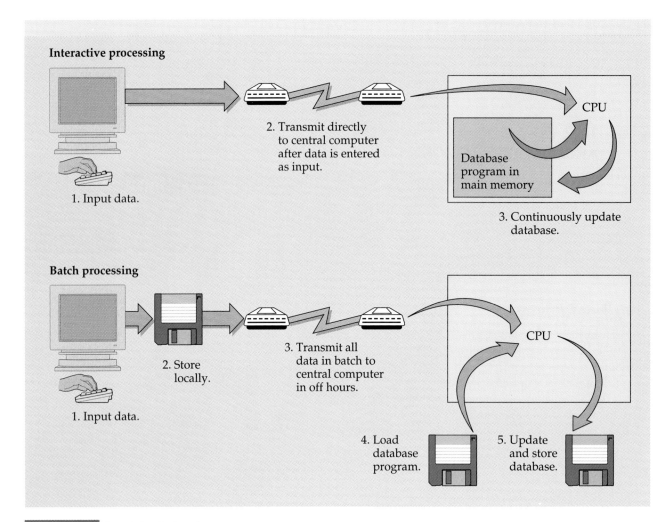

Interactive processing

1. Input data.

2. Transmit directly to central computer after data is entered as input.

CPU

Database program in main memory

3. Continuously update database.

Batch processing

1. Input data.

2. Store locally.

3. Transmit all data in batch to central computer in off hours.

CPU

4. Load database program.

5. Update and store database.

Figure 10.11 *Remote terminals and communications equipment can be used in both interactive processing and batch processing to interface with a central computer.*

processes the entire file at some later time. Batch processing makes more efficient use of a computer than interactive processing for three reasons:

1. A high-speed secondary storage device like a disk drive can transmit data to a CPU much faster than a person can key it in using an online terminal.

2. Data can be transmitted later in the day, after normal working hours, when transmission costs such as telephone charges are cheaper.

3. The database files to be updated, along with the update program, do not need to be online at all times; this makes the central computer available for other applications.

Systems analysts who design remote data entry systems consider factors such as cost, speed, and security when they decide whether to use interactive or batch processing. For example, a department store's accounts receivable system often processes transactions immediately. Processing in this manner creates a charge slip that is the customer's receipt and keeps data such as the customer's available credit up-to-date at all times. On the other hand, interactive processing of an accounts receivable master file for a small organization may be too expensive; it might also be more prone to security problems because employees at specific locations would always have access to the master file. In this instance, batch processing may be preferable.

Remote terminals or micros may also be used to inquire about the status of records in a file. Organizations that process data online need to request information about data stored in a database file linked to a central computer. Stockbrokers, for example, frequently query a central database of stock information when they want to quote a stock price to a customer. To get a price, the broker keys in a stock code at a terminal or micro on his or her desk. The host computer receives this code immediately, accesses the price from the database, and transmits the information back to the stockbroker in seconds or even a fraction of a second.

A display screen and keyboard are almost always essential for inquiry purposes—even for simple queries. Sometimes a printer is also needed to produce hard-copy output. Businesses generally use remote inquiry systems when customers want immediate responses to requests or when managers need information immediately for making decisions. Connectivity enables the responses to inquiries to be transmitted to other devices such as laser printers for high-quality output or fax machines for delivery to other locations.

Typically, systems with remote data inquiry capability require database files to be up-to-date at all times. Remote data inquiry devices are also commonly used for remote data entry. For example, the stockbroker who queries the database for a stock price also needs to buy and sell stocks. Thus, remote data entry and remote inquiry are often part of the same system (Figure 10.12).

CLIENT-SERVER COMPUTING *Client-server computing* is a form of distributed processing that has a server as a host that controls access to resources. The actual processing is handled by the PCs, which are nodes in the network.

IN A NUTSHELL

Distributed processing enables users to:
- Share software
- Share hardware such as printers, faxes, modems
- Share data
- Supervise and monitor computer resources

Figure 10.12 *This stockbroker and his client are working with an information system to retrieve stock prices and other information. The same system can be used to buy or sell stocks and keep brokerage records.*

According to Peter Lewis of the *New York Times*,[1] think of a client-server as a restaurant where the waiter takes your order for a hamburger, goes to the kitchen and returns with raw meat and a bun. As the client, you cook the burger at your table and add your favorite condiments. This results in faster service and the food gets cooked exactly to your liking. The giant, expensive stove in the kitchen can be replaced by lots of inexpensive little grills at each customer's table.

Peer-to-peer networks are another form of distributed processing where any node can act as a server for purposes of sharing resources. This is not as common as standard client-server computing because security risks are higher.

Accessing Information from Networks

ONLINE SUBSCRIBER SERVICES A computer, modem, and telephone line enable any user access to a variety of databases and other resources. For a fee, online **subscriber services** offer access to hundreds or even thousands of databases. Here are some of the better-known subscriber services.

General	*Specific*
CompuServe	Lexis/Nexis (legal)
Prodigy	Westlaw (legal)
Genie Service (GE Network for Information Exchange)	Business (Dow Jones News/ Retrieval)
America Online	
Microsoft Network	
Delphi	

Access to a subscriber service requires you to

1. Enroll or subscribe, that is, pay a startup fee and obtain passwords, log-on codes, and documentation.

2. Pay a monthly fixed-rate service fee.

3. Pay a per-use charge to the subscriber service for the time you are online as well as for services.

4. Pay the telephone company for connect time. Most subscriber services provide access to SprintNet, Tymnet, or some other wide area telephone service so that you can communicate with it using a local telephone number; with some, however, you must make a long distance call.

Some subscriber services offer joint access. For example, Westlaw offers access to Dow Jones Retrieval from within Westlaw itself.

CompuServe is a text-oriented, combined command- and menu-driven subscriber service that has been available for many years. Prodigy, a more recent joint venture between Sears and IBM, is a graphically oriented and completely menu-driven service. Figure 10.13 illustrates the different interfaces for these services. CompuServe, America Online, and Prodigy are currently the market leaders; each has several million subscribers. Prodigy is the least expensive one primarily because it accepts and displays advertisements.

E-mail is available to all subscribers of an online service. Many show business personalities like Jerry Seinfeld, Katie Couric, and Rodney Dangerfield, as well as politicians like Bill Clinton, Al Gore, and Jimmy Carter host question-and-answer sessions on Prodigy or CompuServe.

[1]Harry Newton, *Newton's Telecom Dictionary,* (New York: Computer Select), 1994.

IN A NUTSHELL

SERVICES TYPICALLY OFFERED TO CUSTOMERS OF A SUBSCRIBER SERVICE

Communications and e-mail with other members

News, weather, and sports

Shopping from online catalogs using a credit card

Stock quotes and other business information

Travel services, including the ability to make online reservations

Consumer information from sources such as *Consumer Reports*

Banking, including the ability to make on-line payments

Reference and other educational material including encyclopedias, dictionaries, and databases on a wide range of subjects

Entertainment and games

Shareware and public domain software that you can download

(a)

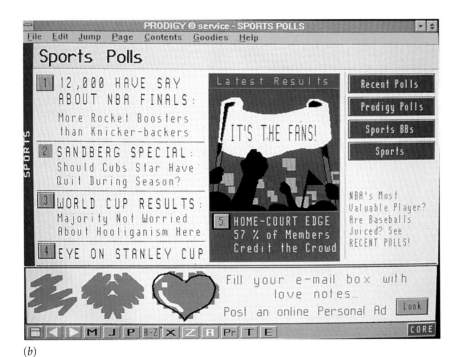

(b)

Figure 10.13 *(a) A CompuServe screen display. (b) A Prodigy screen display.*

Microsoft has a product called Network, which has the potential for being more powerful than Prodigy, more graphics-oriented than CompuServe, and more organized than the Internet. Windows 95 includes the client-server software for accessing this network so that users need not purchase separate software. With Microsoft's significant advantages in distribution, packaging, and insider knowledge of software, many people think that the Microsoft Network is likely to become the leader in online services. See Figure 10.14.

IN A NUTSHELL

ALTERNATIVE TECHNOLOGIES COMPETE

Approximately 150 software developers are now offering CD-ROM titles that include legal data. Using Lexis and Westlaw can cost as much as $240 per hour, while purchasing a CD-ROM subscription can cost as little as $60 per month.

Figure 10.14 *Microsoft Network screen display.*

Critical Thinking

Do you think profit-making organizations should have access to the Internet?

IN A NUTSHELL

Beginning with the 1994 Winter Olympics held in Norway, the results of the games have been published on the Internet. On the first day of the 1994 games, there were 100,000 people who accessed this service.

THE INTERNET The Internet consists of more than 12,000 worldwide interconnected academic, commercial, government, and military networks. Connection to the Internet is available through most universities, government agencies, and medium-to-large businesses, as well as through many online subscriber services such as CompuServe and America Online. Currently there are over 40 million users in 120 countries. The Internet tends to be used mostly by researchers, students, professors, and nonprofit organizations, but it will become more business-oriented in the years ahead.

The Internet provides access to tens of thousands of databases that include newspapers, journals, magazines, books, and public domain software in thousands of subject areas. It also has thousands of news groups that enable users with similar interests to communicate with each other and learn about the latest developments in their areas of interest. In addition, all Internet users can communicate with each other.

Wading through all the services provided by the Internet can be an awesome task. Software products like Mosaic and Netscape provide a front-end interface for navigating through these vast services. Mosaic and Netscape are available on subscriber services. Most browsers can be purchased for less than $100. See Figure 10.15.

Here are some popular Internet terms:

Anonymous FTP	A method of obtaining public domain software from the Internet using the word *anonymous* for a login ID and your Internet address as a password (see below). FTP is an abbreviation for *File Transfer Protocol*.
Archie	A database that lists what is available from anonymous FTP sites.
FAQ	*Frequently Asked Questions* maintained by most user news groups on the Internet.
Gopher	A menu to enable users to "go for" items on the Internet without having to use complex commands and addresses.
Internet address	The format for an Internet address is username@location.domain. Domains include:
	com for business

Looking Ahead

The Internet will include:
- More business-oriented resources
- More use or "traffic"
- Advertisements and "junk" mail
- Increasing numbers of video-based broadcasts and other multimedia products

	gov for government
	org for other organization
	edu for education
	mil for military site
	Outside the United States, the Internet address also includes the country (e.g., username@location.domain.country).
Mosaic	A graphical interface to the World-Wide Web (WWW) (see below).
Veronica	With all the Gopher sites available, locating one that has the information and files you want may be difficult. Veronica enables users to find the desired Gopher site(s).
WAIS	Wide Area Information Servers. A very powerful system for looking up information in databases on the Internet.
WWW	World-Wide Web. A hypermedia system for finding and accessing resources on the Internet. Text-based information is supplied with some words, sound buttons, and video icons highlighted. For more information about a specific topic, click on the highlighted term, button, or icon.

Current concerns about the Internet include:

1. Who will finance the cost of services?
2. Will advertisements get in the way?

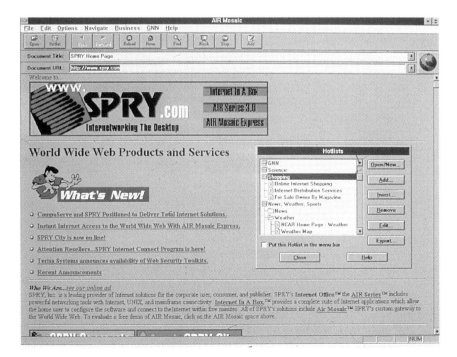

Figure 10.15 *With all the services provided on the Internet, an easy-to-use and fast navigator or browser is essential.*

Critical Thinking

The U.S. government is committed to helping private industry and academia make the Internet available to all citizens. But accessibility may remain a problem for some in rural or poor areas. What the government needs to do is guard against the possibility of an information underclass. What do you think the ethical solution to this problem might be? Would you favor subsidies to such people in order to guarantee universal participation in the Information Superhighway?

●●●●●▶ Looking Ahead

THE INFORMATION
SUPERHIGHWAY

1. Many major computer and telecommunications companies are jockeying for position in this market, which is expected to be worth several billion dollars a year in 1996.
2. The objective of this superhighway is to link virtually everyone in the United States to everyone else.
3. Electronic mail will connect people using sound and full-motion video as well as text.
4. Consumers will be able to connect to the superhighway using devices connected to televisions, phone lines, and wireless products.

3. Will there be a need for a firmer government policy regulating the resources transmitted?

4. What is proper etiquette or "netiquette" for network users? It is currently voluntary rather than prescribed and enforcement is by peer review.
   - What you transmit should be politically correct and in no way offensive to the community of users.
   - Blatant self-serving ads are frowned upon but ads that genuinely provide information are acceptable if they are in good taste.

The Information Superhighway

This term gained widespread popularity when then Senator Al Gore introduced it in the early 1990s and became even more popular when Gore became Vice President and, along with President Clinton, began promoting the concept. Rep. Newt Gingrich has also been a strong supporter. The term "Information Superhighway" is a vague expression that means different things to different people. Its objectives include enhanced Internet availability as well as an interactive cable TV system with video-on-demand for every household in the United States. The concept is based on the belief that the more information we have, the better the quality of our lives. The details of how these services will be provided and paid for have yet to be determined.

BULLETIN BOARD SERVICES Free bulletin board services are also widely available, some for special interest groups such as Mac users, IBM users, or Word-Perfect users, or for members of various clubs or societies. These electronic bulletin boards enable users with similar interests to communicate with one another, keep track of recent innovations in specific areas, and upload and download files.

Interoffice Electronic Mail and Groupware

Electronic mail (e-mail) is the transmission of memos and messages over a network. Users send messages to individual recipients or "broadcast" messages to groups of users on the system. If the recipient is online when the message is being transmitted, a beep will announce that mail has arrived. If the recipient is not online, the next time he or she logs on, a message will indicate that there is mail waiting. Recipients can read, reread, reply to, forward, delete, or save messages. "Folders" can be established so that all mail from, and responses to, spec-

Looking Back ◀ ●●●●●●●●●●●●●●●●●●●●●●●●●●●●●●●●●●●●●●

PRECURSORS TO THE INTERNET

- In 1969, Arpanet was a network developed by the Advanced Research Projects Agency of the Department of Defense. It connected university, military, and defense contractors in an effort to help researchers share information. By 1991, this network along with NSFnet became the Internet, managed in the United States by the National Science Foundation (NSF) and costing the government $20 million a year. The NSF no longer funds the Internet. The cost must be assumed by businesses, universities, private organizations, and governments throughout the world.
- Bitnet—*Because It's Time Network*—began in 1981 as a communications link between the City University of New York and Yale University. It grew to an extensive network of hundreds of sites, mostly universities, from dozens of countries. Bitnet access is now available over the Internet.

ified individuals or groups of individuals can be stored separately. Recipients who are not available can have standard responses transmitted to senders.

Electronic mail has the potential for greatly influencing the ways in which people communicate. For one thing, people need not play "telephone tag" trying to track down each other. Messages can be as detailed as necessary and can include spreadsheets, charts, other documents, and so on. Records of messages sent and delivered can be retained as "ticklers" or to help evaluate the effectiveness of the exchange. People can take time to structure a message so that what is transmitted is exactly what is intended—verbal messages are not always as effective in this regard.

To send or receive e-mail, you must be connected to a network. If the network is active 24 hours a day, you can transmit and receive messages at any hour. Moreover, you can transmit messages to people who may be far away but who have access to the network over telephone lines. If groups of people use the same network—either by accessing their own company's computer or by using a subscriber service, for example—messages can be transmitted over local phone lines with minimum telephone costs, even if other users are not at the same location.

E-mail is available not only to employees within a company, but to anyone who makes use of subscriber services, electronic bulletin boards, or other public networks. One problem with e-mail is lack of cross-communication: users may have access to many e-mail services, none of which permits communication with another. E-mail software, such as Lotus Notes or Groupwise, is designed to ease this problem. It enables users to establish one set of IDs and passwords and a set of folders that can be called in to communicate across different e-mail services.

Groupware further facilitates communicating over a computer network by enabling teams of employees to work together on documents, proposals, spreadsheets, presentations and so on, incorporating their own suggestions and making comments on the suggestions of others. All annotations can either be anonymous or specify user names; annotations can also be date and time stamped. Groupware can be used offline with users at different sites or it can be used online at meetings, with team members sitting around a conference table and typing their ideas into the PCs in front of them. According to an article in *Fortune* magazine, on March 23, 1992, Boeing cut the time required to complete a wide range of team projects by an average of 91%, or to one-tenth what it previously required. The most popular groupware software product is Lotus Notes.

Telecommuting

Telecommuting is the use of computers to access office databases, programs, electronic mail systems, and so forth while away from the office. Managers, professionals, and many other types of employees can work effectively at home or on the road, almost as if they were in the office. Telecommuting has the potential for improving the quality of life of employees by increasing leisure time and by enabling workers to do their jobs on a schedule that better suits their individual needs. It has social benefits as well. Telecommuting can save energy and decrease pollution and traffic congestion. People with disabilities and illnesses can work effectively at home. Employers can hire experts from all over the world without concern for their geographical locations. Studies predict that within 10 years, 42% of the office work force will be telecommuting for part of their workweek.

The common application areas for networks are not mutually exclusive. An organization may use data communications for remote data entry, for inquiring about the status of records in a database file, and for accessing a subscriber service. Connectivity, in its most global sense, relies on multiple uses of networks.

Critical Thinking

In what ways does e-mail *improve* communication between people and in what ways does it *impede* effective communication?

GROUPWARE FEATURES
- Document management
- Group scheduling
- Conferencing
- Electronic messaging
- Workflow automation

Critical Thinking

Mention telecommuting to some office workers and visions of doing twice as much work in half the time come to mind—while some employers envision employees at home watching TV or otherwise avoiding work. What can be done to minimize potential abuses of telecommuting? How can employers measure the benefits of telecommuting?

Self-Test

1. A device called a _____ makes programs and data available to nodes on a network.

2. (T or F) Remote data entry systems can only be used for interactive processing.

3. (T or F) With client-server computing, most tasks are performed by the client.

4. _____ is the transmission of memos and messages over a network.

5. (T or F) Telecommunications is the use of computers to access office databases, programs, and so on by employees while they are away from the office.

10.3 CONTROLLING DATA FLOW WITH COMMUNICATIONS SOFTWARE

Communications software enables computers to communicate with one another. The software controls transmission by indicating the (1) speed of transmission, (2) direction of data flow, (3) method of transmission, (4) number of bits in the computer code, and (5) type of parity, if any. The rules and procedures for exchanging information between computers is called the communications protocol.

Speed of Transmission

Transmission speeds set by communications software indicate how fast data can travel accurately across specific communications channels. Different types of channels can handle data efficiently only at certain speeds. Transmission speed is related to the bandwidth of a channel. There are two common types of bandwidths—baseband and broadband—which determine the capacity of a channel to transmit data. Just as you would not drive 80 miles an hour over a rocky, potholed road, you would not send data through baseband lines at extremely high speeds.

The speed at which data is sent is commonly expressed as a **baud rate,** measured in bits per second (bps). Note that bps stands for the number of bits (not bytes) sent through the line per second. Most modems operate at 1200, 2400, 9600, 14,400, 28,800 or more bps, roughly equivalent to 120, 240, 960, 1440, and 2880 or more characters per second. The computer code for just a character itself typically requires seven or eight bits. Sometimes start and stop bits are added along with a parity bit to control and regulate transmission. In all, a transmis-

---

Solutions

1. file server or host computer

2. F—They can also be designed for batch processing.

3. T

4. Electronic mail (or e-mail)

5. F—The term is *telecommuting.*

SPEEDS OF TRANSMISSION LINES

Type of Line	Example	Characteristics	Range of Transmission Speed
Baseband (voice-grade or midrange)	Telephone	Most commonly used, some noise	300 to 19,200 bps
Broadband (wideband or high speed)	Leased lines, microwave, satellite, fiber optics	More expensive, least noise, can transmit data, voice, and video simultaneously	20,000 to 300,000+ bps and above
Broadband ISDN (ISDN is an abbreviation for integrated services digital network)	Digital lines for voice, data, and video transmission; used in networks connecting high-speed workstations	Most significant benefit is uniform handling of services, allowing one network to better meet the needs of all users	Up to gigabyte range

sion may require 10 or so bits per character. Hence, we say that a 9600 bps modem transmits approximately 960 characters per second.

The speed of the communications line and the baud rate of the modem determine the maximum transmission rate. It is advisable to select a modem with a baud rate similar to the capacity of the transmission channel. It would not be prudent, for example, to use a modem with a baud rate of 9600 bps for transmitting data over a narrow band; similarly, it would be inefficient and unnecessarily slow to use a 1200 bps modem to transmit data over broadband channels.

Direction of Data Flow

Traffic signs direct cars to move in only one of two directions on a street; similarly, data moves only in specific directions through communications channels. Electronic impulses can move in one of three ways: using simplex, half-duplex, or full-duplex communication channels. See Figure 10.16. Communications software sets the transmission protocols that indicate the way data will flow over a communications channel.

Simplex lines allow data to flow in one direction only, like a one-way street. A simplex line functions with a device that only sends or only receives data from a CPU but does not do both; a printer, for example, is a receive-only device that could obtain its messages over a simplex line. An airline monitor that displays departure and arrival information might use a simplex line because data is always transmitted in one direction only—from the CPU to the monitor (Figure 10.17). But simplex lines are clearly very limited and are therefore used infrequently.

A **half-duplex line** permits data to move in two directions, but not at the same time. When the line is being used to transmit data from a terminal to a main CPU, it cannot be used simultaneously to transmit data back from the main CPU to the terminal. Data moves first one way and then the other, but never at the same time. Half-duplex channels work like CB radios, which can send and receive voice messages alternately, but not at the same time.

A **full-duplex line** can transmit data in both directions at the same time. A

TYPES OF CHANNELS

1. Simplex — permits transmission of data in one direction only (e.g., from computer to printer); rarely used now
2. Half-duplex — permits transmission of data in two directions but not at the same time (analogous to CB transmissions)
3. Full-duplex — permits transmission of data in two directions at the same time (e.g., most baseband and broadband transmissions)

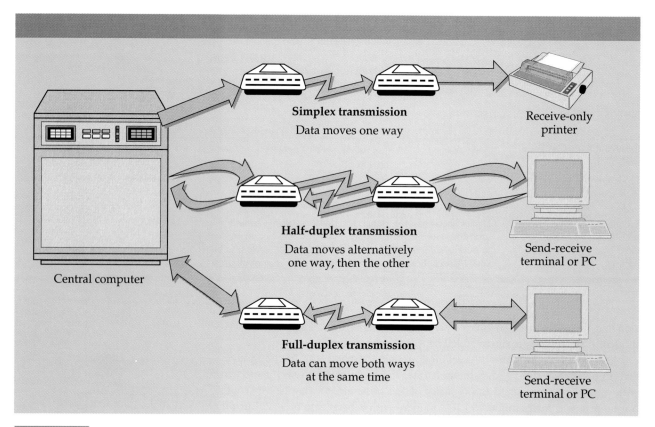

Figure 10.16 *Transmission protocols allow one-way (simplex), alternating (half-duplex), or full two-way (full-duplex) transmission.*

telephone line, for example, can make use of a full-duplex channel. Similarly, the main CPU transmits messages to a node at the same time that the node is transmitting to the CPU. Full-duplex channels are the most frequently used channels in data communications applications.

Figure 10.17 *Receive-only terminals that use simplex lines can be used in a limited number of applications, such as displaying flight information at airline terminals.*

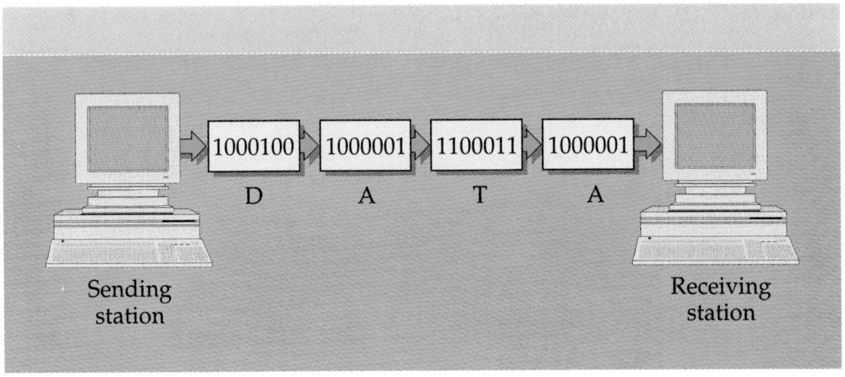

Figure 10.18 *Serial transmission.*

1000100 ⟩ 1000001 ⟩ 1100011 ⟩ 1000001
   D   A   T   A

Sending
station

Receiving
station

Serial and Parallel Transmission

Another factor specified by the communications software package is the method of transmission. Like the baud rate, it affects the speed of transmission. There are two basic methods for transmitting data: serial and parallel.

SERIAL TRANSMISSION In **serial transmission,** each bit is transmitted one at a time in sequence over a single channel. See Figure 10.18. Most peripherals communicate with computers in serial mode through a standard serial interface that attaches to modems.

There are two types of serial modes for sending data: asynchronous and synchronous. **Asynchronous transmission** means that one character at a time is transmitted. The transfer of data is controlled by start and stop bits. This is the least expensive method of transmission and is often used with narrow or low-end voice band channels. **Synchronous transmission** enables blocks of characters called packets to be transmitted in timed sequences. A stop bit indicates the end of data. Synchronous transmission is not only much faster than asynchronous transmission, but it is also more widely used.

PARALLEL TRANSMISSION **Parallel transmission** is a faster method of transmission in which all bits are transmitted simultaneously. See Figure 10.19. Parallel transmission is more expensive than serial transmission because of the large number of cables needed and is usually limited to communications over relatively short distances.

Figure 10.19 *Parallel transmission.*

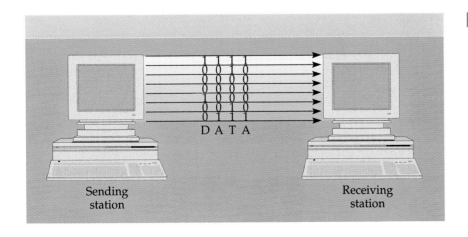

Sending
station

Receiving
station

D A T A

Data Bits in the Computer Code

Computers typically transmit data using the ASCII code which, as noted in Chapter 4, is an abbreviation for American Standard Code for Information Interchange. There are two versions of this code, a 7-bit and an 8-bit version. In order for two computers to communicate with one another, the communications package must include a parameter indicating which ASCII version—7-bit or 8-bit—is being used by each computer.

Parity

In Chapter 4 you learned that parity bits are added to computer codes to minimize the risk of transmission errors. Even-parity computers require each character being transmitted to have an even number of bits on at all times. If the character being transmitted uses an odd number of ASCII bits, then the parity bit is automatically turned on to ensure that an even number of bits are being transmitted. If the character being transmitted uses an even number of ASCII bits, then the parity bit is automatically turned off so that an even number of bits is, in fact, transmitted. Some computers use even parity and some use odd parity; other computers do not use parity bits at all. The type of parity—odd, even, or none—must be specified by the communications software used for interfacing with another computer.

The number of characters that actually get transmitted per second is only partly determined by the baud rate. The actual number of characters transmitted per second depends also on the computer code, parity, and method of transmission being used. Consider, for example, an 8-bit code with parity and one stop bit. This type of transmission requires 10 bits per character. In this instance, a baud rate of 9600 bps would mean a transmission of 960 characters per second. If no parity were used, or both a start and stop bit were included, or the code were 7-bit, then the number of bits per character might not be exactly 10.

An Overview of Protocols

A **protocol** is a set of rules and procedures for formatting and regulating the speed of data transmitted from one device to another. Error handling is also under the control of a protocol.

Communications programs for PCs offer a variety of protocols such as Kermit, Xmodem, and Zmodem to transfer files. On networks, protocols are part of the network software. TCP/IP, an abbreviation for *Transmission Control Protocol/Internet Program*, is a set of protocols used for transmission over the Internet.

In a move toward standardization, the International Standards Organization (ISO) in Geneva, Switzerland has defined a set of communications protocols called the international **Open Systems Interconnection (OSI) standard.** The standard has been endorsed by the United Nations but has not yet become a universal standard because it will take time for countries or vendors to adopt it.

Self-Test

1. The speed at which data is transmitted over communications channels is expressed as a _____.

2. (T or F) A 14,400 bps modem transmits approximately 1440 characters per second.

3. (Simplex/half-duplex/full-duplex) channels are the most frequently used ones in data communications applications.

4. The two basic methods for transmitting data are serial transmission and _____.

5. (T or F) Computers typically communicate with one another using the EBCDIC code.

10.4 NETWORK CONFIGURATIONS

Networks consist of computer hardware as well as the programs used to link the hardware. Network configurations depend on an organization's needs and application areas. Full connectivity of office equipment—telephones, fax machines, and printers, as well as computers—can be achieved through a network configuration. There are two basic categories of networks: local area networks and wide area networks.

The Local Area Network (LAN): A Promised LAN for Sharing Resources

A **local area network (LAN)** is the most common configuration. It is used when computer devices are in relatively close proximity to one another. Although some LANs can connect devices as far apart as 50 miles, most LANs connect devices within several thousand feet of one another. Most often, these LANs have coaxial or fiber optic cables for linkages, but telephone lines or wireless radio waves could be used.

LANs enable organizations to share resources such as software, hardware, and data. They also help schedule, supervise, and monitor the processing of data from remote locations. LANs used in this way have a file server, which is linked to each station or node. As we have seen, this file server can be a RISC-based microcomputer or workstation, or a mainframe, midrange, or minicomputer depending on the complexity of the jobs it must perform.

LAN Software

LAN software interfaces with application software and controls resources. This software must contain an operating system or operating system interface that enables a variety of different programs to be used on the LAN. LAN software also contains communications programs that permit all devices to communicate either with the file server or with each other. In addition, the software contains utilities for monitoring and supervising hardware and software use. Currently, Novell is the leading developer of LAN software.

Installing and controlling hardware and software on a network can be fairly complex. Many organizations employ a network manager or administrator who is responsible for establishing the network, supervising its implementation, and monitoring its activities. See Figure 10.20.

Solutions

1. baud rate, or bits per second (bps)

2. T

3. Full-duplex

4. parallel transmission

5. F—They typically use the ASCII code.

Study Objective

4. Describe common network configurations.

IN A NUTSHELL

PHYSICAL COMPONENTS OF A LAN

1. *Nodes*, which may be input/output devices or micros.

2. *File server* that stores the data and software and controls access to resources.

3. *Network cables* or links such as telephone lines or wireless radio waves that connect nodes to a host or file server. LANs usually employ coaxial cables, either baseband or broadband.

4. *Interface cards* inserted in an expansion slot of the nodes that enable these devices to communicate with other devices.

5. *Cable interface unit* in a separate device that enables signals to be sent and received on the network cables.

Looking Ahead

SOFTWARE SENSATIONS

Novell's acquisitions of both the WordPerfect Corporation and Borland's Quattro Pro make it the second largest PC software company. With Novell software, it is now possible for users to work with a single vendor who can satisfy their networking *and* desktop application needs.

Figure 10.20 *LAN software manages and reports on shared resources.*

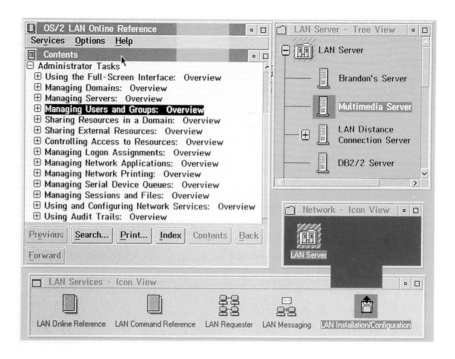

Network Topologies: Star, Bus, Ring, Hybrid

The specific type of network configuration is called the **network topology.** The topology differs depending on how the network will be used. The three basic types of network topologies—ring, star, and bus—are illustrated in Figure 10.21. Each topology has specific features. Hybrid topologies are those that combine the three basic types in one network.

1. Ring
   - This topology is common for LANs that use file servers.
   - It also can be used to connect a series of devices where there is no central computer.
   - Nodes are linked to each other as well as to the file server.
   - A message transmitted from one node to another must pass through the ring from node to node until it reaches its destination.

2. Star
   - All devices can access a host but not necessarily each other.
   - Typically, there are no difficulties if one node is down—it is simply bypassed.
   - The central computer or host monitors all processing.
   - This topology is ideal for networks where branch offices need to communicate with a main office.

3. Bus
   - Nodes share the same bus, or channel, for transmitting to other nodes or hosts.
   - *Ethernet,* a popular type of LAN that interconnects PCs via coaxial cable, has a bus topology.
   - Nodes can access a host as well as each other.

Networks with a file server to enable users to share resources will most likely use a *token* ring topology. IBM's **token ring network** uses twisted pair cables for

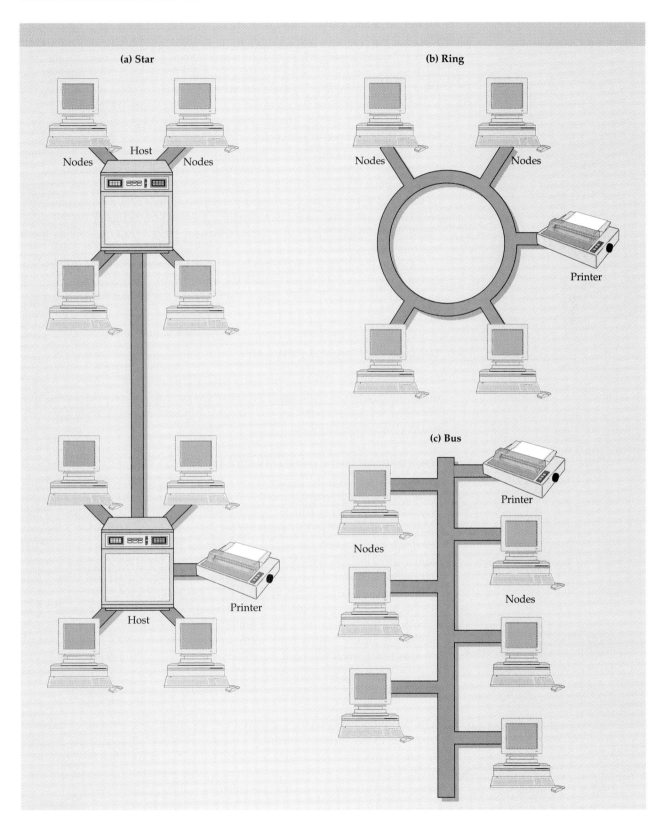

Figure 10.21 *A comparison of star, ring, and bus networks. (a) A star network is most often used with terminals (or PCs) and hosts. (b) In a ring network, all computers are connected in a continuous loop. Data flows around the ring in one direction only. (c) Bus networks are commonly used in Ethernet systems.*

transmission and has become a de facto standard in the industry. A "token" is a special signal that moves from node to node around the LAN. Only one token on the network is available at any given time. When a user at a node on the network wants to transmit or receive data from the file server, it first captures the token; then it completes its transaction. After the transaction is complete, the token is released back to the network for use by other nodes. Think of the tokens as dump trucks revolving around a ring—some are empty and some are full. Some will be dumped at the central site and some must first pick up a load.

Often networks are used by larger organizations for distributed processing. Nodes process data at the local level as well as transmit and receive data from a host computer. Large-scale database management systems are typically accessed by means of networks for distributed processing applications. Such applications are likely to use a star or a bus technology. Networks in which a central computer is accessed by terminals primarily for remote data entry are apt to use a star topology.

A central computer might link several networks, creating a *hybrid* of bus and star topologies. As we will see in the next section, differences in topologies and communication channels among the networks can be handled by a gateway system.

Wide Area Networks (WANs)

Our discussion of LANs has been fairly detailed because that is the type of network you are most likely to encounter at school or at the office. Where local area transmissions and transfers of files are not sufficient, however, **wide area networks (WANs)** are required.

FOR TRANSMISSION OVER GREATER DISTANCES THAN LANs As you may suspect, WANs are similar in concept to LANs except that the technology permits transmission over greater distances. A WAN typically uses private and public telephone lines and fiber optic lines as well as microwave relays and satellites so that individuals at nodes can communicate with a host or with each other over long distances, even around the world. Commercial WANs widely available in the United States include Tymnet and Telenet, which link users to subscriber services. Organizations rent or lease private telephone lines from Tymnet and Telenet and then provide shared resources to computer users at a relatively low cost.

MasterCard's worldwide, private WAN is called Banknet and consists of 14 switching centers, 8 in the United States and 6 in other countries. One major application area for Banknet is *electronic funds transfer* (EFT). Banks around the world that are MasterCard members settle their accounts daily by using the Banknet WAN to electronically transmit transaction data rather than by creating a paper trail of checks, deposit slips, withdrawal slips, and so forth.

FOR NETWORKING LANs Sometimes a WAN is simply a network of LANs. A department store, for example, may have a LAN at each branch store; in addition, the LANs at all stores may be connected to the main office by means of a WAN. Sometimes a WAN simply permits a large number of nodes at different locations to communicate with each other.

GATEWAYS, BRIDGES, AND ROUTERS CONNECT LANs TO WANs AND LANs TO LANs LANs linked to WANs or other LANs require a special device, usually a computer, along with special software. **Bridges, routers,** and **gateways** are devices that route messages from one LAN to another or from a LAN to a

•••••▶ Looking Ahead

GLOBAL NETWORKING

1. The distinctions between LANs and WANs are fading as global networking becomes more popular.
2. The trend toward very sophisticated network management capabilities will grow.
3. Networks will result in more "downsizing"—smaller computers networked to more sophisticated file servers.
4. Wireless networks will enable the world to be even more connected.

WAN. They are used to network systems with different structures and can select the best route based on traffic, transmission speed, and cost.

Routers with high-speed buses may serve as an Internet backbone connecting numerous networks.

Self-Test

1. (T or F) A LAN benefits organizations that have both Macs and IBM-compatibles because it enables resources to be shared among the two environments.

2. (T or F) All networks must have a host or file server.

3. (T or F) A wide area network can consist of a network of LANs.

4. (T or F) It is possible to connect nodes and LANs that have different technologies.

5. (T or F) WANs are used for transmitting data over greater distances than can be handled by LANs.

■■■ 10.5 CONNECTIVITY LEADS TO A SMALLER, SMARTER, AND MORE CREATIVE WORLD

In the previous sections, we considered connectivity in relation to computerized application areas for information processing. As we approach the twenty-first century, computerized devices are likely to be used in a more integrated manner to help people in their businesses and in their personal lives as well. Connectivity is the key to that integration. In this section, we discuss other technologies and application areas that will make the world more connected in the years ahead.

Facsimile (Fax) Machines

A **facsimile (fax) machine** enables us to transmit virtually any document to any location over telephone lines. See Figure 10.22. The sender uses a telephone to dial the receiving fax machine's phone number and then feeds the document through the sending fax machine. The receiving fax machine produces a copy of the document.

Facsimile machines have a scanner that reads and digitizes a document. The document itself can contain illustrations and photos as well as handwritten or typed text. The digitized document is converted into analog form and transmitted over telephone lines. At the receiving end, the analog signals are converted back to digital form thereby producing a copy of the document.

Solutions

1. T

2. F—A ring network connects a series of devices where there is no central computer.

3. T

4. T—This can be accomplished with a gateway.

5. T

Study Objective

5. Identify new technologies that contribute to connectivity.

Figure 10.22 *Fax machines are widely used in business. In this illustration, hungry patrons fax their meal orders to their favorite restaurant.*

The number of fax machines for both business and personal use has increased dramatically during the past few years. Fax machines can be programmed to (1) transmit at off-peak hours when phone rates are lower, (2) transmit to a number of different locations (e.g., each sales office of a company), and (3) accept documents from designated senders only, so that the risk of receiving a "junk fax" is reduced.

Some application areas are already predominantly fax-based; that is, they rely on telephones along with fax machines to communicate with clients. For example, potential customers dial a designated number for information about items. An answering machine instructs them on how to select a specific item—a sales brochure, for example. Typically, the customer is instructed to key specific digits using a Touch-Tone phone. The customer then keys in his or her fax number and the system immediately faxes the information requested. This is called a fax-back system. As phone charges decrease and mail charges increase, fax and fax-back systems for providing information to customers are likely to become more popular.

Some computers have **fax boards** that capture any document or screen display stored by the computer and transmit it via a modem either to another computer with a modem or to a fax machine. See Figure 10.23. Some e-mail and subscriber services enable users to create documents on a PC, upload them to the host, and have them faxed to a receiving party who has either a computer or a fax machine. They are often preferable to fax machines for several reasons:

Figure 10.23 *Fax board for PCs.*

- Security and privacy is better maintained—no one but the sender and receiver sees a copy of documents.

- Junk fax can simply be deleted without ever being printed.

- A PC can store incoming faxes in background mode while other processing is being performed; the PC can also keep a log of faxes sent and received.

- The amount of paper generated and stored in offices is reduced because faxed documents can be stored on disk rather than in hard copy form. This may facilitate the trend toward a paperless office, which is a goal in many organizations.

Most fax boards are internal computer devices, but some companies sell external fax boards for use with portable computers. Fax boards are best used to send *computer-produced* documents. If data is not in a computer file or on a storage device (e.g., a book page, photo, or drawing), it must be scanned (or retyped) and stored before it can be transmitted by fax board.

Networked Fax Machines. Standalone office fax machines, like copy machines, require a staff to feed, monitor, and oversee operations. Many companies are now integrating fax, computer, and network technology to cut costs, save time, and avoid the inconvenience associated with fax transmissions. Users transmit their computer-produced document to a network-based "fax server" which sends faxes, from numerous users, in batch mode. The PC user who has access to a network-based fax server does not have to wait for documents to be printed and then wait on a separate fax line to transmit them. Instead, documents generated on a PC may be uploaded to a fax server for transmission to a recipient. This method of routing also reduces security problems—users need not worry that other office workers are reading their faxes.

Fax servers reduce the need for multiple phone lines. Whereas each standalone fax machine or fax board typically has its own phone line, a network-based server can queue documents to be faxed and transmit them, in batch mode, over

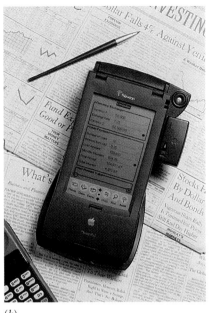

(a)   (b)

Figure 10.24 (a) Wrist-sized cellular phone. (b) Apple's Newton Message Pad is a popular PDA for sending and receiving messages. It has a slide-in PCMCIA radio receiver called a Messaging Card.

one phone line. Fax servers, like all fax machines, can be programmed to transmit documents that are not time sensitive at off hours when the cost is cheaper and the lines are less congested. Some sophisticated fax servers can also scan and route incoming faxes to the appropriate recipient.

Wireless Communications

Wireless communications enables users with a portable PC to communicate with their office from virtually anywhere in the world. Wireless communications facilities include cellular telephones, pagers, and radio modems that can be linked to any computer but are most commonly used with PDAs and subnotebook or notebook PCs. (Many PDAs are specifically designed for use as wireless communication devices.) These devices use radio waves to communicate with a local cell assigned to an individual geographic location. See Figure 10.24.

Transmitting stations are placed at strategic locations in an area, dividing it into cells. Mobile cellular phones, pagers, and radio modems transmit to these stations, which connect the user to a standard phone system. As the caller moves from one cell location to another, computers transmit to stations in adjoining cells.

Smart Phones

Does the rotary dial telephone seem like a dinosaur to you? Now some telephone manufacturers are hoping to make the Touch-Tone telephone a memory too. The caller who has a **smart phone** can automatically pay the heating bill by pushing a button, order a pizza by pushing another, and find out what is on sale at the local supermarket or department store by pushing a third button. See Figure 10.25.

Smart phones contain computer chips that can be programmed for many advanced features and monitors that can visually display data. They have modems and built-in fax capability as well.

AT&T, Northern Telecom, and other telephone companies supporting smart phone development believe that these devices will encourage consumers to shop

ıN A NUTSHELL

In 1994, portable PCs sold 3 million units, which took third place behind cellular telephones and pagers.

Experts predict that U.S. sales of mobile devices—computers, phones, faxes, pagers—will soar from 11 million in 1994 to 21 million in 1999, nearly doubling in a five-year period.

Figure 10.25 *A smart phone can pay bills, do the shopping, and provide us with a variety of information services.*

•••••▶ **Looking Ahead**

INTEGRATING COMMUNICATION CAPABILITIES

AT&T has launched Project Sage, a program to enable telephones to act as central controllers in home-based integrated systems consisting of VCRs, TVs, PCs, fax machines, answering machines, online services, and telephone services. The Sage phone will use PCMCIA plug-in boards to connect to these appliances. AT&T will need the support of cable TV and regional phone companies as well as software developers like Microsoft for a full implementation of this program.

Interactive TV, smart phones, and PCs with enhanced multimedia capabilities all have the ability to improve the quality of our lives and to literally revolutionize the way we communicate. But no single network or industry is likely to corner the market—nor should it! The cooperation of cable TV, telephone HDTV, cellular, satellite, publishing, and entertainment companies will be essential.

and bank at home. For many years, subscriber services have offered consumers the ability to shop, bank, and retrieve data from databases while at home. But consumers have been slow to use this technology.

The new smart phones, however, are expected to make banking and shopping more convenient. Because they are telephones and do not require a separate computer, they seem more user-friendly. Many people believe that telephones may be better suited than computers for home shopping because, unlike the PC, they are already found in almost all homes and people are intimately familiar with them. Smart phones are less likely to intimidate users and they fit more comfortably into the average living room! Developers of the smart phone admit, however, that what they are really doing is disguising a computer to look like a telephone. They hope that the simplicity, price, and convenience of a smart phone will encourage people to use it the way subscriber services are used.

Some of the telephone services offered with the smart phone, such as Caller ID which displays the number of the caller, are designed to spur interest as well. For a cost of $150 to $200, users can have enhanced phone services as well as shop-at-home capabilities.

Interactive TV and High-Definition Television

High-definition television (HDTV) has the potential for converting the TV from a passive, receive-only home unit used exclusively for entertainment purposes, to an interactive device that brings a wide variety of services and information into the home. HDTV is a system that provides wide-screen digital pic-

Figure 10.26 *Interactive processing can be performed using a PC or TV.*

tures with twice the resolution, or sharpness, of ordinary TVs and sound as clear as that on a compact disk.

Because HDTV digitizes all signals including text, graphics, and sound, it has great potential as a fully computerized device that can be used for creating high-quality multimedia presentations for education and entertainment.

Many cable TV and HDTV manufacturers have begun offering on-demand videos and games. Users operate a controller box to obtain the videos they want. Shop-at-home services can also be obtained by using the controller box to place an order or to pay bills. See Figure 10.26.

Videoconferencing and Distance Learning

Videoconferencing systems enable full-motion video and sound to be transmitted over telephone lines. Sound, captured by microphones, and images, captured by cameras, are digitized, compressed, and transmitted to the receiver. See Figure 10.27. The systems include recorders and receivers along with compression/decompression units called codecs, which are similar to modems in that they enable video and sound signals to be transmitted over phone lines but in compressed, digitized form that can be transmitted at high speeds.

Although expensive, videoconferencing equipment can result in a considerable savings in travel expenses for a company and in wear-and-tear on employees. Time-shared videoconferenced facilities are available to organizations at an hourly rate. The cost for such services a decade ago was $2,000 per hour; now it is about $35 per hour. Some companies manufacture PCs with video conferencing capability. Desktop computers may have tiny video cameras, miniature microphones, and video software that can connect you to video networks.

The Information Superhighway and other networks make distance learning an alternative to a traditional classroom experience. **Distance learning** is defined as the use of video and audio technologies in education so that students can attend classes in a location distant from where the course is actually presented. See Figure 10.28. Some of the features of distance learning include:

Figure 10.27 *Videoconferencing systems transmit full-motion video and sound over telephone lines.*

Figure 10.28 *Students in a classroom are being taught by an instructor whose lectures are transmitted over a network. After the lecture, the students get more information from their PCs, which are linked to the network.*

1. The best educators in specific subject areas can communicate with students regardless of geographical location.

2. Students can communicate and interact directly with their peers as well as their teachers and establish truly global relationships.

3. Social distinctions will break down between the "haves" who can afford expensive tuition at high-priced schools and the "have nots" who often must settle for a lower-quality education or none at all.

Distance learning centers have been established throughout the world that enable people at remote locations to learn and communicate via a videoconferencing network. Although such centers are expensive, they greatly increase the availability of education for all people regardless of their geographical location and mobility.

Text, video, and graphic images as well as sound are being transmitted with greater frequency over phone lines. Transmission standards are needed to ensure compatibility and to improve efficiency. Many telephone companies offer *Integrated Services Digital Network* (ISDN) as a set of standards for the digital transmission of voice, video, and data over telephone lines. We discuss this standard in more depth in the next chapter as we summarize the reasons why standards are so important in the computer field.

Self-Test

1. (T or F) Computers can send messages to fax machines if they have fax boards.

2. (T or F) With a smart phone, you can shop at home.

3. (T or F) HDTV has the potential to a make a TV function like an interactive computer.

CHAPTER SUMMARY

Data communications allows us to combine the power and resources of computers no matter where the hardware is located. Connectivity, which brings the world closer together, is accomplished through different types of networks.

10.1 Communications and Connectivity

Connectivity involves a combination of technologies that enable computers to transmit data, voice messages, and video electronically to each other. When computers are located near one another, cables or telephone lines connect the systems. When computers are a considerable distance from one another, a special communications technology called **telecommunications** (or teleprocessing) is required. Connectivity refers to the linking of all types of equipment—telephones, fax machines, and televisions as well as computers—so that resources in a wide variety of organizational and personal areas can be distributed and shared.

A network is the type of configuration that enables devices to communicate with one another. In some networks, remote devices called nodes are linked to one another; in other networks, nodes are linked to a central computer called a host. A file server is a special host computer that makes programs and data available to nodes on a network. **Communications channels** are the linkages between nodes and/or hosts in a network. Types of communications linkages include hardwired cables, telephones, microwave stations, satellite stations, and wireless networks. Three types of cable can be used for hardwired channels: twisted-pair cable, **coaxial cable,** and **fiber optic cable.** When telephones are used for communications, modems are needed to convert computer data, which is in digital format, to an analog format for transmission, and vice versa. Two basic kinds of modems are the direct-connect type and the **acoustic coupler,** which has two cups into which a telephone handset is placed.

A **multiplexer** is a device that collects messages from numerous nodes at one physical location and transmits them collectively at high speeds over a single communications channel. A **front-end processor** is a microcomputer or minicomputer that helps offload the activities performed by a host computer so that it can run more efficiently.

Many telephone companies offer **value-added services,** such as leased telephone lines, which are extra features beyond those normally provided for voice messages.

10.2 Common Application Areas for Networks

Distributed processing refers to the transmission of computer power throughout an organization from a central facility to each user site. Common distributed processing activities include (1) remote data entry and inquiry and

Study Objective
1. Identify the communications linkages that contribute to effective connectivity.

Study Objective
2. Describe the ways in which connectivity can be achieved in organizations.

Solutions

1. T
2. T
3. T

(2) client-server computing. **Remote data entry** means that terminals or PCs are used for entering data at the places where transactions occur, such as in point-of-sale systems; the terminals or PCs are not physically at the same site as the central computer, or host. Client-server computing enables users at PCs to share hardware, software, and data stored under the control of a file server.

Networks are used in other application areas as well. Online **subscriber services** allow a user with a computer, modem, and telephone line to access a wide variety of databases and other resources. The Internet provides access to thousands of databases and user groups and has e-mail facilities as well. The future Information Superhighway is likely to extend these services. Electronic mail *(e-mail)*, the transmission of memos and messages over a network, is a growing business application. Telecommuting is the use of computers to access office databases, programs, e-mail systems, and so forth while away from the office.

Study Objective

3. Explain how transmission specifications and protocols control the flow of data in networks.

10.3 Controlling Data Flow with Communications Software

The speed at which data can travel accurately across communications channels is called the **baud rate,** expressed in bits per second (bps).

Simplex lines permit transmission of data in one direction only. **Half-duplex lines** permit data to move in two directions, but not at the same time. With **full-duplex lines,** data can be transmitted in both directions at the same time. With **serial transmission,** each bit is transmitted one at a time in sequence over a single channel. There are two types of serial transmissions: **Asynchronous transmission** means that one character at a time is transmitted, and **synchronous transmission** enables blocks of characters called packets to be transmitted in timed sequences. With **parallel transmission,** each bit of a character is transmitted over a separate channel. A **protocol** is a set of rules and procedures for formatting and regulating the speed of data transmitted from one device to another. The international **Open Systems Interconnection (OSI) standard** is a set of communications protocols that is an international standard. There are various communications protocols for regulating the transmission of data over a network.

Study Objective

4. Describe common network configurations.

10.4 Network Configurations

A **local area network (LAN)** connects devices that are in relatively close proximity to one another, typically within a range of 50 miles. LAN software controls and monitors computer and data access, ensuring that only designated users and devices can read specified data. One technique for using a LAN is called the client-server method; with this method, a file server does as much processing as possible before downloading. Another method is called the peer-to-peer method.

The term **network topology** refers to the type of network configuration used in a data communications system. IBM's **token ring network** is a topology that has become a de facto standard in the industry; it allows only one node at a time to transmit or receive data from the file server.

A **wide area network (WAN)** uses microwave relays and satellites to enable users at nodes to communicate with a host or with each other over long distances around the world. **Gateways, bridges,** and **routers** contain software and hardware that enable LANs to connect to other LANs and to WANs.

Study Objective

5. Identify new technologies that contribute to connectivity.

10.5 Connectivity Leads to a Smaller, Smarter, and More Creative World

A **facsimile machine (fax)** scans documents, and **fax boards** capture computer screen displays or files. The documents, displays, or files are then transmitted to either computers or other fax machines. Cellular telephones and radio-frequency-based modems permit people in the field to communicate with the home office. **Smart phones** have features that make them similar to home computers. **High-definition television (HDTV)**, a system that provides wide-screen pictures with twice the resolution of TVs and high-quality sound as well, has the potential for converting TVs into interactive computers that bring many services and information into the home. **Videoconferencing**, which can transmit full-motion video and sound over telephone lines, enables people at different locations to see and hear one another and to communicate interactively.

KEY TERMS

Acoustic coupler,   *p. 334*
Asynchronous transmission,   *p. 351*
Baud rate,   *p. 348*
Bridge,   *p. 356*
Coaxial cable,   *p. 332*
Communications channel,   *p. 331*
Distance learning,   *p. 361*
Facsimile (fax) machine,   *p. 357*
Fax board,   *p. 358*
Fiber optic cable,   *p. 333*
Front-end processor,   *p. 336*
Full-duplex line,   *p. 349*

Gateway,   *p. 356*
Half-duplex line,   *p. 349*
High-definition television (HDTV),
   p. 360
Local area network (LAN),   *p. 353*
Multiplexer,   *p. 336*
Network topology,   *p. 354*
Open Systems Interconnection (OSI)
   standard,   *p. 352*
Parallel transmission,   *p. 351*
Protocol,   *p. 352*
Remote data entry,   *p. 339*

Router,   *p. 356*
Serial transmission,   *p. 351*
Simplex line,   *p. 349*
Smart phone,   *p. 359*
Subscriber service,   *p. 342*
Synchronous transmission,   *p. 351*
Telecommunications,   *p. 330*
Token ring network,   *p. 354*
Value-added service,   *p. 337*
Videoconferencing,   *p. 361*
Wide area network (WAN),   *p. 356*

CHAPTER SELF-TEST

1. The term _____ refers to electronically transmitting data from one location to another by means of communications channels.

2. (T or F) Using terminals at remote locations avoids manual transmittal of data, which can be very time consuming.

3. A _____ in a computer is used to send messages to a facsimile machine.

4. What kind of transmission waves do wireless LANs use?

5. A _____ distributes resources in a network.

6. Immediate online processing of data is required only when files must be kept _____ at all times.

7. _____ is a form of distributed processing that enables users to share resources.

8. The _____ is a series of networks accessible to users of subscriber services as well as people in education, business, and government.

9. Most simple data communications systems use either _____ or _____ as a data communications link.

10. _____ cable is the fastest and most expensive communications link available for data transmission.

11. High-speed data communications typically use _____ stations and _____ stations above the earth.

12. The speed of a communications channel is called the _____ rate.

13. When transmission is permitted both to and from a CPU over the same communications line but *not at the same time*, the line is called _____.

14. What is the device that converts signals in digital form to analog form for transmission over telephone lines?

15. What is the device that can collect messages from numerous terminals and transmit them collectively over a single communications line?

REVIEW QUESTIONS

1. Briefly discuss three major ways network technologies are used in a distributed computer system.

2. List seven major communications links for sending data between computers. Briefly discuss two advantages and disadvantages for each.

3. List and describe three common configurations for networks.

4. How many computer networks are used on your campus? What types of networks and configurations are used? How are they being used? Is there access to a WAN? If so, why is it being used?

CRITICAL THINKING EXERCISES

1. Most subscriber services do not fill screen displays with any advertisements but rely instead on pay-per-use customers for their revenues. Prodigy, however, does include ads. The Internet has begun to permit ads as well. Do you think advertisements should be a part of an online service? What if it reduces costs to users?

2. While netiquette on the Internet is a kind way of requesting people to use good taste when communicating, do you think more specific regulations with imposed penalties should be considered?

3. Some people say that the current Internet (and the future Information Superhighway) promotes democracy because it makes information available to all people. Do you agree?

Solutions

1. connectivity or networking
2. T
3. fax board
4. radio
5. host computer or file server
6. current
7. Client-server computing
8. Internet
9. a standard voice-grade telephone line; a cable
10. Fiber optic
11. microwave; satellite
12. baud
13. half-duplex
14. modem or acoustic coupler
15. multiplexer or front-end processor

Case Study

Distance Learning

How well can college students really learn when they study via a computer network? Drexel University is about to find out.

Beginning in the 1994-95 academic year, Drexel undertook a three-year pilot project in computer-supported instruction, conducted by the College of Information Studies. Students and faculty meet only three times during each course and send each other information electronically through personal computers. Delivery of course materials, reviews, assignments, and exams is provided electronically as well. Students encountering difficulties can meet with their instructors as needed, of course, but university officials are hoping the program will offer an opportunity to measure the effects of computer-supported learning and of allowing students the chance to pace themselves as they move through the required syllabi.

Four courses are being offered in the program, each at both graduate and undergraduate levels. They are Formal Methods and Models for Software Design, Human-Computer Interaction, Interactive Simulation for Process Modeling and Reengineering, and Systems Analysis and Design. If the project succeeds, Drexel will look into its potential for other disciplines as well.

Source: Educom Review, July–August 1994, p. 40.

Analysis

1. Do you think students can learn better and faster over a computer network?

2. Would interactive TV be a good substitute for distance learning?

3. What types of courses would lend themselves to this type of education?

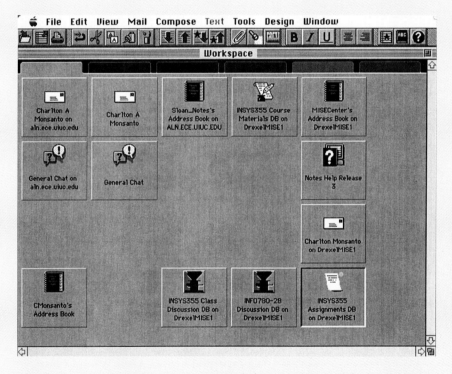

Drexel's computer-supported instruction system includes a vast assortment of online material.

PART FIVE

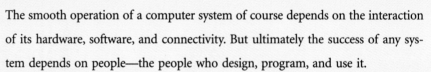

People Power Makes the World a Better Place

The smooth operation of a computer system of course depends on the interaction of its hardware, software, and connectivity. But ultimately the success of any system depends on people—the people who design, program, and use it.

People design and use computers in countless applications, business as well as personal. In addition to improvements in professional productivity, people look to computers for enhancements in **education, entertainment, health care,** and even the performance of **household tasks** (sometimes with a flair). Among those who can benefit most from online shopping services, for instance, are physically challenged and housebound users. So while computers can't shop, play games, or exercise for us, they are already helping to make these activities more efficient.

With their more widespread use, however, computers sometimes bring thorny issues of social responsibility. People's rights to privacy and security need to be protected, now more than ever, as networks proliferate and the information superhighway continues to impact our daily lives. Virtually every day we hear of lawsuits relating to the use of computers to invade people's privacy, or inves-

tigations into computer crimes committed for financial gain or mere personal satisfaction. However powerful a computer system may be, illegal and unethical uses can only be controlled by people, informed of and attentive to the rights and responsibilities of individuals.

Computers can be seductive in their ease and speed of use and in their potentially enormous power. Whether they function as tools to help us **improve and enjoy our lives,** or decrease

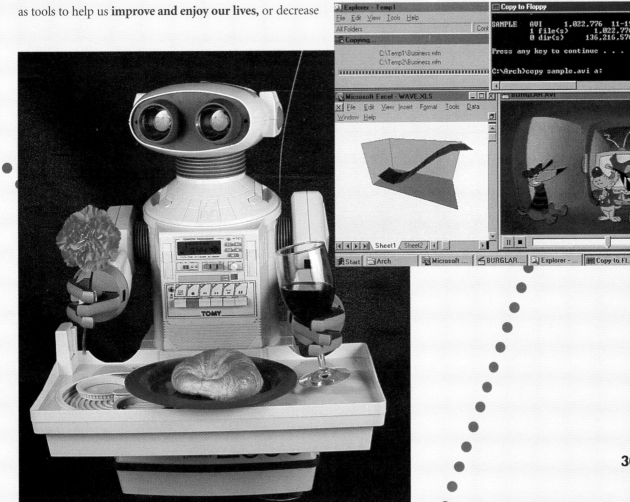

our leisure by making us slaves to our jobs, depends again on people, and on our continued commitment to socially responsible uses of all forms of technology.

CHAPTER 11
Systems Analysis and Design

11.1 THE ROLE OF THE SYSTEMS ANALYST

Making Business Systems More Efficient

In-House Analysts vs Outsourcing

Job Requirements for Systems Analysts

Interfacing with Key Users

Understanding the Systems Development Life Cycle

11.2 INVESTIGATING AND ANALYZING EXISTING BUSINESS SYSTEMS

Collecting Data About the Existing System

Describing the Elements of an Existing System

Using Structured System Charts to Describe an Existing System

Undertaking the Feasibility Study

Developing Alternative Design Strategies

Obtaining Management Approval for a Design Alternative

11.3 DESIGNING A NEW OR REVISED SYSTEM

Prototyping a System

Using CASE—An Automated Design Tool

Designing Components of the New System

11.4 IMPLEMENTATION

Obtaining Management Approval for Implementation

Implementing the New System

Redesigning Tasks Performed by Users

Types of System Conversions

Documenting the System

omputerized business systems called information systems integrate hardware, software, people, and the concept of connectivity so that information produced is accurate, timely, and meaningful. Design of these systems is usually supervised by systems analysts who work closely with users and other computer professionals to produce an effective set of procedures. In this chapter we consider how systems analysts analyze current procedures and then design more efficient ones.

Study Objectives

After reading this chapter, you should be able to:

1. Outline the skills systems analysts bring to the analysis, design, and implementation of new information systems.

2. Describe the analytical tools systems analysts use to create new information systems.

3. Show how systems design tools are used in the building of effective information systems.

4. Describe how new information systems are approved and implemented.

▬▬ 11.1 THE ROLE OF THE SYSTEMS ANALYST

Study Objective

1. Outline the skills systems analysts bring to the analysis, design, and implementation of new information systems.

Every business consists of a series of interrelated functional areas that accomplish an organization's goals. No matter how large or small a business is—whether it is a yacht-building firm or a mom-and-pop grocery store—it consists of functional areas that are organized to achieve business objectives.

Each of these functional areas consists of a set of procedures, or methods, that employees use to complete their tasks or achieve their goals. For example, employees in the purchasing department might have systems for checking the quality of materials, negotiating with vendors, and ordering supplies.

Making Business Systems More Efficient

Managers plan, organize, and control business systems on the assumption that if each system's functional area works efficiently, the entire organization will run smoothly. To keep organizations running efficiently, managers hire systems analysts to examine their procedures and systems and to recommend how to make them more efficient.

Systems analysts design **information systems** that use computers to improve the efficiency of existing business systems. An information system (IS) is a combination of the computer hardware, software, and networked facilities people need to perform business functions. This chapter focuses on traditional information systems, which are computerized business systems for individual functional areas. In the next chapter, we focus on management information systems, which are designed to provide output to managers on a companywide basis—across functional areas.

New systems can be designed for the following reasons:

1. Existing procedures are inefficient.

2. Error rates are too high.

3. Output is not timely.

4. Security or protection of privacy is inadequate.

5. Newer services such as interactive capabilities are needed.

These reasons may lead management to request changes and improvements to existing systems as well.

A new information system may also result in many intangible benefits:

*   Faster response time in answering inquiries from customers, which leads to more efficiency and better public relations.

*   Greater employee satisfaction resulting in lower turnover of staff.

*   More accurate delivery promises to customers.

*   Better availability of stock and fewer out-of-stock situations.

*   Improved quality of products and services.

*   More efficient use of resources and personnel.

*   Better management control over resources.

*   Greater flexibility in dealing with a changing business environment.

*   Improved ability to handle growth.

In-House Analysts vs Outsourcing

Systems analysts may be employees of a company or consultants hired on a contract basis. Increasing numbers of companies are *outsourcing* to satisfy their information processing needs. That is, they hire outside firms to develop and run their information systems on a regular basis.

Regardless of the method used to hire them, systems analysts should all possess similar skills that will help analyze existing procedures and develop new, more efficient ones.

Job Requirements for Systems Analysts

Basic skills that systems analysts should possess include the following:

1. Basic knowledge of business—to understand user needs.

2. Computer proficiency—to supervise development and acquisition of computer resources required for satisfying user needs. Networking skills are also becoming increasingly important.

3. Effective communication skills—for working closely with users, programmers, and other computer professionals.

Interfacing with key users is a critical component that can make the difference between the success or failure of a new design. See Figure 11.1

Interfacing with Key Users

Because many users today are computer proficient, their role in the systems analysis and design process has changed dramatically, particularly in PC-based computer environments. Managers often ask users who have a strong interest and technical expertise in computing to help develop information systems for their work areas. Called key users, these people are intimately familiar with business problems in their own functional area. They also have an understanding of how computers can best be used, so they act as on-the-spot problem solvers. Key

IN A NUTSHELL

Information should be:
*   Complete
*   Accurate
*   Timely
*   Economically feasible
*   Relevant

Looking Ahead

OUTSOURCING ON THE RISE

An increasing number of businesses are outsourcing, that is, using outside consultants for the analysis, design, and implementation of their information processing needs. Their hope is that outsourcing will be cheaper and more efficient than maintaining an in-house staff. Design of an information system as well as implementation and regularly scheduled computer runs may all be performed by outside firms.

Looking Back

"EFFICIENCY EXPERTS"

In the 1950s, systems analysts were often called efficiency experts. Armed with clipboards, *they* determined what systems needed revising—not management; sometimes those recommendations included eliminating a large number of jobs. Many efficiency experts were accused of callousness in making their recommendations. Today, management determines the systems to be revised, and analysts are more sensitive to the sometimes negative image associated with the term *efficiency expert*. As a result, changes in an organization are hopefully being made with less fear and resistance on the part of users.

Figure 11.1 *Systems analysts work closely with employees on all levels to assess the needs and potentials of an information system.*

users often need to learn the techniques of systems analysis and design to assist them in solving business problems quickly.

Throughout this chapter, we will build on the following case study to reinforce general concepts in a specific situation:

Margaret Cotham is an administrative assistant in the MBA office at Metropolitan Graduate School (MGS). Her supervisor asked her to design an information system for downloading student data files from the campus minicomputer to the department's three micros. Such a system could help the office track student progress through the MBA program, schedule future classes, and in general make it easier to compile student statistics. The chairperson of the MBA program decided that he did not have enough money to hire a systems analyst as a consultant, and because several microcomputer database and communications packages were advertised to be user-friendly, he asked Margaret, as a key user, to design the information system. Margaret thought computer systems were interesting and felt that the assignment was a good way to get a promotion, so she eagerly accepted the task. She quickly realized, however, that she was not sure about how to design a new information system. The first thing she needed to do was analyze the current set of procedures as objectively as possible. Before undertaking such an analysis, Margaret needed to understand the life cycle of business systems.

Understanding the Systems Development Life Cycle

Whether entirely new information systems are created or existing ones are improved, each system passes through four basic stages known as the **systems development life cycle:**

1. Investigation and analysis.
2. Design and development.
3. Implementation.
4. Operation and maintenance.

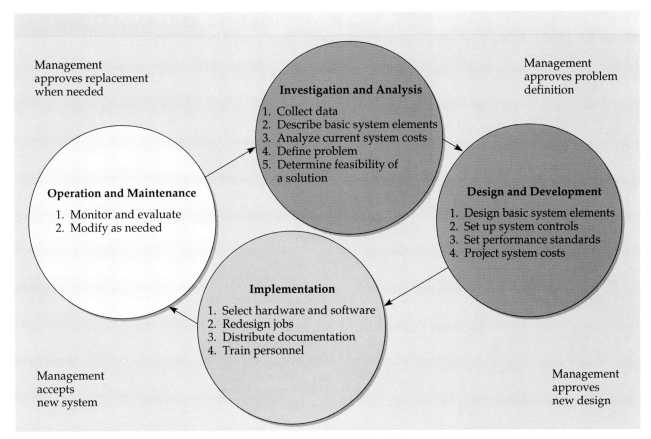

Figure 11.2 *The life cycle of a business system moves from investigation and analysis through design and development, implementation, and then operation and maintenance. Eventually, the business system needs to be replaced with a new system and the cycle is repeated.*

The term *life cycle* is used because, like living organisms, business systems are born (planned and analyzed), grow (are designed and implemented), mature (are operated and maintained), and eventually die or are replaced. During its lifetime, a system must constantly be modified and refined to ensure that it satisfies user needs even if business objectives change. The systems analyst is responsible for overseeing all four stages of the life cycle.

Figure 11.2 provides a detailed schematic of the steps involved in the systems development life cycle, which are discussed in the next section.

Self-Test

1. Give several tangible reasons why analysts are asked by management to examine an existing business system.

2. A systems analyst could be an outside consultant or _____.

3. Name the four stages of the systems life cycle.

4. Name three skills that a systems analyst should possess.

Solutions

1. Current procedures may be too costly, inaccurate, time consuming, and labor intensive, just to name a few.

2. an employee

3. investigation and analysis; design and development; implementation; operation and maintenance

4. basic business knowledge; computer proficiency; communication skills

Study Objective

2. Describe the analytical tools systems analysts use to create new information systems.

11.2 INVESTIGATING AND ANALYZING EXISTING BUSINESS SYSTEMS

Analysts begin designing new or improved systems by first analyzing basic problem areas in existing procedures. Then they present management with the results of their analysis in a document called a **problem definition,** which highlights those areas needing improvement. Before writing a problem definition, analysts must complete the following four steps:

1. Collect data about the existing system.
2. Describe and analyze the elements of the existing system.
3. Determine current costs.
4. Determine whether a new system is necessary and feasible. If so, devise possible design alternatives.

The problem definition must be approved by management before a new design is undertaken.

In the MBA office, Margaret Cotham, the key user who is serving as a systems analyst, needs to write a problem definition that specifically describes the current business system, including costs and any flaws in the system. Her report should outline in broad terms if a new system is feasible and, if so, how she would redesign the old system to eliminate current problems. Because the purpose of the problem definition is to present alternatives rather than a fully defined solution, Margaret needs her boss's approval of the problem definition before she formally begins to design a new system.

Collecting Data About the Existing System

Analysts begin the problem definition phase by gathering as much information as they can about existing procedures and basic problem areas (Figure 11.3). Generally, they use a combination of several methods for collecting data:

Figure 11.3 *Analysts must collect data about an existing system from the users themselves.*

1. Reviewing all written documents on the existing system: These include written procedures and policy statements that indicate how the system is supposed to work, memos, and reports that track the progress of the system.

2. Observation and sampling: Analysts actually observe how tasks are performed and the sequence in which they are performed, both of which shed significant light on a system. The people being observed should be reassured about the purpose of these observations so that they do not feel that their jobs are at risk. Sampling means selecting representative periods in a workday in which observations are performed. This technique is efficient because it decreases overall observation time.

3. Interviewing employees and using questionnaires: The best way to learn about the problems in a system is to have frank discussions with users. After the analyst learns how the system *is supposed to* operate by reading procedure manuals and other documents and after the analysts learns how it actually *does* operate, it is time to discuss the problems from the user's perspective. If there are many key users, the analyst may distribute questionnaires rather than interview all of them.

At MGS, Margaret began by reading the following documents:

- The school's organization chart.
- The school catalog, which outlined degree requirements and formal registration processes.
- Lists of all classes taught in the MBA department.
- Office procedure manuals for tracking student progress.
- All student registration reports.
- All form letters the MBA staff sent to students.
- All MBA department reports regarding students.

Analysts review forms carefully but they recognize that the written records tend to focus on how things *should* be done not on how they actually *are* done. Because what she read was often out of date or did not match what she knew to be common procedures in the office, Margaret quickly realized that she could not depend solely on formal documentation to get a firm understanding of current procedures. As a result, she began to observe employees as they worked to find out how procedures really were carried out.

Critical Thinking

What are some techniques you would use as a systems analyst to minimize the fear and resistance of users?

Describing the Elements of an Existing System

Often the best way to analyze a system is to break it down into its seven components:

1. Objectives or goals.
2. Constraints or limitations (e.g., budgetary, legal, equipment).
3. Output—review output before input to get a clearer picture of what the system should deliver to the user.
4. Input.
5. Processing.

Figure 11.4 *Breaking a business system down into its seven elements helps analysts examine the system's effectiveness and identify problems.*

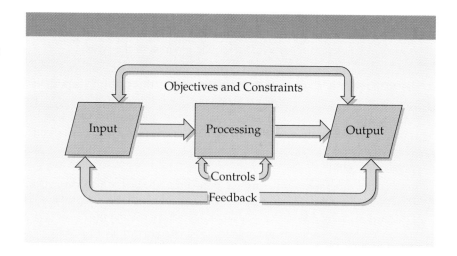

6. Controls.

7. Feedback or methods used to evaluate performance.

Figure 11.4 illustrates these components of a system and the way they relate to one another. Analysts examine them to see how they work and to identify problem areas. Later, if a new system is designed or the current one is redesigned, each of these components will be modified as the need arises.

> Once Margaret had gathered data, she was prepared to describe and analyze the current MBA office system in terms of its components.

OBJECTIVES By the time analysts have finished collecting information, they generally have a good idea of the system's original objectives. Then they look at how the current system actually supports those objectives. They also consider appropriate new goals so that they can begin to create a new system design if it proves feasible to do so.

> Margaret found that the MBA program's long-term objectives are to allow for a 25% increase in student enrollment and the hiring of four new professors during the next five years, to maintain a high quality of service, and to make registration procedures as easy for students and staff as possible. To analyze whether the current system meets the objectives, and to design a system that will meet *new* objectives, Margaret next needs to look at the constraints, or limitations, placed on the existing system.

CONSTRAINTS Every system has its own unique constraints, which are the limitations placed on it. The most common are legal, budgetary, and equipment constraints.

OUTPUT During both the analysis and design phases of their work, analysts consider output requirements *before* input and processing. This is so because the needs of the users—that is, the outputs that will be produced by the system—are the most important elements in the design. Only after output needs have been determined can input and then processing procedures be evaluated.

Figure 11.5 *Processing operations can vary widely. A banking system, for example, needs to provide teller receipts and ATM transaction records as well as detailed check logs, customer balance statements, and balance sheets for all operating levels at the bank, from the teller to top management.*

INPUT After determining the output derived from a system, analysts examine all the incoming data needed to produce the output.

PROCESSING After studying the existing output requirements and input data, analysts inspect the types of processing operations that are being performed on data to obtain the desired results. See Figure 11.5.

CONTROLS AND FEEDBACK When systems are designed, **controls** are developed to minimize errors. Controls include techniques for verifying that the data entered is correct and for cross-checking calculations.

Because errors occur even with the best of controls, techniques are also needed to evaluate performance. These techniques help pinpoint errors in the system and indicate how they are handled once they are discovered. **Feedback** is the process of periodically evaluating a system to determine how well it meets user needs. Analysts need to know all current procedures for adjusting and correcting systems when feedback shows that errors have occurred.

IN A NUTSHELL

A system is defined in terms of its seven components each of which is reevaluated when the analyst designs a new system.

Margaret found that the secretaries in the MBA program were using a personal computer to develop a database of graduates' names and addresses based on program records. Several years ago, MGS's development staff, which solicits funds for the school, installed a sophisticated desktop publishing system, which they linked to the registrar's computers. The development office was now creating the same database as the secretaries, but in booklet form and more quickly and accurately. Nobody had informed the department secretaries! Margaret realized instantly that this was a major problem area.

Using Structured System Charts to Describe an Existing System

After data has been collected and the analyst understands the system in its entirety, a problem definition must be prepared that describes:

1. The existing system.
2. Its basic problem areas.
3. The feasibility of a solution.
4. Suggested design alternatives.

Describing the existing system requires a narrative or explanation along with a pictorial representation of how the system operates. Two common tools for pictorially representing a system are data flow diagrams and system flowcharts.

DATA FLOW DIAGRAMS A tool available to analysts for depicting a system is called a **data flow diagram.** This diagram focuses on the flow of data through a system—where it originates and where it goes. Figure 11.6 illustrates the standard symbols used in data flow diagrams. The process symbol shows what is done to data in the current system—whether it is filed, printed out, forwarded, and so on. The source symbol indicates where data has come from. A destination, or sink, symbol shows where data is going, for example, to a recipient. Vectors illustrate the direction of flow. Storage for the data is indicated by the file symbol.

Figure 11.6 *These are the standard symbols used in a data flow diagram.*

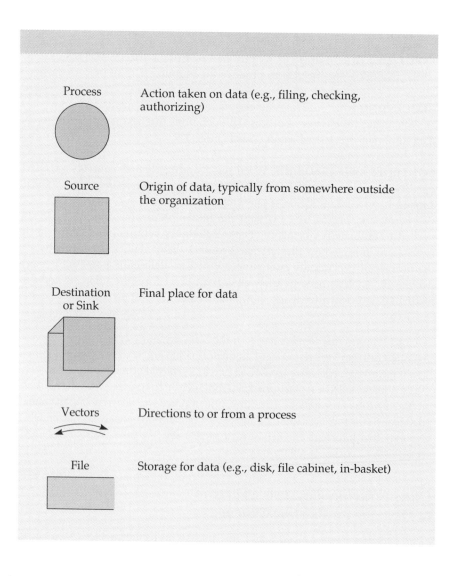

Process — Action taken on data (e.g., filing, checking, authorizing)

Source — Origin of data, typically from somewhere outside the organization

Destination or Sink — Final place for data

Vectors — Directions to or from a process

File — Storage for data (e.g., disk, file cabinet, in-basket)

Figure 11.7 *This data flow diagram shows how a student registers for a class at Metropolitan Graduate School. The necessary databases are indicated on the right.*

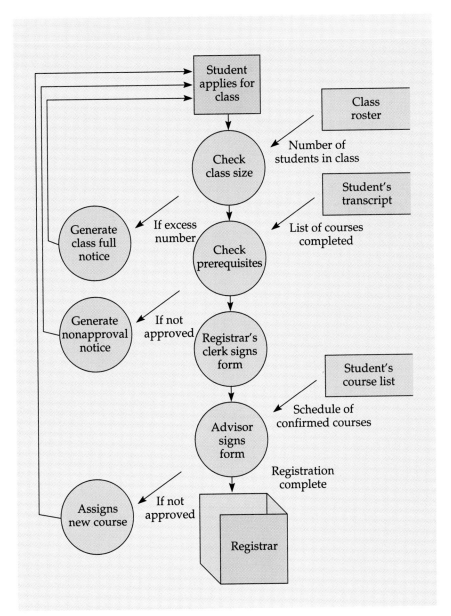

At MGS, a student's course record may be sent by the MBA office (source) to the registrar (sink). A file symbol indicates that the data is stored—in a filing cabinet or on a computer disk. Figure 11.7 is a data flow diagram depicting how a student registers for classes at MGS.

SYSTEM FLOWCHARTS Analysts also need to represent the information flow within the total system in order to depict elements of the system. The **system flowchart,** like its more detailed counterpart the program flowchart described in Chapter 8, shows relationships among inputs, processing, and outputs, in terms of the information system as a whole.

Figure 11.8 illustrates the symbols commonly used in system flowcharts. Analysts draw flowcharts by means of plastic templates or special automated pro-

IN A NUTSHELL

A data flow diagram focuses on the flow of data in a system whereas a system flowchart illustrates the relationships among system elements.

Figure 11.8 *These are the commonly used symbols in a system flowchart.*

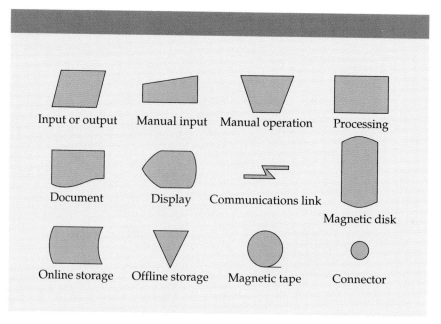

Input or output   Manual input   Manual operation   Processing

Document   Display   Communications link

Magnetic disk

Online storage   Offline storage   Magnetic tape   Connector

Figure 11.9 *This system flowchart shows the process for updating a company's payroll records.*

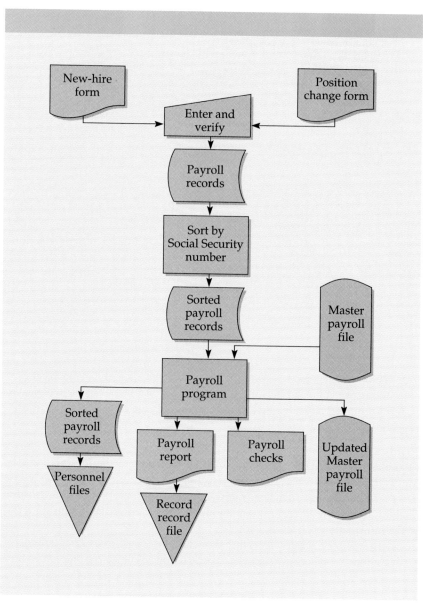

grams. Figure 11.9 is a system flowchart for a payroll system. Note how relatively easy it is to understand the overall processing involved by reading such a flowchart.

Undertaking the Feasibility Study

After the data has been collected and the current system has been described and analyzed, the analyst undertakes a **feasibility study** to determine whether, in fact, the current problems can be resolved and if a solution is feasible given the cost and time constraints established by management. If the analyst believes a solution is feasible, he or she prepares design alternatives for recommendation to management in the form of a problem definition. If no design is feasible, the analyst states this in the problem definition.

Developing Alternative Design Strategies

Once the current system has been described and analyzed, and the feasibility of developing a solution to the problem has been established, analysts generally outline several broad design alternatives for the new or revised system. At this stage in the design process of information systems—especially large ones that interact with other systems—analysts usually describe for management the trade-offs between a new system's cost and its potential benefits. Often, the most desirable system is also the most expensive. Because analysts make recommendations, not final decisions, they provide management with several design alternatives to help them decide whether to invest in extremely effective systems at a high cost or to invest in systems that will cost less but may not be as effective.

Margaret might suggest five design alternatives to her boss (Figure 11.10).

- *Alternative 1:* Purchase a new minicomputer.
- *Alternative 2:* Link three existing personal computers into a network and download data from the campus minicomputer.
- *Alternative 3:* Update and maintain student data records for the department, independent of other campus records.
- *Alternative 4:* Purchase terminals linked to the campus minicomputer.
- *Alternative 5:* Keep doing what they have always been doing: receiving hard-copy reports from campus computers and manually entering data as needed into personal computers for further analysis.

At this stage of the analysis phase, the systems analyst only describes, in general terms, alternative design strategies.

After outlining design alternatives, analysts estimate the cost of designing, implementing, and operating each of them. The most important factor in obtaining management's approval for a new design alternative is to demonstrate that the new design will result in a cost benefit. Performing a **cost-benefit analysis,** which compares the costs of the existing system to costs of a proposed system, is an integral part of an analyst's job. See Figure 11.11.

Obtaining Management Approval for a Design Alternative

After analysts have completed their analysis and have mapped out, in general terms, some design alternatives, they present a formal problem definition to

IN A NUTSHELL

HINTS FOR SYSTEMS ANALYSTS

1. Smaller and simpler systems cost less and have a better chance of functioning properly.
2. A system must fit into the existing environment—it does not stand alone.
3. Computers are good for many tasks, but people are often better at other things, particularly where intuition and experience are needed.
4. Patching small problems over and over again may be a "quick fix," but replacing the overall structure may, in the end, be more efficient.

IN A NUTSHELL

STEPS IN SELLING A NEW SYSTEM DESIGN TO MANAGEMENT

- Define the problem in a problem definition. Be sure the problem definition is:
  1. Nontechnical.
  2. Clear and concise.
  3. Free of spelling or grammatical errors.
- Prepare for presentation of the problem definition.
  1. Notify people in a letter indicating when the presentation will occur.
  2. Discuss the problem definition, prior to presenting it, with key people who are apt to be supportive. Ask them for their opinions.
- Make the presentation.
  1. Know in advance who will be attending your presentation and know something about each person.
  2. Dress for success.
  3. If you are using visuals or electronic slides, prepare in advance and make a trial presentation.

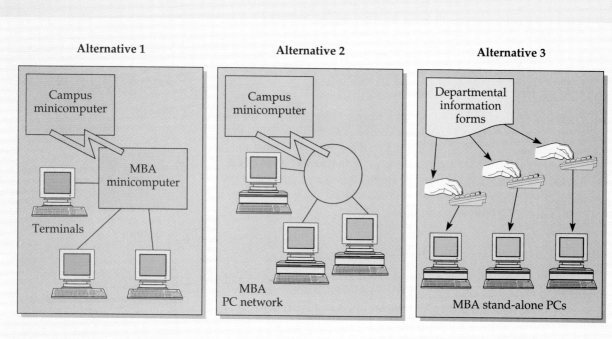

Figure 11.10 *Here are five design alternatives for maintaining MBA records at the Metropolitan Graduate School.*

management. Management uses the problem definition to select a design alternative. The costs outlined by the analyst for the design selected become a constraint on the new system.

In the case of MGS, Margaret's boss decided to approve the previously outlined alternative 2—to link the MBA program's three personal computers into a network and download data from the campus minicomputer. At that juncture, Margaret began designing the new system.

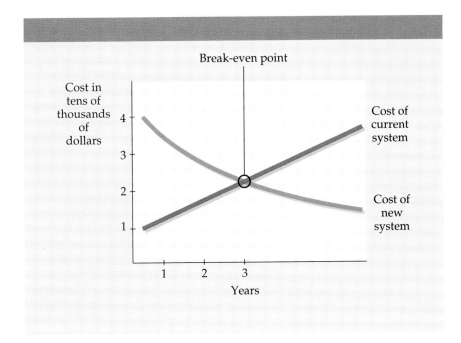

Break-even point

Cost of current system

Cost of new system

Cost in tens of thousands of dollars

Years

Self-Test

1. What are the seven basic components of any system?

2. What are three common types of constraints?

3. Describe the basic methods of collecting data.

4. What are two design tools commonly used to depict elements in a system?

10.3 DESIGNING A NEW OR REVISED SYSTEM

After the analyst evaluates the existing system, determines the feasibility of a solution, and discusses possible design alternatives, management selects a new design. Analysts then begin the design stage by preparing a model of the new system using system flowcharts, data flow diagrams, and other design tools.

Prototyping a System

The systems design process requires a lengthy period of development, and the needs of users may change during that time. **Prototyping** enables analysts to

---

Solutions

1. objectives, constraints, output, input, processing, controls, and feedback

2. legal, budgetary, and equipment

3. reviewing all written documents, interviewing employees and using questionnaires, making observations, and sampling

4. system flowcharts and data flow diagrams

Figure 11.12 *Users and analysts can test a prototype using a computer.*

provide users with all essential systems elements very quickly, before all of the interfaces and software modules have been designed. For instance, an analyst might create an on-screen menu or interactive display for users to try out, and then modify it to incorporate their suggestions—all before the system is actually implemented. See Figure 11.12.

Prototyping is a relatively new systems design tool in which a new information system, or a part of it, is simulated by means of a model constructed with a fourth-generation programming language—usually a CASE tool. **CASE** is an abbreviation for *c*omputer *a*ided *s*oftware *e*ngineering. The result is a working model, although it is not intended for online production. Prototyping is one of the best methods for getting users to view the new systems design and to identify any additional needs or changes that can be made to improve its effectiveness. The user's role in evaluating the prototype is critical. Users also help set performance standards so that the analyst can assess the new design as it is being developed. See Figure 11.13.

Using CASE—An Automated Design Tool

CASE is a systems analysis productivity tool intended to help analysts evaluate existing systems. It is also used to help them design structured, efficient, and well-documented new systems. It is a tool for building information systems. If integrated with a graphics package, for example, CASE tools alleviate the need to draw by hand graphic representations of an existing system's specifications. Similarly, CASE tools assist the systems analyst in designing a new system. They do *not*, however, fully automate the systems development process. Analysts must still control the overall process; CASE tools are used to increase their productivity.

CASE tools help in prototyping and can also help increase productivity with features such as:

- Automatic construction of charts such as data flow diagrams and hierarchy charts.

- Ability to integrate other productivity tools such as project managers, cost-benefit analysis tools, and spreadsheets.

IN A NUTSHELL

BENEFITS OF CASE TOOLS

1. Increased productivity
2. Improved quality assurance
3. Better documentation
4. Facilitates standards (though they are still too limited)
5. Elimination of redundancy because global changes can be made easily
6. Sharing of data flow diagrams and data dictionaries by more than one system
7. Ability to pinpoint inconsistencies in systems design

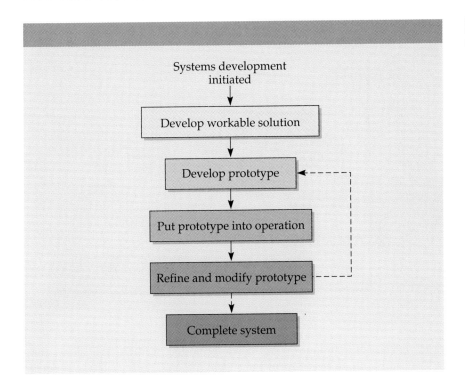

Figure 11.13 *Developing a prototype requires several steps.*

- Quality assurance capability to check for consistency and completeness of a design.
- Ability to share diagrams and data with other systems.
- Rapid prototyping for timely generation of screen displays and output.

Index Technology Corporation's Excelerator was the first CASE product for IBM-compatibles and is the current market leader. Figure 11.14 shows a CASE screen display. It is best used to automate the early phases of the systems development life cycle. Excelerator enables analysts to automatically diagram entire systems, from conceptual overviews down to individual data records. Excelerator uses a

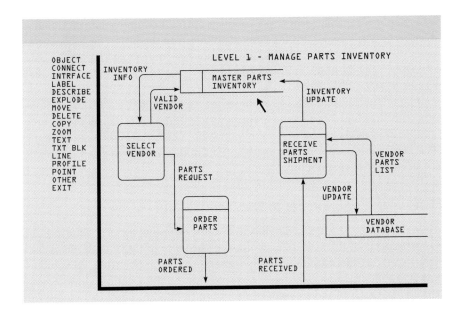

Figure 11.14 *Excelerator is an automated design tool that uses structured design techniques. An Excelerator screen display is shown here. Analysts start with an overview of the system and progress to finer levels of detail.*

Figure 11.15 *A chart produced by Excelerator.*

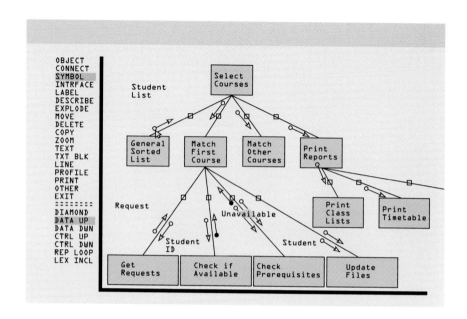

structured design technique—a top-down "explosion" feature—that allows analysts to start with an overview of the system, progress to finer levels of detail, and then explode the whole into different types of graphs and diagrams. Figure 11.15 is an example of an Excelerator data flow diagram.

To appreciate how helpful CASE tools can be, suppose Margaret Cotham needs to determine long-range class enrollments. She decides to begin by analyzing enrollment trends in all business courses at MGS over the past 50 years. Even if she had 10 people to help her, if they worked by hand, they would all be sitting at desks a long time, and it would be difficult to coordinate their work. CASE tools can help identify course names and enrollments and will automatically produce an organized, integrated index of courses. Margaret can choose from many packages for the micro market.

• • • • • ▶ Looking Ahead

MORE CHANGES FOR CASE

• CASE tools will be able to contribute to the entire systems development life cycle.

• CASE will be used to generate source code in a 3GL or 4GL.

• Currently, the main obstacle to widespread use of CASE tools is a lack of standards. CASE tools are often incompatible with each other and do not interface properly with other software products. Eventually, a de facto standard will emerge as it typically does with software and hardware.

Functional capabilities of CASE products are built around a **data dictionary,** which records and maintains the contents of files and the properties of data elements. CASE tools also provide a mechanism for controlling changes to data description specifications and checking the specifications for consistency and completeness.

CASE tools have graphics capabilities for segmenting a system into components and drawing data flow diagrams and structure charts. In addition, some CASE tools even generate limited program code. This reduces the programming effort required to transform the specifications into working systems. CASE tools also help in preparing documentation.

Designing Components of the New System

While the prototype is being developed, the analyst begins the detailed design of all components of the new system, with the assistance of CASE tools where feasible. Recall that there are seven components of a system: objectives, constraints, output, input, processing, controls, and feedback. Analysts designing a new system evaluate each of these components and make modifications as necessary:

1. OBJECTIVES AND CONSTRAINTS Based on the results of discussions with management, analysts begin by defining objectives and constraints for the new system. These may include some of the objectives and constraints of the existing system, but they are also likely to include new elements.

Because the MBA program's long-range goal is to improve administrative services, Margaret and her boss agree that the new information system should meet three new objectives:

1. Students should be able to register for all their classes *in one hour*.
2. The administrative staff should be able to plan the next semester's courses *within the first week* of a new semester.
3. Advisors should be able to determine a student's matriculation status *within 15 seconds*.

Margaret and her boss also agree that she can only spend two months building the new information system and no more than $3,000 on hardware and software. When the system is completed, she will spend 25% of her time maintaining the system and training users.

2. OUTPUT DESIGN Just as analysts considered output before input in analyzing the existing system, they should design output as the first component for a new system. Designing output first helps ensure that users' needs will be satisfied. Analysts review all the reports generated by the current system and discuss with users any additional reports or changes needed from a new design. The design of new output affords the analyst the opportunity to give users exactly what they need.

> **IN A NUTSHELL**
>
> HINTS FOR DESIGNING OUTPUT
> - Summaries are frequently as good as, or even better than, detailed reports.
> - Often data from several reports currently distributed to different people can be combined without adversely affecting the usefulness of the output.

At this stage Margaret sat down with her boss and designed all the new forms and computer screens needed in the new system.

3. INPUT DESIGN After new outputs have been agreed upon, analysts and users determine what new input will be required and what other resources will be needed to create the desired output. Sometimes business systems need to be entirely redesigned to ensure accurate, timely input.

Margaret's boss wanted the new system to generate reports indicating:

- All professors teaching during any semester.
- All professors who teach a particular course.
- All courses a professor has taught over the years.

Although the campus minicomputer could easily provide the first two requests, getting a list of courses that all professors have taught over the years was more difficult. Margaret created a set of procedures that ensured proper input; in this case, the faculty secretary was required to:

- Retrieve the data from file cabinets in storage.
- Create a database on the personal computer.
- Update the database every semester.

Input is stored in database files. When the analyst designs a database file, he or she defines record descriptions, fields within the records, and the size and type of those fields. All the data used by the system is described using a CASE tool. Design of input also includes establishing screen formats and dialogs for data entry.

4. PROCESSING REQUIREMENTS Analysts decide whether batch or online procedures are best suited for processing the data. Whatever processing method is selected, appropriate software and hardware are necessary to convert input to output.

Most analysts use or augment software and hardware that already exists in the organization. Before acquiring new software, analysts must decide whether to purchase it or to have custom programs written, either by in-house programmers or by software consultants who specialize in designing specific kinds of software. Chapter 7 discussed how analysts decide whether to "make" or "buy" software.

Analysts initially attempt to design new information systems by using the computer equipment already in place in the organization. Frequently, a new design may require additional computers or peripherals. If the new design requires its own large computer system, or if it requires the organization's current computers to be upgraded, then the following procedures must be followed:

- Prepare a request for proposal that provides an analysis of existing needs.
- Evaluate the proposals from vendors.
- Select a vendor.
- Make preparations for installing the new system.

Prepare a Request for Proposal. Analysts prepare a document called a **request for proposal (RFP)** to obtain specific technical information and cost bids from vendors and to ask for information about the vendors themselves. A successful RFP includes two parts: (1) the description of the organization's needs, often called a **needs analysis,** and (2) a request for information regarding the vendor and the equipment proposed by the vendor.

5. CONTROLS AND FEEDBACK After all output and input have been designed, and software and hardware have been selected, analysts evaluate what controls are needed to ensure the quality of output. Controls consist of manual as well as computer audit trails to guarantee the reliability of information. Feedback procedures also need to be developed to help evaluate the effectiveness of the new system.

Margaret had to use existing computer facilities when she designed the new system. First, she identified the data she wanted from the campus minicomputer; then she created periodic update schedules for downloading this data to the department's personal computers. To ensure data integrity, she decided to have one of the clerks in the MBA office check every 20th MBA record each month. Margaret also created backup procedures to protect the department's computer system against the possibility of a hard disk failure. To obtain consistent feedback from the system, Margaret planned to meet with users once a month to discuss problems and new ideas and to suggest better ways to use the system.

Once the new system has been completely designed and tested, it can then be implemented.

Self-Test

1. (T or F) Output should be designed before input.

2. _____ enables a new system or part of a system to be tested before the full design has been finalized.

3. An automated design tool used to assist in building information systems is _____.

11.4 IMPLEMENTATION

Obtaining Management Approval for Implementation

In most instances, analysts make another presentation to management after the entire set of procedures has been designed and all programs have been written or acquired. This presentation includes:

- A detailed description of the new system.
- An analysis of the actual design costs and the operating costs of this new system as compared to the costs estimated in the problem definition.
- A plan for converting to the new system.

If management approves the actual design, the analyst can continue with the final phase, implementation. Recall that management originally approved a new design alternative as outlined in the problem definition because they were not satisfied with the existing system. They may not, however, approve implementing a new system if the analyst's plans are unacceptable for some reason (if, for example, original cost estimates differ significantly from actual costs).

Implementing the New System

After receiving management approval, analysts implement the new system. A new information system is likely to require changes to existing files and to the media on which files are stored. The process of creating computerized files for a new system is called **file conversion.** Controls such as the following must be incorporated during this process to ensure the integrity of the new files:

- Comparing record counts and batch totals of key fields before and after conversion to verify that all the data has been converted correctly.
- Comparing and checking randomly selected records before and after conversion.
- Testing the information system with the new files to verify that all file conversions have been completed successfully.

> **Study Objective**
>
> 4. Describe how new information systems are approved and implemented.

Solutions

1. T

2. Prototyping

3. CASE

Redesigning Tasks Performed by Users

To reap the full benefits of the new system, analysts usually advise managers about the need to restructure the jobs of some employees. Every new job description should make use of an employee's skills, maintain individual autonomy insofar as possible, and provide a degree of job satisfaction.

Types of System Conversions

In Chapter 8, we discussed the ways programs are implemented in information systems. Similar methods are used to convert to new information systems. As in

Figure 11.16 *Techniques for converting from one system to another.*

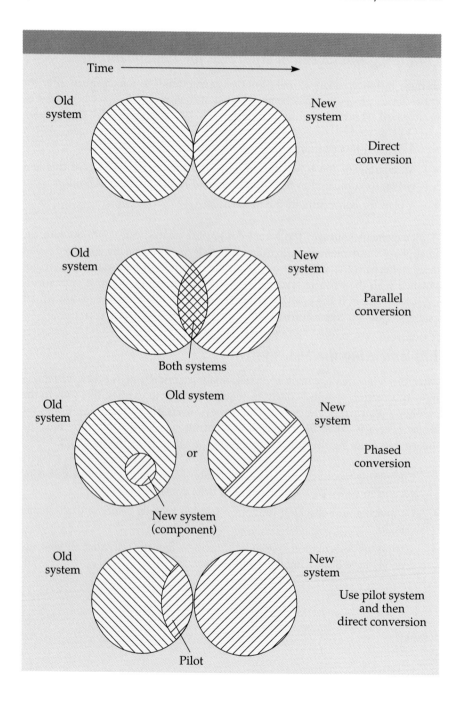

program implementation, the four conversion alternatives are direct conversion, parallel conversion, phased conversion, and pilot conversion. See Figure 11.16.

Direct conversion occurs when a company simply stops using its old system and begins using the new one; there is no overlap between systems. Direct conversion is efficient but risky because any error in the new design is likely to cause serious delays.

In **parallel conversion,** the old system and the new system operate simultaneously for a period of time. Output from both systems is compared to make sure the new system is functioning properly. When the new system is operating satisfactorily, the old system is discontinued. Parallel conversion is a slow but reliable method.

Phased conversion is a gradual implementation. It is particularly appropriate when a large, complex system has been designed in modules that can be run independently. As each module is implemented and refined, it is added to the others in the system. For example, a company might implement the order processing module, then the inventory management module, and finally the accounting module—each module should run effectively before the next is introduced.

Pilot conversion refers to implementation of the entire system in one part of the company, perhaps a single department or a single division. This approach allows the analyst to work out any problems that develop while the scale of implementation is small and manageable.

Documenting the System

While the system is being developed, written procedures for using it should be compiled. Once the system is functioning properly, analysts finalize these written procedures by providing a complete record of the precise operations and techniques it uses, as well as technical specifications for all the hardware and software used. This record is called a **documentation package.** It is usually prepared during the analysis and design stages and finalized during implementation. Because documentation describes all the facets of a new design, it is similar to a procedures manual (although it may consist of several components). CASE tools often help to provide written documentation on the system. If a problem occurs after the system is operational, analysts and users can consult the documentation, which, if it is complete, should provide a solution. Figure 11.17 lists typical elements in a documentation package.

IN A NUTSHELL

ANALYZING AND DESIGNING INFORMATION SYSTEMS

Define the problem.
- Collect data about the existing system.
- Describe the elements of the existing system.
- Use structured system charts to describe the system.
- Undertake a feasibility study.
- Devise possible design alternatives.
- Prepare cost-benefit analyses for design alternatives.
- Obtain management approval for one design alternative.

Design the new system.
- Create a prototype while designing new components.
- Select and/or develop software.
- Select hardware.
- Monitor progress of the new design.

Implement the system.
- Obtain management approval for implementation.
- Implement system.
- Redesign jobs if necessary.
- Prepare and distribute documentation.

Figure 11.17 *A documentation package typically consists of four elements: logical design, physical design, programming, and operations and procedures.*

Logical design elements	Physical design elements	Programming elements	Operations and procedures
• Output specifications • Processing procedures • Systems and program logic • File specifications • Input specifications	• Database and file layouts • Processing procedures • Input formats • Output formats • File conversion plan	• Top-down structure charts • Pseudocode and flowcharts • File and record layouts • Code specifications	• User options • Data entry procedures • Data control procedures • Computer operations

Self-Test

1. The process of creating computerized files for the new system is called _____.

2. Name the four types of conversions.

3. A new system is fully described in the _____ package.

CHAPTER SUMMARY

11.1 The Role of the Systems Analyst

Every business consists of a series of interrelated functional areas that accomplish the organization's goals. To keep organizations running efficiently, managers hire systems analysts who examine business systems and recommend ways in which they can be improved. Systems analysts are basically problem solvers, and the **information systems** they design may or may not involve computers. Analysts can be company employees or outside consultants; *outsourcing* is the term for using outside services to satisfy a company's needs. As information needs increase, key users often use systems analysis and design techniques to help them solve business problems.

Business systems pass through four basic stages known as the **systems development life cycle:** (1) investigation and analysis, (2) design and development, (3) implementation, and (4) operation and maintenance.

11.2 Investigating and Analyzing Existing Business Systems

Analysts begin designing new systems by first understanding the basic problem areas in existing procedures and by presenting their results in a **problem definition.** To write a problem definition, analysts (1) collect data about the existing system, (2) describe and analyze the elements of the system, (3) determine current costs, and (4) devise possible design alternatives if a new system is feasible. The problem definition is the means by which management approval is obtained for a design alternative. Analysts combine several methods for collecting data about the current system: reviewing documents; observing employees at work and sampling; interviewing employees and preparing and analyzing employee questionnaires.

Perhaps the best way to analyze a system is to segment it into its seven component parts: objectives, constraints, output, input, processing, **controls,** and **feedback.** Analysts examine these components to see how they work and to isolate any problem areas. Later, when a new system is designed, each of these components is modified as the need arises. Tools used to pictorially represent an existing system are **data flow diagrams** and **system flowcharts.**

After analyzing and describing the existing system in a problem definition, analysts undertake a **feasibility study** to determine whether a new design is possible given constraints established by management. If a solution is feasible, several broad design alternatives are outlined and the cost of each is estimated. To

---

Solutions

1. file conversion

2. direct conversion; parallel conversion; phased conversion; pilot conversion

3. documentation

measure costs, analysts choose from two basic methods: break-even analysis, which indicates when the new system will start to be cost-effective, and **cost-benefit analysis,** which compares the cost of an existing system to the cost of a proposed system.

11.3 Designing a New System

After analysts have completed a formal problem definition, they present their analysis to management for approval. Once management decides on a new design, analysts prepare a model, or prototype, of the new system using a 4GL to simulate the essential elements of the system. A structured analysis process requires long planning and design periods, and during that time the needs of the user often change. **Prototyping** enables analysts to have users try out parts of a proposed system so that there will be fewer changes when the entire system is implemented. **CASE** tools assist the analyst in designing a structured, efficient, and well-documented new system. They help produce a **data dictionary** that records and maintains the contents of files and the properties of data elements. The new design is defined in terms of the seven basic system components: objectives, constraints, output, input, processing, controls, and feedback.

As part of the design process, software is either purchased or developed. If it is to be developed, either in-house programmers or consultants will be used.

If the new system requires major changes in hardware, analysts prepare a **request for proposal (RFP)** to obtain specific technical information from vendors and to ask for information about the vendor itself. The two parts of a successful RFP are (1) the description of the organization's needs, often called a **needs analysis,** and (2) a request for information about vendors themselves.

Once all seven components of the new system have been designed, management must approve the system. The analyst then implements the system.

> **Study Objective**
>
> 3. Show how systems design tools are used in the building of effective information systems.

11.4 Implementation

Implementing the new system usually requires performing a **file conversion** (i.e., the process of creating computerized files), redesigning tasks performed by users, and converting to the new system by employing one of four approaches. **Direct conversion** occurs when an organization stops using its old system and begins using the new system with no overlap. In **parallel conversion,** the old and new systems operate concurrently, and the output is compared at various stages to make sure the new system is running correctly. When it is, the old system is discontinued. **Phased conversion** involves introducing one module of a large system at a time; **pilot conversion** means the system is used in only one part of the company until all the problems are solved.

Once the system is functioning properly, analysts provide a **documentation package** that details the procedures and techniques used in the new system as well as the technical specifications of the hardware and software.

> **Study Objective**
>
> 4. Describe how new information systems are approved and implemented.

KEY TERMS

CASE, *p. 386*
Controls, *p. 379*
Cost-benefit analysis, *p. 383*
Data dictionary, *p. 388*
Data flow diagram, *p. 380*
Direct conversion, *p. 393*
Documentation package, *p. 393*

Feasibility study, *p. 383*
Feedback, *p. 379*
File conversion, *p. 391*
Information system, *p. 372*
Needs analysis, *p. 390*
Parallel conversion, *p. 393*
Phased conversion, *p. 393*

Pilot conversion, *p. 393*
Problem definition, *p. 376*
Prototyping, *p. 385*
Request for proposal (RFP), *p. 390*
Systems development life cycle, *p. 374*
System flowchart, *p. 381*

CHAPTER SELF-TEST

1. What is the document, prepared by the analyst, that defines in detail all aspects of the existing system?

2. The _____ must work closely with users when creating a new system design.

3. (T or F) Preparing a cost-benefit analysis for a proposed system is usually the responsibility of a cost accountant.

4. Bids from _____ must be compared during a feasibility study.

5. (T or F) The systems analyst's role in an organization is essentially advisory.

6. (T or F) A new design must be based on the existing system's objectives, which cannot be altered in the revised system.

7. (T or F) Legal constraints can generally be modified in the new system.

8. (T or F) If an analyst suggests a new form of output in the system design, the user should not question it because the analyst is more qualified to decide what is best for the system as a whole.

9. (T or F) Systems analysts should always design systems so that computer equipment replaces all manual operations.

10. (T or F) A systems flowchart depicts the relationships between inputs, processing, and outputs for the system as a whole.

11. An analyst must evaluate the way an existing system meets its _____.

12. Name three methods of collecting data about an existing system.

REVIEW QUESTIONS

1. Briefly discuss three methods of gathering data about business systems. Which method do you think is most important?

2. What are the seven components of a business system?

3. Describe four tools used to analyze systems.

4. Briefly describe two common ways analysts measure the cost and benefits of business systems.

Solutions

1. problem definition
2. systems analyst
3. F—It is the responsibility of the systems analyst.
4. computer vendors
5. T
6. F—Objectives can, and frequently do, change.
7. F—Legal constraints cannot be changed.
8. F—Designing output is a joint task of users and analysts.
9. F—New designs can include both manual and computerized components.
10. T
11. objectives
12. review documents, observe employees, interview employees and distribute questionnaires

CRITICAL THINKING EXERCISES

1. Suppose you are a systems analyst planning to interview a key user who you realize has a negative attitude and is unwilling to help. What would you do?

2. Suppose you recommend a new design but management decides to impose additional budgetary constraints, limiting your ability to deliver an effective design. What would you do?

CHAPTER CASE STUDY PROBLEMS

1. In connection with the case study discussed throughout this chapter, do you think Margaret should purchase software or hire someone to write software for the MBA program's new information system? Explain your answer.

2. Which of the five possible design alternatives that Margaret provided would have required an RFP? Write a brief RFP for one of the alternatives.

Case Study

The Changing Role of Information Systems (IS) Departments

Information systems (IS) departments are the areas within organizations that have traditionally been the home of systems analysts as described in this chapter. These IS departments have had the opportunity—if not the need—to reinvent themselves in the last few years, as both software and hardware continue to undergo enormous transformations. With end users calling upon computer networks and telecommunications for more and more of their information needs, systems analysts have had to acquire more expertise in the process of integrating business applications in a networked environment. In fact, in a recent survey information systems professionals ranked knowledge of networks and telecommunications as the most important skill needed for success in their field.

Mastery of the networking of business applications is in fact proving crucial to the survival of some information systems. In addition to analyzing existing software packages, evaluating hardware, and developing in-house applications as in the past, systems analysts today are managing the integration of their firms' networks and databases in an environment in which end users, rather than programmers, are often writing the applications themselves.

The changing role of the systems analyst in business has also resulted in changes to the infrastructure of IS departments themselves. The IS area in many organizations is becoming less of a technical service department and more of a place where managers on the fast track learn important skills they need to reach the top. With its broad view of all

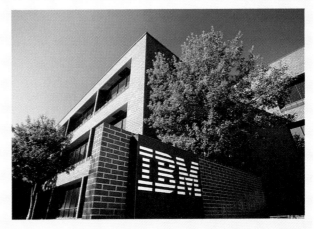

IBM is one of many companies whose IS Department has undergone major changes.

the firm's operating and information systems, its custody of the enterprise's intellectual assets, and its ability to guide the continuous reengineering process that many successful firms are undergoing, the IS department is viewed by many as the launching ground for the next generation of CEOs.

While many analysts within the IS department hope to become top-level executives, other systems analysts see their future in the functional areas of an organization rather than in the IS department. Mastery of networking and integrated

(*Continued*)

Case Study

business applications in environments that are downsizing has resulted in a trend toward decentralization where analysts apply their technical skills solely within specific functional areas. This trend is most evident in the financial industry but many people believe other industries will follow, as businesses continue to reengineer their processes.

Analysis

1. What new skills do systems analysts need to learn to adjust to downsizing and other changes that have been occurring in the information systems departments of large organizations?

2. Do you think the future of IS departments is secure or do you think that the tasks performed by comptuer professionals will be increasingly added to the functional areas instead?

3. If an end user is computer proficient enough to write his or her own application programs, is there any reason for him or her to consult a systems analyst first? Explain your answer.

CHAPTER 12
Database Management
Information Systems

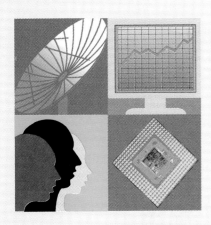

12.1 DATABASE MANAGEMENT SYSTEMS: THE DRIVING FORCE BEHIND MANAGEMENT INFORMATION SYSTEMS

Database Structures

Components of DBMS Software

Issues for the Database Administrator

12.2 MANAGEMENT INFORMATION SYSTEMS

Facilitating Decision Making at All Management Levels

Specialized Management Information Systems

Recall from Chapter 2 that there are two kinds of information systems designed by systems analysts: traditional systems that focus on satisfying the operational needs of each department and management information systems that focus first on providing top-level management with immediate access to data and second on satisfying operating needs. In the last chapter, we discussed traditional information systems and the way they are designed. In this chapter, we look at management information systems.

Regardless of whether organizations have traditional information systems or management information systems, they typically have databases to store the data and database management systems to access and manipulate the data. We concentrate in this chapter on database management systems and their use in management information systems.

Study Objectives

After reading this chapter, you should be able to:

1. **Explain the relationship between the format and features of a database and the value of database management systems.**

2. **Demonstrate how access to databases helps managers make better decisions.**

■ 12.1 DATABASE MANAGEMENT SYSTEMS: THE DRIVING FORCE BEHIND MANAGEMENT INFORMATION SYSTEMS

Study Objective

1. Explain the relationship between the format and features of a database and the value of database management systems.

■ A NUTSHELL

In a management information system, database files are frequently joined, and networks allow access to the data. Traditional information systems in the functional areas have less of a need to interrelate data from different systems.

A database is a collection of files that can be joined. While information systems in each of the functional areas need files to perform their day-to-day operations, management information systems (MIS) need database files to provide companywide information to executives.

A *database management system* (DBMS) is a software package designed to enable users on all levels to access databases. Files can be edited, updated, and joined to provide reports and answers to inquiries.

DBMS software is available for small companies with a handful of PCs and for large organizations with client-server networks.

Database Structures

HOW DATA IS ORGANIZED AND RETRIEVED IN A DATABASE First, let us review the data hierarchy concepts introduced in Chapter 3. You may also want to reread the section in Chapter 6 that deals with data hierarchy. Figure 12.1 is a graphic representation of the relationship of fields, records, and files in a database. The text that follows expands on this terminology and explains the role of the computer professional who administers the database.

Database. An organization may have more than one database, each of which consists of related files. The records and fields within files can be joined or otherwise interrelated for query purposes. An MIS is the type of system most likely to need information linked from numerous database files. A school, for example, may have a database containing the names and authors of all the books in its library,

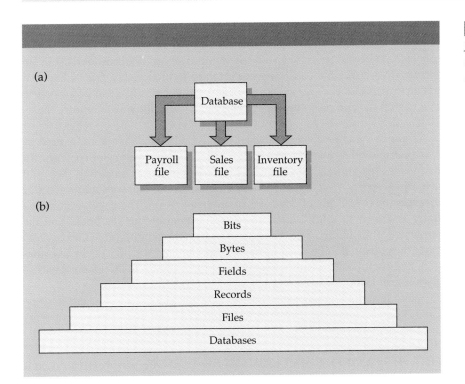

Figure 12.1 (*a*) *A database consists of files that can be linked.* (*b*) *This hierarchy represents the building blocks for turning data into information.*

a short description of each book, a list of books checked out, a list of books on order, and a list of students who are eligible to borrow books. Each list may be in a separate file; the composite group of files makes up the library's database.

The same school might have another database containing information about its employees, including salary, date hired, home address, year-to-date payments, year-to-date deductions, amounts paid to the IRS, and any other information needed to process the payroll. It is likely that the year-to-date payroll and tax deduction information would be in one file, while the rest of the employee information would be in another file. Having the two files, each containing different payroll information, is more efficient than having one master file for this reason: Several different functional groups can access employee data—accounting and payroll as well as the human resources department, for example—and they each may need different data. If a master file contained *all* employee data, that file would be very large, and retrieving data from it could be quite time consuming. Very large files also are far more difficult to access for an MIS in a multiuser environment.

Database File. A database file, often called simply a file, is a collection of records used in a given application (e.g., payroll or accounts payable). A file usually contains many records, each with the same structure. A payroll file, for example, may consist of many payroll records, each with a similar format.

Record. A record is a collection of fields that represents one entity within a file, such as an employee record in an employee payroll file or a customer record within an accounts receivable file (see Figure 12.1b). All the records in a database file generally have the same structure; that is, each record contains the same fields and the fields hold the same type of information. The contents of the fields for each record, however, are different.

Field. A field is a unit of data within a record (see Figure 12.1b). For example, salary and number of dependents claimed would each be a field in a payroll record. Customer name and telephone number fields would be in an accounts receivable file consisting of customer records. A *key field* is one that uniquely identifies each record. Social Security number is likely to be a key field in a payroll file and part number is apt to be a key field in an inventory file.

Database Administrator. Database applications are designed to be used by managers and other users who need output for decision-making purposes or for performing day-to-day jobs such as answering inquiries, updating files, and preparing reports. A computer professional called the **database administrator** manages the overall use of databases in an organization. The database administrator is similar to a head librarian who is responsible for the books and the operation of the library. The database administrator is responsible for the databases themselves, the integrity and validity of the data, security of the information, and the operation and maintenance of the DBMS. Some of the database administrator's duties are illustrated in Figure 12.2.

Keep in mind that database files are those that can be joined or linked while flat files are those that are always handled independently. Before we discuss types of database organizations, we consider flat files and how they are created.

FLAT FILES AND FILE MANAGEMENT SYSTEMS File management systems, which have been widely available for years, are not true database management systems, because data in one file cannot be linked easily to data in another file. Despite this limitation, file management systems are often very useful for storing simple data files on a computer, especially in traditional information systems. For example, you might use a file management system (sometimes called a "file manager") to store your personal address book or a small payroll file. Such systems are too limited, however, for most true database or MIS applications where files need to be linked in some way. Symantec's Q&A and Claris's FileMaker Pro are two examples of microcomputer file management programs (Figure 12.3). Even spreadsheet packages can be used as flat file managers, where columns are used to define fields and each row defines a record.

There are four types of DBMSs that can be used to create, edit, join, query, and report from files. They are hierarchical, network, relational, and object-oriented. We discuss them now in detail.

HIERARCHICAL DATABASES A **hierarchical database** is organized like a tree planted upside down—with the roots at the top. In Figure 12.4, for example, the root field (the top field in the diagram) is the Business Department. It is linked

Figure 12.2 *A database administrator's duties include ensuring data security, controlling the database life cycle, and supporting user needs.*

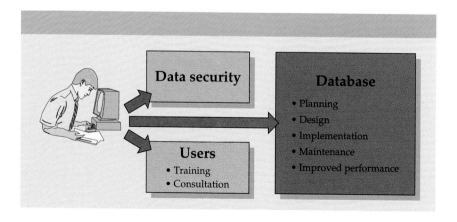

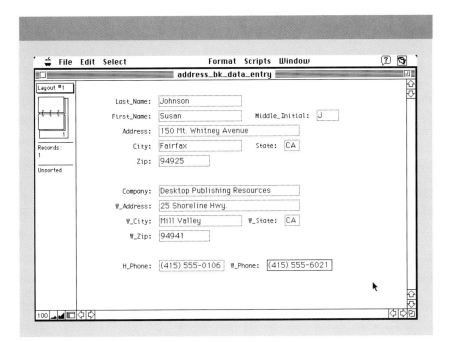

Figure 12.3 *A file management system can be used to create and maintain individual files.*

to its corresponding courses. One branch from the Business Department root field contains the Introduction to Marketing course, another contains the Managerial Accounting course, and the third contains the Business Law course.

Each data item or group of data items shown in the inverted tree diagram is called a segment, which is similar to a file of records. You could consider the segments to be arranged like a family tree. Parent segments (Departments, for example) appear above the child segments (Courses) in the diagram. Each parent segment can have more than one child, but a child can only have one parent. This is called a one-to-many relationship. Each segment lies on a hierarchical path, from the root segment to the branches to the lowest-level child, and a given segment cannot appear on more than one path.

Figure 12.4 *Segments of data in a hierarchical database are organized into levels, where each level is increasingly detailed. Each segment can have only one upward path.*

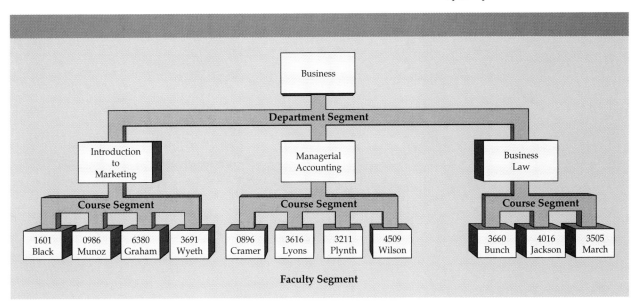

In the hierarchical structure shown in Figure 12.4, faculty members teach courses in only a single department. If a faculty member taught both Business Law and Introduction to Marketing, the hierarchical model would not be totally effective, because the same faculty name would have to appear in two different segments. That violates the rule that a given segment cannot appear on more than one path. Similarly, if there were a Managerial Accounting course in both the Business Department and the Law Department, a hierarchical database model such as the one described would not be ideal.

Certain types of data lend themselves to hierarchical representation. For example, if a retail establishment has a series of stores and each store has its own unique sales staff, then a hierarchical database structure could be used to store salesperson data. There would be no risk that data in one segment might also appear in another segment. Operating systems often store configuration information about hardware, software, and drivers in a hierarchical database.

An example of a hierarchical database management system for mainframes in large organizations is IMS from IBM. The database can be accessed by commands in the IMS query language or by a custom program written in a third-generation language such as COBOL. In general, hierarchical databases have the fastest access time.

NETWORK DATABASES Network and hierarchical databases are similar in the way they organize data according to a parent-child type of relationship. In a hierarchical database, as we have seen, a child can only have one parent, but in a **network database,** a child can have more than one parent. Consider our Business Department root field in Figure 12.4 with its segments. Professors who teach in different areas can be handled easily in a network database. Similarly, salespeople who work in more than one location can have two or more branch (parent) offices in a network sales database. A child with no parent at all is also permitted in a network database. So if Professor Kim Lee in the Business Law Department were on leave, she could be linked to the department segment without being linked to an intermediate course segment.

Figure 12.5 shows the department/course/faculty example for a network database. A network DBMS can create more complex relationships among types

> **IN A NUTSHELL**
>
> A root field in a hierarchical database is like a root or main directory on a disk, and a segment in a hierarchical database is like a subdirectory on a disk.

Figure 12.5 *Segments of data in a network database can have multiple relationships to parent segments on a higher level.*

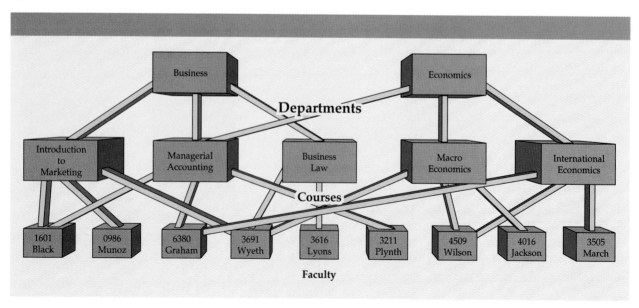

of data and thus is suited to more types of applications. Users are limited, however, to the connections that were originally defined by the application's developer. One disadvantage of both hierarchical and network database models is that relationships among elements must be determined when the system is designed; if there is a need to make changes to those relationships later on because different information is required, then the database must be restructured.

The most popular network database model was developed by CODASYL (Conference on Data Systems Languages), a standards group that also helped shape the COBOL language. Many commercial products use the CODASYL network database model.

RELATIONAL DATABASES Relational databases are the most common type of database structure for all types of computers, from micros to mainframes, and for most types of systems, from traditional to management information systems. In a relational database, key fields within records can be used to link, or join, any number of files. Whereas hierarchical and network database management systems establish the relationships among data elements when the database is being designed, a relational database allows virtually any type of linkage or relation among data elements to be established as the need arises. This flexibility is one important reason why relational databases are so popular. Oracle is number one among client-server DBMS users.

Many DBMS packages based on the relational database model present files in table format: the records are represented conceptually as rows and the fields as columns (Figure 12.6). Data is presented this way because it is often more easily visualized in tabular form. The computer, however, does not actually store files in table form but as a sequential stream of records. Relational databases are designed so that they can display data in table form in any sequence desired.

As we noted, a major advantage of a relational DBMS is that it allows linking, or "relating," of several database files. For example, the payroll department needs employee addresses only once a year, when W-2 forms are mailed. To save

Relational databases are the most popular type of database structure.

Figure 12.6 *A relational database usually presents data in table format, as shown in this screen from a dBASE database.*

10/27/96			Standard Report	Page 1
Customer No.	Last Name	First Name	Address	City
------------	----------	----------	----------------------	----------
1909	Cole	Warren	3434 Washington Blvd.	Indianapol
1913	Mason	John	2421 Prospect Ave.	Berkeley
1969	O'Hare	Ned	4950 Pullman Ave. NE	Seattle
2001	Bowman	Dave	1 Discovery Lane	Pueblo
2306	McGarrett	Steve	5 "O" Street	Honolulu
2589	Thompson	Donald	2339 Broadway	San Franci
3154	Yee	Emerson	2938 42nd Street	New York
3684	Aberdeen	Roxie	15 State Street	Dallas
4158	McDougal	Craig	1 Airport Drive	Chicago
4175	Anderson	Jack	8947 San Andreas	Klamath Fa
5510	Samuelson	Doris	Bull Run Ranch	Aurora
5719	Alland	Mary	17 Norfolk Way	Birmingham
5926	Kern	Glenn	45 Utah Street	Washington

Rows (records)

Columns (fields)

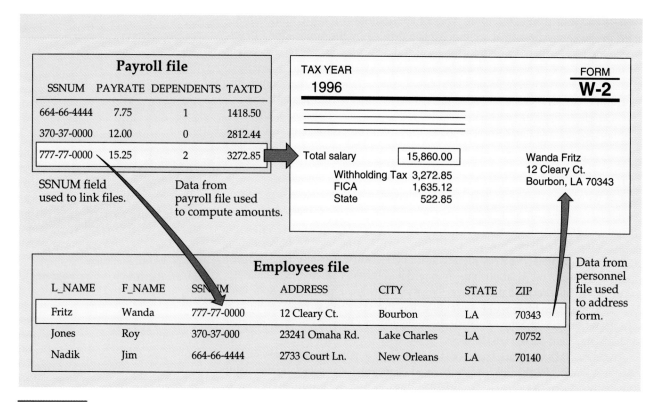

Figure 12.7 *To send W-2 forms, a relational DBMS retrieves salary information from the payroll file and then uses the SSNUM field to locate and retrieve the corresponding employee address from the personnel file.*

space and access time, the payroll file typically includes Social Security numbers but not employee addresses. These addresses are found in a separate personnel file that also includes Social Security numbers and that is accessed only occasionally. The Social Security field, called SSNUM in Figure 12.7, functions as a key field to link the payroll and personnel files so that the application that gen-

Figure 12.8 *This is a sample dBASE program to display linked data from employee and payroll files.*

```
.  SELECT 1
      Selects an initial file work area.
.  USE EMPLOYEES
      Opens the EMPLOYEES personnel file as file 1.
.  INDEX ON SSNUM TO EMPIND
      Indexes on SSNUM field and creates an index file called EMPIND.
.  SELECT 2
      Selects a second file work area.
.  USE PAYROLL
      Opens the PAYROLL file as file 2.
.  INDEX ON SSNUM TO PAYIND
      Indexes on SSNUM field and creates an index file called PAYIND.
.  SET RELATION TO EMPLOYEES INTO SSNUM
      Relates SSNUM for both files.
.  GO TOP
      Goes to the top of the first record in the linked files.
.  DISPLAY ALL FIELDS SSNUM,TAXTD,ENAME,EDEPT
      Displays fields where SSNUM in EMPLOYEES file = SSNUM in
      PAYROLL file.
```

```
Record#   ssnum          taxtd  a->ename                  a->edept
      1   302123456    1234.56  SMITH, JOHN               PURCHASING
      2   456341234     456.34  OSBORNE, GLENDA           DP
      3   567349876     876.54  JONES, MARY               ACCOUNTING
      4   876126598    2345.87  DAVIS, LINDA              DP
      5   987341256     734.66  WHITE, WILLIAM            DRAFTING
  .
  .
  .
```

erates W-2 forms can retrieve employee addresses from the personnel file. Both files are indexed on the SSNUM field. Recall from Chapter 6 that an index for a disk file contains the key field for each record and the disk address of the corresponding record. This index provides a fast way for the DBMS to access the desired data randomly without scanning a file from beginning to end. The user supplies the key field of the record to be accessed. The computer looks up the disk address of the record with that key field from an index and then accesses the record directly.

Suppose you want to produce a screen display containing employee names, departments, and taxes withheld to date so that you could visually check payroll data. Figure 12.8 shows one way to access and display the required data with dBASE, a micro-based DBMS that uses the relational model. Notice that dBASE's programming language uses English words in abbreviated sentences. The names assigned to files and fields in this example are also abbreviated but are easy to understand: SSNUM is Social Security number, PAYIND is payroll index, and so on.

The resulting table would look like the one in Figure 12.9. It contains all the data needed for inquiry purposes. The data in the table cannot be edited directly, however, because it is not a formal file; rather, it is a linked relation of two files that is temporarily stored for purposes of providing needed output.

Windows-based relational DBMSs for IBM-compatibles are even easier to use. Icons are available for selecting files, joining files, positioning record pointers, and displaying fields.

Let us take a look at another application for a relational DBMS: how the IRS might set up files to verify that taxpayers are declaring all their interest income (Figure 12.10). The IRS has a file of data from bank records as well as a file of data from income tax returns submitted by each taxpayer. The bank file

Figure 12.9 *This is the linked file created by the program in Figure 12.8. It can only be viewed or printed; it cannot be edited.*

Figure 12.10 *Here, the IRS uses Social Security numbers to compare individual reporting of bank interest income with bank records.*

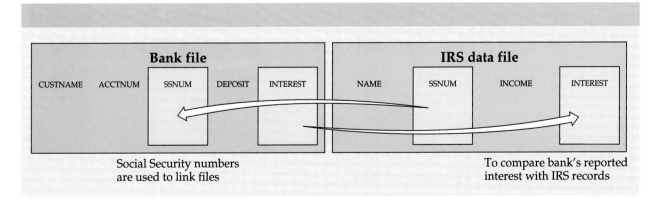

Bank file					IRS data file			
CUSTNAME	ACCTNUM	SSNUM	DEPOSIT	INTEREST	NAME	SSNUM	INCOME	INTEREST

Social Security numbers are used to link files

To compare bank's reported interest with IRS records

Table 12.1 *Database Management Systems for Mainframes*

Relational	Network
Oracle	Adabas
DB2	IDMS
Ingres	Object-oriented
Hierarchical	OpenODB
Focus	
IMS	
RAMIS	

Table 12.2 *Popular Database Management Systems for Micros*

Product	Manufacturer
dBASE	Borland
Access	Microrim
FoxPro	Microsoft
Paradox	Borland
Oracle	Oracle
Sybase	Sybase Inc.

consists of customer records with fields for customer name, bank account number, Social Security number, total deposits for the past year, and total interest earned. The taxpayer file contains records that include fields for taxpayer name, Social Security number, reported income, and reported interest earned from bank deposits. The Social Security number is the key field used to link these two files. Linking the two files enables the IRS to compare each taxpayer's total interest earned for the year with the reported interest earned. In this way, any returns in which reported interest is less than actual interest can be flagged.

OBJECT-ORIENTED DATABASES Most database management systems today use the relational model, but **object-oriented databases** are gaining considerable ground. Object-oriented database management systems use objects as elements within database files where an object consists of text, sound, video, graphics, and other images. Objects in an object-oriented DBMS can also mix differently structured records alongside one another. See Figure 12.11. Perhaps most importantly, objects in a database inherit characteristics, or attributes, from their parents; in this way, attributes need only be defined once—at the highest level.

Consider an automobile inventory application in which objects contain information about cars and car parts, including prices, suppliers, transaction data, and customer information. The database includes text descriptions as well as color images of car parts. The object-oriented DBMS can display a "tree" depicting all of the objects and their hierarchical relationships to each other. For example, specific types of cars inherit parts such as a motor, chassis, and so on from major classes of cars. Color can be used in any way desired; items displayed in red, for example, could be out of stock. By means of an object-oriented DBMS, car parts can be viewed, combined, assembled, and so on.

Object-oriented systems are becoming very popular and are likely to have a considerable impact on the computing field in the years ahead, especially as multimedia techniques improve. The ability to display a video or a photo—even create sound—along with textual data on an object can be very useful.

Table 12.1 lists some of the better-known database management systems currently available for mainframes. Table 12.2 includes a similar list for micros. There are many packages available for all categories of computers.

Figure 12.11 *An illustration of how different forms of data can be integrated in an object-oriented database. This screen shows order information along with actual illustrations of the products ordered.*

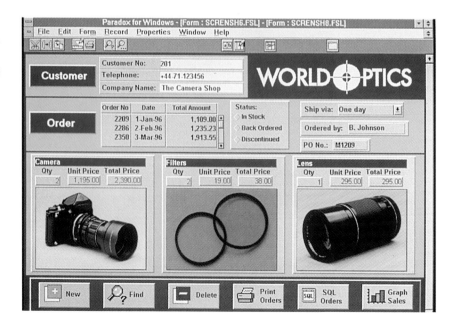

Components of DBMS Software

Database management systems enable users to establish and use databases for a wide range of customized applications. There are six basic components in a DBMS (see Figure 12.12).

1. DATA DICTIONARY A data dictionary specifies features of the data, how data can be accessed, who has access, and so on. Typically maintained by a database administrator, the data dictionary minimizes errors. As data is entered, the dictionary ensures that values fall within specified ranges.

2. DATA DEFINITION LANGUAGE (DDL) The **data definition language (DDL)** describes the technical specifications for the elements in the data dictionary and the relationships among them. Each DBMS package has its own DDL.

3. DATA MANIPULATION LANGUAGE (DML) OR QUERY LANGUAGE A **data manipulation language (DML)** or query language enables users to request data

Figure 12.12 *The six components of a database management system allow organizations to set up and use their databases for a wide range of customized applications.*

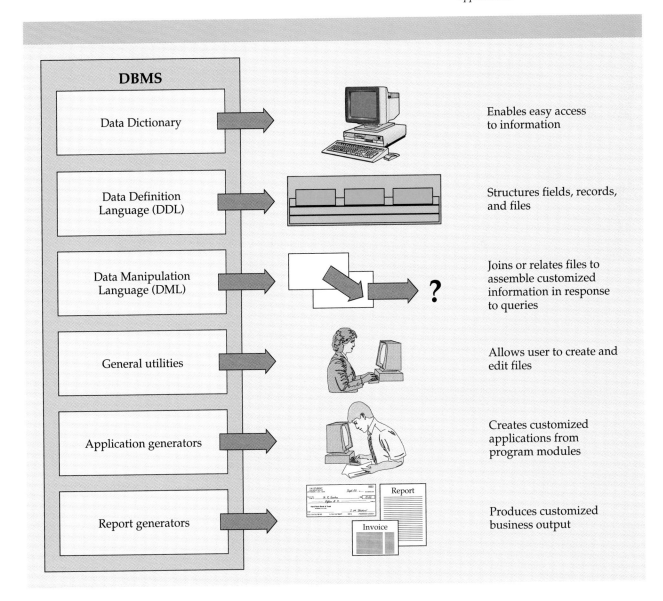

An SQL screen display that reports on the status of specific records in a database.

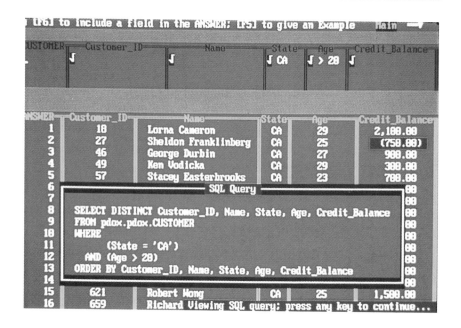

IN A NUTSHELL

FEATURES OF A DBMS

1. Multiuser accessibility.
2. User-friendly interface.
3. Ability to link files in different functional areas.
4. Controls that protect databases from unauthorized use and monitor the access of databases.

from a database file and to update the data in the file. Some DBMSs have their own proprietary query languages and some also permit users to use standard query languages or DMLs written for other packages. **SQL,** an abbreviation for Structured Query Language, is one that is widely used with many DBMSs. QBE, an abbreviation for Query By Example, is also widely used. Query languages use basic English words such as APPEND, MODIFY, and DELETE to update database files.

Many database management systems also enable users to write programs in a 3GL such as COBOL to access data in the database file.

4. UTILITIES Utilities are the components of a DBMS that allow you to maintain the database by editing data, deleting records, creating new files, and so on. Utilities enable users to control the input procedure by establishing ranges for data items entered, types of acceptable data, and so on. They can also help create user-friendly screen displays for data entry or data retrieval.

5. APPLICATION GENERATORS The application generator is the component of a DBMS that allows users to create applications without actually writing pro-

---

Looking Ahead

USING NATURAL LANGUAGE TO QUERY A DATABASE

In the future, you will be able to use a "natural query language" to query a database over the phone or on a computer terminal and receive your answer in conversational English. A natural query language enables you to use standard English without following any specific programming rules. It is as natural as speaking to another person. Here is a fictitious example of an interactive dialog between a user at a terminal and a computer. The computer's responses are in italics.

- How much does John make?
- *John who?*
- Smith.

- *I've got two John Smiths, one in Purchasing and one in Sales.*
- The one in Sales.
- *$40,000 plus commissions.*
- How much was his commission in 1993?
- *$32,456.67.*

If you are a science fiction fan, you are probably familiar with the concept of natural language interfaces. They are likely to be in full use for database management systems within the next few years. Some current query languages have begun to approach this level of natural communication.

grams. It is really a collection of program modules. A user requests specific tasks and the application generator selects the appropriate program modules.

6. REPORT GENERATORS The report generator makes it easy to ask for and design hard copy output in the form of reports and graphs. It permits users to define row and column heads, to generate report headers identifying the full report, page headers at the top of each page, and so forth. In summary, DBMS report generators enable users to create readable and attractive reports on short notice and with little computer expertise.

As you learned in Chapter 7, application generators and report generators are also regarded as fourth-generation programming languages because they permit people without programming experience to develop computer applications. Moreover, users need only learn English-like commands, rather than program logic, to have the computer execute procedures.

Issues for the Database Administrator

A DBMS is used to create, edit, update, and report from database files. The relative ease with which data can be manipulated using a DBMS sometimes results in errors; for example, unauthorized users may gain access or data entry workers may make errors. So the use of a DBMS actually increases the need for security and for minimizing the risk of entering invalid data. The database administrator is the computing professional who must address these issues.

SECURITY Most organizations have hardware and software controls that (1) protect databases against unauthorized use and (2) monitor overall computer activities. In addition, many database management systems offer their own security software to help minimize unauthorized access and to prevent loss of data.

Regardless of the type of information system and DBMS, security measures are necessary to minimize risks. It is unrealistic, however, to expect such measures to be able to eliminate *all* risks.

Most database management systems have log-on security, which prevents unauthorized users from accessing the DBMS. The database administrator defines which files, which records, and which fields within records each user or department can access. In addition, the administrator may assign various access levels that define who can read files, update records, delete records, or add data. Most DBMS products can protect a file so that it is only readable by the person who "owns" or shares it. Data in a DBMS is often protected by encoding it in a special way, a technique called **encryption.**

The more users who have access to a DBMS, the greater the security risk and the greater the need for monitoring file access.

DATA INTEGRITY Maintaining **data integrity** means ensuring that a system is uncorrupted by invalid data. Despite all efforts, simple data entry errors will inevitably occur. A DBMS can never eliminate all of them, but it can succeed in minimizing them. For example, the DBMS cannot find an invalid date such as 11/30/96 when it should be 11/29/96 or a price entered as $12.00 instead of $12.50. It can, however, flag clearly invalid entries such as a date of 11/31/96 (November has only 30 days). Similarly, it can flag a negative price as an error.

The cost of recovering or restoring files containing corrupted data can be very high, especially if many records are affected. The database administrator is responsible for training users in good practices, ensuring that applications are designed to protect data integrity, and controlling access to limit the risks of corrupting data. In addition, the administrator implements feedback and control mechanisms to check the reliability of the database on a periodic basis. The database administrator also participates in the selection and evaluation of the database management system.

SELECTING A DBMS Several factors should be considered when an organization chooses a database management system:

- Compatibility with existing hardware and software.
- Type of database models—relational, hierarchical, network, or object-oriented.
- Suitability of the DBMS for specific applications.
- Purchase or lease price and maintenance costs.
- Response time for queries, indexing, sorts, and so on, given the existing hardware and the size of the files.
- Number of simultaneous users permitted by the DBMS.
- Restrictive limitations on database, file, or record sizes.
- The number, type, and quality of query languages and/or programming languages that can be used.
- Capability and ease of use of the application generator and report generator.
- Security features.

Self-Test

1. In relational databases, records are often displayed as _____ in a table and fields are often displayed as _____.

2. (T or F) A file manager is generally more powerful than a relational database.

3. In a hierarchical database, how many parents does a child have?

4. (T or F) Object-oriented database management systems use objects to store graphics, video, and even sound as part of a record.

5. What are two key issues a database administrator faces?

Solutions

1. rows; columns

2. F—With file management systems, data in one file cannot be linked easily to data in another file.

3. one

4. T

5. security and integrity of databases

12.2 MANAGEMENT INFORMATION SYSTEMS

Facilitating Decision Making at All Management Levels

Throughout this book we have emphasized that information is data processed in such a way that it can be used as a basis for decision making. To be useful, information must be complete and concise, accurate, timely, economically feasible, and relevant.

An information system that provides useful information to managers from the top levels on down is referred to as a management information system (MIS). An MIS may use not only the data in an organization's own databases but also data from external database services such as company profiles and stock analyses. The principal goal of an MIS is to deliver to managers the timely and relevant information that they need for effective planning and managing.

Study Objective

2. Demonstrate how access to databases helps managers make better decisions.

HOW AN MIS DIFFERS FROM A TRADITIONAL INFORMATION SYSTEM

All managers need information to help them make decisions and to assist them in achieving their business objectives, but the kind of information required differs at each level of management. For example, the day-to-day operational information that a line supervisor requires may not be of value to a vice president responsible for long-range planning. An MIS integrates all of an organization's information, from the highest organizational level to the operating level, so that it is capable of satisfying the needs of top-level management first and then those of the operating staff.

The traditional approach to designing information systems, discussed in Chapter 11, treats each functional area or business system as a separate unit. Analysts design operational-level systems based on the assumption that if each functional area within an organization operates efficiently, the organization as a whole will run smoothly. Although these traditional operational-level systems are designed to satisfy the requirements of lower-level managers and operating staff, they often do not provide the information top-level managers need.

In contrast, the MIS approach focuses on the organization as a whole with one set of specific corporate objectives that originate from top management. The MIS approach assumes that if the system meets the information needs of top managers, more detailed information will "trickle down" the organization to meet the needs of lower-level managers. For instance, if the main objective of an MIS is to provide top managers with sales forecasts, middle managers in each functional area should be able to obtain summary reports from the data that was used to compute the sales forecasts. Similarly, first-line managers can receive transaction reports, using the same data but in a more detailed way (Figure 12.13). Such an approach is often referred to as a top-down approach because it is designed to satisfy top-level needs first and foremost.

FUNCTIONS AND LEVELS OF MANAGEMENT

We saw in Chapter 2 that an organization consists of functional areas that work together to meet the overall goals of the organization. Typical functional areas, or departments, are marketing and sales, manufacturing, accounting and finance, and research and development—all necessary components of a business. Organizations consist of a hierarchy of top managers, middle managers, and first-line managers, or super-

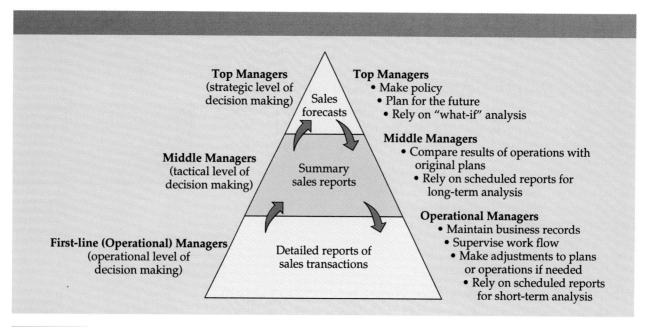

Figure 12.13 *A top-down MIS approach focuses on information to meet the needs of top-level managers first. Reports for lower levels of management can then be generated from the same data.*

visors, who work within or integrate the activities of these functional areas. A typical organization chart is shown in Figure 12.14.

A manager's level determines what kind of information he or she needs. To be effective, an MIS must provide information appropriate for each level of management. It does so by providing top-level management with the information it

Figure 12.14 *Within a typical organization, information flows vertically down organizational lines as well as horizontally among departments.*

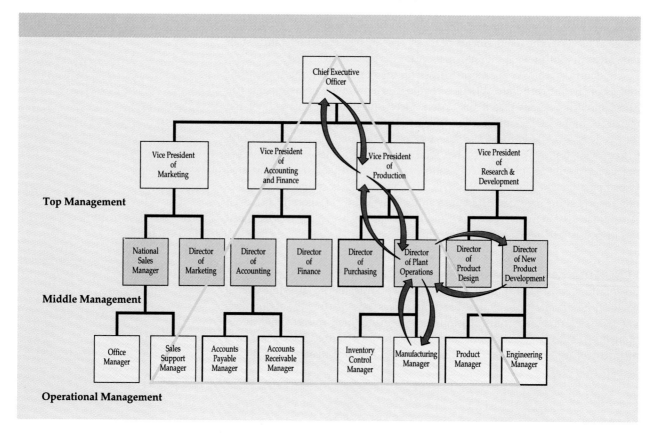

needs and then using that information in a more structured and detailed manner to satisfy the needs of lower-level personnel.

Specialized Management Information Systems

Three types of management information systems—decision support systems, executive information systems, and expert systems—are growing in popularity for business applications. We discuss these here.

DECISION SUPPORT SYSTEMS A well-designed MIS provides whatever information managers need in the form most useful to them. But typically the information supplied by an MIS to all levels of management is *structured* information. In general, structured information requires managers to know in advance what they want the system to provide.

A **decision support system (DSS)** goes beyond providing well-designed structured reports to managers. A DSS is a *flexible* information system that allows top-level managers to access both corporate and external databases and to create their own reports and applications, even their own specialized databases. With a DSS, a manager is able to address problems that are not structured and problems that may not have been anticipated when the system was designed.

The five goals of a decision support system are to:

1. Specifically address the decision-making needs of the top levels of management.

2. Address problems that were not previously thought about when the management information system was developed.

3. Make available to the decision maker analytical tools for financial planning and forecasting.

4. Enable decision makers with only a minimal amount of computer expertise to use the system, that is, to make interaction as "natural" as possible.

5. Enable decision makers to access corporate data in any way they want and to perform what-if analysis with ease.

Critical Thinking

Think of some situations in business where unanticipated needs for information from an MIS might develop.

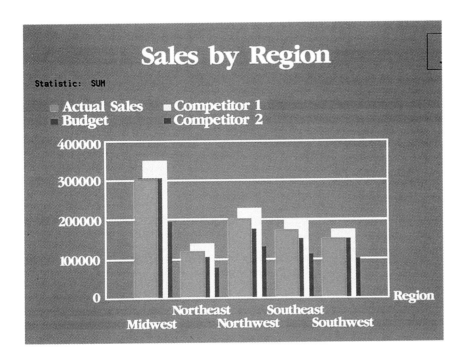

Financial analysis tools help to develop decision support systems.

Executive information systems are customized for each executive.

EXECUTIVE INFORMATION SYSTEMS A DSS provides tools to the organization's managers so they can develop their own applications. One weakness of the DSS approach, however, is that the tools are relatively sophisticated and require some computer expertise. Top-level managers who lack either the time or the inclination to learn how to use these tools need something different if they want to apply the power of the computer to their needs as decision makers.

An **executive information system (EIS)** is a custom-designed DSS for individual managers. The EIS tends to be used at the highest management levels, whereas a DSS is used mainly by middle managers. The basic distinctions between decision support systems and executive information systems follow:

- A DSS is typically designed generically for middle-level managers and is used by many managers for different purposes. An EIS is usually designed for the unique needs of a single, high-level executive and takes his or her skills and needs into account.

- A DSS, while relatively easy to use, requires some training before a manager is effective at tasks such as building applications or creating a financial model. An EIS requires no computer training; the analyst designing the system creates the needed models and menus so that the executive is free to simply ask for exactly the information required to make corporate decisions.

- Because a DSS is developed generically for a number of managers, it is much less expensive to develop than an EIS, which is designed for a single executive (or for a small group of executives).

Executive information systems use the same tools as decision support systems, but computer professionals design the systems so that they are customized for individual executives. An EIS is usually implemented on very sophisticated minicomputer or microcomputer workstations, but the systems analyst creates a turnkey system, which is one that requires little or no computer knowledge on the part of the user (Figure 12.15). You need only turn the computer on (e.g.,

Figure 12.15 *This executive information system allows the user to access customized reports, update data, and generate standard or custom charts from a simple menu.*

Executive information systems provide top managers with the type of information they need in the form that suits them.

"turn the key") to access the EIS. Four design factors are essential for an EIS system:

An EIS must not be too technical. An EIS should present information to executives in a way that hides the technical communication links between all the hardware and software that might be accessed to compile a report.

An EIS must be individualized. Each executive has an individualized style of decision making that is based on his or her training and experience. An effec-

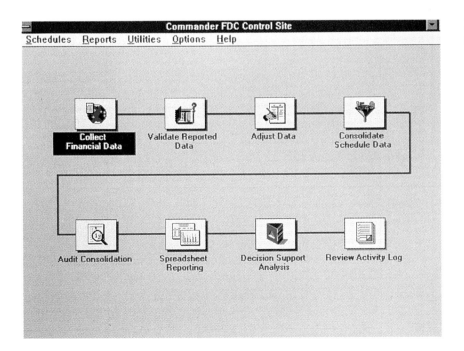

This is how a customized executive information system main menu may appear.

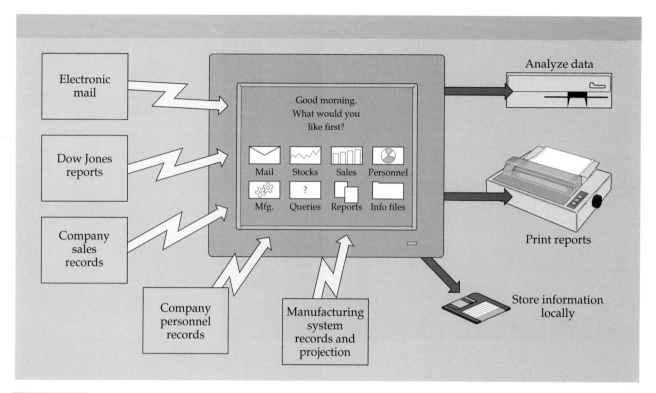

Figure 12.16 *A typical executive information system assembles data from various sources and makes it available for use at the executive's computer.*

tive EIS provides only the information the executive is likely to use when making decisions. Executive information systems often use individualized databases as well: subsets of the corporate database, databases developed from industry statistics, sources outside the company, and online database services.

An EIS must be relevant, complete, and clear. An EIS should contain only information that is relevant for a specifc executive, and the information should be displayed in comparative forms, where possible, such as in ratios, exception reports, and historical perspectives. Extraneous or irrelevant information impedes a manager's ability to use the system effectively and efficiently.

An EIS in Practice. To see how a high-level EIS might operate in practice, let us look at a system devised for the chief financial officer (CFO) of a large consumer products corporation (Figure 12.16). When this CFO turns on her workstation in the morning, the EIS software activates the communications link between the workstation and the mainframe and connects the workstation to the "command center" mainframe system. A menu then appears on her screen that enables her to:

- Read memos, reports, and messages that have come in over the electronic mail system since she last logged on.
- Review selected financial data that she has marked for close scrutiny.
- Review external data, such as economic indicators, competitive information, or financial markets, that are downloaded automatically to the EIS database.
- Analyze sales and financial results with a wide range of "push-button" statistical tools that can explore ratios, trends, and relationships in the data.
- Review reports generated by existing corporate information systems that have been linked to the EIS via a network.

IN A NUTSHELL

EXECUTIVE INFORMATION SYSTEMS AREN'T JUST FOR MAINFRAMES ANYMORE

A recent study revealed that 60% of all organizations surveyed had implemented an EIS on a desktop PC, workstation, or a network of PCs. The benefits cited included lower cost, less dependence on general management information systems for development of applications, and faster response time.

- Select and download corporate data to microcomputer disks in forms readable by popular spreadsheet packages.
- Access personnel data to keep tabs on who's who in the organization and how each functional area is performing.
- Track the progress of key projects and development schedules.

EXPERT SYSTEMS Expert systems consist of a database and software that simulate the knowledge and analytical ability of an expert in a particular field. For example, analysts at the American Express Company (AMEX) built an expert system that uses a computer to quickly determine customer credit limits and to approve requests for additional credit. The system helps the company provide better service to customers by allowing its staff to approve credit more quickly. Because the AMEX credit card has no fixed spending limit, it had been difficult for the staff to determine appropriate levels of credit for each customer. Each time a customer made a large purchase, a merchant telephoned AMEX to authorize the charge. An AMEX employee had to search through as many as 13 databases for more information about the customer and then make a judgment call. The expert system, called Authorizer's Assistant, now performs that search and makes recommendations to the credit employee, who makes the final authorization decision. The entire process takes only seconds (while the merchant is on the phone); it had previously taken as much as half an hour.

See Figure 12.17 for an illustration of the relationships among MIS, DSS, EIS, and expert systems.

Uses for Expert Systems. Expert systems are best suited for problems that need to be solved repetitively and that require some decision making. The best applications for expert systems are often those in which employees who are highly trained, well paid, or have very specific expertise cannot always be available on site to make critical decisions quickly. See Figure 12.18. Although expert systems are expensive to develop, the cost must be weighed against the cost of keeping highly trained decision-makers readily available at widely scattered locations.

There are other ways in which expert systems help solve business problems:

1. Fast decisions.
2. Low cost because only a limited number of experts are required.
3. Decision making is standardized.

ın A NUTSHELL

COMMON APPLICATION AREAS FOR EXPERT SYSTEMS

- Diagnosis
- Planning
- Monitoring
- Instruction
- Interpretation
- Control

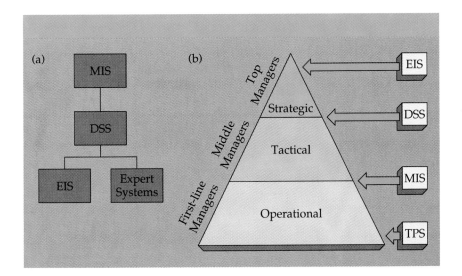

Figure 12.17 (a) Relationships among information systems. (b) How information systems best suit the needs of various levels of management. (TPS stands for transaction processing system and is a type of traditional information system.)

Figure 12.18 *Expert systems in business help users determine whether a client is a good credit risk.*

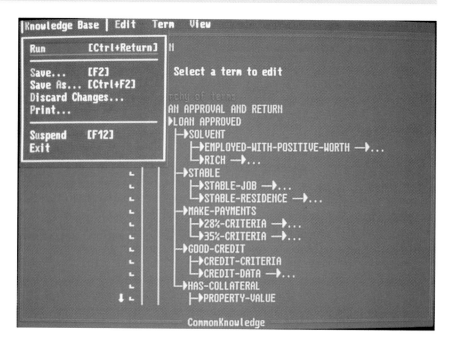

Components of an Expert System. An expert system has four basic components: a knowledge base, an inference engine, subsystems, and a user interface (Figure 12.19).

The **knowledge base** is the heart of the system. It translates the knowledge from human experts into rules and strategies and is developed by a computer professional called a **knowledge engineer.** Unlike a database, which consists of static relationships among fields, records, and files, a knowledge base is always changing as it reflects the advice of human experts. In fact, as more information is supplied, the basis for making decisions or the decisions themselves may actually change.

The knowledge engineer encodes knowledge by means of a variety of approaches. The most common way is to use rules that express knowledge in an IF-THEN format: IF a patient's symptoms are lung infection, fever, and a cough, THEN he or she has an 80% probability of having pneumonia. Expert systems often assign probabilities, because like human experts, they cannot be 100% sure. The person who obtains the computerized results must weigh the risk of delaying treatment against the risk of making the wrong diagnosis.

The **inference engine** is the software that draws conclusions. It examines existing facts and rules to make its conclusions. The inference engine also adds new facts if it finds them consistent with present information and rules. For example, if it noticed that most of the patients meeting the criteria for pneumonia also shared another symptom, this symptom would be added to the knowledge base. In addition, the inference engine controls the way the knowl-

Figure 12.19 *The principal components of an expert system are the knowledge base, the inference engine, the subsystems, and the user interface.*

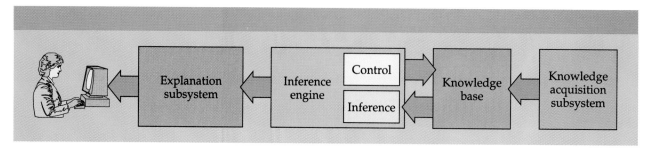

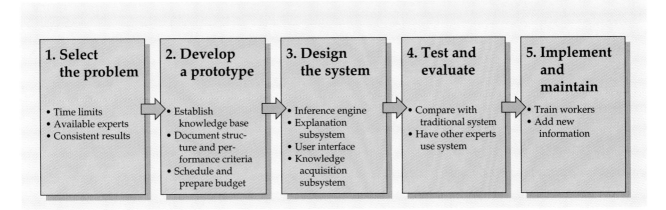

Figure 12.20 *The five phases of development for an expert system.*

edge base is searched. A search can be a time-consuming process if the knowledge base is large and complex.

Two subsystems assist knowledge engineers in updating the knowledge base and explaining to users how a recommendation was made. The knowledge acquisition subsystem helps the knowledge engineer define and encode the expert's problem-solving ability, and it also allows the engineer to easily insert knowledge in the system or delete it if the need arises. The explanation subsystem describes to users why the system has chosen to ask a certain question or how it has reached certain conclusions.

Ideally, expert systems should communicate information using a *natural language interface.* This type of interface lets users conduct dialogs with the computer that seem as natural as talking to another human being.

Steps for Developing an Expert System. Nontechnical managers with the proper tools can build a small-scale expert system. Sometimes the knowledge of experts in the company can be incorporated into the database developed for the expert system. Large expert systems require a team of knowledge engineers and generally a year or more to develop. Development consists of five phases that parallel the steps in the systems development life cycle (Figure 12.20).

IN A NUTSHELL

COMPONENTS OF AN EXPERT SYSTEM

1. Knowledge base
   a. The database at the heart of the system.
   b. Developed by a knowledge engineer.
   c. Translates knowledge from human experts into rules and strategies.
2. Inference engine
   a. The software that draws conclusions.
   b. Controls the way the knowledge base is searched.
   c. Has the ability to "learn"—change decisions based on new information.
3. Subsystems
   a. The knowledge acquisitions subsystem.
   b. The explanation subsystem.
4. User interface
   a. Permits dialogues between user and machine.
   b. Natural language interfaces enable users to ask open-ended questions.

EVOLUTION OF INFORMATION
SYSTEMS

This graph provides a historical view of
the evolution of types of information
systems from the 1950s through the
1990s. As you can see, expert systems
are a relatively recent innovation.

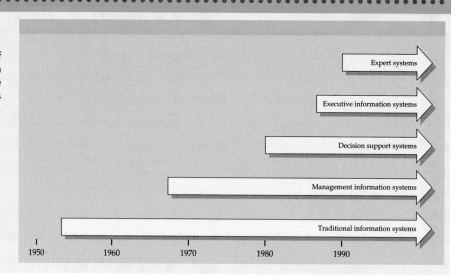

1. *Define the problem.* To avoid wasting development time and money, knowledge engineers first identify a suitable subject for an expert system. Good opportunities for expert systems are those that require expensive or rare experts to make fast decisions consistently over a long period of time.

2. *Develop a prototype.* A prototype is a small-scale model of an expert system. During this step, knowledge engineers learn everything about the problem they can from books and reports, and they help the human experts convey their knowledge about solving certain tasks. Knowledge engineers also select the best tools for building the expert system. The most flexible design approach is to use one of the artificial intelligence programming languages such as LISP or Prolog. Alternatively, the engineers may choose a commercially available expert system shell such as Gensym's GZ or Knowledge Garden's Knowledge Pro; they then enter the decision-making rules to create a knowledge base. Knowledge engineers develop a detailed design document that estimates the number of rules to be included, a more precise statement of performance criteria, and a detailed schedule and budget for the entire project.

3. *Design the complete system.* Now the knowledge engineer and the expert fine-tune the knowledge base by creating additional rules that are capable of handling the more subtle aspects of the problem. At this point, the knowledge engineer begins to turn development over to the experts and to monitor the project rather than actively participate in it. In turn, the expert, with all the insight and experience gained during the development process, starts to implement the expert system.

4. *Test and evaluate the system.* Once the knowledge engineer and expert believe the system is complete, they test it. Results obtained should be evaluated according to the performance criteria specified during prototyping. For example, a medical diagnostic system's recommendations can be evaluated by comparing diagnoses with bacterial culture tests performed later. Testing may result in further refinements of rules entered into the knowledge base. Other experts may also be invited to experiment with the system in other working situations.

5. *Implement and maintain the system.* After the first four steps have been completed, it is time to integrate the expert system into the workplace and provide training for prospective users. Maintenance of the system is an ongoing process. A major benefit of expert systems is that knowledge engineers can

continue to add new information or modify existing information. As a result, expert systems have much more flexibility and are eventually more accurate than information systems developed using more traditional approaches.

Self-Test

1. A business system whose primary objective is to provide useful information to managers from the top level down is called a _____.

2. (T or F) One basic difference between a DSS and an EIS is that the EIS is simpler to use.

3. Name four basic design requirements for executive information systems.

4. What kinds of tasks are best incorporated into expert systems?

CHAPTER SUMMARY

A database management system (DBMS) provides users with the ability to create, edit, update, and report from database files. Database management systems are used in both traditional and management information systems (MIS). An MIS uses a DBMS primarily to provide top-level management with company-wide information; only after management needs are met do operating staff needs—the major concern of traditional information systems—get addressed. This is called a top-down approach to information processing.

12.1 Database Management Systems: The Driving Force Behind Information Processing

Data in a database is stored in files that contain records; each record stores individual units of data called fields. Database management systems can join, or link, files in a database; in contrast, file management systems have flat files that cannot be linked.

A **database administrator** is the computing professional who manages the database and protects it from unauthorized access and poor database practices.

The four database structures are hierarchical, network, relational, and object-oriented. A **hierarchical database** has a tree structure with branches that are viewed as segments. "Parent" segments can have "child" segments, but a child segment can belong to only one parent segment, which limits the applicability of this kind of database. A **network database** is similar, but a child can have many parent segments, which enables records to be linked to numerous files. With both of these types of databases, however, the relationship among elements must be known in advance. In a **relational database,** which is the most common database form, key fields of records in different files can be linked to create a table that relates the files. Relational databases are more flexible than hier-

---

Solutions

1. management information system

2. T

3. it requires no technical knowledge; it is individualized; it evolves with the executive; information is relevant, complete, and just what the user needs

4. those performed by highly trained and well-paid decision makers; those that require decisions to be made very quickly

archical or network databases. **Object-oriented databases,** which use objects as elements within database files, can combine text, graphics, sound, video, and other images and have great potential for the future.

Database management systems typically include six components: (1) a data dictionary that defines relationships among elements, (2) a **data definition language (DDL),** which defines the technical specifications of the database, (3) a **data manipulation language (DML)** (or query language) that allows users to create custom applications, (4) utilities for performing basic database functions, (5) an application generator for creating applications without writing programs, and (6) a report generator for creating custom reports. Some systems also have their own proprietary DDLs. **SQL** (Structured Query Language) is a standard query language used with many database management systems.

To keep databases secure, database administrators sometimes use **encryption** techniques. They also must focus on **data integrity** to ensure that the database is not corrupted by invalid data.

12.2 Management Information Systems

Management information systems are designed according to the top-down approach. Rather than focusing on the business needs of each functional area, the top-down approach views an organization as though it were one complete unit with one set of specific corporate objectives.

A manager's level in the organization dictates what kind of information he or she needs. Broadly speaking, lower-level managers generally require information derived from operational-level business systems. Middle-level and top managers use **decision support systems (DSSs)** to meet their quantitative and analytical needs; a DSS is often designed to be used by managers across all functional areas. Top managers may use a specialized form of DSS called **executive information systems (EISs).** These systems are individually tailored to deliver specific financial, reporting, and planning information needed by a particular executive.

An EIS has four basic design requirements: (1) it must be easy to use, (2) it must be individualized, (3) it must evolve with the executive, and (4) it must provide information that is relevant, complete, and clear.

Expert systems, another type of specialized MIS, consist of a database with software that processes and distills the knowledge of an expert in a particular field. Expert systems can apply expertise without bias and tell users what assumptions were made to make a decision and what line of reasoning was used. An expert system consists of four components: the **knowledge base,** the **inference engine,** two subsystems (the knowledge acquisition subsystem and the explanation subsystem), and the human interface (usually a natural language interface). A **knowledge engineer** is the computer professional who develops the knowledge base for an expert system.

Study Objective

2. Demonstrate how access to databases helps managers make better decisions.

KEY TERMS

Database administrator, *p. 402*
Data definition language (DDL), *p. 409*
Data integrity, *p. 411*
Data manipulation language (DML),
  p. 409
Decision support system (DSS), *p. 415*

Encryption, *p. 411*
Executive information system (EIS),
  p. 416
Hierarchical database, *p. 402*
Inference engine, *p. 420*
Knowledge base, *p. 420*

Knowledge engineer, *p. 420*
Network database, *p. 404*
Object-oriented database, *p. 408*
Relational database, *p. 405*
SQL, *p. 410*

CHAPTER SELF-TEST

1. (T or F) Operational-level systems analysis focuses on the top-down approach to designing information systems.

2. (T or F) In a company that has implemented an MIS, information systems for individual departments usually function independently.

3. What does SQL mean?

4. (T or F) The database administrator is responsible for maintaining the data dictionary.

5. (T or F) A data dictionary contains technical information about the data stored in each record and how to access the information.

6. DBMS stands for _____.

7. What do we call the computer professional who builds expert systems?

8. What types of tasks are well-suited for expert systems?

9. (T or F) In hierarchical databases, each parent segment can have many children segments; this is called a one-to-many relationship.

10. (T or F) A file manager is generally more powerful than a relational database.

11. In a hierarchical database, how many parents does a child have?

12. (T or F) A top-down management information system uses separate databases for top management and operational-level departments.

13. What do we call a DSS specially designed for executives?

REVIEW QUESTIONS

1. Why is a file manager not a true database management system?

2. What are the major differences between relational, hierarchical, network, and object-oriented databases? What are the advantages and disadvantages of each?

3. Describe the three levels of management. In general, what kind of information is most useful to managers at each level? Explain your answer.

Solutions

1. F—An MIS uses a top-down approach.

2. F—Information from various departments is combined to form the MIS database.

3. Structured Query Language

4. T

5. T

6. database management system

7. knowledge engineer

8. those that need to be performed quickly and repetitively

9. T

10. F

11. one

12. F—The same databases are used, but different kinds of information are generated as appropriate for each level of decision making.

13. executive information system (EIS)

4. Explain the roles of the four major components of an expert system: the knowledge base, the inference engine, the two subsystems, and the human interface.

5. Your mother bakes the best chocolate cheesecake in the world. You would like to build a cheesecake business based on your mother's baking skills. Give three reasons why her baking ability is a good candidate for an expert system. Illustrate your reasons with three specific examples of how personal judgment and expertise might be reflected in an automated recipe for chocolate cheesecake.

6. In what situation do you think a network database would be better than a hierarchical, relational, or object-oriented database?

7. Make a list of all the database management systems you can find advertised in computer magazines; include their prices. Identify the kind of database model of each—relational, hierarchical, network, or object-oriented.

CRITICAL THINKING EXERCISES

1. Comment on the following use of a decision support system:
A database management system lists the likely financial outcomes of patient conditions. The $400,000 system that has already been installed in twenty hospitals gives an estimate of how much time and money should be provided to each patient in intensive care. This illustrates a trend in the medical field to move toward risk management and financial justification for treatment.

2. A recent study found that corporations that routinely handle personal information, such as people's medical, financial, and purchasing history, operate without policies aimed at protecting an individual's privacy. The study also found that even when such policies do exist, they are frequently not followed. Moreover, it seems that executives are not proactive in creating information privacy policies; instead they wait for an incident such as an illegal or unethical act that could result in legal action before they address the issue. If you were an executive at a company, what steps would you take to minimize the risks associated with an invasion of privacy?

Case Study

Touch-Tone Eases College Registration

Now you can register for college from the comfort of your own home—if you attend the University of Oregon, San Jose State, or one of the other schools currently using Touch-Tone course registration systems. With Touch-Tone registration, students electronically enroll in the classes of their choice by pressing buttons on their phones in response to "voice" instructions.

For example, at California's San Jose State University (SJSU), students who call the TOUCH-SJSU registration system are greeted electronically and prompted to enter a term code: 2 for spring or 4 for fall. Then they are asked to key in their Social Security number and a personal identification number (PIN) that has been assigned to them. To add a class, the student presses 2 and the five-digit code for that class. To drop a class, the student presses 3 and the code.

The system can also delete from class lists the names of students who have not paid their tuition. The university estimates that in its first semester of use, TOUCH-SJSU saved more than $60,000 in computer costs alone, not to mention savings in labor and student wear-and-tear.

At the University of Oregon, the Touch-Tone registration system, named Duck Call after the school's mascot, began operating in May 1991. Before that, registration had always taken two full days, adding up to a total loss of eight teaching days per year (a quarter system). Another inconvenience was that registration had always been held on the two days before each quarter began, which made it difficult for administrators to make scheduling changes because professors were not readily available. Now registration proceeds at a more leisurely pace. Students can use Duck Call 14 hours a day for several weeks before the new quarter begins, and faculty members and administrators have more time to make adjustments to schedules when necessary.

Registering for college using a Touch-Tone phone saves time and energy.

The registration procedure with Duck Call, which takes each student only a few minutes, provides university administration with statistical information that can be used for making decisions on class size and growth of students' majors. Developed by the Periphonics Corporation of Bohemia, New York, as was TOUCH-SJSU, Duck Call can handle up to 32 simultaneous phone calls.

Analysis

1. What uses can you envision for Touch-Tone telephones in business application areas?

2. What types of reports can the Touch-Tone system generate for the university administration to help them make decisions?

3. Cite positive and negative implications of Touch-Tone systems.

CHAPTER 13
Social Issues in Computing

13.1 PROTECTING THE PRIVACY OF USERS
Privacy Issues Relating to E-mail
Privacy Issues Relating to Database Access
Privacy Legislation
Public Interest Groups

13.2 MAKING INFORMATION SYSTEMS AND NETWORKS MORE SECURE
What Is Computer Crime?
Legal Concerns
Minimizing Security Problems
The Clipper Chip: When Privacy and Security Concerns Clash

13.3 MAKING INFORMATION SYSTEMS MORE SOCIALLY RESPONSIBLE
Managing the Work Environment
Do Computers Result in Unemployment or Worker Dissatisfaction?
Computer Professionals and Social Responsibility
Developing, Promoting, and Supporting Standards
The Impact of Computers on the Quality of Life

T hroughout this text, we have seen that effective computerization has many advantages for individuals as well as organizations. But sometimes computer use needs to be controlled or monitored to protect an individual's rights, an organization's files, and the proper relationship between the individual and the organization.

Study Objectives

In this chapter we will explore privacy, security, and other social issues. After reading this chapter you should be able to:

1. **Identify personal, legal, and ethical issues raised by the proliferation of information systems and computer networks.**

2. **Justify the integral part that security must play in the development and use of information systems and computer networks.**

3. **Describe how information systems networks affect the quality of life.**

13.1 PROTECTING THE PRIVACY OF USERS

Privacy and security issues raise legal as well as ethical questions. Where breaches in privacy or security result in violations of a law, legal issues are involved. Where breaches result in a violation of a commonly accepted standard of behavior, but do not break an existing law, ethical issues are involved. Any society that promotes social responsibility needs to be concerned about both the legal and ethical behavior of people.

The problems associated with keeping a network secure so that it protects people's right to privacy need to be addressed seriously if connectivity is to be accepted widely and used effectively. The more accessible a network is, and the more options available on it, the greater the security risk. As networks proliferate, which they will in the years ahead, and as more and more people have access to them, the risks are likely to increase as well.

Because the entire field of connectivity is so new, there are very few laws to deal with violations of privacy. State governments and the federal government, however, are becoming increasingly sensitive to the issues and have begun to enact appropriate legislation.

Privacy Issues Relating to E-mail

With 20 million employees in the United States currently using computers for e-mail, the potential for policy disagreements and lawsuits with regard to privacy issues is great. Currently, no federal law addresses the rights and obligations of e-mail users, and state laws are often inadequate.

Many companies have been taken to court over privacy issues relating to e-mail. Because established policies are not in place and clear-cut laws do not exist, employees and employers often find themselves in disagreement as to what privileges e-mail users should have.

In one classic case, Epson America, Inc., a computer manufacturer, fired an e-mail administrator because she alleged that the company read employees' e-mail messages and she believed that to be an invasion of privacy. She, and the e-mail users involved, filed a class-action suit claiming that under a California statute, interception of electronic communications without the consent of all

---

Study Objective

1. Identify personal, legal, and ethical issues raised by the proliferation of information systems and computer networks.

Critical Thinking

Some employers think that e-mail generated at the office is company property and that it is acceptable for managers to read messages intended for their staff. Do you agree? Should there be laws governing e-mail?

parties was prohibited. But the judge ruled in favor of the company stating that the statue cited did not cover e-mail in the workplace.

In general, courts seem to be taking the position that intra-office e-mail is the commercial property of the organization and is not covered by the First Amendment right of free speech. Employees who feel their privacy is invaded when employers read their e-mail would like the same protection that covers mail sent through the U.S. Post Office, but most courts disagree. Regardless of how future cases are resolved, employers should establish their own guidelines for use of e-mail.

A related issue regarding e-mail is copyright protection. If an individual receives an e-mail message, does he or she have the right to disseminate or use the information it contains without permission? Proper "netiquette," a term used to describe network etiquette, would suggest that one ask the sender for authorization before using or forwarding messages.

Online subscriber services face privacy issues as well. Should messages be screened? What action should be taken against offensive transmissions?

Transmissions such as pornography or criminal solicitations that are clearly illegal are handled by the law. But subscriber services also face legal action when monitoring is not vigorous enough and face charges of invasion of privacy when monitoring is too rigorous.

Privacy Issues Relating to Database Access

Privacy concerns have become even more widespread as the use of computers for storing public access databases increases. Because of the proliferation of large databases, it is easier for companies to gather information about individuals and organizations, information that might not otherwise be readily available or feasible to compile. Many individuals and consumer groups have sought to enact laws that would limit access to computerized databases.

Consider reporting agencies that have access to credit information for large numbers of individuals. For a fee, they will provide organizations with an individual's credit history. Besides the threat to privacy, the credit searches performed are not always accurate. Any data captured by computer could be obsolete or it could simply be wrong. Correcting such data can take a long time, and in the interim a person's credit rating and chances for getting a loan could be seriously affected.

The *Privacy Journal* recently published articles about 200 people who lost their jobs or suffered in other serious ways because databases containing credit information were incorrect. TRW, Equifax, Trans Union Corp. and other credit reporting agencies are now required by law to provide any person, on request, with his or her own credit history, free of charge. Now you can know in advance what the report will reveal to others, and you have the opportunity to make corrections. This change has reduced the negative impact that inaccurate credit histories have had on people's lives.

Several recent cases illustrate how computerized databases can invade an individual's privacy. For example, indictments were brought against police officers who sold criminal histories from the National Crime Information Center (NCIC) databases. Other indictments were brought against several employees of the Social Security Administration who were bribed by "information brokers" to perform computer searches through the records of 140 million workers. The market for improperly obtained information from the NCIC and the Social Security Administration databases includes private investigators and creditors who are trying to locate people, lawyers who are deciding whether to bring lawsuits against certain individuals, and employers who are deciding whether to hire, fire, or promote prospective or actual employees.

When organizations put together profiles on people based on information compiled from many sources, the information can reveal personal habits or spending patterns that might otherwise not be available. Lotus Development Corporation recently terminated development of a CD-ROM product (called Lotus MarketPlace: Household) that was to make available to companies a database of names, addresses, and life-style profiles on 80 million Americans. Lotus received so many complaints and such bad publicity about this database that it decided it would be prudent to simply terminate the project. There are other companies, however, building products that use confidential personal data including credit, medical, and legal records to create mailing lists.

Minimizing the problems associated with invasion of privacy is not easy. One mechanism, of course, is to enact laws. We discuss next legislative measures enacted and planned to alleviate some of these problems, but passing laws is just one method to protect people's rights. Public awareness of privacy issues and pressure placed on businesses by an informed society are equally important.

Privacy Legislation

The Fair Credit Reporting Act of 1970 gives individuals the right to review and correct credit reports. It also prohibits credit agencies from sharing personal information with anyone except those who have a "legitimate business need." Privacy advocates are not satisfied, however. They say the law fails to clearly define the term *legitimate business need,* so they call for clarification of the 1970 act.

Sometimes people need protection from government organizations as well as credit agencies. The Freedom of Information Act of 1970 guarantees citizens the right to see all of the information about them that is held by federal agencies such as the IRS and the CIA. A person can request any files on record by writing to each agency individually. The agency must supply the information unless it is deemed vital to national security or it invades someone else's privacy. Similar legislation has also been enacted by many states.

The Crime Control Act of 1973 is designed to ensure that criminal records are accurate and complete. People who have criminal records on file in a law enforcement agency have the right to review their file to ascertain its accuracy. Moreover, when a criminal record is sent from one law enforcement agency to another, it must be complete. That is, it must include details about the arrest, whether the person was prosecuted and, if so, the final verdict.

The Privacy Act of 1974 restricts the way the federal government can use information about its citizens. The law allows some data matching from different databases at different agencies, but the information must be used in a way that is consistent with the purpose for which it was originally collected—whatever that means! The Right to Financial Privacy Act of 1978 is more specific: It establishes strict procedures for federal agencies that seek to examine an individual's bank account.

Regulations proposed by the European Community attempt to control the types of data that international corporations can collect. The regulations are designed to avoid disputes between countries with conflicting rules about data use. Because many European countries have stricter privacy rules than the United States, the European Community guidelines could force U.S. businesses that deal with customers abroad to change their own practices.

Currently businesses often provide some individual and statistical data when requested, but because of public pressure they do so cautiously. The most recent relevant legislation is the Computer Matching and Privacy Act of 1988, which requires government agencies to obtain legal authorization before matching data in their databases.

The United Kingdom has a law called the Data Protection Act that requires all organizations maintaining computerized personal data on individuals to register with the Data Protection Registrar.

Public Interest Groups

Public interest groups recognize the need for public awareness, legislation, and protection of rights. Their members are social and political activists who have concerns about the impact of computing on society.

The most important public interest group for computing professionals and enthusiasts is the Electronic Frontier Foundation (EFF). The EFF was formed in 1990 by Mitch Kapor, a founder of Lotus 1-2-3, and Grateful Dead lyricist John Perry Barlow. It is an organization actively involved with social and political issues relating to computing and communications.

The Electronic Frontier Foundation is dedicated to ensuring that the rights and responsibilities of individuals as specified in the U.S. Constitution are applied to network users including the Internet community. The EFF is also active in establishing policies for those who will travel the information superhighway.

Preservation of privacy is a major concern of the organization, which has been a privacy advocate in many court cases defending the right of privacy for users of e-mail and online publications.

Social and political positions of the EFF can be obtained by contacting:

EFF
1667 K St. NW Suite 801
Washington, DC 20006
202-861-7700
Internet: ask@eff.org

The EFF has been successful in the political arena as well as in the courts. Rep. Edward Markey (D–MA) has incorporated some of its platform into his National Information Infrastructure (NII) proposal (H.R. 3636). Al Gore has also supported the EFF position on many issues.

Another organization that lobbies for privacy rights is Computer Professionals for Social Responsibility.

Self-Test

1. (T or F) Several federal laws specifically address the rights of e-mail users.
2. (T or F) Credit reporting agencies are now required by law to provide individuals with their own credit histories, free of charge.
3. (T or F) Federal agencies can share information about U.S. citizens without any restrictions or limitations.
4. (T or F) Under the law, personal record-keeping systems may be kept secret from the public.

Figure 13.1 *Sometimes computers can reduce crime rates. Here the Internet is used to help locate missing people and suspected criminals.*

13.2 MAKING INFORMATION SYSTEMS AND NETWORKS MORE SECURE

The existence of large databases that include personal information raises important social issues. We have just analyzed one such issue: privacy. People need assurance that their personal information, such as employment and credit history, will be used appropriately. More laws need to be passed and enforced to protect privacy.

Security is another relevant issue. Businesses need safeguards that protect computer systems and their data from damage or unlawful use. First, security measures are needed to protect hardware, software, and data from natural disasters such as fire, flood, and earthquakes. Second, security measures are also needed to guard against computer crime, which can take the form of sabotage and espionage as well as theft.

Computer crime has become a serious threat for all organizations, including the federal government. The proliferation of networks makes the problem even worse. We will focus on computer crime and measures that organizations use to protect themselves from such crime; these methods also help to protect data from natural disasters. See Figure 13.1.

Study Objective

2. Justify the integral part that security must play in the development and use of information systems and computer networks.

Solutions

1. F—Currently, no federal law addresses this issue.

2. T

3. F—The Privacy Act of 1974 allows some data matching, but the information must be used in a way that is consistent with the purpose for which it was originally collected. The Computer Matching and Privacy Act of 1988 is even more stringent.

4. T

What Is Computer Crime?

One recent study of 283 businesses and government institutions found that more than half are victims of computer crime each year. Records show that while a bank robber armed with a gun steals an average of $1,600 from a bank, the white-collar criminal armed with a computer steals an average of $100,000! These statistics for white-collar crimes may, in fact, be low, because many organizations such as banks, fearing a loss of customer confidence, do not report all the crimes that occur. The statistics may also be low because many crimes go undetected.

Computer crime can be as relatively "innocent" as the unauthorized use of computers for personal purposes, for example, for creating greeting cards or calendars or for playing computer games. On the other hand, it can be as serious as using computers to send corporate financial assets to a private Swiss bank account.

Computer crime is difficult to detect and even more difficult to prevent. Detection and prosecution are hampered because (1) it may take many months or even years before the crime is discovered, (2) it is difficult to gather evidence and prove culpability, (3) the laws governing computer crimes are not as clear-cut or well-tested as other types of laws, and (4) often organizations like banks, credit card companies, and investment houses are reluctant to report the crime. **Computer crimes** can be separated into four types:

1. Theft of computer time.
2. Tampering with programs or data.
3. Theft of data and assets.
4. Illegal copying of software.

THEFT OF COMPUTER TIME As we have seen, theft of computer time may be as relatively innocent as a student doing a term paper on a computer at work or as serious as someone stealing thousands of dollars of processing time for personal profit. Sometimes an employee will moonlight as a software developer and do programming at his or her employer's computer site—often on company time! Most people would view this as unethical, but it is also, strictly speaking, a theft. The FBI recently revealed that in AT&T's MIS Department, unscrupulous managers leased the company's computers to others and kept the lease payments—a total of $30 million!

TAMPERING WITH PROGRAMS OR DATA You may have seen the movie *Disclosure,* which includes virtual reality databases that Michael Douglas actually "walks through" while Demi Moore attempts to delete files that Douglas needs. Or perhaps you are familiar with the classic 1983 movie *War Games* in which an amiable teenager changed his grades in the high school computer by using a modem at home and then almost caused World War III by "breaking into" a Department of Defense computer. See Figure 13.2. Unfortunately, tampering with programs or trying to delete them happens all too often. Sometimes the crime is committed for profit or gain, and sometimes just for fun. In 1989, a Cornell University student broke into the Internet international computer research network and sabotaged files in thousands of computers. The perpetrator, whose father was, ironically, a computer security expert, was sentenced to three years probation and a $10,000 fine and had to perform 400 hours of community service.

Newspapers frequently print stories about hackers who break into public and private databases for the technical challenge involved. Hackers have even

Figure 13.2 *In* Disclosure, *Michael Douglas "walks through" virtual reality databases while Demi Moore tries to delete files that Douglas needs.*

planted computer viruses that tie up CPUs by commanding them to do such time-consuming tasks as attempting to calculate the precise value of pi, thereby crippling enormous data networks. As we saw in Chapter 7, a virus is a self-replicating computer code that winds its way through a system, possibly transferring itself to other systems or disks. It can destroy data and programs, cause the system to crash, or simply send mischievous messages to the user. Some hackers infect systems for fun while others engage in industrial espionage.

There are over 600 known viruses. The *Joshi* virus, for example, changes the hard disk drive's partitions so that it gains access to, and damages, the system. *Stoned* is a virus that infects the default drive and any floppies put into the machine. Another type of virus is the *Jerusalem* virus, which adds itself to a program repeatedly until the program is too large to be loaded.

Junkie, a virus first detected in the Netherlands, has recently spread throughout the world. It is particularly dangerous because it is encrypted, making it difficult to spot by virus scanners. Each time it replicates, it infects the drive and executable files on disk. It was first discovered in packaged software, unlike most viruses that are spread through downloaded or shared files. Another virus is called a "logic bomb" because it destroys all files that are run when the computer shows that the date is a Friday the thirteenth. You may also have heard of the infamous *Michelangelo* virus, which has a trigger date of March 6—the birth date of the famous artist. *Smeg* erases a user's hard disk between 4 and 5 PM local time each Monday.

Any of these viruses can be "caught" from an infected program that is uploaded to the system by disk. The best protection against viruses, as with all computer crime, is to impose hardware and software controls to prevent their spread. Many programs are available that not only detect but rid a system of a virus. Despite the proliferation of viruses, however, a recent survey revealed that only 85% of computing sites use **antiviral software** as protection.

The problem with viruses is apt to get worse before it gets better, especially as the capacities of computers increase and as more users download software from the Internet and other sources. A virus can slowly erode the integrity of a file or an entire storage device without anyone knowing it. In other cases, a virus can encrypt data, and when the time is right, transmit it to an unknown receiver, for example, a corporate raider. For those of you with personal computers, we strongly recommend that you always use a virus protection program when you boot up or download files. Some operating systems, utilities, and desktop man-

Figure 13.3 *Who commits computer crimes? Source: Executive Information Network.*

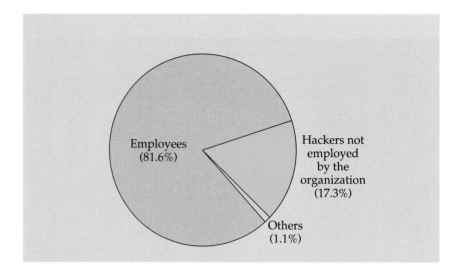

agers now come bundled with such software. We will discuss other methods of protection later in this chapter.

THEFT OF DATA AND ASSETS Legally called embezzlement, computer theft often involves a trusted employee who cannot resist the temptation to steal. See Figure 13.3. All too often, the theft is amazingly easy to carry out. For example, the chairman of the board and some of the executive officers of the now infamous Equity Funding Corporation—a publicly held mutual fund and insurance company—used terminals to enter insurance policies for nonexistent people. By entering bogus data over a period of years, they greatly increased the company's apparent assets. Of the 97,000 insurance policies maintained by the computer, almost two-thirds were fictitious policies with a face value of $2.1 billion! Because the company appeared to be more profitable than it actually was, the stock of Equity Funding was greatly inflated; consequently, the officers, who were large shareholders, were able to sell their shares at considerable profits. The fraud went undetected because auditors consistently accepted as beyond question the computer printouts that listed policyholders. The crime was uncovered only after a former employee revealed the scheme. It became a classic case of how easy it is to use a computer fraudulently if proper controls have not been implemented.

As users of the Internet proliferate, problems of viruses and theft of documents have increased. Encrypting transmissions and educating people about the need for virus protection software are methods used to alleviate the problem.

ILLEGAL COPYING OF SOFTWARE Are you "stealing" when you make a copy of word processing software for a friend? The law says you are. Yet many normally law-abiding people who would not dream of shoplifting, see nothing wrong with making a copy of a $300 word processing package and giving it to a friend, despite the fact that such an action is in violation of the U.S. Copyright Law. Making unauthorized copies of software is clearly unethical as well as illegal, yet it is so widespread that estimates suggest there may be as many as 10 illegal copies of a program for every legitimate copy sold.

To prevent "software piracy," manufacturers sometimes develop **copy-protected software,** which means that the programs cannot easily be copied to other disks or can only be copied a limited number of times, generally twice. Copy-protected software is becoming rarer, however, as vendors respond to complaints from legitimate users that copy protection is a nuisance. Copy protection can make it difficult to do legitimate copying, such as creating backup disks or recovering from hard disk failure. In fact, the lack of copy protection is often a selling feature for many packages.

Ironically, software piracy may become less of a problem in the future, if viruses abound. Any experienced computer user will be more likely to load into his or her computer only those programs that come packaged with a warranty from the manufacturer, because a program that has "been around" is more likely to be infected.

Legal Concerns

Because computer crime is on the rise, many of the laws to protect organizations and individuals from such crimes need to be clarified or revised.

Legislators have been trying for years, without much success, to enact laws at the federal level to curb computer crime. The major stumbling block is the lack of legal definitions for *property* and *value* as they relate to computerized information. In 1986, however, the federal government passed the Computer Fraud and Abuse Act, which makes it a felony to intentionally access a federal computer without authorization and cause damage over $1,000.

As we have seen, one way to help clarify laws is to have the judicial branch of the government rule on key cases. But companies are reluctant to prosecute because a trial might draw attention to weaknesses in their computer's security system. Prosecutors are also reluctant to take computer criminals to court because computer crime laws are so vague it is difficult to build and win cases.

Because the federal government has not enacted effective laws in this area, many states are beginning to pass stronger legislation that protects companies from crimes such as computer theft and deliberate destruction of data.

Minimizing Security Problems

Precautions and controls can be employed to protect hardware and software from illegitimate use. Several of the critical ones are outlined in Table 13.1. Users with their own PCs should:

1. Use an antiviral program (e.g., McAfee's Viruscan, Norton Antivirus, or one that comes with your operating system) each time the computer is turned on.
2. Avoid downloading of programs from electronic bulletin board systems or other networks that do not screen for viruses.
3. Always make backups.
4. Not use bootlegged software.
5. Be educated about dangers.
6. Avoid using programs whose origin is unknown.
7. Purchase only sealed packages of software.

Figure 13.4 summarizes some of the ways employees could use computers improperly.

The Clipper Chip: When Privacy and Security Concerns Clash

Privacy and security are two social concerns that are sometimes at odds with each other. An example is the recent controversy over the Clipper Chip proposed by the National Security Agency (NSA). NSA wanted this encryption chip installed in all telephone and data networks, as well as in ATMs, cable TV boxes, and fax machines. The chip would provide some measure of security by encoding or encrypting data so that it could not be accessed by unauthorized users. Every Clipper Chip would have a "back door"—a serial number to identify a key that could decode whatever the chip had encoded. With a court order government security agencies could gain access to the key for monitoring any suspected criminal activities.

Figure 13.4 *Here are some of the numerous ways in which people could use computers, data, or software improperly.*

Disgruntled employee could

• Sabotage equipment or
  programs

Competitor could

• Sabotage operations
• Engage in espionage
• Steal data or programs
• Make copies of records,
  documentation, or screen
  displays

Data entry operator could

• Insert data
• Delete data
• Bypass controls
• Sell information

Clerk/supervisor could

• Forge or falsify data
• Embezzle funds
• Engage in collusion with
  people inside or outside the
  company

System user could

• Sell data to competitors
• View private information

Operator could

• Copy files
• Destroy files

User requesting reports could

• Sell information to competitors
• Receive unauthorized
  information

Engineer could

• Install "bugs"
• Sabotage system
• Access security information

Data conversion worker could

• Change codes
• Insert data
• Delete data

Programmer could

• Steal programs or data
• Embezzle via programming
• Bypass controls

Report distribution worker could

• Examine confidential reports
• Keep duplicates of reports

Trash collector could

• Sell reports or duplicates
  to competitors

Control Access to Hardware and Software

- Lock physical locations and equipment.
- Install a physical security system.
- Monitor access 24 hours a day.

Backup Data and Programs

- Make incremental backups, which are copies of just the changes to files, at frequent intervals.
- Make full backups, which copy all files, periodically.
- To protect files from natural disasters such as fire and flood, as well as from crimes and errors, keep backups in separate locations, in fireproof containers, under lock and key.

Implement Network Controls

- Set access controls to decrease employee errors and crime, hacker break-ins, and other external wiretaps.
- Monitor username and password use—require changes to passwords periodically.
- Encrypt data.
- Install a callback system.
- Use signature verification to ensure user authorization.

Separate and Rotate Functions

- If functions are separate, then two or more employees would need to conspire to commit a crime.
- If functions are rotated, employees would have less time to develop methods to compromise a program or a system.
- Perform periodic audits.
- Protect against natural disasters.
- Install uninterruptible power supplies and surge protectors.

Protect Against Viruses

- Use virus protection programs.
- Use only vendor-supplied software, or public domain or shareware products that are supplied by services that guarantee they are virus-free.

Table 13.1 *Security Measures to Protect Hardware and Software*

Fingerprint readers are used to protect computers, software, and networks from unauthorized use.

The proposed Clipper Chip has proven to be rather controversial.

So in addition to providing a measure of security, the Clipper Chip, like a wiretap, would have the potential for invading an individual's privacy. Government agencies argue that we must be willing to give up a degree of personal privacy for safety and security.

As you might expect, there is a great deal of controversy over this chip. Here is a classic case of how security and privacy concerns can clash.

Self-Test

1. (T or F) Virus detection is typically performed using hardware controls.
2. (T or F) Rotating job functions within an organization minimizes the threat of computer crimes.
3. (T or F) Once a computer crime is detected, it is relatively easy to find the perpetrator.
4. (T or F) Both hardware and software controls are necessary to effectively minimize security risks.

▬ 13.3 MAKING INFORMATION SYSTEMS MORE SOCIALLY RESPONSIBLE

Study Objective

3. Describe how information systems networks affect the quality of life.

Managing the Work Environment

A computer's data and programs need to be protected for both legal and ethical reasons. It is also important to ensure that computers in the office are used in a socially responsible way. When computers are used appropriately, they have the potential for improving people's quality of life. We discuss here some elements that can have an impact on the quality of life.

ERGONOMICS The widespread use of computers in the workplace has created a number of new organizational issues in areas such as health and safety. Consider what happened to a telephone company that installed an automated telephone system for its operators. Operator productivity suddenly decreased because:

*   Light reflecting onto terminal screens from a large bank of windows bothered the operators. Although the windows were a much desired change for the operators, the bright, natural light was sometimes so intense that it caused eyestrain.

*   The operators' workstations were designed for the average operator. There was little, if any, flexibility for changing the position of the screen, keyboard, or desk to satisfy individual tastes and needs.

Solutions

1.   F—Software is typically used.
2.   T
3.   F
4.   T

- Each operator was given a U-shaped desk with side panels for privacy. Many operators had been more comfortable seeing their colleagues while they worked and now felt cut off from their peers.

As noted in Chapter 5, ergonomics is the science of adapting machines and work environments to people. Ergonomically designed workplaces provide the best physical environment for people using computers and other technology. Ergonomics has the potential for improving the quality of life of employees and for reducing health hazards such as repetitive stress disorders including muscle, nerve, and circulatory problems caused by using a computer.

Ergonomically designed offices have:

- Reduced Office Glare. Perhaps the most obvious problem in the work environment, and the one easiest to deal with, is office lighting. Improper lighting conditions create glare on video display terminals. There are two common ways to reduce glare: provide indirect lighting, which may eliminate the problem, and provide antireflection filters that reduce glare on the screen and also reduce the intensity of the screen image. The trend in many organizations is to eliminate all direct overhead lighting, such as fluorescent lights, and to substitute softer, indirect lighting in its place.

- Reduced Sound Pollution. Well-planned offices eliminate distracting sounds yet make provisions for private conversations. Because noise created by keyboards, printers, and even the computer itself can be annoying and distracting, an effective noise control plan focuses on three areas: efficient sound-absorbing materials on furniture, walls, ceilings, and floors; sound-masking devices such as printer covers; and well-designed office layouts.

- Ergonomically-Designed Workstations. Workstations should be designed to allow users the greatest economy of movement. As shown in Figure 13.5, factors such as reach lengths, arm angles in keyboarding, and eye viewing angles all contribute to the comfort of employees performing necessary

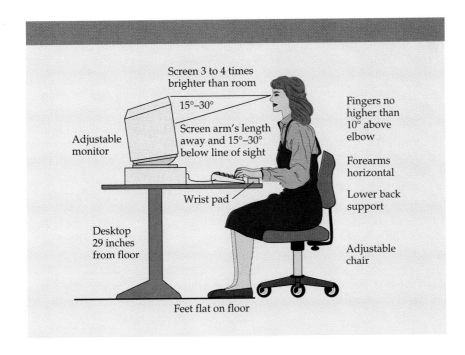

Figure 13.5 *Ergonomically designed workstations are intended to make the user comfortable and to reduce health problems.*

Screen 3 to 4 times brighter than room

15°–30°

Screen arm's length away and 15°–30° below line of sight

Adjustable monitor

Wrist pad

Desktop 29 inches from floor

Feet flat on floor

Fingers no higher than 10° above elbow

Forearms horizontal

Lower back support

Adjustable chair

office tasks. A wrist pad or wrist supports, which are available for ergonomically designed keyboards, should be provided. Poor workstation design will ultimately result in user fatigue, a high rate of error, health problems, and slow task performance as well as employee dissatisfaction.

- Radiation-Free Monitors. As we saw in Chapter 5, another hotly debated issue is whether monitors emit harmful radiation. Numerous studies have failed to detect radiation above acceptable levels, but not everyone is satisfied with these findings. Questions center around the long-term biological effects on users of low-level radiation from computer monitors. Many people are concerned about whether prolonged exposure of pregnant women to these devices can cause birth defects. Until conclusive evidence is available to resolve these issues, a corporate policy requiring periodic testing for malfunctioning monitors that emit radiation above established safety limits might be appropriate.

Many people are also concerned about the potential radiation risk from wireless networks. This is likely to be addressed as well in the next few years.

Employee experiences with computer systems affect their attitude toward new technology. In a poorly managed computer environment, employees may believe that their computer system displaces workers, adversely affects their health, and limits their freedoms. In a well-planned environment, employees may believe that computers provide new opportunities, enhance employee control over tasks, and improve their decision-making ability. The perception of the effects of computers in a given business depends on the leadership and vision of the company's managers as well as on the attitude of computer professionals who plan and develop information systems.

Critical Thinking

Should employees have a role in the use of monitoring procedures? Some companies post individual performance data; is this likely to motivate people? Are high-level achievers likely to be ostracized by other employees? What impact do you think monitoring will have on overall productivity and the quality of the work performed?

COMPUTER MONITORING Two objectives of managing the work environment are (1) to improve job satisfaction for employees and (2) to make the office setting ergonomically sound. Another goal is to monitor the productivity of the work force—a goal that is not very popular among employees and could adversely affect their quality of life.

Computer monitoring of data entry clerks, reservation agents, insurance claim processors, and customer service agents is widespread. Typically, network software or the software for processing transactions includes monitoring utilities that compile usage statistics about each terminal or PC linked to a host. Many insurance companies are installing document management systems that include "work flow software," which keeps track of how documents are handled by different levels of employees and where bottlenecks occur. A recent survey by the Communication Workers of America, which focused on 762 video display terminal users at telephone companies, indicated that such electronic monitoring of work flow dramatically increased the level of stress and stress-related pain, as shown in Figure 13.6.

Thus, while some monitoring devices are designed to test for ergonomically sound work environments, many others are actually designed to monitor computer workers themselves. This has prompted some unions to compare today's office environment to "sweatshops" where constant supervision and the need to meet minimum levels of productivity are the norm.

Critics of monitoring devices want legislation to limit electronic "surveillance" of employees. They also want laws to require employers to notify workers that they are being monitored. Employers claim that notifying workers would

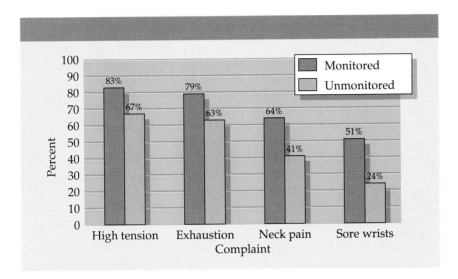

negate the results because normal patterns of work are likely to be altered when people know they are being watched. Congress is considering a bill introduced by Sen. Paul Simon and currently called The Privacy for Consumers and Workers Act, that would limit employers' rights to monitor production and require that workers be notified by a flashing light or tone when they are being monitored.

Do Computers Result in Unemployment or Worker Dissatisfaction?

Most recent studies demonstrate that mass unemployment resulting from automation is rare. In total, more jobs have been generated by computers than have been eliminated by them. Nonetheless, in some areas computers have substantially reduced the work force—in automated factories and typesetting companies for instance. In general, computers need an operating staff, and when they generate growth, this means an increased need for labor. Many publishing firms, for example, once feared that desktop publishing would result in fewer opportunities for publishers. But the evidence suggests otherwise. As many as 10,000 new publishing companies with desktop publishing capability emerged in the past decade.

Computers have minimized tedious tasks that workers once performed. As a result, one might think that the average worker has it easier today than a decade ago. But this is not always true. Some studies suggest that workers displaced by computers who are retrained to perform computer-related jobs in their organizations tend to find the new tasks less satisfying.

Moreover, as we have seen, many companies now use computers to monitor their workers' productivity, which often increases the level of stress at work. Workers who sit and look at a computer screen all day have health problems that range from eyestrain to muscle strain to fears about the effects of radiation. Computer phobia adds to the stress as well: Many people continue to be afraid of computers and fear the depersonalization that they may bring. Computer professionals and computer users should be sensitive to such concerns, be informed about measures to allay them, and help future users understand and appreciate some of the benefits of computing.

Computer Professionals and Social Responsibility

What happens if a computer professional fails to satisfy the needs of the user? What happens if the information system developed is so poor that processing errors are rampant and huge delays occur? If the professionals responsible for a poorly designed information system work for the organization, then their jobs could be in jeopardy. If outside consultants were responsible, users may be able to bring legal action to recoup any losses resulting from the poor design, but it is difficult to prove liability in such instances. In fact, the reasons for poorly designed systems may not always be the fault of the designer. Users may have supplied incorrect information or too little information, or the needs of the organization may have changed. What is clear, however, is that because unsatisfactory information systems do exist, lawsuits abound and resolving them equitably continues to be problematic.

Whether or not users can take legal action against computer professionals for a poor design, these professionals bear an ethical responsibility to provide users with systems that function properly. That is, ethical conduct goes beyond merely adhering to laws. For example, what should you do if you learn that a system you helped develop invades privacy? Or how responsible are you if you are part of a team that creates a software package with known bugs? There are no simple answers to questions such as these. Many people with high ethical standards have argued against holding computer professionals totally responsible for their work, because the way an information system is used may not be under the developer's control. Some people claim that, just as Alfred Nobel cannot be held accountable for the immoral use of his invention of dynamite, computer professionals should not be held accountable for programs that are used illegally or unethically. (How's that for an analogy?)

Most professionals have a code of ethics that sets broad standards for professionals where such standards may not be covered by specific legislation. As the debate over the issues goes on, many computing organizations believe that a code of ethics is needed to enable computer professionals to police themselves before the government finds it necessary to pass strict laws. Two types of certification are currently available for computing professionals: Certificate of Data Processing (CDP) and Certified Computer Professional (CCP). Both certifying organizations have a code of ethics.

Developing, Promoting, and Supporting Standards

Throughout this text, we have discussed the lack of hardware and software standards in the computing field and how this lack has adversely affected computerization. The absence of transmission standards, for example, impedes the effectiveness of networks.

We saw in Chapter 10 that the ISDN (Integrated Services Digital Network) has as its goal the implementation of a universal standard for transmission of voice, data, and video information to people and organizations throughout the world. ISDN standards are being developed by a standards committee within the United Nations called the International Telecommunications Union. The standards being considered relate to physical interfaces, communications protocols, message formats, and services offered. Telephone companies, hardware and software suppliers, and service organizations that agree to adhere to these standards will develop systems that permit ISDN users ready access to a wide variety of network-based information services. Once a standard is widely accepted, then more appropriate procedures for controlling access can be implemented. It is often difficult, however, to convince users to adopt a standard, especially if it means they will need to change their procedures.

Many people advocate a National Information Act to develop new technology standards and to consolidate telecommunications control under a single agency. With the seven "Baby Bell" telephone companies formed as a result of the AT&T breakup, and recent court decisions that give these Baby Bells the right to provide information services, national regulation may become a necessity in order for standardization to be achieved.

The Impact of Computers on the Quality of Life

Despite widespread use of computers, the predictions that they would completely alter the way we live and work have not really materialized. There are, however, specific areas in which computers have had a dramatic impact on the quality of life.

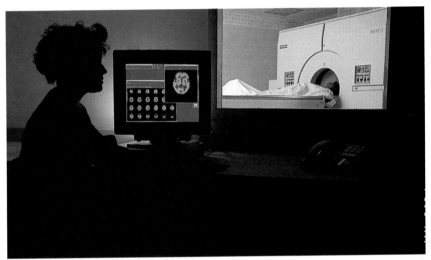

Figure 13.7 *(a) Here, an MRI is used to display a cross-section of a patient's brain. (b) This computerized device automatically tests blood for a variety of illnesses and diseases.*

(a)

(b)

COMPUTERS IN MEDICINE When we think of improved quality of life, we tend to think first and foremost of health. A sound body and mind are prerequisites for a satisfying life. Computers have had a very significant impact on the quality of medical services. The following are just some of the ways that computers have improved services provided by the medical field:

- Computerized tests such as CAT scans and MRIs provide doctors with information that would otherwise require surgery. See Figure 13.7.

- Computerized devices such as pacemakers, artifical organs, and prostheses have enabled tens of thousands of people to live a longer and fuller life.

- Medical records stored in hospital information systems improve the quality of patient care. They are not only more accurate but they can facilitate proper treatment. They keep track of medicines and tests administered, dietary needs, patient history, and so on.

- Clinical databases that maintain vast records on people with various symptoms and illnesses have made it possible for researchers to more effectively diagnose and treat diseases.

- Expert medical systems and telecommunications help to provide care to patients who are in remote locations, far from available medical facilities.

- Computerized devices provide improved mobility for the physically challenged, as we will discuss in the next section.

Proposed health care reforms will rely heavily on computers to store patient information. The government is considering the distribution of smart cards that would contain medical and insurance data on all people in the United States.

While computers used in medical application areas are clearly beneficial, issues of privacy and security remain relevant social concerns.

COMPUTERS AND PEOPLE WITH DISABILITIES On the whole, people with disabilities have benefited greatly from computer technology. See Figure 13.8. Scanners convert printed text to verbal output for the visually impaired. Voice

Figure 13.8 *Computers have many benefits for the handicapped. (a) This is a computerized braille telesensory system for enabling the visually impaired to read. (b) Touch screens make it easier for people with motor or coordination problems to use a computer for learning or just playing games.*

(a)

(b)

recognition equipment converts speech to printed or displayed output for the hearing impaired. People confined to their home can be productive by working on computers that offer access to an office and all its resources.

Visually and hearing-impaired students can use computers with special adapters for learning at home or even in a classroom setting. People with other physical disabilities can use special pointing devices, pens, or touch screens instead of keying devices for interacting with a computer. These input devices are easier to manipulate and require less manual dexterity than a keyboard. In short, computers are very useful tools for improving the quality of life for people with physical handicaps. They can be used to communicate, to perform job-related activities, and to help the disabled learn.

Through artificial intelligence technology, computers can also be used as medical aids to compensate for certain disabilities. Vision systems have sensors built into special glasses; computerized walking sticks help blind people "sense" the presence of large objects and even determine what the objects are. Computerized devices—some experimental and some in widespread use—also help the physically impaired become more mobile. Some of these devices are implanted in limbs and actually cause muscles to flex so that movement can occur. In other cases, wheelchairs, prostheses, and other "smart" equipment can be programmed to help the disabled person be more ambulatory.

The federal government estimates that the lifetime cost of an unemployed disabled person to the country is more than 1 million dollars. Thanks to computerized devices, many disabled people will be able to lead more productive lives. The Americans with Disabilities Act of 1992 requires organizations that do not provide access and work for the disabled to cease discrimination. As a result, companies have become more attuned to the ways in which computer technologies can be used by the disabled to enhance their contribution to the workplace and to improve their overall quality of life.

COMPUTERS AND THE GOVERNMENT Most government agencies depend heavily on computers. Some, like NASA, simply could not exist without them. See Figure 13.9. Linking databases has become a necessity for the government—

Figure 13.9 *(a) NASA's space program would not be possible without computers. (Continued on next page.)*

(a)

Figure 13.9 *(b) Total government spending on information technology, measured in billions of dollars. Source: Federal Sources, Inc.*

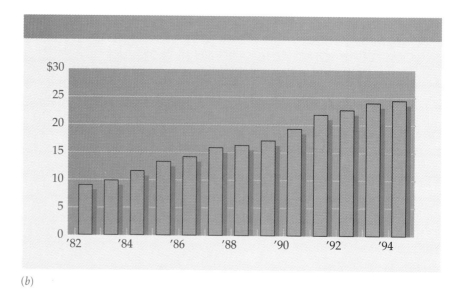

(b)

Critical Thinking

The Brady handgun law requires the government to inform dealers if a customer has a criminal record. The NCIC could also flag people who have had dishonorable discharges from the military or a record of mental illness where violence was involved. Should the Brady law apply to these people as well?

on both the local and national level. The National Crime Information Center (NCIC), which has 10 million criminal records on file, needs to be far more accessible to local law enforcement agencies. NCIC 2000 is a project designed to provide police cars with online access to criminal records by the year 2000. The project will also provide police cars with mobile fingerprint scanners. A suspect's fingerprints will be scanned and transmitted to the NCIC and any criminal activity on file for that suspect will be immediately sent to the officer. See Figure 13.10.

The success of the 1993 Brady handgun law will depend on better accessibility to the NCIC. Currently, the nation's 285,000 licensed gun dealers require that a potential customer who wishes to purchase a gun wait five days, during which time the dealer calls a hotline to request a computer search to determine whether the customer has a criminal record. NCIC 2000 will eliminate the five-day waiting period—gun dealers will be able to access the criminal files immediately.

Figure 13.10 *Local law enforcement officers can access the NCIC from their police cars.*

Another government agency that would benefit from better integration between the national and local level is the Internal Revenue Service. Currently, IRS magnetic tapes are mailed to state agencies for matching of records. The IRS has developed an Electronic Management System that will provide online exchange of tax data with state governments by 1998. The Computer Matching and Privacy Act of 1988 permits this use of files, but many other government agencies need prior court approval before matching databases.

While the scope and size of government agencies necessitates computer use, citizens need to be concerned that their privacy is not invaded when databases on individuals are used.

COMPUTERS AND LEISURE TIME The Industrial Revolution dramatically altered the fiber of society during the last two centuries. The Information Revolution and the Communications Revolution are likely to have as profound an impact on people today and in the future. Changes resulting from such major technological breakthroughs affect not only the socioeconomic infrastructure, but the very quality of our lives. The leisure time we have is greater and activities that we can pursue during our free time are more exciting.

Computers have given us more leisure time by performing many menial tasks that we would otherwise need to do ourselves. The use of computers for fast computations probably springs to mind, but "smart" devices that regulate our cars, household appliances, and the very air we breathe are also part of that Computer Revolution—and they have a significant impact on how much we enjoy life. As we have seen, medical tests, surgical implants, and prostheses based on computing devices give us more leisure time by improving the quality of our lives and the length of our lives as well.

Other aspects of the Computer Revolution that have the potential to improve our quality of life include:

1. Telecommuting—Using a computer at home instead of commuting to work reduces stress, increases the amount of leisure time, and puts less strain on the environment—if fewer people travel to an office, pollution is reduced, there is less need for fuel, and problems associated with mass transportation are abated. Employees often find they work more diligently and are more productive when they work at home. Some employers still worry, however, that distractions in the home will decrease a worker's productivity—this belief has been an obstacle to the spread of telecommuting.

2. Computers make it possible to customize or individualize activities so that they meet your specific needs. For example, you can access news from online subscriber services and tailor it to an individual format. In this way, you can receive a customized electronic newspaper with test and video clips on local, national, and international news, the arts, sports, and so forth, and select the kind of priority and coverage that interests you most. See Figure 13.11.

3. Videos on demand will not only be available any time and any place you want, but you will be able to watch digitized images of yourself—or anyone else you want—in the leading role. See Figure 13.12. How's that for customized entertainment?

4. If you like to travel, you can experience a virtual reality trip by viewing an interactive video or CD-ROM. Using a subscriber service or the Internet or other network, you can ask questions, make reservations, get tourist information, and so on. In addition, you can use a car equipped with electronic maps or travel information to help you on your trip. See Figure 13.13.

Figure 13.11 *Prodigy screen display.*

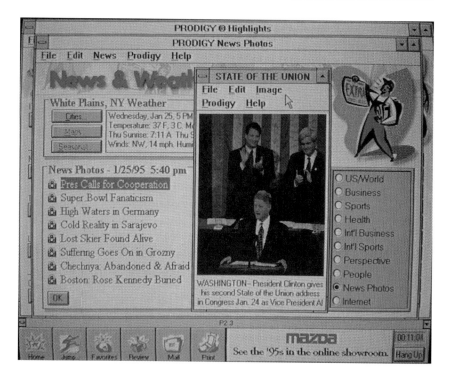

5. If you like to play games, the variety of available software is endless. See Figure 13.14. Interactive shop-at-home options make ordering from catalogs virtually obsolete and traveling to a store a waste of time. Interactive kiosks at stores make shopping more pleasant. See Figure 13.15.

6. Robots improve the quality of life by accomplishing tasks too dangerous for people to perform and also by performing normal household tasks. See Figure 13.16.

Figure 13.12 *Lunching with a dinosaur.*

Figure 13.13 *CD-ROMs, electronic maps, and travel guides are available to provide tourists with information on services and attractions at tourist locations.*

Quality of life, then, as measured by an increase in leisure time and leisure-time activities, can be enhanced by computers. But computers could also have a negative impact on the quality of our lives if we, as citizens, are not attuned to their potential disadvantages:

Being Online Twenty-four Hours a Day. Communications technologies now make it possible for people to be accessible 24 hours a day via standard telephones, cellular phones, wireless devices, fax/modems, and PCs. While beneficial

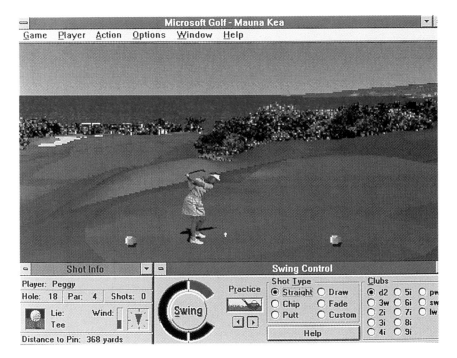

Figure 13.14 *Computers are used for some leisure time activities like game-playing as well as for household functions.*

Figure 13.15 *In-store information kiosks with touch screens help people make selections.*

in certain situations, such availability could actually have a negative impact on the quality of our lives. Surely you have seen people out for a leisurely evening of dining or watching a ballgame—with a cellular phone glued to their ear! This may improve an individual's ability to make a deal with a client, for example, but it is not likely to enhance the person's quality of life.

COMPUTERS IN EDUCATION For many years now, people have been predicting that computers could profoundly impact the ways in which individuals learn and, by so doing, improve our ability to educate people. Numerous projects have demonstrated the effectiveness of computers for (1) teaching through the use of tutorials, (2) reinforcing learning through the use of drill and practice exercises, and (3) providing an interactive educational experience that uses virtual reality or simulations where hands-on training would be too expensive or too risky—

Figure 13.16 *Robots can replace people for (a) high-risk tasks or (b) tedious jobs.*

(a)

(b)

Figure 13.17 *Virtual reality simulations help people learn to fly planes.*

such as teaching pilots to fly and to respond to emergency situations, teaching chemists how to conduct delicate experiments, or teaching interns to diagnose and treat various illnesses. See Figure 13.17.

A number of recent advances in computing have made the use of tutorials, drill-and-practice exercises, and simulations even more effective. PCs with multimedia capabilities can expose students to much more than text-based information—graphics, animation, sound, video, hyperlinks, and interactivity really enhance the educational experience, making learning more challenging and rewarding. There is CD-ROM and laser-disc-based software to teach youngsters reading, writing, and arithmetic, as well as many other subject areas. See Figure 13.18. There are also highly sophisticated edutainment packages such as SimCity, SimEarth, and SimAnt that enable players to "pretend" they are controlling a specific environment such as a public transportation system or an urban area. Players learn to be managers, planners, investors, and financiers. Such software helps people become better decision makers and improves their overall ability to be effective managers.

CD-ROMs and laser discs with virtual reality simulations improve not only decision-making but also a person's understanding of an environment. Would-be archeologists can put on goggles, gloves, and headsets that launch them into a simulated dig; would-be firefighters could find themselves in an "explosive" situation from which they must extricate themselves and others—the hardware and software makes it feel like you are actually there and the experience is as close to real-life as is possible. The feelings, the responses, the computer's analysis of the decisions you make, all enhance the educational process. Computers, then, have had, are having, and will undoubtedly continue to have a profound impact on learning.

There are also other benefits of computing in education. As we have seen, the physically challenged can use computers to express themselves, interact with others and, in general, communicate better.

Distance learning is a concept that enables people at remote locations to access an electronic classroom and learn along with others. Those who cannot attend an actual class can still benefit from the educational experience. Such uses of computing in education not only enhance learning but make it more widely available.

Critical Thinking

Do you think that a lesson on John F. Kennedy that includes excerpts from some of his speeches or a lesson on Hamlet that includes monologues by Sir Laurence Olivier improves learning? Are students likely to remember better? Are they likely to be more informed about subjects if multimedia systems are used as teaching tools?

Figure 13.18 *Here, a laser disk provides the focus for an interactive, computerized classroom lesson on astronomy.*

COMPUTERS MAKE THE WORLD MORE CONNECTED Online subscriber services, CD-ROMs with libraries of information, the Internet, and the coming information superhighway will bring to an individual's desk the resources equivalent to what is available in the Library of Congress and other vast specialized databases. Advanced search-and-retrieval techniques make these resources easily accessible. You no longer need to wade through dozens or hundreds of sources when looking for information about a specific subject. All such information is available by means of a few keystrokes or by selecting a few entries from menus. When such services become commonplace in the home, classroom, and office, then learning about any topic will itself become an easier and more rewarding experience—the process is already well underway and it is possible that within a decade libraries themselves will become obsolete! See Figure 13.19.

Cost still remains a problem, however. Hardware, software, and connectivity expenses are decreasing over time, but educating large numbers of people is still expensive and adding computer-based training as a component is sometimes not practical.

THE OFFICE OF THE FUTURE Some of us have observed firsthand the dramatic changes that have occurred in the office environment during the past years. For example, typewriters and ledgers have been replaced by personal computers with word processing and with spreadsheet software. Sophisticated voice-mail systems, telephone equipment, and e-mail and groupware software permit office personnel greater latitude in communicating with their colleagues.

The office of the future is likely to be as different from today's office as the current office is from that of the past. Some of the changes predicted are:

- The number of employees who work at home, in the field, and on the road will increase. Wireless LANs already permit personal computers to communicate with an organization's databases from virtually anywhere.

- Multimedia brought to the desktop with video and audio capabilities will enable employees to obtain information from databases in more meaningful ways.

Figure 13.19 *CompuServe provides many methods for obtaining information from the Internet as well as many other databases.*

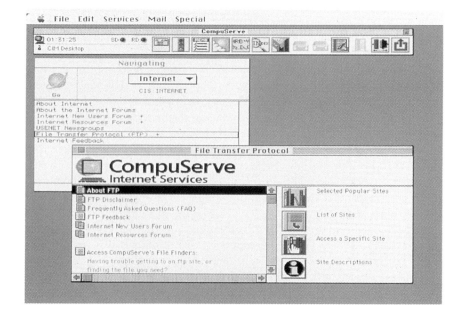

- Customized workstations will allow employees to create their own work environment, one that suits their individual needs and style.

- At meetings, notepads will be replaced by pen-based computers that will enable users to handwrite notes at the computer with the pen. Presentations will no longer be in the form of hard-copy reports; instead they will employ multimedia tools and will be available to all who need to view them via a computer.

- Computers themselves will not only be smaller but more natural. You will be able to talk to your computer in a normal voice and obtain either verbal or displayed responses—whichever you prefer. There will be fewer add-ons, because phones, modems, faxes, and so on, will be built in.

- The vast databases at an employee's disposal will soon be accessible using a more meaningful search-and-retrieval technique that will enable people to conveniently retrieve the precise information they desire. Such availability has already led us to become a more global society.

- Smart Messaging Services will integrate services currently available. Many people have access to e-mail over local-area networks or wide-area networks. Some have access to multiple e-mail facilities. If you use intra-office e-mail service, the Internet, and a separate online subscriber service, you might need to access all three and learn three different protocols to retrieve messages. Moreover, if you use wireless devices such as cellular phones, pagers, and personal digital assistants, you need to spend additional time responding to messages from these sources.

  Companies like IBM, AT&T, and Motorola offer "smart" messaging services that act as brokers linking LANs, WANs, cellular phones, PDAs, and pagers. With these services, you can link your communication devices so that all e-mail can be accessible through one routing system using one protocol.

One of the original objectives of bringing computers to the office was to eliminate paper documents or at least to minimize their use. But that goal has not yet been fully realized. Indeed, many office workers believe that far more paper is generated now than before. When people have a great deal of information at their fingertips, they are apt to want to capture it on paper. After all, children are still growing up with paper. Will they, as most adults nowadays do, still trust paper more than a flickering screen or a disk that cannot be read without a machine?

The pundits believe—or hope—that paper will be virtually nonexistent in the future. All mail will be received electronically as either text, verbal messages, or even video. Any documents that need a signature will be displayed on a screen, signed by means of a stylus, and operated on using image processing software; that is, the document will be displayed on a screen, you will add your signature by writing to the screen, and the signed document will be safely stored on an optical storage device.

The point is that a customized, paperless office could be achieved tomorrow *if* that became a major goal of organizations. At the moment, most of us still prefer the use of paper for some applications—banking, for instance. Because of personal preferences, the likelihood of becoming paperless in the near future is remote. The likelihood of becoming less paperbound is, however, much more feasible. Moreover, image processing systems are widely available to capture forms and other documents and store them on disks for easy access. This technology as well is likely to decrease the amount of paper generated in an office.

IN A NUTSHELL

Fifty percent of all office workers in the United States use a computer. Fifty percent of all PCs in the United States have access to a network.

▶ Looking Ahead

THE WELL-CONNECTED OFFICE

In the future, intelligent, bundled office machines will have integrated telephones, fax machines, photocopiers, color printers, and computers. These super machines will be linked to corporate databases as well as external databases, thereby providing access to enormous amounts of information.

Self-Test

1. What do we call the science of adapting machines and work environments to people?

2. (T or F) Numerous studies have demonstrated conclusively that there are no long-term biological effects of low-level radiation from video display terminals.

3. (T or F) Overall, more jobs have been generated by computers than have been eliminated by them.

4. (T or F) In general, businesses have been slow to accept the virtues of telecommuting as an alternative to working in an office.

5. (T or F) In general, most consumers view micros as essential devices for the home.

CHAPTER SUMMARY

The proliferation of information systems and computer networks has raised many issues about privacy and security that involve legal as well as ethical questions. In addition, sociological questions concerning the effects of computers on the quality of life in this Information Age must be addressed.

<table>
<tr><td>

Study Objective

1. Identify personal, legal, and ethical issues raised by the proliferation of information systems and computer networks.

</td></tr>
</table>

13.1 Protecting the Privacy of Users

As a result of the widespread development of information systems and computer networks, many legal issues have arisen that were neither anticipated nor addressed when various privacy laws were enacted. Consider, for example, privacy issues related to electronic mail. Currently, no federal law addresses the rights or obligations of e-mail users. State laws are vague with regard to liability if an individual's e-mail messages are intercepted. Because laws differ from state to state, an individual's rights can vary dramatically, depending on which state's laws apply if a lawsuit is brought.

The existence of large databases has raised other privacy concerns. Many organizations and government agencies maintain databases containing individual credit histories, income statements, criminal records, and so on. What rights does an individual have if, for example, hackers illegally gain access to financial databases and then sell the information to market research companies, telemarketing firms, or companies that buy mailing lists? Although laws have been enacted on the federal level to protect an individual's privacy, many of these laws are considered inadequate by privacy advocates.

<table>
<tr><td>

Study Objective

2. Justify the integral part that security must play in the development and use of information systems and computer networks.

</td></tr>
</table>

13.2 Making Information Systems and Networks More Secure

Businesses need security measures (1) to guard against computer crime, which can take the form of sabotage, espionage, and theft, and (2) to protect hardware, software, and data from natural disasters such as fire, flood, and earthquake.

Solutions

1. ergonomics

2. F—There has been no conclusive evidence to that effect.

3. T

4. T

5. F

Computer crime is difficult to detect and even more difficult to prevent. **Computer crimes** include (1) theft of computer time, (2) tampering with computer programs or data, (3) theft of data and assets, and (4) illegal copying of software. The prevalence of viruses makes it prudent for organizations as well as individuals to use **antiviral software** as a protection. To prevent software piracy or the making of unauthorized copies, software vendors sometimes sell copy-protected software. **Copy-protected software** means that the software cannot easily be copied to other disks, or can only be copied a limited number of times.

Organizations must take other precautions and institute controls to protect their hardware and software. Such measures include (1) controlling physical access to the computer system, (2) creating backup copies of data and software, (3) implementing network controls such as data encryption and callback systems, (4) separating and rotating functions among employees, and (5) using mechanisms for protection against natural disasters.

13.3 Making Information Systems More Socially Responsible

Study Objective

3. Describe how information systems networks affect the quality of life.

Ergonomics is the science of adapting machines and work environments to people. Ergonomically designed workplaces provide the best physical environment for people who use computers and other office technologies. Problems that are typically addressed include (1) reducing glare on video display terminals, (2) reducing sound pollution, (3) designing ergonomically sound workstations to reduce user fatigue and discomfort, and (4) reducing hazards to health.

Some organizations use monitoring devices and/or software to measure the productivity of employees. Critics of monitoring devices want legislation that will significantly limit electronic surveillance of employees.

The use of computers has raised some serious social issues. We must also consider, however, the areas where computers have already improved the quality of life for many people. When computers are used as tools for the disabled, for computer-based training, for providing in-home services, and for enhancing leisure time, they can indeed enhance one's quality of life.

KEY TERMS

Antiviral software, *p. 435*
Computer crime, *p. 434*
Copy-protected software, *p. 436*

CHAPTER SELF-TEST

1. (T or F) Most privacy advocates believe that existing federal laws adequately address privacy issues related to the proliferation of large databases.

2. (T or F) Computer crime is difficult to detect and even more difficult to prevent.

3. A _____ is a self-replicating computer code that is typically designed to destroy data and programs or cause other damage to a computer system.

4. Software vendors sometimes sell _____ software to prevent it from being copied to other disks or to limit the number of times that it can be copied.

5. (T or F) As a rule, prosecutors have had little difficulty in prosecuting computer criminals under existing criminal laws, even though these laws do not specifically address computer crime.

6. Creating _____, or making extra copies of programs or data, safeguards against the loss of programs or data.

7. _____ is the science of designing workplaces to provide the best physical environment for people who use computers and other technology.

8. (T or F) Telecommuting has the potential for reducing energy consumption and improving the quality of life.

9. (T or F) Computer-based training is most widely used for simple tutorials and self-tests of the drill-and-practice variety although multimedia systems are likely to change that in the future.

10. (T or F) Telecommuting enables people to work at home and still have access to their company's resources.

11. (T or F) The presence of computers in offices has led to the virtual elimination of paper documents.

12. (T or F) The lack of transmission standards has sometimes impeded the effectiveness of networks.

REVIEW QUESTIONS

1. Discuss major privacy issues that have resulted from the proliferation of large databases.

2. Why are detection and prosecution of computer crimes so difficult?

3. Discuss techniques that an organization can use to protect its hardware and software from computer crimes and natural disasters.

4. Discuss how computers help the handicapped.

5. It is illegal to make copies of licensed software. What can colleges and universities do to convince students that software piracy is wrong? What can colleges and universities do to minimize the practice on campus?

CRITICAL THINKING EXERCISES

1. Most U.S. manufacturers of computing devices are against the Clipper Chip because it adversely affects their ability to compete internationally. The Chip not

---

Solutions

1. F—Because the field of connectivity is new, there are few relevant laws.

2. T

3. virus

4. copy-protected

5. F—The lack of legal definitions for computerized information is a problem.

6. backups

7. Ergonomics

8. T

9. T

10. T

11. F—The paperless office has still not been attained.

12. T

only adds cost to a computing device but foreign customers would not want to purchase products that give the U.S. government the potential to access sensitive data. Do you think the Clipper Chip is a good idea?

2. Some people criticize the Electronic Frontier Foundation for accepting contributions from communications companies. They feel that this will compromise the EFF's ability to fight for an individual's civil liberties. What do you think?

3. The controversies concerning a person's first amendment rights have been both frequent and heated. Should pornographic material and discriminatory comments sent over networks be censored? Should individuals always be free to exchange views with one another the way they can over a telephone or by mail? Junk faxes and junk e-mail also pose a problem. Some users want legal protection from unsolicited messages over networks. What do you think?

4. Speakers at a recent computer conference in Sydney claimed that Australian schools have been faster to accept technological development than most other countries, especially the United States. What aspects of Australia's geographical location might make this so?

5. It is possible that, in the near future, the information superhighway could make local video stores obsolete. Telephone and cable companies are currently arranging to offer movies on demand so that customers can dial up what they want to see from a catalog of films. No longer interacting with a video store clerk may seem like an unimportant example of loss of interpersonal communications, but it may be part of a larger trend. Do you think it possible that connectivity could cut us off from one another?

Case Study

The Microsoft Home of the Future

In a tongue-in-cheek forecast of the computerized home of the future, writer Gil Schwartz suggests that all the potential needs and wants of twenty-first-century citizens will be anticipated—and met.

In this brave new world, in which Schwartz imagines that every product and service imaginable will be provided by a subsidiary of Microsoft, you can open the automatic gates to your Microhome with a remote radio-frequency mouse pointer installed in your own fingertip and double your garage space by pressing the Dblespace button next to the trash compression algorithm. Tiny microphones embedded everywhere in the house respond to your voice patterns, and the ROM database, which contains information about you and your family and resides in your basement, enables your home to conform itself to your comfort, automatically providing the kind of background music (or noise) you enjoy and adjusting the heating and cooling of your home to suit your preferences.

Every room houses a holographic communication and entertainment pod, and through the process of atomic realignment your cybernetic food preparation suite can offer you any dish ever created, instantly. You can feast on re-quarked record albums and packing crates, and when you're through just press the "clean up countertops" button

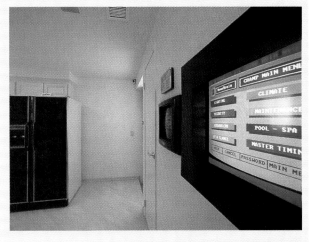

A computerized "smart" home.

on the order pad implanted in your wrist.

Instead of working, you can enjoy a full day of leisure every day, as long as you remember to respond to at least three interactive marketing and opinion polls daily. After that, you can access any book, magazine, newspaper, movie, or TV show in the world, like *Jurassic Park XIV* or a come-

(Continued)

back tour by a cryogenic Mick Jagger. You can even download the day's news directly into your brain where an upgradable chip has already been installed. When you feel the need for fresh air you can stroll outside for a sampling of chemically reozonated atmosphere and some "ice cream" and maybe watch the stars come out above the Great Federal Superdome. At day's end, you and your significant other can relax in your sleep chamber, enjoy a little virtual-reality lovemaking, and drift off into the dreams of your choice while your video ceiling panel displays a calming screen saver.

All this can be yours, says Schwartz, if you have the money to pay for it, and if you want it. Do you?

Analysis

1. What aspects of the Microsoft home of the future have real potential to improve the quality of life?

2. What aspects of the Microsoft home of the future could negatively impact society?

APPENDIX

An Overview of the History of Computing

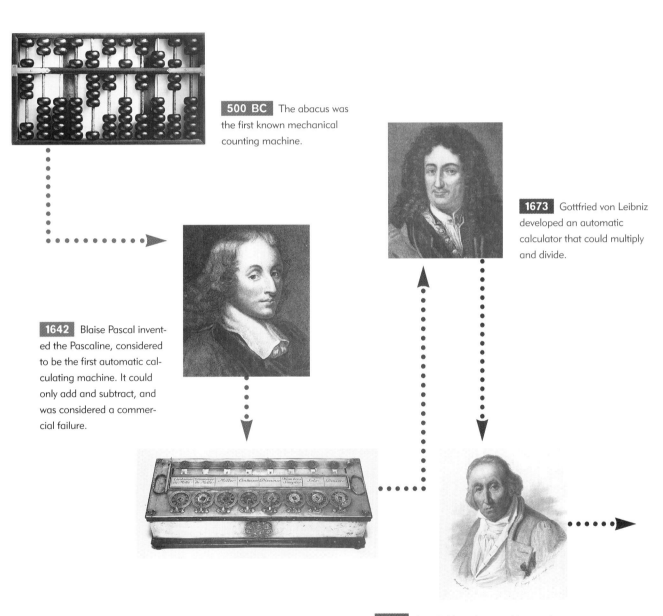

500 BC The abacus was the first known mechanical counting machine.

1642 Blaise Pascal invented the Pascaline, considered to be the first automatic calculating machine. It could only add and subtract, and was considered a commercial failure.

1673 Gottfried von Leibniz developed an automatic calculator that could multiply and divide.

1804 Joseph-Marie Jacquard invented a punched-card loom attachment that revolutionized the French silk-weaving industry by automating the process of entering input data. The principles used in Jacquard's loom were later applied to many computing devices.

1822 Charles Babbage began work on his Differential Engine, abandoned it, and then conceived the idea of an Analytical Engine, which, in principle, contained concepts now found in modern computers.

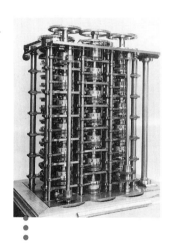

1884 Herman Hollerith, a statistician with the U.S. Census Bureau, introduced his electromechanical punched-card system to compile the 1890 census. Hollerith's company grew and merged with other companies, and eventually became the International Business Machines Company (IBM).

1833 Augusta Ada, Countess of Lovelace and daughter of the poet Lord Byron, worked closely with Babbage to show that it was possible to program the Analytical Engine with a single set of cards that specified a series of instructions.

1939 John Atanasoff and Clifford Berry designed a prototype for their ABC (Atanasoff Berry Computer), which was intended to be a special-purpose electronic digital computer.

1951 The UNIVAC, the first commercially available stored-program, electronic digital computer, was developed by John Mauchly and J. Presper Eckert.

1943 John Mauchly and J. Presper Eckert began work on the ENIAC, the first operational general-purpose electronic digital computer. It was completed in 1946.

1946 The concept for a stored program computer was introduced by John von Neumann and his associates.

```
STATEMENT
NUMBER
1 2 3 4 5 6 7 8 9 10 11 12 13 14 15 16 17 18 19 20 21 22
C       LINEAR REGRESSIO
        READ (2,2) N,XES
      2 FORMAT (I5,F10.5
        XSUM=0.0
        YSUM=0.0
        XXSUM=0.0
        XYSUM=0.0
        DO 6 I=1,N
        READ (2,4)X,Y
      4 FORMAT (2F10.5)
        XSUM=XSUM+X
        YSUM=YSUM+Y
```

1957 Fortran, the first high-level programming language for scientists and engineers, was introduced by IBM.

```
INPUT "ENTER THE EMPLOYEE'S NAME"; NAMES
INPUT "ENTER THE HOURS WORKED"; HOURS
INPUT "ENTER THE PAY RATE"; PAYRATE
REM
REM CALCULATE GROSS PAY
LET GROSSPAY = HOURS * PAYRATE
REM
REM PRINT RESULTS
PRINT "EMPLOYEE NAME:        "; NAME$
PRINT "HOURS WORKED:         "; HOURS
PRINT "PAY RATE:             "; PAYRATE
PRINT "GROSS PAY             "; GROSSPAY
END
```

1964 BASIC programming was introduced at Dartmouth College by Thomas Kurtz and John Kemeny.

1964 Control Data Corporation introduced the first supercomputer, the CDC 6600.

1967 MacHack, a program written at MIT, was the first to play chess so successfully it could enter tournaments and win at the novice level.

1971 The first expert system, DENDRAL, was completed. It was used as an "expert" chemist to determine the structure of molecular compounds.

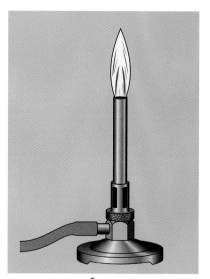

1965 The first commercially available minicomputer, the PDP-8, was introduced by the Digital Equipment Corporation.

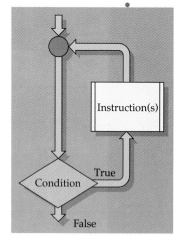

1968 Edsger Dijsktra introduced the concept of structured programming, which became a standard for third-generation languages.

1971 Intel introduced its first microprocessor chip, developed by Ted Hoff.

1977 The Apple II computer was introduced. It was developed by Stephen Wozniak (left) and Stephen Jobs (right).

1975 Bill Gates and Paul Allen establish the Microsoft Corporation. Gates (pictured here) is currently chairman of the board of Microsoft.

1980 The now defunct Ashton-Tate, developer of dBase, the most popular database management system for PCs, was founded.

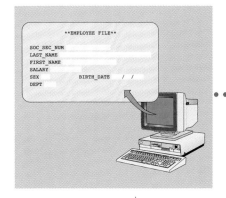

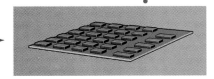

1974 Intel announced its microprocessor, later used in the original IBM computers and their compatibles.

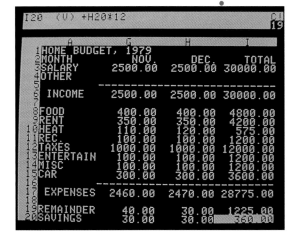

1979 VisiCalc introduced the first commercial spreadsheet program designed for inexperienced users of PCs. Its success helped to drive the PC market to greater heights.

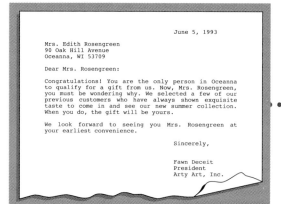

```
                                        June 5, 1993

Mrs. Edith Rosengreen
90 Oak Hill Avenue
Oceanna, WI 53709

Dear Mrs. Rosengreen:

Congratulations! You are the only person in Oceanna
to qualify for a gift from us. Now, Mrs. Rosengreen,
you must be wondering why. We selected a few of our
previous customers who have always shown exquisite
taste to come in and see our new summer collection.
When you do, the gift will be yours.

We look forward to seeing you Mrs. Rosengreen at
your earliest convenience.

                                        Sincerely,

                                        Fawn Deceit
                                        President
                                        Arty Art, Inc.
```

1982 WordPerfect announced its word processing package, which became the biggest selling package of its kind.

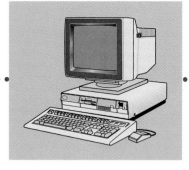

1980 The installed base of micro-computers reached 700,000—one year before the IBM PC was introduced.

1980 WordStar shipped its first word processing package. Productivity tools made it to the top in 1980.

1982 Compaq Inc. was founded. Their original luggables proved that PCs did not have to be desktop—or IBM!

1982 Hayes brought the 300 bps smart modem to the PC market, and it became an instant success.

1981 The IBM PC was introduced and quickly made it to the top of the microcom-puter market and, with it, Microsoft's DOS operating system.

1982 The breakup of AT&T created a new market for corporate networks by making it feasible for companies to create their own wide area communication networks.

1983 IBM PC Jr. was introduced for the home market. It became that company's Edsel and died in 1985.

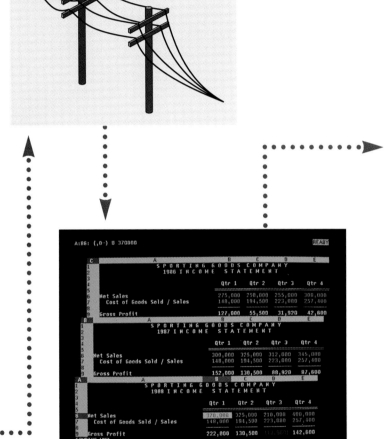

1983 Lotus Development Corporation was founded. Their spreadsheet software, which cost $340,000 to develop, became the best-selling program for the PC.

1984 IBM AT was introduced. Operating at 8 MHz, this 80286 16-bit computer ushered in the next generation of micros. In that same year, Apple unveiled the Macintosh (pictured above).

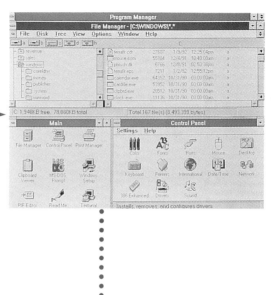

1985 The first Windows graphical user interface was introduced by Microsoft.

1984 Hewlett-Packard introduced the laser jet printer for PCs, which produced high-resolution output without the noise of an impact printer.

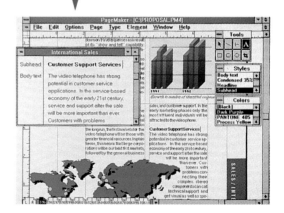

1985 Desktop publishing had a banner year, with the new Aldus PageMaker at the forefront.

1985 The 80386 chip was introduced but did not appear in a computer until a year later.

1986 Compaq beat IBM to the market with the first 80386 computer.

1987 IBM and Microsoft announced the OS/2 operating system.

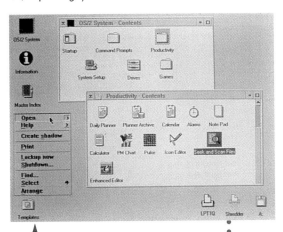

1988 A new category of smaller notebook PCs, led by NEC's 4.4 pound UltraLite, appeared.

1987 IBM replaced the original PCs with the PS/2 Line.

1988 The first million-transistor microprocessor was introduced by Intel for the RISC (reduced instruction set computer) device. It became the technology standard for workstations.

1990 The 10-year partnership between IBM and Microsoft began to fall apart as Microsoft promoted Windows for DOS and IBM promoted its OS/2 operating system.

1990 80486 computers became the models to beat.

1992 The Pentium computer was announced; CD-ROMs became a popular storage medium; object-oriented programming grew dramatically; and multimedia standards were set.

1991 IBM and Apple agreed to share technology and develop software and hardware platforms together.

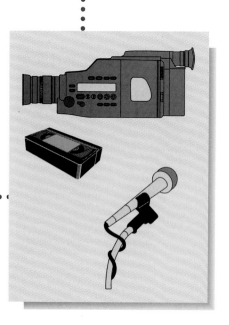

1989 Multimedia was highly touted but it took years to catch on, because software and hardware products initially were very expensive, and development costs were high.

1993 Multimedia hardware and software for creating and running presentations, tutorials and games with sound, video, and animation became a priority with most PC users.

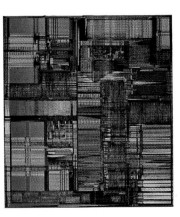

1995 The Power PC which can run Mac and IBM-compatible software, along with fast, Pentium-based IBM-compatibles became the market leaders in 1995.

1994 The number of users of the Internet and subscriber services such as America Online, CompuServe, and Prodigy exceeded 30 million.

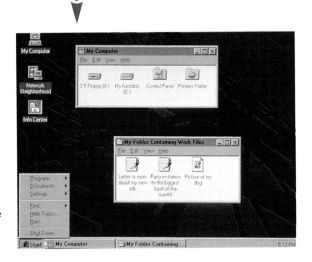

1995 Windows 95 becomes the leading operating system for IBM-compatibles.

GLOSSARY

The terms here include those in the key terms lists at the end of each chapter as well as other computer-related terms discussed in the text.

Absolute addressing Copying a cell address in a spreadsheet formula so that it remains constant in every new location in which the formula appears; contrast with relative addressing.

Access rate Measures the time needed to locate data on a secondary storage device; typically measured in thousandths of a second.

Acoustic coupler Type of modem that has two cups into which a telephone handset is placed to transmit and receive computer data.

Ada Third-generation programming language that uses the structured concepts first used in Pascal; an extremely powerful and sophisticated language specifically designed for real-time and embedded systems.

Address register Temporary storage in the control unit of the CPU that holds the main memory address of (1) data to be processed or (2) the next instruction to be executed.

Analog signal Signal in the form of electronic waves that is often transmitted over telephone lines.

Antiviral software Programs designed to detect and disable viruses.

Application A specific use of a computer such as for payroll or inventory.

Application generator Software that generates application programs from descriptions of the problem and the processing required.

Application package Type of prewritten software designed for business or personal use that can be purchased off-the-shelf.

Application programmer Computer professional who writes, debugs, and documents programs for specific business tasks.

Application software Any program designed to satisfy a user need.

Architecture The technology used in a computer for processing data.

Arithmetic/logic unit (ALU) Part of the CPU that performs arithmetic and comparison operations.

Artificial intelligence Simulated human decision making by means of a computer.

ASCII Acronym for *American Standard Code for Information Interchange*; the computer code widely used by micros and for data communications, where each byte consists of 7 or 8 bits.

Assembler Program for translating an assembly program into machine language.

Assembly language Second generation programming language that uses symbolic instruction codes and symbolic names for storage areas; it is a programming language that is most machinelike and least user-friendly.

Association for Computing Machinery (ACM) A society for computer science professionals.

Asynchronous transmission Type of transmission in which one character at a time is transmitted over communications channels.

Audio response unit Output device that provides verbal responses which simulate the human voice; the output actually consists of prerecorded messages or phrases.

Audit trail Printout that lists all changes made to a file; produced for checking or control purposes.

Automated design tool A technique for analyzing and developing information systems.

Automatic teller machine (ATM) Interactive input/output device in which data entered at the point of transaction can either automatically and immediately update banking records in an online operation or store the transaction and update banking records later in batch mode.

Auxiliary storage Same as secondary storage.

Backup A copy of secondary storage files that is maintained in case something happens to the original.

Band printer Type of line printer that uses a flexible, stainless-steel print band that is photoengraved with print characters.

Bandwidth Transmission capacity of a computer or communications channel, measured in bits per second.

Bar code reader Device that reads or scans either the Universal Product Code on merchandise or other types of bar codes and transmits the data as input to a computer.

Baseband Communication technique in which data is transmitted over only one communications channel at medium speed.

BASIC Acronym for *Beginner's All-purpose Symbolic Instruction Code*; an easy-to-learn third-generation programming language.

Batch processing Type of processing in which input is read at fixed intervals as a file and operated on all at once; contrast with interactive processing in which input is operated on as soon as it is transacted.

Baud rate Speed at which data is transmitted over communications lines; it is commonly expressed in bits per second (bps).

Benchmark test Performance test that compares the capabilities of various computer devices.

Binary numbering system Numbering system in which there are only two possible digits: 0 and 1. Digital computers use binary codes to represent letters, digits, or special symbols.

Bit Short for binary digit—a single on- or off-state signal; characters are represented in a computer by 7- or 8-bit codes.

Bit-mapped graphics Graphic images created by painting and other programs in which the images consist of patterns of dots. Contrast with vector graphics.

Bits per inch (bpi) A measure of the density of data recorded on a magnetic disk or tape.

Bits per second (bps) Speed at which information is transmitted over communications lines.

Block Section of a data file that can be moved, copied, or placed anywhere in the same file or in a different one.

Blocking Process whereby records are placed as a unit or block on a disk or tape to make more effective use of the physical space on that disk or tape.

Boilerplating Word processing feature in which a section or block of a standard text can be used in many documents.

Bootlegging of software Making an unauthorized version of a program.

Break-even analysis Cost study that indicates when a new system design will start to be cost-effective.

Bridge Interface for connecting similar networks.

Broadband Communication technique in which data, voice, and video transmission can be transmitted at high speed along numerous channels.

Bubble memory *See* magnetic bubble memory.

Budgetary constraints Limits imposed on the time and money allocated to a business system.

Buffer Temporary print area where a queue of files to be printed is placed so that they can be printed while other processing is being performed.

Bulletin board system Service that enables people with PCs and modems to communicate with one another.

Bundled software Programs supplied along with the hardware by the manufacturer or vendor as part of a package.

Bus Special electronic path that carries data between the control unit, arithmetic/logic unit, and main memory.

Bus configuration Type of network topology in which each node can access not only the host computer but every other node as well.

Business system Integration of tasks and procedures in each functional business area.

Byte One storage position in main or secondary storage used to store a letter, digit, or symbol.

C Third-generation programming language that incorporates the advantages of both assembly language and high-level languages; the UNIX operating system was written in C.

C++ An object-oriented version of C.

Cache memory Type of memory that can double the speed of a computer; it stores and retrieves the most frequently used data in readily accessible form.

Callback system Security method to ensure that a user on a phone line is calling from an authorized telephone number.

CASE tool Acronym for *C*omputer *A*ssisted *S*oftware *E*ngineering; a systems analysis and design productivity tool for building information systems.

Case-insensitive program A program in which you can type commands or instructions using either uppercase or lowercase letters and get the same results.

Cathode ray tube (CRT) The most common type of screen or monitor used to display instructions and computer responses; can be either monochrome or color.

CD-ROM (compact disk read-only memory) Type of storage medium that uses the same technology as audio CDs. CD-ROMs cannot be written to—they can only be read. The disks are suitable for storing large amounts of fixed data (680+ MB) for frequent reference.

Cell Intersection of a row and column in a spreadsheet program.

Central processing unit (CPU) Part of the computer system that controls all computer operations.

Centralized processing A single computer facility that serves all or most of the computing needs of an organization.

Chain printer Type of line printer that uses characters linked together on a chain as its print mechanism. The chain spins horizontally around a set of hammers and when the desired character is in front of the selected print position, the corresponding hammer strikes the paper into the ribbon.

Character A unit of data consisting of a single letter, digit, or special symbol.

Chip Integrated circuit that can hold millions of electronic components.

Client-server computing One method of using a LAN in which a file server does as much processing as possible before downloading to nodes.

Clip art Database of graphic displays that can be added to documents.

Clock speed Rate at which a computer can process data, as determined by the CPU's clock; in micros, it is measured in megahertz (MHz).

Coaxial cable A cable used for hardwired communications channels because it can carry large amounts of data.

COBOL Acronym for *CO*mmon *B*usiness *O*riented *L*anguage; a third-generation business-oriented programming language that is machine independent, relatively easy to maintain, and English-like.

Command Instruction given to an operating system or application package.

Common carrier A company that furnishes communication services to the general public.

Communications channel Linkage between nodes and/or hosts in a network.

Compiler Program for translating a source program into an object program. Compiling is a separate step that is completed before a program is run on the computer.

Compression Technique for storing files so that they require less storage space on disk.

Computer-aided design (CAD) Highly sophisticated drawing technique whereby engineers and architects use software to create complex drawings.

Computer-aided manufacturing (CAM) Technique whereby engineers use software to design the manufacturing components in a factory or production facility.

Computer crime Use of a computer to steal, embezzle, or defraud.

Computer literate Being aware of computers, how they operate, and how they are used for personal and business purposes.

Computer system Group of devices that reads data, processes it, and produces information.

Configure To specially equip a computer system so that it includes components or devices designed to meet specific needs.

Connectivity Concept that enables different computer systems along with other technologies to interact with one another.

Context-sensitive help A level of on-screen help in which the displays pertain specifically to what is currently being done in an application.

Continuous-form paper Printed paper with small holes on either side that allow it to be fed through the printer without interruption.

Control listing Printout listing all changes made to a file; produced for checking purposes.

Controls Actions taken to minimize errors; they include techniques for verifying that data entered is correct.

Control unit Component of the computer's CPU that monitors the operations performed by the entire system.

Coprocessor Special chip that can be added to, or built into, microcomputers to speed up certain kinds of operations; for example, a math coprocessor speeds up the processing of mathematical operations for applications such as statistical analysis.

Copy protection Preparing software in such a way that the programs cannot be copied to other disks or can only be copied a limited number of times; copy protection is designed to prevent bootlegging.

Cost-benefit analysis Study that compares the cost of an existing system to the cost of a proposed system.

CPU *See* central processing unit.

Cursor Small blinking underline or rectangle that indicates where your input will actually appear on the screen.

Cursor control keys Keys on a terminal or microcomputer keyboard with arrows pointing in four directions; the arrows are used for positioning the cursor on the screen.

Custom program A set of instructions designed to meet the specific needs of users; it is written by a programmer within an organization or by an outside consultant.

Cutting and pasting Technique for moving, copying, or deleting blocks of text; first you define a block of text so that it can be "pasted" to another place.

Daisywheel printer Type of impact printer that prints fully formed characters from a flat disk that has petal-like projections containing individual characters.

Data Raw facts to be processed by a computer.

Data definition language (DDL) Set of technical specifications for a database's fields and the relationships among data in the database.

Data dictionary Descriptions of fields, records, and files in a database and the relationships among them.

Data encryption Encoding data so that it cannot be understood unless it is first decoded; used to protect data from unauthorized access.

Data file Collection of records in a specific application area.

Data flow diagram Tool used by analysts to depict an existing information system or one that is being developed; emphasis is placed on where data originates and where it goes during and after processing.

Data integrity The need to keep databases from being corrupted by input or programming errors or by deliberate attempts to tamper with the data.

Data manipulation language (DML) Computer language that is typically a proprietary part of a database management package and that allows users to create custom-designed applications. Query languages are types of data manipulation languages.

Data Processing Management Association (DPMA) A society for business computer professionals.

Database Collection of related files that are stored electronically and can be linked, joined, or cross-referenced.

Database administrator Individual responsible for organizing, designing, and maintaining the database and all other data used by the organization.

Database file Collection of data in a specific application area; database files can be linked or joined for reporting purposes or for providing responses to inquiries.

Database management system (DBMS) Software used to create, edit, and update database files and to inquire about the status of records in those files.

Debit card A form of bank card that is used for payment transactions. The instant you make a purchase with your debit card, the money is extracted from your bank account and placed in the bank account of the seller.

Debugging Finding and correcting all logic and coding errors, or "bugs," in a program.

Decentralized processing Computer facility in which each business department within a company has its own computer system intended to accomplish its goals more directly.

Decision support system (DSS) Flexible management information system that allows managers to access corporate and other databases and to create their own reports and applications, even their own specialized databases. Such systems are used by managers to help them make decisions.

Default Standard setting or assumption made by a software package; default settings can be changed by users if the need arises.

Density Number of characters that can be represented in an inch of disk or tape.

Desk-checking Process in which a programmer manually traces through a program visually checking for syntax errors.

Desktop accessory A program that performs a function usually associated with an object found on a desktop. Such accessories include a calendar, calculator, and clock. Windows comes with a variety of desktop accessories.

Desktop computer The most widely used type of PC in business; typically, it is a single-user device.

Desktop publishing Software tools offering advanced capabilities that allow users to do page design for publications such as newsletters, magazines, and books.

Device driver A piece of software that expands an operating system's ability to work with peripherals.

Digital audio tape (DAT) Type of tape that can store a large amount of data very compactly.

Digital computer Electronic computer that processes data in discrete form as on-off electronic pulses.

Digital signal Signal in the form of an on-off electronic pulse.

Digital video interaction (DVI) Technique for compressing video images so that they can be stored more compactly for computer processing.

Digitizer tablet Input device for converting illustrations into digital form.

Direct-connect modem Type of modem built into a computer or directly attached to it by cable.

Direct conversion Method of converting from an old information system to a new one in which the company simply stops using the old system and immediately begins using the new system (no overlap).

Direct file Method of database organization in which a key field itself is used to calculate each record's address, thereby eliminating the need to look for the record in an index.

Disk Type of secondary storage in which data is recorded as magnetized bits and is randomly accessible at high speeds.

Disk cartridge Storage medium that combines the advantages of both diskettes and hard disks; cartridges are portable like diskettes yet store as much data as some hard drives.

Disk drive Device that gives the CPU access to programs and data stored on disks; widely used for secondary storage.

Disk organizer Application package that enables users to manage data and program files on their disks.

Disk pack Older type of disk used for some midrange and mainframe computers; consists of removable sets of hard disks.

Diskette *See* floppy disk.

Distance learning The use of video, audio equipment, and computers in education so that students in remote locations can attend courses given at a central site.

Distributed processing Integrated computer facility that allows individual users within a business to process data locally and to communicate with a central computer in the company; combines the advantages of centralized and decentralized environments while minimizing their disadvantages.

Document Letter, report, or other text produced with a word processing package.

Document viewer A program that enables users to read any document, regardless of the program or platform used to create it.

Documentation package A set of manuals that details the procedures and techniques used in a new information system as well as the technical specifications of the hardware and software.

DOS The operating system for IBM micros and their compatibles. *See* PC-DOS and MS-DOS.

Dot-matrix printer Impact printer that creates characters using a rectangular grid of pins which press against a carbon ribbon to print on paper.

Download To copy files maintained by the host to remote or local nodes, which are typically microcomputers.

Downsizing Strategic plan in which applications are moved from large computers to smaller ones.

Drum printer Type of line printer that uses a cylindrical steel drum embossed with print characters to generate output.

E-mail *See* electronic mail.

EBCDIC Acronym for *Extended Binary Coded Decimal Interchange Code* (pronounced *eb-c-dick*). The standard 8-bit computer code for most IBM and IBM-compatible mainframes.

EEPROM Acronym for *electronically erasable programmable read-only memory*. A ROM chip that allows program information to be changed by software without removing the chips from the computer.

Electroluminescent (EL) display Type of flat-screen technology used in display screens that do not depend on cathode ray tubes; often used in laptop computers.

Electronic mail (e-mail) Productivity tool that enables users to electronically send, store, and retrieve messages that would otherwise be delivered verbally or by mail.

Electronic spreadsheet Software productivity tool that uses a row-and-column format for storing data and performing calculations; any data that can be displayed in row-and-column format, like ledger sheets used by accountants, can be prepared with this tool.

Embedded system Computers built into other systems, such as those in a video cassette recorder or on an airplane.

Encryption *See* data encryption.

EPROM Acronym for *erasable programmable read-only memory*. A ROM chip that must be removed from the computer if reprogramming is desired; a special process is required to erase old programs from EPROM chips.

Equipment constraints Limits on the type of computer hardware and other devices that can be used by a business system.

Ergonomics Science of adapting machines and work environments to people.

Ethernet A local area network used for connecting computer devices, typically within the same building. Ethernet operates over twisted pair and coaxial cable at speeds up to 10 million bits per second.

Even parity Method of verifying the accurate transmittal of data by checking to ensure that an even number of bits in a byte are always in the on state at any given time. Some computers use even parity and others use odd parity.

Exception report Report that calls attention to unusual situations in which certain predefined conditions occur.

Execution cycle CPU processing time during which instructions are executed and results produced.

Executive information system (EIS) Specialized form of decision-support system that requires no expertise on the part of the user and is often designed around the information needs of a single executive.

Expansion slot Receptacle on the main circuit board in which add-on units can be inserted.

Expert system Software that simulates the knowledge and analytical ability of an expert in a specific field; helps users make decisions.

Facsimile (fax) machine Machine that scans documents and transmits them to either computers or other fax machines.

Fax board Board that captures documents or screen displays stored by the computer and transmits them via a modem either to another computer with a modem or to a fax machine.

Feasibility study Study undertaken to determine if a new systems design is possible given current constraints.

Feedback Process of periodically evaluating a system to determine how well it meets user needs.

Fiber optic cable Communications channel using light impulses that travel through clear flexible tubing half the size of a human hair to transmit data at very high speeds with few or no errors.

Field Unit of information contained in a record (e.g., Social Security number or name).

Fifth-generation language (5GL) Nonprocedural programming language for querying databases or developing expert systems; typically uses artificial intelligence techniques.

File Collection of related records.

File allocation table (FAT) Table on a disk that keeps track of the disk address of each file; permits fast access of files on a disk.

File conversion Process of creating computerized files as part of implementing a new system.

File extension One to three characters added to a filename that helps to identify it; for example, Lotus for Windows files are automatically given a WK4 file extension so that they are easily identified as worksheet files.

File management system Set of programs for storing simple data, such as a personal address book in which one file need not be linked in any way to data in another file. Also called a file manager.

Filename Name given to a file; it is typically from one to eight characters long. Windows 95, OS/2, and the Macintosh operating system permit longer names.

File server Special host computer that makes programs and data available to nodes on a network.

Financial planning language (FPL) Fourth-generation programming language that uses sophisticated mathematical, statistical, and forecasting methods for analyzing data.

Firmware Read-only memory chips that contain permanent, nonvolatile instructions.

First-generation language Another name for machine language; it was the earliest type of programming language developed.

Fixed disk Another term for a hard disk.

Fixed-head disk drive Storage device that contains one or more hard disks and stationary access arms with separate read/write mechanisms for each of the tracks on the disks.

Flash card Credit card–sized memory card that fits into a slot of some portable computers; used in place of disks in very small computers.

Flat file A file that cannot be linked or joined to another file.

Flat-screen technology Technology such as liquid crystal display, electroluminescent display or gas plasma that is used in a display screen instead of a cathode ray tube; often used in laptop computers.

Floppy disk Portable disk on which data is stored; most commonly found in 5¼-inch and 3½-inch diameters; same as a diskette.

Flowchart Pictorial representation of the logic flow in a program or a system; illustrates major elements and how they are logically integrated.

FORTRAN Acronym for *FORmula TRANslator*; a third-generation programming language best suited for scientific and engineering applications.

Fourth-generation language (4GL) An easy-to-write, nonprocedural programming language that simply states the needed output using English-like terms without specifying each step required to obtain that output.

Friction feed mechanism Print mechanism that moves paper through a printer by pressure between the paper and the carriage.

Front-end processor Microcomputer or minicomputer that helps offload the activities performed by a host computer so that it can run more efficiently.

Full-duplex line Communications channel that permits data to move in both directions at the same time (e.g., a telephone line).

Function key Any one of the keys numbered F1 through F10 or F1 through F12 on a microcomputer; each key typically performs a specific operation depending on the software package being used.

Gas-plasma display Form of flat screen technology for laptop computers that sandwiches a neon/argon gas mixture with grids of vertical and horizontal wires.

Gateway Hardware that connects small local area networks to mainframes or wide area networks.

Gigabyte (GB) One billion storage positions in main memory or auxiliary storage.

Graphics software Programs with tools for drawing, charting, and presenting graphics and illustrations.

Groupware Software that is used to serve a group of users working on a related project.

Hacker Computer user who illegally or unethically accesses a computer system.

Half-duplex line Communications channel that permits data to move in two directions, but not at the same time, like a CB radio.

Hard copy Output that is printed on paper.

Hard disk Rigid disk mounted permanently in a disk drive for storing data; can typically store hundreds of millions of bytes or more.

Hard disk drive Storage device that can typically store hundreds of millions of characters or more.

Hardware Set of devices that perform information-processing functions.

Head crash Loss of all data on a hard disk when a read/write head collides with a disk recording surface.

Hierarchical database Database organized like an upside-down tree with the root, or main segment, at the top in a one-to-many, or parent-child, relationship. Each data item or group of data items shown in the tree diagram is called a segment.

Hierarchy chart Program planning tool that graphically illustrates how programs are segmented into subprograms, or modules, and how the modules relate to one another.

High-definition television (HDTV) High-quality TV and sound system that can be used for converting TVs into interactive computers by bringing many services and information resources into the home.

High-level language A symbolic programming language that is similar to English, such as COBOL or BASIC; third-generation languages are high-level languages.

Host computer Central processor in a network.

Hyperlinking The linking in a multimedia package of sections and components such as text, graphics, animation, sound, and video.

Hypermedia Multimedia objects such as sound and video clips that can be hyperlinked.

IBM-compatible A PC based on the original IBM PC architecture.

Icon Graphic symbol displayed on a video screen representing files or commands that a user can select.

Illustration package Painting or drawing software.

Image processing system System whereby software and hardware input actual images of documents, store them, and retrieve them when needed.

Impact printer Printer that uses some form of strike-on method, as a typewriter uses, to press a carbon or fabric ribbon against paper.

Importing data Copying files or portions of files into other files that may have been created using different programs.

Incompatibility Situation in which hardware or software produced for one computer system cannot be used with another system.

Index File that contains two lists: the disk address of each record in the main file and the corresponding key field for that record.

Indexed file File that uses a method of organization in which data is created along with an index which keeps track of the physical location on disk of each record; the most common method of file organization when records need to be accessed randomly.

Inference engine In an expert system, the software that examines facts and rules to draw conclusions.

Information Data that is processed or operated on by a computer.

Information processing Set of procedures for operating on data and producing meaningful information.

Information superhighway An integrated network that will someday enable everyone to access databases and send and receive e-mail.

Information system System that uses computers to improve the efficiency of existing business operations.

Inheritance A feature of object-oriented programming where objects within a class share the same attributes.

Ink-jet printer Type of nonimpact printer in which tiny dots are shot onto paper to form characters; well suited for graphics applications.

Input Incoming data read by computers.

Input device Component of a computer system that accepts data from the user (e.g., a keyboard or mouse).

Insert mode Mode available with software packages so that when you are editing text you can add characters rather than replace them.

Institute for the Certification of Computer Professionals (ICCP) Organization that certifies computer professionals.

Instruction cycle CPU processing time during which the control unit fetches an instruction from primary storage and prepares it for processing.

Instruction register Temporary storage location within the CPU for processing data.

Integrated circuit A chip that can hold millions of electronic components.

Integrated package Software that combines the features of the four productivity tools (word processing, spreadsheet, database management system, e-mail) into a single package so that users need to learn only one common interface and so that they can easily move from one application to another.

Integrated Services Digital Network (ISDN) An international standard for the transmission of both voice and data over communications lines.

Interactive debugger A feature of some compilers that enables programmers to easily debug programs online.

Interactive processing Immediate processing of data as soon as it is transacted.

Internet A computer network that enables users within governments, academic institutions, and businesses to (1) send messages around the world to each other and (2) access a variety of databases.

Interpreter Translator program that converts instructions written in a high-level language into machine language one statement at a time as the program is being run on the computer.

Iteration One of the four logic structures in programming in which a program executes a series of steps repeatedly. Also called a looping structure.

Joy stick Device used to position a cursor (similar to a mouse); minimizes the need for keyboarding.

Jukebox Device that can make available a number of optical disks.

Justification Ability of a word processing package to align both left and right margins.

Kernel Part of the operating system that manages the computer's resources including the CPU, primary storage, and peripheral devices; also called the supervisor.

Keyboard Common input device for entering data and instructions; similar to a typewriter.

Key field A main field that uniquely identifies each record and that is used to create an index for fast, random-access retrieval of records.

Kilobyte (K) Approximately 1,000 storage positions (actually 1,024 bytes) in main memory or auxiliary storage.

Knowledge base Part of an expert system that translates the knowledge from human experts into rules and strategies.

Knowledge engineer Computer professional who creates a knowledge base in an expert system.

Laptop computer Portable computer weighing 11 pounds or less.

Laser printer Nonimpact printer that produces high-quality output.

Legal constraints Limits on the design of an information system due to legal requirements, such as compliance with the rules for Social Security payroll deductions.

Letter-quality printer Printer capable of high-quality output. Each letter is composed of solid lines, just like typewriter output. Contrast with dot-matrix printer.

Light pen Special device that uses a light-sensing mechanism to transmit signals to a computer; typically used for selecting items from a menu.

Line printer Type of impact printer that prints an entire line at a time. These include band printers, chain printers, drum printers, and dot-matrix printers.

Linkage editor Utility program that links an object program to a computer so that it is ready to run.

Liquid crystal display (LCD) Type of flat screen in which a current runs through liquid crystals sandwiched between two sheets of polarized material.

Local area network (LAN) System of connecting devices that are in relatively close proximity to one another.

Logic error Mistake in a program that occurs because instructions are not sequenced properly or because the wrong instructions are used.

Longitudinal parity Method of verifying the accurate transmission of data in which a check byte is added to the end of each record; each bit of the check byte is used to preserve the appropriate parity of each bit position in each byte of the record.

Looping One of the four logic structures in programming in which a program executes a series of steps repeatedly. Also called an iteration structure.

Machine cycle The time during which the processing of a single instruction occurs.

Machine language Computer's own internal language; all programs must be in machine language to be executed.

Macintosh operating system A user-friendly operating system that uses windows and icons for selecting commands and processing data in a multitasking environment.

Macro Collection of instructions that can be executed as one unit to facilitate the processing of data.

Magnetic bubble memory Type of memory frequently used in addition to, or in place of, integrated circuits because it is nonvolatile; information is stored in a magnetic film as a pattern of oppositely directed magnetic fields.

Magnetic ink character reader (MICR) Device used by banks to read or scan the magnetic ink digits and symbols printed at the bottom of checks.

Magneto-optical (MO) disk Erasable compact disk that makes use of combined optical and magnetic technologies; can store hundreds of megabytes of data.

Mail merge A word processor feature that allows letters and a name and address file to be linked so that the letters are personalized.

Mainframe First computer used in business; widely used as a host or central computer in mid-sized and large companies.

Main memory Another term for primary storage; used for storing programs and data.

Maintenance programmer Computer professional who modifies existing programs to ensure that they are current and working efficiently.

Management information system (MIS) Information system designed to integrate the information needs of the entire organization, beginning at the top, with the companywide goals set by high-level managers.

Master file Main collection of records relating to a specific application area.

Megabyte (MB) Approximately 1 million storage positions in main memory or auxiliary storage.

Megahertz A measurement of a computer's speed equal to a million ticks of a computer's clock; in general, the more megahertz per second, the faster the computer.

Memory board Extra memory that fits on a main circuit board; used to enhance a computer's primary storage.

Memory management A component of systems software that allocates and controls the effective use of a computer's memory.

Menu List of choices displayed on the screen from which required operations can be selected.

Microcomputer Smallest and least expensive type of computer system; used mainly by one individual at a time.

Microjustification Feature of word processing packages that pro-

duces automatic adjustment of spacing between characters on a line so that the text has flush right and left margins.

Microprocessor The CPU of a PC along with main memory and other components; typically contained on a single board.

Microsecond One millionth of a second.

Midrange computer Same as a minicomputer.

Millions of instructions per second (MIPS) Measurement of a computer processor's speed.

Minicomputer Computer system that is midway between a mainframe and a micro in terms of size, cost, and processing power.

MIPS *See* millions of instructions per second.

Modem Device that enables data to be transmitted over telephone lines by converting digital signals to analog signals and vice versa.

Modula-2 Structured, high-level programming language developed as an alternative to Pascal.

Module Subprogram contained within a main program that performs a fixed set of operations.

Monitor TV-like screen that displays user instructions and the computer's responses. Also called video display terminal (VDT) or cathode ray tube (CRT).

Monochrome monitor Display screen with only one color, typically green or amber against a black background.

Morphing Transforming one image into another.

Motherboard Main circuit board of a computer that contains the microprocessor, battery-operated clock, and other components.

Mouse Handheld device with one or more buttons on the top that is slid around the desktop to electronically move the cursor on the computer screen, thereby eliminating the need to type commands.

MPC (Multimedia PC) A minimum specification for multimedia PCs. MPC computers must be an 80386 or higher, have 4+ MB of RAM, a VGA monitor, a CD-ROM drive, and Windows 3.1 or Windows 95.

MS-DOS The operating system for IBM-compatible micros.

Multifunction drive Drive that can read or write either WORM-CDs or erasable optical disks.

Multimedia Use of text, video, graphics, animation, and sound to communicate, make presentations, educate, store database files, and so on.

Multimedia authoring tool A program used to create a multimedia product such as a game, tutorial, simulation, or sophisticated presentation.

Multiplexer Device that collects messages from numerous nodes at one physical location and transmits them collectively at high speeds over a single communications channel.

Multiprocessing Linking of two or more CPUs so that different instructions or different programs can be executed simultaneously.

Multiprogramming Ability to store and process more than one program in a computer concurrently.

Multitasking A variation of multiprogramming implemented on many high-end microcomputers that allows the user to access several programs at the same time.

Multiuser system Computer system shared by many users.

Nanosecond One billionth of a second.

Natural language Method of interacting with an expert system or database that allows users to conduct dialogs with the computer that seem as natural as talking to another human being.

Near-letter-quality (NLQ) printer Dot-matrix printer that produces relatively high-quality output but not quite as good as that produced with fully formed characters.

Needs analysis Description of an organization's needs.

Network System that permits the sharing of resources such as computing power, software, and input/output units by different computers.

Network database Similar to a hierarchical database except that more than one parent per child is permitted and a child with no parent is also permitted.

Network operating system Set of control programs that works in conjunction with the normal computer operating system to facilitate basic network management functions such as transmitting files, communicating with other systems, and performing diagnostics.

Network topology The specific type of configuration used in a network.

Node Terminal or computer at a remote location that is linked to a host computer in a network.

Nonimpact printer Printer that produces images by methods other than the strike-on method; thermal, ink-jet, and laser printers are nonimpact devices.

Nonprocedural language Another name for a fourth-generation programming language; languages are called nonprocedural because they only specify the output required, not the procedure by which the output is to be obtained.

Nonvolatile memory Type of memory typically composed of magnetic bubbles so that data stored in it can be retained for some time even after the power is shut off.

Notebook computer Portable computers weighing 7 pounds or less.

Numeric keypad Section of a keyboard containing numbers; used to make numeric data entry easier.

Object-oriented database Database that can link not only text but graphics, photos, video, and sound; objects consisting of data and functions are used to make information available.

Object-oriented programming Type of programming in which both the data and the set of operations that can act on that data are treated as one unit; object-oriented programs are designed to facilitate the use of reusable code.

Object program Program that has been translated into machine language.

Odd parity Method of verifying the accurate transmission of data in which an odd number of bits must always be in the on state at any given time. A computer is said to be an even-parity or odd-parity computer.

Offline Data entry in which data is entered on computers or terminals that are not connected to the main CPU. Used for collecting data for future batch processing.

Offload To reduce one computer's tasks by having those tasks handled by a second computer.

Online Data entry in which input entered is immediately used by the computer for updating files or answering inquiries.

Open Systems Interconnection (OSI) model A set of communications protocols defined by the International Standards Organization.

Operating systems software A set of control programs that moves data in and out of storage and monitors the running of application programs; a main component of systems software.

Optical character reader (OCR) Input device that scans data, eliminating the need for a keying operation. *See* bar code reader, optical mark reader, and optical scanner.

Optical disk Direct access storage medium that can store 600 MB or more. CD-ROMs and WORM disks are types of optical disks.

Optical mark reader Device that detects the presence of pencil marks on predetermined grids. Used to read test answer sheets and market research forms. Also called a mark-sense reader.

Optical scanner Device that scans text and graphics from typed or handwritten entries, eliminating the need for keying in the data.

OS/2 An operating system for IBM-compatibles.

Output Outgoing information produced by a computer.

Output device Part of the computer system that produces processed data or information. Monitors and printers are output devices.

Outsourcing Use of outside services to satisfy some or all of an organization's information processing needs.

Packaged program Program designed for a wide range of users and sold or leased by computer vendors, consultants, or software houses.

Page printer Nonimpact printer that uses a laser, thermal, or ink-jet technology to print a page at a time.

Palmtop computer Handheld portable computer weighing approximately a pound.

Parallel conversion Method of converting to a new design in which the old and new systems are used concurrently and output is compared at various stages to make sure the new system is running correctly.

Parallel processing Use of multiple CPUs to process data.

Parallel transmission Method of transmitting data in which each bit of a character is sent over a separate channel.

Parity bit A single bit attached to each byte to verify that data is being transmitted correctly.

Partition Section or portion of primary storage or disk space set aside for some purpose such as running an application program.

Pascal Third-generation programming language that is relatively easy to learn and is highly structured.

PC-DOS The operating system specifically for IBM micros.

PDA *See* Personal Digital Assistant.

Pen-based system A computer, usually a notebook, palmtop, or PDA, that can accept input using a stylus or pen; commonly used for filling out forms or taking notes.

Peripheral Input or output device.

Personal computer (PC) Same as a microcomputer.

Personal Digital Assistant (PDA) A very small computer used for desktop tasks and communications.

Personal information manager A software package that combines the features of project management software and desktop organizers for a manager's personal use.

Phased conversion Method of converting to a new design in which a gradual or stepwise implementation of the new system is used.

Picosecond One trillionth of a second; used to measure computing speed.

Pilot conversion Implementation of an entire system in only one part of the company until all problems are solved.

Pixel A tiny point of light or picture element on a screen or monitor.

PL/1 High-level programming language designed to meet the needs of both business and science; it combines the advantages of FORTRAN and COBOL.

Plotter Printer that produces high-quality line drawings in color by moving either pens or electrostatic charges with different colors of ink over paper.

Point-of-sale (POS) terminal Input device used in retail establishments to enter data at the point where a transaction is made.

Polling Method of controlling transmissions in a LAN ring configuration so that two computers are prevented from sending a message at the same time.

Port Sockets for plugging peripherals into a computer.

Portability Ability to run the same program on two or more types of computers.

Portable microcomputer Compact and lightweight computer that is easy to transport.

Presentation graphics package Set of packaged programs for producing graphic representations of data for business presentations.

Primary storage The main memory of a computer where data and programs are stored for processing.

Printer The most common output device for PCs; used to obtain printed or hard-copy reports.

Problem definition A report that presents the results of an analysis of the basic problem areas in an existing system.

Procedural language Another name for a third-generation programming language; the term *procedural* means that the programmer must develop the logic necessary to carry out each procedure.

Processing Manipulation of data by computer that results in quick and efficient information.

Processor The CPU of a computer along with main memory and other components; typically stored on integrated circuit boards.

Productivity tool Application package designed to help users perform day-to-day business tasks and to assist them in decision making; a spreadsheet package, a DBMS, a word processing package, and an e-mail package are considered productivity tools.

Program Set of instructions that inputs data, processes it, and produces output information.

Program file Software typically stored on a secondary storage device such as a disk.

Programmer Computer professional who writes, debugs, and documents programs.

Programmer analyst Computer professional who serves as both programmer and systems analyst and is responsible for integrating new software into an information system.

Program testing Execution of a program with different sets of data to find and eliminate errors.

Project management software A set of programs that allows users to set up schedules and allocate personnel and resources for projects.

PROM Acronym for *programmable read-only memory*; a ROM chip that can be programmed to perform user-defined tasks.

Prompt Message or blinking cursor that appears on a screen and requires action by the user.

Protocol Standard set of rules that regulates the way data is transmitted between two computers.

Prototyping Technique used by systems analysts whereby users experiment with parts of a proposed system in order to minimize the need for changes when the entire system is implemented.

Pseudocode Program planning tool that uses key words to depict the logical control structures to be used in a program.

Public domain software Noncopyrighted programs that developers make available free of charge. Same as freeware.

Pull-down menu A submenu that is superimposed over a main menu, from which the user can select more specific entries.

Query language Type of fourth-generation programming language that allows a user to retrieve information from databases.

QuickTime An operating system extension developed by Apple to enable users to incorporate video into their multimedia applications.

Random-access memory (RAM) The part of primary storage that stores programs and data during processing.

Read-only memory (ROM) Memory chip that permanently stores instructions and data.

Read/write head Mechanism used to read data from or write information to a disk (or tape).

Real-time processing Type of processing in which the interaction between user and computer is very fast; that is, there is no perceived delay between sending an inquiry and receiving a response.

Record Unit of information pertaining to one item in a file; a collection of related fields.

Register Special storage area in the arithmetic/logic or control unit of a CPU that is used to process data.

Relational database Type of database that presents files in table format to the users, that is, with the records as rows and the fields as columns; relational databases enable files to be linked together and are known for their flexibility.

Relative addressing Copying a cell address in a spreadsheet formula so that it adjusts for the columns and rows being copied to; contrast with absolute addressing.

Remote data entry Method of processing in which terminals or PCs are used for entering data at the place where transactions occur.

Remote job entry Method of processing in which users enter and run programs from terminals or PCs linked to a host computer.

Report generator Component of a database management system that produces customized reports using data stored in a database.

Request for proposal (RFP) A document prepared by a systems analyst to obtain specific technical information and cost bids from computer vendors.

Resolution Crispness of the characters or images on a monitor or screen.

Reusable code A goal of structured programming in which a module or combination of modules can be used in more than one program.

Reverse video Display screen feature for highlighting data in which background and foreground colors are reversed.

RGB monitor Color monitor in which the pixels each have a dot of red, green, and blue that can create many hues and colors.

Ring network Network configuration that connects computers in a circle of point-to-point connections with no central host computer.

RISC computer RISC is an acronym for *reduced instruction set computer*. RISC technology makes it possible for CPUs to have fewer and simpler instructions programmed into ROM but still have the capability for performing complex tasks by combining simple instructions; a reduced instruction set greatly reduces processing time.

ROM *See* read-only memory.

Root directory Main directory on a disk drive.

Router Hardware used to route messages from one LAN to another or from a LAN to a WAN.

Runtime program A program capable of running or "playing" a file but not capable of editing the file. Presentations are often made using a runtime version of a presentation graphics package.

Scanner (optical scanner) Device that converts images, pictures, and text into machine-readable data.

Scrolling Text that flows rapidly past on the screen.

Search and replace A word processing feature that searches for a specified word or phrase and replaces it with another, either automatically or after pausing for the user to verify the change.

Secondary storage A set of devices that stores data and programs in electronic form so that they can be accessed by computer. Also called auxiliary storage. Examples of auxiliary storage are floppy disks and hard disks.

Second-generation language Another name for assembly language, which is one step removed from machine language.

Sector A wedge-shaped segment of a track on a disk.

Sequence structure One of the four logic structures in programs whereby statements are executed in the order in which they appear.

Sequential file File that is stored in some sequence or order and that can only be accessed sequentially.

Serial printer Impact printer that prints one character at a time.

Serial transmission Method of transmission in which each bit is transmitted one at a time in sequence over a single channel.

Shareware Software typically distributed through bulletin boards, subscriber services, or the Internet free of charge on a trial basis; if you use it, you are asked to pay for it and you receive additional documentation.

Shell The user interface to an operating system that is contained in a separate software module; COMMAND.COM is the program that provides the command-driven user interface to DOS.

Simplex line Communications channel that permits data to flow in one direction only, such as from CPU to printer.

Site license The right to have multiple users at a site access or copy a single software product; the manufacturer agrees to sell or lease the rights to a fixed number of copies of the software for a set price.

Smart card Storage medium the size of a credit card that contains a microprocessor capable of recording and storing information.

Smart phone A telephone with built-in computing power for sending messages, making bank transactions, placing orders, and performing other computerized tasks.

Soft copy Output that is produced on a screen.

Soft-sectored diskette Diskette with a small hole near the center hub that tells the disk drive where the tracks begin. These diskettes do not have sectors already defined when you buy them and must, therefore, be formatted.

Software Total set of programs that enables a computer system to process data. Consists of both operating system and application programs.

Software development cycle Steps involved in creating a program. These include developing the program specifications and designing a solution; coding the program and translating it into machine language; debugging, testing, installing, maintaining, and documenting the program.

Software engineering The formal techniques for designing and developing software.

Sound board Circuit board that can generate a variety of sounds and audio responses.

Source data automation (SDA) Process of computerizing the procedures that convert source documents to machine-readable form.

Source document Document such as a purchase order, vendor invoice, or payroll change report that contains data to be used as input to a computer.

Source program Program written by a programmer in symbolic language; it must be translated into machine language before it can be executed.

Spooling Process of transmitting output that is to be printed to a disk first, in a high-speed operation, so that the CPU can do other processing while the output is printed from disk.

Spreadsheet package A program that can represent data in column-and-row format and can manipulate and present that data in a number of ways.

SQL Abbreviation for *structured query language*; a nonproprietary data manipulation language that has become a standard for many database applications.

Star network A network configuration in which one or more small computers, or nodes, are connected to a host computer that coordinates the transmission of data from node to node.

Statistical package Type of software that performs data analysis such as determining standard deviations and variances.

Status line A display line, usually at the top or bottom of the screen, that an application package uses for providing key information about the current settings for that application.

Storage capacity Amount of data a storage device or memory unit can hold; most often measured in megabytes or gigabytes.

Storage device Part of the system that permanently stores programs and data so that they can be used again later.

Stored-program device A computer that requires a set of instructions to be entered and stored before data can be processed.

Structure chart *See* hierarchy chart.

Structured analysis Top-down method of systems analysis for describing a system.

Structured programming Standardized approach for creating a program using logical control constructs that make the program easier to write, read, debug, maintain, and modify.

Structured walkthrough A concept in which a group of programmers manually step through the logic of a program to help dubug it and to evaluate its structure.

Subdirectory Directory accessible from the root directory on disk; each subdirectory contains related files.

Subnotebook computer A laptop computer that weighs less than five pounds.

Subprogram Set of instructions that fit together as a unit; same as module or routine.

Subscriber service Service that allows a user with a computer, modem, and telephone to access a wide variety of databases and other resources.

Suite A set of productivity tools (word processing, spreadsheet, DBMS, e-mail, and others) sold as a unit by a manufacturer for a reduced price.

Summary report Report that contains totals rather than detailed data; typically used by either the operating staff or by managers for decision making.

Supercomputer The fastest, largest, and costliest of all computer systems; used mainly for scientific and industrial research, by the government, and for networking.

Supervisor *See* kernel.

Swapping Process using virtual memory that permits a very large program to be executed by a computer with limited storage capacity; parts of the program are loaded into memory at different times, overlaying parts that have already been executed.

Symbolic language Programming language that uses instructions such as ADD or + instead of complex operation codes and allows the programmer to assign symbolic names to storage locations.

Synchronous transmission Method of transmission that enables blocks of characters called packets to be sent in timed sequences.

Syntax error Error that occurs when the programmer violates the grammatical rules of the programming language.

System interrupt Temporary suspension of some programs so that others can use the resources and devices of the computer.

Systems analyst Computer professional who studies the information needs of various groups in an organization and works with user groups to design, develop, and implement a new system.

Systems development Designing and implementing of information systems.

Systems development life cycle The five basic stages through which a business system passes: investigation and analysis; design and development; implementation; operation and maintenance; and replacement.

Systems flowchart Diagram that shows the relationships among inputs, processing, and outputs in a system.

Systems programmer Computer professional who develops operating systems, compilers, and other programs designed to maximize the processing efficiency of the computer system.

Systems software Set of programs, including the operating system, that supervises and controls the overall operations of a computer system.

Telecommunications A communications technology in which data is transmitted over telephone, microwave, or satellite lines.

Telecommuting Technique whereby employees with PCs in their homes can do word processing, access corporate data, and send messages to colleagues without having to be physically present in the office.

Template A shell of an application such as a spreadsheet which includes all the necessary design elements so that the user need only enter data.

Terabyte A trillion storage positions in main memory or auxiliary storage.

Terminal Any input/output device or PC that is not at the same site as the CPU; it usually has a keyboard and monitor.

Test data Data that closely resembles expected input data; used to test a program's logic.

Text editing A feature of a software package that enables you to make changes to a file; standard feature of a word processing package.

Thermal printer Type of nonimpact printer that creates whole characters on specially treated paper that responds to patterns of heat produced by the printer.

Third-generation language (3GL) A high-level, symbolic programming language that uses English-like commands to instruct the computer. Also called a procedural language.

Time-sharing Technique whereby a large computer can be used or shared by many organizations or individuals.

Token ring network A topology that allows one node at a time to transmit or receive data from the file server; it has become a de facto standard in the industry.

Top-down design Type of system design that is organized around the goals and informational needs of top managers.

Touch screen Screen that enables the user to select entries and choose commands by simply making contact with the screen to point to, or highlight, the desired item.

Track Invisible concentric circles on a disk that are segmented into wedge-shaped units called sectors.

Trackball Pointing device like a mouse; the user rotates a ball to position or move the cursor.

Tractor feed mechanism Printer mechanism that uses sprockets to feed continuous-form paper; the holes on the sides of the paper are inserted into the sprockets.

Traditional systems approach An approach to designing information systems that assumes that if each business system within an organization functions efficiently, then the organization as a whole will run smoothly.

Transaction file File of changes to be made to the master file.

Transaction processing Form of interactive processing that enables a user to input data and complete a transaction on the spot.

Transaction report Report that contains detailed information of business transactions; usually used by the operating staff.

Transfer rate Speed at which data is transferred from disk to main memory; it is typically measured in megabytes per second.

Transmission protocol Procedure that is part of communications software; used to set the speed at which data can travel accurately across communications channels.

TSR program Abbreviation for *t*erminate and *s*tay *r*esident; some programs are loaded into main memory and remain there available for use while other software is being run.

Twisted-pair cable The typical telephone wires used in homes and also used for computer connections; the cable consists of two individual copper wires that are twisted to make them stronger.

Typeover mode A feature of application packages in which text that is currently on the screen will be replaced by the new text entered. Contrast with insert mode.

Universal Product Code (UPC) Bar code found on most consumer goods that indicates the manufacturer of a product as well as the product itself.

UNIX operating system An operating system written in the C programming language that can be used on many different sizes and types of computers.

Update Procedure for keeping a file of records current; includes operations to add new records, delete obsolete records, and make changes to existing records.

Upload To send data and programs to a central computer from a mini or micro.

Upwardly compatible Term used to indicate a family of computers for which software run on lower models in the family can also be run on higher models.

User Someone who uses a computer.

User-friendly Term describing hardware and software that is easy to use.

User interface Part of the systems software that permits interaction between the hardware and the user.

Utilities Component of a database management system that allows the user to maintain the database by editing data, deleting records, creating new files, and so on; can also be programs that perform standard procedures such as sorting files, merging files, and so on.

Value-added service Extra services offered by telephone companies.

Vector graphics Type of graphic image created by a drawing program in which images are produced by using combinations of lines, arcs, circles, squares, and other shapes or objects rather than dots. Contrast with bit-mapped graphics.

Video display terminal (VDT) A TV-like screen that displays instructions and the computer's responses. Also called cathode ray tube (CRT) or monitor.

Video for Windows A Microsoft product that enables Windows users to play video files.

Videoconferencing Using video transmissions, computers, and telephones to enable people to communicate with each other over long distances without the need to travel to central locations.

Virtual machine Processing concept whereby the real machine simulates a number of virtual machines, each capable of interfacing with its own operating system, so that it functions as though there were a number of separate systems.

Virtual memory Type of memory that allows the computer system to operate as if it had more primary storage than it actually does by segmenting the application program and storing parts of it in auxiliary storage. Also called virtual storage.

Virtual reality An area in artificial intelligence that immerses users in a 3-D computer-generated environment and enables them to interact with that environment.

Virtual storage *See* virtual memory.

Virus Software added to operating systems or application programs that can destroy the product and damage files in a computer.

Visual Basic A version of the Basic programming language that is object-oriented and that uses visual programming techniques.

Visual programming An object-oriented technique that allows menus, buttons, graphics, and multimedia elements to be selected and used by a program.

Voice recognition equipment Devices that can interpret spoken messages; they minimize the need for keying data and result in user-friendly interactions.

Voice response unit Output in the form of verbal responses.

Volatile memory Type of memory composed of microprocessor chips in which programs and data are lost when the computer is turned off or loses power.

Wand reader Handheld optical reader for scanning typewritten fonts, optical character fonts, and bar codes.

What-if analysis Using a spreadsheet or other software package to make hypothetical changes to data in order to determine the impact of those changes.

Wide area network (WAN) Similar to local area networks but used where nodes are far from the central computer and each other; uses microwave relays and satellites to enable people at nodes to communicate with a host or with each other over long distances around the world.

Windows Software package that serves as a graphical user interface for DOS (Windows 3.11 or earlier) or as a full operating system (Windows 95); facilitates multitasking and maximizes the efficient use of the computer.

Wireless transmission Method for connecting computers to other computers or input/output devices; usually uses light beams or radio waves for transmission.

Word A group of consecutive bytes in storage; refers to a unit of data that can be processed at one time.

Word processing package Productivity tool used to enter, edit, and print documents.

Word wrap A feature of word processing packages that brings words down to the next line if there is no room on the current line, so that margins are aligned properly.

Worksheet Another term for an electronic spreadsheet.

Workstation High-powered supermicro; commonly used for generating graphics or as a file server in a small network.

WORM (write once, read many) disk Optical disk that can be written on one time only; typically used for storing reference or archived data.

Write-protect notch An indentation in a diskette that can prevent data from being changed on that diskette; cover the notch and you will not be able to write to the diskette.

WYSIWYG Acronym for *what you see is what you get*; word processing, desktop publishing, spreadsheet, and many other packages are capable of displaying text exactly as it would appear printed.

INDEX

A

A/UX, 308
Absolute addressing, 472
Access time (rate), 185, 186, 211, 472
ACM, *see* Association for Computing Machinery
Acoustic coupler, 334, 363, 472
Action (program), 228
Ada (language), 280–281, 289, 472
Ada, Augusta, 280, 281, 462
Address register, 472
Addresses, diskette, 188–189
AIX, 308
Allen, Paul, 465
ALU, *see* Arithmetic/logic unit
America Online, 96, 97, 342, 471
American National Standards Institute (ANSI), and programming language standards, 276
Analog computer, 115–116
Analog signal, 472
Analytical Engine, 281
ANSI, *see* American National Standards Institute
Antiviral/anti-virus software, 222, 248, 250, 435–436, 437, 457, 472
Apple, 39, 40, 41
Apple Macintosh computers, 43
AppleShare, 309–310
Application, 472
Application generator, 284, 289, 472
in DBMS software, 410–411
Applications packages, 61–66, 472. *See also* Applications software; Productivity tools
Applications programmer, 472
Applications software, 9–10, 23, 472. *See also* Applications packages; Productivity tools; Software
Architecture, computer, 121, 135, 472. *See also* Computers, architecture of
Arithmetic/logic unit (ALU), 109, 113, 134, 472

Arpanet, 346
Artificial intelligence, 216–217, 237–240, 252, 472
expert system shells, 238–239
expert systems, 237–239
neural networks, 239–240
virtual reality, 239
ASCII, 118–119, 135, 472
communications software and, 352
Ashton-Tate, 465
Assembler, 288, 472
Assembly language, 274, 288, 472
Association for Computing Machinery (ACM), 472
AST computer, 44
Asynchronous transmission, 351, 364, 472
Atanasoff, John, 462
Atanasoff-Berry Computer, 37
Atari computer, 39, 41
ATM, *see* Automatic teller machine
Audio response unit, 472. *See also* Voice response unit
Audit trail, 147, 176, 472
Auditor, job of, 51–52
Authorware, 229
AUTOEXEC.BAT, 318
Automated design tool, 472
Automatic teller machine (ATM), 157–159, 177, 472
Auxiliary storage, 472. *See also* Secondary storage

B

Babbage, Charles, 280, 281, 462
Backlit panel, 165
Backspace key, 69
Backup, 472
programs for automatic, 222
Band printer, 170–171, 472
Bandwidth, 472
Banking industry, uses of source data automation, 157–160
Bar code reader, 7, 177, 152, 472
Baseband, 472

BASIC (Beginner's All-purpose Symbolic Instruction Code), 276–278, 289, 463, 472
Batch file, 318
Batch processing, 130–131, 135, 472
Baud rate, 348–349, 364, 472
Benchmark test, 245, 252, 472
Bibliographies, creating in word processing programs, 76
Binary digit, *see* Bit
Binary numbering system, 115–118, 135, 472
Bit-mapped graphics, 232, 251, 473
Bitnet, 346
Bit, 116–118, 135, 472
    stored on disk, 186
Bits per inch (bpi), 195–196, 473
Bits per second (bps), 473
Block (of text), 99, 473
    highlighting, 71, 76, 473
Bob (program), 245
Boilerplating, 76, 99, 473
Bootlegging of software, 473
Bpi, *see* Bits per inch
Bps, *see* Bits per second
Break-even analysis, 473
Bricklin, Dan, 63
Bridge, 356–357, 364, 473
Broadband, 473
Bubble memory, 473
Budgetary constraint, 473
Budgeting, use of spreadsheets for, 62
Buffer, 317, 322, 473
Bulletin board service, 346, 473
Bundled software, 294, 321, 473
Bus, 113–114, 134, 473
    configuration, 473
    EISA, 126
    ISA, 125
    MCA, 125–126
    PCI, 126
    topology, 354
    width, 125–126
Business systems, 11–19, 24, 46–53, 473. *See also* Information systems
    avoiding dissatisfaction with computers, 16–19
    benefits of using computers, 14–16
    information processing environments in, 46–49
    MIS approach to, 49–51. *See also* Management information systems
    systems analysts and, 13–14
    systems development and, 17–19, 46. *See also* Information systems
    types of computer systems in, 46–53
    user needs and, 49–51
    when to purchase, 53
Byte, 33, 54, 116–118, 473

C
C (language), 279–280, 289, 473
C++, 264, 281–282, 289, 473
CA-Realizer, 284
Cache memory, 127, 135, 473
CAD, *see* Computer-aided design
Callback system, 473
CAM, *see* Computer-aided manufacturing
Carterfone decision, 336–337
CASE (computer-aided software engineering), 386–388, 395, 473
Case-insensitive program, 473
Cathode ray tube (CRT), 177, 473
cc:Mail, 224
CD-ROM (compact disk read-only memory), 67, 201–208, 212, 473
    applications of, 214
    as a storage medium, 205–206
    Computer Select and, 205
    graphics packages and, 205
    image processing with WORM disks, 207
    and multimedia software, 202–206
    networking drives, 206
    published databases and, 204–205
    virtual reality and, 202, 204
    WORM CDs and drives, 206–208
CDC 6600, 463
Cells, in electronic spreadsheets, 62, 100, 473
Cellular telephone, 359, 364
Central processing unit (CPU), 2, 6, 7, 23, 473. *See also* Microprocessors
    arithmetic/logic unit (ALU), 109, 113
    control unit, 113–114
    data representation and, 115–121
    functions of, 109
    how data is processed, 108–115
    primary storage in, *see* Main memory
    registers, 114

typical operations performed by, 109

Centralized information processing, 46, 47, 55, 473

Chain printer, 170, 473

Character, 111, 134, 473

Character printer, 168, 177

Child segment, in hierarchical database, 403–404

Chip, 109–110, 121–123, 134, 473
  comparison among chips, 124
  Pentium computer, 110, 122, 470

CISC computer (complex instruction set computer), 40

Claris Corp., 66

ClarisWorks, 66

Client-server computer/computing, 31, 55, 341–342, 473. *See also* Mainframes
  distributed (networked) environments and, 47–48
  hard disks and, 190–191

Clip art, 236, 251, 473

Clipper Chip, 437–438

Clock speed, 123–124, 473

Coaxial cable, 331–333, 363, 473

COBOL (Common Business Oriented Language), 276, 289, 473

Colmerauer, Alain, 286

Commands, 69, 78, 99, 473

Commodore computer, 39, 41

Common carrier, 473

Communications channel, 331–338, 363, 473

Communications controller, 335–336

Communications hardware, 331–338

Communications software, 348–352
  ASCII code and, 352
  asynchronous transmission, 351
  baud rate, 348–349
  full-duplex line, 349–350
  half-duplex line, 349
  parallel transmission, 351
  parity, 352
  protocols and, 352
  serial transmission, 351
  simplex line, 349
  synchronous transmission, 351
  wireless transmission of data, 337–338

Compact disk read-only memory, *see* CD-ROM

Compact disk, 34

Compaq, Inc., 39, 44, 466

Compel (software), 228

Compiler, 282–283, 289, 473

Compression/decompression program, 318, 473

CompuServe, 96, 247, 342, 471

Computer-aided design (CAD), 215, 233–234, 251, 473

Computer-aided manufacturing (CAM), 233–234, 251, 473

Computer-aided software engineering, *see* CASE

Computer art, 215

Computer code, *see* ASCII, EBCDIC

Computer crime, 17, 433–437, 457, 473

Computer Fraud and Abuse Act (1986), 437

Computer literate, 5, 473

Computer monitoring, in the workplace, 442–443

Computer operator, 51–52

Computer Professionals for Social Responsibility, 432

Computer professionals, social responsibility of, 444

Computer Select (CD-ROM), 205, 206

Computer system, 6, 23, 473
  business system, 11–19, 46–53, 473
  development, 17–19
  network, 12

Computer virus, 248–250

Computers:
  analog, 115–116
  architecture of, 121–129
    bus width, 125–126
    clock speed, 123–124
    devices for improving processing power, 127–129
    expansion slots, 126–127
    main circuit board, 126–127
    processing speed, 124
    word size, 125–126
  avoiding dissatisfaction with, 16–19
  benefits of using, 14–16
  data processing methods, 129–132
  digital, 115
  government and, 447–449
  history of development, 37, 461–471
  impact on quality of life, 445–455
  in education, 452–453

Computers (*continued*)
  in medicine, 446
  leisure time and, 449
  memory, units of storage, 33
  office of the future and, 454–455
  people with disabilities and,
    446–447
  power of, factors affecting, 126
  processing power of, 32–35
    input/output devices and, 33–35
    main memory, 33
    memory size, 33
    MIPS, 33
    peripherals and, 33–35
    processing speed, 33
  types of, 30–32, 36, 39–45. *See also*
    Personal computers
Computing, history of, 37, 461–471
Configuration of computer systems,
  6–7, 23, 108, 473
Connectivity, 2, 12, 24, 45, 474. *See
  also* Networking
  communications and, 330–331
  e-mail and, 64
  operating systems software and,
    294
Context-sensitive help, 70, 99, 474
  hyperlinking and, 227
Continuous-form paper, 168, 177, 474
Control listing, 147, 176, 474
Control program, *see* Kernel
Control unit, 109, 134, 474
Controls, 474
  and implementing new
    information systems, 390, 394
Conversion software, *see* Document
  viewers
Coprocessor, 122, 135, 474
Copy protection, of software, 248,
  436–437, 457, 474
CorelDRAW, 205
Cost-benefit analysis, 383, 394, 474
CPU, *see* Central processing unit
Cray Research, 38–39
Cray-2 supercomputer, 124
Credit cards, *vs.* debit cards and
  smart cards, 160
Cross-platform compatibility, 40
CRT, *see* Cathode ray tube
Cursor, 69, 474
Cursor control keys, 69, 474
Curtis, Walt, 139
Custom programs, 3, 9–10, 219, 257,
  474

developers of, 257–258
software development cycle,
  259–267
software development, techniques
  for standardizing, 267–272
Cutting and pasting, 99, 474
Cyberspace, 65. *See also* Information
  superhighway

D
Daisywheel printer, 168, 177
DAT, *see* Digital audio tape
Data, 5, 23, 474
Data automation, *see* Source data
  automation
Data collection devices, 155–157
  fax machines as, 155–156
  pen-based systems, 156–157
  portable, 155–156
  telephones as, 155–156
  wireless communications
    equipment, 155–156
Data compression/decompression,
  318
Data definition language (DDL), 409,
  424, 474
Data dictionary, 388, 395, 409, 474
Data encryption, 474
Data entry operator, 51–52
Data file, 474
Data flow diagram, 380–381, 394,
  474
Data integrity, 411–412, 424, 474
Data manipulation language (DML),
  409–410, 424, 474
Data Processing Management
  Association (DPMA), 474
Data processing methods, 129–132
  batch processing, 130–131
  interactive processing, 131–132
Database administrator, 51–52, 402,
  423, 474
  issues concerning, 411–412
    data integrity, 411–412
    security, 411
    selection of databases, 412
Database file, 63, 100, 401, 474
Database management system
  (DBMS), 63–64, 99, 210, 400,
  474
  capabilities of, 88–89
  components of DBMS software,
    409–411
  how to use, 89–95

network database, 404–405
object-oriented database, 408
query language and, 95–96
reasons for popularity of, 95
relational database, 405–408
structure of database, 400–408
types of, 402–404
uses for, 64, 89
Databases, 63, 99, 327, 400–401, 474
  access to and privacy issues,
    430–431
DBMS, *see* Database management
  system
DDL, *see* Data definition language
Debit card, 159, 160, 177, 474
Debugging, 264, 287, 474
Decentralized information
  processing, 46, 47, 55, 474
Decision support system (DSS), 415,
  424, 474
Default, 69, 99, 474
Dell computer, 44
Delphi, 342
DENDRAL, 464
Density, tape and disk, 195–196, 211,
  474
Desk-checking, of software, 264,
  287–288, 474
Desktop accessory, 221, 251, 474
Desktop computer, 40, 55, 474
Desktop publishing, 251, 474
  use of clip art in, 236
Device driver, 318, 322, 474
Difference Engine, 281
Digital audio tape (DAT), 474
Digital computer, 115, 135, 474
Digital Equipment Corporation
  (DEC), 37
Digital signal, 474
Digital video interaction (DVI), 474
Digitizer, 161–162, 177, 474
Dijsktra, Edsger, 464
Direct-connect modem, 475
Direct conversion, 393, 395, 475
Direct file, 210, 212, 476
Director (software), 229
Disk cartridge, 191, 475
Disk drive, 7, 34, 54, 186, 475
  fixed-head disk drive, 192, 192,
    211, 476
  for mainframe computer, 191–192
  read/write head for, 188, 193
Disk operating system, *see* DOS
Disk organizer, 475

Disk pack, 186, 192, 211, 475
Diskette, 34, 54, 186, 475
  addresses, 188–189
  protecting data on, 188
  soft-sectored, 187
  write-protecting diskette, 187
Disks, 34, 475. *See also specific types of
  disks*
  organizing data files on, 209–210
Distance learning, 22, 361–362, 367,
  475
Distributed information processing,
  46, 47–48, 55, 339–342, 475
Distributed information processing,
  and client-server computing,
  47–48
DML, *see* Data manipulation
  language
Document processor, 172
Document viewer, 234, 252, 475
Documentation, 10, 19, 24, 266, 393,
  395, 475
Document, 62, 99, 475
DOS (disk operating system), 9, 23,
  295, 296–299, 475
Dot-matrix printer, 168, 177, 475
Downloading, 191, 211, 475
Downsizing, 31, 55, 58, 475
DPMA, *see* Data Processing
  Management Association
Drawing program, 232–233
Drum printer, 170–171, 475
DSS, *see* Decision support system
DTP, *see* Desktop publishing
DVI, *see* Digital video interaction

E
E-mail, *see* Electronic mail
Easytrieve Plus, 284
EBCDIC, 118–119, 135, 475
Eckert, J. Presper, 37, 463
EDLIN, 299
EFF (Electronic Frontier
  Foundation), 432
EEPROM, 112, 113, 136, 475
EIS, *see* Executive information system
EISA bus, 126
Electroluminescent (EL) display, 475
Electronic boardroom, 22
Electronic classroom, 22
Electronic communications, etiquette
  of, 103
Electronic Frontier Foundation
  (EFF), 432

Electronic mail (e-mail), 219, 326, 346–347, 475
  communications software for, 224
  e-mail packages, 64–65, 96–98, 99
    Lotus cc:Mail, 97
    Microsoft Mail, 97
  privacy and, 429–430
  subscriber services and, 342
Electronic music, 215
Electronic spreadsheets, *see* Spreadsheets, electronic
Electronically erasable programmable read-only memory, *see* EEPROM
Embedded system, 475
Encryption, 411, 424
End key, 69
ENIAC, 37, 463
Enter key, 69
EPROM, 112–113, 136, 475
Equipment constraints, 475
Erasable programmable read-only memory, *see* EPROM
Ergonomics, 166–168, 177, 440–441, 475
Error checking, with parity bits, 119–121
Error control procedures, for data entry, 147–147
Ethernet, 475
Even parity, 120, 135, 352, 475
Excelerator (CASE software), 387–388
Exception report, 163, 177, 475
Execution cycle, 114–115, 134, 475
Executive information system (EIS), 416–419, 424, 475
Expansion slot, 126–127, 135, 475
Expert system, 21, 24, 252, 419–423, 475
  components of, 420–421
  steps for developing, 421–423
  uses for, 419
Exsys, 239
Extended Binary Coded Decimal Interchange Code, *see* EBCDIC
Extended Industry Standard Architecture (EISA) bus, 126

F
Facsimile (fax) machine, 357–359, 364, 475
  networked, 358
FAT, *see* File allocation table
Fax boards, 34, 358, 364, 475

Fax machine, *see* Facsimile machine
Fax-modem, 34
Feasibility study, 394, 475
  systems analysis and, 383
Feedback, and implementing new information system, 390, 394, 475
Fiber optic cable, 331, 334, 363, 475
Field of data, 90, 100, 402, 475
Fifth-generation language (5GL), 285–286, 475–476
File allocation table (FAT), 322, 476
File conversion, 391, 395, 476
File extension, 476
File management system, 476
File processing, overview of concepts, 141–143, 184
File server, 31, 476
File-Maker Pro, 402
Filename, 99, 476
  creating, 68
File, 63, 99, 476
  creating, 68
  organizing, 209–210
  retrieving, 68
Financial planning language (FPL), 476
Firmware, 112, 134, 476
1st Class (expert system shell), 239
First-generation language, 476
Fixed disk, 186, 476
Fixed-head disk drive, 192, 211, 476
  read/write head for, 193
Flash card, 199–200, 476
Flash memory, 113
Flat file, 90, 99, 402, 476
Flat-screen technologies, 165–166, 476
Floppy disk, 34, 54, 186, 476. *See also* Diskette
Floptical disk/drive, 208
Flowcharts, in software development, 260–261, 287, 476
Format conversion, software for, 222
FORTRAN, 275–276, 289, 463, 476
Foster, Ed, 325
Fourth-generation language (4GL), 283–284, 476
FPL, *see* Financial planning language
Frankston, Bob, 63
Freeware, *see* Public domain software
Friction feed mechanism, 476
Front-end processor, 335–336, 363, 476

Full-duplex line, 349, 364, 476
Function key, 70, 476
Fylstra, Dan, 63

G

Gas-plasma display, 165–166, 476
Gates, Bill, 465
Gateway, 356–357, 364, 476
GB, *see* Gigabyte
Genie Service, 342
Gigabyte (GB), 33, 476
Gore, Al, and support of EFF, 432
Graphic analysis, of spreadsheet data, 62–63
Graphical user interface (GUI), 43, 45, 296–306, 299, 311, 321
Graphics software, 228, 230–234, 476
   CAD/CAM packages, 233–234
   computer-aided design, 233–234
   computer-aided manufacturing, 233–234
   drawing programs, 232–233
   illustration packages, 231–233
   for multimedia presentations, 228
   painting programs, 232
Graphics, bit-mapped, 232
Groupware, 64, 65, 96–98, 100, 219, 476
   communications software for, 224
   Lotus Notes, 97
   Novell Groupwise, 97
   resolving incompatibility across platforms with, 224–225
   work teams and, 103
GUI, *see* Graphical user interface

H

Hackers, 17, 24, 248, 252, 435, 476
Half-duplex line, 349, 364, 476
Handheld computer, 42–43
Hard copy, 163, 177, 476
Hard disk drive, 189, 476. *See also* Disk drives
   external, 189–190
   head crash on, 189, 211, 476
   internal, 189
Hard disks, 34, 54, 186, 476
   and client-server computing, 190–191
   vs. diskettes, 190
Hardware, 2, 6, 476
   new developments in, 20–21. *See also* Smart devices
   when to purchase, 53

Hardwired cable, 331–332
Hayes (modem), 466
HDTV, *see* High-definition television
Head crash, 189, 211, 476
Help feature, in software, 70
Hewlett-Packard, 39, 44, 468
Hierarchical database, 402–404, 423, 476
Hierarchy chart, in software development, 261–262, 287, 476
High-definition television (HDTV), 328, 360–361, 365, 476
High-level language, 274–283, 476
Hitachi, 38
Hoff, Marcian E. (Ted), 110, 464
Hollerith, Herman, 143, 462
Home key, 69
Hopper, Grace Murray, 265
Host computer, 331, 476
Hybrid topology, 354–355
Hyperlinking, 227, 251, 476
Hypermedia, 476

I

I/O device, *see* Input/output device
IBM, 38, 39, 40, 41
IBM AT, 467
IBM PC, 9
IBM PC Jr, 467
IBM-compatible computer, 9, 43–44, 476
ICCP, *see* Institute for the Certification of Computer Professionals
Icon, 9, 149, 477
Illustration package, 231–233, 251, 477
Image processing, 173–174, 177, 477
IMIS (Integrated Management Information System), 58
Impact printer, 168–171, 177, 477
Importing data, 72, 477
IMS, 404
Incompatibility, 24, 477
   resolving across platforms, 224–224
   software and hardware, 9
Index, on a disk, 477
Indexed file, 209–210, 212, 477
Indexes, creating in word processing programs, 76
Industry Standard Architecture (ISA) bus, 125
Inference engine, 420, 424, 477

Information, 5, 23, 477
Information overload, 18
Information processing, 5, 23, 477
Information processing
    environments, 46–49
  centralized, 46, 47
  comparison of environments, 47
  decentralized, 46, 47
  distributed, 46, 47–48
  networked, 46, 47–48
Information superhighway, 12, 15,
    22, 64, 65, 96–98, 477. *See also*
    Internet
  supercomputers and, 38–39
Information system, 372, 394, 477.
    See also Business systems
  designing a new or revised system,
    385–390
    prototyping, 385–386
    using CASE tools in, 386–388
  implementing new, 391–393
  problem definition in, 376–384
  role of systems analysts in, 372–375
  social responsibility issues,
    440–455
  staff/department, changing role of,
    397–398. *See also* MIS staff
  types of systems conversions,
    392–393
Inheritance, 271, 288, 477
Ink-jet printer, 172, 177, 477
Input, 5, 23, 477
Input devices, 2, 6, 7, 23, 141–151,
    477. *See also* Data collection
    devices; Source data automation
  bar code reader, 7, 177, 152, 472
  disk drive, 7, 34, 54, 186, 475
  fixed-head disk drive, 192, 211, 476
  joy stick, 150, 176, 477
  keyboard, 7, 34
  keying device, 143, 146
  light pen, 150
  for mainframe computers,
    191–192
  mouse, 34, 148–149
  optical mouse, 148
  page scanner, 7
  rollerball, 148
  terminal, 30, 34, 54, 155, 177,
    164–165, 480, 482, 483
  touch screen, 149–150, 176
  trackball, 148
  voice recognition unit, 7, 160–161,
    177, 483

Input/output unit, *see* Peripheral
Insert key, 69
Insert mode, 69, 477
Institute for the Certification of
    Computer Professionals (ICCP),
    477
Instruction cycle, 114–115, 134, 477
Instruction register, 477
Integrated circuit, 109, 134, 477. *See*
    also Chip
Integrated Management Information
    System (IMIS), 58
Integrated package, 65–66, 99,
    219–220, 477
  vs. suite, 220
Integrated Services Digital Network
    (ISDN), 362, 444, 477
Intel, 121, 464, 469
Interactive debugger, 265, 288, 477
Interactive processing, 131–132, 135,
    477
Interactive television, 328, 360–361
Internet, 12, 22, 65, 97, 100, 247, 327,
    344–346, 471, 477
  communications software for
    accessing, 224–225
Internet-in-a-Box, 225
Interpreter, 282–283, 289, 477
INTUITY, 255
ISA bus, 125
ISDN, *see* Integrated Services Digital
    Network
Iteration, 269–270, 477

J

Jacquard, Joseph-Marie, 461
Jobs, Stephen, 41, 310, 465
Joshi virus, 435
Joy stick, 150, 176, 477
Jukebox, 477
Junkie virus, 435
Justification, 477. *See also*
    Microjustification

K

K, *see* Kilobyte
Kapor, Mitch, 432
Kemeny, John, 463
Kermit, 97
Kernel, 293–294, 321, 477
Key field, 477
Keyboard, 7, 34, 54, 477
  Backspace key, 69
  Cursor control keys, 69, 474

End key, 69
Enter key, 69
Home key, 69
Insert key, 69
PgDn key, 69
PgUp key, 69
Keying operations, minimizing errors in, 146–148
Kilobyte (K), 33, 477
Knowledge base, 420, 424, 477
Knowledge engineer, 420, 424, 477
Kurtz, Thomas, 463

L
LAN, *see* Local area network
Laptop computer, 40–41, 477
Laser printer, 172, 177, 468, 477
LCD, *see* Liquid crystal display
Legal constraint, 378, 477
Letter-quality printer, 477
Lewis, Peter, 342
Lexis/Nexis, 342
Licensing agreement, 247–248, 252
Light pen, 176, 477
Line printer, 170, 477
Linkage editor, 316, 322, 477
Liquid crystal display (LCD), 165, 477
LISP, 285
Loading program, 67–68
Local area network (LAN), 353, 364, 477
  software for, 353
  topologies for, 354–356
Logic error, 288, 477–478
Longitudinal parity, 478
Looping, in a program, 269–270, 478
Lotus Development Corporation, 97, 224, 467
Lotus Notes, 97

M
MacHack, 464
Machine cycle, 114, 134, 263–264, 273–274, 287, 478
Macintosh operating system, 304–306, 478
Macro, 72, 99, 478
Magnetic bubble memory, 478
Magnetic disk, 7, 34, 54, 186, 475. *See also* disk
Magnetic ink character reader (MICR), 157, 177, 478
Magnetic media, for secondary storage, 186–208

Magnetic tape, 193–194
  as a backup medium, 194
Magneto-optical (MO) disk, 207–208, 212, 478
Mail merge, word processing program and, 77, 478
Main circuit board, 110, 136
Main memory, 2, 6, 7, 33, 54, 111–113, 478
  and CPU, 109
  firmware and, 112
  random-access memory (RAM), 111–112
  read-only memory (ROM), 112–113
  sizes of, 111
  volatile *vs.* nonvolatile, 111
Mainframe computer, 30, 36, 44–45, 54, 478. *See also* Client-server computing
Maintenance programmer, 266, 288, 478
Management information system (MIS), 49–52 400, 413–423, 478. *See also* Database management system; MIS staff
  decision support system, 415
  executive information system, 416–419
  expert system, 419–423
  functions and levels of management and, 413–415
  vs. traditional information system, 413
Markey, Edward, 432
Master file, 141, 478
Mauchly, John, 37, 463
MB, *see* Megabyte
MCA bus, 125–126
McCarthy, John, 285
Megabyte (MB), 33, 478
Megahertz (MHz), 124, 478
Memory board, 478
Memory card, 199–200, 207, 211
Memory management, 315, 322, 478
Memory size, 33
Menu, 69, 99, 478
Michelangelo virus, 435
MICR, *see* Magnetic ink character reader
Micro Channel Architecture (MCA) bus, 125–126
Microcomputer, 31, 39–44, 45, 54, 478

Microcomputer (*continued*)
  as desktop computer, 40, 55, 474
  multitasking on, 44
  portable, 40–43
  workstations, 39–40
Microfilm, 173
Microfloptical, 34
Microjustification, 79, 99, 478
Microprocessor, 2, 110, 134, 478
Microsecond, 124, 478
Microsoft, 66, 219, 224, 342, 465
Microwave transmission of data,
    337–338
MICR, *see* Magnetic ink character
    reader
Midrange computer, 30–31, 37–38,
    54, 478
Millions of instructions per second
    (MIPS), 33, 54, 124, 478
Minicomputer, 30–31, 37–38, 54, 478
Minitab, 237
MIPS, *see* Millions of instructions
    per second
MIS staff, 51–52
  auditors, 51–52
    computer operators, 51–52
    data entry operators, 51–52
    database administrators, 51–52
    network managers, 51–52
    programmers, 51–52
    systems analysts, 51–52
MIS, *see* Management information
    system
Modem, 34, 54, 326, 333–334, 478
  radio, 326, 359, 365
Modula-2, 278–279, 289, 478
Modular programming, 268
Module, 263, 478
Monitors, 34, 54, 164–168, 478
  health-related issues and, 166–168
Monochrome monitor, 478
Morphing, 478
Mosaic, for using the Internet, 225
Motherboard, 126, 135, 478
Motorola, 121
Mouse, 54, 69, 148–149, 478
  optical, 148
  rollerball, 148
  trackball, 148
MPC (Multimedia PC), 478
MS-DOS, 478. *See also* DOS
Multifunction drive, 478
Multimedia, 478
Multimedia authoring tool, 478

Multimedia computing:
  authoring packages, 229, 251, 478
  examples of, 28
  presentation, graphics packages,
    216
  recommended equipment for, 203,
    204
  software for, on CD-ROM,
    202–206
  software packages, 226–230
  systems, 21, 24, 174–175, 177–178
  virtual reality in, 204
Multimedia computer, 3, 470
Multimedia PC, *see* MPC
Multiplexer, 335–336, 363, 478
Multiprocessing, 313–314, 478
Multiprogramming, 55, 311–313, 478
  vs. multitasking, 44
Multitasking, 55, 313, 478
  vs. multiprogramming, 44
Multiuser system, 30–31, 39, 54, 478
  supermicro as, 39

N
Nanosecond, 33, 54, 124, 478
National Crime Information Center
    (NCIC) databases, 430–431, 448
National Information Infrastructure
    (NII) proposal, 432
National Semiconductor, 139
Natural language, 285, 289, 478–479
NCIC, 430–431, 448
Near-letter-quality (NLQ) printer,
    479
Needs analysis, 390, 395, 479
Netscape, 225
NetWare, 309–310
Network (Microsoft's online
    subscriber service), 342
Networked information processing
    environment, 46, 47–48. *See also*
    Distributed information
    processing
Networking, computer utilization
    capabilities and, 45
Networks, 12, 24, 479
  accessing information from,
    342–346
  application areas for, 339–347
  collections of, *see* Information
    superhighway
  computer, 326
  configurations for, 353–357
  databases, 404–405, 423, 479

electronic mail, 346–347
groupware, 346–347
information superhighway, 12, 15,
     22, 64, 65, 96–98, 346, 477
managers, 51–52
operating systems, 309–310, 479
telecommuting, 347
topologies, 354–356, 364, 479
Neural network, 239–240, 252
NeXt Computer, Inc., 41, 310–311
NextStep, 310–311
NLQ printer, *see* Near-letter-quality
     printer
Nodes, 331, 479
Nomad, 284
Nonimpact printer, 168, 171–172,
     177, 479
Nonprocedural language, 275, 283,
     286, 289, 479
Nonvolatile memory, 111, 134, 183,
     479
Norton Utilities, 299
Notebook computer, 40–41, 55, 469,
     479
Novell Groupwise, 97
Numeric keypad, 479

O

Object program, 264, 287, 479
Object-oriented database, 408, 424,
     479
Object-oriented programming,
     271–272, 479
OCR, *see* Optical character reader
Odd parity computer, 120, 135, 352,
     479
Offline operation (data entry), 130,
     135, 479
Offload/offloading, 38, 54, 479
Online operation (data entry), 132,
     135
Open Systems Interconnection (OSI)
     standard, 352, 364, 479
Operating environment, *see* User
     interface
Operating systems software, 8–9, 23,
     293–296, 479
  Apple Macintosh, 9
  batch files and, 318
  connectivity and, 308–311
  file allocation tables and, 319–320
  for microcomputers, 296–308
  for pen-based computers, 306–307
  for Power PC, 306

functions and features of, 293–296
  memory management and, 315
  network operating systems,
       309–310
  subdirectories and, 319–320
  translator programs, 316
  utility functions, 316–318
Operating systems. *See also* DOS;
     Macintosh
     operating system; OS/2; UNIX;
     Windows
  multitasking and, 44
  processing efficiency and, 311–320
Optical character readers (OCRs),
     151–155, 177, 479
  bar code scanner, 152
  optical mark reader, 153–154
  optical scanner, 154–155
  wand reader, 152–153
Optical disk, 173, 479
Optical mark reader, 153–154, 177,
     479
Optical scanner, 154–155, 177, 479
Optical storage media, 201–208
OS/2, 44, 304, 469, 470, 479
  OS/2 Warp, 304
OSI standard, 352, 364, 479
Output, 5, 23, 162–164, 479
  types of, 163–164
Output devices, 2, 6, 23, 164, 175, 479
  document processor, 172
  fax-modem, 34
  modem, 34, 54, 326, 333–334, 478
  monitor, 34, 54, 164–168, 478
  multimedia system, 174–175
  plotter, 172, 177, 180, 480
  printer, 7–8, 34, 168–172. *See also*
       under specific printer types
  sound board, 172, 173, 177, 481
  terminal, 30, 34, 54, 155, 164–165,
       177, 480, 482, 483
  video monitor, 8
  videoconferencing with, 175
  voice response unit, 172–173
Outsourcing, 48, 56, 373, 479

P

Packaged program/software, 9–10,
     23, 219, 479
Page printer, 479
Page scanner, 7
PageMaker, 236
Pager, 359
Palmtop computer, 479

Paperless office, 18, 455
Parallel conversion, 393, 395, 479
Parallel processing, 479
Parallel processor:
  mainframe and, 36
  supercomputer and, 39
Parallel transmission, 351, 364, 479
Parent segment, in hierarchical
    database, 403–404
Parity bit, 120, 135, 479
  error checking with, 119–121
Parity, in communications software,
    352
Partition, 312, 321, 479
Pascal (language), 278, 279, 289, 479
  object-oriented, 281
Pascal, Blaise, 461
Password protection utility, 222
PC Marketing Council, 203, 204
PC-DOS, 479
PC, see Personal computer
PCI bus, 126
PCMCIA card, 129, 199–200
PDA, see Personal Digital Assistant
PDP-8, 463
Peer-to-peer network, 342
Pen-based computer/system, 41,
    42–43, 150, 156–157, 55, 306–307
  operating systems for, 306–307
Pentium chip/computer, 110, 122,
    470
Peripheral Component Interconnect
    (PCI) bus, 126
Peripherals, 54, 108, 142, 479
  networking, 108–111
Personal Computer Memory Card
    International Association, see
    PCMCIA cards
Personal computers (PCs), 5, 23, 30,
    31, 54, 479
  Apple Macintosh, 43
  client-server computing and, 31
  growth of in U.S., 42
  IBM-compatible, 9, 43–44, 476
  Power PC, 9, 40, 44, 122–123, 471
Personal Digital Assistant (PDA),
    42–43, 223, 479
  operating systems software for,
    306–307
Personal information manager
    (PIM), 223, 251, 479
PFS:WindowWorks, 219
PgDn key, 69
PgUp key, 69

Phased conversion, 393, 395, 479
Photo CD, Kodak, 206
Picosecond, 33, 54, 480
Pilot conversion, 393, 395, 480
PIM, see Personal information
    manager
Pipeline (software), 225
Pixel, 165, 480
PL/1, 480
Plotter, 172, 177, 180, 480
Point-of-sale (POS) terminal, 155,
    177, 480
Pointing device, see Mouse
Polling, 480
Port, 108, 134, 480
Portability, 480
Portable microcomputer, 55, 480
Portable programming language, 288
POS terminal, see Point-of-sale
    terminal
PostScript, 236
Power PC, 9, 40, 44, 122–123, 471
  operating systems for, 306
PowerPoint, 228
Presentation graphics package, 228,
    251, 480
Primary storage, 480. See also Main
    memory
Printer, 7–8, 54, 168–172, 480
Privacy:
  computer networks and, 429–432
    Computer Matching Act (1988),
      432
    credit reporting agencies, 430
    Crime Control Act (1973), 431
    database access, 430–431
    electronic mail, 429–430
    Fair Credit Reporting Act
      (1970), 431
    Freedom of Information Act
      (1970), 431
    Privacy Act (1974), 431
    privacy legislation, 431–432
    public interest groups, 432
    vs. security, 437–440
  and interactive information
    processing systems, 132
Problem definition, 376–384, 394,
    480
Procedural language, 275, 283,
    288–289, 480
Processing, 5, 480
Processing speed, 124
Processor, 480

ProComm, 97
Prodigy, 96, 247, 342, 471
Productivity tools, 10, 23–24, 60, 480.
    See also Software
  common features of, 67–72
    basic commands, 69–71
    creating and retrieving files, 68
    data entry, 69
    function keys, 69, 70
    importing files, 72
    loading programs, 67–68
    macros, 72
    search and replace, 71–72
    status lines, 68–69
  evaluating products, 245–246
    benchmark tests for, 245
    tips on, 96
  types of, 61–66
    communications software, 224
    database management systems,
      63–64, 88–96, 219
    electronic mail, 64–65, 96–98, 219
    electronic spreadsheets, 62–63,
      80–88, 219
    groupware, 64, 65, 96–98, 219
    word processing, 61–62, 73–80,
      219
Program, 6, 8, 23, 480. *See also*
    Software
Program file, 480
Program testing, 264–265, 288, 480
Programmable read-only memory,
    see PROM
Programmer, 51–52, 480
Programmer analyst, 287, 480
  software development and, 257
Programming:
  languages used in, 273–286
  techniques for standardizing
    software development,
    267–272
Project management software, 251,
    480
Prolog, 285–286
PROM, 112, 136, 480
Prompt, 147, 176, 480
Protocol, 352, 364, 480
Prototyping, 385–386, 395, 480
PS/2 personal computer, 304, 469
Pseudocode, 261, 287, 480
Public domain software (freeware),
    246–247, 252, 480
Pull-down menu, 99, 480
Punched card, 143

Q
Q&A, 402
QBASIC, 299
QBE, 284, 410
Quality of life, impact of computers
    on, 445–455
Quark Xpress, 236
Query-By-Example (QBE), 284, 410
Query language, 100, 284, 409–410,
    480
Quicken (software), 244, 245
QuickTime, 480

R
Radio modem, 326, 359, 365
Radio Shack, 39, 41
RAM card, *see* Memory card
RAM, *see* Random-access memory
Random-access file organization,
    209–210
Random-access memory (RAM),
    111, 134, 480
Read-only memory (ROM),
    112–113, 134, 480
Read/write head, 211, 480
  for fixed-head disk drive, 193
Ready-Set-Go!, 236
Real-time processing, 480
Records, in a database file, 90, 401,
    480
Reduced instruction set computer,
    see RISC computer
Registers, 114, 134, 480
Relational database, 405–408, 423,
    480
Relative addressing, 480
Remote data entry, 339–341, 364, 480
Remote job entry, 480
Report generator, 284, 289, 411, 480
Request for proposal (RFP), 390, 395,
    480
Resolution, 165, 177, 480
Reusable code, 271, 288, 480–481
Reverse video, 481
RFP, *see* Request for proposal
RGB monitor, 481
Ring network, 481
Ring topology, 354
RISC computer, 40, 44, 55, 469, 481
  vs. CISC, 122–123
ROM, *see* Read-only memory
Root directory, 319, 322, 481
Roussel, Philippe, 186
Router, 356–357, 364, 481

RPG (Report Program Generator), 276
Runtime program, 229–230, 251, 481

S
SAS, 237
Satellite transmission of data, 338
Scanner, 7, 152, 154–155, 177, 479, 481
Screen saver, 222–223
Scrolling, 481
SDA, see Source data automation
Search and replace, 71–72, 99, 481
Second-generation language, 481
Secondary storage, 183, 211, 481
    criteria for evaluating, 184–185
    magnetic media for, 183, 186–200
    magneto-optical storage, 207–208
    maintaining disk and tape files, 195–197
    optical storage media, 201–208
    safeguarding files, 196–197
Sector, on disk, 187, 481
Security
    of database management system, 411
    computer networks and, 433–440
    computer networks and, vs. privacy, 437–440
    information systems and, 17
    and interactive data processing systems, 132
Segment, in hierarchical database, 403–404
Sequence structure, 481
Sequential file, 209, 481
Serial printer, 168, 177, 481
Serial transmission, 351, 364, 481
Shareware, 246–247, 252, 481
Shell, 308, 481
Silicon Graphics, Inc. (SGI), 40
Simplex line, 349, 364, 481
Simply Money, 244
Site license, 248, 252, 481
SmallTalk, 281
Smart card, 20, 139, 159–160, 198–199, 211, 481
Smart devices:
    appliances, 16
    cards, 20, 139, 159–160, 198–199, 211, 481
    cars, 16, 20
    phones, 20, 359–360, 365, 481
    houses, 20, 459–460

Smeg virus, 435
Social responsibility issues, information systems and, 440–455
Soft copy, 163, 177, 481
Soft-sectored disk/diskette, 211, 481
Software, 2, 6, 8–10, 23, 481
    acquiring, 246–247
    application, 9–10, 23, 60
    application packages, 60–61, 70
    artificial intelligence, 237–240
    automatic backup, 222
    business packages, 240–242
    consumer packages, 243, 244
    custom, 10, 23, 60, 219
    desktop accessories, 221
    desktop publishing, 234–236
    development cycle, of custom programs, 259–267, 287, 481
    document viewers, 234
    expert systems, 21
    industry-specific, types of, 241–242
    innovations in, 21
    integrated packages, 65–66, 219–220
    licensing and copy protection, 247–248
    make or buy decision, 244–245
    multimedia systems, 21, 226–230
    operating systems, 8–9, 23, 60
    overview of, 60
    packaged, 9–10, 23, 60, 219
    password protection utility, 222
    personal information managers, 223–224
    productivity tools, 10, 23–24, 60, 480
    programmers, 8
    project management, 223–224
    public domain, 246–247
    screen savers, 222–223
    shareware, 246–247
    statistical packages, 237
    suites, 66, 99, 219–220, 251, 482
    system optimizers, 221
    unerase utility, 222
    versions of, 245
    virus detection programs, 222
Software development cycle, 259–267, 287, 481
Software documentation, see Documentation

Software engineering, 266, 288, 481
Sorting, 317
Sound board, 172, 173, 177, 481
Source data automation (SDA), 151–162, 176–177, 481
Source document, 142, 176, 481
Source program, 264, 287, 481
Spelling checker, in word processing software, 74
Spencer, Kenneth L., 291
Spooling, 317, 322, 481
Spreadsheet package, electronic, 62–63, 219, 481
    entering data in cells, 84–88
    history of, 63
    software capabilities, 80–83
    using commands, 85–88
    uses of, 62–63
    VisiCalc, 63, 465
SprintNet, 342
SPSS, 237
SQL, *see* Structured Query Language
Standards, concerning computers and computer use, 444–445
Star network, 481
Star topology, 354
Statistical package, 252, 481
Status line, 68–69, 481
Storage capacity, 185–186, 211, 481
Storage device, 6, 23, 481
Stored-program device, 8, 23, 481
Structure chart, *see* hierarchy chart
Structured analysis, 481
Structured programming, 268–270, 288, 481–482
Structured query language (SQL), 96, 284, 410, 424, 481
Structured walkthrough, 482
Subdirectory, 190, 482
Subnotebook computer, 40–41, 55, 482
Subprogram, 482
Subscriber service, 96, 342–343, 364, 482
Suite, 66, 99, 219–220, 251, 482
    vs. integrated package, 220
Summary report, 163, 177, 482
Sun Microcomputer Systems, 40
Supercomputer, 30, 38–39, 482
    information superhighway and, 38–39
Supermicro, 39–40
Supervisor, *see* Kernel

Swapping, 314–315, 322, 482
Symbolic language, 264, 287, 482
Synchronous transmission, 351, 364, 482
Syntax error, 264, 288, 482
System flowchart, 381–383, 394, 482
System interrupt, 312–313, 321, 482
System optimizer, 221
Systems analysis, 51–52
    designing components of new system, 388–390
        constraints, 388
        controls and feedback, 390
        input design, 388–389
        objectives, 388
        output design, 388
        processing requirements, 389
    feasibility study and, 383
    problem definition in, 376–384
    structured systems charts and, 379–383
Systems analyst, 13–14, 372–375, 482
Systems development, 17–19, 24, 46, 482
Systems development life cycle, 482, 374–375, 394
Systems programmer, 295, 321, 482
Systems software, 482

T
Table of contents, creating in word processing programs, 76
Tape drive, 193–194
TCP/IP, 309
Telecommunications, 330, 363, 482
Telecommuting, 21, 24, 482
Telephone:
    carriers, 336–337
    and data communications, 333–337
    Touch-Tone college registration example, 427
Television:
    high-definition, 360–361
    interactive, 360–361
Template, 100, 482
Terabyte, 111, 482
Terminal, 30, 34, 54, 482. *See also* Point-of-sale (POS) terminal; Video display terminal
Terminate and stay resident program, *see* TSR program
Test data, 482
Text editing, 73, 99, 318, 482

Thermal printer, 171–172, 177, 482
Thesaurus, in word processing
     software, 74
Thinking Machines, Inc., 38
Third-generation languages (3GLs),
     274–283, 482
Time-sharing, 48, 56, 482
Token ring network, 354–355, 364,
     482
Toolbox, 229
Top-down design, 482
Top-down processing, 49
Top-down programming, 270–271
Touch screen, 149–150, 176, 482
Trackball, 482
Tracks, 482
     on disks, 186
     on tape, 195
Tractor feed mechanism, 168, 482
Traditional systems approach, 482
Transaction file, 141, 482
Transaction processing, 132, 135, 482
Transaction report, 164, 177, 482
Transfer rate, 12, 185, 186, 482
Translator programs, 264, 283, 316
Transmission protocol, 482
TSR program, 482
Turing test, 237
Twisted-pair cable, 331–332, 363,
     483
Tymnet, 342
Typeover mode, 69, 483

U
Unemployment rate, impact of
     computers on, 443
Unerase utility, 222
UNIVAC, 463
Universal Product Code (UPC), 177,
     483
UNIX operating system, 44, 295,
     308–311, 483
UPC, see Universal product code
Update (procedure), 141, 483
Upload/uploading, 191, 211, 483
Upwardly compatible, 54, 483
User interface, 294, 321, 483. See also
     Graphical user interface
User-friendly, 9, 11, 23, 483
     screen displays, 146–147
Users, 5, 13–14, 483
     data entry operators, 13
     operating staff, 13
     power users, 61

Utilities, 483
     in DBMS software, 410

V
Value-added services, from telephone
     carriers, 336–337, 363, 483
VDT, see Video display terminal
Vector graphics, 232, 251, 483
Ventura Publisher, 236
Video display terminal (VDT),
     164–165, 483
Video for Windows, 483
Video monitor, 8
Video software, 230
Videoconferencing, 22, 177–178,
     180–181, 361, 365, 483
Virtual machine, 314–315, 322, 483
Virtual memory, 314–315, 322, 483
Virtual reality software, 217, 239,
     252, 483
Virtual storage, see Virtual memory
Viruscan, 437
Virus, 248, 252, 435–436, 483. See
     also Antiviral/antivirus software
VisiCalc, 63, 465
Visual Basic, 264, 282, 289, 291, 483
Visual programming, 272, 288, 291,
     483
Visual Xbase, 284
Voice recognition equipment, 7,
     160–161, 177, 483
Voice response unit, 172–173, 177,
     483
Volatile memory, 111, 134, 183, 483
Volatile vs. nonvolatile computers,
     136
von Leibniz, Gottfried, 461
von Neumann, John, 463
VP-Expert, 239

W
WAN, see Wide area network
Wand reader, 152–153, 177, 483
Westlaw, 342
What-if analysis, 483
Wide area network (WAN), 356–357,
     364, 483
Windows, 23, 44, 299, 468, 470, 483
Windows 95, 44, 302–304, 471
Windows for Workgroups, 301
Windows NT, 301
Wireless communications, 359, 483
Wireless networks, 336–338
Wirth, Niklaus, 278

Word, 118, 135, 483

Word processing software, 61–62, 73–80, 98, 483

capabilities of, 73–74

commands in using, 78

entering text in a document, 78–80

multilingual, 78

Word size, 125–126

Word wrap, 79, 99, 483

WordPerfect, 466

WordStar, 466

Worker dissatisfaction, impact of computers on, 443

Worksheet, 99, 483. *See also* Spreadsheet

Workstation, 39–40, 55, 483

RISC computer *vs.* CISC computer, 40

vs. standard microcomputer, 39

WORM (write-once, read-many) CDs, 206–208, 212, 483

Wozniak, Stephen, G., 41, 310, 465

Write-protect notch, 483

Write-protecting disk, 197

WYSIWYG, 80, 99, 235, 483

X

XENIX, 308

PHOTO CREDITS

Part One Opener
Page 3 (top): Robert Frerck/Woodfin Camp & Associates. *Page 3 (center):* David Chambers/Tony Stone Images/New York, Inc. *Page 3 (bottom left):* Charles Allen/The Image Bank. *Page 3 (bottom right):* Lonnie Duka/Tony Stone Images/New York, Inc.

Chapter 1
Figure 1.2a: Courtesy International Business Machines Corporation. *Figure 1.2b:* © Courtesy NCR. *Figure 1.3a:* Jon Feingersh/The Stock Market. *Figure 1.3b:* Bob Daemmrich/The Image Works. *Figure 1.4:* Daniel Bosler/Tony Stone Images/New York, Inc. *Figure 1.5b:* Courtesy Apple Computers. *Figure 1.5c:* Courtesy Waggener Edstrom. *Figure 1.6:* Loren Santow/Tony Stone Images/New York, Inc. *Figure 1.7:* Fujifotos/The Image Works. *Figure 1.8:* © Roger Ressmeyer/Ressmeyer-Starlight. *Figure 1.9:* Courtesy Sony Electronics Inc. *Figure 1.10a:* Frederic Pitchal/Sygma. *Figure 1.11:* Billy E. Barnes/Stock, Boston. *Figure 1.12a:* Richard Pasley/Stock, Boston. *Figure 1.12b:* Bernard Annebicque/Sygma. *Figure 1.13:* © Roger Ressmeyer/Ressmeyer-Starlight. *Figure 1.14:* Sygma. *Figure 1.15:* HMS Images/The Image Bank. *Page 28:* Courtesy *L.A. Times.*

Chapter 2
Figures 2.1 and 2.3: Courtesy International Business Machines Corporation. *Figure 2.4:* Courtesy Hewlett Packard. *Page 35 (far left):* Courtesy Microsoft. *Page 35 (center left):* Courtesy Digital Equipment Corp. *Page 35 (center right):* Courtesy International Business Machines Corporation. *Page 35 (far right):* David Parker/Science Photo Library/Photo Researchers. *Page 37:* Courtesy Moore School Computer Museum, University of Pennsylvania. *Figure 2.5:* Courtesy International Business Machines Corporation. *Page 39 (far left):* Courtesy Silicon Graphics. *Page 39 (second from left):* Courtesy International Business Machines Corporation. *Page 39 (center):* Courtesy Toshiba. *Page 39 (center right):* Bruce McAllister/Gamma Liaison. *Page 39 (far right):* Courtesy Sharp Electronics Corporation. *Figure 2.6:* John Greenleigh/Courtesy Apple Computers. *Page 41 (top):* Courtesy Apple Computers. *Figure 2.7b:* John Greenleigh/Courtesy Apple Computers. *Figure 2.7a:* Courtesy GRID. *Figure 2.9:* Courtesy Apple Computers. *Figure 2.10:* AST Computers. *Page 47:* Courtesy International Business Machines Corporation. *Page 58:* Courtesy United Nations.

Chapter 3
Figure 3.2: Courtesy Microsoft. *Page 63 (bottom):* Courtesy Daniel Bricklen. *Figure 3.3:* Courtesy Borland International, Inc. *Figure 3.4:* Courtesy Microsoft. *Figure 3.5:* Courtesy Lotus. *Figure 3.10:* Courtesy Microsoft. *Figure 3.18:* Courtesy Wordstar Institute. *Figures 3.22 and 3.38:* Courtesy Borland International, Inc. *Figure 3.39 and Page 103:* Courtesy Lotus.

Part Two Opener
Page 105 (top): Steve Dunwell/The Image Bank. *Page 105 (top center):* Sautelet/Jerrican/Photo Researchers. *Page 105 (bottom center):* Gamma Liaison. *Page 105 (bottom):* Christian Zachariasen/Sygma. *Page 106 (top):* David Brooks/The Stock Market. *Page 106 (center left):* Courtesy *L.A. Times.* *Page 106 (center right):* Paul Van Riel/Black Star. *Page 106 (bottom):* Tim Bieber/The Image Bank.

Chapter 4
Page 110: Courtesy Intel. *Figure 4.2:* Courtesy Intel. *Figure 4.3:* Courtesy Motorola. *Figure 4.4:* Paul Silverman/Fundamental Photographs. *Figure 4.5:* Courtesy Hewlett Packard. *Page 122:* Peter Silva/Picture Group. *Figure 4.16a:* William McCoy/Rainbow. *Figures 4.17 and 4.18:* Courtesy International Business Machines Corporation. *Figure 4.20a:* Laima Druskis/Stock, Boston. *Page 139:* Thomas Craig/FPG International.

Chapter 8
Page 265 (right): Courtesy Digital Equipment Corp. *Page 281 (left):* Courtesy New York Public Library. *Page 281 (center):* The Science Museum. *Figure 8.6:* Courtesy Lisa Passmore. *Page 281 (right):* Courtesy International Business Machines Corporation. *Page 291:* Courtesy Microsoft.

Chapter 9
Figure 9.2: Courtesy Paul Constantine. *Figure 9.3:* Courtesy Mike Green. *Figure 9.4a:* Courtesy Microsoft. *Figure 9.5:* Courtesy Waggener Edstrom. *Figure 9.6:* Courtesy Waggener Edstrom. *Figure 9.7:* Courtesy International Business Machines Corporation. *Figure 9.8:* Courtesy Paul Constantine. *Figure 9.9:* Courtesy General Magic. *Page 308:* Courtesy Marge Graham. *Figure 9.10 and Page 325:* Courtesy International Business Machines Corporation.

Part Four Opener
Page 327 (top left): The Image Bank. *Page 327 (top right):* Eric Lars Bakke/Black Star. *Page 327 (bottom left):* Peter Menzel. *Page 327 (bottom right):* Mark Gamba/The Stock Market. *Page 328 (top):* Courtesy International Business Machines Corporation. *Page 328 (center):* Charlie Westerman/Gamma Liaison. *Page 328 (bottom left):* Hank Morgan/Rainbow. *Page 328 (bottom right):* Courtesy Samsung Electronics America.

Chapter 10
Figure 10.1: David Weintraub/Photo Researchers. *Figure 10.6:* Courtesy Hayes Microcomputer Products, Inc. *Figure 10.8:* Tim Davis/Photo Researchers. *Figure 10.9a:* Mikki Rain/Science Photo Library/Photo Researchers. *Figure 10.10:* Courtesy BellSouth Cellular Corp. *Figure 10.12:* Courtesy International Business Machines Corporation. *Figure 10.13a:* Courtesy CompuServe, Inc. *Figure 10.13b:* Courtesy Prodigy Service Co. *Figure 10.14:* Courtesy Microsoft. *Figure 10.15:* Courtesy Spry Inc. *Figure 10.17:* Chris Sorensen/The Stock Market. *Figure 10.20:* Courtesy International Business Machines Corporation. *Figure 10.22:* Louis Psihoyos/Matrix International, Inc. *Figure 10.23:* Courtesy Digiboard. *Figure 10.24a:* David York/The Stock Shop. *Figure 10.24b:* Courtesy Apple Computers. *Figure 10.25:* AT&T Archives. *Figure 10.27:* Stock, Boston. *Figure 10.26:* John Barr/Gamma Liaison. *Figure 10.28:* Richard Pasley/Gamma Liaison. *Page 367:* Courtesy Drexel University.

Part Five Opener
Page 369 (top left): Shahn Kermani/Gamma Liaison. *Page 369 (top right):* Stephen Derr/The Image Bank. *Page 369 (center right):* Courtesy Waggener Edstrom. *Page 369 (bottom left):* Shahn Kermani/Gamma Liaison. *Page 370 (top):* Brooks Kraft/Sygma. *Page 370 (center left):* Mel Digiacomo/The Image Bank. *Page 370 (center right and bottom):* Dan McCoy/Rainbow.

Chapter 11
Figure 11.1: Courtesy International Business Machines Corporation. *Figure 11.3:* Tim Brown/Tony Stone Images/New York, Inc. *Figure 11.5:* Courtesy International Business Machines Corporation. *Figure 11.12:* Picture Group. *Page 387:* Bob Daemmrich Photography.

Chapter 12
Figure 12.11 and Page 410: Courtesy Borland International, Inc. *Page 415:* Courtesy SAS/Graph Software. *Page 416 (top):* Courtesy International Business Machines Corporation. *Figure 12.15:* Courtesy DacEasy, Inc. *Page 417:* Courtesy Comshare. *Figure 12.18:* Courtesy Wang Laboratory. *Page 427:* Steve Niedorf/The Image Bank.

Chapter 13
Figure 13.1: James Kesyer. *Figure 13.2:* © 1994 Warner Bros. *Page 439 (top):* Spencer Grant/Photo Researchers. *Page 439 (bottom):* Courtesy Mykotronx. *Figure 13.7a:* Will & Deni McIntyre/Photo Researchers. *Figure 13.7b:* Walter Bibikow/The Image Bank. *Figure 13.8a:* Dan McCoy/Rainbow. *Figure 13.8b:* Melchior DiGiacomo/The Image Bank. *Figure 13.9a:* Nieto/Jerrican/Photo Researchers. *Figure 13.10:* Robert E. Daemmrich/Tony Stone Images/New York, Inc. *Figure 13.11:* Courtesy Prodigy Service Co. *Figure 13.12:* G. Vormwald/Sygma Photo News. *Figure 13.13:* Ben Van Hook/Black

Star. *Figure 13.14:* Courtesy Waggener Edstrom. *Figure 13.16a:* Alexis Puclos/Gamma Liaison. *Figure 13.16b:* Shahn Kermani/Gamma Liaison. *Figure 13.15:* Courtesy International Business Machines Corporation. *Figure 13.17:* Steve Lehman/SABA. *Figure 13.18:* James Wilson/Gamma Liaison. *Figure 13.19:* Courtesy CompuServe, Inc. *Page 459:* © Roger Ressmeyer/Ressmeyer-Starlight.

Appendix
Page 461 (top left): Courtesy New York Public Library. *Page 461 (top right):* Courtesy Monroe Systems for Business. *Page 461 (bottom left):* Courtesy International Business Machines Corporation. *Page 461 (left center):* Courtesy International Business Machines Corporation. *Page 461 (bottom right):* Courtesy New York Public Library. *Page 462 (top left):* Courtesy New York Public Library. *Page 462 (top center):* Courtesy The Science Museum. *Page 462 (bottom left):* Courtesy The Science Museum. *Page 462 (right center):* Computer Museum, Inc. *Page 462 (bottom right):* Computer Museum, Inc. *Page 463 (top left):* Courtesy Moore School Computer Museum, University Pennsylvania. *Page 463 (top right):* Sperry Univac, Div. of Sperry Corporation. *Page 463 (bottom left):* Institute for Advanced Study, Princeton, NJ. *Page 464 (bottom right):* Courtesy Intel. *Page 464 (left):* Courtesy Digital Equipment Corp. *Page 465 (top):* Courtesy Apple Computers. *Page 465 (center):* Courtesy Microsoft. *Page 465 (bottom):* Courtesy Apple Computers. *Page 466 (bottom):* Courtesy International Business Machines Corporation. *Page 467 (left):* Courtesy Lotus. *Page 467 (top right):* Courtesy International Business Machines Corporation. *Page 467 (right center):* Courtesy Compaq. *Page 467 (bottom right):* Courtesy Apple Computers. *Page 468 (top):* Courtesy Aldus Corporation. *Page 468 (bottom):* Courtesy Microsoft. *Page 469 (top left):* Courtesy International Business Machines Corporation. *Page 469 (top right):* Courtesy Compaq. *Page 469 (bottom left):* Courtesy International Business Machines Corporation. *Page 469 (bottom right):* Courtesy Intel. *Page 470 (left):* Courtesy Compaq. *Page 470 (right):* Courtesy Tandy Corporation. *Page 471 (top right):* Courtesy International Business Machines Corporation and Courtesy Intel. *Page 471 (bottom left):* Courtesy America Online, Inc. *Page 471 (center right):* Courtesy Apple Computers. *Page 471 (bottom right):* Courtesy Waggener Edstrom.